Reconstructing Lenin

RECONSTRUCTING LENIN

An Intellectual Biography

TAMÁS KRAUSZ

translated by BÁLINT BETHLENFALVY
with MARIO FENYO

MONTHLY REVIEW PRESS
New York

Library of Congress Cataloging-in-Publication data available
from the publisher
ISBN pbk 978-158367-449-9
ISBN cloth 978-158367-450-5
—

Monthly Review Press
146 West 29th Street, Suite 6W
New York, New York 10001

www.monthlyreview.org

5 4 3 2 1

The publication of this book was made possible by the generous support of the National Cultural Fund of Hungary and by the Foundation for Russian Language and Culture.

Contents

Preface

MARX'S FAMOUS THESIS, "The knell of capitalist private property sounds. The expropriators are expropriated,"[1] was derived from the contradictions of "modern society." But it was Vladimir Ilyich Lenin who first gave this thesis the bearings of an applied program and objective. Even seen from a distance of decades, the first conscious historical experiment aimed at realizing a "stateless" society (communism), the Russian Revolution, which eliminated the capitalist system of labor, labor distribution, and social classes, is the lasting achievement of Lenin and his revolutionary associates. At the same time, as founder of the Soviet state, Lenin is inextricably bound up with the seven decades of Soviet history that sprang from this antistate, anticapitalist experiment.

Even though, for more than two decades, there have been no large organizations, movements, or political parties in Europe of national or international consequence that are promoting *social revolution* or either "state" or "stateless" *socialism* in any form, the disputes about Lenin in political theory and specialized areas of historiography have not abated either in Russia or in the rest of the world. Since 1991 it has been clear that the major, community-oriented, socialist perspectives have faded from political practice globally. In such periods, not only historians but intellectual and political groups engaged in surmounting modern bourgeois society along humanist lines attempt to consider the causes of their marginalization, while taking stock of their traditions. They seek to understand the precedents of these traditions—their sources and their roots, and how thought and praxis changed the course of civilization.

In this all-encompassing story, Lenin—along with Plekhanov, Martov, Kautsky, Rosa Luxemburg, George Lukács, Gramsci, a long list—certainly had a fundamental role that cannot be overlooked, even in the twenty-first century. Nonetheless, we are aware that socialist revolutionaries—people whose actions were directed at laying the foundations of a communal-humanist alternative to capitalism—are not held in any great esteem in modern historiography. The historian can be a typical example of the "servile intellectual." This gives ample reason to keep a strong hold on objectivity, which any historian will need in order to avoid following the fashionable views of the times and preserve a critical approach. Research into Lenin's legacy has been pushed to the peripheries of current *academic* literature, but of course this does not mean that new books and studies about Lenin and his lifework do not appear daily.[2] While it is obvious that Lenin's Marxism was essentially of a political nature, and shaped his political struggles, it also had a grasp on virtually all the definitive problems of his age—problems that are undeniably still being reconsidered, under completely new conditions.

These interpretations, however, not only preserve the old misconceptions but add the prejudices of our own times. The problem lies in Lenin himself. His legacy allows for a variety of interpretations because, in reality, a "variety" of Lenins existed, and in spite of the inner unity and coherence of his actions he waged a constant struggle upon and within himself. For instance, the immediate pressures of the movement as he tried to escape the clutches of the secret police in 1917 dictated a stance quite different from the theoretician whose concern was to liberate all of humankind. Still another Lenin stands before us during the civil war, at the peak of power, "submerged" in the terror; and contours of yet another Lenin emerge if we consider his "revolutionary and theoretical legacy" after 1922, with his gaze fixed in the distance as he lies seriously ill. There is room for both the Lenin of autumn 1917, who aimed to sweep all state power off the board (think of *The State and Revolution*), and the Lenin who came after October 1917, a politician and statesman trying to organize the Soviet state. Nonetheless, to subsume Lenin's theoretical work under his pragmatic political measures, often dictated by mere necessity, is to commit a serious methodological error. And as we shall see, distortions of this kind can be carried through on the basis of rather different, even contradictory, worldviews. Meanwhile, notwithstanding all of Lenin's "inner struggles," there existed a line of intellectual development that holds his lifework together. This book explores "the difference and the unity" between these "various" Lenins.

The subject of this book is not unprecedented within the Hungarian field of Lenin research. A publication by Georg Lukács of what he called "an occasional study" on the "unity of Lenin's thought" came out as early as 1924.[3] His 100-page essay is an autonomous philosophical work of extraordinary value, and as such still has its own independent life.[4] This book, however, has a different purpose: to reconstruct the history of ideas in Lenin's thought, his sociological and theoretical views. It may seem that the present historical constellation is not suited for an objective approach to Lenin research, but in fact the opposite is true. No current political topicality, no matter its weight, drives the issue as it pleases through the gates of history—and the historical sciences.

On the other hand, there are indeed books that seem to have been written for no "logical reason" since they are so alien to the "spirit of their times"; their subject seems obsolete. Yet in many a case the opposite may turn out to be true at some future time (as in the case of Ervin Szabó, Trotsky, or Bukharin). And if the *history* of the Lenin phenomenon is given some thought, the timeliness of research on him may become clear. The recent memory of innumerable studies, brochures, and books appearing on Lenin's life and work during the decades of state socialism still haunts Hungary. The first Hungarian historian to speak about Lenin seriously was Gyula Szekfű. In a memorial speech in January 1948, as Hungarian ambassador to Moscow, he spoke in recognition of Lenin's significance as a statesman and state builder, and the speech soon appeared in print.[5] Lenin's works were published in an incredible variety of forms and in great volume in the years that followed. During the 1960s, a list of works by Lenin available in Hungarian filled a volume.[6] Of course, the universal, "systematized" interpretation of Lenin, the "canonical text," was a Russian monopoly until 1989. This is an obvious explanation for why a single *comprehensive* Lenin interpretation was not published in Hungary, unless we count the official Soviet biographies, which were published in all east European languages.[7]

The Lenin centenary was, in a sense, an event of great consequence. It seemed like a turn of some sort, even from a Hungarian vantage point. The time was, after all, the aftermath of 1968 and the rise of the "new left." It may be found rather surprising, but in 1970, the one hundredth anniversary of Lenin's birth, Professor György Ránki held a *critical* Lenin seminar in the history department of Debrecen University (Hungary) as part of the academic "memorial celebrations," while his teaching assistant, a young Lajos Menyhárt, addressed the Lenin theme in line with his own main interests. At "literary evenings," students from the Kossuth Lajos University of Sciences and Eötvös Lóránd University made declarations denouncing the social inequalities of the day with demonstrations of a leftist critique of the prevailing system. For the Hungarian intelligentsia, the "literary" "Lenin" of the Hungarian writer László Gyurkó crowned the memorial celebrations. His *Lenin, Október* (Lenin, October) elevated the leader of the revolution from the clichés of boring propaganda publications.

In fact, a sort of reevaluation had already begun in the 1960s.[8] The first widely influential and scientifically discriminating Lenin biography was written by a leftist American intellectual, Louis Fischer.[9] An excellent book even in comparison with the literature up to that time, it not only contested the official Soviet portrayal of Lenin—hallmarked by P. N. Pospelov—but presented the outlines of a new Lenin interpretation backed up by a wealth of serious literature on the subject. As well as taking up the usual historical themes, the book brought Lenin's "role as a dictator" and the relationship with his revolutionary associates into the foreground, topics still taboo in the Soviet Union (and more widely Eastern Europe) of the 1960s. While a Russian translation of Fischer's book was published only in London,[10] it did not remain without some influence within the "world socialist system," though of course no serious effect upon the intellectual life of the Soviet Union can be attributed to it.

In spite of the centennial year celebrations, no new Lenin analyses of any depth or seriousness enriched the Soviet *Lenin personality cult*, perhaps partly in reaction to the openness of the earlier Khrushchev years. But details were addressed during the 1970s—within the given limitations of an officially restricted pool of sources and following the required ideological line—with at times highly valuable results, as individual events were processed with a "positivist" approach and in unbelievable minutiae.[11] In the 1980s, Perestroika opened the floodgates, leading to well-known changes: the personality cult of Lenin was buried under the crumbling state socialist system of the Soviet Union, along with its legitimizing ideology of "Marxism-Leninism" that was built on Lenin and propped up by an enormous institutional system, culture, and the efforts of a mass of scholars to substantiate and sustain the system.[12]

It is not surprising that the study and science of history has become even more politicized since Perestroika, and *writing history* on the subject has been transformed into a *political venture*. The new system cried out for a legitimizing ideology. Documents that had not been entered into the "complete works" of Lenin for reasons and aspects dictated by the cult of Lenin, and unknown even to scholars specializing in the subject, came to light, one after another. Moreover, their publication, and the reorganization of the field on these new grounds, had commercial aspects. The scramble for the publication and media presentation of each document had begun. The "anticult of personality" took the form of a media show—new swill filled the old flask.

The features peculiar to this development in political commerce became increasingly apparent, with serious historians quickly taking due notice. The new trends were of course not difficult to make out, as the rhetoric, logic, and message of the 1950s returned in a new guise and with new functions; what had been dramatic then was rather slapstick now. As pointed out by Eric Hobsbawm in regard to its bearing on Europe, the initiators of this turn in events were to be found among the old former Marxists/Communists in France, who had turned out brilliant historians: "Though the 1950 International Congress of Historical Sciences attracted young Marxists, numerous excellent, later anti-communist historians who were hard-line young Communist Party activists—such as François Furet, Annie Kriegel, Alain Besançon, Le Roy Ladurie—stayed away. I only had the good fortune of getting to know them in their post-Communist periods."[13] A similar turn in Hungarian philosopher Ágnes Heller is also mentioned,[14] and one might append a whole list of Hungarian authors if their intellectual achievements on the subject of Lenin were not so embarrassingly poor.

In Russia, where the figure of Lenin also gained an important place in the new ideological constellation, a somewhat different situation evolved. With little delay the "iconoclastic" approach in the Western manner also took hold in Russia under the leadership of the suddenly "righted," former Marxist-Leninist, exegetists. For a classic example one need look no further than the 1994 book by D. Volkogonov, formerly the director of the central political office of the Soviet military, titled *Lenin*,[15] or A. G. Latishev's less famous work, *Lenin Revealed*.[16] At the same time a number of accomplished works grounded in new concepts and views on the history of the Russian Revolution and Bolshevism also appeared,[17] and were briefly outlined by O. V. Volubuyev.[18] The new conceptualization offers only a marginal account of Lenin the theorist, a sort of "dogmatic Marxist," while casting him basically as a pragmatic politician.

Fashionable postmodernism, with its own disappointed "leftism" and neo-conservative traditional attitudes, situates Lenin in the narrative of "terrorism and dictatorship." In Hungary, the influence of R. Pipes's portrayal of Lenin, rooted in the Cold War sensibilities of the 1950s, probably has the widest following—next to an almost complete lack of more serious or deep interest.[19] Borrowing from postmodern terminology, the "deconstruction" of Lenin is complete, which means, in the "official" language of our times, that the "Leninian narrative" has been resituated in the cul-de-sac of history, as has "terrorism" (understood as any radical opposition to capitalism) in general. This currently fashionable classification is conceptually more indistinct and misleading than any experiment devoted to rationalizing Lenin since his death.[20]

Practically the whole range of Lenin documents falsified or suppressed in the Soviet period are to be found in the volume *V. I. Lenin—The Unknown Documents, 1891–1922*.[21] The author of the conclusion, V. Loginov, does, however, remark that the publication must not be given greater importance than it deserves, as its 422 documents are virtually a drop in the ocean of the 24,000 documents contained by the fifty-five-volume collected works of Lenin, volumes of the *Leninskiy Sbornik*, the multivolume *Decrees of Soviet Power*, and the *Biographic Chronicle*, all world-renowned Soviet publications of primary source material.[22] Another incredible fact should be noted: in the fifty-five-volume collected works of Lenin, quoted or otherwise used are over 16,000 books, brochures, articles, journals, documents, and letters. "The sources are quoted in over 20 languages. Lenin's Kreml office had over 10 thousand books and newspapers, many of them works of literature."[23]

Undoubtedly some general social interest for objective approaches to studying Lenin has remained, though in Russia this usually stems only from a sort of defensive footing, the politico-historical and psychological causes of which need not be addressed here.[24] The "anti-personality cult" that came to the fore immediately after the change of regimes could not really come to grips with the phenomenon of Lenin's positive image surviving alongside a deep-rooted nationalism and traditional patriotic values in the wider population.. In fact, according to a sociological survey in 1994, at the height of Lenin's unmasking, Lenin was the second most popular historical figure in the country (33.6 percent), following Peter the Great (40.6 percent).[25]

A strange obscurity surrounds the fact that Lenin's "personality cult" was built independently of, and even against, his express wishes, which are hidden even today. The matter becomes highly distinct in light of documents that reflect the political and socio-psychological emotions and reactions following Lenin's death, especially the GPU's (State Political Directorate) reports on the general mood. The attraction of Lenin's "strong personality" amid the fear of upheaval and sudden change is reflected in the various documents, not only where the workers caught up in the spirit of the revolution are concerned,[26] but also among the rural populace. This is how Lenin first emerged as "protector of the Russian people" against foreign aggressors (especially Jews, of course); all of these feelings were also colored by strong religious sentiment. Those in power used the formula "Lenin is the party, the party is Lenin" in their attempts to strengthen and conserve the revolutionary legitimacy of the new system. Meanwhile, in opposition to this personality cult (and those in power), an antipathy for Lenin (the anti-personality cult) also took shape, fed likewise by social and religious roots.[27] In fact, the burial ceremony and the raising of the mausoleum, with the embalming and public display of the corpse, was also a show of devotion for the "good father." That event has a literature all its own.[28] In the background, a kind of naïve messianic hope, conviction, and belief animated the growing cult of Lenin. A multitude of workers and peasants associated their hopes for a better world with the leader of the revolution; they saw the realistic, material realization of a just society, and the ideals related to this, embodied in him. Everything added to this by the Communist majority—their effort to "nurture-teach" and enlighten, and their will for power—was its modern ideological cement. The slogan about "devotion to the cause" rang out even at Lenin's funeral. The typical circumstance of workers competing for the right to participate in Lenin's burial ceremony—in a −22°F January freeze—was not necessarily a result of top-down organization, and soon topical songs about Lenin as a folk hero and oracle began to spread.[29]

This belief in the future was incarnated in the way people related to Lenin, exemplified by the formative effect it had on the inner worlds of the young heroes at the time of his death, in Vera Panova's *Sentimental Novel*:

> They stood on the corner, while the icy wind whistled, chafed at them as they shuffled in their flimsy boots, teeth chattering as they talked: What was Ilyich like? Had they ever seen him though? Yugay had seen him at the third congress of the Komsomol. But Lenin meant so infinitely much in their lives. Not just in years past, but in the coming years, forever, it was impossible to count how much he meant to them. He would always be there, whatever happened. This is how they felt, and this is how it was to be. And forever entwined with him, their greatest role model, they would have liked to know all the details about him, what he looked like, his voice, his walk, what were the things he kept in his room, about his relations to comrades, to his family. All spoke together, telling the others what they knew or whatever came to mind.[30]

Later, the official state socialist cult doctrine of Stalinism was built on the same earnest revolutionary fervor, without the "two layers" ever being clearly distinguished in historical terms. It is evident that scholars looking for a path between the "cult" and "anticult" are not motivated purely by professional goals. Lenin's whole legacy is so bound up with the practical political dimensions of "changing the world" that some anticapitalist movements still give currency to the "Leninian legacy," as demonstrated by the theoretical initiative of S. Žižek (earlier of the Slovenian opposition) and the remaining Marxist theorists in the New Left circles, as well as numerous Trotskyite reflections.[31] While examining the various manifestations of Marxism's life processes and its "neo-" and "post-" Marxist forms, Göran Therborn, in discussing Žižek's work, gave special emphasis to Žižek's passionate defense of tradition-destroying Marxism as opposed to "conformist liberalism." "Žižek's exhortation to 'repeat Lenin' posits an openness to the possibilities for radical social change in an apparently hopeless situation, following disastrous defeat—in Lenin's case, World War I and the breakup of the Second International."[32] Today, in a completely different historical situation, the historical and scientific preconditions of such an initiative are worth a thought. This is one of the subjects to which this volume seeks to join its argument.

From this standpoint, Lenin is once again part of an intellectual and political—though seemingly peripheral—search for the way ahead, whose trajectory, depth, potential, and perspective are still difficult to judge. It is nevertheless certain that where the history of *socialism* as an intellectual and sociopolitical movement of the twentieth century is concerned, Lenin's work cannot be bypassed.

Two extreme *methodological* approaches have also come to the fore in Lenin studies. One of these approaches derives the historical progression of socialism from the views of Lenin (or indeed Marx), albeit history—as the later chapters of this book should hopefully make clear—was not the "realization" or embodiment of their views. Such approaches lead to the reproduction of Lenin interpretations in terms of salvation history, with a diametrically opposite prognosis.[33] A second approach, marked for example by a new trend in American historical literature that studies primarily the "cultural foundations" of the evolving Soviet system—in contrast to adherents of the totalitarianism concept—emphasizes that the "ideas" and "myths" of Marxism, as well as Marxist ideologies and political goals, gained relevance as expressions of historical structures and mentalities. In other words, this approach does not extrapolate the significance of Marxism among historical processes from any kind of individual commitment, exceptional personality, or fall into damnation, but rather from, for example, "the geopolitical ambitions of Russia," or "the sense of special calling," the particular characteristics of everyday routine and style of command, and other factors of cultural history.[34] How could the Bolshevik party have fought the tsarist secret police had not its organization been somewhat similar to it?

Then there is a third approach that is a "twin" to totalitarianism that stands out for its old-fashioned mechanistic determinism. It considers the historical process as a logical series of events without alternatives, the "consummation of socialism," in which Lenin always recognized the right choice and decided accordingly.[35] In Hungary, the case of István Dolmányos shows that this portrayal of Lenin and the revolution stems not from the abilities of the historian but the spirit of the times.[36]

It is also evident that Lenin's legacy belongs to the curious pages of the history of Marxism-Leninism. Of course, it is possible to observe and interpret this group of phenomena through perspectives gained from any "narrative" or "paradigm."[37] Yet a key to its understanding can only be found in Lenin's own theoretical "paradigm," his Marxism, because it is only possible to adequately capture the stimuli, motivations, and performance of his politico-theoretical thought within this conceptual framework. For Lenin will never conform to "extraneous" normative expectations, as his lifework was directed at radical change of the *existing* and simply cannot be interpreted independently of this objective.

Meanwhile, the stumbling blocks of such an immanent analysis are also evident, as the collapse of the state socialist system discredited those basic concepts in the Marxist tradition that are central to the intellectual legacy of Lenin: social class, working class (proletariat), class struggle, class consciousness, class point of view, class movement, etc.[38] While the eradication of *class* and concepts associated with it in the post-1989 world came with the appearance of numerous new theories and paradigms, their scientific standing—put euphemistically—is more than relative. The problem is that the relationships and structures that dictate stratification in social development now stand out for their class-specific bearing just as they did over the past two hundred years. It is important not to mix up the concepts of class *in itself* with class *for itself*, or neglect the differences between the two (as they were, incidentally, under state socialism as well); this slip of meaning is used so often that it need not even be illustrated with an example. The range of terms offered by new social and political theories to replace class include "household," "producers and consumers," the "antagonisms," "population," "profession," among others (not to mention the terms cultivated by racist theories). Conflictual relations between individuals and social groups, with manifold roots—in economics, social history, and society—tower over the concept of class even today. For who would deny the existing opposition between those with property and those without, the contradictions raised by a place in the hierarchy of production, the facts of social exclusion? The whole system of wealth disparity is at constant work in human relations, its stark reality reflected as an everyday experience in terms of distribution. In the final count it is social emancipation that is at stake in the conscious or unconscious struggle through social contradictions and class conflicts. In other words, the historical development of society can be grasped unambiguously, even in purely empirical terms, through the concepts related to class, the opposition between work and capital, the distribution of labor in society and its terms, though it cannot be described wholly and exclusively by these—unless we fall back on pre-Marxist, vulgarly materialist sociology. But what reason would there be to do such a thing?

These concepts are not dogmas into which any mass of historical facts can be condensed. They are only an approach. *Culture* and *language* as primary sources and points of departure for any approach raise issues that are, of course, not infertile. But while language and words are given a virtually magical, mystical significance, and raised as independent entities to the status of absolutes that stand above relations in society, historical facts are relativized and the historical account dissolves into narratives. Thus, with a conceptualization of history in which social groups, interests, and objectives, as well as social and power struggles, are only narratives, the success of the revolutionary narrative—history, that is, the reconstruction of the past—is a functional precondition of who can speak to the population in the most accessible and most convincing idiom. This approach to history dissolves history itself, as it were, down to the remembered past and makes a cohesive "retelling" of history or a study of its inner coherences impossible. According to this "postmodern" view the success of the Bolsheviks was made possible by their formulation of an "effective" revolutionary narrative, which stayed the course in the memories of individuals and groups. But history approached as "representation" and "myth" makes for an "institutionalization" of the revolution in which the search for the causes of action on a social scale dissolves, and traditional (Marxist and non-Marxist) historiography is tamed as a "discarded" narrative.[39] Naturally, this does not call the justification of postmodernism into question; it only serves to call attention to the fact that serious hazards for historiography follow upon abandoning the positions of "traditional" investigative historiography.[40] The calling into question of historiography as a science is a problem that dates back decades. Followers of this movement advanced a sort of "discursivity," "inspiration," "theoretical terminology," "free thought," or "personal philosophy" as opposed to science. This formulation was used against Marc Bloch above all, as early as the 1970s, by Raymond Aron, Henri-Irenée Marrou, Paul Veyne, and others. This was followed by an American initiative, the "linguistic turn" in historiography, whose European followers also tried to lay the foundations of a deconstruction of the conceptual apparatus of this science.[41]

Aware as we are of the "linguistic problem," it, of course, cannot be solved by means of trashing the Marxist paradigm, which came about in a historical way, for the sake of the paradigm of "modernization." If we use the Western forms of development to examine different courses of development, we find ourselves contradicting centuries-old rules of scientific historical investigation. For this reason we make an effort to keep our distance from the "propagandistic" messages of the language of the age under examination, though some "reconstruction" of that "archaic language" spoken by revolutionary Marxism seems unavoidable as a consequence of the fundamental task set for this book, the *historical contextualization* of Lenin's legacy. It would be disappointing if we had no success in "digging up" some historical elements of the viable theoretical culture hidden under the legitimizing ideology of the old state socialist system, particularly and primarily (but not exclusively!) from the field of historical science.

The basic task of the historian, as mentioned earlier, is first of all to place the examined historical series of events, processes, or historical "experience" into its original context. This task needs particular emphasis where a "phenomenon" as controversial as the "Lenin phenomenon" is concerned. And though the systematization and appropriation of his views, work, political and theoretical legacy began immediately after his death (or in fact, already in the last period of his life[42]), the notion of Leninism is still used today,[43] with widely divergent connotations. There is no argument between the various ideologies and movements with different worldviews that Lenin brought such an original intellectual and political "product" (though not alone, and not in and of itself) into being, without which the history of the twentieth century cannot be analyzed or interpreted. It is no coincidence that serious historians avoid all *analogies* when it comes to Lenin. In the balance, this is determinedly not because Lenin's performance is held to be unique and unprecedented in world history (this can be one of the reasons), but because it is absurd to propose a Marxist Robespierre, or Marxist Atatürk, or any other even more absurd parallels. Let us hope this relatively extensive book explains why such analogies are pointless.

Accordingly, a Lenin monograph that seeks to grasp—in a predefined and comparative sense—his work as a whole, or at least aims to discuss the complete work, will meet a variety of challenges beyond those already discussed. Above all, one must note that in the course of analysis, an event, a problematic issue, or a given work or line of thought by Lenin is bound to come up in different chapters, framed in different arguments. All works that are compelled to apply a chronological and thematic exposition to their subject simultaneously face this difficulty. This "composite method" is an added burden for an author in the development of the subject. However, if successful, it can strengthen the inner coherence of the work and elucidate deeper correspondences in the evolution of Lenin's thought. Such an attempt at a historical reconstruction of Lenin's views in the field of social theory must dispense with a variety of details. In the course of time many questions that were thought of as fundamental are no longer of interest, and other questions that were earlier given virtually no significance have just recently gained importance in the light of the early twenty-first century. Not only has the Soviet state—which was celebrated by Soviet historians and politicians as Lenin's greatest historical achievement—itself since collapsed, but the realization has also dawned that what had been brought into being was wholly different from what was planned by the first "Leninian generation" of revolutionaries. Even the real content and compass of the "plan" have faded, with the latest, truly valuable, and perhaps most extensive survey of Lenin's legacy from R. Service's pen completely "unsettling the picture." It is interesting that the latest literature on the subject in a certain way returns the reception of Lenin to the level of the Stalin era, in that it takes Lenin's intellectual and theoretical legacy into account mechanically, purely as an ideology of legitimization. The basic methodological drawback of this approach is that it uncouples the theoretical and practical elements that belong together: Lenin's theoretical discoveries and definitive political decisions. At the same time the substantial and insubstantial are mixed up, and in place of uncritical glorification we find Lenin's "rectification": seventy to eighty years after the fact we learn—at extraordinary length—more about what a British professor would have done in Lenin's place and how Lenin should have conceived of the world in theoretical terms than what Lenin actually thought and did.[44] The author of this book would prefer to avoid these methodological pitfalls and do so, moreover, in hope of consigning all uncritical justifications to final eradication.

Needless to say, determining the suitable proportions for the weight of each subject gave the author cause for much consideration. The issue of whether or not Lenin's influence upon the course of events, and the role and weight of his political decisions, is exaggerated has come up in the case of other scholars as well.[45] If I were to apply self-criticism to my work immediately upon completion of this volume, I would bring up the fact that while in the case of Lenin there is a constant effort to bring the theory and political practice into organic correlation, I nevertheless got a sense that in certain questions—due in particular to the way in which the question is put—I unwittingly exaggerated the theoretical footing on which Lenin's political actions stood. At the same time, I do not think that this "exaggeration" leaves a mark on the inner proportions of the work as a whole, or the historical logic of its argument. This is also the point at which I must submit that the author grappled constantly with his own prejudices, but never gave up hope of reassembling the mosaics he "disassembled."

I may personally have been profoundly disparaged by him because of the existing differences between us. . . . But in the moment of death one has to evaluate the whole man, not just a few years of his life, nor just a few aspects of his work, and must put aside all personal grudges. Our differences should not blind us to the importance of his passing. He was such a colossal figure, only a few of whom are to be found in world history.

—KARL KAUTSKY

He often took harsh positions in opposition to us. . . . However these differences of opinion are silenced at Lenin's grave, as we join in lowering our flags, flourishing our banners in awe of the genius of his will, his cause, which revolutionized the world as a whole.

—OTTO BAUER

In him could be found Razin and Bolotnikov, even Peter the Great. Our descendents will untangle this genealogy in future monographs. . . . Years pass, new generations take the place of the old and the bitter offences, mortifying personal attacks inflicted upon millions of feeling, suffering Russian people by this man who had worn a blood-soaked halo, and risen so fatefully over all Russia will be quelled. Then everyone will once and for all come to understand that Lenin—our Lenin—is Russia's own son, a national hero in the likeness of Dmitriy Donskoy, Peter the Great, Pushkin and Tolstoy.

—NIKOLAY USTRYALOV

1
Who Was Lenin?

FAMILY

LENIN DID NOT CONCERN HIMSELF a great deal with his family tree. He had no interest in his ancestors' deeds, couldn't care less about their descent, and so he knew hardly anything about them.[1] A great majority of Lenin's revolutionary associates were of educated backgrounds, some of noble descent. For instance, G. V. Plekhanov or Chicherin, and Felix Dzerzhinsky who was born of the Polish lesser nobility. Others, such as Zinoviev and Kamenev were of middle-class backgrounds, or an expressly educated background, like Bukharin—eighteen years Lenin's junior—to mention only a few of his most famous companions from various periods. Stalin, whose father was a manual laborer, counted as a rarity. Kalinin, who had worked the lines as an industrial laborer, was an exception. The fact that there were few workers among the founders of the Russian Social Democratic Labor Party explains a great deal about the progression of Russian affairs and the well-known social specificities of social democracy within it. Revolutionaries from *raznochintsy*, or "mixed-class" intelligentsia background, were legion however. These figures often arose from lower social layers than the strata occupied by, among others, the father of Vladimir Ilyich Ulyanov, or "Lenin."

Vladimir Ilyich was born in Simbirsk, on 22 April 1870 of the Gregorian calendar used in Russia since 1917. His christening, according to the rites of the Eastern Orthodox Church, took place on 28 April. Situated on the banks of the Volga, Simbirsk was a typical Russian city with the usual curious contradictions: quiet, dusty, provincial, multinational, with over thirty thousand inhabitants. It was established in the seventeenth century to defend "Muscovy" from eastern onslaught.[2] Statistics dating to the end of the nineteenth century list 57.5 percent of the city's population as petty bourgeois, which meant that they were neither peasants nor laborers, but also did not belong to the ruling classes. Today they would be termed middle-income small business owners, though then they were artisans, merchants, and grocers.

Simbirsk could also pride itself for two high schools, a seminary for priests, a Chuvash school, a Tatar madrasah, the great Karamzin Library, Goncharov Library, and a theater.[3] Most houses in the city were made of wood. Historical accounts mainly refer to Simbirsk's wood-processing industry; however, the settlement was granted the status of capital within its governorate, and thereby became the administrative and military center.

In line with this, the city's population was divided into three segments: the nobles, the merchants, and the petit bourgeois. Seventeen percent of the total population belonged to the armed military (though the city had lost its military significance a long time back), 11 percent were peasant, 8.8 percent noble, and 3.2 percent merchants made honored citizens, or *pochotniy grazhdanin*. Eighty-eight percent of the population was of the Eastern Orthodox faith (which did not necessarily mean they were of Russian nationality), 9 percent of the population was Muslim, and the rest was composed of Mordvin, Tatar, and Chuvash people as well as a small Jewish community of four hundred.

The historical memory of the city's perseverance against the Tatars was strong, and this must have played a role in securing a local garrison for the town in the 1870s. Lenin may have known that the Eastern Orthodox peasants of Simbirsk had taken part in Stenka Razin's uprising of 1670 and Pugachev's a century later (1774). Simbirsk's elderly even remembered the house where Pugachev had been kept shackled. A small group of exiles also lived in the city or in its precincts.

The Ulyanov family moved to Simbirsk in 1869, renting a flat near the prison. Lenin was born here. As they were newly settled, and on account of her German-Lutheran upbringing, his mother, Maria Alexandrovna, did not readily find company in Simbirsk. Nor would it have been easy to fit in with the city's gossipy, pretentious petty bourgeois, and his mother most likely was preoccupied with the endless work of caring for her large family at home.[4]

The university town of Kazan lay to the north of Simbirsk. Penza to the southwest counted as a larger city, and the Volga connected Lenin's birthplace to Sizran and Saratov, and finally to the Caspian Sea into which the Russian River issues. Lenin's grandfather, Ilya Nikolayevich Ulyanov, came from the city of Astrakhan. His family tree was also typically Russian in that it was ethnically and socially mixed. At the time of Vladimir Ilyich's birth his father looked forward to a brilliant career by the standards of the time, though he was past forty and had two children. Ilya Nikolayevich was known to be an extremely hardworking, ambitious, and talented man. He first became a state school inspector at the Simbirsk Governorate, and later he was appointed director of the district's state schools. He was noted as a Simbirsk intellectual of some consequence.

Ilya Nikolayevich was born into a poor urban middle-class family.[5] Lenin's paternal grandfather, Nikolay Vasilyevich Ulyanin (later Ulyanov), was a serf in the governorate of Nizhniy Novgorod. When he was freed from serfdom to work in the city, he settled in Astrakhan, learned the tailor's trade, and was accepted into the order of middle-class citizen in 1808. Ilya had been a late arrival. At his birth, Nikolay was in his sixties and mother past forty-three. Anna Alekseyevna, Vladimir Ilych's paternal grandmother, was the daughter of a christened Kalmyk according to certain sources, but little is known about her. The fact that Ilya Nikolayevich, the son of a serf who became a tailor, attained the title of nobility counted as an extraordinary social elevation. This development undoubtedly had an effect on the life of Vladimir Ilyich Ulyanov-Lenin, since he himself became a noble as a result.[6]

Ilya Nikolayevich graduated with a silver medal from the Astrakhan high school in 1854. With the financial support of his childless elder brother, he went on to complete his education at the Faculty of Mathematics and Physics at Kazan University. He was offered a position on the faculty upon his graduation.

He began his teaching career at the Boarding School for Nobility in Penza, where he received the title of Honorary Councilor in 1860. He was appointed inspector for state schools in 1869.[7] The wife of one of his colleagues, Ivan Dmitriyevich Veretennikov, introduced him to one of her relatives, the teacher Maria Alexandrovna Blank, to whom he got engaged in 1863, and married soon thereafter. They moved to Nizhniy Novgorod on the banks of the Volga, already a city of significant historical tradition and commercial-industrial importance.

Ilya Nikolayevich was probably acquainted with the rebellious messages of the revolutionary generation of 1860, which included Herzen, Chernyshevsky, Dobrolyubov, and Pisarev, though he never lent himself to activities aimed at overturning the autocracy and would have been even less in favor of the principle of revolutionary terrorism that gained hold of his eldest son two decades later. He did, however, believe in constraining bureaucratic autocracy, the elevation of the poor, and, in general, Russian culture.

The father's *raznochinets*, or mixed-class background, was important from this point of view, for many people of these origins became opponents of autocratic rule, members of the opposition, or revolutionaries as they rose to the upper levels of society. But Lenin's father was neither revolutionary nor part of the opposition, and as a teacher he was focused on making education available to children from the lower layers of society. Lenin's sister, Anna Ilyinichna, called her father a "peaceful Narodnik" whose "favorite poet was Nekrasov," reflecting his democratic mentality.[8] Being a religious person he did not rebel against the Eastern Orthodox Church, and though he was by no means a bigoted or fanatical believer, he attended regularly. Religious festivals were observed by the family and the children were christened, though they were not forced to attend church. Lenin's father accepted Alexander II's reforms, and was sorry when the tsar became the victim of assassination in 1881.

The state schools and the so-called Sunday Schools took up a great deal of Ilya Nikolayevich's energies. In order to check on hundreds of village schools spread over vast distances he would be away from home for weeks. He often came into conflict with the prejudices, and at times opposition, of the conservative nobility in his travels. Alexander II decreed the closure of the Sunday Schools two years later, saying that some of these schools spread "harmful notions" about property rights and impiety.[9]

Ilya Nikolayevich was seriously engaged with pedagogy. He worked doggedly, and his untiring efforts were acknowledged by the authorities and highly respected by his colleagues.[10] In spite of his frequent absences he remained in the thoughts of his children as a loving father. He embodied authority in the family, a circumstance related to the great changes the lives of his children underwent after his death. In brief, they all came to be revolutionaries.

The eldest daughter, Anna, was born in 1864; followed by Alexander Ilyich, known as Sasha; then Vladimir Ilyich, called Volodya; then Olga, who passed away early; and Nikolay, born 1873, who lived only a few months; in 1874 came the younger brother Dmitriy, who secured a diploma in medicine; and finally Maria in 1878. The siblings grew up in harmony, in a home that was comfortable (a cleaning lady and a cook were the family help and Volodya also had a governess) and spacious. The older children lived in their own rooms and the younger ones shared a room. A sense of solidarity within the family came naturally, but thanks to their upbringing this was extended to life beyond the family as well, and the children turned out to be helpful young adults who were sensitive to others' difficulties. Ilya Nikolayevich took frequent walks in the forest with his children, where—in Anna's description—"he often sang banned student songs for his children."[11]

Valuable paintings did not adorn the walls of their house, but there was a piano and a large library of books. Anna Ilyinichna explained this peculiar simplicity as a continuation of *raznochinets* cultural traditions.[12] This background was the source of a dedication to learning and social improvement, which came from both sides of Lenin's family. All of the children went to institutions of higher education.

The children's mother played an exceptional role in all their achievements. By the values of the age, Maria Alexandrovna, née Blank, came from a "better family" than her husband. She was born the fifth child of a doctor, A. D. Blank, in

1835. She lost her mother at a young age, and traveled around the country with her father, as he had made a name in the medical use of baths and thermal water therapy (balneology), working as a pioneer of his field in the governorates of Smolensk, Perm, and Kazan.

The question of grandfather Blank's ancestry has been an issue of fierce argument in historical circles, especially after the breakup of the Soviet Union. His possible Jewish extraction would mean that Lenin was one-quarter Jewish, which within the framework of current attitudes would explain—in the view of present-day anti-Semitic trends—"a great deal." The notion takes us back to the well-known Black Hundreds tradition. Among historians the issue goes back a long way. Shub and Volskiy (Valentinov) locked horns over the issue decades earlier, and the second denied the Jewish descent of Lenin's grandfather.[13]

The origins of the Blank family were the subject of serious study by Lenin's two sisters, and later by M. S. Shaginyan, A. G. Petrov, M. G. Shteyn, V. V. Tsaplin, and others. Anna Ilyinichna Ulyanova, for whom research into the origins of her family was a profession, documented clear evidence of the Jewish descent of her maternal grandfather in 1932. On 28 December 1932, Stalin heard her report on her discovery and ordered absolute silence on the matter, though Anna could not understand why "the communists need to hide this fact." She turned to Stalin once more in 1934 for permission to publish the documents, but Stalin remained inflexible.[14] Lenin's sisters and wife thought that admitting the truth would be an argument against anti-Semitism, but Stalin was of the opposite opinion and feared an exacerbation of the negative tendencies in anti-Semitism.[15] The study of Lenin's family tree remained dangerous ground in the Soviet Union for decades.[16]

Recent historiography has established that Lenin's great-grandfather, Moshe Itskovich Blank, moved to Zhitomir from Lübeck after coming into conflict with the local Jewish community at the beginning of the nineteenth century. A letter he wrote to Nicholas I shows that Moshe was not only christened but switched to the Eastern Orthodox Church and became an anti-Semite. His recommendations to the tsar that Jewish religious practices and codes of dress be restricted and that a prayer for the tsar and his family be prescribed was heard in 1854, when the restrictions and modification to the prayers were introduced. (There were, of course, more aggressive Jewish anti-Semites in Russia—V. A. Gringmut, a founder and leader of the Black Hundreds Union of the Russian People in Moscow, the most widely known among them.) Lenin's great-grandfather converted his son Israel to the Eastern Orthodox faith, christening him Alexander. This grandfather of Lenin died on his Kokuskino estate the same year Lenin was born.[17]

Aleksandr Dimitriyevich married the daughter of Baltic-German (Groschopf) and Swedish-Lutheran (Estedt) parents, Anna Yohannovna Groschopf, and their daughter Maria Alexandrovna was Lenin's mother. Maria's godparents were high-ranking personalities from court circles. After their mother's death, her sister Ekaterina Nikolayevna von Essen took Maria into her patronage. Her father acquired hereditary nobility, as did her husband, and thus she herself became noble, though the title appeared only on the paternal line.

Maria's father bought the famous Kokuskino estate in 1848, approximately 500 hectares with 39 serfs and a watermill, where his grandchildren later spent many summers. Maria's wedding on 25 August 1863 was also hosted on the estate.[18] The doctor from Lübeck soon made himself at home in the region, and the peasants in the neighborhood often turned to him with their ailments, whether great or small.

Vladimir Ilyich was afforded all that a family in the intelligentsia in contemporary Russia could provide a child. Though looking after many children, his mother was always especially attentive to "Volodya" as she called him, whose abilities revealed themselves at an early age. He could read and write at the age of five. He also had much to learn from his mother, who spoke numerous languages—especially German—and would often play the piano with Volodya and his siblings. This may well have fueled Vladimir Ilyich's passion for serious music, the exceptionally high respect and zeal he had for books, and his receptivity to culture in general.

In addition to a copious list of pastimes as a child, Volodya Ulyanov liked to play war games, and cut the toy soldiers out of cardboard paper himself. He took the side of Union forces led by Lincoln against the hated slave owners of the South. *Uncle Tom's Cabin* was a favorite book, which he read innumerable times. With his mother, he created a handwritten family newspaper and Maria Alexandrovna even made the clothes for the children herself. The boy also liked to sing, especially the poems of Heine set to music, and Valentine's aria from Gounod's *Faust,* as remembered by his younger brother, Dmitry.[19] He learned to play chess from his father at a young age, and countless reminiscences relate how often he sat down for a game of chess until the end of his life.[20] The children's recreation also included long vacations. The Ulyanov family spent some time in the summer of 1877 on holiday with paternal relations in Stavropol, and other summers were usually spent on the Kokuskino estate or with their relatives in Astrakhan.

On 1 (14) February 1887 at the request of I. N. Ulyanov, the consistory issued the birth certificate of his son, Volodya.[21] It may have been needed for his enrollment in school. The Church did not leave a marked impression on Volodya's personality in spite of mandatory classes in theology. Perhaps one reason for this is that a significant segment of the Eastern Orthodox Church's priests in the lower orders were not literate, which represented a severe limitation on cultural emergence.

In spite of all the differences in the intellectual and cultural background of the paternal and maternal sides of his family, a kind of harmony came into being in terms of both intellect and worldview. Looking at Lenin's childhood, nothing out of the ordinary can be found. He had a predilection for taking toys apart, and "examined" dolls also from the inside, a circumstance that later prompted approaches using a method of banal psychology to project into the personality of Vladimir Ilyich, even at that "tender age," some sort of "pitiless," "tyrannical" trait.

The literature on the subject of Vladimir Ilyich's childhood emphasizes his gradually developing sense of order and exemplary school career, characteristics in which his elder brother Alexander may have played a role. Both parents were hardworking and orderly, with a hint of pedantry about the mother. Oblomov, the protagonist of the novel of the same name by Goncharov—son of Simbirsk, and a much loved author in the family—is the symbol of a different Russian mentality: laziness, indifference, weakness of will, and lack of belief in the future. Later on, Lenin would frequently mention Oblomov as a symbol of the "Russian nobility."

While according to some interpreters, Vladimir Ilyich had a "phobic" hatred for the Russian nobility and educated middle classes—perhaps based on his father's accounts of his contempt for the privileged even as a child—this so-called phobia presumably fed on Russian literature itself. He was deeply influenced by Saltykov-Shchedrin, Gogol, Turgenev, Chekhov, and Tolstoy. Indeed, in this literature, "educated Russian society" was motionless, indecisive, idle, egotistic, and irresponsible.[22] With these typical traits the nobility mostly defined where the limits of the autocracy's ability for renewal could be drawn. A Russia of "Oblomovs" and "Uncle Vanyas," in addition to the Black Hundreds' Purishkeviches, did not show any positive alternatives within this society. Turbulence among intellectuals and the appearance of Turgenev-style "nihilists" who rejected everything only signaled disorganized and sporadic dissatisfaction, however, and gave the impression of a bad alternative to "Oblomovism" and "idleness." Nihilism never attracted Lenin.

The emancipation of the serfs in 1861 brought some change to the backwardness of provincial social life, but few areas in the last third of the nineteenth century exposed as many social problems as rural and small-town education. While the experiences gathered by Lenin's father obscured the alternative of adapting to the power structure of an autocratic regime, the northern European cultural roots of the mother—with a grandfather from Lübeck and a grandmother of Swedish-German-Baltic descent—made change even more remote.

Many of Lenin's memoirists recount the feeling of warmth in the family, their sense of "solidarity." The siblings helped each other devotedly, greatly encouraged by their mother, especially when their father was away.[23] Anna Ilyinichna described their mother as a strong-willed, energetic, and active woman with a strong preference for justice. These characteristics were inherited most of all by her eldest son, Alexander.[24] His mother was devoted to Volodya, and helped him in exile and emigration with enduring faith till her last days.

As a teacher, Maria Alexandrovna was effectively the home tutor for each of her children. She did not teach professionally on account of the large family. From the age of five, a governess also came to instruct Volodya, and for four years, until 1879, she practiced German and French with the children, in line with their mother's instructions.

From 8 to 14 August 1879, Volodya took his entrance exams for Simbirsk's "classical" elementary school. The academic council of the school exempted the nine-year-old Volodya from all fees in view of his father's ten years of employment with the Ministry of Public Education. He stood out among his classmates with his exceptional talent and diligence.[25] He received excellent marks in every subject in second grade. According to all accounts, he read a great deal. He was a considerate child, but had only a few friends he met with after school. The principal of the school was Fyodor Kerensky, father of Alexander Kerensky, who would be the prime minister of the Provisional Government thirty-eight years later, in 1917.

Of his siblings, Alexander, whom he helped with his chemistry experiments,[26] had the greatest influence on him.[27] They often played in the garden, engaged in a game of chess, or enjoyed breaks on the banks of the Volga. Louis Fischer notes that although Volodya imitated his brother in many ways, as younger brothers often do, there were significant differences in matters of principle, behavior, and looks. The siblings paired off according to year of birth: Anna played most with Sasha, Volodya with Olga, and Dmitri with Maria, as mentioned by Anna Ilyinichna herself.[28]

EDUCATION

Vladimir Ilyich did not develop his political views during his years at school, nor could he have heard much concrete detail about political developments in the country from his parents. He found Thiers's multivolume work on the French Revolution—incorporating the bourgeois concept of class struggle—on his mother's shelf. It is frequently mentioned in the literature that the execution of his older brother Alexander had a significant effect on shaping the political perceptions, interests, and views of the seventeen-year-old Volodya. His sister Anna was also imprisoned, though not as a member of an underground organization. The voluntary martyrdom of their brother imposed a certain moral responsibility upon the siblings, along with their mother. The possibility of rebellious youth arriving at a compromise with the absolutist system vanished following the execution. Appeasement was ruled out by the traditional Russian critical approach to the system, Narodnik and pro-Western intellectual trends, and the influence of the European social democratic and revolutionary movements.

The critical point of departure and first stage of Lenin's political-intellectual progress was not Marx. Contrary to legend, he only became acquainted with the first chapters of Marx's *Capital* at the age of nineteen. His desire to study the third volume of *Capital* as late as 1894 is documented,[29] and his study of Marx became a lifelong pursuit. When discussing Lenin's relationship to Marx, well after Lenin's death, Krupskaya mentions that "at the most difficult moments, at the turning points of the revolution, he would take up the rereading of Marx." According to Krupskaya, this turn of phrase was "characteristic of him. He always 'consulted' Marx."[30]

A literary encounter held responsible for Lenin becoming a revolutionary, elaborated upon numerous times in the course of his life, was the novel *What Is to Be Done?* by Nikolay Chernyshevsky in which the protagonist, Rakhmetov, is a revolutionary.[31] During one summer he read the book five times. This would most likely have been the summer that followed his expulsion from Kazan University, when by his own admission he gorged himself on books.

Other sources indicate Vladimir Ilyich read Chernyshevsky's book by the age of fourteen. According to the famous memoirs of Volskiy, the defected Bolshevik of 1904, he spoke about it during his exile in Kokushkino:

> My favorite author was Chernyshevsky. I read everything that was published in the *Sovremenik* to the last line, and not only once. Thanks to Chernyshevsky I made my first acquaintance with philosophical materialism. He was the first to reveal Hegel's role in the development of philosophical thought, and the concept of dialectical method, which made it much easier to acquire Marx's dialectics, came from him.[32]

Throughout his life, Lenin declared that next to Marx, Engels, and Plekhanov, Chernyshevsky had the greatest influence upon his thinking. He even sent him a letter in 1888, and was terribly disappointed he did not receive an answer.[33] Some writers argue the "Rakhmetov model" was decisive in encouraging the romantically inclined Volodya to become a revolutionary.

Indeed, Lenin's physical and spiritual-moral stamina are proof of the influence of the Rakhmetovian model. It is important to note that in contrast to Rakhmetov,

Lenin was not an ascetic. He enjoyed exercise in the conscious development of his physical strength and was also a sportsman, with expertise in skating, hill climbing, and skiing. He was also a good swimmer, bicyclist, gymnast, marksman, and hunter. He experimented for a while with weightlifting.[34] At that time in Europe, physical training was at its zenith in Germany in particular, and attention was given to displays of strength by the new nation-states. Lenin's dedication to sport was an expression of his affinity with European modernity as opposed to the "lethargy" that characterized his own country.

While still in school, Lenin read Pushkin, Lermontov, Gogol, Turgenev, Nekrasov, Saltykov-Shchedrin, Tolstoy, Belinsky, Herzen, Dobrolyubov, and Pisarev, and extensively in foreign classical literature.[35] He often returned to these books, even composing literary and political observations in relation to them in later periods of his life.[36] This literary tradition played a serious role in young Lenin's becoming a professed revolutionary, since he could recognize the Russia he knew and his own experiences in these readings. His first actual revolt against autocracy came at the age of fifteen or sixteen when he broke with the Eastern Orthodox Church, which was the strongest intellectual and organizational foundation of absolutism.

Even as he received evaluations such as "abundantly talented, diligent and precise" in his school report of May 1885 (at high school he always had the highest grades, even in divinity), and perhaps under the influence of his brother, Volodya was reexamining the value of autocracy and unconditional subordination to the "force of authority" that permeated everyday life in Russia. This authority demanded reverence, a slavish spirit, and corporal punishment, often applied to whole villages. It was the standard legal procedure until 1905.

Lenin's open break with religion fits into this context. When his father complained to one of his guests that his children avoided attending church a guest's comment was that boys like this "should be beaten, and beaten again!" (*Sech, sech nado!*) After the guest's outburst Volodya ran out to the courtyard, tore the cross from his neck and threw it to the ground. Thirteen years later, Vladimir Ilyich related this story to Krupskaya while in Siberian exile.[37] It was not so much an expression of rebellious feeling toward his father as a child's instinctive spirited resistance to a conservative order.

In January 1886, Lenin's father unexpectedly died of a cerebral hemorrhage. His death put the family in complete disarray. Alexander was already at university in St. Petersburg, drawing the attention of his teachers by his talent for biology. Yet what turned out to be more important than science for him was that the student body in the capital was already resolutely looking for an alternative to autocracy. Led by the brave disposition of the romantic revolutionary, Alexander did not shrink from putting his own life at risk for the cause. In 1887, as a member of a terrorist group, he became a participant in an attempt on the life of Alexander III. The assassination attempt was a failure and the young man was arrested on 1 (13) March. Alexander remained true to his principles even to the end, and went to the gallows without asking for a pardon in spite of his mother's pleadings.[38] He was executed on 8 May.

In May and June 1886, Vladimir Ilyich took his final high school examinations with excellent results, and was awarded the gold medal as the best student.[39] The family was deeply wounded by Sasha's execution[40] and its accompanying social rejection. The liberal "educated society" of Simbirsk turned its back on the whole family, not even commiserating with them in their grief, which left its mark upon Vladimir Ilyich. "They crossed to the other side of the street," as Lenin would later write.[41]

Vladimir Ilyich left his birthplace when he was admitted to the Faculty of Law at Kazan University on 13 August. Fyodor Kerensky wrote an appreciative characterization of the student, who had gained some fame after the execution of his elder brother, calling Vladimir an "exceptionally talented, diligent and precise student" who "has not once expressed himself or acted in a way as to shake the high opinion of him held by his teachers and superiors either at the high school or outside of it."[42] He had high standing among his classmates as well.

Hardly had he begun his studies at university when he became among the first to join the burgeoning student campaign against the "University Act," which blocked the education of children coming from the lower social classes. In September he joined the Simbirsk-Samara *zemlyachestvo*, a civil organization he could not in theory have been a member of because he had signed an oath upon enrollment at the university stating he would not join any society.

Any sort of ethical commitment to autocratic rule was at this stage a matter of the past for Vladimir Ulyanov.[43] The formation of a new revolutionary ethic was now the issue, for which he would find an organizational framework in local revolutionary circles, illegal Marxist or Narodovolets activist groups. Vladimir Ilyich was arrested on 4 December for his participation in a day of demonstrations. He was immediately barred from university, and three days later the authorities assigned Kokuskino as his place of residence.[44]

He read throughout the period he was under strict police surveillance.[45] Over the course of nearly a year, the old authors were followed by new ones: Dobrolyubov, Uspensky, Narodnik economists such as V. P. Vorontsov, Mihaylovsky, (Nikolai-on) N. F. Danielson, who translated *Capital* into Russian in 1872. He also read the famous Russian and international journals, such as *Sovremennik*, *Russkoya slovo*, *Kolokol*, *Otechestvenniye zapiski*, *Vestnik Evropi*, and *Russkoye bogatstvo*.

But Lenin's first meetings with representatives of revolutionary organizations were equally if not more important. This is about the time Lenin joined a Marxist circle whose founder, N. Y. Fedoseyev, was arrested in July 1889. Lenin referred to him as the first "Marxist of Samara" with great respect many years after his death.[46] An intellectual adventure of critical importance to his future began in 1888–89, as he meticulously worked his way through the first volume of *Capital*, and then undertook a study of Darwin's theory of evolution, while also discovering British economics. In spring the family traveled to the recently acquired Alakayevka estate, which Maria Alexandrovna bought in January-February of 1889 with money she received from the sale of the house in Simbirsk.[47] It was here Lenin became acquainted with A. P. Sklyarenko, one of the first organizers of the revolutionary circles of Samara. He met the Narodovolets M. V. Subanayev at Sklyarenko's house. He learned a great deal from the Narodovolets—in general and from their political history—about techniques for organizing revolution, the "conspiratorial arts," and maintaining contact between prison and the world outside, which later became very useful.

At the end of 1889, he continued his analysis of *Capital* at Sklyarenko's house. He took a trip to the Volga region with the Sklyarenko group in May 1890 and visited the house of A. P. Nechayev in Yekaterinovka. He had a conversation with Nechayev's father about the stratification of the *obshchina*, the beginnings of agricultural capitalism, and its consequences.[48] Volodya would have heard a great deal about S. G. Nechayev, the inexhaustibly energetic revolutionary who even won over his prison guards. Volodya was ten when Nechayev, the leading figure of the Narodnaya Rasprava (People's Reprisal) movement, died in the Peter and Paul Fortress. He came to represent a whole generation of late nineteenth-century revolutionaries, even though Dostoevsky's novel *Devils* took a toll on Nechayev's reputation as being quite off the mark concerning the realistic possibilities of "gratifying the people."

To mention Nechayev, a figure of the revolutionary conspiracy and a brave member of the resistance, as one of the "original sources" for Lenin would be going too far, for at this point Lenin was not a "conspiratorial" revolutionary in the Nechayev or Tkachov vein. It may well be that both current Russian monarchist conservatism and liberalism attempt to reduce him—on the grounds of Dostoevsky's ethically sound critique of nihilism—to a Nechayevist-Blanquist type.[49] This formula has a historiographic tradition reaching from the work of Berdyaev to N. Valentinov, from D. Shub to Tibor Szamuely and L. Schapiro. These form the conceptualization of the Leninian revolutionary who is not derived from the "incorruptible" revolutionary, Chernyshevsky's Rakhmetov, but Dostoevsky's unbridled and amoral Raskolnikov or his distorted Nechayev appearing as the devil.[50]

Lenin's intellectual-political-moral outlook was shaped by numerous movements and traditions. Apart from Chernyshevsky and Marx, there were the Russian Narodovolets and the intellectual legacy of the so-called revolutionary democrats, the French Enlightenment, French Revolutionary Jacobinism, Russian Jacobinism, as well as Western European socialist-social democratic economic and political thought. Lenin found his way to a new social democratic worker's movement through a critical appraisal of Russian nihilism and the rejection of terrorism as a form of resistance. He was no longer a rebel, but a revolutionary. Furthermore, he became the original model for a revolutionary; that is, in purely historiographical terms he was singular. His early interest in the sciences, aptitude for theoretical thought, and his instinctive conjoining of theory and revolutionary practice made him the perfect revolutionary. Deliberation and rational thought distinguished him even at nineteen, for he never gave in to any manner of sentimental, exhibitionist moralization, or sermonizing Christian humility.

The older Marxist P. N. Skortsov had some influence upon Lenin's thought at this time. In December 1892, a circle of illegal Marxists was formed under his leadership, with the participation of M. I. Semyonov, M. I. Lebedeva, and others. In Alakayevka he also met Sklyarenko and I. H. Lalayants,[51] who schooled him in the basics of theoretical and organizational activity.

The first action of a political nature Lenin participated in was the "civil initiative" to alleviate the famine of 1891. It provides a perspective on later falsifications of incidents in Lenin's life. V. Vodovozov[52] presented the case (after Lenin's death) that the ethical grounds for action were completely alien to him in the famine of 1891, and some historians have taken this account for granted.[53] This account is used to prove Lenin's "merciless inhumanity," taking the view that the twenty-one-year-old's aim was to starve the peasants.

From a current perspective, it may seem that a young doctrinaire revolutionary would indeed have taken a stance of noncooperation with the "educated layers of society" in the "official elimination" of hunger at the time of the famine, choosing to participate in an independent initiative instead. Recalling the conversations of the young people in Samara, Vodovozov writes that for Vladimir Ulyanov "these discussions about aid for the hungry were psychologically speaking no more than expressions of pathetic sentimentalism, which was much too typical of our educated people." According to Vodovozov, Lenin was only interested in the people from the point of view of how useful they were in overthrowing the autocratic system.[54] Vodovozov came into conflict with Vladimir Ilyich in Samara, and that argument apparently left a deep mark upon his spirits.[55]

Vladimir Ilyich found any sort of cooperation with the authorities unacceptable. As such, he did not think of actions aimed at relieving the conscience to be either examinations of the problem, or even less, solutions to the problem, but the opposite, its concealment. Naturally he never questioned the significance of the campaign, as he himself emphasized in a later paper, "A Draft of Our Party Program":

> Precisely today, when the starvation of millions of peasants is becoming chronic, when the government that wastes millions on gifts to the landlords and capitalists, and on an adventurist foreign policy, is haggling for pennies off the grants to the starving. . . . . The Social-Democrats cannot remain indifferent spectators of peasant hunger and the death of peasants from starvation; there have never been two opinions among Russian Social-Democrats as to the need for the most extensive help to the starving.[56]

While the liberals danced and had balls and concerts for the "benefit of the hungry" in 1891, writes V. Loginov, the social democrats—among them Lenin—were engaged in unmasking precisely this waste of money, and participated in independent protests.[57]

During this time, Lenin as well as his mother submitted petitions to continue his university education. On 9 (21) May 1888—when his mother's petition for allowing her son to resume his studies at Kazan University was refused by the Minister of Education[58]—she turned to other universities. Two years later she finally succeeded. Her son could take examinations at St. Petersburg University. At the end of August 1890 Lenin arrived in St. Petersburg—for the first time in his life—to take the examinations at the Faculty of Law. He lived in the city from the end of March 1891 till 9 May preparing for his exams, which he passed with complete success in April.[59] At this point another tragedy struck the family: Olga died of typhus in St. Petersburg. After his younger sister's funeral, Lenin traveled to Alakayevka with his mother, from where he often visited Samara. He spent the summer reading, studying intensely, and after the autumn exams, on 15 November he received a First-Class Diploma from the Faculty of Law.[60]

Lenin worked as a lawyer for a brief time, but did not give up his critical study of the economic theory and history of Narodism. In 1892 he was granted permission to work independently, under continued police surveillance, at the court in Samara.[61] He had a legal practice from January 1892 to August 1893.[62] His cases, twenty-four in all, were mostly successful and he managed to lessen the sentence in every trial.

A case in which he defended a tailor on trial for blasphemy gained fame after the Revolution of 1917. Zinoviev later jocularly recounted the types of defensive tactics he employed. On one occasion he was not willing to defend a rich merchant even for a higher fee, though quite a few peasants accused of theft appeared among his defendants. At any rate, the trials enriched his knowledge of the real world. He defended merchants, and even a husband who tortured his wife, though in that case finally withdrew from calling for a lower sentence. He based his defenses on grounds of principle. He would not have become a good lawyer as his guiding principles were social, guided by ethical laws, and formed all of his decisions from the perspective of the economically downtrodden.

The matter of his family's good economic situation was a factor in his intellectual development, and his mother's sound money management meant that each sibling had some support.[63] After her husband's death, his mother received a pension of 1,200 golden rubles, and money had been set aside from the Kokuskino estate.[64] The Simbirsk city bank held another 2,000 rubles left by Ilya Nikolayevich. The Kokuskino estate was rented out. Not counting this income, the original value of the land was 3,000 rubles. In addition, Maria Alexandrovna had formerly inherited some money upon the deaths of her father and the elder brother of her husband. Vladimir Ilyich did not live off his family after giving up his legal practice, as conjectured by some modern commentators, but set himself up as an independent intellectual. His first publications did not bring significant sums, but the second printing of his *The Development of Capitalism in Russia* in 1908, which he completed in exile, made him 2,000 rubles in royalties.[65] This does not mean that he could have lived comfortably without his mother's constant support. Vladimir Ilyich never lived in great style; indeed he was very frugal, having become accustomed to a spare existence in his youthful years, as documented by numerous letters he wrote to his mother. This excerpt from his correspondence is an illustrative example:

> I am now, for the first time in St. Petersburg, keeping a cash-book to see how much I actually spend. It turned out that for the month 28 August to 27 September I spent altogether 54 rubles 30 kopeks, . . . It is true that part of this 54 rubles was spent on things that do not have to be bought every month (galoshes, clothes, books, an abacus, etc.), but even discounting that (16 rubles), the expenditure is still excessive. . . . Obviously I have not been living carefully.[66]

In the summer of 1893 Lenin was working on a draft of his *What the "Friends of the People" Are and How They Fight the Social-Democrats* while attending illegal debate circles to attack Narodism, as well as lecturing on the works of Marx. In the beginning of 1894, he read Chekhov's short story *Ward 6*, published only in November 1893, and the work had an extraordinary impact upon him. He told

Anna Ilyinichna: "When I read the short story last night I simply became sick, I could not remain in my room, I got up and went out. I felt like I was also shut into ward no. six."[67]

A move from Samara to St. Petersburg—via Nizhniy Novgorod and Moscow—in August 1893 was a turning point. In St. Petersburg he spent a good part of his time in libraries, but soon found serious company among the students of the Institute of Technology. The members of the Marxist circle he joined included revolutionaries that would be tied to his whole career as a revolutionary and politician: L. B. Krasin and S. I. Radchenko, G. M. Krzhizhanovsky, V. V. Starkov, P. K. Zaporozhets, A. A. Vaneyev, M. A. Silvin. Their first impression of him, and a surprise for these friends-to-be, was how extraordinarily well prepared he was. His brilliant knowledge of economic literature, including the works of Marx and Engels, his fascinating readiness to debate, warm spirit, and firm conviction and passion all immediately secured him high esteem.[68]

Lenin visited family in Moscow in January of 1894, where, as had become his custom, he looked up the illegal Marxist groups. Remarkably, even the Okhrana (secret police) agent spoke highly of his debate with Vorontsov in the report he wrote for his superiors. This was the young man's first public appearance in Moscow. Upon his return to St. Petersburg, workers established contact with him: it was no longer only him looking up others; they were finding him.[69] He was quick to become known and respected in other groups that had revolutionary zeal, such as Klasson's "salon," a Marxist debate forum. This was where, toward the end of 1894, he first met Nadezhda Krupskaya. She was to become his wife in Siberian exile.[70] Visiting Krupskaya, who lived with her mother on the Nevsky Prospekt, was among his weekend pastimes. He also met the so-called legal Marxists Petr Struve and M. I. Tugan-Baranovsky at Klasson's salon. After a few years of agreement with these well-known intellectuals a lifelong political struggle set in. It literally became a battle of life and death with Struve, who ended up in the counter-revolutionary camp serving under Denikin and Wrangel.

The historical debate between Lenin and Struve[71] was loaded with psychological associations,[72] but in the 1890s these seemed as if they could be kept under control. The fact that Lenin and Struve were once friends was generally (but not always!) denied or passed over in early Soviet historiography.[73] Lenin himself later related their first meeting when, in 1907, he republished his critique of Struve's book. This was originally a lecture titled *The Reflection of Marxism in Bourgeois Literature*, based on discussions held in Klasson's flat by the Neva. The group included those social democrats—especially the groups of Lenin and Martov—who would later form the organization League of Struggle for the Emancipation of the Working Class.[74]

The many evenings Struve and Ulyanov spent together in discussion of current economic and political issues in the company of friends (and girlfriends) in 1895–96 indicate a budding friendship. Struve's later statement about Lenin's early "enmity" is therefore unfounded.[75] Lenin appreciated Struve's widely acknowledged achievements, such as the party program he drafted for the First Congress of the Russian Social Democratic Labor Party (RSDLP) held in Minsk in 1898. In this period Petr Berngardovich (Struve) sent innumerable books to Vladimir Ilyich in exile in Shushenskoye and oversaw the publication of a number of his works.[76] Until Lenin appeared on the scene, Struve was the highest figure of authority among the Marxists of St. Petersburg, but he soon fell from that pedestal. Since Vladimir Ilyich was the younger brother of the Ulyanov who had been executed for an assassination attempt upon the tsar, he had the kind of recognition among young rebels that Struve could never achieve. Additionally, Lenin spoke more clearly and lectured better than Struve, who even as he matured remained a dull lecturer and even worse speaker. Nor could Struve match Lenin in organizational matters. In a nutshell, after his arrival on the scene, the students' idolatry of Struve was transferred to Lenin.[77]

Along with the usual study of the works of Marx and Engels, Lenin worked on the second edition of his *Who the Friends of the People Are* in the summer of 1894. The work gained him national renown, especially in revolutionary youth circles. He followed student actions closely, asking Maria Ilyinichna, in a letter dated 13 December 1894, about the famous affair with Klyuchevsky, when he was whistled off the podium at the university. This incident ended with the arrest of fifty students, some of whom were banished from Moscow.[78]

Two important events took place in 1895. The first was a trip Lenin made to Switzerland, Germany, and France, leaving Russia on May 1 and returning on 9 September. In his extended travels he gained the acquaintance of Russian social democrats living in exile, among them foremost were G. V. Plekhanov and the Group for the Liberation of Labor. While in Berlin, he looked up Wilhelm Liebknecht, one of the leaders of German social democrats, with Plekhanov's recommendation letter: "I recommend to you one of our best Russian friends...." He also spent time in the library: "I am so far pleased with Berlin," he wrote to his mother. "I am still working in the Königliche Bibliothek and in the evenings I wander about studying the Berlin mores and listening to German speech."[79]

The Russian secret police kept a watch on Vladimir Ilyich, considered a number-one target among the social democrats. But when he brought illegal literature through the border in a double-bottomed suitcase, the report from the border-control secret police gave an account that nothing was found upon the closest possible examination of the baggage.[80] Not only did this trip widen the scope of the revolutionary Lenin's horizons, it also enabled him to acquire new organizational and literary contacts throughout Europe that he would later so desperately need.

Lenin was arrested on the night of 8 December 1895 because of his work with the League of Struggle for the Emancipation of the Working Class. Along with his political comrades, he was taken to the House of Preliminary Arrest. With this, the years of Lenin's imprisonment and exile had begun. He was given fourteen months of solitary confinement to be followed by three years of Siberian exile.[81]

THE PERSONALITY OF LENIN AS A YOUNG MAN IN EXILE AND AS AN ÉMIGRÉ

When Vladimir Ilyich was imprisoned, he was already a social democrat and Marxist. At the time, these terms were interchangeable, at least in Germany and Russia. He considered these positions to be a natural part of the path leading to revolution. Correspondence is a way of life in prison, exile, or emigration, and thus his letters to his family serve as primary sources for information about this period.

In her foreword to the 1931 publication of Vladimir Ilyich's letters, his sister Anna Ilyinichna Ulyanova-Yelizarova emphasized how little attention her brother gave his personal problems, being much more absorbed in the "common cause" he served.[82] Through necessity, Ulyanov-Lenin became a great letter writer. His letters are mainly occupied with his theoretical and scientific work,[83] and his family members did everything in their power for Vladimir Ilyich to have access to all the literature prison regulations would allow. His letters are especially valuable in terms of understanding and mapping Lenin's personality.[84] His younger sister, Maria Ilyinichna, emphasized how important family was in Lenin's life.[85] Even his fabled punctuality, remarked upon in virtually every biography, was a family trait:

> One of Vladimir Ilyich's familiar traits was great precision and punctuality, as well as strict frugality in general, and especially where personal expenses were concerned. He probably inherited these traits from his mother, to whom he was similar in many aspects of his character. Our mother was German on the maternal line and all of these attributes were amply present in her.[86]

Molotov's opinion that few German traits could be found in Lenin, though he was "precise, devilishly organized," reflects a later experience. This tradition of orderliness, stemming from the maternal side, was deeply rooted in Lenin's personality. He hated half-done jobs.[87] Perhaps it was this practical trait, this "orderliness," that played a major role in his adapting to the most difficult circumstances and remaining productive. It was as if he raced against time throughout his life.

In prison, Lenin adapted to the conditions of solitary confinement, isolation, and the cold with incredible speed. The young man of twenty-five consciously prepared himself both intellectually and physically for the circumstances of prison and exile. He conceived of prison as a place that provides relatively favorable conditions for academic and theoretical work. With regard to prison conditions, he gave assurances to his sister Anna—who had come to know the conditions prevalent in the St. Petersburg house of detention at the time of her brother Alexander's trial. In a letter dated 12 January 1896, he stated, "I now have everything I need, and even more than I need." Continuing from this, he wrote:

> My health is quite satisfactory. I even get my mineral water here—it is brought to me from the chemists' on the day I order it. I sleep about nine hours a day and see various chapters of my future book in my sleep.[88]

There was something grandiose in this self-confidence, which was combined with an ability to see the humorous side of his position. This humor never let him down. A knowledgeable writer in the field of Lenin studies is right to point out that a person without a sense of humor will not say, when leaving prison, that his departure is premature, as he has not collected enough material from the metropolitan municipal library for his work on economic history and he still has more to read.[89] The literature dealing with Lenin's personality describes his fundamental nature as "high-spirited"; he was very much a lover of life. He dealt with everything that was important to him with complete devotion. He was a passionate politician but also a sportsman who never gave up. N. Volskiy (Valentinov) writes that Lenin did not like dispassionate, morose individuals, but favored keen, good-spirited revolutionaries. Socially he was usually at the center of attention, because he always spoke with great gusto and had a loud laugh, like a child. He preferred to converse with people who had already won recognition in the eyes of other social circles. It is interesting that in spite of his passionate convictions, he took defeat, when he had to, with generous composure, though naturally preferring not to lose. He had an aptitude for self-reflection because he was not vain; it was simply not one of his habits to speak about himself.[90]

Angelica Balabanoff's writing stands out among objective character portraits of Lenin. Before she broke with Bolshevism she worked with Lenin in various periods, from the war years in Zimmerwald to the establishment of the Comintern (she became its secretary). Regarding Lenin the man, she writes: "Primarily, Lenin was free of all egocentrism, he was absolutely indifferent to what was said or written about him." In contrasting him with Trotsky, she emphasized that "Lenin explained and taught; Trotsky decreed and ordered. This difference revealed itself more clearly after their rise to power. Lenin remained the same, though millions of men—followers and opponents—were in his power."[91] Trotsky "always watched himself in the mirror of history," whereas such self-advertisement was alien to Lenin. Lenin—unlike Lev Davidovich incidentally—not only understood humor but was also able to laugh at himself.[92]

His confidence and self-assurance came partly from being always the best, or among the best, in his academic studies. His incredible talent for analysis and synthesis, and his excellent memory, predestined him to become an outstanding figure in a branch of the sciences or politics. Vladimir Ilyich was not the least bit inhibited and was able to relate to everyone in an unaffectedly natural way without bias. Nothing was more foreign to his nature than hypocrisy, posturing, and false modesty. Whether he was speaking to a minister or a laborer it was all the same to him. Only the subject of the conversation, and its political or theoretical significance, counted. In order to establish strong personal relations he did know how to captivate people, as evidenced in numerous reminiscences. However, his belief in himself was coupled with modesty.[93]

An interesting alloy of tough and gentle traits came to the fore in the younger Ulyanov's personality, undoubtedly with a predominance of the former. It was a typical characteristic, virtually from childhood, to get to grips with an argument even with those closest to him. However, in times of need he would rush to their assistance. These characteristics were especially apparent during his periods in exile and emigration, between 1895 and 1917.

As pointed out by his sister, a manifest attribute of Lenin's character "is the permanence of his attachment, his enduring, unchanging attitude toward the same people in the course of many long years . . . the permanence of his affection; the steadiness and stability of his character are clearly delineated in his letters."[94] He did not have many friends with whom he used the informal manner of speech exhibited in letters to his family, however Martov, Krzhizhanovsky, and Lepeshinsky were such friends. His circle included a few women, including Inessa Armand, who he grew rather close to. Later, Kamenev and Zinoviev became his closest political students.

His relationship with Martov was a "special one." Lenin was attracted by the colorful vibrant personality and intelligence of Yuli Tsederbaum (Martov), whom he frequently mentions in his letters of the exile years.[95] It is widely known that he inquired about Martov's health in a warm and concerned manner as late as 1922, though by then they had been unappeasable political opponents for nearly two decades.[96]

The most accurate description of his disposition would be an amalgam of sanguine and choleric. According to Krupskaya's memoir, Vladimir Ilyich became a reserved person as a consequence of his brother's execution. Even in childhood he had loved to be alone, reading by himself. This did not mean he was not sociable, only that he desired complete control of his private life, which he did not want to lay bare to anyone. He despised nothing more than gossip and meddling in other people's private lives; he considerd such behavior unpardonable.[97] In her account of Vladimir Ilyich, Anna Ilyinichna mentions that he had been a "sober boy" even at a young age.

Lenin's rational means of looking at his prison experiences allowed him to write to his imprisoned brother, a doctor, and give him a lesson on how complete physical debilitation and sickness could be avoided through exercise. He relates some of his advice to Dmitry in a letter to his mother dated 7 February 1898:

> It's bad that in two and a half months he has already begun to look puffy. First—does he stick to a diet in prison? I suppose not. In my opinion that is essential. Second—does he do physical jerks? Probably not, either. Also essential. I can at least say from my own experience that *every day*, with great pleasure and profit I did my gymnastics before going to bed. You loosen up so well at times that it makes you warm even in the worst cold, when the cell is like an ice-well, and after it you sleep better. I can recommend to him an exercise that is very convenient (even if funny)—bow to the ground *50 times*. I set myself that stint and was not embarrassed when the warder watched me through the peephole and was amazed that a prisoner who had never expressed a desire to attend the prison church should suddenly have become so pious![98]

There was no room for mystical impulses in Lenin's thought. He did not belong in the category of revolutionaries "with a cause," but instead embodied the rational, predictable fighter. The constant police surveillance he endured never distorted his personality. He considered it in the same vein as adverse weather conditions and preserved this equanimity even while he was in prison.

He left the St. Petersburg prison on 14 February 1897, and soon departed for exile in distant Siberia. The journey to Shushenskoye village took weeks. He did not have a single complaint; in fact he was rather satisfied with the location of his exile.[99] En route, while taking a rest at the Ob train station, he could only muster a complaint about how much this "private trip"[100] to eastern Siberia was costing him. In a letter dated 2 March 1897, he writes:

> I still have two more days' journey ahead of me. I drove across the Ob in a horse-sleigh and bought tickets to Krasnoyarsk. . . . I had to pay 10 rubles for a ticket and 5 rubles for luggage for something like 700 versts! . . . Now there is less uncertainty and I therefore feel better.[101]

Hardly a week had passed in Shushenskoye when he wrote to Manyachka (M. I. Ulyanova) to exult that he had gained access to "the famous local library belonging to Yudin," who gave him a hearty welcome. "I see from the newspapers that in the spring fast trains will be coming here—8 days from Paris to Krasnoyarsk, which means six days from Moscow. It will then be much more convenient to correspond."[102]

In reading his letters of this period it becomes apparent that nature, new landscapes, and new people had become a source of interest. After weeks of travel, he writes to members of his family: "I am going to the village of Shushenskoye. . . . It is a big village with more than fifteen hundred inhabitants, where there are the Volost council, the office of the zemstvo assessor (he is the same as a superintendent of police in Russia, but has greater powers), a school, etc. The village stands on the right bank of the Yenisei, fifty-six versts to the south of Minushinsk." They traveled by ship until Minushinsk. His friends Krzhizhanovsky and Basil had been directed to another place, the village of Tesinskoye. For different reasons, he would later be happy that he was sent to a place relatively distant from the other exiles. The landscape of Krasnoyarsk around the river Yenisei reminded Vladimir Ilyich of the Swiss mountains and the Zhiguli peak. He jokingly recommended the settlement to his brother with an offer to go hunting together, "if only Siberia can manage to make a sportsman out of me."[103]

In almost every letter he describes the books he is reading at the time, as well as the ones he is in dire need of. For example, he wrote to Anyuta (10 December 1897, from Shushenskoye to Moscow):

> I am now reading the French translation of Labriola's *Essais sur la conception matérialiste de l'histoire*. It is a very sensible and interesting book. The idea came to me that you ought to translate it. . . . It goes without saying that only the second part is suitable for translation. . . . If something is left out, it will not by any means detract from this extremely clever defense of "our doctrine" (Labriola's expression).[104]

Of course, the phrase was used to deceive censorship, and the defense of Marxism is what was meant. The results of this reading resurface in his study opposing the "bureaucratic and fiscal utopias" that appeared in a volume published in St. Petersburg a year later.[105]

His first letter from Shushenskoye to his mother and sister Maria (dated 18 May 1897) overflows with descriptions of "artistic beauty," and he adds, "the shooting here, apparently, is not at all bad."[106] The name of his love, Nadezhda Konstantinovna Krupskaya—who was arrested in the same case as Vladimir Ilyich albeit much later, on 12 August 1896—came up often in his letters. In his letters from 19 October, 10 December, and 21 December 1896 (from Shusha to Moscow, addressed to his mother, Manya, and Anyuta), he wrote to his relatives that Nadezhda Konstantinovna might join him soon, for she had received permission to choose Shushenskoye instead of northern Russia.[107]

In a letter written on 10 May 1898 he informed his mother of Nadezhda Krupskaya's arrival: "At last, Mother dearest, my visitors have arrived. They got here on the evening of 7 May, and on that very day I was clever enough to go shooting, so they did not find me at home.... As for me—Yelizaveta Vasilyevna exclaimed, 'Oh, how fat you're getting!'; and so, you see, you could not wish for a better report!" They at once set about organizing the wedding, as the precondition of Nadezhda's moving to the place had been their immediate official joining in matrimony. Vladimir Ilyich would have liked the whole family to come to Siberia, but this was a bit of romantic wishful thinking:

> By the way, Anyuta asked me who I was going to invite to the wedding; I invite all of you, only I do not know whether it would not perhaps be better to telegraph the invitations! As you know, N.K. has been confronted with a tragicomic condition—she must get married *immediately* (sic!) or back to Ufa! Since I am not at all disposed to allow that, we have already begun "bothering" the authorities ... so that we shall be able to marry before the Feast of St. Peter; ... I am inviting the people from Tesinskoye (they are already writing that I shall certainly need witnesses) and I hope they will be allowed to come.[108]

In his next letter of 7 June we learn that the marriage can only be held on 10 July—due to the bureaucracy. On this day, the priest married them in the Shushenskoye church. Lenin tried to talk his mother into the trip but also warned her: Krupskaya's mother is worried that the lengthy journey would be too tiring for her.[109] After all, Maria Alexandrovna was sixty-three years old.

Lenin's correspondence shows that even everyday problems were brought into some sort of association with one another. Questions he posed here and there, elaboration of difficulties, reveal a great deal about the period and its conventions. It shows Lenin's complete ability to exchange views on any facet of life when he chanced upon a serious partner in conversation or correspondence. From wages for "domestic help" in Switzerland to finding a place to live, from hunting to the habits of his friends, "every little thing in life" held interest for him.[110]

According to some recollections, everyday monotony brought the greatest difficulty to the lives of exiles. Vladimir Ilyich "solved" this problem by purchasing a dog.[111] It is common knowledge that Lenin also liked cats; evidence in photographic and even cartoon form can be found for this, and at any rate, a love for animals was part of his nature. His devotion to the game of chess may also have alleviated the monotony; he wrote about this favorite pastime almost ecstatically. In his letters written with Krupskaya, sent from Shusha and Minushinsk to Podolsk in December 1898, they informed Maria Alexandrovna and the family about New Year's Eve celebrations in Minushinsk.[112] Lenin liked to sing, especially revolutionary songs, but he would also launch into an aria. Of course, sad events also come up in the letters. Certainly Fedoseyev's case must have weighed most heavily upon Vladimir Ilyich, for it was not by chance that he remained in Shusha with his wife and mother-in-law, finding a long-drawn-out close company of intellectuals difficult to bear. He was not prejudiced about this either, but did not like the constant "soul searching."

In this context the term *intellectual* is a synonym for oversensitivity, individualistic exhibitionism, jealousy with regard to partners, and the unremitting slander of competitors. Vladimir Ilyich's caution, his protection of the integrity of his private life, was edified by Fedoseyev's fate. As he related it to his family through Anyuta, it came about that the elder friend of Vladimir Ilyich was slandered: "he stole the money of the exiles." He wrote: "N.Y.F. does not write to me and does not even answer, although I have written him two letters. Scold him for that if you write. I have heard of the 'scandal' in Verkholensk—some disgusting scandalmonger has been attacking N.Y. No, don't wish me comrades from among the intellectuals in Shushenskoye—I'd rather not! When N.K. arrives there will be a whole colony anyway."[113]

The details of Fedoseyev's suicide emerge in Lenin's letter of 15 July 1898 to Anyuta: "I had a letter from the doctor yesterday, about N. Y.— he shot himself with a revolver. He was buried on 23 June. He left a letter for Gleb [Krzhizhanovsky], and manuscripts, also for him. They say he asked me to be given a message to the effect that he 'died full of faith in life and not from disappointment.'"[114] In a letter dated from a few weeks later, Lenin returned to the matter: "For people in exile, these 'exile scandals' are the worst thing of all, but I would never have believed that they could assume such proportions! The slanderer was exposed a long time ago and condemned by all comrades, but I never thought that N.Y. (who had some experience of exile scandals) would take it so much to heart." He later also wrote to the family that the exiles had started a collection for a gravestone for Fedoseyev.[115]

While the private sphere was in some respect inviolable and sacrosanct for Lenin, he never really sympathized with those revolutionaries who were led to the movement by a desire for the unrestricted, unbridled freedom of the individual. He subordinated his private life to the political cause and expected others to do so. He conceived of the freedom of the individual only as a part of some "collective" (be it a party, organization or "cause"). By the terms of his value system, discipline ("the minority subjects itself to the decisions of the majority"), solidarity with the community, belonged to the inner essence of the individual, or it *should* belong there, to be exact.

As the end of his exile approached, the sad eventuality of the young couple's separation arose, as Nadezhda Konstantinovna's term of exile had not yet elapsed. They had lived happily, which was partly due to the many household burdens taken on by the mother-in-law. The literature usually emphasizes that Nadezhda Konstantinovna was an atrocious housewife; she did not like to cook or do household chores, and lived like a typical intellectual. Vladimir Ilyich would sew his own buttons unless Yelizaveta Vasilyevna took care of these tasks. Nor did Krupskaya distinguish herself as an "organizer of parties or socialite" even later as an émigré. However, this is only half true, for in reality—though she did not like housework—she did take care of many things around the home, even when young. For example, on 11 September 1898 she wrote to Manyachka that Lenin had left for a week to go to Krasnoyarsk, and "[d]uring Volodya's absence I intend: (1) to carry out full repairs to his suits; (2) learn to pronounce English."

The truth is that Vladimir Ilyich did not expect her to excel in household matters; he was much more in need of a wife who was at home in intellectual and organizational issues.[116] They co-translated Sidney and Beatrice Webb's *The History of Trade Unionism* purely to boost their earnings. Vladimir Ilyich did not care to spend his time on such effort as it drew him away from his work on publications in the fields of economics and economic history and politics. They both were highly attentive to each other to the end of their lives, and this was true even of the period in which tender feelings bound Vladimir Ilyich to Inessa Armand.

Apart from love, they had an enduring shared cause and shared interests, which shaped the exemplary solidarity between them. At times of illness this solidarity is especially well documented on both sides. In the beginning Vladimir Ilyich was hardly ever sick. He was fit and athletic as a young man. He had a strong, short and stocky physique. Nadya was a very beautiful girl, but a thyroid issue soon led to Graves' disease, an autoimmune disorder that affected her eyes and remained a problem throughout her life. She dressed cleanly and simply, avoiding all conspicuousness.

When the term of exile elapsed in February of 1900, Vladimir Ilyich petitioned—and signed his petition as "hereditary nobleman"—in vain for permission to have his wife travel with him to Pskov, so he would not have to spend the remainder of the exile in Ufa.[117] On his way to the newly appointed place of residence in Pskov as he returned from exile, Vladimir Ilyich could finally visit his family in Moscow.

Frequent apprehension by the authorities gave the thirty-year-old revolutionary the incentive to coalesce the social democratic movements from abroad—around a journal to begin with—under the theoretical leadership of Plekhanov, who was the head of the Liberation of Labor Group. On these grounds he left the country with Martov and Potresov. The authorities were satisfied with this development, in the belief that the three would cause less trouble at home. However, they still took Lenin and Martov into custody for three weeks on the way from Pskov to St. Petersburg.

Establishing the journal required a great deal of energy and detailed organizational work. Lenin's accounts of his first months in exile revolved around this. In the spring of 1901 he happily announced to his mother the imminent arrival of Nadya and his first impressions of culture in Munich. He also expressed interest in Moscow's cultural events.[118]

The journal *Iskra* (Spark) became influential and was taken seriously by Russian revolutionaries—in spite of its intellectual idiom—and played a vital role in the Second Congress of the Russian Social Democratic Labor Party. It also brought a decisive turn in Lenin's life.[119] A personal matter, the alteration of his name, also signaled the major change the *Iskra* period meant in his life.

Between 22 May and 1 June 1901, a locally posted letter containing materials for the journal was received at *Iskra*'s illegal printing house. No one recognized the last name signed under the letter: *Lenin.* On 24 May 1901, he signed another letter to G. D. Lejtejzen using this alias, and then two more to Plekhanov on 21 October and 11 November. The alias *Lenin* only gained real renown when the second and third issues of the first Russian social democratic theoretical and scientific journal *Zarya* (published on 8 or 9 December 1901 in Stuttgart) printed the third of Vladimir Ilyich's three articles—"The Persecutors of the Zemstvo and the Hannibals of Liberalism," "Review of Home Affairs," and "The Agrarian Question and the 'Critics of Marx.'"[120] This one was signed *N. Lenin.*

Not even the most meticulous research has yet revealed from whence the name derives.[121] Soviet historiography has generally associated the choice of this name with the river Lena, just as it attributed Plekhanov's alias (Volgin) to the Volga. The family name *Lenin*, though not frequent, still has its occurrences, and Shteyn takes ample account of these families in his quoted book. Krupskaya also commented that she did not know the origin of the name. Though Ulyanov used over 150 aliases, this is the only one that remained in use. Trotsky assumed the name of one of his prison wardens, and came to be known under this name, though he used a number of aliases during the *Iskra* period of which, perhaps, the alias "Penn" is best known, but Kamenev, Zinoviev, and Stalin were also aliases used in the movement.

Time, which passed slowly in exile, was replaced by the hectic, exciting period of the professional revolutionary in another exile, with the libraries of the metropolises, organization of the party and the social meetings, gatherings, and conferences taking center stage. Adapting to émigré life, with its nomadic existence necessitated by party and political matters, always carried a degree of uncertainty for the young couple. Due to tough police scrutiny, the editorial board of *Iskra* (with Potresov and Vera Zasulich) first had to move from Switzerland to Munich, and then to London in 1902.

Lenin's letters from this period evince a keen interest in comparing the distinctive features of western and eastern European agricultural development to Russia's, but he also observed the curious differences in everyday life with some excitement.[122] This interest stretches through to the second period of emigration as well, which is inseparable from certain emotional motives. Though not in the least sentimental, Lenin would often be assailed by homesickness. This tendency is also easily followed in his correspondence.[123]

Lenin and Krupskaya made an effort to live quietly, modestly, and also to entertain themselves; it was a time given almost as much to music and theater as to the library.[124] This relative calm was typical of the period leading up to the Second Congress of the Russian Social Democratic Labor Party and the Bolshevik-Menshevik split. Lenin's writing at the time was mainly aimed at organizing and establishing the illegal party of the professional revolutionaries (his famous book, *What Is To Be Done?*, is treated in detail in chapter 3).

Following the great arguments and split at the congress, a nervous exhaustion took hold. For example, when the fractious battles broke out again in March of 1912—after the January party conference, where the first Bolshevik Central Committee was formed—Lenin's complaints to his younger sister read as follows:

> Among our people here, by the way, there is more bickering and abuse of each other than there has been for a long time—there probably never has been so much before. All the groups and sub-groups have joined forces against the last conference and those who organized it, so that matters even went as far as fisticuffs at meetings here. In short, there is so little here that is interesting or even pleasant that it's not worth writing.[125]

Vladimir Ilyich was not able to take the political battles and party struggles halfheartedly. Politics was a passion for him just as any other matter he took seriously. As one biographer writes, "He even picked mushrooms passionately."[126] Lenin argued with intensity, almost always "over-spicing" his position with epithets and metaphors denouncing his opponent's views to undermine his opponent's argument. The words "stupid," "idiotic," "cretin," and "degenerate" occur no less than a hundred times in his *Collected Works*.[127] Innumerable sources bear testimony to the fact that he sometimes fell into near ecstasy, was in a sense "unsettled" by arguments when the stakes were high. Anna Ilyinichna's writings also mention these "nervous exhaustions."

Many—and it must be stressed, quite wrongly—misconstrue Lenin's effect on people. They explain his public role as based in some sort of obsession with power, a desire to capture or keep a grip on power, and similar motives. While the role of power cannot be divorced from serious political debate, the decisive factor in Lenin's case was personal conviction. This small man was charismatic. After his death, even friends who had by then become his sworn enemies, such as Potresov, admitted this.

In opposition to this was the distorted image of him presented by Struve. Struve's Lenin was a "misanthropic" figure whose valuation of a human being was commensurate to his immediate political goal: "he looked down upon people, he was cold and merciless, his love of power was inexorable." Struve took late revenge on his onetime rival by portraying him as someone incapable of compromise and full of hatred.[128]

On the other hand, the Lenin who emerges from Potresov's much-cited memoirs is not a cold-blooded, calculating politician, but rather an extremely charismatic leader. He also stressed the importance of conviction and inner faith where Lenin's influence on people was concerned:

> Neither Plekhanov, nor Martov, or anyone else was endowed with the mysterious ability that just radiated from Lenin, with which he had a hypnotic effect on people, one could say, he ruled over them. Plekhanov was respected, Martov was loved. But people only followed Lenin unswervingly, as a single indisputable leader, because Lenin had what was rare, especially in Russia, a will of iron, inexhaustible energy coupled with fanatical faith in the movement and the cause, with no less faith in himself. This peculiar sense of being chosen with regard to his will once also bore an effect upon me.[129]

Rosa Luxemburg made a similar observation in 1907. According to Clara Zetkin, at an international conference, "Rosa Luxemburg, who possessed an artist's eye for the characteristic, pointed Lenin out to me with the remark: 'Take a good look at him. That is Lenin. Look at the self-willed, stubborn head. A real Russian peasant's head with a few faintly Asiatic lines. That man will try to overturn mountains. Perhaps he will be crushed by them. But he will never yield.' "[130]

After the momentous and exhaustive arguments at the congress, which entailed a break with all his old friends, Lenin was left on his own. Even Plekhanov—with whom Lenin had virtually "fallen in love"[131] a few years before—had taken the side of the Mensheviks in 1904. Lenin was once again disappointed in his "great teacher."

In the course of setting up *Iskra* he had felt emotionally alienated by Plekhanov's magisterial manners and authoritarian style. At the same time, under the influence of his meetings with Plekhanov, Lenin spoke of the "physical power of the mind" in relation to him. His clash with Plekhanov almost made him ill. Nevertheless, he respected both Plekhanov and Martov.

That Lenin could have been some sort of "coldly calculating," "manically *raskolnik* [schismatic]" figure goes against all historical information in this regard,[132] but he was undoubtedly a man who did not stray from his convictions on the revolutionary path. After Lenin turned his back on *Iskra*, the Bolsheviks brought the journals *Vperyod* and *Novaya Zhizn* to life in 1904 and 1905 respectively, which had a popular base among Russian organizations. But 1904 was a dark year in terms of Lenin's family history, as his mother, who lived in Kiev, was left practically on her own after all three of her children who lived with her were put under arrest.

THE 1905 REVOLUTION AND THE SECOND EMIGRATION

The revolution also turned a page in Vladimir Ilyich's life. It became a test for him, just as he would later call 1905 a test for 1917. His circle of contacts widened. One example is his friendship with A. A. Bogdanov, who gained notice as a philosopher and economist a few years earlier and joined the Bolsheviks. But he also cultivated a deeper relationship with Gorky[133] and Lunacharsky, to mention a couple of the intellectuals who were to become the most famous, their names more lasting than those of workers such as Babushkin, who died young.

Vladimir Ilyich worked in St. Petersburg in the 1890s. In the outbreak of the 1905 Revolution, his life grew very busy. The spring was "taken up" by preparations for it and the Third Party Congress itself, at which Lenin raised the question of armed uprising for the first time in the history of the party. Prior to this he had studied these issues as a complex of theoretical and practical questions.[134] Though he did not immediately return to Russia upon news of the revolution, he produced an incredible volume of literary work, with a succession of Russian publications of his writings.

After the declaration of the tsar's October Manifesto on 17 October, which represented a form of political "liberalization" of the existing authoritarian system, on 2 November he set out for Russia from Geneva, via Stockholm to St. Petersburg. His wife followed ten days later. For a time, he and Krupskaya stayed on Nevsky Prospekt, but they had little time for a private life as upon his arrival in St. Petersburg, Lenin immediately dug himself into his editorial and organizational work.[135]

In mid-November, with M. N. Lyadov mediating, Lenin invited the leaders of the German Social Democrats—Kautsky, Rosa Luxemburg, and Karl Liebknecht—to take part in publishing *Novaya Zhizn*.[136] Lenin and Krupskaya had of course not abandoned the paper's illegal approach. On 23 November the St. Petersburg Censorship Committee ordered legal prosecution of the editor-publisher of *Novaya Zhizn*, N. M. Minsky, because the journal published Lenin's article "The Dying Autocracy and New Organs of Popular Rule."

Late 1905 to early 1906 was a period of revolutionary upsurge and quick decline. The December armed uprising in Moscow opened new avenues of thought, on the one hand, but the scope of potential action narrowed, with a warrant for Lenin's arrest issued at almost the same time the uprising was being put down. This time, he was prosecuted for his brochure *The Tasks of the Russian Social-Democrats* and later writings. The authorities confiscated copies of these publications and made similar arrests in many other cities.

In the beginning of January, Vladimir Ilyich, arriving in Moscow from St. Petersburg hoping to more closely examine the consequences of the armed uprising, had consultations with representatives of numerous local Bolshevik organizations. On 23 January, he met A. M. Gorky in Helsinki, in the home of V. M. Smirnov. This is a moment to note[137] because the "author of the workers" had over the years become rather important in Lenin's life, being his most serious connection to revolutionary literature, the new Russian art.

In February, the police confiscated practically all of his writings and went so far as to issue a warrant for his arrest in Finland. His organizational work for the party remained highly active in St. Petersburg, and he appeared as speaker at scores of party events. Lenin and Krupskaya moved to the Finnish town of Kuokala, from where he frequently commuted to St. Petersburg. In the first half of March he returned to Moscow and participated in the preparations for the Fourth Congress of the Russian Social Democratic Labor Party. He traveled to Stockholm in the beginning of April for the "congress of unification," which rather than unifying the party drove it into a deeper schism.

Unquestionably, 9 May 1906 came as a most peculiar turning point in Lenin's career. It was his first opportunity to speak in front of a real mass rally of three thousand people, many of them workers, and moreover in St. Petersburg (in Countess Manina's palace). The chair presiding over the meeting had doubts about giving a completely unknown person the chance to speak, however, when informed that the person in question was the leader of the Bolsheviks he gave in. This was Lenin's only appearance at a mass meeting until 1917. Krupskaya worried throughout the debut along with him.[138]

The "unknown" speaker ascended the podium under the alias of Karpov, with stage fright, an ashen face, and slightly burred speech. He gestured a lot but spoke very persuasively. In all, it was a successful first appearance. Lenin effectively revealed to his audience that the liberals, supposedly standing alone by the revolution, had in fact cooperated with the government and he also condemned the "tsarist executioners" of the counterrevolution.

> He spoke and gestured passionately, as if seeking with his whole body, a flow of words emanating. He believed what he said and lived the significance of his words as he spoke them. He liked it when he was heard through, and not interrupted with questions, and in fact he listened to his debate partners with great attention. . . . He was ready with an immediate retort in the course of a speech or a discussion, himself in constant motion, stepping back and forward, at times coming really close to the conversation partner. If he spoke to a crowd, he looked slightly above the gathering, obviously in order to avoid being disturbed by single dissonant expressions or interlocutions.[139]

These are all documented in original recordings on film. Lenin never became a great orator, but he could transplant his inner conviction to others.

In July he met his mother in the St. Petersburg suburb of Sablino, but the visit was cut short by the dissolution of the First Duma. In the course of the summer he met many people whose importance would come to bear upon the future, among them Rosa Luxemburg, Felix Dzerzhinsky, and V. D. Bonch-Bruyevich. He was reading Bogdanov's book titled *Empirionism* in his free time, having received it as a gift from the author he would soon be "moving in with" in Kuokala, on the way to a second period of emigration.[140]

With a huge literary and organizational output, Lenin was not left much time to rest. At the end of April 1907 he escaped from the pressure in Russia—he was charged with party matters in connection with the Fifth Party Congress among others—to travel to London, with a short stay in Berlin, where he again met with Luxemburg, Kautsky, and Gorky. He was joined on his trip to London by Gorky, reading the writer's novel *Mother* on the way, which only served to deepen his feelings of friendship toward him. He took care of the writer's accommodations and, against the wishes of the Mensheviks, made him a fully participating delegate.[141]

In June, the St. Petersburg police authorities pressed Finland for Lenin's extradition. After participating in the Stuttgart International Socialist Congress in July–August, while in conversation about prospects with Lunacharsky, Vladimir Ilyich plotted his personal course. This would involve further stay in Finland, close to St. Petersburg, because "reactionary forces will rule" for the coming three to four years. At the same time he invited Lunacharsky to become a permanent contributor to the "central paper," the *Proletary*.[142] The financial and organizational concerns of the paper would be a heavy burden in the near future, but these issues were not apparent at the end of 1907, and all spare energy was directed at managing the next emigration.

Under increasing persecution by the police authorities Lenin left Russia. On 8 December, together with A. A. Bogdanov and I. F. Dubrovinskiy, the Bolshevik Central Committee gave them the task of traveling abroad and organizing the continued publication of the *Proletary*.[143] Vladimir Ilyich crossed to the island of Nauvo in an adventurous, or rather reckless, venture over the barely frozen ice of the Gulf of Finland, guided by Finnish peasants. He was fortunate on this occasion. He and Krupskaya left Stockholm on 3 January 1908, arriving in Geneva on 7 January.[144]

The second period of emigration, which proved far more oppressive than the first, now began. Much of this could be foretold from the way counterrevolutionary forces gained the upper hand in 1907. Vladimir Ilyich's sister conveyed a sense of this period in her biography of Lenin:

> After the freedom of the years 1905 and 1906, this second emigration proved more difficult than the first. The intellectuals and vast strata of youth, as well as many workers, were overtaken by feelings of fatigue and bitterness. The all-embracing approach to social problems was replaced by personal ones, with questions on sexual life and mysticism, a philosophy leaning toward religion. Yet disillusionment showed itself in much more grim guises as well: among younger people—who provide the most sensitive reading of social life—a veritable epidemic of suicide was rife.[145]

A growing number of Vladimir Ilyich's party members turned away from politics, and the mad passion and intensity of the arguments he sustained with his best comrades drained his energy. At the same time, the philosophical and organizational debates, polemics of an economic and, after Tolstoy's death, of even a literary nature, honed his political skills and shaped his perceptions as a thinker.

The period of the Great War was the most difficult they had ever faced. Serious financial hardships burdened their everyday lives. Yet Lenin also had some beautiful experiences during this time. His friendship, and even love, for Inessa Armand[146] proved an emotional gift of a lifetime. The relationship also had a positive bearing upon Lenin's political activity. In the summer of 1911 Lenin organized a party school for workers arriving from Russia, in Longjumeau, near Paris, while expending great efforts towards founding both the legal and illegal workers' press. In 1912 he was elected a member of the International Socialist Bureau. He launched the Bolshevik *Pravda* in May of this year, after the independent Central Committee of the Bolsheviks was organizationally established in Prague in January.

Lenin's name came to be known throughout Europe as one of the main organizers in the international antiwar movement. His studies hit the benchmark of international significance. His views formulated at this time, on the subjects of Russian historical development, the national question, the structure of the capitalist world system and unequal development, as well as his imperialism theory and philosophical exposition against neo-Kantian Machism and in defense of Marxist dialectics, are all subjects of debate to this day.

This period of hardship prepared Lenin for his "masterwork": his role in the revolution yet to come and bringing the Soviet Union into existence. During this time, the general mood was mostly subject to the battles between the factions, which—it must be stressed once more—wore out Lenin's nerves. Luckily he could always count on Nadezhda Konstantinovna's understanding.

A feeling of political loneliness must certainly have weighed upon Lenin. Dispute and contention had already become acute within his faction by 1908, and contrary to the assumption of some present-day authors, the stakes, politically, organizationally, and theoretically, were indeed very high. With little exaggeration, apart from Kamenev and Zinoviev, he had little day-to-day contact with any Bolshevik revolutionaries. As before, Vladimir Ilyich felt attached to his old friends, even if not at all costs, as demonstrated by his quarrel with Bogdanov. He did all that he could, in the midst of the most heightened political arguments, to hold on to Gorky's sympathy.

Lenin aimed to unite the various factions and movements—with different leaders—under the banner of social democracy but he was not ready to make concessions in matters of principle that might result in the defeat of the "cause" itself. A tenacious warrior of this sort could hardly count on his adversaries' understanding; it is enough just to turn to the unappeasable arguments with Trotsky for evidence of this. These conflicts of the second emigration plainly show that Vladimir Ilyich had become a complicated personality. If he distanced himself politically from someone he also suspended personal contact. Anyone on the general staff of the Bolshevik Party (not to mention the Mensheviks) could testify to this. Krupskaya called attention to an interesting contradiction: "His personal commitments never influenced his political stances. However much he loved Plekhanov or Kamenev, politically he broke off with them." It was this special trait "which made such a break so incredibly hard for him."[147]

Yet these rifts were almost never on personal grounds. Revenge and personal hatred meant so little in terms of motivation that "all was forgotten" as a result of political overtures. For a better understanding of this mechanism, the Lenin-Trotsky relationship may be cited once more. Even at the time of their greatest discord, emotionally speaking, he was not without an empathy, the nature of which would be difficult to explain. For example, when his relationship with Trotsky was at a low point, Kamenev, who had become Lev Davidovich's brother-in-law, presented a letter from "little Judas [Yudushka] Trotsky" asking him for the financial support of the Bolsheviks, which Lenin agreed to.[148]

As a backdrop to these strained relationships, Geneva itself was not too calming to his nerves either. As early as 14 January 1908 he had written to his younger sister: "We have been hanging about in this damned Geneva for several days now. . . . It is an awful hole, but there is nothing we can do. We shall get used to it."[149] This may have been more a matter of mood, since when they had first arrived in Geneva four years earlier with the aim of "settling there," he gave his mother the following account from the mist-filled city: "altogether a good Russian winter's day. . . . So we are beginning to get to know Switzerland and its scenery."[150]

It was not the city he had problems with, for he did not feel any better in Paris when they relocated their base at the end of the year.[151] Prior to this move, while visiting Gorky in the second half of April, they spent some time as tourists in southern Italy, took a look at Naples, Pompeii and its surroundings, and ascended Vesuvius. In May he traveled to London and worked on his book on empirio-criticism at the British Museum for a few weeks. In Paris, while continuing his theoretical and political work—including a heightening of the struggle between the factions, experimenting with the establishment of an alternative "Party School," and giving frequent lectures and participating at conferences—he familiarized himself with the city's cultural life. They had rented a three-room apartment in Paris, with one of the rooms occupied by Manyachka. The *Proletary*[152] was also relocated to Paris. Lenin even had a chance to give in to his passion for chess in the course of meetings with Bogdanov. It was on such an occasion they played their famous match, immortalized in a photograph, which much to Lenin's dismay ended in Bogdanov's victory.

Nonetheless, this period took a heavy toll on Vladimir Ilyich's nerves. There were no signs of revolutionary upswing in evidence either in Russia or among the exiles, and as a result, his disillusionment increased. In February 1910 his opinion was:

> Paris is a rotten hole in many respects. . . . I am still unable to adapt myself *fully* to it (after living *here* for a year!) but I nevertheless feel that only extraordinary circumstances could drive me back to Geneva![153]

It was a typical immigrant syndrome: "Nowhere at home, sweet home." Complaints about the struggle between the factions can be found in almost every private letter. The fact that many Russian immigrants lived on a minimum subsistence level is a repeatedly cited problem in his correspondence. He wrote, with regard to the penury of M. F. Vladimirski: "The émigrés here are very poor. My work is going extremely badly. I hope to get over this period of intense squabbling." He refers to the so-called 1910 Unifying Plenary Session of the RSDLP (Russian Social Democratic Labor Party) Central Committee, where the opposition between the factions of the party became even more pronounced.[154]

The greatest difficulty the couple faced in Paris was navigating its excessive bustle, the traffic congestion, and the huge amounts of time spent commuting. Vladimir Ilyich normally rode to the libraries on his bicycle. They both enjoyed bicycling. "Nadya and I often go cycling," he wrote to his mother in August 1909. But he had trouble with this as well. On one occasion his bicycle was stolen; another time he had an accident that ended in a lucky escape for him. It happened after a particularly enjoyable New Year's Eve party,[155] so his January got off to a bad start: "I was riding from Juvisy when a motorcar ran into me and smashed my bicycle (I managed to jump off)." Lenin wrote in this letter that he had wanted to see the airplanes, which interested him greatly, to be found at the aerodrome twenty kilometers outside Paris.[156] Though he escaped the accident unscathed, the "usual" nervous exhaustion overpowered him for days. He did, however, win the ensuing compensation case so that at least the cost of the bicycle was remunerated.[157]

Though they continued to live very economically, and Lenin was also supporting his sister who needed an appendectomy, a little money was left over for concerts and theater. He even mentioned it to his sister: "I have begun to pay more attention to the theater; I have seen Bourget's new play *La barricade*. Reactionary but interesting."[158] They were especially on the lookout for Russian pieces of course. In his letters, wherever they go—more so if the trip went well—Russia and the Volga were the grounds for comparison.[159]

In the summer of 1910, he and his family went to the sea for holidays, to Pornic on the Bay of Biscay. After the break he traveled to the Congress of the Second International in Copenhagen, where the problem of cooperatives was tackled as one of the main unavoidable issues as far as the prospects for socialism were concerned. At the time, however, he was immersed in study of the system of Stolypin, and the problems of the development of the Russian state and Russian agrarian circumstances.

Following the congress, on 4 September, he went to Stockholm to take a rest and finally met with his seventy-five-year-old mother. This meeting was their last. Maria Ilyinichna remembered it as follows:

> It was also in Stockholm that Mother for the first and last time heard Vladimir Ilyich speak in public; it was at a meeting of worker exiles. When we left, Vladimir Ilyich accompanied us to the boat—he could not go aboard the vessel because it belonged to a Russian company and he might have been arrested on it—and I still remember the expression on his face as he stood there looking at Mother. How much pain there was in his face! He seemed to feel that this was the last time he would see her. And so it was. Vladimir Ilyich did not see any of his relatives again until he came to Russia after the February Revolution, and Mother died shortly before it, in July 1916.[160]

At the same time, many in Russia experienced Tolstoy's death as a great blow. In the autumn of 1910 all intellectual and political elements were engaged with the event. In Lenin's view Tolstoy was without doubt the greatest genius among all the Russian writers he adored. For him, Tolstoy was not only a writer but a particular sort of "institution" who took on the official church, gave the peasant land from his own estate, and established a tradition for the anarchist community. His personal courage was undoubted. He defied all authority and had been excommunicated by the Russian Orthodox Church.

Lenin's literary spheres of interest defined the way he related to Tolstoy. The concerns that governed his judgment were not aesthetic; nonetheless, the writers he liked were almost all artists of universal import. Indeed, his dedication to Russian literature only deepened in the years of emigration, which may partly be explained by the homesickness that assailed him in the periods of exile. In a letter to Vladimir Ilyich's mother in Vologda, sent from Krakow in December 1913,[161] Nadya seemed to register this persistent mood exactly, apropos of a Beethoven concert given by a string quartet:

> For some reason the music made us terribly miserable, although an acquaintance of ours [a reference to Inessa Armand], an excellent musician, was in ecstasies over it. . . . If there is anything we thirst for here it is good literature. Volodya has practically learned Nadson and Nekrasov by heart and an odd volume of *Anna Karenina* is being read for the hundredth time. We left our literature (a tiny fraction of what we had in St. Petersburg) in Paris and here there isn't a Russian book to be had anywhere. At times we read with envy the advertisements of secondhand booksellers offering 28 volumes of Uspensky or 10 volumes of Pushkin, etc., etc.
>
> Volodya, as luck would have it, has become a great fiction-lover. And an out-and-out nationalist. You cannot get him to look at the pictures by Polish artists at any price but he has picked up, for instance, a catalogue of the Tretyakov Gallery that some acquaintance had thrown away and is always burying himself in it.[162]

Lenin valued literary works mainly on the basis of their social and political impact, but the fact that he never promoted bad writers indicates that he had aesthetic judgment when it came to quality. His main concern was whether a given literary work teaches the reader about history and the world as it is. On these grounds he did not read works from writers who were indifferent to the problems of the social elevation of the working classes. He approached literature from a political and class point of view. He normally recognized talent, but he was not really interested in an artist whose talent was expressed in the "aestheticization" of the counterrevolution, or artists who locked themselves in the ivory tower of literature. Important writers such as Bunin, Gumilev, Akhmatova, Gippius, or Tsvetayeva may not even have been mentioned once in Lenin's writings. Just as he did not think of himself as a philosopher—a thought he voiced in a letter to Gorky written in early 1908—so he did not consider himself an oracle in matters of literature or aesthetics. Indeed, he did not make statements on issues of aesthetics. In general, he defended classical works in literature and the fine arts and their traditions, especially the social footing of painting, whether attacked from the left or the right. To him, avant-garde negation seemed "anti-dialectic," an insensitivity to the historical continuum. Thus, in line with his "agitprop" perspective, he was mostly critical of this trend.

His theoretical works, political articles, and speeches successively evoke the creations and protagonists of Russian writers. Lenin's works cited Krilov's 29 fables and Gogol's 24 protagonists countless times. Other authors have determined that Lenin's most quoted writer is Saltykov-Shchedrin, but a profusion of literary figures appear in Lenin's writings, raised to the status of symbols, from Pushkin to Nekrasov and Chekhov, as well as such eminent personalities of world literature as Shakespeare, Molière, and Schiller.[163]

Though his literary references are almost too numerous to be counted, the only writer in Lenin's work whom he actually analyzed and "systematized" in a theoretical sense was Tolstoy. Between November 1910 and February 1911 he wrote as many as four articles or studies about the work, the merits, and mistakes of the deceased writer. Of course he recognized the exceptional talent in Dostoevsky as well, but considered him a reactionary writer who had reconverted to Russian Orthodoxy, embellished the "oriental" streams of development, and, in the final analysis, applied his talent to the service of the monarchy. Whether this judgment is right or wrong (for example, he could have used a thing or two from Dostoevsky's romantic critique of capitalism!), he always spoke with great admiration of Tolstoy as a writer in spite of the fact that he rejected his political philosophy.

At the core of Lenin's criticism, an effect also of his experiences as a European émigré, is that as opposed to "Occidentalism" in a sense Tolstoyism is:

> [A]n ideology of an Oriental, an Asiatic order. Hence the asceticism, the non-resistance to evil, the profound notes of pessimism . . . Tolstoy is true to this ideology in his Kreutzer Sonata too when he says: "the emancipation of woman lies not in colleges and not in parliaments, but in the bedroom."[164]

In the obituary he wrote for Tolstoy, Lenin "integrated" the lifework of Tolstoy—albeit he rejected it in *philosophical terms*—into the history and present of the Russian Revolution for the way it "reflected its universal significance." This integration also served as part of his own development. For Lenin, the epoch of preparation for the revolution gained form in Tolstoy's "inspired rendition."

The Leninian evaluation harks back to the paternal heritage of "enlightened instruction." Tolstoy's valuable works must be made available to the wide public because the writer lifts his voice against a system which condemns:

> millions and scores of millions to ignorance, benightedness, drudgery and poverty. . . . He succeeded in conveying with remarkable force the moods of the large masses that are oppressed by the present system, in depicting their condition and expressing their spontaneous feelings of protest and anger. . . . Tolstoy's works express both the strength and the weakness, the might and the limitations, precisely of the peasant mass movement.[165]

However far Lenin went in fighting Tolstoy's anarchism, he glorified Tolstoy's description of the police state and his denial of private property, and distanced himself from the purely moral resistance that denied politics.[166] His approach to literature was shaped primarily by what his socialist revolutionary conviction dictated: Vladimir Ilyich was occupied by questions of whether the workers will be able to understand literature and art; will they read; will they go to museums? Only an enthusiastic revolutionary attributes such significance to works of art, to the idea of art.

Lenin was hardly the best judge of human character. At times he "could fall in love" with people just because he projected onto them the traits he imagined a "working-class revolutionary" would have. He had a certain naiveté about people of the proletariat until his party came to power. This is how he committed the error of making the worker R. Malinovsky a Central Committee member and Duma representative, while that individual had been one of the best informers of the tsar's Okhrana. Naturally, not all of his human relations had to end in disappointment. The year 1910 was also the one in which the most important relationship of the later years of his life, with Inessa Armand, was taking shape. Vladimir Ilyich made her acquaintance in 1909.[167] Nadezhda Konstantinovna related their coming to know each other in her memoirs:

> Inessa Armand arrived in Paris from Brussels in 1910 and immediately became an active member of our Paris group. Together with Semashko and Britman (Kazakov) she was elected to the presidium of the group and started an extensive correspondence with the other groups abroad. She had a family of two little girls and a boy. She was a hot Bolshevik, and before long our whole Paris crowd had gathered round her.[168]

Soviet historiography suppressed the intimate-romantic side of the relationship between Lenin and Armand so doggedly as to even truncate the form and content of his letters in the publication of his collected works. Those sections in which they expressed tender feelings for each other fell prey to extreme censorship.[169] For decades this gave extra value to Krupskaya's memoirs as a source. Her account records how Inessa Armand purchased the house in Longjumeau in which the pupils of Lenin's Party School were lodged, and how she opened a canteen where Lenin and Krupskaya themselves ate. After the Lenin household moved to Cracow,[170] Inessa Armand traveled to Russia on an assignment from Lenin. There she was soon arrested,[171] and only freed upon the intervention of her divorced husband who posted bail for her. She escaped the country before her court hearing, traveling to Lenin, who was in Poronino.

> [W]hereas in Cracow we lived together in a small close and friendly circle. Inessa rented a room in the same house where Kamenev lived. My mother was greatly attached to her. Inessa often came to have a chat with her, or sit and smoke. Things seemed cozier and more cheerful when Inessa was there. We were completely absorbed by party cares and affairs. Our home life was more like that of students, and we were very glad to have Inessa. During this visit of hers, she told me a great deal about her life and her children, and showed me their letters. There was a delightful warmth about her stories. Ilyich and I went for long walks with Inessa. Kamenev and Zinoviev called us the "gadding party." We used to go for long walks outside the town, to the meadows—called blon in Polish. Inessa in fact took the pseudonym of Blonina. She loved music, and persuaded us all to attend the Beethoven concerts. She was a good musician herself and played many Beethoven pieces very well. A particular favorite of Ilyich's was the *Sonate pathetique,* and he always asked her to play it.[172]

There must be some credibility to the words, "[h]e could never have loved a woman whose views differed from his own, who was not his comrade in work," if Krupskaya has written them.[173] Their mutual feelings of love, plainly evident in their letters, were not only based on completely matching worldviews but also their similar "organizational and cultural" backgrounds. "I am sure that you are one of those people who develop, grow stronger, become more vigorous and bold when they are alone in a responsible position," Lenin wrote to Armand in July 1914.[174]

As a result of Inessa's ability to speak fluently in five languages, Lenin often chose her to accompany him to international congresses and conferences.[175] However, Lenin stayed with Krupskaya. He did not want to unsettle his life, which was indivisible from the party, the cause in general, and the revolution. Nadezhda Konstantinovna was a part of this. Whether someone else in his place would have taken the risk, it cannot be said. Among Lenin's considerations, the cause of the revolution was always first. Lenin had the ability to hold together the most complex of personal relationships if the cause—or "larger politics"—so required.

Lenin stayed in Poronino in June of 1914 while Krupskaya had an eye operation in Bern. With the beginning of the war on 18 July 1914, Lenin and family were forced to move from Poronino. This was not a simple venture because for Lenin the war began with his arrest. After all, he was residing within the borders of the Austro-Hungarian monarchy and a Browning handgun was found in his possession in the course of a house search on 7 August 1914. Viktor Adler, the famous Austrian Social Democrat leader, interceded on his behalf with the minister of internal affairs to have him freed, stressing that he was a sworn enemy of the tsar's order. He was kept in prison for twelve days altogether. In the meantime, Vladimir Ilyich could not at first believe that on August 4 the German Social Democrats had voted in favor of war loans. On this day, Rosa Luxemburg pronounced her famous phrase: "German Social-Democracy has become a stinking corpse."

Lenin and Krupskaya relocated to Switzerland—Bern in fact—on 5 September.[176] The local Bolshevik group, however, was practically penniless; 160 francs remained in the party coffer by autumn of 1914.[177] At home, Bolshevik Duma representatives (Badayev, Shagov, Muranov, Petrovsky, Samoylov), who held out for Lenin's stance rejecting Russia's participation in the war, were arrested and then sent into exile. At this time Lenin undertook deep theoretical work mainly in the fields of economics and philosophy. At the secret conferences held in Zimmerwald and Kienthal by the international movement Lenin and his circle were able to elaborate their principles and ideas regarding the war.

Lenin and Inessa continued to correspond intensively during the war even after they "split up" at Lenin's behest.[178] The trio lived together for a few months in the autumn of 1915 in Sörenberg, in the sanatorium of a little mountain village not far from Bern. There had been an international conference on women in Bern the preceding spring. A theoretical debate about "free love" had arisen between them in this period, based on the draft brochure prepared (and sent to Lenin) by Inessa. In a letter dated 17 January 1915, Lenin described the demand for "free love" as "not really a proletarian but a bourgeois demand," because in his opinion what Armand subjectively means by "freedom of love" is not what is important. Lenin wrote about the prevalence of the "*objective* logic of class relations in affairs of love."[179]

Lenin supported Inessa's argument clearly and categorically where it posited that the freedom of love can only be spoken about in a shallow middle-class sense if the relationships of those in love are detached from material-financial considerations. It follows that Inessa's line of argument does not accept the identification of free love with adultery. Lenin's thesis was the following: under freedom of love the "women of the bourgeoisie" understand "freedom from the more serious aspect of love, from childbearing"; it is the freedom of adultery. Quoting Inessa, Lenin engaged in polemics with her:

> "Even a fleeting passion and intimacy" are "more poetic and cleaner" than 'kisses without love' of a (vulgar and shallow) married couple. That is what you write. And that is what you intend to write in your pamphlet. Very good.
>
> Is the contrast logical? Kisses without love between a vulgar couple are *dirty*. I agree. To them one should contrast . . . what? . . . One would think:

> kisses *with* love? While you contrast them with "fleeting" (why fleeting?) 'passion' (why not love?)—so, logically, it turns out that kisses without Love (fleeting) are contrasted with kisses without love by married people. . . . Strange. For a popular pamphlet, would it not be better to contrast philistine-intellectual-peasant (I think they're in my point 6 or point 5) vulgar and dirty marriage without love to proletarian civil marriage with love (adding, *if you absolutely insist*, that fleeting intimacy and passion, too, may be dirty and may be clean).[180]

The problem of applying class theory in relation to the private sphere of love has sprung numerous debates; however, the arguments between the two people involved here perhaps also document their unfading love.

In the course of 1916, when he and his wife lived in the greatest financial difficulty since their exile, Lenin sought to offer support to his friend and comrade in a row of solicitous letters. On 7 April, for example, he writes the following letter to Inessa from a sanatorium in the hills near Zurich, where he was convalescing with his wife. Inessa was preparing to travel from Paris to Switzerland:

> My dear friend, We are surprised and worried that we have no news of you. We sent the book and the money on 25 March. Since then, unlike on most occasions, we have not received an answer from you. Could it be that you are working on your dissertation with such dedication? I wish with all my heart that it is successful, but still there is no need to take it to complete exhaustion. Why not write us a few lines. We send you our greetings and wish you all the best. Your own, Lenin.[181]

Lenin inquired about Armand's health persistently. On 25 July 1916, for example, he wrote: "I wish you all the best and beg you to *take a cure*, so that you may be *quite* fit by winter. Go south, to the sunshine!!"[182] Vladimir Ilyich's devotion to Inessa was to remain a lifelong commitment, and he himself always supported her children, a role taken over by Nadezhda Konstantinovna after his death.

Lenin's contact with other women always remained within the bounds of petit bourgeois conventions and courtesy. Any kind of sexist attitude was alien to him. This behavior stemmed partly from his upbringing and at the same time from his personality and convictions. Though very few women became really close to him, he took women as seriously as men when it came to political debates, and never differentiated between the sexes in this sense. That is to say, he did not derive the relationship of men and women from "naturally ordained" or primary "power" relations. Liberal feminism as conceived today remained alien to his whole approach and mental apparatus in terms of theory and the philosophy of history, in that he deduced the oppression and disenfranchisement of women from the role of capital, the capitalist system, and the "hierarchizing" characteristics of the labor market.

IN POWER

Though Lenin became hesitant around the turn of 1916/17 whether the outbreak of the Russian Revolution was for the best, he set about arranging his return home immediately upon news of the February Revolution. Finally, thirty-two Bolsheviks returned to St. Petersburg through Germany in the famous "sealed train."[183] As they departed from Zurich, a group of Mensheviks and Esers organized a small demonstration of protest against Lenin at the train station.[184] As it turned out, after their return, Inessa settled in Moscow while Lenin settled in St. Petersburg.

The true story of 1917's significance in Lenin's life was not a fairy-tale rise to the highest seat of power, but that of great ordeals, with his life often hanging by a thread. The events that felt most miraculous were his return to Russia and the victory of the October Revolution.[185] The districts of St. Petersburg where workers stayed—the St. Petersburg soviet—burst into terrific activity in anticipation of Vladimir Ilyich's arrival home in the evening hours after twelve years in exile. By midnight, soldiers and workers in the tens of thousands awaited the train, and of course Lenin especially, at the Finland Station.

Upon his arrival he gave speeches amid waves of loud cheers, accompanied by strains of the *Marseillaise* and the *Internationale* as they proceeded further into the city. This was the moment when Lenin became a real "champion of the people." As he cried out at the end of his speech, "Long live the socialist revolution!" this signaled that the sense of timing of the future leader of the revolution was on a different footing, where its evaluation and perspectives were concerned, from those of the official Soviet leaders (and for a period of time, even that of the leaders of his own party). The legendary armored car took him to the Kshesinskaya palace, where the Bolshevik Central Committee and the St. Petersburg party committee had their headquarters. Lenin and Krupskaya settled into the flat of his sister and her husband, Mark Yelizarov, where they spent their nights until the "days of July."

When protests on 3 July almost led to the outbreak of the revolution, those in power turned to the usual tools for suppression: outlawing the party of the "ultrarevolutionaries"; in this case, the Bolsheviks. Lenin was forced underground, though the idea that he should appear in court was voiced by some of the leading figures of the party. Stalin opined that it would be better if he were not to appear, because the Kadets would beat him to death before he ever got to the court. Vladimir Ilyich constantly changed flats within the capital, then changed residences a number of times, finally reaching Finland through Sestroretsk. He landed first in Razliv, in the neighborhood of St. Petersburg, in the company of Zinoviev, and with visits from Ordzhonikidze, Stalin, Sverdlov, and Dzerzhinsky. The place became famous for the fact that Lenin essentially wrote the whole of *State and Revolution* here. The bounty placed on his head did its work, however, and personnel of the authorities began to show up in the vicinity. In the end, he moved out of Razliv on August 8, helped by Shotman, Rahya, and Yemelyanov, and left the country disguised as a stoker on a steam locomotive. The "book with the blue cover" was shortly in Shotman's safekeeping. Lenin instructed him to hand over this work to the Central Committee in the event of his apprehension.

Upon arrival in Helsinki, Shotman set Vladimir Ilyich up in the apartment of a Finnish social democrat, who was then captain of the Helsinki police force. It was a rather fine solution in its conspiratorial aspect.[186] Lenin continued to change residences in the Finnish city. He did not cease to work, writing throughout these days on the run, receiving the dailies and by complicated, conspiratorial routes he kept in continuous touch with the capital.

Lenin's famous letters about the uprising and the possibility and necessity of taking hold of power were composed in these circumstances. He felt that he had arrived at the meaning of his life; the proletarian revolution was at hand. When the soviets convened the "Democratic Council" in September and elected the "Preparliament," it became clear that one way or another the question of power would become the issue of heightened, if not armed, struggle within the shortest period of time. The polarization (from curtailments of democracy to the Kornilov revolt) advanced relentlessly, marking out the basic alternatives that Lenin had already traced out in April (in his *April Theses*). The romantic descriptions of his return that were the staple of history books a few decades ago in the Eastern Bloc were essentially true to historical fact.[187]

Still underground, Lenin showed up in Petrograd in early October, and participated in the truly momentous Central Committee meeting of 10 October where the resolution about armed uprising was passed. The meeting was convened at the flat of Sukhanov, a Menshevik intellectual whose wife supported the Bolsheviks. Only Kamenev and Zinoviev, Lenin's closest political pupils, opposed the armed uprising. In the end, they "spilled the beans" to the press. This took a toll on Lenin's feelings, so much so that he brought it up repeatedly years later. Meanwhile his other relationships, such as with Trotsky, who joined the Bolshevik Party in

August 1917 and played a part in the revolution that Lenin held in high esteem, took a turn for the positive. Everyone already saw Lenin as the leader of the proletarian revolution even before his election to any official function.

Lenin, in spite of his reluctance, was unanimously elected the Chairman of the Council of People's Commissars (the Soviet government). He was not surrounded by any kind of official "cult." He was pressed into nearly ceaseless polemics on the most varied and crucial issues with his dearest friends and colleagues holding the same principles from the first minute to the last.[188] He would often lose these arguments. Lenin was not the official leader of the party even in October, he was simply a member of the Central Committee, and then of course he also became a member of the tighter overseeing body established in 1919, the Politburo. The charismatic leaders of the people are initially not elected, or even appointed, but raised by the masses and their immediate political surroundings. This is called "popular legitimation."

In 1919, Lenin was the engine of the establishment of the Communist International, just as he played a fundamental, instigating, and organizational role in the creation of the Soviet Union. This is when he became a revolutionary, politician, and statesman all at once. Lenin embodied all that was necessary in the Russian Revolution for its survival: his organizational drive focused on decisive fields; he was inspiring to the masses; he had great political flexibility, uncompromising plebeian and internationalist commitment, and stamina; he was self-sacrificial.

As one of his official biographers noted, Lenin never showed any sign of despondency or panic, even at the most critical junctures during or after the period of the revolution. Within his select circle of family and friends, and even in some writings, he expressed doubts regarding the possibility of achieving the main aims of the revolution in the short term. His energy, strength of will, and his passion for life infused his surroundings and became a sort of incitement to significant masses of workers, which was partly instrumental in the party's, or the Soviet government's, ability to suddenly change tack in its politics whenever this proved necessary.[189] Getting the Peace Treaty of Brest-Litovsk with Germany ratified in March 1918 took a long and tenacious battle on Lenin's part, affording the soviet in power a much needed, though brief, respite. The policies introducing War Communism or the New Economic Policy (NEP) were the results of similar sudden realizations and turning points.

Lenin's private life after the revolution is indivisible from the political history of Soviet power. His wife continued to work in the field of pedagogy and general education after 1917, employed by the commissariat of Lunacharsky. The lifestyles of his siblings, such as those of old revolutionaries, did not differ much from Lenin's. The revolution occupied them twenty-four hours a day.

October did not bring change for Lenin, for as with the fate of the revolution his life also hung by a thread. Day and night he and his comrades were on the lookout for any chances of survival. They coursed between ingenious political ploys and commonplace mistakes to reach the summer of 1918, the outbreak of civil war, and a new chapter of the life-and-death struggle.

Lenin's eating habits were as humble as those of any Soviet citizen working in a factory or an office. Soup, bread, fish, and tea made up his daily intake. He forwarded all gifts of food he received from workers and peasants to child care institutions. His humble way of life did not stem from self-righteous pretense, but from his plebeian view of life and revolutionary worldview, which "did not permit him to eat when others starved." His dearest colleagues would sometimes smuggle a piece or two of bread into his drawer, which he would not have guessed was above the rationed amount.[190] Among many of his set approaches from before October, his "idées fixes," foremost remained the desire to enlighten and educate the masses, and to establish libraries.[191] To begin with, he did not believe the revolution had a good chance of surviving under the conditions created by the world system of capitalism, so he sought to set up records of the federation of workers' and peasants' soviets and its cultural and political aims in as short a time as possible. The statues of Marx and Engels, the revolutionaries, the murderers of the tsar (Perovskaya, Zhelyabov and their companions, but not his brother), the great writers and artists (Gogol, Dostoevsky, Tolstoy, Saltykov-Shchedrin, and, of course, Chernyshevsky) erected at the time all had this purpose. And as he never raised his voice as an "expert" in matters of art, he also refused to officially formulate his antipathy toward the avant-gardists. He declared the significance of art, and its humanizing, "civilizing" function frequently and in general terms.

Right from the start, Lenin signified "enemy number one" to the greatest variety of political forces. After the coalition partners in the Soviet government rebelled in the spring of 1918, Lenin became the prime target of the latest form of terrorism. His life was fundamentally transformed by the three assassination attempts made on him.

Anyone seeking to understand Lenin's life and thought must see that at all costs for Vladimir Ilyich, even after October, revolutionary action remained at the epicenter of his life. For him, life was one with the revolution. He had made this clear at an earlier date, when on 20 November 1911 he gave a speech at the grave of Marx's daughter Laura and her husband Paul Lafargue, representing the RSDLP.[192] The couple had taken their own lives because in their declining years they felt they had become superfluous to the revolutionary movement and their lives had thus lost meaning.

This feeling must have also taken hold of Lenin eleven years later, in December 1922, when he partially lost his ability to move and therefore, his ability to work. The memoirs of Krupskaya and Molotov inform us that Lenin wanted to give up his life. He asked Stalin for poison (potassium cyanide, as was used by the Lafargues) to end his emotional torture. It is another matter that Stalin twice promised to satisfy his wish, though he refused to complete the "task" at the meeting of the Politburo on 30 May 1923, with no one taking it on in his stead.[193]

No special apparatus was established to protect Lenin's life. This may well not have been the result of any "Russian slovenliness," even if it did factor into many things. The true cause of this can be assigned to the fact that Lenin, led by the military, social, and institutional spontaneity of the revolution, was not yet thinking of its bureaucratization. This would come up as the problem of a later period, but by then it would be without his leadership.

In a collectivist spirit, Lenin thought in terms of class and class contradictions. Numerous assassination attempts were made on him. Even in the attempts on his life he saw the immediate results of class-typical actions, while appropriating no special significance to his own person. It was true, however, that individualist solutions, such as the institution of personal guards, were not at the time reconcilable with the revolution itself.

In December 1917 a neurotic student "strayed" into Lenin's room in Smolni (which was not even properly guarded!), but did not shoot him. Only after he had left and wanted to return (having this time been apprehended by a guard) did the gun go off in his pocket. Luck was on Lenin's side on more than one occasion.

The first real attempt at an assassination occurred in Petrograd on 1 January 1918, when, as he returned from a meeting and turned off Simeonovsky Bridge onto the Fontanka, his car came under fire. Fortunately, the bullets "skidded off" or got lost in the armor plating of the De Luna Belville, though some broke through the hood and the windshield. Lenin was saved from getting wounded by Fritz Platten, who shielded the president of the Russian government with his own body. Lenin did not even consider the event worthy of an investigation. As Platten later recounted, "Lenin noted, no Russian Bolshevik can avoid such peril today."[194]

The most dangerous attempt on Lenin's life was made on 30 August 1918 by Dora (Fanni) Kaplan. In the morning, Lenin was informed that a terrorist had shot the captain of the Petrograd Cheka, M. S. Uritsky. He immediately sent Dzherdzinsky to Petrograd to investigate. In the evening, ignoring the express dissuasion of his younger sister, he left for the workers' meeting at the Mikhelson factory. Thousands of workers were to assemble and he would draw their attention to the closing of the new front opened by the Czechoslovak Army. Kaplan fired three shots from point-blank range; one bullet struck his neck.

Though seriously wounded, Lenin appealed for calm and composure among the workers surrounding him. When they arrived at the Kremlin, his driver, S. K. Gil, wanted to have him taken up on a stretcher. Lenin demurred, asking only that his jacket and overcoat be brought by someone. He took the stairs to his third-floor flat while leaning on his comrades.[195]

Hardly a year had passed, and in the lean period of War Communism Lenin became the victim of another assault. After he had given his famous speech from the balcony of the building housing the headquarters of the Moscow Soviet, in which he protested the murders of Rosa Luxemburg and Karl Liebknecht, on 19 January 1919, he departed for Sokolnyk in the company of Maria Ilyinichna, where he was to take part in the Christmas festivities with the children of the forest school. Lenin enjoyed the company of children, perhaps because he could have none himself due to his wife's autoimmune deficiency. A curious intermezzo interrupted the outing. The automobile was attacked by bandits—typical, given the civil war conditions of general insecurity—and the occupants were compelled at gunpoint to hand over the vehicle, their wallets, and their papers.[196] Lenin was ready with a "compromise," and was even forced to give up his loaded handgun.

After the robbery they found their way to the soviet of Sokolnik by foot, and Lenin called Peters, one of the leaders of the Cheka, and informed him of the events. Fortunately for Lenin the bandits did not realize who they had apprehended. However, the story found its way into Lenin's famous brochure, *Left-Wing Communism: An Infantile Disorder*, discussed in the chapter on compromise. What counts as a brave deed in a particular epoch? Is it worth sacrificing ourselves and others for aims that cannot be achieved? The personal drama passed into the field of politics and political ideology through such questions.

Meanwhile, he was forced to give up most of his sports activities and was unable to play chess after 1917 because it required too much in the way of mental energy. Gorki, a town in the neighborhood of Moscow, became his place of respite, where he could hunt once in a while or take walks, but mountain climbing had to be relegated to the domain of beautiful memories. Lenin spent his spare time reading, but though he had a library of nearly ten thousand books in the Kremlin,[197] he regularly borrowed books and journals from the libraries in Moscow, devouring the foreign arrivals with a special gusto. He received a significant volume of journals and books from Berlin in the first half of 1923, including various works of V. Shklovsky, I. Ehrenburg, S. Prokovich, and G. Landau. He undertook a major work in theory and politics in February 1923—with a sudden and marked turn for better health, after his earlier paralysis. He had three volumes of Hegel and a work by Plekhanov brought from his library in the Kremlin to Gorki on 19 October. This very same day he traveled to the Kremlin for the last time, to "bid his office farewell."[198]

Lenin was at once very "modern" and conservative, in matters of art just as in his manner of dress and questions of taste. He abhorred the superficiality and snobbism of the "all-negating" revolutionaries. His tastes in literature and music were defined by the classical tradition, as was his dress code. The slightly worn but spotlessly clean suit, waistcoat, overcoat, tie, and famous peaked cap accompanied him on virtually all his travels. In such matters, his wife had much the same approach, a well-worn woman's jacket and worn-out heels. Her simple costume is now on exhibit in Gorki.

At the same time Lenin stood up for freedom of lifestyle, apparent from the fact that a decree signed by him in Soviet Russia was the first in the world to end the criminality of homosexuality. Chicherin, the commissar for foreign affairs, did not make a secret of the fact that he loved men, and many others did not hide their sexual orientation either. It is another matter that under Stalin, as of March 1934, homosexuality came to be considered a medical disorder and an offense.[199]

Lenin's physical strength did not fail him for a long time. He hardly knew what "exhaustion" meant until he was overtaken by serious illness. In the hundred days running up to the October Revolution, while constantly on the move under the threat of illegality—in huts, wash houses, and such—he wrote an average of five to six printed pages of text (with about 2,800 characters per page), by hand of course, every day on the most critical political and theoretical questions of the revolution. This includes his brochure, *State and Revolution*. This is an achievement even in merely physical terms. Lenin exceeded this achievement with the scale of activity he put into state building, party affairs, the Comintern, and other organizations after 1917. Until the point at which he lost his speaking and writing ability, over a period of five years, he wrote over ten volumes of theoretical work, political publications, documents, letters, and notes.

Lenin read in a number of languages, practicing them until his last days. The last foreign language he began studying—he had already mastered German, French, English, and a number of Slavic languages—was Bulgarian. The last book he enjoyed, which his wife read to him and he kept on his bedside table, was one of Jack London's works. He also took bearings on the literature brought out in the first Soviet period, though he was not attracted by revolutionary rhetoric. Toward the end he "made peace" with the formally innovative poetry, not because of its revolutionary romanticism but for its debunking of Soviet bureaucracy and its "self-annihilating continuity of meetings." He preferred not to share his experiences of literature with others. He read for his own pleasure, and the thought of foisting his own tastes onto anyone else never crossed his mind. Everything new from film to the fine arts aroused his interest, but he still remained a puritan. In 1921 he even wanted to provisionally close the Bolshoi Theater for a lack of funds, but his fellow commissars, with Lunacharsky at the helm, voted down his strange idea.

Lenin's health did not suddenly go into its final decline at the end of 1922. Painful, often tortuous headaches and sleeplessness assailed him for a very long while. In hindsight, doctors noticed symptoms that he may have inherited through his paternal line.

Ilya Nikolayevich Ulyanov (1832–1886) had also lived a short life. He was just four months past fifty-four when he died; his son lived nine months less. Vladimir Ilyich resembled his father in his physical makeup: emotional, energetic, early to mature. Both were equally prone to early arteriosclerosis, which often induces cerebral hemorrhaging.[200] This was the ultimate cause of his death.

Lenin's constitution took the pressures of unbelievable physical and mental strains until March 1922. He had already asked for a month's holiday on 8 July 1921, complaining to Gorky that he was tired, and later excusing himself to Lunacharsky for the same reason, citing his sleeplessness. In February 1922, following the Third Congress of the Comintern, it once more became doubtful whether he could continue to take part in the work at all. On 23 April the bullet that had lodged itself in his body during the Kaplan attempt was finally removed. Due to his strong physique he recuperated from the operation in a matter of days, but even this did not bring relief from his suffering. The first brain hemorrhage, resulting from the cerebral arteriosclerosis, brought him down on 26 May.[201]

He gave a serious speech in the Bolshoi Theater in October 1922 at the pan-Russian Congress of the Soviets, which was proof of his unequalled willpower but did not mean he was able to perform as he did before, as his sentences were now sometimes falling apart. He suffered two attacks on 13 December, and then, following another seizure during the late night of the 15th, his right hand and right arm became paralyzed. While these symptoms would at times recede, this was in fact the beginning of the end.

Nevertheless, he continued to dictate his opinions and matters relating to his personal succession to his secretary. This was, as it were, a preparation for the party congress in which he was unable to participate.[202] As a consequence of Lenin's illness, Stalin's ambitions were reinforced, and as a result of a strange episode between them, their private relationship became strained.

On 23 December, Krupskaya complained to Lev Borisovich Kamenev, who had earlier nominated Stalin to the post of secretary general, with the following words:

> Dear Lev Borisovich,
> Concerning the brief letter written by me at Vladimir Ilyich's dictation with the doctors' permission, Stalin phoned me yesterday and addressed himself

> to me in the crudest fashion. I have not been in the party for just a day. In the whole 30 years I have never heard a single rude word from one comrade. The interests of the party and Ilyich are not less dear to me than to Stalin.

She went on to ask Kamenev to protect her "from rude interference in my personal life, unworthy brawling and threats. . . . I have no doubt about the unanimous decision the control commission Stalin threatens me with, but I have no strength and no time to waste on such stupid squabbles."[203]

Nadezhda Konstantinovna only told Lenin about the incident at a much later date, upon which Lenin angrily wrote a top-secret letter to Stalin on 5 March 1923, with copies delivered to Kamenev and Zinoviev. A number of researchers believe that the letter is a document of a break in their relationship, and in fact, already reflects Lenin's opinion that Stalin was a "bad choice" for general secretary. In a much-cited note dated 4 January 1923, he gave a statement including a characterization of Stalin.[204] Though proposing a dismissal of Stalin ("Stalin is too rude, and this fault, entirely supportable in relations among us Communists, becomes insupportable in the office of General Secretary. Therefore, I propose to the comrades to find a way to remove Stalin from that position and appoint to it another man . . ."), he did not name anyone in particular as his successor, even emphasizing the negative features of the revolutionaries characterized.[205] The fact that his earlier favorable opinion of Stalin had changed was also reflected in the 5 March letter described above, in which he calls on Stalin to ask for his wife's forgiveness posthaste. In the event there is no such apology, he proposes an immediate breaking off of relations.[206]

The last months of Lenin's life were passed under serious psychological trials, not to mention physical pains. The emotional problem for him was not caused by having to take leave of his life, but the circumstance by which he came to be isolated from the politics that meant life to him, his influence on public affairs, while continually becoming more aware of the difficulties stemming from the inner contradictions of the new system. The most important of these was perhaps the national question.

One day after issuing the letter calling on Stalin to apologize, Lenin turned to the directorate of the Georgian Communist Party in the matter of the so-called Georgian Affair to offer his support and protection from Stalin, Ordzhonikidze, and Dzerzhinsky. He wrote: "I am following your case with all my heart. I am indignant over Ordzhonikidze's rudeness and the connivance of Stalin and Dzerzhinsky. I am preparing notes and a speech in your matter."[207]

At the end of his life, one might say, Lenin was fighting a battle on two fronts to keep the Soviet state alive: on the one hand, geared toward rooting out the bourgeois intellectual circles with ties to the old system and putting the church in its place, while on the other, to—less successfully, it should be noted—censure and beat back the party's own nationalists and bureaucrats. His failure distressed him terribly.

Two days before his death he went hunting for the last time in the surrounding forests in a wheelchair, but he could not himself hold a gun. It would have naturally crossed his mind that he was saying goodbye to the life from which he had received fulfillment: revolution. Yet he was disappointed as his death approached, for the *work* remained a torso and not an entire body.

Lenin was not yet dead when his fellow revolutionaries and colleagues in leading positions began to fight over his intellectual and political legacy. When the Left Opposition was formed in October 1923, with the leadership of Trotsky, even Lenin would have had to recognize the inevitable development of this process. Lenin became so agitated when the Thirteenth Party Congress resolution denouncing Trotsky was read on the day before his death that his wife, in a benevolent lie, had to tell him that "the resolutions were passed unanimously."[208] Not long before Vladimir Ilyich's death his wife also read to him a tract by Trotsky in which Lev Davidovich compared Lenin's significance with that of Marx.

His condition got acutely worse at 5 p.m. on 21 January 1924, his fever rising to 105.8°F. At 6:50 p.m., due to paralysis of the breathing organs, he died. At 7 p.m., Maria Ilyinichna informed the members of the Political Committee in Moscow by phone of Lenin's passing.[209] On the day after his death the Central Committee of the Bolshevik Party made the following proclamation addressed to the members of the party: "Since Marx there has not been as gigantic a figure in the history of the great movement for the liberation of the proletariat as our leader, teacher and friend who has just passed away."[210]

Although the embalming and exhibition of his corpse in the mausoleum was completely alien to his spirit, as his wife noted at the time, it was normative by the historical standards that characterized the stage at which the "Leninian experiment" was finally arrested. Not a single official document that shows any party or state leader opposing the exhibition of Lenin's embalmed body in the mausoleum has emerged. The fact of the embalming of the corpse and the establishment of the mausoleum was officially proclaimed on 25 March 1924, thereby raising the cult of Lenin to official status.[211]

The task of a bourgeois professor is not to lay bare the entire mechanism, or to expose all the machinations of the bank monopolists, but rather to present them in a favourable light.

—V. I. LENIN, *IMPERIALISM, THE HIGHEST STAGE OF CAPITALISM*

LCW, VOL. 22, 219

2
Russian Capitalism and the Revolution

THE CHALLENGES AT THE TURN OF THE CENTURY

AT THE BEGINNING OF the twentieth century, 82 percent of Russia's mostly peasant population lived in the European governorates. A bare 13.4 percent of the total population of 125.7 million lived in cities. The birth rate was rather high, with nearly a quarter of the population below the age of nine. By 1914, despite rapid capital investment, industrial development, and a significant increase in the urban share of the population, agrarian overpopulation did not decrease.[1] Even today the depth of capitalist penetration remains a matter of contention among historians, especially given that Russia was a continent-sized empire composed of 140 nations. This situation is more easily approached after a close examination of the contemporary philosophical-intellectual consequences of the economic development, without which no historian can analytically grasp the history of the Russian revolutions.

From the last third of the nineteenth century, that is, from the Peasant Reform of 1861 onwards, the fundamental issue of educated discourse within intellectual life was the nature of Russia's newly developing, autocracy-supported capitalism.[2] Both émigré and local writers from Herzen to Dostoevsky, Kovalevsky to Klyuchevsky, Marx to the young Lenin, were engaged in understanding the particularities of the new form of development in Russia, each drawing political inferences in line with their convictions.

From the 1890s to the first Russian revolution, the fundamental question can be summed up as follows: what are the parameters of the new advances of capitalism, brokered with the direct investment of foreign capital? Embedded within this question is another: what are the roots of "agrarian capitalism"? The upsurge of heavy industry in Russia's two main cities and their larger surrounding areas, as well as in the prosperous, highly profitable mining regions, gave the Russian intelligentsia food for thought regarding the perspectives offered by the new system. After all, the multinational Russian empire was loosening at its seams, a process hastened by the aspirations of awakening ethnic nationals.

Considering the natural consequences of the capitalist upsurge—urban squalor, the slow yet capitalist transformation of agriculture, economic and social differentiation, the broadening of unemployment, prostitution, poverty, and the proliferation of crime—a number of inferences can be drawn. The already existing animosities in Russian society were clearly exacerbated by the first Russian revolution, with its bourgeois democratic goals and partial results. These include the appearance of legal political parties, the "tsar's constitution," the Duma, the peasantry starving for land, a nobility and large landowning aristocracy fearful of losing its social status. The crisis of the reigning autocracy can thus be expressed as the new problems borne by the ascent of the middle classes and the revolutionary activity of the modern labor movement. The resolution of this crisis was demanded by the course of history.

The first Russian revolution expressed all the fundamental contradictions of the new form of development: the failure of imperial politics, the humiliating defeat suffered in the Russo-Japanese War (which revealed the military weakness of the empire), and the increasingly desperate social problems endangering social and political unity from within. There were traditional forms of social resistance such as hunger revolts, peasant land grabs, and strikes. At the same time, there was also the establishment of soviets and an armed workers' uprising (in December 1905). A certain dynamic unfolding of events can be observed. With the weakening of the autocratic framework, many wings of the social democratic movement were thinking of ways to advance the revolution further. At this point, with the growing radicalization of the revolution, the overtaking of the capitalist system as a whole appeared possible.

After the defeat of the first revolution, the contradictions in Russia's development were grouped around three basic issues: (1) the new autocracy; (2) the alternatives presented by the agrarian reforms of Stolypin and Russian economic development; and (3) political solutions to agrarian land distribution and industrial development. This final issue defined the internal conflicts of the revolutionary workers' front.

Though the total defeat of the revolutionary goals in 1907 prompted constitutional-monarchist bourgeois solutions for the educated society, the Russian intelligentsia was divided on how such a "wedding" should be imagined. Intellectuals who fell back upon autocracy, such as the conservative liberals grouped around the *Vekhi* volume (Berdyaev, Struve, Bulgakov, Frank, and others), tried to wed bourgeois development under the cloak of religious philosophy to Russian statehood, hegemony (*derzhavnosti*), Russian Orthodoxy, and the monarchy. The Western-oriented liberals in Miliukov's Kadet Party fantasized about constitutional monarchy. The extreme-right Black Hundreds—with their focus lost in a distant past—wanted "monarchist renewal" propped up by terror and violence. That is, they wanted to mobilize the masses with organizational tools for mass movements that had not been seen before, and "completely exterminate" social democracy. The so-called Octobrist bourgeois and conservative right, in an expression of the essentially peculiar nature of the Russian bourgeoisie, were not willing to give up their close "covenant" with the tsar and the large-landowning aristocracy. Those in the peasant party, the Esers, were also divided between those who supported Russian bourgeois development and antimonarchist terrorists.

These developments, arguments, and struggles were also reflected in the ongoing conflict between the Social Democrats and the various movements. Vladimir Ilyich Lenin was a decisive figure in these struggles. At the center of this theoretical work stood his increasingly differentiated conclusion that Russia was unavoidably on the verge of revolutions that would shape the future of the world.

Lenin's lines of thought, historical analysis, and theoretical arguments, along with numerous other writings and investigations about Russian capitalism, form a cohesive whole internally and in terms of methodology. This is in spite of the fact that political events and aims have considerable weight in his process of analysis. Immediate political concerns, however, did not negatively impact the quality of his thought and theory; at times, in fact, they served as inspiration. The theoretical and methodological coherence of his investigations is surprising, given that Lenin had not even finished his university education when he had already emerged from his first study of Marx. He undertook his systematic study of the Russian conquests of the capitalist system in parallel with these studies, around 1891–1892.

What is capital? What does its essence consist of? Is there a reasonable alternative to it? Is a restoration of traditional society in any way possible? These questions had to be raised at the time, in opposition to the Narodniks and all movements that saw capitalism as something independent of, and alien to, the Russian spirit and Russia's historical conditions. This is when Marxism made headway in Russia, triggering a Copernican turn in the history of Russian scientific thought, and especially the way the young generation of intellectuals in revolt against autocracy thought.

Lenin's ideas in the fields of political theory and organization came to be formulated organically through the historical, economic, theoretical, and political study of Russian capitalism, and more broadly, the capitalist system. This analysis "gave rise" to the new *mass movement* of the proletarian type, and the mapping of a revolution to come.

It was through analysis of the *system* that the recognition dawned that the enemy was not the person of the tsar or the capitalist proprietor, but tsarism, the *system*, and capitalism itself, with its impersonal social conditions, complex network of associations, and the totality of its differentiated social-economic structures and relationships.[3] By extension, this realization led to an appreciation of the value of the workers' movement and a rejection of the tradition of terrorist actions in Russia.

The question that the twenty-year-old Lenin had already framed was: how is it possible to fight the system successfully if its characteristics and rules of existence are not revealed, understood, and debated in public? The young man accepted Hegel's maxim that slaves are no longer slaves when they come to a consciousness of their slavery.

BREAK WITH NARODISM

Lenin was not yet twenty-three years old when he completed the first drafts of his work on the development of Russian capitalism.[4] These early writings and other reviews, articles, lectures— among them the famous pamphlet *What the "Friends of the People" Are, and How They Fight the Social-Democrats* (1894),[5] which conclusively refuted the Narodniks' economic and political approach—were all, according to Lenin's later communications, preparatory labor for *The Development of Capitalism in Russia*. This book, his main work in Russia's economic history, is the single historical text to have been developed with a truly specialized scientific approach.[6] These scientific investigations played an exceptionally important role in the crystallization of Lenin's political and theoretical thought.[7] It needs only to be remembered how thoroughly the writing of this work occupied him in prison, with chapters appearing to him there in full measure, and how he first requested the specialized books he used as source texts from his family when he was in exile.[8]

Though Lenin had a diploma in law, as the years progressed, in addition to serious studies in the fields of agriculture and statistics, he acquired knowledge of economics, history, and scientific methodology. In his research, he consciously strove to link specialized scientific methodology and knowledge with the economic and historical theory and method applied by Marx. Lenin left the old, positivist, sociological approach to history and science behind. These were the grounds on which he criticized the parochialism of certain scholars of the age, those with narrow-minded empirical approaches divorced from other sciences and theory, which left the system as a whole out of consideration and raised "segmentation" and "singularity" to the status of absolutes.

Young Lenin's Marxist approach already showed in his early notes dealing with V. E. Postnikov's volume on agricultural history. He could sense that if a given subject—for example the peasant question—was "artificially" extracted from the *whole* system of references the "fullness of the representation is lost." Using a mixed approach of economic history, theory, and political economy, Lenin placed the nature and system of relations in peasant farming within the context of the flourishing system of capital as a whole, in order to capture the essence of capitalism conceptually.[9] He strove in all consciousness to recreate the real historical and sociological context of the matters being examined.

His early conceptualization of capitalism also took off from the production of commodities and the specific *historical* forms of the division of labor on whose particular form of differentiation it was based. He approached capitalism as a social system, a "social economy," in which the relation to capital, value-added production, maximization of profit, and accumulation of capital is the dominant social association. He saw the fact, a fundamental peculiarity of capitalism, that competition in the market transformed the human being himself, human labor, into a common commodity (wage laborer). He took account of this system, which he already had interpreted as a world system at a young age, in a great variety of historical forms.[10]

Lenin discovered a general economic and social theory outlined in the Marxian legacy, and used its coherent system of concepts to capture the fundamental factors of modern bourgeois society and the tendencies of its universal development.[11] Various political streams could find at long last a link with Lenin's approach, unlike with the Narodnik worldview, which had dominated opposition thinking in Russia for decades. Of course, it was not just Lenin, but a number of other revolutionary writers who were speculating about these problems.

For example, Martov, who was arrested alongside Lenin, set about a methodical critique of Narodism in 1896 when he was behind bars. The following year it was published in the first legal Marxist journal, *Novoye Slovo*.[12] Martov saw the difference between his and Lenin's approach as ideological, in that Lenin compared the "declining Narodism of the 1890s" to the revolutionary Narodism of the 1870s, while Martov himself "attentively traced the whole evolution of legal Narodism" and closely examined the basic contradiction in which the "revolutionary/utopist movement rejecting every sort of 'bourgeoisie' and the whole capitalist mode of production strained against the adaptive opportunism of its reformist tendencies."[13] However, the difference between them lies in the fact that Lenin was primarily occupied with the economic views of Narodism.

What the "Friends of the People" Are elicited a significant response and not only on account of its political bite. In opposition to positivist sociology, it emphasized that the plain "collection of material" and the "plain description of phenomena" are among the worst legacies of the old approach to science.[14] In Lenin's interpretation, the question closest to the heart of the new conception of science was how the commodity system of the social economy develops, and how Russian agriculture becomes subjected to the capitalist market system.

Even the lead-in to *What the "Friends of the People" Are* is extremely interesting. What was the reason for Marx to speak about "modern society" when all economists before him had spoken about society in general? In what capacity does the concept of the "modern" come into play, and by what criteria does he differentiate this modern society from other societies?

Here Lenin sketched the basic concepts of the Marxian theory of social form (social formation, mode of production, relations of production, etc.), emphasizing the economic predetermination of social structure.[15] Apart from the universal characteristics of capitalism, he was interested in the *concrete* transformation from traditional society to capitalism, and especially the commodity structure of the Russian capitalist economy. Contradicting the Narodniks, Lenin proved that "Russia *has entered* the capitalist path,"[16] while at the same time joining battle on "the second front" against the liberal approach (mainly Mikhailovsky's), which then still made its case as Narodism, informing contemporary readers that in Russia "there is no proletariat," but that a system *of its own kind* is about to be born.[17]

Lenin saw the greatest economic and social problem—from both a theoretical and scientific perspective—in the social and economic differentiation of the peasantry, which could be directly associated with the spread of rural wage labor. His attention was drawn to the fact that the Russian peasant most often did not even use the land allotted to him in important agricultural areas ("belonging to him" as its owner within the village community). Due to the lack of tools needed to work the land, he rented it out or was alienated from it on some other account. Lenin looked for the causes of the wide differentiation of the peasantry in capitalist competition and production in general, as well as technological development: "the appearance of a mass of non-farming households and the increase in their numbers, are determined by the struggle of economic interests among the peasantry." The main instrument in this battle is the limitation of the costs of production, which follows the growth of the size of the economy.[18]

In the course of his studies of the causes of peasant differentiation, Lenin arrived at the question of market economy: "The fundamental cause of the struggle of economic interests arising among the peasantry is the existence of a system under which the market is the regulator of social production."[19] He combined the problem of peasant differentiation and the formation of the market economy in his second work, *On the So-Called Market Question*.[20]

This is where Lenin first discussed the general aspects of capitalism and the particular aspects of Russian capitalism in the context of the dialectic of the particular and the general. The question was put as follows: "Is the development of capitalism in Russia necessary?" Behind this question was a conviction that the historical ground had once and for all slipped from under the feet of Narodism, and that the Narodniks were incapable of understanding why, despite the destitution of their social strata, the Russian peasantry remains "silent." That is, why it does not listen to the nation-saving ideals of the Narodnik "preachers" who thought they had a calling.

From a political and scientific perspective Lenin believed the most harmful and naïve Narodnik prejudice was to oppose poverty to the way capitalism works.[21] The political significance of this scientific and theoretical problem is immediately clear, for if capitalism did not have roots in the empire of the tsar, then Marx, Marxism, and social democracy were not applicable to Russia. Lenin's scholarly work was focused wholly on disproving this thesis. The Narodniks saw Russia as if the old, natural economic system would still have been a viable alternative in the face of capitalism. He considered the main mistake of the Narodniks and the first Marxists to be that they conceived of capitalism—and its essential feature, exchange—as a matter of chance "rather than a particular, defined system within the economy."[22]

So in accordance with his approach, Lenin did not view *poverty* as an anomaly of the system, whereas the Narodniks saw it as some sort of remediable "accident." The market economy, the accumulation of capital, concentration, and market competition that permeated everything, in addition to technological development, constantly renews whatever is outdated in capitalism's structure of labor distribution. In the process, as a consequence of crises, from time to time the system undercuts the subsistence of millions of people chained to this structure. When the Narodniks invested market issues with morals, they drew attention away from the real nature of the system. As opposed to this, Lenin focused on structural transformation and the proletarianization of broad masses within society. This process—the current term being *restructuring*—was conditional upon the dissolution of the united peasant class, the village community, the *obshchina*.

In his earliest writings he had already detected the presence of precapitalist economic components that did not "belong there," which he later himself considered a basic problem (*mnogoukladnosti*). In *What the "Friends of the People" Are*, which was written with a primarily political objective, he addressed the historical peculiarities of Russian capitalism. In *The Development of Capitalism in*

Russia, his analysis of the combination of the corvée and the capitalist economy after the reforms of 1861 represents a fully mature part of the work. Even in the title of the book he had signaled that with the broadening of the internal market, the manufacturing industry eliminates the isolation of precapitalist rural Russia.[23] The peasant—having been left, so to say, without land in the wake of the 1861 reforms—becomes a proletarian by remaining tied to agriculture,[24] a fact that proved a truly Russian phenomenon with far-reaching social and political consequences. Lenin's burgeoning polemic against liberalism contributed fundamentally to the differentiation of his stance. The first allies of liberalism—be it of a Slavophile-Narodnik or Western-oriented derivation—emerged from the circles of the "legal Marxists."

BREAK WITH LIBERALISM

Lenin's meeting with Pyotr Struve in 1894 marked the beginning of his debate with liberalism, which was to last nearly three decades. At the time, the liberal movement was still "maturing" in the guise of "legal Marxism"[25] from which, in part, it had emerged. The fundamental theoretical and political issue was how to relate to the new capitalist system along with a critical stance where the Narodist approach to capitalism was concerned.[26]

Lenin made distinctions between the different non-Marxist critiques of capitalism. For example, he wrote an appreciative review of Hobson's *The Evolution of Modern Capitalism*, published in Russian translation in St. Petersburg in 1898 while he was still in exile. Lenin considered Hobson's works describing capitalism critically, and found some of his statistical investigations valuable. For example, Hobson recognized that the role of female labor in modern industry was significant and worthy of elaboration. What Lenin took issue with was Hobson's lack of clarity concerning the theory and basic concepts of modern capitalism, such as the notion of capital or the problem of "savings." However, Lenin was confident that Hobson's empirical research would direct the course of his thoughts toward Marx.[27]

While he interpreted Hobson's "reformism" as an interest in Marxism, he perceived Struve's "Bernsteinism" as distancing him from Marxism. In this case the theoretical split preceded the political one. Even then, Bernsteinism already meant a rejection of the overthrow of the system by revolutionary means, a separation of the political and the economic struggle of the working class, and a narrowing down of "class war" to economic struggle.

The amicable gestures did not in essence influence Lenin's statements about Struve's views, though he obviously did not force the arguments over the edge, making sure not to offend Struve.[28] For a long time, however, Lenin and Struve had been in agreement, in that they believed capitalism would make headway under any circumstances, adding that the less it meets with the resistance of old forms and the more completely it erases these, the better conditions it provides for the labor movement. During this time Lenin widely expressed his regard for Struve's journalistic talent. Their cooperation even extended to *Iskra*, until Struve set out to establish the liberal emigrant periodical *Osvobozhdeniye*[29] at the turn of 1901. For a moment, there still seemed a chance for them to take a common anti-monarchist position. In his private letters, however, Lenin had begun using the epithets "traitor" and "Judas" to describe Struve's turn against social democracy.[30]

At this juncture, Lenin immediately discarded the reformulation of capitalism's emergence that, instead of looking at regional-historical causes, set out from an ahistorical distinction between "good" (Western) capitalism and "bad" (Russian) capitalism. Rather than allowing for a scientific approach, this point of view opened the floodgates for moralizing justifications for the system. Lenin ridiculed Struve, who spoke on behalf of the Russian bourgeoisie, because he also invested this class with a *calling* and such characteristics as "brooding over the future."[31]

A similar criticism is outlined in his notes to Sergei Bulgakov's *Capitalism and Agriculture*, published in 1900, although in Lenin's view Bulgakov is "guilty" of mistakes more of the "Narodnik type." Lenin was mainly critical of Bulgakov's illusions with regard to the following: the development of Russian agriculture could "circumvent" capitalism; the small-holding peasant agriculture, as an independent framework, could be "brought back" after capitalism had faced a crisis.[32]

The work with the greatest significance in Lenin's intellectual development of this period was Kautsky's *Die Agrarfrage*,[33] which he studied and annotated in February and March of 1899 during his time in Shushenskoye. Marxist literature dealing with agriculture was certainly not plentiful at the time. Scholarly investigations by "academic socialists"[34] drew more attention. Kautsky took a close look at basic issues, from land rent to various other problems of agrarian capitalism, and the overweening power of large holdings over small.

It is interesting to see where the different priorities in their approaches parallel at this early stage. Lenin, unlike Kautsky, is already focused on the poorest peasantry, those who are most hurt by the capitalization of agriculture. Lenin also took a different stance on the nationalization of land, not accepting Kautsky's thesis that the state would be worse than private capital at land husbandry. He also rejected Kautsky's thesis that nationalization would not benefit the working classes, as it would only serve to strengthen bourgeois government.[35]

Unlike Lenin, Kautsky did not envision either a communist revolution or a dictatorship of the proletariat, though he did demonstrate the characteristics of wage labor in agriculture and pointed out the significance of self-defense struggles taken up by the peasantry and small-holders, which was very much to Lenin's liking. However, Kautsky recommended a sort of neutrality of the peasanty toward the working classes. Kautsky's anti-utopian, scientific, and theoretically excellent work helped Lenin a great deal in presenting the Russian and eastern European peculiarities in relation to the advance of capitalism. Additionally, it gave him inspiration to expose the Russian illusions concerning small-holder peasant agriculture and directed his attention to the points of conjunction between Narodniks and the liberals.

Lenin sensed that Narodnik reasoning and Struve's argument coincided at a point: "That question is a very relevant one, since Mr. V. V. [V. P. Vorontsov] (and all Narodniks in general) have always compared the Russian order of things with some 'English form' of capitalism and not with its basic features, which have a different appearance in each country." In Struve, for example, the Russian national peculiarity is shown as a trait that is embodied in the circumvention and distortion of capitalism. In contrast, Lenin emphasized that a general theoretical concept of capitalism exists that is not present in either the Narodnik or the "quasi-liberal" position. Struve also points to the "domination of exchange economy," but does not take into account the other feature of capitalism, that surplus value is appropriated by "the owner of the money, the capital."[36] This Narodnik-liberal utopian vision carried such significance for Lenin because he believed that his opponent interpreted Russian capitalism as something taking place in the future instead of something existing in the present; that is, "not as something already and definitely established," as if one of the features of capitalism were "well-being."[37] These divergent theoretical approaches had vastly different political implications.[38]

Some of the aspects of the romantic, nostalgic Narodnik conception of the capitalist system are also featured in the other "stray path": the "liberal deviation." Lenin discovered these similarities in Struve's argument on the state. According to Lenin's interpretation, there is nothing more misleading than taking the state as the "organization of order" to be an analytical starting point, since the most characteristic trait of the state is what Engels emphasized in his day: "Is a public power distinct from the mass of the people?" This has become, at root, the instrument upholding the system of capital and capitalism in general. Lenin argued, "the distinguishing feature of the state is the existence of a separate class of people in whose hands power is concentrated." In agreement with Marx, Lenin thought that the modern state is embodied in the bureaucracy: "In modern society the bureaucracy is the particular stratum which has power in its hands. The direct and intimate connection between this organ and the bourgeois class, which dominates in modern society, is apparent both from history . . . and from the very conditions of the formation and recruitment of this class."[39]

One of the particular characteristics of the "opposition" taken up by the Russian bourgeoisie and its ideological-political representatives by the end of 1903 was that the nationalist bourgeoisie ought to demonstrate its "bravery" and close ties to the "nation's soil" by adding a "Narodnik extension" to liberalism. Lenin wrote: "The Russian bourgeoisie plays at Narodism (and sometimes sincerely) just because it is in opposition, and not yet at the helm of state." Similar to the main trends of Narodism, Lenin explained the "Bernsteinian" unification of liberalism and socialism as the phenomenon of "play imitation of political opposition." That is, as mere tools for the ideological expulsion of revolutionary social democracy and *opposition to the system.*[40]

The true and final split between Marxism and liberalism came with the 1905 Revolution, which presented the following questions in Russian society: in what way should the transformation of autocracy be tackled; how can the democratic federal republic be established; and what should it entail (democratic freedom rights, constitution-founding congress, an eight-hour workday)? With the radicalization of the revolution the problem of transition from "democratic revolution to socialist revolution" (permanent revolution) came to the fore. Serious questions needed answers, such as how to resolve the agrarian issue, the confiscation and redistribution of the estates of the landed gentry, and demands for social and legal equality. The question of a more distant future also surfaced, and was formulated as follows: should there be self-government or revolutionary dictatorship?[41]

These problems provoke a closer examination of the formation of, and relationships between, the political forces of the time. This includes the role of the parties in the revolution, and the development of the social democrats and the "leftist block" (worker-peasant union). The creation of the worker-peasant union was questioned in the contemporary political language as follows: whose side does social democracy take in the struggle against autocracy—the bourgeoisie or the poor peasantry? This question already carried the seeds of the split within social democracy. The first split, at the turn of the century, took place between Lenin and Struve. That is, between the Marxists and the so-called legal Marxists watered down by liberalism.[42]

Russian Distinctiveness and the World System

Lenin had already explored the developmental peculiarity of Russia in his work *The Development of Capitalism in Russia.* Russia was embedded in the global economy—the phrase "semi-peripheral integration" was used—with its pre-capitalist forms preserved as enclosures under capitalism in order to reinforce a subordination that was, among other things, quite suitable to Western capitalist interests. He saw an organic relationship between the "union" of precapitalist and capitalist forms and the concept of tsarist "internal colonization," as well as the devouring of peripheral regions by the center in Russia, through the growth of the Russian market.

A distinct "center–periphery relationship" evolved in light of the facts dictated by "internal colonization" (the border regions including the steppes were earlier the "colonies" of the central, long-populated parts of European Russia).[43] Lenin wrote:

> The extensive development of commercial crops was possible only because of the close economic ties of these colonies with central Russia, on the one hand, and the European grain-importing countries, on the other. The development of industry in central Russia and the development of commercial farming in the outer regions are inseparably connected and create a market for each other.[44]

Capital appropriated the grain and milk markets, thereby rendering all of Russian agriculture subservient to it. Lenin, somewhat exaggerating the level and extent of the development of capitalism, identified this with Russia as a whole. Lenin showed at a very early stage—and this was one of the discoveries that would become a building block of his theory of imperialism—that in the merciless, competitive fights for external markets, "state support, and utilizing state enforcement powers was the ignition to the imperialist period and a defining feature of imperialism."[45] In his work entitled *Once More on the Theory of Realization*, Lenin presented the problem of the market as a question of the *world economy*, the *world system*. He advised capitalism's critics, "do not stop at the traditional separation of the home and foreign markets when analyzing the question of capitalism. This distinction, groundless from a strictly theoretical point of view, is of particularly little use for such countries as Russia."[46]

Lenin returned to this question in his extensive comments on Rosa Luxemburg's *The Accumulation of Capital* in 1913, while living in Poronino.[47] While Luxemburg's accumulation theory posed the problem of the realization of surplus value in the new stage of the development of capitalism in an original way, Lenin shifted emphasis to the recapitalization of the realized surplus value. This would become the fundamental problem of the "period of imperialism," and is deeply intertwined with "the central issue of international exploitation in the world system of imperialism."[48] Goods are always produced for a world market in "pure" capitalism, therefore the problem of the market is part of the process of production. The accumulation of capital and export of goods and capital are part of the same process, indivisible from that which chains the so-called backward countries to the capitalist center. Here, Lenin and Luxemburg are of the same opinion, that the industrialization of the "backward countries and regions" itself subjugates or "colonizes" these territories through the "mediation"[49] of loans. As it later becomes clear, divergent political solutions are born of disparate theoretical views, inasmuch as Lenin did not share Luxemburg's belief that the capitalist system could "collapse."[50]

In his theorization, Lenin connected the features of the world market—today it would be called globalization—with the demise of traditional forms of village community. By way of example, he made reference to the cheap grain from the North American prairies and the Argentinean pampas that had flooded the market. The peasants proved powerless in the face of such competition, with the result that "industrial scale grain production" forced patriarchal agriculture to abandon vast tracts of land.[51] A primary conclusion that can be drawn from Lenin's analysis is that overcoming the patriarchal conditions of slavery itself "certifies" the expansion of capitalism. While the ineluctable facts of history make a return to any traditional form of society impossible, the remnants of obsolete social formations will often fuse with the modern system.

The scientific discovery of this alloy of a variety of forms of production and divergent historical structures is what strengthened Lenin in his conviction that Russia was a region of "overdetermined contradictions" (Althusser). Such contradictions can only be resolved on the *path of revolution*. Lenin only became conscious of the net of correspondences in which the local particularities of capitalism and of the possible overthrow of the tsarist monarchy were conjoined in the course of over a decade of scientific research and political struggle.[52] These investigations led him to the discovery of something of great significance, which was summed up in his thesis of Russia and "the weak link in the chain of imperialism."[53]

To begin with, questions linking the *obshchina* and the *state* were addressed. Going along with Plekhanov, Lenin wrote of the irreversibility of the dissolution of the *obshchina* in his *Friends of the People* (1894), and broke away from Marx's indulgent supposition that in the framework of a European revolution the *obshchina* could fulfill a progressive function as one of the structures of communist society.

The Narodniks also dallied with this Marxian idea—adapting it to their worldview—though in practice what they experienced on their rounds of villages forced them to concede "the naïveté of the idea of the *muzhik*'s instincts being communist."[54]

In writing about the advantages of *bourgeois development* in Russia—with regard to the overlapping old and new forms of exploitation—Lenin stated that the bourgeois democracy provided better conditions for the Social Democrats' political struggle, and more freedom in self-organization, but he had already come to think that they did not have a social base worthy of note. Aware of the peculiar way society was structured in Russia, he took the long-term perspective for the still sparse working class into consideration when determining the goals of the revolution. He related this to the noted "congestion" of economic and political forms of development in Russia, the revolutionary spirit characteristic of the Russian workers as a group, and a complete lack of European bureaucratic organization. Furthermore, he was able to examine the historical phenomenon of "small capitalism," including in his calculations the effect it had on the thinking of the oppressed classes, and the role it would play in the formation of the "workers' socialism" that would oust the Narodniks' "peasant socialism" in early twentieth-century Russia.

> The breakup, the de-peasantization of our peasants and handicraftsmen, which can be depicted accurately thanks to the admirable material provided by Zemstvo statistics, furnishes factual proof of the correctness of precisely the Social-Democratic conception of Russian reality, the conception that the peasant and the handicraftsman are petty producers in the "categorical" meaning of the term, that is, are petit bourgeois. This thesis may be called the central point of the theory of WORKING-CLASS SOCIALISM as against the old peasant socialism, which understood neither the conditions of commodity economy in which the petty producers live, nor their capitalist differentiation due to these conditions. . . . This mass of small rural exploiters represents a terrible force, especially terrible because they oppress the isolated, single toiler, because they fetter him to themselves and deprive him of all hope of deliverance; terrible because this exploitation, in view of the barbarism of the countryside due to the low labor productivity characteristic of the system described and to the absence of communications, constitutes not only robbery of labor, but also the Asiatic abuse of human dignity that is constantly encountered in the countryside. Now, if you compare this real countryside with our capitalism you will understand why the Social-Democrats regard the work of our capitalism as progressive when it draws these small, scattered markets together into one nationwide

> market, when, in place of the legion of small well-meaning blood-suckers, it creates a handful of big "pillars of the fatherland," when it socializes labor and raises its productivity, when it shatters the subordination of the working people to the local blood-suckers and subordinates them to large-scale capital. This subordination is progressive compared with the former—despite all the horrors of the oppression of labor, of gradual extinction, brutalization, and the crippling of the bodies of women and children, etc.—because it AWAKENS THE MIND OF THE WORKER, converts dumb and incoherent discontent into conscious protest, converts scattered, petty, senseless revolt into an organized class struggle for the emancipation of all working folk, a struggle which derives its strength from the very conditions of existence of this large-scale capitalism, and therefore can undoubtedly count upon CERTAIN SUCCESS.[55]

Even at this early stage Lenin connected the inevitable unfolding of Russian socialism with Marx's idea of "world revolution," though in his consideration, the Russian revolution would be the first push for world revolution.[56] In theoretical and intellectual terms, Lenin prepared the ground for the new wave of revolutions beginning in 1905, but he overestimated the universality and depth of the revolutionary movement, the vulnerability of centralized capitalism, and the revolutionaries' ability to integrate antagonisms. Marx made the same "mistake" a half century earlier, in a period similarly overrun with revolutions (and called the first European revolutions by E. J. Hobsbawm, in his work *The Age of Revolution*).

It should be apparent that Marx thought the whole capitalist system as it is, with its own technical and cultural basis, apt for the realization of a communal society. Lenin, in "semi-peripheral Russia," was "impelled" by this "traditional" attitude to develop a mindset that examined the sociopolitical forces and interests that moved revolutionary and counterrevolutionary outbreaks in the period of the revolution.

In the years following the failure of the first Russian revolution, Lenin made the *particularities of the circumstances of the development* of Russian capitalism the subject of even more systematic study.[57] The defeat of the revolution motivated him to more closely study the transforming role and nature of the (autocratic) state: how it was becoming relatively independent; the "Bonapartist" separation of the state from the ruling classes (which, as he thought, made any form of serious cooperation with the bourgeoisie on the part of the working classes impossible); the heavy concentration of industrial capitalism that went hand-in-hand with the concentration of the main political forces. The main alternatives of agrarian development came to be outlined in his thought.

In debates with friends and comrades from 1901 to 1911, Lenin emphasized that the tsar's monarchy had wrested some independence from the ruling classes, and that though in the aftermath of 1905 "tsarism took a few steps toward becoming a bourgeois monarchy," the bureaucratic machine preserved its relatively independent system of interests opposing the landed aristocracy on the one hand, but even more so, the bourgeoisie. In the beginning of the twentieth century, tsarism wanted to preserve its own existence and its competitiveness on the international scene by "soliciting the entry" of foreign capital into Russia. But in 1905, as it wrestled the peasantry and the insurgent, mainly agricultural proletariat, tsarism had to face the fact that it had lost its social base.[58]

Particularity appeared in Lenin's thinking not only in relation to development in Russia, but also in regard to and comparison with Western development. For example, the theoretical interpretation of center–periphery relations appears early and often in Lenin's work. The first investigation took shape in 1899, in the introduction to *The Development of Capitalism in Russia*, where he emphasized how palpable were the identical main features in the spread of capitalism in Western Europe and Russia, "notwithstanding the tremendous peculiarities of the latter, in both the economic and non-economic spheres."[59] He referred to the widespread use of wage labor in agriculture, and, in general, to freely deployed wage labor, the introduction of technology, and the increasing division of labor, which do not contradict the peculiarities of capitalism in Russia previously discussed but mark out the universal coordinate system for the peculiarities. At the same time, the "disconnection" of social development from economic development in the literature of the day proved to be misleading, and from the point of view of those setting out a political strategy, absolutely disorienting. One need think only of the misunderstandings engendered in certain wings of the Mensheviks and among the liberals with regard to the nature of the revolutionary process. They erroneously interpreted economic development exclusively in terms of the Western European experience.[60]

After the outbreak of the First World War, Lenin returned to his methodical investigation of the nature of the world system of capital in his book on imperialism,[61] some aspects of which must be discussed here—though out of sequence in terms of our timeline. Lenin had observed some of the impressive elements in the processes of "new capitalism," or "imperialism," which he discussed summarily in his article "The Taylor System—Man's Enslavement by the Machine."[62]

During the First World War, when Lenin developed his theory of imperialism,[63] in certain ways he anticipated the modern line of inquiry about a *hierarchical world system* while focusing on its economic and political features.[64] In the age of collusion between industry and bank capital, he emphasized the trend of exporting capital rather than commodities, which makes the amassing of extra profit possible in Western countries due to *unequal development*. In this way he pointed out the system of dependence built on debt, in the course of which Great Britain, for example, "grants loans to Egypt, Japan, China and South America," while her military-political power "protects her from the indignation of her debtors," and "her navy plays here the part of bailiff in case of necessity."[65]

He came upon the important realization—subsequently characterizing his stance in regard to the whole revolution—that with the new level of concentration of capital, the universal spread of finance capital "throws a close network of dependent relationships over all the economic and political institutions of present-day bourgeois society without exception."[66] This development is expressed in the monopolization of colonialist politics.[67] The specific features of imperialism as an economic and political world system became apparent in regard to all of its aspects during the First World War. The fact that Lenin recognized the *extraordinary expansion in the economic role of the state* and its *interconnectedness with capital—finance capital to put it more exactly*, which gained such special significance in the hierarchic organization of the capitalist world system and in the universal war carried on to secure the colonial periphery—is a fundamental factor in his estimation of the possibilities for the revolution of 1905, and revolution in general.[68] Elsewhere, he reformulated it as "wherever finance capital becomes very strong, so does the state."

Taking into account the stock shares in the possession of the world capitalist system's major economic players (Britain, the United States, France, and Germany) in 1910, Lenin established that there is a hierarchy that brings about a chain of mutual dependence: "in one way or another, nearly the whole of the rest of the world is more or less the debtor to and tributary of these international banker countries, these four 'pillars' of world finance capital. It is particularly important to examine the part which the export of capital plays in creating the international network of dependence on and connections of finance capital."[69] In an article of October 1913, "Capitalism and Workers' Immigration," Lenin already noted the mass expatriation of people for the global immigration of labor, which he considered a new form of exploitation. He charted the development of rising expatriation and international migration based mainly on U.S. sources.

The United States witnessed the arrival of over a million people annually between 1905 and 1909, with reinforcements to the U.S. labor supply mainly coming from Russia. A significant portion of these Russian immigrants "had participated in various strikes in Russia, [and] introduced into America the bolder and more aggressive spirit of the mass strike." Based on his observation of this emigration phenomenon, Lenin theorized that the basic aim of the rapidly developing industrial countries was to minimize the price of labor by luring immigrant laborers away from their home countries by the promise of higher wages. With this the competition between wage workers is heightened in various regions of the world system: "Capitalism has given rise to a special form of migration of nations. The rapidly developing industrial countries, introducing machinery on a large scale and ousting the backward countries from the world market, raise wages at home above the average rate and thus attract workers from the backward countries . . ." With this the competition between wage workers is heightened in various regions of the world system (with the "classical" examples of this best evidenced in the present stage of globalization).

> Emancipation from the yoke of capital is impossible without the further development of capitalism, and without the class struggle that is based on it. And it is in this struggle that capitalism is drawing the masses of the working people of the *whole* world, breaking down the musty, fusty habits of local life, breaking down national barriers and prejudices, uniting workers from all countries in huge factories and mines in America, in Germany, and so forth. America heads the list of countries which imports workers.[70]

Looking at it from a current perspective, this was a rather mechanical deduction of the international unification of labor from the globalization of capital. However, there was a surprising clarity of vision regarding the United States' potential for being the motor of global development in the twentieth century.

Lenin expanded this analysis in the brochure "New Data on the Laws Governing the Development of Agriculture," originally written in 1915 and published in 1917. In this iteration he also offered a historical comparison with European and Russian development:

> The U.S.A. is unrivalled either in the rate of development of capitalism at the turn of the century, or in the record level of capitalist development already attained; nor has it any rival in the vastness of the territory developed with the use of the most up-to-date machinery, which is adapted to the remarkable variety of natural and historical conditions or in the extent of the political liberty and the cultural level of the mass of the population. That country, indeed, is in many respects the model for our bourgeois civilization and is its ideal.[71]

As Lenin realized, the integration of the colonies in world politics would recompose the very nature of the world system. In the modern age, the universal mechanism of capitalist production worked continuously in the background of these processes, inevitably "integrating" the subjected peoples.

Lenin was perhaps first amongst Marxists to outline in a clear theoretical way that the colonies, in the age of free-enterprise capitalism, were,

> drawn into commodity exchange but not into capitalist production. Imperialism changed this. Imperialism is, among other things, the export of capital. Capitalist production is being transplanted to the colonies at an ever increasing rate. They cannot be extricated from dependence on European finance capital. From the military standpoint, as well as from the standpoint of expansion, the separation of the colonies is practicable, as a general rule, only under socialism; under capitalism it is practicable only by way of exception or at the cost of a series of revolts and revolutions both in the colonies and the metropolitan countries.[72]

Lenin's recognition of the "victims" of colonization establishing independent *national movements* in addition to the workers' movement—thereby the national question gaining significance on a world scale, pointing far afield of Europe—is to be addressed later. Here it need only be noted that, historically speaking, even in this question Russia falters at a "midway" stage. While Lenin attributes great importance to the hierarchic structure of the world system elsewhere, he nonetheless underestimated, when considering the unification of the workers of the world by capital, the strength of factionalism, the cultural and linguistic obstacles, the psychological and political barriers, and the economic and social potency of central capitalism.

The Political Factors Determining Russian Capitalism in 1905

By 1901 Lenin suspected, or was quite aware, that the "ruling class" (current terminology would use dominant, or hegemonic) in the Russian bourgeois democratic revolution would be the proletariat.[73] The foremost reason for this was the political insignificance of the bourgeoisie at the time. It was dependent on tsarism, and lacked autonomy in relation to both tsarism and foreign capital. As a result, those members of the peasantry who lost their livelihoods because of capitalist development would come forward to join the working-class alliance (the politics of the leftist block),[74]displacing the bourgeoisie and the large landholding gentry. At the time, these realizations were considered by many to be some sort of "Leninist heresy," even in Western Marxist circles, as if the Russian peasantry was still a sort of reactionary pulp.

Lenin considered the agrarian interests of the peasantry part and parcel of the question of power and economy in Russia. He rejected the Mensheviks' suggestion that the agrarian question could be resolved through municipalization, with land as the property of local governments. Lenin and the Bolsheviks thought in terms of the *nationalization* of the large landholdings because this was to their thinking the *best means to expropriate* the estates and unseat the monarchy.[75] The direct political content of the debates addressed the question of who would receive the land-rent: the local governments controlled by the nobility or the state. After the defeat of the 1905 Revolution, Lenin struck this note with regard to the agrarian program:

> Theoretically, nationalization is the "ideally" pure development of capitalism in agriculture. The question whether such a combination of conditions and such a relation of forces as would permit of nationalization in capitalist society often occur in history is another matter.[76]

The rejection of small private holdings was not merely the effect of some social-democratic doctrinaire attitude, but was based on the historical grounds that the Prussian form of agrarian development, with its specific internal features, did not pertain to Russia's situation. That the Social Democrats stood for an agriculture based on collectives and voluntary cooperation, which was viewed as the only alternative to capitalist agricultural development, was an entirely different matter.

The experiences of 1905 helped to clarify the whole picture. The peasantry—to put it euphemistically—stood for agrarian land distribution. In reaction to the peasant uprisings of 1902–1903 and the revolutionary agrarian movements of 1905–1907, the tsar's government (from Witte to Stolypin) strove to quicken the demise of the village community by encouraging a well-to-do peasant layer secured by private landholdings. On Stolypin's initiative the tsar soon issued a decree, on 9 November 1906, giving every head of household who owned land the right to take his farmstead into private ownership and out of the land commune. He could also demand that the plot be sliced out in one piece as opposed to several smaller and noncontiguous parcels. Barely two million peasants left the village community in the almost nine years preceding the First World War.

After the failure of the revolution, Lenin wrote *The Agrarian Program of Social-Democracy in the First Russian Revolution, 1905–1907*, in which he took positions on basic political questions concerning Russia's agricultural conditions with the expertise of a scholar.[77] Again, it is the group of issues Lenin chose as central that would be very important for the future. The "decisive link in the chain" was the peasants' struggle for land in determining Russian village life:

> Ten million peasant households own 73,000,000 dessiatins of land, whereas 28,000 noble and upstart landlords own 62,000,000 dessiatins. Such is the main background of the arena on which the peasants' struggle for the land is developing. On such a main background amazing technical backwardness, the neglected state of agriculture, an oppressed and downtrodden state of the mass of peasantry and an endless variety of forms of feudal, corvée exploitation are inevitable. . . . The size of the landholdings outlined by us in no way corresponds to the scale of farming. In the purely Russian gubernias large-scale capitalist farming definitely drops into the background. Small-scale farming preponderates on large latifundia, comprising various forms of tenant farming. . . . The mass of the peasants, crushed by feudal exploitation, are being ruined and some of them let their allotments to "thrifty" farmers.[78]

In accordance with these circumstances of "medieval likeness," Lenin established—in contradiction to all other trends—that the basic political conflict of the Russian village was between the great masses of peasantry and the owners of large estates supported by tsarism. This conflict could only be resolved when at last the peasantry appropriated the land possessed by the landowners.

Lenin was accused of taking an agrarian position, which prompted the following reply to his critics: "My picture . . . does not deal at all with the terms of the transfer of the land to the peasants. . . . I have taken only the transfer of the land in general to the small peasants and there can be no doubt whatever that this is the trend of our agrarian struggle."[79] Elsewhere he argued against his agrarian comrades. He said that agrarian reform was not on the historical agenda for the moment, as its formulation would create misunderstandings. Specifically, it might seem to represent the interests of the wealthy, who were the capitalists in the eyes of the poor peasant. The suitable political and class power relations did not yet exist.[80] Later, he explored in extensive detail the conditions under which nationalization might lead to land division, and to what degree it might "'whet the appetite' for the socialization of the whole of social production."[81]

Lenin had already grasped that land division was unavoidable in the future, perhaps "not as private property, but for economic use."[82] This foreshadowed the land decree of October 1917 that implemented agrarian land division through nationalization. Lenin considered two possible trends: the bourgeois, capitalist transformation of latifundia, which would "substitute bourgeois for feudal methods of exploitation"; and the more radical, truly revolutionary transformation, which would open the gates to smallholding peasant agriculture and lead to its free development "along the path of capitalist economy."[83] The latter case would mean the "transformation of the patriarchal peasant into the bourgeois farmer."

Lenin considered Stolypin's reforms "progressive" for their destruction of the feudal chains and their acceleration of the evolution of capitalism. In contradiction to Plekhanov and the Mensheviks, he refused any and all forms of political support for these reforms and excluded any possibility of cooperation with the bourgeoisie. Beside this, he considered the bloodthirsty Stolypin a "modernizer" and a "market economy" guardian of the autocracy, rather than its opponent.

Lenin had seen these political, tactical, and strategic debates through with the Mensheviks, when Russia was still moving toward the revolution, as evidenced by his *Two Tactics of Social-Democracy in the Democratic Revolution* (published in the summer of 1905 in Geneva). The Bolsheviks emphasized the *worker* side of a revolution that is bourgeois-democratic in its aims, and the participation of the Social Democrats in the powers of government, while the Mensheviks relegated to the working class the role of "extreme left." According to Lenin, a victorious revolution brings about the regime of the "democratic dictatorship of the proletariat and the peasantry."[84] This would be a dictatorship that could lead the country, through internal and external circumstances beneficial for development, to a new "socialist phase" of the revolution while repressing the forces seeking to restore autocracy.

Even at this stage Lenin considered the relatedness of these two phases of the revolution:

> We all contrapose bourgeois revolution and socialist revolution; we all insist on the absolute necessity of strictly distinguishing between them; however, can it be denied that in the course of history individual, particular elements of the two revolutions become interwoven?[85]

The Russian bourgeoisie had no interest in the radicalization of the revolution and its completion. Rather, it had hopes that the revolution could be reined in. During the 1905 Revolution and especially after its defeat, Lenin lashed out at the liberals: "After October 1905, all that the liberals did was to shamefully betray the cause of the people's freedom. . . . The revolution exposed the liberals very quickly and showed them in their true counterrevolutionary colors." Hopes that the autocracy could be combined with actual representation of more or less broad masses of the people existed not only among the ignorant and downtrodden inhabitants of various out-of-the-way places. Such hopes were not absent even in ruling spheres of the autocracy.[86]

In January of 1917, speaking to an audience of young Swiss workers—and remembering 1905 on the eve of a new revolution—Lenin explained the political insignificance of the Russian bourgeoisie, its subjection to the tsar, and to the Western European bourgeoisie. In this instance Lenin was also arguing with Max Weber about the nature of the revolution:

> Even in the freest, even in the republican countries of Western Europe, the bourgeoisie manages very well to combine its hypocritical phrases about "Russian atrocities" with the most shameless financial transactions,[87] particularly with financial support of tsarism and imperialist exploitation of Russia through export of capital, etc. . . . The bourgeoisie likes to describe the Moscow uprising as something artificial, and to treat it with ridicule. For instance, in German so-called "scientific" literature, Herr Professor Max Weber, in his lengthy survey of Russia's political development, refers to the Moscow uprising as a "putsch." "The Lenin group," says this "highly learned" Herr Professor, "and a section of the Socialist-Revolutionaries had long prepared for this senseless uprising.". . . In reality, the inexorable trend of the Russian revolution was toward an armed, decisive battle between the tsarist government and the vanguard of the class-conscious proletariat.[88]

At the same time he took on members of his own party for their polemics. Many who believed in the struggle against the system found even the mere formulation of bourgeois democratic demands pointless, that its realization was impossible under capitalist conditions. Lenin, on the other hand, saw the bourgeois democratic demands as important and specifically suited to the conditions of Russian capitalism. Not because it was possible to realize them in the "periphery" of the Russian capitalist system, but for their potential to disrupt this framework.

He was fully aware, for example, that the democratic republic "logically" contradicted capitalism since it officially put the rich and the poor on the same footing and this equality before the law only cloaked the existing antagonistic economic inequalities. He was also aware this contradiction between the economic system and the political structure in the age of imperialism, when free competition is replaced by the rule of monopolies, makes the achievement of every democratic right more difficult:

> How, then, is capitalism reconciled with democracy? By indirect implementation of the omnipotence of capital. There are two economic means for that: (1) direct bribery; (2) alliance of government and stock exchange. (That is stated in our theses—under a bourgeois system finance capital "can freely bribe and buy any government and any official.")[89]

Though Lenin was of the opinion that "'wealth' in general is fully capable of achieving domination over any democratic republic by bribery and through the stock exchange," this did not necessarily mean that the fight for democracy should be abandoned in claiming socialism. To Lenin's political mind the precondition of any successful attack upon capital was the creation of as wide a support of the masses (the "leftist block," that is, "the alliance of the workers and the landless poor peasants") as possible. He argued for the importance of the struggle for democracy with the members of his party, and he only became more convinced of its significance following the experiences of 1905. The *worker's revolution*, as a precondition of socialism, seemed possible in a single country. According to Lenin's line of argument, however, a socialist system could not be realized on a purely "Russian basis." His argument about permanent revolution with Parvus and Trotsky also concerned this matter in major part, in that they judged the problem of "transition" between the two revolutions differently.[90]

Lenin was the first, along with Rosa Luxemburg, to realize that in historical terms a new form of revolution had taken place in 1905.[91] This event was "proletarian in its tolls and character" (in other words, political mass strikes and armed uprising), bourgeois democratic in its aims, and at the same time open to socialist revolution. Lenin saw precisely the limitations of the revolution, most clearly apparent in the "weakness" of its social carriers: "loyal God-fearing subjects—led by the priest Gapon, streamed from all parts of the capital" to the tsar. While the naïve, illiterate Russian masses "learned" from the unfolding events with tumultuous speed, "the uneducated workers in pre-revolutionary Russia [also] proved by their deeds that they were straightforward people awakened to political consciousness for the first time."[92] Yet the Russian workers' and peasants' radical revolutionary action was not enough to insure that the structures of self-government (strike committee, soviets, workers' committees, etc.) would remain standing.

As a "new type" of revolution, this event finally lifted Russia onto the stage of "modern" history. In Lenin's words, "dormant Russia was transformed into a Russia of a revolutionary proletariat and a revolutionary people." Interwoven in this scene were: the land grab movement of the peasants in revolt against patriarchal conditions; the revolution of the industrial laborers; and the freedom struggles flaring up among the repressed peoples of Russia. All this unfolded in the course of 1917, which meant that the revolutionaries could not yet attain from the experience itself the necessary depth of understanding about them. Meanwhile, it is obvious that Lenin could give expression to the Western European urgency of the revolution in any form but that of a logical hypothesis, and that to back it up, he could not chart an analysis of even nearly as great a depth as he had done for the possibilities of Russian development.

THE HISTORICAL DEBATE: THE NATURE OF THE AUTOCRATIC STATE

By the time of the 1905 Revolution, Russian social democracy had been thoroughly engaged in theoretical and scientific debates that raised to consciousness those particularities of Russian historical development that defined the events, limits, and possibilities of the contemporary political class struggle, as well as the more significant trends of the revolution's development. The debate on the autocratic state proceeded in phases. The original point of departure was the Slavophile approach, dating to the early nineteenth century, which posited a "Russian exceptionality" with the "state being alien to the spirit of the people," or even the "omnipotence of the state" in the form of the "*obshchina*, which preserved Russian virtues."[93] The "Westernizer," or *zapadnik* group, formed in opposition to the Slavophiles. They soon relegated the "Russian peculiarities" to the category of *backwardness* as compared with the West. At the end of the nineteenth century, this debate turned into the polemics of the liberals and the Marxists. In the early twentieth century, following the first Russian revolution, the treatment of autocracy became the grounds of fractious contention even among the various wings of the social democratic movement. The political stakes of historical analysis were so high that arguments arose even among the Bolsheviks with regard to the nature of the autocratic state and the right theoretical-political conclusions to draw from it.

By the time Lenin joined the fray, Plekhanov had drawn up—on the basis of Hegel, Marx, and Engels,[94] as well as Russian historians M. M. Kovalevsky and V. O. Klyuchevsky—a Marxist position with a liberal approach to history in relation to the Russian autocratic state and on the issue of the *obshchina*. This was opposed to Miliukov and the so-called state school's position, where the main influences were Comte and Spencer.[95] This set of issues became a serious matter of discussion in social democratic circles during the first Russian revolution, when they had to clarify their relationship with the bourgeoisie and peasantry.

In April 1905, the Bolsheviks convened the Third Party Congress in London with the purpose of taking a stance on these issues. The Mensheviks clarified their point of view at a rival conference in Geneva, and then debated the Bolsheviks at the Fourth and Fifth Congresses of 1907 in London. In tandem with these debates, the subject was addressed in numerous political works.

Engrossed in the polemics of the agrarian debate with Lenin, Plekhanov once again highlighted that "Asian stagnation," the "*kitayschina*," played a defining role in the development of Russian peasantry. He insisted that Lenin did not understand his historical analogy of twentieth-century Russia to eleventh-century China. He argued, "the history of Russian agriculture is similar more to that of the world of Eastern despotism, such as India, Egypt or China, than that of Western Europe."[96] In a certain sense, Plekhanov retreated from his earlier position, as presented in his *Our Differences* (1885), that the question of the taxed village community—which descended directly from Peter the Great—should be examined in the comparative context of Russia and the East but also pinpointed a determinative characteristic in Russia's peculiar "oscillating line of development" between the East and the West. In particular, it stressed the destructive force of Western development where it concerned Russian serfdom.[97]

At the conference, Lenin reminded Plekhanov that if land was nationalized in Muscovite Russia, it was done in a period when Asian modes of production were dominant in the economy. However, at the beginning of the twentieth century, when the dominance of capitalist modes of production in agriculture needed to be addressed, not much was left of Plekhanov's argument. Plekhanov mixed up the two types of nationalization—which Lenin, not without cause, called a mistake worthy of a popular comedy[98]—and considered the "Asiatic aspect" of the capitalist mode of production (in contrast to all other historicizations) an ancillary phenomenon. The political stake in this theoretical debate about economic formations was the choice between the Bolshevik concept of the *nationalization* of land and the Menshevik idea of *municipalization*. The historical evaluation of the Russian state came to maturity within the framework of political debates born from the 1905 Revolution and its downfall.

The agricultural reforms of Stolypin that served to make the rural regions available to the spread of capitalist private property signaled change both in the policy of the autocracy and in its very nature. Lenin interpreted this as resolute steps on the autocracy's "path toward becoming a bourgeois monarchy." Three contentious questions were raised in the process.

The first is represented by the neo-Slavophile and "statist" worldview of the *Vekhi* circle, which defended the autocracy under the mantle of religious philosophy. The main ideological objective of the essays that comprised *Vekhi* was to "save the Russian state at all costs" against "renegade intellectualism."[99] In Struve's formulation, state socialism provided justification for both the foreign policy ambitions of the autocracy and the patriotic mobilization of the intelligentsia to defend the autocratic state.[100] Thus, it became the forerunner of the edict that intellectuals accept Russia's commitment to the war as a matter of their own responsibility. The Miliukovist wing of liberals opposed the diffusion of Vekhist religious philosophy in scientific questions, but did not side with the conclusions of the revolutionaries and the overthrow of the autocracy either. Russian Marxists saw the advance of the "Russian Bismarck" in Vekhism,[101] while a sort of Westernized evolution of autocracy seemed to have been envisioned in Vekhism.

The analyses of the Russian Marxists were differentiated from the liberal approaches by two main features. The first was the extension of the theory of class struggle to the historical analysis of the Russian state, in that they did not speak about the Russian state in general but examined the various forms in which it had existed and its class character. Second, they brought the development of the Russian state into correlation with the given economic factors, especially the specificities of the development of capitalism in Russia. Both the Bolsheviks and the Mensheviks strove to interpret the Russian historical process independently, in line with their own political schemes.[102]

Trotsky's analysis came to the conclusion that, unlike in the West, where an "equilibrium of the economically dominant classes" had been achieved, in Russia the social weakness and political insignificance of the ruling classes "made bureaucratic autocracy a self-contained organization [*Samodovleyushchiy*]." In this sense Trotsky placed Russian tsarism after 1907 somewhere between European absolutism and Asiatic despotism. Inasmuch as he emphasized the demiurgic role of the autocratic state in economic life (and at the same time "prophesied" a colossal role for the state in the case of a socialist takeover), Trotsky discovered a key to understanding the evolution of the tsar's autocratic state.[103] P. P. Maslov, the leading Menshevik economist, saw the main obstacle to modernization as the landed aristocracy's blocking of the Stolypin reforms, and the fact that most of the foreign capital entering the country in the form of government bonds was not directed at the modernization of production.[104] Lenin was in agreement with this analysis.

The Mensheviks had not grasped the fact that the economic role of the Russian state began to grow when capitalist development took off precipitously. This peculiar contradiction of the archaic and modern within the autocratic state was reflected in a paradigmatic way. It gained expression in the *high level of independence of the state*, and the political weakness and shapelessness of the social groups upon which it was built.

Bolshevik historian M. Alexandrov Olminsky[105]—a close colleague of Lenin in publishing *Pravda* and other Bolshevik journals—together with famous Bolshevik historian M. N. Pokrovsky collaborated on an analysis of the historical role and function of the Russian state that contained a vulgarized account of the class struggle.[106] For Olminsky, the prime enemy was the historical sciences' liberal conception of the state. He strove to prove that with the Russian state, absolutism signifies the political power of the nobility, and the autocratic state is *directly* at the service of the economic interests of the landholding nobility. In consequence, all views discussing an opposition of the state and the nobility are merely expressions of the liberal-Miliukovist[107] doctrine that the state is *above class*. He even attacked Kautsky's *The Driving Forces and Prospects of the Russian Revolution* (1907) because the author "underestimated the power of the popular masses." Kautsky conceived of history not as the history of the masses, but as the history of monarchs.[108] Olminsky treated a variety of historical forms of the state as absolutism, the constitutional monarchy and the democratic republic at the same level, on the grounds that all "were the political organization of one or more classes."

The problem with such a vulgarized approach to the state and class struggle is not that it is simplified and unscientific, but that no acceptably articulate revolutionary politics could be built upon such a notion. Lenin had to take an opposite position to this view and the political deductions that followed from it. He did this with some reluctance, since Olminsky was a valued member of the Bolshevik Party.

To gain some understanding of the historical circumstances of this approach, it is necessary to see that polemics against a liberal approach to history were practiced by certain historians who wanted to prove at any cost that for centuries capitalism had been progressing in Russia contiguously with developments in the West. They found Marx at fault for his alleged "liberal leanings." David Ryazanov published an abridged translation of Marx's famous work, *Revelations of the Diplomatic History of the 18th Century*, and a critical examination at the end of 1908 in German (published in Russian in 1918). Ryazanov did not like Marx looking for the "cradle of Muscovy" in the "bloody swamp of Mongol slavery," because this conception contradicted the thesis of Russia's capitalistic past, and he assumed it could be used to justify and strengthen the liberal view of the "demiurgic role" of the Russian state.[109] The resulting image of Marx as a "naïve democrat or liberal" could not have met with Lenin's approval.

Behind the theoretical and historical errors of certain Bolshevik ideologues and historians, Lenin discovered the "left-wing" *Otzovist* movement that had arisen in his own Bolshevik faction. This movement underestimated the political significance of the Social Democrats in the Duma and even wanted to recall the representatives. Apart from its theoretical and methodological weaknesses, the position taken by Olminsky and others made it impossible in political terms to prepare the *transitional demands* for, and *transitions* to, the final revolutionary goal. The approach questioned the grounds of the whole political struggle for the republic and democratic human rights.

For similar reasons, Lenin waged a polemical battle against a platform that had come to the fore in Trotsky's *Pravda*, one that opposed the RSDLP resolution of December 1908. Taking a position similar to Olminsky's, the first thesis of this platform stated that:

> the regime established on 3 June 1907, represents, "in fact, the unrestricted domination of the feudal-type landed nobility." It goes on to point out that they are "disguising the autocratic and bureaucratic nature of their domination with the pseudo-constitutional mask of a State Duma that actually possesses no rights." If the landowners' Duma "actually possesses no rights"—and that is true—how, then, can the domination of the landowners be "unrestricted"? The authors forget that the class character of the tsarist monarchy in no way militates against the vast independence and self-sufficiency of the tsarist authorities and of the "bureaucracy," from Nicholas II down to the last police officer. The same mistake, that of forgetting the autocracy and the monarchy, of reducing it directly to the "pure" domination of the upper classes, was committed by the *otzovists* in 1908–09 . . . by Larin in 1910, it is now being committed by some individual writers (for instance, M. Alexandrov), and also by N. Rikov who has gone over to the liquidators.[110]

In his *Draft Resolution on the Present Moment and the Tasks of the Party* of December 1908, Lenin captured the change caused by the *coup d'état* of 3 June and the establishment of the Third Duma. The upper classes and monarchy were now aligned in defense though in constant battle with each other:

> The alliance of tsarism with the Black-Hundred landlords and the top commercial and industrial bourgeoisie has been openly solidified and recognized by the *coup d'état* of 3 June and the establishment of the Third Duma. Having of necessity finally taken the path of the capitalist development of Russia, and striving to keep to a path which would preserve the power and the revenues of the feudalist landlords, the autocracy is maneuvering between that class and the representatives of capital. Their petty disputes are made use of for the maintenance of absolutism.[111]

As early as November 1908 Lenin described the Bonapartist traits of the "new" system in formation. In his article "The Assessment of the Present Situation," he projected the inevitability of the "confiscation of all landed estates" if the established system and the reforms of Stolypin, with their shared aim of transforming land owned by village communities into capitalist private property, came up against opposition. Both the peasantry and the landed aristocracy were unhappy with their end of the deal, and the interests of the latter allowed for the assassination that ended Stolypin's life in 1911. The Bonapartist mechanism of power settled upon these social and political conflicts.[112]

Lenin estimated the maximum "success rate" of Stolypin's reforms in "the emergence of a stratum of consciously counterrevolutionary Octobrist peasants" (i.e., the bourgeois conservative political faction) while the decisive majority of peasants remained in the revolutionary camp. This balance of forces could not find expression in the Duma, but "the faked majority of Black-Hundred representatives plus the Octobrists" as determined by the existing electoral law and in line with the Bonapartist tendencies could not hide the increasingly obvious contradiction between the "Black-Hundred autocracy, which virtually reigns supreme, and the window-dressing of a bourgeois 'constitution.'"[113]

Lenin projected his argument with his opponents in two directions: to the matter of the transformation of the social character of the monarchy and about Bonapartism on the one hand, and the question of determining the stream of Russian agrarian development on the other. In an article written at the end of 1911, Lenin marked out the new sociopolitical arrangement after the revolution. He highlighted interrelations between "old and new" motifs of development. For the evolution of the monarchy he referred to the Stolypin reforms, and proposed connections between the leading circles of the autocratic bureaucracy and the merchant and industrial bourgeoisie would be an important factor:

> Only people who have never given a thought to the new [innovations] brought by the first decade of the twentieth century, who understand nothing about the interdependence between the economic and the political relations in Russia and about the significance of the Third Duma can deny that this connection exists, deny that the present agrarian policy is bourgeois in character, deny in general that "a step" has been taken "toward the transformation into a bourgeois monarchy.". . . While "drawing strength" from the support of the upper ranks of the bourgeoisie the bureaucracy is not recruited from the bourgeoisie, but from the old, very old . . . landed and office-holding nobility.[114]

Lenin drew attention to the effect the bureaucracy had on the Russian bourgeoisie. It gave the function of the bourgeoisie an altogether feudal character. According to Lenin, it also gave this relationship a new definition:

> [I]f there is a difference between the bourgeois character of the Prussian Junker and the American farmer (although both of them are unquestionably bourgeois), there is a no less evident and equally great difference between the bourgeois character of the Prussian Junker and the "bourgeois

> character" of Markov and Purishkevich. Compared with the latter, the Prussian Junker is quite a "European."[115]

Lenin's differentiated views applied to the development of the monarchy are surprising mainly to those who treat the historical references and groundwork of his political writings as subsidiary, and who deliberately or unwittingly overlook the coherence of Lenin's political and historical-theoretical analyses. Yet, by 1902 Lenin had whittled down the peculiar development of autocracy as a "relatively independently organized force" to the special interests of the "plenipotentiary powers of the chinovniks." This trend has centuries-long roots which, by the early twentieth century, included certain traits of not only "Asiatic despotism" but the latest in terms of European civilization.

In thinking about the development of Russian capitalism, in addition to its "being multisectored" (*mnogoukladnosti*)—the stratified existence and buildup of a variety of forms of production and society—Lenin gave consideration to the preponderance of "Octobrist-Purishchevist," "Asiatic," trade-usurer exploitation.[116] He interpreted the agricultural conditions as another form of "mixed development," characterized by the new "American way" in combination with the "Asiatic" or Turkish traits that had survived the Stolypin reforms. Lenin approached the development of modern Russian capitalism as a medieval phenomenon. He referred to this form of imperialism as "military-bureaucratic." He located its basic contradiction along the fault lines of "progressive industrial finance capitalism" and the "most savage village."[117]

During this period, Lenin also addressed the political struggle against the so-called liquidators (a political concept and movement for the liquidation of illegal party structures on behalf of the legal parties). In a somewhat simplified form, the Menshevik liquidators had the most to gain from the political exaggeration of the "European" lines of development, insofar as they counted upon the "delayed" repetition of Western development in Russia. Although he rejected liquidatorism and was opposed to the liberal conception of history, Plekhanov nevertheless adopted Miliukov's account of the historical evolution of the Russian state. His argument adhered to the Menshevik conviction that Russian capitalism was capable of following the "European model," though he contradicted it by emphasizing the survival of Asiatic modes of production in the case of development. Antithetically to Lenin, he overestimated by far the role of "noncapitalist" forms in Russian development.[118]

Even during the debates of the first party program in 1902, Lenin had held its author responsible for the same striking contradiction: "Plekhanov only spoke about capitalism in general terms" and left the question of a "specifically Russian form of capitalism" in the dark, for this kind of analysis "must serve as a lead for agitation against Russian capitalism." As Lenin put it, "the declaration of war has to be addressed directly to Russian capitalism" in order to solder together theory and practice.[119] As discussed earlier, these methodological-theoretical differences between Lenin and Plekhanov were reflected in their assessment of Asiatic modes of production. Plekhanov did not relinquish his earlier position, which perceived the struggle between "Asianness" and "Europeanness" in Russian history, even fitting February and October 1917 into this scheme. Unlike Lenin or Trotsky, Plekhanov did not base his approach on a combination or accumulation of the two trends of development, but chose to starkly contrast them, making absolutes of the historical categories in their pure form. This was like the "pure" capitalism of Ilminsky or Pokrovsky, which got no further than a one-sided identification of Russian and European lines of development. In fact, the idea that the February Revolution fit into the political "Europeanization" of Russia, while October, indeed quite to the contrary, reinstated the "Eastern," "Asiatic," or "peculiarly Russian," has once again become fashionable since the collapse of the Soviet Union.[120]

Based on his early historical studies, Lenin clarified that opposed interests and political conflicts within the ruling classes, and certain groups they include, must not be underestimated, because as demonstrated by the events of 1905 and 1917, the road to revolution was in part paved by these conflicts. Lenin distinguished between two trends within the "landowner camp," later defined by historiographers as the "Bonapartist" and "legitimist" movements.[121] The "Bonapartists" accepted a few of the consequences of the revolution with Stolipyn (or rather his reforms) at the helm, while also ready to make concessions to the conservative bourgeoisie and the progress of capitalism. A loyalty toward the old monarchy was characteristic of the landowner "legitimists" with an expression of their political interests that defended the autocracy even from the monarchy itself, as did the Black Hundreds' Purishkevich and Markov.

Lenin did not consider the way liberalism joined Stolypin's economic policy—that is, the experiment of further capitalizing the villages—extra-systemic, for (with reference to the experiences distilled from French Bonapartism by Marx and Engels) the defensive tactics of the propertied classes against the proletariat do not disappear from the agenda even if the bourgeoisie keeps the nobility under pressure. There is a transition from absolute monarchy to bourgeois monarchy, which is the last stage of the bourgeois revolution. To protect its economic interests the bourgeoisie relinquishes a significant political power (in deference to the large-landowning aristocracy, the tsar's bureaucracy, etc.). The liberals would rather share power with the Black Hundreds than to join the fray of democracy—as

Lenin put it at the end of 1911 and the beginning of 1912, in the *Prosveshcheniye*. The "Struveist-Vekhist and Miliukovist bourgeoisie" will choose Purishkevich over the democratic mass movements:

> The liberal's job is to "threaten" Purishkevich so as to get him to "move over" a bit, to make more room for the liberals, but making sure at the same time that this does not obliterate from the face of the earth all the economic and political foundations of Purishkevichism.[122]

The essence of Bismarckian-Stolypinist Bonapartism lies not just in alignment with the bourgeoisie and the landowners, but in the process of the monarchy's assuming bourgeois traits, the tsar's monarchy having conformed to the needs of capitalist development.[123] At the same time Lenin had the clear insight that the Russian autocracy, tsarism—in direct contrast to the system of Bismarck—"in view of its impotence in the face of the world competition of the modern capitalist states and being pushed more and more into the background in Europe" had come into alliance with the most reactionary forces:

> [I]n alliance with the reactionary nobility and the growing industrial bourgeoisie, [tsarism] is now endeavoring to satisfy its predatory interests by means of crude "nationalist" politics, directed against the inhabitants of the border regions, against all oppressed nationalities . . . and, through colonial conquest, against the peoples of Asia (Persia and China) who are waging a revolutionary struggle for freedom.[124]

Lenin's analysis of Russian capitalism links with his outline of the capitalist world system. This analysis—as will be shown in chapter 4—gains more depth and becomes more differentiated in the course of his theorization of the concept and phenomenon of imperialism. In the end, it was this analysis that determined the intellectual framework for Lenin's work within the movement and that defined the other applications of his theoretical practice.

[T]he "spontaneous element," in essence, represents nothing more nor less than consciousness in an embryonic form. Even the primitive revolts expressed the awakening of consciousness to a certain extent. The workers were losing their age-long faith in the permanence of the system which oppressed them . . .

[T]here could not have been Social-Democratic consciousness among the workers. It would have to be brought to them from without. The history of all countries shows that the working class, exclusively by its own effort, is able to develop only trade union consciousness, i.e., the conviction that it is necessary to combine in unions, fight the employers. . . . The theory of socialism, however, grew out of the philosophic, historical, and economic theories elaborated by educated representatives of the propertied classes, by intellectuals . . .

—V. I. LENIN, *WHAT IS TO BE DONE? LENIN'S SELECTED WORKS*

LCW, VOL. 5, 374–5

3
Organization and Revolution

LENIN'S BOLSHEVISM: POLITICS AND THEORY[1]

LENIN INHERITED FROM MARX THE notion that "capitalism can be overthrown by way of revolution." From the 1890s onward, Lenin was motivated to understand just how the capitalist system might be overthrown—by what means, methods, and in what organizational form. In this chapter we will discuss Lenin's views regarding how to "seize power" and "integrate the masses" into the party. During his Siberian exile (1897–1900), Lenin began to formulate plans for how to organize the working class and for revolutionary organization in general.

What Is To Be Done?— *Party and Class Consciousness*

On 29 January 1900 (February 10), six days after Lenin was released from exile in Siberia, he settled in Pskov. In July, he was finally able to meet with G. V. Plekhanov, the father of Soviet Marxism, in Switzerland. He also met with his future fellow editors, Potresov, Axelrod, and his friend Martov, who had also just been released from exile. By December 1900 they launched the first issue of *Iskra*, the illegal paper of the Russian Social Democracy.[2]

As the Russian representatives of Marxism, all of them considered the paper a potentially revolutionary, underground intellectual source of social democracy as well as its official publication.[3] Although the party had been inaugurated during the First Congress held in Minsk in 1898, its actual incorporation did not occur until the Second Congress in Brussels in 1903, and continued in London when the party program and the bylaws were adopted.[4]

By the mid-1890s Lenin recognized that under capitalist conditions, "intellectual" circles and revolutionary cells—in other words, the small organizations that utilized the methods of workshops—tended to dry up and become absorbed, like a pond in the desert. They became defenseless prey of the Okhrana and certainly did not present a serious challenge to the regime. Yet Lenin and friends were fully aware of the social consequences of the rapid evolution of capitalism, including the soaring of the Russian workers' movement.

The organization of social democracy, based on various discrete revolutionary groupings, had begun as early as 1895. This trend assumed a more concrete form in the underground Militant Association for the Liberation of the Working class in December of that year. The young Marxists were cautious in their approach to the old traditions of the Narodniks and of the Narodovoletz, and avoided any direct ideological confrontation. In turn, the Narodovoletz abstained from any acts of terrorism and propaganda about their views of Russian economic development.[5]

Even before his three years of exile—a sentence he received precisely for his role in forming the association—Lenin enjoyed great public support. From Zurich, Plekhanov and Axelrod had expressed their esteem for Lenin and his efforts on behalf of the workers' movement in Petrograd. It is clear from his responses that Lenin was already aware that social democracy could find roots in Russia only if the Marxist intellectuals developed organic contacts with the spontaneous and promising workers' movement, the representatives of which were actively seeking contacts with these young revolutionary intellectuals.[6] Lenin had been studying Russian economic history in exile. In the aftermath of his release, he functioned primarily as a party militant as the organizer, editor, and author of *Iskra*.

Once Lenin settled abroad, he immediately proceeded to sketch the factors and processes that would lead to a centralized organization based on conspiratorial principles—the creation of a truly social democratic party under the prevailing autocracy. In *What Is To Be Done?* (1902) Lenin confronted the Russian version of Bernstein's reformism, or more precisely, the "economist" movement congregated around the *Rabocheye Dielo* (the paper of the Russian Social Democrats in exile).

This pamphlet, regarded for decades as the basic document of the Communist Party, failed to include a systematic party philosophy yet it served as the ideological foundation of a hitherto nonexistent social democratic party.[7] The title itself indicated both a continuation and a break with Narodnik revolutionary traditions (see Chernyshevsky's *What Is To Be Done?*).[8]

What Is To Be Done? elicited intense debates among Marxists. The editors of *Iskra* on the whole accepted the theses of this work, which outlined the framework and structure of the party's operation. Lenin cannot be blamed that during the Stalinist period the work was essentially canonized for the sake of ensuring the leading role of the party and consolidating party discipline. Taken out of historical context, however, its intent and purpose were generally falsified. The debates on this pamphlet continue to this day because every workers' movement runs into it as a "tradition" in its own right.

One of the most insightful students of this problematic, Lars T. Lih, was able to identify the basic reasons for this development.[9] Lenin appears as a modern-day missionary, as a preacher, as the man of the "Great Resurrection," of "Enlightenment," who has faith in the power of the word and is able to transmit his faith to the workers across national boundaries, and is capable of "converting" them. This interpretation, however, according to which this "modern proselytizer" is nothing but an elitist and a megalomaniac intellectual, is not based on historical analysis, and does not place Lenin in historical context, whereas Lih begins with an account of the historical circumstances, how the working class "resurrects" and, because of its activism—as Lenin recognized—may achieve "hegemony" among wage workers around the world.[10] The principal premise in *What Is To Be Done?* is quite specific and historical: a revolutionary party capable of overthrowing the autocracy requires an underground organization built on volunteer activity. This can only be a party of "professional revolutionaries" who are familiar with the rules of conspiracy, the revolutionary consequences of Marxist theory, the history and "logic" of political and armed struggle, and are aware of the means at the party's disposal. The objective of the party's organization is socialism, but only in the long run. Its immediate political and economic goal is social revolution. The historical stage preceding socialism, to use Marx's term, is *the dictatorship of the proletariat*. According to Lenin, the historical role of the party is to function as the leader and the catalyst of a movement already in existence, the embodiment of a trend shaping the Russian revolutionary workers' movement.

What Is To Be Done? is a by-product of the debate within social-democratic circles at the time. The theoretical starting point was first and most succinctly identified in *Credo*, the pamphlet co-written by Yekaterina Kuskova and Sergei Prokopovich in 1899.[11] By Lenin's estimation, *Credo* stressed the economic struggles of the working class and diminished its daily political struggles, thus importing the debate into Bernstein's revisionism. Almost as a matter of course, the argument led to the issue of the revolutionary nature of the working class.

From 1902 onward, Lenin's basic goal was to define "the role of social democracy with regard to spontaneous mass movements."[12] In other words, how do the "working masses become mature enough to be able to overthrow tsarist autocracy"? Similar views had emerged among the social-democratic economists (principally with Martinov), but Lenin focused his arguments against the vulgar economic arguments that distinguished the economic and wage struggles of the working class from their political demands. These economists cited Eduard Bernstein's direction of German social democracy to substantiate their arguments. In the name of spontaneity and "self-education," they saw the workers merely in the guise of trade resistance and labor union consciousness.

Lenin, for whom social democracy was the party of social revolution, viewed the essence of Bernstein's reformism in the precept that social democracy must be transformed from the party of social revolution into a "democratic party of social reforms." Bernstein denied that "socialism can be scientifically justified," hence he removed the prospect of "socialist revolution" from the agenda. As we know, this thesis remains the ideological starting point of modern social democracy and its successors.

In *What Is To Be Done?* we find an acute awareness that behind this confrontation between the "revolutionary party" and the "party of reforms" lies further conflict between their relationship to the *state* and *revolution*, and to bourgeoisie and capitalism. Marx had already rejected the Vollmar concept of "state socialism."[13] The "state socialism" of Bernstein (or Vollmar) posits the possibility of the parliamentary triumph of social democracy as the ultimate goal instead of socialism or the socialist revolution. Likewise, the camp of Russian economists tried to excise the *revolutionary* transition leading to socialism. Underlying the political conflict, therefore, we find conflict over the views of Bernstein, who "denied the theoretically antithetical nature of liberalism and socialism, denied the theory of class struggle."[14]

At the very center of Lenin's party-building thesis was the issue of how the working class could achieve class consciousness. According to his analysis the working class is subject to bourgeois society not only in its generality, but also concretely, since all preconceived notions associated with the capitalist system find their way into the deepest consciousness of workers. The working class is unable to spontaneously rid itself of these preconceived notions. During the first years of his exile in Western Europe, Lenin found that the regime thrusts notions sustaining capitalism into the workers' consciousness—for example, by means of propaganda or the media. From this he came to the conclusion that there "cannot be a revolutionary movement without a revolutionary philosophy." This would apply to everyday propaganda efforts and the theories underlying agitation, with local and national conditions taken into consideration. Lenin was perfectly aware that "the tasks Russian social democracy had to face are tasks no other socialist party in the world has had to face as yet."[15]

Regarding connections to be made between "the spontaneity of the masses" and the "consciousness of social democracy," Lenin and Bolshevik philosopher Bogdanov each recognized, in his own way, that the periods of preparation for revolution—some shorter, some longer—are most essential when the working class is "enabled." But learning the "logic" of political struggle, the nature of the forces participating in it, cannot occur spontaneously. As a result of his analyses, Lenin came to the final conclusion that, in general, under a bourgeois regime it is not possible for the workers to develop a social democratic consciousness. Later, in 1907, in the aftermath of the revolutionary experience, he gave up this thesis. In fact he admitted that under the changed circumstances, the proletarian masses might enter the party alongside the "professional revolutionaries."

To what extent *Iskra* and Lenin's concept of the Russian Social Democratic Party was tailored to the labor movement can be discerned unequivocally in his pamphlet *One Step Forward, Two Steps Back (The Crisis in Our Party)*, published in 1904. Here he rejects the charge that he identified social democracy as a secret conspiratorial organization:

> This quotation shows how out of place it was for Comrade Martov to remind me that the organization of revolutionaries should be enveloped by broad organizations of workers. I had already pointed this out in *What Is To Be Done?*—and in *A Letter to a Comrade* I developed this idea more concretely. . . . Every factory must be our fortress.[16]

Of course, Lenin argued that "conspiracy" is but one special tool to be used under a certain set of circumstances rather than the foundation of a party.[17] In *One Step Forward, Two Steps Back*, Lenin sketches out a network of legal and underground organizations dedicated to enlisting workers in a social-democratic movement. Lenin's basic objective in creating these networks of agents was to facilitate communication and political activity between different segments of an oppressed society.[18] Generally speaking, Western scholars locate the roots of Lenin's conception of social organization and socialism in *What Is To Be Done?*[19]

Lenin maintained his views on the significance of enlightenment and education and never denied that day-to-day struggle serves at least as much of a "self-educating" purpose as "teaching and learning." This is "theoretical consciousness," as Lukács was to phrase it later in *History and Class Consciousness* (1919–1923).[20] In *What Is To Be Done?* however, the "assigned consciousness" is not represented by a sterile proletariat (as in Lukács's text) "but by the historical experience of every country."

Since this consciousness had to be injected from the outside, as "the working class could only achieve a unionist consciousness on its own," it should come as no surprise that Lenin ascribed an enormous role to the revolutionary vanguard. This is not so much the consequence of the Narodnik influence but rather the specific and contradictory nature of Russian capitalism; for example, the "youth" of the working class, its spontaneous radicalism, and its cultural backwardness. What appeared as a virtue in the eyes of Lukács was a problem for Lenin. He knew very well that "in Russia, the theoretical doctrine of social democracy arose completely independently of the spontaneous growth of the working-class movement. . . . It arose as a natural and inevitable outcome of the development of thought among the revolutionary socialist intelligentsia."[21]

This evolution also reflects that in building up the party, Lenin started out from the experiences of the Russian workers' movement, and the direct logical outcome was centralization and conspiracy. He was aware of the negative impact of this situation, of its "Asiatic features"[22] when—in arguments against sectarian attitudes—he urged the inclusion of the masses in politics. Lenin viewed the "issue of the relationship between the professional revolutionaries and the purely workers' movement"—the general strike being the meeting point between party and movement—as one of the most important achievements of the movement. He did not conceive of a general strike as a "secret" action, even though he felt that a small number of professional organizers would be required to technically prepare the participation of thousands. Yet anyone with revolution as their calling would have to organize this struggle "to be launched taking into consideration the rules of the art." Thus Lenin combined or connected several relationships simultaneously: the trade or occupation to which the worker belonged, professional organization and conspiracy, ideological and political farsightedness within the sphere of the new political theory, and Marxism.[23]

From the point of view of "professional preparedness," Lenin politically and ideologically assessed the two old revolutionary tendencies, Narodism and anarchism. As early as 1901, he argued that these approaches could not provide answers to the challenges posed by the new bourgeois society. His main objection was that Narodism did not understand the features of the new Russian capitalism and hence resorted to old, reactionary romantic utopias to attempt to transform the existing regime. As for anarchism, which rejected politics altogether, Lenin contended its adherents did not understand the historical evolution that could lead to socialism and did not perceive the "causes of exploitation," nor did it have "an understanding of the *class struggle* as the creative force for the realization of socialism." He referred to anarchism as the "absurd negation of politics in bourgeois society" which would, in the long run, end in the "subordination of the working class to bourgeois politics in the guise of negation of politics."[24]

Lenin felt that neither approach—nowadays we would refer to them as "premodern" solutions—would lead to any positive outcome in the organization of the workers. As for the question, "What is there in common between economism and terrorism?" his answer was their similarities were rooted in "subservience to spontaneity." He wrote, "Those who are not, and cannot be, roused to excitement even by Russian tyranny will stand by 'twiddling their thumbs' and watch a handful of terrorists engaged in single combat with the government"[25]

There is even a detailed discussion of the consciousness of class struggle in *What Is To Be Done?* The participation of workers in everyday politics depends primarily on understanding the development of political forces at work in class relations, without which the proletariat remains a mere tool of capital.[26] Lenin undoubtedly exaggerated the role of "understanding" theories of knowledge and of scientific truth in history and politics, and paid less attention to resolving the complicated connections of various interests. The reason for this was that "to be submerged in the details" could become an obstacle to revolutionary organizing and lead to the "death of action." His views regarding revolutionary organizing also reflect that the "revolutionary nucleus" must first of all be clear about this fact. At the same time he was also aware that the workers were not preoccupied with theoretical issues, because existential difficulties would spur them to revolutionary action. As we shall see, Lenin remained very critical of anarchist movements even later on, not because of the competition (albeit this may have played a role) but rather as a matter of principle and tactics.

Lenin conceived of the underground organization of the revolutionaries as composed of "people who make revolutionary activity their profession (for which reason I speak of the organization of revolutionaries, meaning revolutionary social democrats)."[27] This is not surprising, since under an autocratic regime, laurels can accrue only to "professionals" and even then not very often. Consider, for instance, the regrettably well-oiled machine of the Okhrana, or Bulat Okudzhava's *The Adventures of Shipov*, which revealed the operation of the secret police from the inside. If it hoped to succeed, the party of the organization of the revolutionaries must not only become secretive, but must even appear, in a sense, as the alternative to the secret police.[28]

The professionalism on which the lives of the workers and of the professional revolutionaries depended made no allowance for naïveté or dilettantism.[29] Lenin wrote about this sense of professionalism with regard to the party: "In *form* such a strong revolutionary organization in an autocratic country may also be described as a 'conspiratorial' organization."[30] He considered such an organization as the most important instrument of an anti-tsarist revolution that "prepares" the great historical transformation and "works out" the transition between the daily political and economic struggles and the revolutionary goal. In this mindset, he wrote of "rejecting an immediate *call* for assault."[31] Thus the party itself becomes the most important organization in the hands of the working class during the transition.

As already mentioned, Lenin conceived of the organizational conditions for the party's foundation, and the achievement of its goals, in terms of a "network of agents" that provided connections among various types of workers' movements. He believed that without such a network the uprising was not possible.[32] Only these forms of contact would have the result of "creating *real* party unity; for without such contacts it will be impossible collectively to discuss the plan for the uprising and to take the necessary preparatory measures on the eve, measures that must be kept in the strictest secrecy."

Lenin viewed everything in terms of the planning and execution of the ultimate goal, the "preparation of the entire nation for an armed uprising." It was no accident that with regard to *Iskra*, "the 'plan for an All-Russian political newspaper,' far from representing the fruits of the labor of armchair workers, infected with dogmatism and bookishness . . . is the most practical plan for immediate and all-round preparation of the uprising."[33]

It was already apparent in the debates at the party congress (see below) that all basic principles, such as democratic centralism or the vanguard—which became mere notions of political science for future generations—could be justified only in terms of the growth of the movement. The revolution of 1905 marked a sudden yet decisive shift for the party. It transformed from a party built on conspiracy into a true mass movement, with a membership of over 160,000.

The concept of democratic centralism as the "law" of party bureaucracy was a product of a later historical period—the combination of power, pragmatism, and a messianic "future expectation." It is easy enough to define the basic concept of democratic centralism: democracy in reaching decisions and unity in implementing them. The difficulty resides only in how to apply this basic principle to small propaganda groups that do not have an organic relationship with the working class. That is, groups whose constituencies are not created from among the most class-conscious members of this class through a hard-fought process of selection.[34] The Russian Social Democratic Party, and later the Bolshevik Party, benefited from real feedback thanks to its close relations to its *social base*. The Social Democratic Party, at least *potentially*, was a real mass party from the beginning. It had an ideology and an organization chart, for example, that were recognized by politically conscious members of the working class in 1905 and 1917 as valid expressions of their politics. This consciousness, however, was soon in conflict with the official position of the party in view of the truly impossible demands of self-liberation. There was no guidance offered in *What Is To Be Done?* since its author could not have been thinking from the perspective of a future "party state."

The party as vanguard meant simply that the organization must find roots as part of the social class and incorporate all progressive and revolutionary elements (that is, "those who are first to mount the barricades") as mentioned in the *Communist Manifesto*. This description of vanguard, of course, has no real kinship with the structure that came about in a later period, the bureaucratic embodiment of the "Stalinist state party," in spite of the fact that the latter kept referring to Lenin and its so-called origins in 1903. Regarding its own ideology and politics, it considered Bolshevism as originating in that year.

Those attending the Second Congress of the Russian Social-Democratic Labor Party were driven by the shared conviction that the principal task of this Congress was to elaborate a platform and an organization for the direction of the workers' movement—a party that would deal with tactical issues in a united manner. In view of this shared intention, the Congress's organizing committee elaborated ground rules. The eighteenth point of these rules was formulated as follows:

> [A]ll decisions of the Congress and all the elections it carries out are decisions of the Party and binding on all Party organizations. They cannot be challenged by anyone on any pretext whatever and can be rescinded or amended only by the next Party Congress. . . . This provision in fact expressed the *free will* of all the revolutionaries. . . . It was equivalent to a *word of honor* mutually pledged by all the Russian Social-Democrats.[35]

The party's handling of tactical issues in a united manner proved more complicated than that. The personality and power struggles among individuals—even revolutionaries, since we are not speaking of saints—often overrode the covenant of the *word of honor*.

The 1903 "Party Split"

In the debates held at the Second Congress, it was consistently argued that the party of the proletariat could only stand on the basis of "common interests." Just as the general capitalist state expresses the general interests of the capitalist class at the expense of special interests, for the sake of eliminating all inequities resulting from class, the mission of the revolutionary party must be the embodiment of the totality in the interest of the movement as a whole. For the first time in the course of the debate over organization, in 1903 the delegates took a stand on the final goal ("the dictatorship of the proletariat") on the basis of class consciousness. This goal was included in the party program as a joint resolution by Plekhanov and Lenin.

Parvus represented a dissenting voice. The principal disagreement was not about the assessment of conspiracy; nevertheless, Parvus—who was on the periphery of the Mensheviks—placed this issue at the heart of his later disagreements with Lenin.[36] Even though every tendency at the Second Congress argued in favor of an underground party, Parvus described Lenin as a "one-sided author who does not admit nuances," who "evolved into a political anti-Struve" and who "recognized only one style of movement, namely forward."[37] Yet Parvus himself came up with just such an abstract template to explain everything regarding permanent revolution, and this abstraction marks history's view of him even to this day.

It was the Western European model that Parvus seemed to have in mind, as he tried to apply the formula he superficially borrowed from Marx regarding permanent revolution to the Russian case. This idea, which reached maturity during the revolution of 1905, proved irrelevant to Russian reality because it underestimated those tactical considerations without which the connections between theory and practice cannot be clearly understood. Parvus wrote, "indeed, Lenin looks at tactics from the point of view of toppling autocracy and the immediate victory of the revolution, whereas I look at it from the point of view of the organization of the army of social revolution which would render revolution uninterrupted."[38]

The abstract character of Parvus's thought becomes even more obvious from an open letter he addressed to Lenin on 2 December 1904. He chides Lenin, on the one hand, because the latter felt a political compromise with the liberals was permissible for the sake of overthrowing autocracy. Parvus, however, feared that the revolutionary masses might fall under the influence of the liberals and become disabled, unable to pursue the goal of permanent revolution. On the other hand, he criticized Lenin for breaking with the Mensheviks.[39]

Lenin's extreme vehemence in every party debate exacerbated and polarized the stands taken, with all the ensuing negative consequences. He dismissed all stands that were inconsistent, vague, unclear, ambiguous, or poorly thought out, as politically and structurally unacceptable. He tried to set all the important issues simultaneously within the network of theory, organization, and politics. Parvus, however, was not the most typical challenger of Lenin and for a while he influenced the ideas of Trotsky.

One year after the fateful Second Congress, Lenin's *One Step Forward, Two Steps Back*, which reflected on this congress, was published in Geneva.[40] With this relation acknowledged, the old notion that the Bolshevik-Menshevik split occurred in 1903 must finally be discarded. In that year there was merely the first stage of a schism that underwent a lengthy process. Indeed, Lenin proposed the "party split" itself was only one of the political processes that shaped increasingly divergent political tendencies. When Lenin spoke of the origins of Bolshevism as a "political stream of ideas," he deliberately avoided use of the term "organizational."[41]

The debate between Martov and Lenin (and their respective disciples) that became so famous regarding ground rule number one at the Second Congress—namely who could or could not qualify as a member of the party—never really became an issue. We know that Lenin felt the requirements for membership should be stricter than those advocated by Martov, and should entail active participation in carrying out the program. Even today not everyone knows whether the break occurred at the time of the nomination of the Central Committee, the decision over offices,[42] when Lenin's followers—namely Kryzhanovsky, Lengnyik, and Noskov—made it into the Central Committee by majority vote. That is, the Bolsheviks versus the Mensheviks.[43] Consequently Martov lost his "equilibrium" to such an extent that he gave his "mandate" as one of the elected editors of *Iskra*.

There were sociological and psychological reasons for the breakup of the organization. However, in *One Step Forward, Two Steps Back* Lenin entertained a digression about the "significance of the mentality of the intelligentsia." According to him, differences in mentality were bound to hamper consolidation, at least until the time the workers took control of the party. He explained that it was not only due to psychological factors that the minority at the congress was unable to accept the outcome of the balloting:

> The minority was formed of those elements in the Party *who are least stable* in theory, *least steadfast in matters of principle*. It was from the *right wing* of the Party that the minority was formed. The division into majority and minority is a direct and inevitable continuation of that division of the Social-Democrats into a revolutionary and an opportunist wing . . . which did not appear only yesterday, nor in the Russian workers' party alone, and which no doubt will not disappear tomorrow. . . . Comrade Martov's mistake was a minor one (and I said so even at the Congress, in the heat of the struggle); but this minor mistake *could (and did)* cause a lot of harm because Comrade Martov was pulled over to the side of delegates who had made *a whole series of mistakes*, had manifested an inclination towards opportunism.[44]

Among those who attended the congress there were many who disagreed with the tendency represented by *Iskra*. Their principal spokespersons—including V. P. Akimov (Mahnavec), Ryazanov, those of the Bund—could not possibly be the allies of Martov, as a matter of principle.[45] Akimov, who tended to be a reformist, was the one who pointed out that the views of Lenin and Plekhanov diverged on the point of organization:

> The one who says that social democracy accelerates the development of the consciousness of the proletariat is obviously expressing an idea that is diametrically opposed to the notion of the one who argues that creating a socialist consciousness among the proletariat has to come from the "outside" since he feels that the working class cannot get beyond the doctrine of unionism, from its own resources.[46]

Among other factors, Martov's personal reaction prompted Lenin to muse about "spineless intellectuals" and vituperation within the party. The "psychology of the typical intelligentsia"—based on Kautsky's article about Franz Mehring—could be contrasted with the psychology of the proletarian formed and regulated by heavy industry.[47] By "average intellectual" Kautsky meant the professional based in bourgeois society, who gave the class of intelligentsia its character and who, to a large extent, stood in "contrast to the proletariat."

This contrast is of a different kind than the "contrast between work and capital"; it is not economic, but social. It is a matter of "sensibility and thought process" deriving from the fact that the two social groups work under different divisions of labor. As a consequence of this, "the proletarian as an isolated individual is nothing" but "feels powerful as a member of a strong organization," and fights with the greatest sense of self-sacrifice, without considering personal glory. The intellectual feels altogether differently, for individualism is a consequence of his or her work relations:

> [H]ence the freest play for his individuality seems to him the prime condition for successful activity. It is only with difficulty that he submits to being a part subordinate to a whole, and then only from necessity, not from inclination. He recognizes the need of discipline only for the mass, not for the elect minds. And of course he counts himself among the latter. . . . Nietzsche's philosophy, with its cult of the superman, for whom the fulfillment of his own individuality is everything and any subordination of that individuality to a great social aim is vulgar and despicable, is the real philosophy of the intellectual, and it renders him totally unfit to take part in the class struggle of the proletariat. An ideal example of the kind of intellectual the socialist movement needs was Liebknecht. . . .[48]

Lenin's *One Step Forward, Two Steps Back* prompted Trotsky to prepare an essay—cited in anti-Leninist literature even today—where he described Lenin's concept in this work as a collection of "organizational, bureaucratic and Jacobinist prejudices."[49] In the evolving conflict of tendencies, a third stream was making its appearance between economism (a passive approach, a conservative political quietism) and the tradition of the old *Iskra* (an isolated intellectual trend out of touch with the workers). He saw the party's function as representing the "will of the class" and providing an organized form for its "consciousness." As a consequence he formulated his now famous resolution, which interpreted Lenin's concept and practice as a "substitute for proletarian politics" (adding attributes such as "Blanquist," "antidemocratic," etc.).

Trotsky also rejected the notion that the revolutionary intelligentsia was called upon to import class consciousness into the proletariat from the outside.[50] If we shed the polemical stamp and all the simplifications from Trotsky's arguments, it turns out that, for Lenin, the party is a structured political institution with a military and bureaucratic hierarchy. In contrast, Trotsky posits an abstract notion of "proletarian self-directed activity" as the main inspector of history, a militant materialist idea.

In 1904, Trotsky was still the Saul in party matters. The proletarian communitarian ideology he stressed challenged the features in the Social Democratic Party functioning under autocracy. It was no accident that Trotsky rebelled against Lenin's factory analogy. Trotsky integrated the party individual into the proletarian community by reducing it entirely to the "general existential needs of the proletariat."[51] Yet to untie the workers' party from the structure of the specific mode of production ultimately leads the party and its very organization to the collapse of organization, to individualist perceptions.

Lenin seldom returned to the experiences of the congress from a psychological point of view, which may be due to the fact that the political contradictions could be perceived ever more clearly during the revolution and through the experience of the failure of the revolution. An assessment of political tendencies from September 1907[52] explains how the Mensheviks became an organized political faction: "during the first period of the Russian revolution (1905–07) [it] pursued its own distinct policy—a policy which *in practice subordinated the proletariat to bourgeois liberalism*."[53] It was precisely in order to place the workers' movement on its own footing during the revolution that he rejected collaboration with bourgeois liberalism, because the latter tried to reach a compromise with the tsarist regime.[54]

Perhaps the Menshevik position drove him to exaggerate his arguments.[55] It was during this congress that the notion of forming a left bloc with the landless peasantry replaced the notion of working with the liberals, albeit most of the Mensheviks never accepted this notion. Hence we may refer to this congress as the "second" permanent rift within Russian Social Democracy, even though Lenin would continue to seek to restore collaboration with Plekhanov and vice versa.

Never again did Bolsheviks and Mensheviks unite at a joint congress. The years 1905–07 signaled the final rift.

In his debates with the anarchists in November and December 1905, Lenin said that, as a prerequisite for collaboration, only those who were in agreement about the basic objective of the organization were capable of collaborating within a militant organization. Consequently, this was also Lenin's response to the 23 November resolution of the Executive Committee of the Soviet of the Workers' Deputies, which rejected the request of the anarchists to be included on the committee because "anarchists do not recognize political struggle as a method for achieving their goals." Lenin agreed that the anarchists "should not be admitted into that body, for it is not a workers' parliament, nor an autonomous organ of the proletariat." Had it been a parliament then anarchists could not be excluded.[56]

Lenin considered the workers' soviet as the political arm of the uprising and an institution of the revolution. The soviets and similar popular organizations (strike committees, the soviet of the soldiers, railroadmen's union, etc.) were the product of the workers' autonomous agency. As Lenin wrote about the uprising of December 1905, "It was not some theory, not appeals on the part of someone, or tactics invented by someone, not party doctrine, but the force of circumstances that led these non-party mass organs to realize the need for an uprising and transformed them into organs of an uprising."[57]

The dissension within the Social Democrats around Lenin's thesis led to the split and ultimate dissolution of the Russian Social Democratic Party, because "within a militant association there is room only for those who fight for the objectives of the association." The issue of organization could never be dissociated from political issues—nor from the attitudes and positions associated with these issues—not even after the collapse of the revolution. When the Social Democratic Party broke up it seemed it would drown in the struggle of the factions. Indeed, the history of the party between 1907 and 1917 is one of failed attempts at reunification and further splits.

Already in 1906, at the congress in Stockholm, delegates debated the desired reunification. This was followed by the "second" break at the congress in London. The collapse involved the further split of the Mensheviks into the absolutist so-called liquidators and the group of "party builders" led by Plekhanov.[58] The Bolsheviks, too, broke into splinter groups. The so-called Otzovists turned against Lenin—they were the ones who, under the leadership of Bogdanov, demanded the recall of the Social Democratic delegates from the Duma and insisted on the tactic of boycotting elections. Indeed, there were further attempts at reunification and further splits.[59] This kind of sectarianism, of organizational ostracism, smacked of the intolerance of "religious denominations."

It was a kind of defense mechanism against the impact of counterrevolution; it is not a Russian "peculiarity."

Early in 1908, in his work entitled *Marx's Historical Significance,* Kautsky raised the issue of combining socialism and the workers' movement, in accordance with Marxist traditions, as "the unity of theory and praxis."[60] Not only did this greatly impress Lenin; this was a necessity if the proletariat was ever to overthrow capitalism and liquidate itself as a social class. Here Kautsky becomes key to an understanding of Lenin. In this text Kautsky points out that socialist objectives were voiced before Marx, "yet they were only able to establish sects, the proletariat was disjointed because everyone of the socialists stressed his or her own particular manner of resolving social issues. There are as many sects as there are solutions."[61] A similar phenomenon could be observed after 1907.

The "disorganization" of social democracy did have a positive by-product, however. The party base began to spread in the direction of organization by occupation which, after the counterrevolutionary dismantling of the soviets, remained the sole root of social democracy among the proletarian masses. According to Kautsky, it was not the theoretical discussions that led to "splitism" within Russian social democracy, even if the ideological background of the final split became clear and evident later on:

> Never has there been a Marxist or a Marxist group which initiated a split simply for the sake of theoretical divergence. Where there has been division, it was always both practical and theoretical, it was always tactical or organizational conflict, and the theoretical aspect was merely the scapegoat on which to heap all the sins.[62]

One of the most interesting and least known episodes of the split among the Bolsheviks was the debate between Lenin and Bogdanov.[63] The issue was what should happen to the party if the movement experiences a low tide.

LENIN AND BOGDANOV

The Political-Organizational Conflict

The treason of the intellectuals following the defeat of the 1905 Revolution involved the switching of sides, drifting over to the ranks of the new counterrevolutionary regime, and acquiescence. The mere existence of the Vekhists, ex-leftist "legal Marxist" intellectuals, was a manifestation of this phenomenon. Educated people abandoned in droves what seemed to them the sinking ship of the revolution. They were "going under into a private sphere," retreating into small circles and societies, turning away from politics, and adapting their philosophy to the opportunities offered by the counterrevolution. This state of affairs was clearly expressed in Machism and empirio-criticism becoming fashionable philosophies, in the "molding together" of Marxism and idealism, in God-searching and God-building, with many of Lenin's comrades from his own political faction in the lead.

In the process of the disintegration of social democracy, the split within the Bolshevik bloc came from the left. Interpreted differently, it could be said that Lenin broke with the group or groups to his left, the Otzovists and the Ultimatists, who came under the influence of new fashions in philosophy. While it became typical of other social democratic circles to give up every revolutionary end goal in favor of certain possibilities that legality offered, in one group of Bolsheviks (the circle including A. Bogdanov, A. Lunacharsky, Bazarov, Gorky, et al.) the dedication to end goals grew even stronger. A complete personal dedication to the end goal entailed turning away from reality and found expression in transcendent philosophical experimentation. This mindset was further colored by the so-called immigrant disease, which under conditions of isolation, favors divisiveness, self-justification, and infighting. The reaction is not rare among revolutionaries when a sudden low tide in revolutionary fervor sets in.

In response to all of this, Lenin began reorienting himself toward political realities. He "converted"—accepting the facts of the new situation—to the world of parliamentary struggles. He dedicated himself to the purpose of making the Social Democratic representatives in the Duma propagate revolutionary tactics and strategies until the coming of the new revolutionary surge. The other wing of the Bolsheviks, represented by Bogdanov, rejected the "dissolution" of revolutionary politics in parliamentary politics. It was not as if, in the manner of the politically understood "extreme left," they had the socialist revolution on their immediate agenda. They aimed rather to preserve the "pure" socialist image of the future in the given political-historical conditions, not letting it be "contaminated" by disgraceful *realpolitik*.[64] For them, the contemptibly trivial arguments between various social democratic groups about the Duma and their own organizational disintegration seemed to be merely the pitiful, disillusioned reflexes of the counterrevolutionary period, which should be understood as transitory. In the present, to remain pure meant almost exclusively to prepare for the *future*.

These two differing attitudes within Bolshevism had become apparent even before the revolution. Around Lenin and Bogdanov, the internal split of the Bolsheviks into the "Leninists" and the *Vperyod* group formed by Bogdanov and his followers was, in a certain sense, already conditionally outlined in organizational terms at the so-called conference of the twenty-two Bolsheviks.[65] Within the Bolshevik faction, the *Vperyod* of August 1904 did not seem like a force that would determine the way forward in this period of the revolution, when the unity of the movement needed to be grounded. If the events of the split are to be recapitulated, indeed the point of departure must be 1904, signifying that seemingly even then the Bolsheviks were at odds among themselves in their approach to politics.

Nearly a decade later Lenin summed up the organizational evolution of Russian Social Democracy, Menshevism, and Bolshevism in a short essay. He outlined the history of Bolshevism in the following way:

> The main practical divergences between the two trends in the autumn of 1905 were over the fact that the Bolsheviks stood for boycotting the Bulygin Duma while the Mensheviks favored participation. In the spring of 1906, the same thing happened with regard to the Witte Duma. First Duma: the Mensheviks stood for the slogan of a Duma (Kadet) Ministry; the Bolsheviks, for the slogan of a Left (Social-Democratic and Trudovik) Executive Committee that would organize the actual struggle of the masses, etc. . . . At the Stockholm Congress (1906) the Mensheviks won the upper hand, and at the London Congress (1907), the Bolsheviks. In 1908–09 the *Vperyod* group (Machism in philosophy and otzovism, or boycotting the Third Duma, in politics—Bogdanov, Alexinsky, Lunacharsky and others) broke away from the Bolsheviks. In 1909–11, in fighting against them,[66] as well as against the liquidators (Mensheviks who denied the need for an illegal Party), Bolshevism came close to the pro-Party Mensheviks (Plekhanov and others), who had declared a resolute war on liquidationism.[67]

The split between the two trends of Bolshevism issued from questions of a very practical nature. Bogdanov and his group condemned participation in parliamentary, "bourgeois" politics. Lenin, on the other hand, set the struggle for political power as the main task of the party. He was not occupied with creating and implanting an idea of the future of socialism; he thought of this more as a development to be expected from the period following the revolution. Instead he was preparing the organizational and political-intellectual grounds for a revolution that would be capable of overthrowing tsarism. This divergence in approach came to the fore in numerous differences in questions of tactics as well.

The historical framework Lenin provided was not unequivocal on whether it was Bogdanov or himself who broke with "old Bolshevism" and its "boycott tactics." Lenin's "anti-boycott" turn came during the April 1906 unification congress in Stockholm, at which sixteen Bolshevik representatives voted for participation in elections to the Duma. This was the first appearance of—in the Bogdanovists' usage—Bolshevik "centrism." The Leninist Bolsheviks had voted against participation in the elections at the December 1905 conference in Tammerfors, upholding the boycott policy. The conflict between the "parliamentarian" and "revolutionary" political trends continued at the London Party Congress. The dissolution of the Second Duma in June 1907, the arrest of the sixteen Social Democrat representatives, and the legal restrictions placed on participation in the elections exacerbated the conflict. When the party reexamined its Duma policy at the All-Russian Party Congress of 21–23 July (3–5 August) 1907 in Kotka (Viborg), Lenin and Bogdanov stood for quite opposite tactical approaches. Lenin thought of the boycott tactic as politics suited to revolutionary upswing.[68] In a situation that did not verge on revolution, a different politics was demanded.

According to Bogdanov's interpretation of the time, Lenin was culpable of the same "class cooperation" as Plekhanov and Axelrod, which follows automatically from parliamentary politics. In 1909, as his political-strategic project to consolidate a social-democratic movement that encapsulated both parliamentary politics—including all its tools—and revolutionary propaganda, upholding the promise of revolution, were blocked by the liquidators on the right and the otzovists on the left, Lenin resumed cooperation with Plekhanov. When Plekhanov resigned from the editorial board of the Menshevik newspaper *Golos Sotsial-demokrata* in December 1908, an organizational integration with Lenin's group once more seemed a realistic possibility.

The Bolshevik party paper, the *Proletary*, edited by Lenin, was definitely an important aspect of the balance of forces turning in favor of Lenin. However, from Bogdanov's perspective, the rapprochement with Plekhanov in any form was viewed as "treason." The ideological and political debates were exacerbated by financial disagreements, which inevitably became the subject of acrimonious discussions in exile. While it may be true that the two factions of the Bolsheviks were competing for control of the *Proletary* paper and its financial resources,[69] we must not exaggerate its impact on the Bolsheviks' split.

The Bolshevik centrist (BC) faction came into existence at the London congress. The "financial and technical committee" was established through the "military technical office," which included Bogdanov, Krasin, and Lenin among its members.[70] On 13 (25) June of 1907, a group led by Kamo—with the participation of Stalin—robbed 241,000 rubles from the bank in Tiflis. At Kuokkala in July/August, Kamo remitted 218,000 rubles from this booty to Krasin. In connection with this action, Biggart raised the issue, what would have happened if Lenin had not had access to such financial resources? Indeed, financial independence made it possible for him to break with the comrades.[71] In reality, however, financial matters were not the main aspect of the split.

By the time Lenin ceded the *Proletary* to the control of the Duma faction at the end of 1907, and worked with Dubrovinski against Bogdanov, the ideological and political disagreements were clear. Lenin, however, did not feel the time had come for a definitive political break. The philosophical debate had to take second place to political expediency. All this was not worthy of prolonged debate, and neither was the fact that Bogdanov subjected his famous party schools in Capri and Bologna[72]—where the "cultural development of the working class" was the focus of study—to the interests of his own faction.

In vain, *Proletary* resolved to remain neutral in the philosophical debate, but by April 1908 it became clear that the two approaches could not be reconciled. Of course, each tendency endeavored to promote its own approach.[73] In view of Lenin's essay "Marxism and Revisionism" in his volume on Karl Marx, which attacked empirio-monism, the ideological and political debate degenerated to a point where Bogdanov resigned as editor. He felt there was no contradiction between empiriomonism and the basic ideology of the Bolshevik faction. Lenin, Dubronski, and others assumed that Bogdanov had created "an official opposition" within the editorial office.[74] At the same time Lenin and company excluded Bogdanov from the Bolshevik center in June 1909. The "left Bolsheviks" responded by creating the *Vperyod* at Capri in December 1909, reflecting somewhat nostalgically the paper published in 1904 under the same title and, by the same token, implying that they were the repository of true Bolshevism.[75]

The Philosophical Background of the Political Debate

Lenin preferred not to conflate ideological debates with tactical disagreements. In fact, from a methodological point of view he expressly disapproved of this procedure. Some of his letters to Gorky in February–March 1908 are evidence of this disapproval. On 25 November, he wrote:

> To hinder the application of the tactics of revolutionary social-democracy in the workers' party for the sake of disputes on the question of materialism or Machism, would be, in my opinion, unpardonable folly. We ought to fight over philosophy in such a way that *Proletary* and the Bolsheviks, as a faction of the *party, would not be affected by it.*[76]

Lenin felt compelled to read many essays on such themes since the infighting among the factions continued to grow sharper. It soon forced him to commit the very stupidity that he warned against in his letter to Gorky. He formulated the pertinent philosophical thesis with his accustomed clarity: Marx cannot be complemented with Kant, he argued, for Marx's philosophical concepts have no Kantian "agnostic" roots.

Lenin's later turn toward Hegel in 1914 explains his stance in 1908, namely that the Kantian complement advocated in the 1880s was the very embodiment of a philosophical and theoretical revision of Marxism, from the Narodniks all the way to Bernstein.[77] Marx's Hegelian sources acquired importance through the use of the dialectical method, yet the philosophical problematic of dialectics remained the background to the debate between Lenin's "empirionism" on the one hand, and Lunacharsky and companions' "religious atheism" on the other. It turned out that Plekhanov, and subsequently Lenin, had pointed out the philosophical disagreement with Bogdanov and his followers already in 1903–04. These disagreements were made more explicit upon personal encounter with Bogdanov.[78]

By then the tactical and factional struggles within the party had become imbued with philosophical arguments.[79] Lenin believed he could kill two birds with one stone: he could defend the materialist philosophical position while carrying forward, or at least reinforcing, the political and ideological views of his faction. He could count on the backing of Plekhanov in this undertaking, since it was a matter of defending traditional "bourgeois materialism" in the face of Machism.[80] Actually, the *functional materialism* we find in Marx and Engels—which ties philosophy to revolutionary practice, reconciling dialectics with epistemological and ontological perspectives, and which ultimately transformed philosophy into "theory" by linking it to the workers' movement—could not gain importance in the debates around Machism.[81] Something else was at stake in the debate.

In order to defend "bourgeois materialism" Lenin gave up his reservations regarding philosophical debates. In his empirio-criticism Lenin was mobilizing not so much the Marxist philosophical tradition, but rather that of Plekhanov, in which materialism is formulated within a framework of monist reflection theory. In this work a kind of "biological determinism" relegated historical materialism into the background. This was likewise made clear by the political nature of the philosophical debate.[82]

Eventually there were debates about the work's philosophical import. Noteworthy among them is Gramsci's interpretation and Pannekoek's critique that "resorts to sociology." Even in his definition of matter, Gramsci was already engaging in polemics against a narrow-minded metaphysical focus, disconnected from social reality:

> Clearly, for the philosophy of praxis, "matter" should be understood neither in the meaning that it has acquired in natural science . . . nor in any of the meanings that one finds in the various materialistic metaphysics. . . . Matter as such therefore is not our subject but how it is socially and historically organized for production, and natural science should be seen correspondingly as essentially an historical category, a human relation.[83]

In Lenin's *Materialism and Empirio-Criticism: Critical Remarks on a Reactionary Philosophy*, published between 29 April and 4 May 1909 by Zveno in Moscow, it is difficult to find the dividing line between philosophy and political polemics, much as in the case of the Lenin-Bogdanov debate. Strictly speaking, Lenin did not write a philosophical work, nor was it his intention to write one. Instead, within the framework of ideological polemics, the work is focused on the nature of Marxist philosophy and its functions. Lenin had revealed his political intentions in a letter to Anna, written from Paris, on 9 March 1909.[84]

The Bolsheviks, meaning to break with "traditional" parliamentary politics, experimented with creating a party school under Bogdanov's direction, which would have functioned as a kind of organization headquarters, challenging the Bolsheviks around Lenin. This is what eventually led to the "excommunication" of Bogdanov.[85] The political and philosophical endeavors of Bogdanov meant a different kind of "culture," a different school of politicking, for Social Democrats and for his own Bolshevik faction. The attributes most frequently used to qualify their politics were *otzovism* or *ultimatism*. Their theoretical-philosophical endeavors were described as *proletarian culture, proletarian science,* and *proletarian art*. These were rooted in the syndicalist and Sorelist tradition associated with Lunacharsky, who was interested mainly in aesthetics.

Indeed, Lunacharsky initiated a new philosophical experiment as manifested in his concept of "God-building." In 1907, he published an essay about "scientific socialism . . . as the new, highest form of religion." His intention was to use "religious atheism" to teach the proletariat about faith in the good and in happiness. This was a form of "God building" referring to socialist culture, which viewed Lenin as the "narrow practitioner" of the Second International, oriented toward practical politics.

The future-oriented and hyper-developed "revolutionary consciousness" of Lunacharsky, Gorky, and even Bogdanov, announced a new kind of communitarianism. This "collectivist philosophy of action" attempted to anchor the consciousness of the proletariat to a utopian and messianic type of socialism.[86] In its theoretical construct, "proletarian culture" smacks of a "philosophy of hope." God building appears as a yearning for harmony, and socialism itself becomes a quasi-religion. Of course, Lenin was exaggerating when he suspected some kind of doctrinaire religion. In this case it was a matter of instrumentalizing emotions and aesthetic passions to mobilize socialism as an ideology.

In his December 1905 essay "Socialism and Religion," Lenin deconstructed the relationship between the proletariat and religion. He examined the origins of religion in general, its social functions, and the issue of working along with religion. He advocated collaboration with priests who did not attack the objectives of the workers' movement on "Christian grounds." He argued:

> Impotence of the exploited classes in their struggle against the exploiters just as inevitably gives rise to the belief in a better life after death as impotence of the savage in his battle with nature gives rise to belief in gods, devils, miracles, and the like. . . . Religion is opium for the people.[87]

For Lenin, separation of church and state signified that the state abstains from any kind of support for the church and ceases to keep track of the religion of its citizens. Social democracy fights against the "religious dumbing down" of the people on the basis of its atheism. Beyond the scientific enlightenment of the workers, he made two important observations that the literature on Lenin "forgets" to reveal. One of these was that he felt it was prejudicial for anyone to try to dispel religious biases purely on the basis of enlightenment; these can only be dispelled once the oppressive regime itself is overcome. Even the official program of the party opposed any declaration of atheism. Moreover, the practical unity of the political struggle of the workers transcended all ideology, including all atheistic pronouncements:

> Unity in this really revolutionary struggle of the oppressed class for the creation of a paradise on earth is more important to us than unity of proletarian opinion on paradise in heaven. That is the reason why we do not and should not set forth our atheism in our Program; that is why we do not and should not prohibit proletarians who still retain vestiges of their old prejudices from associating themselves with our Party. . . . Everywhere the reactionary bourgeoisie has concerned itself, and is now beginning to concern itself in Russia, with the fomenting of religious strife—in order thereby to divert the attention of the masses from the really important and fundamental economic and political problems.[88]

At the same time, Lenin continued the debate against "God building," and not just as a matter of organization or for factional reasons. In the personal letters he wrote to Gorky in November 1913 we find the framework of an analysis replete with passionate arguments regarding the ontological, epistemological, power psychology, and political propaganda aspects of religion. He scolded Gorky and the "God builders" because they were "integrating," or absorbing, the most potent, hence the most damaging, rival ideology to social democracy.

This ideology was none other than religion and the concept of God. These have proved themselves as important and effective tools for keeping the population in ignorance, even in bourgeois democratic countries like Switzerland and the United States:

> In the freest countries . . . particular zeal is applied to render the people and the workers obtuse with just this very idea of a clean, spiritual, built-up god. Just because any religious idea, any idea of any god at all, any flirtation even with a god, is the most inexpressible foulness, particularly tolerantly (and often even favorably) accepted by the *democratic* bourgeoisie—for that very reason it is the most dangerous foulness, the most shameful "infection."[89]

Lenin assessed the impact of religion on the consciousness of the workers primarily from the viewpoint of socialist propaganda and universal enlightenment. He saw this impact as the most important ideological tool of autocracy and of the ruling class.[90]

Sociologically speaking, God building could be ascribed primarily to the existential circumstances of the petite bourgeoisie: "from the point of view not of the individual, but of society, the essence of *all* God building is that the vacuous petite bourgeoisie gazes at the mirror enamored of itself. . . ." This stratum is everywhere alike, it is not specific to Russians. As Lenin wrote to Gorky, "the Jewish, Italian, English spirit are all the same, the awful spirit of the petit bourgeois is equally repulsive everywhere." Lenin underlined the words several times to encourage Gorky not to sugarcoat and decorate this nauseating state of the spirit by means of his own writing, on the path to "God building."[91]

In another letter written in November 1913 he gave it even harder to Gorky, revealing his own perceptions of religion still more clearly. He was reacting to Gorky's concept of God, according to which God is the "complex of ideas formed by tribe, nation, humanity which awaken and organize social feelings in such a way as to tie the individual to society, to bridle animal individualism." Lenin referred to this as the worst kind of Christian Socialism and that Gorky, in spite of all his good intentions, had degenerated to the point of repeating "the hocus-pocus of the priests," in that if "you eliminate from the idea of God everything about it that is *historical and drawn from real life* (filth, prejudices, sanctified ignorance and degradation, on the one hand, serfdom and monarchy, on the other), and instead of the reality of history and life here is substituted in the idea of God a gentle petit bourgeois phrase (God = 'ideas which awaken and organize social feelings')."[92]

Lenin objected that it was "the dumb impotence of man intimidated by class oppression" that was responsible for the reproduction of the concept of God from one day to the next, and that his friends were thus "rendering this impotent fear *permanent, putting class struggle to sleep*." For Lenin, one could imagine no greater crime than this on the part of Marxists. Moreover, the idea of God did not tie the individual to society but, on the contrary, "tied up the oppressed classes by means of their faith in the divine nature of the oppressors."

Lenin placed any popular understanding or religion within the framework of "stupidity," "ignorance," "awkwardness," "class oppression," and "manipulation."[93] Philosophically speaking, he rejected Gorky's notion that philosophical idealism "'always has in view only the interests of the individual.' Did Descartes have the interests of the individual more in mind than Gassendi? Or Fichte and Hegel as compared with Feuerbach?" He even went so far as to tell Gorky that his investigations did not satisfy basic methodological requirements: "Your definition is bourgeois (and not scientific, not historical) because it operates with sweeping, general, 'Robinson Crusoe' conceptions in general, not with definite *classes* in a definite historical epoch." Gorky's "sociology" and "theology" upset Lenin greatly, and not simply because of its factionalism. On the contrary, he felt it was evidence of a degeneration of class consciousness in his own milieu.[94] If the task of the party is to uphold class consciousness, then perhaps we can understand Lenin's edginess: he felt the theoretical and ideological issue had a very practical aspect.

This pure, "sterile," almost aestheticized, consciousness seeking a path to the people, to the workers, also permeated Gorky's "ideal of God." It reached its highest conceptual level in the case of Bogdanov. Reading his *Tektology*, or his recently discovered "The decade of my excommunication from Marxism," written in 1914, becomes noteworthy on account of its dilettante solutions and the problematic theoretical underpinnings of its proletarian science.[95]

Empirio-monism elicited Lenin's ire mainly because it discarded the issue mandatory for Marxists, namely, the need to choose between materialism and idealism. Bogdanov offered his own science of organization by way of a solution but it did not fit well into the history of Marxist philosophy.

Much of Bogdanov's correspondence reveals that he understood the philosophical attacks directed against him primarily as political attacks.[96] In a letter written from the editorial offices of *Proletary* in early April 1909, he protests with indignation that the office, which has ample financial means at its disposal, "does not tolerate nuances of ideas that are not in complete agreement with the official line." Bogdanov accused Lenin and company—not without grounds—that they were preventing, by bureaucratic means, the launching of the party schools because they saw it as a competitive venture.[97]

The party schools in Capri and Bologna were in operation between August and December 1909, and again from November 1910 to March 1911. They were a partly successful experiment in that Bogdanov and his followers delivered their ideas regarding the chances of the workers' movement in Russia to activists from the working class. Yet in January 1910, when Bogdanov lost his position on the Central Committee, the *Vpreyod* group was recognized within the party as a "literary publishing venture." In a letter addressed to Rikov at the time, Lenin acknowledged—not without a note of envy—that Bogdanov and company were a powerful force.

In 1910 Bogdanov's earlier followers—Alexksinsky, Pokrovsky, and V. Menzhinsky—united in their opposition to the cultural Marxism of Bogdanov and Lunacharsky, and published an article in *Vperyod* that labeled the theory of "proletarian culture and science" as revisionist. Pokrovsky, tired of the continuous useless debates, left the *Vperyod* group. In January 1911, Bogdanov himself took the same step. Ideological and organizational disagreements dispersed the entire Bogdanov faction.[98]

The organizational struggles cannot cover up the deeper causes of the division within the ranks of the Bolshevik faction. No matter how hard Lenin and Bogdanov fought against each other, Bogdanov gave up the struggle on his own accord by admitting that he was unable to adjust to the daily struggles in party politics, or to the realization of his philosophical ideas in action. In vain, the circle in Geneva appealed to him to return to *Vperyod* in March of 1912. He replied:

> Lately it has become increasingly clear to me, reinforced directly by my work experience, that the revolutionary cultural task has enormous significance. I decided to dedicate myself to it. When the moment is ripe, when there will be persons and means, I will devote all my strength to create "the alliance of Socialist culture" which, I assume, will not turn into a party faction, and will not compete with political organizations.[99]

On 17 January 1914, in a letter to the editors at *Novaya rabochaya gazeta*, Bogdanov wrote that he would no longer write on matters of party politics. He would deal only with tasks of "scientific dissemination."

Bogdanov's extensive publications about Marx and tektology turned out to be ideological experiments with no practical applications. It is not surprising, therefore, that he never returned to party politics. In summarizing his views on the issue of the "cultural hegemony of the working class," Bogdanov believed that the immediate task facing the Bolsheviks, even in the period of autocracy, was to create a *proletarian culture* that would be freer and more creative than bourgeois culture. He could not conceive of socialism without such cultural emancipation. Bogdanov opposed Lenin's rapprochement to Plekhanov even from this angle, fearing that this would amount to "Menshevik opportunism." Presumably, the *Vperyod* group was created explicitly to prevent such a rapprochement.[100]

In spite of their ideological and political differences, both Lenin and Bogdanov believed in the prospect of an armed revolutionary uprising. Bogdanov ascribed a greater role to a *purely socialist* class consciousness, whereas Lenin was more prone to emphasize the practical and "technical implications of anticapitalist and antiautocratic ideas." Where Bogdanov stressed the significance of a pure socialist prospect centered on proletarian culture, Lenin rejected the possibility of an independent proletarian culture. He argued—even after October 1917—that the primary task was the appropriation of the "proper" achievements of bourgeois civilization. The objective being the elimination of class society, by the time the proletariat might conceivably develop its authentic class culture it might not even exist as a class. This is why for Lenin, Bogdanov's "antipolitical" arguments appeared useless under the circumstances, regardless of their apposite theoretical considerations.

In July 1909, Bogdanov delivered an address to his Bolshevik comrades in the name of those comrades who had been removed from *Proletary*'s expanded editorial board. He expressed his regret that "a sufficiently strong and influential nucleus has not evolved within the proletariat, one capable of completely assimilating socialist education, and capable of transmitting the greatest consciousness into every action experienced by the masses of workers."[101] This thesis was at the root of Bogdanov's organizational conclusion, where he said: "We must elaborate a new kind of party school capable of providing party education for the workers . . . and contributing reliable and conscious leaders for all aspects of the proletarian struggle."

In his *Report to the Bolshevik Comrades on behalf of the Expelled Members of the Expanded Editorial Board of the* Proletary, published on 3 July 1909, Bogdanov wrote: "the movement of the masses had to be kept on a strictly revolutionary course."[102] He engaged in an analysis of the "Lenin phenomenon" on several subsequent occasions. In a letter addressed to the Geneva circle of the *Vperyod*, dated 23 June 1912, he expressed disappointment that Lenin used the slogans of the revolution as a politician would (democratic republic, confiscation, etc.)

to "enhance his own revolutionary reputation, yet I have no doubt that Lenin's candidates [for the Duma] kept these slogans in their pockets for the duration of the campaign." He claimed that the supporters of the *Vperyod* were acting the same way, but without really understanding the problem: "Everywhere the election campaign . . . is conducted in a purely Menshevik fashion." In this letter, Bogdanov used the term *politics* with utter contempt, implying the worst besmirching of revolutionary purity.[103]

In a letter written on 11 December 1912, Bogdanov expressed that he felt, precisely because of this despised "politicking," that in Russia the social democratic intellectuals will unavoidably "unite with the Leninists." "It is useless to even mention the 'radicalism' of the general mass of our social democratic intellectuals. No, this is not pessimism." He described this surrender of social democracy to politics as opportunism, the "domination of bourgeois ways of thought over proletarian experience, the bourgeois means of political struggle over the defense of proletarian interests."[104] His stated reason for withdrawing from the *Vperyod* was because he did not wish "to waste his energies uselessly." He was also not so naïve as to believe that he would be able to express his ideas freely. He rejected the idea of working together, for the group had "irrevocably rejected the program of *Vperyod*, whereas its program rests entirely on diplomatic intrigue, first with Plekhanov, then with Trotsky, then with the Mensheviks."[105]

In a letter dated 9 June 1913, he wrote critically about the merger of the "Vperyodists and the left-wing Leninists":

> by Leninism I do not mean personal relations with Lenin, but rather the general idea of politics and political methods which he represents better than anyone else. For the Vperyodist the politics of Social Democracy expresses the organization process which takes place within the working class. For the Leninist, be he the most left-wing (as are many of the Otzovists), politics is a separate, independent profession, subject to its own laws, capable of evolution more or less independently from general class organization processes. For the Vperyodist, [politics are] an element of the revolutionary culture, which evolved earlier and more broadly than other aspects of culture, depending on the historical circumstances. For the Vperyodist, politics and its meaning are always measured by class. . . . For the Leninist, politics are political, which can be successful at the group, at the circle, or even at the individual level; the art of politics is like the art of the good chess-player, placing the right piece in the right place at the right time to win the match.[106]

Bogdanov attacked the rapprochement of Lenin and Plekhanov on these grounds, in spite of the two distancing themselves from both the left and right wings. Bogdanov would have liked to see the Vperyodists break with the left Leninists on the grounds that their lines did not mesh.[107]

There is a peculiar contradiction in Bogdanov's line of thought. While he rejected "politics as a profession," he made no mention of politics below the level of class, or of those individuals on the technical and organizational side of the movement who practiced it as a profession. He also made no mention of the problem of those who viewed politics as he did, those who "give up" the revolution as practice in their everyday struggle (which at the time included armed uprisings).

What is the use of retreating from "dirty politics" then, if during the professional, expert preparation of revolution or uprising, revolutionaries cannot reject the institutions of mass politics, including parliament? How could they reject the inner, favorable workings, when they are essential to fighting an armed uprising? As the founder of "organizational science," it seems odd that Bogdanov did not ask himself: how can Bolshevism succeed in present-day Russia, if the workers cannot make everyday connections with reality, transitions between the instinct, interests, and long-term socialist goals, except at the party schools or at meetings? It was precisely the organizational achievement of the Leninists that drew attention to the unavoidable problems.

Bogdanov's conceptualization of the relationship between theory and practice reminds us necessarily of Lukács's "identity of object and subject, or the 'mandated class consciousness' which occurs historically only at specific moments, during the brief periods of revolution." Lukács consciously accepted one-sided interpretations for the sake of action. This derived from the view that the vanguard has the right, in bourgeois politics, to act on behalf of the proletariat. After that, the revolution would eventually take care of things.

In other words, the real problem was not the acceptance of expertise or participation in bourgeois politics, but rather the contradiction—outlined almost inadvertently—which was to prove almost insoluble: domination by experts over the apparatus of the movement as a whole. In light of this, neither Lenin's empiriocriticism nor Bogdanov's philosophy contributed anything to the development of Marxist theory and politics.

In 1912 the Mensheviks raised the issue as to why the political organization of Lenin, and of the Bolsheviks who sided with him, prevailed in Petrograd, Russia's capital. It was only later that Martov understood why Lenin and his followers were able to control many of social democracy's structures and organizations.[108] In 1912, the worker voters of the Duma elected six Bolsheviks and not a single Menshevik. Later, Martov noted, in a letter to Potresov, that the defeat of the Mensheviks in the elections to the "workers' courts . . . demonstrates once again that the Mensheviks became aware of the growing threat of the Leninists late, and overestimated its temporary decline."[109] In addition to *Pravda*, in April 1912 the Bolshevik newspaper *Zvezda* was printed in 29,000 copies. The Mensheviks only able to manage the weekly paper *Zivoe Djelo*, although in May they published *Nievski golos* as a daily. *Pravda* sold twice as many copies in 1913–1914 as the Menshevik paper.

The series of defeats for the Mensheviks continued in 1913 during the elections in the metalworkers' union at Petrograd, where once again the Bolsheviks got the majority. The successes of the Bolsheviks can be understood not in the organizational achievements mentioned by Martov, but rather in that the Bolsheviks' aiming to connect the short-term—and even daily—demands of the workers with prospects for the "proletarian dictatorship." Their success rested on their ability to weave together legal "mass work" with underground organization.

A renewed rise of the workers' movement was cut short by the explosion of the Great War and the nationalist flood, which, from 1916 on, "rehabilitated" Lenin's Bolshevism. The revolution of February 1917, the analysis of its consequences, and the historical and empirical justification of Lenin's organizational thinking dovetailed into the October Revolution. Bogdanov's "intellectual debating clubs" played no historical role precisely when the historical situation seemed most favorable for them.[110]

The End of "Ideological Redemption"

When the "party split" of 1903 took place Trotsky went into immediate action to "reunite" the party.[111] This venture did not succeed, in spite of all his efforts, even though everyone was intent on remaining united. Perhaps Lenin was the first one who grasped that the Russian Social-Democratic Labor Party could not be reconstituted in its original form. In 1908 Trotsky created his "workers' newspaper" as the paper of the Spilka Ukrainian Association, the *Pravda*. The paper was so well edited that Lenin, "jealous" of its success, decided to give the Bolsheviks' paper the same name. Trotsky, sensing an important particularity of social democratic evolution in Russia, namely its intellectual feature and the predominance of intellectuals among its leaders, announced "that the workers had to take control of their own party entirely" since "the workers' representatives in the soviets and especially in the labor unions had acquired invaluable experience in organization structure and self-government."[112] Later, in the same paper, it is written that the "dispute between Menshevik and Bolshevik, not to mention the split, is incomprehensible to the masses."[113]

Of course, Lenin would have been willing to reconcile the various tendencies only if the deciding force, the initiative, remained with him. It should be noted that during these debates Lenin received significant political and literary support, from Kamenev and Zinoviev in particular (we cannot dedicate space to their analysis here).[114] Trotsky viewed Lenin in the context of his "dictatorial" objectives and personal motives; this was how he interpreted the party conference of January 1912. The first Bolshevik Central Committee formed there, which he considered to be a first step to creating a party "from above." He referred to this as a "party split" in the record of the August 1912 conference he organized (which proved to be a fiasco).[115]

In March 1912 Trotsky's *Pravda* announced the creation of the "RSDLP Organizational Committee," which would serve as the rallying point for every viable Social Democratic formation.[116] He identified Lenin's faction as one group that was an obstacle to unification, since Lenin had called a meeting of his own faction for January.[117] Even at this point it was not possible to be above the factions. There were so many tendencies, from the Vperyodist to the liquidator, that there were at least three potential parties. In his "bulletin" about the conference, Trotsky wrote as follows: "The Central Committee fell apart on the impact of internal discussions, the Leninist group unfurled the banner of 'two parties' and mobilized the most intransigent and divisive elements of the Bolshevik faction under this banner."[118] Trotsky recognized that he did not leave a remnant of organizational achievement behind himself, whereas the Lenin conference, which seemed so inconsequential, turned out to be historic. This became clear five years later when even Trotsky, unlike most leaders of the Mensheviks who never went beyond the slogan of a bourgeois democratic republic, joined forces with Lenin.

For Lenin, the most important of the underground activities was to preserve an underground organization, the political goal of which would be to manage the "transition" to a democratic and proletarian revolution. The underground party (or rather, its nucleus) became a point of crystallization for the Russian workers' movement, which would ultimately integrate the revolutionary tendencies into a great organization when the regime in power experienced a crisis and collapsed. In August 1917, the provisional underground organization "found its way" to the Bolshevik party, signifying, at least symbolically, a new mass party born of the revolution.

Yet the true practical critique of the party conception of Lenin and the Bolsheviks was the European revolutionary upsurge. Later, the revolutionaries—including Lenin of course—noted in disappointment that the radicalization of the proletariat in Western Europe did not take place, or took place only partially. It was not enough to bring about the revolution. According to the young Lukács in his *History and Class Consciousness*, the "reasons for the *surprising ideological crisis*"[119] of the proletariat are due to the Menshevism of the working class, its "economism," the role of the "worker-aristocrats," and its "bourgeoisification." This does not sufficiently strike at the "root of the issue." Aware of the "limits of revolutionary spontaneity," Lukács found the solution in the Communist Party, in the increase "of the decisive role" of Leninist organization.[120]

Between 1902 and 1922, the basic problem, in various ways, was how far the party's "decision-forging role" could extend. The issue became clear only years later, after the Stalinist period, when the old Lukács was searching for the "weak points" in Lenin (and, in his own earlier position as well).[121] The old Lukács, in contrast with the young one, did not locate the basic problem in the backwardness of "the proletariat's ideology," but rather in the changing character of the capitalist economy and its impact on mentality and consciousness:

> Lenin's grandiose concept, contrasting Marx with the present in a truly revolutionary way . . . *concentrates too exclusively upon revolutionizing the ideology* and as a result does not direct the ideology sufficiently toward the object to be revolutionized, change in the capitalist economy.[122]

We have not yet uncovered the economic origins of labor union consciousness or the revolutionary political class consciousness of the proletariat. The historical and economic nature of their difference remains largely hidden. It seemed that the "ideological redemption" was the revolution itself. But the failure of the European revolution to materialize, and the isolation of the Russian Revolution, created a new historical foundation for the "ideological redemption" of the workers.

The social revolution can come only in the form of an epoch in which are combined civil war by the proletariat against the bourgeoisie in the advanced countries and a whole series of democratic and revolutionary movements, including the national liberation movement, in the undeveloped, backward and oppressed nations.

Why? Because capitalism develops unevenly, and objective reality gives us highly developed capitalist nations side-by-side with a number of economically slightly developed, or totally undeveloped, nations.

—V. I. LENIN, *A CARICATURE OF MARXISM AND IMPERIALIST ECONOMISM*, LCW, VOL. 23, 60

4
The War and the National Question

DISINTEGRATION AND DIALECTICS

AFTER 1907, LENIN WAS ABLE to draw a practical lesson from the overall defeat of the 1905 Revolution: the autocratic regime could be shaken only by *revolutionary* means. Revolution as a possibility permeated the foundations he laid in his economic theory *for the end, the "disintegration" of capitalism*. However, this theory, which appears rather deterministic at first glance, was formulated at the highest possible scientific level in Rosa Luxemburg's famous book, *The Accumulation of Capital* (1913). One of the underlying notions is that capital's global expansion and accumulation meets such obstacles because of the shrinking size of the world's not yet capitalized economies. As a result, the whole system becomes untenable and collapses. Luxemburg makes the assumption that in the process of disintegration, the "revolutionary proletariat" will instinctively and spontaneously recognize its own interests, which will be expressed in a resurrection of internationalist solidarity and revolution.

Undoubtedly the Great War gave the problem its urgency, independent of the degree to which the initial theoretical thesis was misguided, for disintegration was an everyday experience during the war. Luxemburg had worked over the problem in her earlier debate with Bernstein by exaggerating Marx's theory of crisis. She found a "solution" to the correspondence between the development of the capitalist credit system and the crisis in the unavoidable destruction of the capitalist system itself: "Credit reproduces all the fundamental antagonisms of the capitalist world. It accentuates them. It precipitates their development and thus pushes the capitalist world forward to its own destruction."[1] However, Luxemburg underestimated Bernstein's realization that the overarching capitalist, the state itself, can at least mitigate the crisis.

From the start, Lenin was at odds with the way Luxemburg conceived of disintegration. Before he read her book, in January 1913, he submitted a request to the editors of the *Bremer Bürger-Zeitung* that a copy of their review of the book be sent to him in Cracow. He went on to express his pleasure at the journal's point of view on the question of whether noncapitalist parts of the world are required to realize surplus value.[2]

Years later, in the early 1920s, Marxist circles were still engaged in debate about whether there existed a point of development beyond which capitalism would unavoidably and automatically crumble.[3] Many agreed with Luxemburg, believing that the prospects for capital accumulation could be explained by imperialist expansion and its constraints. This theoretical proposition manifested itself in the political notion that once expansion stops, there will be fewer opportunities for accumulation and forces opposing the system will spontaneously rise around the globe. In contrast, Lenin's theory of imperialism stated that capital accumulation has no limits, as capital always creates the conditions of a new cycle of accumulation through its own destructive nature (wars, technological transformations, etc.).

For those who accepted Luxemburg's theory of accumulation, counting on the inevitable disintegration of the capitalist system seemed to underestimate the role of *organization* and its immanent component, *class consciousness*. Even Georg Lukács's *Lenin Pamphlet* (1924) rested on the disintegration theory of capitalism. Lenin, however, spoke about the "overthrow" of capitalism rather than its disintegration, thus emphasizing the active, conscious element in the process.[4] He based his theory of imperialism on the more concrete and essential *class consciousness*, something that followed from the new traits of capitalist development and the higher organization of its operation. This only serves to deepen our appreciation that during the imperialist epoch the whole question of "opportunism" turned on the issue of "revolutionary consciousness."[5]

Lenin's research and theoretical work on the question of organization remained in a certain sense "bookish," limited to academicism until the 1905 Revolution, and in the view of some authors, all the way up to 1917.[6] In fact, the practical relevance of his "fustily bookish" Marxism found justification during the first Russian Revolution and the subsequent world war, and revealed its true worth only later.

The 1905 Revolution transformed Lenin's thought and actions primarily because he came into immediate contact with real workers and their mass movement. Though his writings from the period still show some theoretical hair-splitting while discussing matter-of-fact processes—for example, his construct based on the "worker-peasant democratic dictatorship of the proletariat"—he was nevertheless first to react to the outbreak of war in 1914.[7] Thus his "antiquarian" Marxism would serve as a theoretical and practical prerequisite for the Bolsheviks' rise to leadership during the second Russian Revolution in 1917–1918.

In the years preceding and following the war, Lenin wrote excellent analyses of the new traits of capitalist development. After his death, Lenin's estate worked for decades to categorize his papers by fields of specialization and to systematize an archive of his writings according to ever-changing political trends,[8] including those years left unmarked by his Hegelian turn. This period began with the notes he took while reading Hegel's *Science of Logic* in 1914–15.[9]

Whatever significance we attach to this turn, its quality, depth, indeed its very existence, are still matters of debate among Marxists and non-Marxists. It can be said that it matured over a number of years in global political developments as well as in the development of social democracy—inclusive of Lenin's career as a politician and thinker—and found expression in concentrated form during the First World War. Though all artificial periodizations of Lenin's work and achievements may be deemed hair-splitting, there is no doubt that he was the first to recognize the practical significance of *methodology* in the Marxian theoretical heritage and consciously make it serve applied action.[10]

From the point of view that the outbreak of the Great War brought to the surface the widely accepted and un-Marxian Bernsteinism and its spread within the International, a shift in social democracy certainly did take place. This is something Lenin identified and decried at a very early stage, and at the same time revealed the non-revolutionary political strategy and evolutionist worldview of his German "idol," Karl Kautsky.

In the case of Kautsky, Lenin was mostly willing to turn a blind eye. First, he did not wish to engage in political battles on an international scale, since on a number of issues Kautsky's authority could be advantageous to the Bolsheviks. Second, he did not yet see his own allies in the International, though Rosa Luxemburg, Karl Radek, and Anton Pannakoek's criticisms of Kautsky preceded his own, as Lenin acknowledged in *State and Revolution*.[11] Kautsky's attitude to the war gave Lenin a clear picture of how the pope of social democracy was lost to the cause of revolutionary politics. This made a showdown with Kautsky unavoidable.

The showdown with Bernsteinism, as well as the opportunistic decay of the International, was inspired by Lenin's "rediscovery" of Hegel.[12] His notes show that this turn away from Marxism in the form of Bernsteinism was philosophically interlocked with a Kantian/neo-Kantian change of direction at the end of the century.[13] His rehabilitation of Hegel, however, was part of a redirection away from the Second International toward a course of revolutionary momentum. Lenin's reading of Hegel in line with the new situation moved Marx into a theoretically and politically more dynamic mode. Lenin's debate with Plekhanov was part of the same process. The influence of Plekhanov's critique of Hegel's idealism drew a devaluation of the significance of dialectics that was a "bourgeois ('mechanistic,' 'contemplative') materialism," which may have been a philosophical link between Bernstein and Plekhanov.

Though much of the above was scarcely discussed in the Soviet Union, for decades Lenin was portrayed as a constantly evolving thinker who, being at one with history and vice versa, was never "surprised" by it. Only in the aftermath of 1968 did a more nuanced image of Lenin emerge, mainly in Western Europe, though it was contradictorily framed in a new reductionist approach to Lenin's figure.[14] Much later, pre- and post-regime change in Eastern Europe, one of the interpretative frameworks of Lenin's theoretical achievement was determined by his "de-Hegelianization vs. Hegelianization."

Another post-regime-change portrait of Lenin depicts a purely pragmatic politician, someone who perhaps consciously combatted the Marxist writers emphasizing the significance of his "Hegelian shift" as his most important theoretical legacy.[15] On the one hand, Lenin was sublimated as a dialectical theorist and tactician of the revolutionary "leap," and on the other, he was depicted as a "gradualist-evolutionist" thinker and politician.[16] There are even writers who consider him both a dogmatic sectarian and power-oriented pragmatist at the same time.[17]

Whatever the philosophical truth, Kevin Anderson's "Hegelian" position has come to encapsulate the historical perspective of Lenin's philosophical-theoretical "shift." Anderson writes: "we need to celebrate the fact that the Russian Revolution's principal leader, Lenin, was the first Marxist after Marx to place the dialectic back where it belonged, at the center of Marxist theory."[18] In the end, whether Lenin is classified as dogmatic for the way he deduced his politics from abstract philosophical principles, or as pragmatic for his political moves that he prepared on philosophical grounds, is the result of dated schematic approaches.[19]

Robert Mayer calls attention to the fact that one unchanging tactical principle existed for Lenin: the interests of the working class. This defined his whole strategic way of thinking. Lenin states as much in his famous article on Marx commemorating the thirtieth anniversary of his death, "The Historical Destiny of the Doctrine of Karl Marx," published in *Pravda* on 1 March 1913.

However, Lenin's conception of the proletariat is too homogenous in this context. Though he theoretically engages with the methodological significance of dialectics, he does not thoroughly study the "complex system" of proletarian interests in Western Europe, a fact that cannot simply be accounted for by his contempt for bourgeois sociology. Rather, it is his failure to apply Marxist tools more acutely. His objective was effectively to bring the "anticapitalist unity of the proletariat" into strong relief. When Lenin referred to the workers, he usually had the most skilled laborers in mind.

Lenin formulated the essence of "Marxist teaching" in the first sentence of this article: "The chief thing in the doctrine of Marx is that it brings out the historic role of the proletariat as the builder of socialist society."[20] With this, he effectively distanced himself from both *Narodnik* "national socialism," with its eyes in the past, and bourgeois liberalism. Adherents of the Narodnik school of thought did not comprehend "the materialist basis of historical movement, inability to single out the role and significance of each class in capitalist society, concealment of the bourgeois nature of democratic reforms under diverse, quasi-socialist phrases about the 'people,' 'justice,' 'right,' and so on." Next to these political forces incapable of breaking with the past he defined *liberalism*, which mustered its way into the ranks of social democracy as a movement that preached "renunciation of the class struggle" in the name of "social peace." He labeled this the politics of "peace with the slave-owners": "Liberalism, rotten within, tried to revive itself in the form of socialist opportunism."

He also called attention to the fact that it was not easy to see through this opportunistic movement as no one took the step of openly making a break with Marxism, for it would be identical with a plain denial of proletarian interests.[21] Let us not forget the "banality" by which the Mensheviks still considered themselves the orthodox Marxists of Russia. Lenin's argument was somewhat weakened by the fact that he often neglected to differentiate between right-wing social democracy ("Bernsteinian opportunism") and liberalism, or disregarded the lines drawn between them.

Lenin's objective was to have dialectics, as a methodology of action, "engrafted" into the organizational and political activity of "everyday mass struggle." In doing so he hoped to avoid the fate of so many of the groups in revolt who did not prepare for these battles and were driven by their lack of experience of mass struggle to "despair and anarchy." It was Lenin who brought the "unity and interaction" of political praxis back into Marxism. He approached dialectics as the philosophical-theoretical and practical instrument or method, in social and historical terms, for overtaking the capitalist system.

A more extensive study, "The Three Sources and Three Component Parts of Marxism,"[22] was published in the Bolshevik journal *Prosveshcheniye* in March 1913. In early 1914, Lenin also published it as an entry, under "Marx," in the *Granat Encyclopedia*. Here dialectics was discussed not so much for its practical political significance but mainly in its scientific capacity.

Citing Hegelian sources, he saw Marx's place in the history of philosophy based in his development of materialist dialectics, which is "the doctrine of development in its fullest, deepest and most comprehensive form, the doctrine of the relativity of the human knowledge that provides us with a reflection of eternally developing matter." He considered historical materialism Marx's other great accomplishment in this field: "The chaos and arbitrariness that had previously reigned in views on history and politics were replaced by a strikingly integral and harmonious scientific theory, which shows how, in consequence of the growth of productive forces, out of one system of social life another and higher system develops."[23]

In these writings, Lenin encapsulated the socio-philosophical and political-economic essence of Marxism in a clear and popular form, along with the consequences of the theory about surplus value for practical politics and the "doctrine of class war." For example, he affirmed:

> Marx's philosophical materialism alone has shown the proletariat the way out of the spiritual slavery in which all oppressed classes have hitherto languished. Marx's economic theory alone has explained the true position of the proletariat in the general system of capitalism.[24]

Lenin approached Marxism as a historical formation, which he evaluated as an actual revolution in the history of nineteenth-century thought, comprising all its significant achievements—German philosophy, the English school of political economy, and French socialism. He considered Marxism the "apex of civilization" and was among the first to realize that Marxism would be one of the mainstreams of scientific thought in the twentieth century.

Also in 1913, he studied Marx and Engels's correspondence, and found the four-volume German-language publication left much to be desired. Its editors, Eduard Bernstein foremost among them, followed their own current political objectives rather than those of their subjects. The 1,386 letters contained in the volumes were often abridged and lacked scholarly annotation. Lenin made notes of approximately one hundred letters. He summarized his findings in an extensive article published in November 1920 in *Pravda*. Once again, he drew attention to dialectics:

> If one were to attempt to define in a single word the focus, so to speak, of the whole correspondence, the central point at which the whole body of ideas expressed and discussed converges—that word would be dialectics. The application of materialist dialectics to the reshaping of all political economy from its foundations up, its application to history, natural science, philosophy and to the policy and tactics of the working class—that was what interested Marx and Engels most of all, that was where they contributed what was most essential and new, and that was what constituted the masterly advance they made in the history of revolutionary thought.[25]

In accord with the considerations dictated by the work, Lenin—unlike in *empirio-criticism*—highlighted the superiority of dialectic materialism over the mechanistic, "evolutionistic" approach. This piece is a de facto intellectual precursor to his study of Hegel's dialectic.

While continuity is to be seen as the definitive tendency for his interest in dialectics, there are clear shifts of emphasis where some problems are clearly given more prominence and the significance of this must not be underestimated. These points are fundamental to understanding Lenin's theoretical-political accomplishment during the war.

Lenin's endeavors to acquire the "dialectical approach" from 1890 onward are thoroughly documented in the Soviet historical and theoretical literature. The curiosity of the matter lies in a repeat of the debate in the 1990s. The debate concerns the relationship of Lenin and Hegel, just as it did a century earlier.

Lenin did not acquire and interpret dialectics through Marx alone. He was also educated in the "harsh school" of Russian circumstances, in a sense through Chernyshevsky and even more so through Plekhanov, who had their own way of interpreting the question of dialectics though they never attributed it with the theoretical and practical significance Lenin did. He conceived of dialectics not only as an instrument of "scientific contemplation" but also an organic component in "transforming the world."

Commenting on Plekhanov's philosophical legacy in the *Philosophical Notebooks*, and his critique of Kant specifically, he branded everything that followed more along Feuerbach's line of interpretation of materialism than the Marxist, dialectical materialist line, as "vulgar materialism":

> 1. Plekhanov criticizes Kantianism (and agnosticism in general) more from a vulgar-materialistic standpoint than from a dialectical-materialistic standpoint, *insofar* as he merely *rejects* their views *a limine* [from the threshold], but does not *correct* them (as Hegel corrected Kant), deepening, generalizing and extending them, showing the *connection* and *transitions* of each and every concept. 2. Marxists criticized (at the beginning of the twentieth century) the Kantians and Humists more in the manner of Feuerbach (and Büchner) than of Hegel.[26]

Needless to say, the Russian revolutionary tradition was led by explicitly pragmatic organizational motives. It could be said that discounting Plekhanov, Russia had no great Marxist thinker or philosopher at the turn of nineteenth century, which followed—with some simplification—from the particularities of the historical region. (Outstanding revolutionary organizers, ideologists-historians, sociologists and even economists, who were carriers for the ideology of the movement are however proportionally numerous: we needs must think only of Martov and Maslov, Stalin and Yaroslavsky, Martinov and Bogdanov, Pokrovsky and Olminsky, Trotsky and Radek, Preobrazhensky and Bukharin, etc.) Lenin's early interest in dialectics was at once theoretical and activist. Even then, however, Lenin categorically rejected the dominance of philosophy and morality over practice. His attitude to philosophy was best expressed by Marx's thesis on Feuerbach: "The philosophers have only interpreted the world, in various ways; the point is to change it." For Lenin, dialectics was a "contribution" to the issue of "change."

Every time these theoretical-methodological questions came to the fore in Lenin's work, some great historical turn was under way. This made him look for the practical steps, mediations, and transitions that would lead toward socialist revolution. He considered politics—for example, those based on the theory of permanent revolution developed by Parvus and Trotsky, or the unbounded dedication of the anarchists to extreme finalities—to have been deduced from abstract principles. He took a critical stance against all theories that placed limitations on, or blocked the revolutionary movement's sphere of activity, or added to the isolation of the workers' movement by way of hazardous lone-wolf actions. In the same spirit he rejected terrorism, the abstract form of being a revolutionary independent of any given situation, which acted upon the speculative creed of "always and everywhere be more revolutionary than anyone else."

Lenin did not pick up Hegel's *The Science of Logic* all of a sudden, "out of nowhere," in September 1914,[27] on his return from Poronino to Bern. He read the book through in the university's municipal library, finishing on 17 December 1914. In these four months, Lenin took extensive notes. There was no other book notated by him so exhaustively, numbered continuously, page by page, from 1 to 115.[28]

There was a great deal to think through theoretically, for as we have seen the First World War proved to be a catastrophic turn of events for much of the twentieth century.[29] Lenin's "Hegelian digression" can therefore be considered as preparation for this turn of events and the practical-political tasks that would stem from it. Hegel's *Logic* unmistakably provided Lenin with a stimulus—so far as his notes testify—to analyze and conceptually capture the new historical situation and to adapt politically to the new set of conditions. A quintessential turn in his thinking took place and found expression primarily in the epistemological approach being supplemented, and to a degree contradicted, by a historical, ontological, and "functional" examination of problems of importance in relation to politics and the movement.[30]

As opposed to most of his interpreters later, Lenin never understood dialectics as a "collection of eternally valid, abstract laws and principles." For him, dialectics was actually a "critique of abstract reason" that helped him draw practical wisdom from the field of political relations. This was also the spirit in which he earlier turned to Aristotle, who perhaps had even greater influence on his thinking than Hegel.[31]

Lenin's study of the dialectic of the *objective* and the *subjective* made a more exact analysis of political relations possible, and this allowed his epistemological approach to be supplemented with an ontological perspective.[32] In his famous article on Karl Marx, written in 1914, Lenin reveals that apart from Labriola, among his sources, the "book of an Hegelian idealist, Giovanni Gentile, *La filosofia di Marx*, is noteworthy. The author deals with some important aspects of Marx's materialist dialectics which usually escape the attention of the Kantians, Positivists."[33]

Antonio Gramsci interpreted Lenin's dialectical reconstruction of the "correlation between theory and praxis" as "the theoretical-practical principle of hegemony," which was "Ilyich's greatest theoretical contribution to the philosophy of praxis" in that it advanced "[t]he realization of a hegemonic apparatus, insofar as it creates a new ideological terrain."[34] The "quiet" differentiation and crystallization of this new revolutionary worldview was carried on through the war years. Lenin's practical-tactical flexibility became manifest in the famous arguments that he took up with Luxemburg, Bukharin and Pyatakov, mainly on the national question, the revolutionary strategy, and the social-democratic politics of alliance. If Lenin's theoretical legacy is seen in the context of twentieth-century history, it may be said that every critical turn that followed in the history of state socialism returned to him (e.g., the Twentieth and Twenty-second Congress of the CPSU, Perestroika), and not just because those in power and those seeking change were using Lenin to legitimize what they wanted to do.

Indeed, at the end of the 1960s—in antinomic relation to May 1968, the Soviet invasion of Prague, Hungarian economic reforms, and the hundredth anniversary of Lenin's birth—the contemplative-methodological questions of "revolutionary transformation" in Lenin's oeuvre became a focal point for Marxist theorists. Additionally, Georg Lukács's theoretical-philosophical work of the 1920s and 1960s had some influence on the experimental reconstructions of Leninian dialectics, especially by making the concept of *totality*, reflection on the whole, a central question.

In 1971, the year of Lukács's death, István Hermann endeavored an anti-Stalinist reading of Lenin on the basis of "instructions" from Lukács. He did so without maintaining the boring justifications of the system typical of the period, though he positioned himself in opposition to his teacher's denouncement of Soviet intervention. It is no accident that Lukács's by now well-known *Demokratisierung Heute und Morgen* (1968) could not be published in Hungary until 1988. Hermann had a genuine grasp of certain links between the thought of Hegel and Lenin:

> The Hegelian category of the all-encompassing moment—if transposed into praxis—is no more than the theoretical expression of Lenin's category of the *next link* . . . going further, Lenin, no doubt partly on account of Hegel's influence, concentrated on THE WHOLE, ON TOTALITY in his thoughts, theoretical and political activity, connecting the theory and praxis of consciousness and the changeability of the world.[35]

Lenin had indeed thought through the overtaking of capitalism and setting *all of humanity* free as a historical possibility. It is in this regard that he was esteemed as a theorist of action, the person who, after Marx, repositioned praxis once again in the center.

LENIN AND THE GREAT WAR

Lenin himself provides the key to an understanding of his attitude toward the Great War. He perceived events as a coherent system that cannot be broken down without violating scientific standards. The political starting point for Lenin, as always, was an examination of the opportunity for revolution. For him the Great War was the universal and simultaneous embodiment of "endless horrors" and the collapse of the system. Lenin considered this rare conjunction in world history as favorable for revolution, for he was convinced that the war in Europe, and particularly in Russia, might directly elicit the coming of the revolution and sweep away tsarist autocracy. Of course, it could happen that the war—in disregard of Lenin's practical prediction, but in consonance with his theoretical discovery—would entail the "uneven" development toward revolution. But it was merely an unproven assumption on his part, and we will return later to this problem that he correlated the war's revolutionizing effect with the European proletariat being ripe for a world revolution. He gave up this conviction, at least in its more rigid form, in 1918.

Whether one may speak of a revolutionary situation at the beginning of the war, as the troops marched into battle with a song on their lips "to defend their respective nation," has received ample attention from historians.[36] Yet it was simply Lenin's genius, or premonition, that signaled the coming of the revolution—and, in fact, he had his moments of doubt, as in December 1916. We may include P. N. Durnovo, the tsar's former minister of police, among those who had the same premonition. In February 1914, in a memorandum to the tsar, he described Russia's participation in the coming war as leading inevitably to the collapse of the monarchy and its revolutionary overthrow.[37]

The principal point of attack against Lenin, from any political direction (even today), is that the Bolshevik leaders tended to relate the coming of the revolution in Russia to the military victory of Wilhelmian Germany.[38] Although Lenin ultimately proved correct, placing revolutionary politics and the collapse of the tsarist regime on the agenda at that time was not realistic from the standpoint of traditional realpolitik. It was precisely in opposition against such a standpoint that Lenin elaborated his stand on theory and organization.

He devised specific slogans—often quoted and just as often distorted—at the start of the war and during its first phases that he was to repeat until the victory of the October Revolution. Namely, he urged that soldiers, workers, and peasants should seize weapons not against their own brothers, the wage slaves of other nations, but rather turn them against the reactionary and bourgeois governments and parties of the world.[39] In regard to Russia, Lenin felt his organizational base in the Bolshevik Party was solid, although he admitted there were "honest socialists" elsewhere in Europe. For instance, the Serbian socialists who never gave up their antiwar line. Of course, there were antiwar groups in many socialist or social-democratic parties, but the most influential group was to be found in the Russian Duma, formed by the Bolshevik faction. Their very first statements referred to "a war of depredation," insisting that it would dovetail into a revolution. By the time Lenin extricated himself from Poland to go to Switzerland at the beginning of September 1914, he was advocating a return to a revolutionary plan, in opposition to "social chauvinism." He wrote, "The conversion of the present imperialist war into a civil war is the only correct proletarian slogan."[40]

Lenin was bent on demonstrating two things, day in and day out. First, that the contradictions of the tsarist monarchy would lead to revolution as a consequence of military defeat. Lenin argued that the Russian revolution could be the prerequisite for a European revolutionary surge. In an unpublished essay dating from early September 1915, titled "Russia's Defeat and the Revolutionary Crisis," he wrote:

> The situation is almost like that in the summer of 1905, prior to the Bulygin Duma, or in the summer of 1906, after the dissolution of the First Duma. There is, however, actually a vast difference, viz., that this war has involved all Europe, all the most advanced countries with mass and powerful socialist

> movements. The imperialist war has linked up the Russian revolutionary crisis, which stems from a bourgeois-democratic revolution, with the growing crisis of the proletarian socialist revolution in the West. . . . *The Russian bourgeois-democratic revolution is now not only a prologue to, but an indivisible and integral part of, the socialist revolution in the West.*[41]

The second was that the military blocs confronting each other were not carrying on a "defensive war"; the pretense of "defending the homeland" was nothing more than justification for an imperialist war.[42] In his article "On the Two Lines in the Revolution," published in the 20 November 1915 issue of the *Social Democrat*, he traced the evolution of Menshevik and Bolshevik concepts since 1905. Here he noted the decisive liberation of the overwhelming masses of peasants from the dominant influence of the spirit of the monarchy. He also found that the conditions for the acceleration of the revolutionary trend depended on whether social democracy was successful in neutralizing the psychological and political impact of wartime chauvinism.[43]

After the parliaments approved the wartime budgets—but still during the first weeks of the war—Lenin formally broke with the "social chauvinist" and "centrist" tendencies within social democracy. He formulated a completely coherent position in this regard, explaining both theoretically and politically the reasons for his break with social democracy. It was his solid conviction that there could be no compromise with the "management" of the war. As we have seen on other occasions, from the beginning of the war Lenin's revolutionary strategy allowed for no compromise with the pro-war factions or with "pacifist half-solutions." He was convinced that the social-democratic workers' movement around Europe had to be placed on a new footing. Since "official social democracy" proved deaf to this proposal, Lenin addressed his words directly to the masses of soldiers who were treated as cannon fodder in an attempt to voice their concerns.

Lenin conceived of these writings, which came close to the genre of "manifesto," as part of the revolutionary development in the *subjective sense*. The organizational break with the "centrists" and his call for the creation of a new International may be considered new and important elements in this political line. His political behavior is described by some Marxist historians—for example, Anderson and Hermann—as Lenin's elaboration of the radical concept of subjectivity, which he derived from Hegel at the beginning of the war.

With the outbreak of the war, Lenin became aware of the historical conditions conducive to the awakening of the consciousness of the individual and of the masses that would form the basis for a "sudden" turn in revolutionary politics. He expressed the conviction—in both theoretical and practical terms—that the objective conditions can be altered, in the sense that even as few as ten persons may confront the war because the potential of millions joining in is already contained in those conditions. It was this turn that led in September 1915 to the Zimmerwald Conference of antiwar Socialists. That is, to the intimation of the idea of a Third International. Even if the revolutionary left was in a minority vis-à-vis the "centrists," they were able to prevail at the Zimmerwald conference, labeling the bloodbath consuming millions and clarifying the basic causes and objectives of the war as an *imperialist war*.

The formation of the International Socialist Committee signaled to the world that they were preparing an alternative to the social-chauvinist domination of the International throughout Europe.[44] We must remember that the "break" had serious consequences, for it weakened the pacifist forces within the International. Thus, the organizational break seemed to be taking a sectarian position,[45] as it has appeared in the historical literature ever since. Many failed to understand why Lenin adopted such an "uncompromising" position.

In examining his writings following the outbreak of the war, we must think not in terms of the wartime or pacifist logic of traditional socialist or social-democratic thinking, or its minor and major factions, because these do not show an exodus from the war. We must look instead for the direct political strategy of revolution, which included the basic issue of "winning over" the armed masses of soldiers, workers, and peasants. The old social democracy was no longer adequate for the purpose, and Lenin felt the time had come for preparing the revolution on an *international scale*. This involved determining a new political and organizational framework—at the international level—down to the specific slogans. The other requirement was to create a focal point of practice and organization around which a Europe-wide revolutionary trend could crystallize.

In his assessment of the Zimmerwald conference,[46] Lenin made it clear that the correct organization was the one that was really and truly convinced that "the war is creating a revolutionary situation in Europe, and that all the economic and sociopolitical circumstances of the imperialist period are leading up to a revolution of the proletariat." In other words, Lenin thought of the enlightenment of the proletariat and placed it in the spotlight as part of the formation of a revolutionary situation. He referred to the 1905 Revolution, or rather its having been "*foreseen*," as an integral part of the dawning of a new revolutionary situation. It was essential to the prehistory of the revolution itself: "*Before* the revolution, revolutionaries foresee it, realize its inevitability, make the masses understand its necessity, and explain its course and methods to the masses."[47]

In his debates with Kautsky, Martov, and Axelrod in the autumn of 1915, Lenin made mention of all these aspects. Judging by their language they may even be representative of internationalism, as in the case of Martov and Axelrod, but as regards true or so-called Basel internationalism, Lenin assumed a proletarian revolutionary orientation. The "centrists," however, did not consider the organization or the political connotations. In other words, the break with the Second International did not occur.[48]

As early as 1914 Lenin assessed the events surrounding the outbreak of the war as the bankruptcy of every form of the International and of opportunism.[49] This was when he formulated his thesis regarding the transformation of the war into civil war, in such a way as to conform to the Basel resolution. Thus the realpolitik approach did not fit with Lenin's stand, at that time or ever. The Mensheviks often accused him of ignoring the actual mood of the working class in Western Europe, and their "faith in the victory of the war."[50]

According to Lenin's analysis, the arguments of the loose coalition of antiwar pacifist forces did not have any progressive content, for the truly antiwar and revolutionary forces "would not understand it." There could be only one alternative for him: the old International must be allowed to die. As Rosa Luxemburg put it upon receiving the news of the passing of the military budget requests, "German Social Democracy is a putrid corpse." Therefore with this declared death, the gathering of revolutionary forces could begin.

To avoid basic issues was the biggest sin in Lenin's eyes, perhaps even bigger than the acceptance of social chauvinism. He first formulated this in a response written to V. Kosovski, not published at the time; the latter had proposed in a Bundist paper to form the new International from these opposition elements in the various socialist parties' papers. Lenin did not even want to hear about such unstructured international collaboration, as he explained in one of his writings, reflecting on how "opportunism had soared in Europe over the past decades."[51] This strong ideological orientation—particular to Marxism, and especially to Russian Marxism—was truly important under the circumstances, and was to propel events, and result in action.

As we have seen, Lenin himself assumed the possibility of a coming cataclysm long before the outbreak of the war. Yet he was still caught by surprise in August 1914, as was the entire world, including the workers' movement. An even greater surprise and disappointment for him was how easily the most significant groups of social democracy, from Plekhanov to Vandervelde, gave in to pro-war politics. Even the anarchists were affected by the "war mood." Distinguished theoreticians like Kropotkin, Cornelissen, and Malato placed themselves at the service of the anti-German war.[52] Of course, this "nationalist and chauvinist degeneration" of many socialist tendencies only appeared to be "without antecedents." It may suffice to mention the cases of Pilsudski or Mussolini, who provide obvious examples of how working-class politics and internationalist solidarity could be replaced by nationalist and patriotic ideologies as a result of the yearnings of nation-states.

Lenin's political objective was to sharpen the contradictions, to make the new revolutionary turn even easier to perceive. He felt that the analysis of the "operations" of economic conflicts of interest, particularly at the global and national levels, was of decisive importance, for without it the analysis of the nature and prospect of the war could not be done. Lenin's every ideological and political thesis was embedded in this analysis.

It is worth noting that in his foreword to Bukharin's *Imperialism and World Economy*,[53] he wrote extensively about Kautsky's ultra-imperialist theory, which weakened the prospects of revolution. As we know, Kautsky discussed the prospect that with the formation of capitalist trusts, the great monopolies of finance capitalism will unite in a single trust. Lenin detected in this analysis the ideas of the followers of Struve and the "economism" of the apologists of the establishment who were ready to "surrender to capitalism" or "reconcile" with it. Lenin classified Kautsky's ultra-imperialism—the international union of "imperialisms, distinct by nation," which would practically eliminate war and sharp political conflicts—among the naïve utopias, which not even Kautsky could actually believe in, especially since the Great War was already underway. Under the circumstances, this theory meant nothing more than to offer comfort to those who believed in the possibility of "peaceful capitalism." Indeed, Kautsky believed that imperialism could be "improved" and reshaped into a "more pacific form."[54] This "theory, disparate from all sense of reality" did not belong, according to Lenin, among prophecies that had any chance of realization, for the inner contradictions of capitalism in some periods inevitably lead to its collapse, the war being the most obvious example. Lenin harshly criticized Kautsky's concept of imperialism, describing it as some kind of expansionism.

Lenin considered imperialism to be a structural transformation of society and politics. Kautsky's vision, according to Lenin, is "just a petit-bourgeois *exhortation* to the financiers that they should refrain from doing evil."[55] Thus the war appeared to him as an important stage in that collapse.[56] On the basis of similar methodological reasoning, Lenin viewed the slogan of a European United States propounded by Trotsky and others with grave misgivings. Particularly if such a new federal structure was not based on socialist and communitarian principles but on the subjection of the weak by the strong, as a new form of concentration of capital. The new imperialist and destructive evolution of the capitalist system is incapable of liberating itself from the contradictions (national and socioeconomic oppression, dire poverty, exploitation, monopolist competition for markets, etc.), and these would negate any union of states resulting from overcoming the nation-states: "The unequal development of economy and politics being an immutable law of capitalism."[57]

It should be noted that at the time, the Bolsheviks were engaged in fierce debates about the nature of imperialism, as can be seen in a letter from Bukharin to Lenin in the summer of 1915. Bukharin objected strongly to the publication of an article by Pokrovsky in *The Communist* where, by his estimation, the historian (Pokrovsky) did not understand the innovation imperialism represented in the historical development of capitalism. He also criticized Zinoviev's argument because the latter seemed unaware of the new historic direction in the politics of colonialism.[58]

Lenin scored decisive political points in his debate with Pyatakov, a close associate of Bukharin. He rejected discussing the foreign policy aspect of imperialism, in that it placed too much emphasis on expansion. Instead, he derived the new stage of development from monopoly capitalism replacing competition. According to his formulation: "Democracy corresponds to free competition. Political reaction corresponds to monopoly. 'Finance capital strives for domination, not freedom,' Rudolf Hilferding rightly remarks in his *Finance Capital*."[59] He argues politics cannot be dissociated from economics. Even if the two areas are governed by the same set of laws it is necessary to make distinctions, otherwise it is not possible to wage a political struggle.

According to Hilferding and Lenin's assessment, after the imperialist turn, the direction of development is "*from* democracy *to* political reaction." In fact, Lenin even talks of it as the bid to "replace democracy generally by oligarchy."[60] The radical elimination of "liberal self-regulation" for the sake of increasing profit rates can be guaranteed with difficulty, or not at all.

The assumption of identity between economics and politics—the sin often committed by "abstract internationalists"—becomes an unacceptable methodological shortcoming. Lenin emphasized that complete "economic annexation" may take place even without political annexation, and there were many examples of such an occurrence in world economic development. It often happened, even in that period, that an independent nation-state became the economic vassal of a stronger state. Thus it was obvious to Lenin that the finance capital of a strong power may buy out the competition even in politically independent countries.[61]

Equally significant from the point of view of methodology was Lenin's understanding of the "national" aspect of war:

> This is a war between two groups of predatory Great Powers, and it is being fought for the partitioning of colonies, the enslavement of other nations, and advantages and privileges of the world market. . . . Whether Germany

> or Russia wins, or whether there is a "draw," the war will bring humanity fresh oppression of hundreds and hundreds of millions of people in the colonies, in Persia, Turkey and China, a fresh enslavement of nations, and new chains for the working class of all countries. . . . The war is filling the pockets of the capitalists, into whose pockets gold is pouring from the treasuries of the Great Powers. The war is provoking a blind bitterness against the enemy, the bourgeoisie doing its best to direct the indignation of the people into such channels, to divert their attention from the *chief* enemy—the government and the ruling classes of their own country.[62]

In spite of the document's pathetic, agitating, and "populist" tone—as with practically all of Lenin's political writings—it has the purely theoretical foundation, in this case manifested in the economic and class approach to war. Even present-day analyses of the Great War attempt to deconstruct this dual analysis by means of a "philosophy" based on political considerations (dynastic, or occasionally "democratic").[63]

The interpretation of the Great War as a "democratic war" has resurfaced in contemporary historiography. In its classical form it is precisely a "renegade" former Marxist historian, François Furet, who developed this concept most thoroughly. In a long essay, which obscures rather than clarifies the "change in paradigm" of Kautsky, Furet dismisses the "Leninist" or "Marxist" narrative. More importantly, he breaks the intellectual link that had tied liberalism and "communism" together for decades, in spite of all their basic contradictions. Furet combines conservatism and liberalism under the flag of conservatism in order to bring this "united front" against the threat of "totalitarian dictatorship"—that is, the threat of fascism and communism. In Furet's rendering, contemporary history appears as the struggle between democracies and dictatorship. One ideological tool of this process is to disguise the Great War in democratic garb. The political and theoretical message of this conceptualization is that the bourgeoisie has become the victim of "revolutionary passion."

Furet's text argues that we must discard the oversimplification of the Great War traced back to Hilferding, Rosa Luxemburg, and Lenin. In Furet's analysis, the Bolshevik leader derived the war from the capitalist system. That is, from such common and "primitive" things as the pursuit of profit and surplus value, the struggle for accumulation, and the redistribution of markets—the most basic elements of this struggle being the monopolies and the great powers. If we disregard the "crude simplification" of "economism," we can get around two basic issues: the real reasons for the explosion of passions and the issue of responsibility for the war. Furet primarily and ultimately blames the people and public opinion for the war. Until then traditional historiography had described the people as victims. The spark that caused the fateful conflict, writes Furet, "even technically, can be ascribed to diplomatic activity, essentially to the common understanding of people, something the governments had been counting upon." The "social consensus" on which the governments were depending came about almost automatically.[64]

Of course, the "discovery" of the democratic nature of the war cannot be claimed by Furet, but rather—as Lenin already pointed out—by Kautsky. In a work dating from 1910 Lenin had warned about the possible "bourgeois interpretation" of the war, consisting of its "democratization." The slogan of "defense of the fatherland" and the myth of a democratic war are complementary. According to Lenin, these slogans serve only to justify robbery:

> In a war between Germany and England the issue is not democracy, but world domination, i.e., exploitation of the world. That is not an issue on which Social-Democrats can side with the exploiters of their nation . . . presenting it as a democratic war, is to deceive the workers and side with the reactionary bourgeoisie.[65]

Written toward the end of 1915, Lenin's essay "Opportunism and the Bankruptcy of the Second International" contains his fully developed theoretical analysis of the "defense of the fatherland." It is an important contribution to methodology, since Lenin rejected the subjective explanations of the betrayal by the International. He felt it would be "impossible," "ridiculous and unscientific" to blame the collapse of the International on the personal policies advocated by Kautsky, Guesde, or Plekhanov. Rather, the event warrants "the study of the economic significance" of the given policy.[66]

According to Lenin, the social background of the ideology of "defense of the fatherland" also derives from "economic facts":

> What is the *economic* implication of "defense of the fatherland" in the 1914–15 war? The answer to this question has been given in the Basel Manifesto. The war is being fought by all the Great Powers for the purpose of plunder, carving up the world, acquiring markets, and enslaving nations. To the bourgeoisie it brings higher profits; to a thin crust of the labor bureaucracy and aristocracy, and also to the petite bourgeoisie (the intelligentsia, etc.) which "travels" with the working-class movement, it promises *morsels* of those profits. The economic basis of "social-chauvinism" (this term being more precise than the term "social-patriotism," as the latter embellishes the evil) and of opportunism is the same, namely, an alliance

> between an insignificant section at the "top" of the labor movement, and its "own" national bourgeoisie, directed against the masses of the proletariat.[67]

In addition to the economic factors, Lenin ascribes the mass impact of "patriotic ideology" to wartime delusions, enthrallment, and intimidation. He also referred to Kautsky's earlier—and, at that point, still Marxist—view in *The Road to Power* (1909). This text became the foundation of the antiwar and internationalist resolution of Basel, according to which "the era of 'peaceful' capitalism had passed, and that the epoch of wars and revolutions was at hand."[68]

When the war broke out, Marxist analysis and theory were set aside and replaced with the ideology of "defense of the fatherland," attempting to "prostitute" the working class. To those who accused him of being sectarian, he responded with an ironic reference to the antiwar protests: "I suppose these Berlin women workers must have been led astray by the 'Bakuninist' and 'adventurist,' 'sectarian' (see Kolb and Co.) and 'reckless' manifesto of the Russian Party's Central Committee, dated November 1."[69] He reiterated that the slogan of "defense of the fatherland" was simply an imperialist justification of the war.[70] Yet his writing does not allow us to reconstruct his line of argument as to how a large mass of the Western proletariat might extricate itself "from opportunistic ideological and political influences." It is a peculiar contradiction in Lenin's case that his political arguments, and his economic and sociological observations regarding revolutionizing the working class, failed to reinforce one another but rather weakened them instead. Unfortunately, he never brought this contradiction into light.

By the fall of 1916 Lenin's theoretical arguments regarding the nature of the war, its causes, motivations, and consequences were enunciated in complete form. There had been debates with the official position taken by the International, with nationalists of various hues, including Russian nationalists, and with his own "abstract internationalist" comrades. On the basis of his critique of the "national" and the "global" views, he tried to demonstrate to Bukharin, Pyatakov, and Luxemburg that the "defense of the fatherland"[71] argument should not be attacked in general but that "the focus should be on how this slogan is used as cosmetics to beautify the present imperialist war."[72]

In the case of anti-imperialist national uprisings the slogan "defense of the fatherland" is appropriate, revealing wartime relations between the oppressor and the oppressed nations from the point of view of the latter. As Lenin himself wrote, "P. Kievsky never noticed that a national uprising is also the 'defense of the fatherland'—every nation that rises up is defending itself against the oppressing nation, is defending its language, its homeland, its fatherland." He outlined the class content of the slogan, that in cases where "the bourgeoisie of the oppressed nations . . . enters into reactionary compacts with the bourgeoisie of the oppressor nation behind the backs of, *and against*, its own people . . . the criticism of revolutionary Marxists should be directed not against the national movement, but against its degradation, vulgarization, against the tendency to reduce it to a petty squabble."[73] In his debates with the Polish internationalist socialists he formulated a similar stance: "a war *between* imperialist powers or groups of powers, when *both* belligerents not only oppress 'foreign peoples' but are fighting a war to *decide* who shall have a *greater share* in oppressing foreign peoples!"[74]

The concept that the creation and destruction of nation-states was a matter of specific economic and political power relations, of wars and struggles involving many political and economic factors, derived from his social analysis. And this is true even though, in the age of imperialism, the fights and schisms of the great powers and the corporations are a determining factor in the formation, and ultimately, the fate, of smaller nation-states. The demand for the right of self-determination of nations as a basic political doctrine derives, almost automatically, from this anti-imperialist theory.

THE NATIONAL QUESTION AND NATIONAL SELF-DETERMINATION—"TWO CULTURES"

> The more democratic the system of government, the clearer will the workers see that the root evil is capitalism, not lack of rights. The fuller national equality (and it is *not* complete without freedom of secession), the clearer will the workers of the oppressed nations see that the cause of their oppression is capitalism, not lack of rights, etc.
>
> —V. I. LENIN, *A Caricature of Marxism and Imperialist Economism*[75]

There is no basis for which it could be said that Lenin's interest in the national question was rooted in any form of personal obligation. Private experiences cannot be ruled out. It would be hard to find a single revolutionary reminiscence or significant literary work from the beginning of the century that doesn't mention the various manifestations of contempt for other peoples, national absolutism, and chauvinist oppression that marked the tsar's empire, whether in everyday life or the clouded strata of politics. Lenin was naturally also aware of the repressive character of autocracy where the national minorities were concerned. Russia was in such a state that an intellectual of the period simply could not skirt the *national question*. Russian literature as a whole stands witness to this, from Dostoevsky to Tolstoy, Saltykov-Shchedrin to Korolenko, and later, Babel to Sholokhov. The multinational empires, be it the Russian Empire, the Austro-Hungarian Empire, or the Turkish Empire, each came up against the varied and increasingly resolved endeavors of the revived national movements.[76]

According to the 1897 census, at the turn of the century the incomparably multinational Russian Empire was home to 128,924,289 persons. The people living in the Asian regions made up approximately 10 percent of the total population of the empire. This means that the people of Central Asia together with the Caucasians were fewer in number at the turn of the century (and later) than the urbanized population of the empire in 1913 (who made up 18 percent of the total population).[77] It is typical of the mixed ethnicities of cities that, for example, forty-five nationalities were kept on account in Kharkov, while the populace of Odessa spoke fifty different languages.[78] It is evident that revolutionary organization in metropolises faced a tangle of ethnic and social problems and conflicts. The ethnic repression that was inseparable from the "Russifying" tendencies of tsarism also did not leave the workers "intact."

Meanwhile, Lenin would have seen on an international level that social democracy found the national issue of some interest at the start of the century, inasmuch as the International was aware that the national movements and nationalism exerted pressure in the formation and fortification of nation-states. In 1896, the London Congress of the Second International acknowledged *the right of nations to self-determination* and linked this resolution to the aims of the proletarian revolution. They did not, however, point out the east European specificities of the national question and the complexity of the whole issue. At the beginning of the century, this problem could not be evaded by the Russian workers' movement either.

The national question only interested Lenin as a basic problem of party politics and organization, though gradually he came to recognize the wider scope of the issue. Close to a hundred studies and articles, many of which are polemical[79] and written specifically on the national question before the October Revolution, show his thorough engagement with the subject and its significance. A careful examination of his works on the national question would deserve a separate study. However, it must certainly be indicated here that Lenin's legacy on the subject, dating between 1912 and 1916, demonstrates the inquisitive perception and depth of scientific specialization. By 1912 he was already arguing that the *national question* would be of exceptional importance for the following period, and he counted foremost on the national movements and social revolutionary movements coming together.

The national question and more particularly the right of self-determination of nations found an articulate political assertion and definition for the first time at the Second Congress of the Russian Social-Democratic Labor Party (RSDLP) in 1903.[80] The forty-six attending delegates came from virtually every corner of the empire, from a total of twenty-six social-democratic organizations. The relationship of the party and the nationalities and the role of the Jewish workers' association (*Bund*) and its role were also subjects of debate within the RSDLP. On the initiative of Lenin, Plekhanov, Martov, and other leading party intellectuals, a resolution passed at the Second Party Congress that took a firm stand on the question of the *Bund*.[81] The resolution rejected the federative restructuring of party relations based on nationality, on the principle that the party of the Russian working class—being a party based on class—cannot be divided into national sections.

The party, according to the ninth clause of the Party Program, declared—and was the first to do so among east European social democrats—that it recognized *the right of nations to self-determination*.[82] Lenin's writings and related party papers affirm, however, that the recognition of the right to self-determination and secession is not to be mixed up with the question of whether it is expedient for a given nation to become a sovereign state. In his perception, the recognition of the right to self-determination in bringing about a sovereign nation-state, that is, secession from the empire and any other institutional state formation, is in general a fundamental democratic civil right that "cannot be not recognized by any social democrat." In the arena of politics this is the sole means of self-defense for the oppressed ethnic minorities in the face of Great-Russian chauvinism.

The recognition of the right of nations to self-determination also joins that trend with capitalist development, or perhaps the historical opportunity of capitalist development, which means that under the pressure of their inner contradictions the east-European empires dissolve into nation-states. The swift spread of capitalism and bourgeois transformation economically undermined and destroyed the empires originating from feudal mores, and along with the vitalization of the national markets they awoke various forms of nationalism. At the level of movements, the scattering of old state structures and the dissolution of class conflicts in "national unity" were their most important goals. This is why the program emphasized that under capitalist conditions, the inner development of the workers' movement demanded an agenda that would establish the nationally unfettered unity of the workers' movement.

Lenin expressed his theoretical solution for this seemingly complex contradiction in his writings dating from late 1913 to early 1914. He outlined his now-famous thesis that in capitalist development two simultaneous tendencies are in evidence as far as the issue of nationalism is concerned. The first involves the "the awakening of national activity and national movements," "the struggle against all forms of national oppression" and for the nation-states, the "national markets."

The second historical tendency is the development of economic, trade, scientific and other links between nations, and the toppling of national borders in accord with the integration of the global interests and expansion of international capital.[83] Though Lenin believed that "both are universal laws of capitalism," he counted on the amplification of integrationist tendencies with the development of the capitalist system, and registered the "confirmation" of this in his book on imperialism. Only during the war would he face the full significance of the problem that capitalism had shifted into a new destructive phase. In the context of revolutionary class struggle, this makes the national question central to "the politics of working class alliance." It was Lenin's intention that the political program of the social democrats took both tendencies of capitalist development into account. He advocated for "the equality of nations and languages and the impermissibility of all *privileges* in this respect," in conjunction with an "uncompromising struggle against contamination of the proletariat with bourgeois nationalism, even of the most refined kind."[84]

His whole theoretical-economic and political concept for the national question was determined by a thought already examined in relation to imperialism, born from his recognition of the *hierarchical tripartite subdivision of the world system* on the basis of the "law" of unequal development. Upon studying the national question and the problem of the right of nations to self-determination, Lenin outlined the basic structure of the world system as follows:

> In this respect, countries must be divided into three main types: First, the advanced capitalist countries of Western Europe and the United States of America. In these countries the bourgeois, progressive, national movements came to an end long ago. . . . Second, Eastern Europe: Austria, the Balkans and particularly Russia. Here it was the twentieth century that particularly developed the bourgeois-democratic national movements and intensified the national struggle.

The colonial countries were placed in the third group, where the formation of nations was still in process.[85] He reached the realization of the "law" of unequal development on the basis of the variation in historical epochs and regions, the basic differences in modes of production and economic systems.

In the process, once again, of "reviewing" Marx he came to a decisive conclusion from the point of view of the revolution:

> The social revolution cannot be the united action of the proletarians of all countries for the simple reason that most of the countries and the majority of the world's population have not even reached, or have only just reached,

> the capitalist stage of development. . . Only the advanced countries of Western Europe and North America have matured for socialism.[86]

Lenin considered it an important development that the banks and large monopolies began "liberating" the small states and colonies that are not part of the core from their national variety of local capitalist production and oppression. Though the freedom struggles in the colonies had just begun, Lenin already foresaw that in some way they would be forced back into the circumstances of the colonial period, inasmuch as these internationally organized capitalist institutions would dissolve, incorporate the nation-state as their own economic institution, and turn it into one of the functions of globalized capital and its institutions.

The Russian Empire under the tsars appeared as a mixture of semi-periphery and periphery. Autocratic Russia was in a subsidiary position vis-à-vis the capitalist core, but it was also a colonialist power with its colonies integrated in terms of state organization. The centrifugal energy of the national movements unfolding at the end of the nineteenth century in the Russian Empire moved the social democrats, virtually from the beginning, to seek the unification of the workers' movement unhampered by questions of national origin. This was the highest objective as revolutionary goals were concerned.

Lenin's "strategic place of prominence" incorporated the recognition of nations to self-determination as one of the special circumstances on the path to revolution, the noted "critical" alliance with the national movements.[87] The novelty of Lenin's approach to internationalism as opposed to that of traditional social democracy—this includes Luxemburg among other theorists—was that he built the demands for the elimination of national oppression, inclusive of linguistic and cultural oppression, into the "universalist" concept of class struggle as a separate set of issues.[88]

In his study about the right of nations to self-determination written in the spring of 1914—once again polemical with regard to Luxemburg's position[89]—Lenin castigated the political considerations rejecting national self-determination that had been derived from abstract principles. A key concept of social democracy was at stake here; virtually all opponents of tsarism, from the local national minorities to participants of the colonial movements in the midst of their national struggles, would benefit from it.[90]

In these writings Lenin correlated national demands "purified" of nationalism with culture, aiming to outline the two ways "national culture" could be approached[91] as clearly as possible: "Marxist," "democratic," and "socialist" on the one hand, bourgeois on the other. In autumn 1913, he wrote about the way bourgeois "national culture" functioned:

> The national culture of the bourgeoisie is a fact (and, I repeat, the bourgeoisie everywhere enters into deals with the landed proprietors and the clergy). Aggressive bourgeois nationalism, which drugs the minds of the workers, stultifies and disunites them in order that the bourgeoisie may lead them by the halter—such is the fundamental fact of the times.[92]

As he put it when the world war broke out: "Russian liberalism has degenerated into national liberalism. It is vying in 'patriotism' with the Black Hundreds; it always willingly votes for militarism."[93] All gradations disappear as the actualities of the war polarize the "two cultures."

His study *On the National Pride of the Great Russians,* which came out after the war began in December 1914, was a rebuttal against liberal and conservative accusations of social democracy being rootless and unpatriotic. It clearly marked the socially progressive national culture. For Lenin, this meant a dedication to Russian humanist culture on a broad social scale, one that the Russian people could truly be proud of. This culture stands in opposition to the whole historical achievement and the interests of tsarism and the Russian bourgeoisie, the landed gentry, and the priesthood. In Lenin's thought, "national pride" was related with the concept of *freedom*, the ability of the majority of the people to rise from servitude:

> We are full of a sense of national pride, and for that very reason we particularly hate our slavish past (when the landed nobility led the peasants into war to stifle the freedom of Hungary, Poland, Persia and China), and our slavish present, when these selfsame landed proprietors, aided by the capitalists, are loading us into a war. . . . Nobody is to be blamed for being born a slave; but a slave who not only eschews a striving for freedom but justifies and eulogizes his slavery . . . such a slave is a lickspittle and a boor, who arouses a legitimate feeling of indignation, contempt, and loathing. . . . We say that the Great Russians cannot "defend the fatherland" otherwise than by desiring the defeat of tsarism in any war, this as the lesser evil to nine-tenths of the inhabitants of Great Russia. For tsarism not only oppresses those nine-tenths economically and politically, but also demoralizes, degrades, dishonors and prostitutes them by teaching them to oppress other nations and to cover up this shame with hypocritical and quasi-patriotic phrases.[94]

A letter Lenin wrote in reply to Stepan Shahumyan dated December 1913[95] elucidates his commitment to the cultivation of the Russian language and culture. He stands by the idea of the centralized state (he will continue to do so until 1918), not least on account of the need to hold the workers' movement together. However, on the matter of the national question, he turns to Switzerland as the sole felicitous, democratic example of decentralization under capitalist conditions. He addresses the following question to Shahumyan: "We are evolving a national program from the proletarian standpoint; since when has it been recommended that the worst examples, rather than the best, be taken as a model?"[96]

Lenin held firmly the conviction that a people's linguistic or cultural freedom should not be the least bit infringed, and viewed the problem as part of the framework of fundamental democratic rights. For this reason he did not accept any official state language, for it strengthens the chauvinism of the "greater nation"—the Russifying policies of the tsar in the given situation—and exacerbates the inequalities and subjugation already rampant in everyday life. He was primarily led by the political and theoretical consideration that democratic considerations must be taken in evidence where the national issue is concerned.[97]

Lenin considered the Austro-Marxist political and ideological concept of *cultural-national autonomy* a concession to nationalism that constrains the democratic efforts of the national movements. He argued it exposed the movements to the church and its priests, and at the same time restricted the organization of workers, including the internationalist principles and praxis of the workers' movement. Wherever opinion lies regarding Lenin's argument against Otto Bauer's concept of cultural autonomy, it is certain that it draws attention to biases, insofar as the Austrian Social Democrats did not recognize the right of the people or nations to self-determination until 1918.[98]

Lenin always approached the role and character of national movements from a *historical* and *class* perspective. He did not support the struggle of each and every small country fighting the great imperialist powers. He also had a strictly imposed condition: the uprising of any class more reactionary than the bourgeoisie of the center countries is not to be supported.[99]

In line with this approach, he described national oppression as a specific form of class oppression, with its own economic and sociocultural roots. The national issue was a matter of sociopolitical, and cultural-economic emancipation. A solution for the national question—he wrote—was that even under socialism, "the possibility becomes *reality* 'only'—'only'!—with the establishment of full democracy in all spheres, including the delineation of state frontiers in accordance with the 'sympathies' of the population, including complete freedom to secede. And . . . an accelerated drawing together and fusion of nations that will be completed when the state *withers away*."[100]

The picture would not be complete if it were not noted that Lenin tried to reach an understanding of the political behavior of the Western working classes. In trying to comprehend the reasons for the "prostitution" of Western social democracy, Lenin also looked at the economic, political, and intellectual factors of the relationships between the oppressing and oppressed countries.

He studied the situation of the working class in America through Isaac Hourwich's book *Immigration and Labor* (1912). In the context of "dominant" and "oppressed" nations, he explained the opportunist changing of sides by a majority of the working masses in the following concentrated form:

> (1) *Economically*, the difference is that sections of the working class in the oppressor nations receive crumbs from the *super-profits* the bourgeoisie of these nations obtains by extra exploitation of the workers of the oppressed nations. Besides, economic statistics show that here a *larger* percentage of the workers become "straw bosses" than is the case in the oppressed nations, a *larger* percentage rise to the labor *aristocracy*. That is a fact. To a *certain degree* the workers of the oppressor nations are partners of *their own* bourgeoisie in plundering the workers (and the mass of the population) of the oppressed nations. (2) *Politically*, the difference is that, compared with the workers of the oppressed nations, they occupy a *privileged* position in many spheres of political life. (3) *Ideologically*, or spiritually, the difference is that they are taught, at school and in life, disdain and contempt for the workers of the oppressed nations. This has been *experienced*, for example, by every Great Russian who has been brought up or who has lived among Great Russians.[101]

Lenin was among the first of the Marxists and social democrats to come to an understanding of the real historical significance of the colonial question. His most important political conclusion was that colonial and national movements inevitably become intertwined—with each other and the European labor movement—if imperialist oppression creates common interests in the world system. In the process of this realization Lenin seems to have underestimated his earlier observation about how the "labor aristocracy," and the labor movement of the European center countries in general, had come to a relatively privileged position as the result of the exploitation of the colonies. This privilege ensured their support for the conservation of the capitalist system. He also determined that the great imperialist powers recruit groups "adherent to the system" from the leading circles of the national-colonial movements and prostitute them.[102]

With reference to the blurred boundaries between the colonial and national movements in Russia, Lenin denounced "Russia's internal colonialism":

> But what of Russia? Its peculiarity lies precisely in the fact that the difference between "*our*" "colonies" and "our" oppressed nations is not clear, not concrete and not vitally felt! . . . The sheer absurdity of trying to discover some serious difference between oppressed nations and colonies in the case of Russia should be especially clear to a Russian socialist who wants not simply to *repeat*, but to *think*.[103]

Among the allies of revolutionary social democracy, the role of national self-determination as both a political principle and ideology had grown. This question set off major disputes among those closest to Lenin. He argued with Bolshevik friends who shared his principles (the "abstract internationalists" Pyatakov, Bukharin, Radek, and Luxemburg), for they underestimated the required research and exploration of "mediations" and "transitions" to the revolutionary end goal and the possibilities of the moment.

In Lenin's interpretation, this movement showed a two-way distortion similar to that of "economism": a "right-leaning" distortion that rejected the "liberation of the oppressed peoples, the fight against annexations," and a "left-leaning" distortion that revealed itself in a resignation from the "struggle for reform and democracy," a retreat from mass movements, and a sectarian splintering of the group.[104] These debates were repeated with the Polish internationalist socialists, where he branded the rejection of the right of nations to self-determination a "betrayal of socialism."[105] To reject the principle is to support "a *form of political oppression*."

Lenin considered national self-determination a fundamental issue of democracy that the revolutionaries "may not undercut!" He believed that going against the politics of imperial realignment of borders by force, a socialism that would later come to power should return to the democratic traditions of establishing borders. If such a tradition ever existed in the capitalist system it is not clear, but it is certain that "returning" to such a tradition in Russia was not an option.

When Lenin found a correlation between democracy and socialism, he was nonetheless well aware that capitalism works *democratically* only under specific historical conditions: "In general, political democracy is merely one of the possible *forms* of superstructure *above* capitalism (although it is theoretically the normal one for 'pure' capitalism." He goes on, in fact, to emphatically underline that capitalism and imperialism "develop within the framework of *any* political form and subordinate them *all*. It is, therefore, a basic theoretical error to speak of the 'impracticability' of *one* of the forms and of *one* of the demands of democracy."[106]

On this issue, he stood by his conviction that the internal requirements for core capitalism ("pure" capitalism) must be applied as requirements on the periphery of the system as well, independently of whether or not they can be realized. It is a matter of some interest that he viewed the demands of states for self-determination and independent self-government a part of the "democratic *world* movement in general."

> In individual concrete casts, the part *may* contradict the whole; if so, it must be rejected. It is possible that the republican movement in one country may be merely an instrument of the clerical or financial-monarchist intrigues of other countries; if so, we must *not* support this particular, concrete movement, but it would be ridiculous to delete the demand for a republic from the program of international Social-Democracy on these grounds.[107]

It can therefore be said that in Lenin's view, bourgeois democracy is the export of the power relations and institutions representing the interests of a given world power. At the same time, he felt the transformation of autocracies into democracies must be fought for.

In studying the views Marx and Engels formulated in regard to the Hungarian Rebellion of 1848, and evaluating the experiences of 1848–49, Lenin came to the conclusion that the only reason Marx and Engels opposed the national movements of the Czechs and the South Slavs was that they turned against the "Hungarian national liberation and revolutionary-democratic rebellion," taking the side of the tsar. Lenin wrote: "Marx and Engels at *that* time drew a clear and definite *distinction* between 'whole reactionary nations' serving as 'Russian outposts' in Europe, and 'revolutionary nations,' namely, the Germans, Poles and Magyars." The lesson Lenin drew from this was not that Marx wished that some peoples would simply disappear from history, as some of Marx's later interpreters would try to present it, but gleaned that "the interests of the liberation of a number of big and very big nations in Europe rate higher than the interests of the movement for liberation of small nations; that the demand for democracy *must not be considered in isolation* but on a European—*today we should say a world—scale*."[108] This line of thought "means that the democratic interests of one country must be subordinated to the democratic interests of *several and all* countries," so that in the interest of the success of the general world movement it may overcome the interest of its fraction, allowing in the end, the universal interests of socialism to gain the upper hand.[109]

This last realization was one of the thoughts that led to the establishing of the new International, as the world war piled up examples of situations in which partial interests dominated the whole. The weakness of Lenin's stand was that he had not yet come to an analytical solution for determining who would "subordinate" the rather heterogeneous interests arising in a "democracy" to the broader interests of the revolutionary groups and movements in larger nations.

What he was able to offer in practice, apart from recognition of secession, was the "internationalist education of the working class."[110] It is not hard to imagine how limited the scope for an "internationalist education" was in the summer of 1916, yet a concept for this field was already in place for those times when social democracy gains direct "access" to the rebellious workers and peasants who by then had come to hate the war.

Taking Poland and Ireland as examples of the contradictions found in the provincialism of small nations, he showed where the demands for the right to secession should be supported and were not. According to his logic, social democracy in the case of Poland does not need to raise the banner of national secession as an actual demand because it may become the "lackey of one of the imperialist monarchies" as a result. In the case of Ireland, however, Lenin came to exactly the opposite conclusion. Referring to the Irish rebellion then in progress, he said the social revolution cannot be conceived of without the rebellions of the small European nations and the colonized peoples, which are in social terms inherently anti-imperialist, as was the Irish rebellion of 1916. Such rebellions assist the "struggle of the socialist proletariat against imperialism," because they undermine the internal social-political stability of the colonist imperialist powers. They can therefore become close allies of the labor movement in their revolutionary struggle: "A blow delivered against the power of the English imperialist bourgeoisie by a rebellion in Ireland is a hundred times more significant politically than a blow of equal force delivered in Asia or in Africa."[111]

Lenin's keenness on such a "revolutionary redemption" suggests that he had not considered the full sway of political consequences from anti-Russian feeling built up in the Polish people. This does not mean that his comrades proved more "sensitive" to this issue. After all, in his writings Lenin opposed Russian internationalists-—such as Trotsky and Martov—on the national question for the very reason that their position was too inflexible with regard to these sorts of political expectations. With regard to their recognition, in principle, of the right to self-determination, Lenin wrote:

> Take Trotsky's articles "The Nation and the Economy" in *Nashe Slovo*, and you will find his usual eclecticism: on the one hand, the economy unites nations and, on the other, national oppression divides them. The conclusion? The conclusion is that the prevailing hypocrisy remains unexposed, agitation is dull and does not touch upon what is most important, basic, significant and closely connected with practice—one's attitude *to* the nation that is oppressed by "one's own" nation.[112]

Lenin envisaged a proactive relationship on the part of the laborers of the oppressive nation, in support of the secession, the "liberation" of the dependent, oppressed and colonized people.

Under the conditions of political freedom that followed the February Revolution, Lenin and the Bolsheviks soon found themselves faced by virtually the whole array of practical problems involved in the national question. P. Miliukov, the foreign minister of the Provisional Government and a leading figure of the Kadet Party, clearly stated at the Eighth Party Congress in May of 1917 that the "division of the country into sovereign, independent units is considered by the Party as absolutely inadmissible." He went on to add, "At the present moment the Party of the People's Freedom does not consider that the creation of state-territorial organizations would be the right solution."[113] A radically opposite position had been outlined at the famous Bolshevik Party Congress in April 1917, but a federation, as a realistic historical formation, did not come up.[114]

The conference emphasized that the actual realization of secession and the propaganda leading to it are not a goal of the workers' revolution. To the contrary, the basic objective of the socialist revolution is to ultimately "establish the universal socialist soviet state"—in the spirit of the Poronino Resolution formulated by Lenin and adopted by the Central Committee in September 1913. On the basis of a proposal by Stalin, the resolution of the conference declared recognition of the following: the right of people to secession; territorial autonomy for those peoples who wish to remain within the boundaries of the given state; separate laws for national minorities, guaranteeing free development; and the indivisible and unified party serving the proletariat of all nationalities.[115]

At the same time, the abstract internationalist group of Pyatakov, Dzerzhinsky, and Bukharin was still thinking in terms of an international revolution undivided by national delineations. The concept lacked a more thorough historical-political appreciation of Russian (and east-European) specificities. Pyatakov accounted for this universalism as follows: "Drawing upon the analysis of the new period of imperialism we can say that there is no struggle for socialism other than the struggle under the banner that declares, *down with all borders*, all struggle to eliminate borders, even the thought of any other struggle cannot even be entertained."[116]

Lenin distanced himself from every aspect of this stance, for in practice it proved completely inadequate. By his estimation, it lacked transitional demands and showed disregard for the ethnic and peasant movements of Russia:

> Comrade Pyatakov simply rejects our slogan, saying that it means giving no slogan for the socialist revolution, but he himself gives no appropriate slogan. The method of socialist revolution under the slogan "Down with frontiers"

> is all muddled up. We have not succeeded in publishing the article in which I called this view "Imperialist Economism." What does the "method" of socialist revolution under the slogan "down with frontiers" mean? We maintain that the state is necessary, and a state presupposes frontiers. The state, of course, may hold a bourgeois government, but we need the Soviets. But even Soviets are confronted with the question of frontiers. What does "Down with frontiers" mean? It is the beginning of anarchy. . . . The "method" of socialist revolution under the slogan "down with frontiers" is simply a mess. . . . If Finland, Poland or Ukraine secede from Russia, there is nothing bad in that. What is wrong with it? Anyone who says that is a chauvinist. One must be mad to continue Tsar Nicholas's policy.[117]

In the fourth article of their platform, the "abstract internationalists" stated the following: "The slogan of 'national self-determination' is most of all utopist (not possible to realize under the conditions of capitalism) and damaging, in that it inculcates illusions." The *neutral stance as a general rule* with regard to national movements indicated here was still formulated on a purely theoretical basis by Pyatakov, Bukharin, and Bosh. The outcome, as a result, was truly sectarian: "Social democracy cannot establish *minimal* demands in the field of current foreign policy."[118] This debate was no obstacle, however, for close cooperation between Bukharin and Lenin at the end of 1916 and even the beginning of 1917, when Bukharin organized the internationalist group of Russian emigrants in America.[119]

One of Lenin's political pupils, Lev Borisovich Kamenev, emphasized that in speaking about the right to self-determination, there can be no socialist or democratic party without recognition of the right of nations to self-determination. Any other stance serves only to sanctify the imperialist divisions actuated before and during the war. Kamenev noted: "History has taken such a turn that for any democratic party to reject this slogan would be suicide."[120]

The Mensheviks took a relatively positive position. In an article written by Plekhanov for the 16 June 1917 issue of *Yedinstvo*, he criticized the Provisional Government and incited the recognition of "Ukraine's right to autonomy" by all means. In his case, the recognition of the right of nations to self-determination in principle, and the offer of "autonomy" in practice, served the purpose of Russia "building the strongest possible unity with Ukraine in the face of German militarism, by leading the Ukrainian Rada to relinquish their aim of secession from the Russian state."[121]

Finally, the resolution accepted at the congress of the Unified RSDLP (or Mensheviks) in August 1917 stated—at variance with Plekhanov's position—that the party takes a stand on the side of the "principle of cultural-national autonomy" and rejects a federation. The platform accepted at the May–June 1917 council of the so-called national socialist parties still held this position.[122] Apparently the dissolution of the traditional framework on which Russia was built was highly unpopular—independent of national belonging—among the Mensheviks as well. The goal of preserving the bourgeois republic, preventing the further radicalization of the revolution, isolating the proletarian revolutionary trend inspired by the Bolsheviks, and arresting the collapse of imperial structures brought almost every group within the Menshevik camp on board.

The dissolution of the empire strengthened the natural aims of the revolution for the Bolsheviks. They rejected the preservation of the old structures, considering them incapable of being reformed. After October, Lenin arrived from a support for centralization to an agreement with the creation of a federative-state structure on the ruins of the old empire through these arguments.[123]

The degree to which the abstract theoretical point of view penetrated the mindset of many leaders of the party is clearly shown by the fact that seven out of nine members of the section taking a position on the national issue were in support of Pyatakov's proposal for the resolution, though they ultimately voted against it at the conference.[124] After October, the national-ethnic issue, burdened with new conflicts, played a central role in Lenin's work in building the state, with the creation of the Soviet federative-state becoming his principal and all-consuming mission.

The reason why the omnipotence of "wealth" is more certain in a democratic republic is that it does not depend on defects in the political machinery or on the faulty political shell of capitalism. A democratic republic is the best possible political shell for capitalism, and, therefore, once capital has gained possession of this very best shell . . . it establishes its power so securely, so firmly, that no change of persons, institutions or parties in the bourgeois-democratic republic can shake it.

—V. I. LENIN, *THE STATE AND REVOLUTION*, *LCW*, VOL. 25, 393

5
The State and Revolution

The Impact of Lenin's The State and Revolution *and Its Historical Context*

LENIN'S *THE STATE AND REVOLUTION: The Marxist Theory of the State and the Tasks of the Proletariat in the Revolution*, was written in August–September 1917 and first published in the following year. It is perhaps the most influential, most read, and most highly valued work written by Lenin.[1] The significance of this short book is unquestioned even by those biographers and analysts of his legacy who look upon it, from a theoretical point of view, as an insignificant hack job.[2] Not even those critics who give it an ahistorical examination, marking it off as some sort of specialized work, or one that "had not been validated by history, and therefore held no interest," can bypass it. The fundamental subject of the work and its field of interest cover *the intersection of state and class relations in Marxist theory*.

Back in 1970, Tibor Hajdu pointed out that the significance of *The State and Revolution* could not be disputed. Its author had "unearthed, partly on his own and partly in the footsteps of other Marxist scholars, forgotten ideas of Marx" in order to theoretically better capture the outlooks of the socialist revolution.[3] Virtually the same finding was made by Bukharin, who was earlier criticized in this very field by Lenin, in a lecture he gave on communism at the beginning of the 1920s.[4]

The twentieth century saw political movements built worldwide[5] upon this unfinished work by Lenin. Not only Communists read the volume like a bible—until Stalin slapped it out of their hands on the grounds of his statist conviction—but antistatist, anticapitalist parties and movements at large thought it merited in-depth study. This is primarily on account that it sketched an attractive socialist future, which brought high social-communal values into the sphere of politics.

Obviously there must be a "secret" to the little book's success if its historical influence goes far beyond any other work of the same field, though the others may have been better worked out. The book is easy to read, with a clear exposition of its logic, and it covers the requirements of a scientific-theoretical exposition just as well as that of a political pamphlet. It is a passionate work fully in the spirit of the struggle that is both a call for the implementation of the proletarian revolution and a classical summation of the fundamental aims of the revolution. Moreover, it outlines a concept of state revolution that reconstructs Marx and Engels's most important writings addressing this question in order to mobilize *tradition* for the realization of the commune-like state. Its use as a "handbook" for revolutionary movements is no coincidence. After all, the subtitle of the book bears the practical intention of becoming the handbook of the revolutionary workers: "The Marxist Theory of the State and the Tasks of the Proletariat in the Revolution."

The significance of the book in world history is that—in more senses than one—it became *the philosophy of the October Revolution.* The revolution is presented through its immediate objective (seizing power) and end goal (voluntary partnership of free communities) at once, with political revolution shown as the initial momentum in social revolution. Although it predates the revolution, its perspective became an integral part of the critical theory with which later developments were approached, even later becoming vulgarized in the utopist fashion, especially in the Marxist-Leninist propaganda during the period of state socialism. Decades later still, in the dominant ideological "narrative" of the anti-utopist world of regime change, this work of Lenin's came to be sublimated in the guise of the pipe-smoke–clouded dreams of a doctrinaire fantast, which all "serious" intellectual trends were (and are) expected to ridicule.

Two main tendencies can be observed among the more notable analyses. One approach understood it as an intrinsically coherent and consistent theoretical work (for example, Neil Harding, Kevin Anderson), grounded in libertarian ideals and principles. The other approach takes in the historical circumstances and consequences following from the revolution and historicizes these as if *The State and Revolution* had been the intellectual inspiration behind, and expressions of, an authoritarian turn and development (for example, A. J. Polan, Robert Service).[6]

Of all Lenin's works, *The State and Revolution* has had the most interesting afterlife. The Marxist flank, and actually almost every system-critical and anticapitalist movement, has used it as its own. The text can be applied in opposition to both capitalist and Stalinist conceptualizations of the state, inasmuch as the Marxist end goal of the state's demise was (and is) a stated aim of the Russian Revolution and the universal socialist revolution.

The idea of transposing *The State and Revolution* into different historical contexts surfaced in the last phase of state socialism, especially in the Weberian, liberal analysis, with the aim of setting up the book as the historical precursor to the Stalinist period and the Stalinist interpretation. The conclusion to this line of thought was that the Soviet state and its institutions were crystallized in this work by Lenin as the ideological underpinning of the Communist monopoly on power. This is how Lenin's text became "an active agent and component in the realization of the coming future." A causal relationship between Lenin's work and the development that followed the revolution came to be posited. That is, between *The State and Revolution* and Stalin's Gulag. This position sets out to eliminate the difference between the "autocratic" Lenin of *What Is To Be Done?* and the "libertarian" Lenin of *The State and Revolution*, with proof to the effect that the same "authoritarian" philosophy and politics are at the heart of both texts.[7]

Later Marxist criticism showed the ahistorical and "presentist" ideological traits that characterize the approach A. J. Polan subscribes to. It also demonstrated that the Weberian analysis accounts for the "unification of the executive powers and legislative powers in labor associations" as an authoritarian concept, because it paves the way for theoretical and political critiques of bourgeois democracy.

This thesis is where any liquidation of independent bureaucratic structures begins and ends if it seeks to transcend the confines of bourgeois democracy, or any kind of dictatorial power.[8] *The State and Revolution* speaks plainly. It frankly declares its party alliance and class commitment, a fact that sent shudders down the spine of scientific officialdom even then. This finds expression in an oft-quoted formulation of Lenin's regarding the essence of politics:

> People always have been the foolish victims of deception and self-deception in politics, and they always will be until they have learned to seek out the *interests* of some class or other behind all moral, religious, political and social phrases, declarations and promises.[9]

The most "modern" of the analysts focus their criticism on the fact that Lenin "widened the scope of his interpretation of the then current inner struggles of the party to make global principles out of them."[10]

The usual question of "value-neutrality" in the social sciences originating in Weberian thought comes up as a problem here. Yet the scientific formulation of this critique hides two distortions. First, it inverts the implications of cause and effect. In Lenin's case, his interpretation of the "inner party struggles" and the class aspect followed from universal principles. Second, these social scientists generally present themselves as if they stood above class perspectives and the established system, and view themselves in the role of judges who, unlike Lenin, do not represent a party line in the name of social justice but expound objective scientific truth.

In the case of Lenin it would be the quintessence of ahistoricity if we were to overlook the fact that the personality under discussion was a revolutionary politician for whom science and theory were *tools* for the realization of political and social goals. Lenin often quoted Marx on how "theory is merely the guide to action," and unlike many scholars in hiding at the time, he put forward the premises of his worldview in spite of the consequences. It should come as no surprise that Lenin takes traits of such a scientific field to task if they are apologetic with regard to the system.

Neither Marx's nor Lenin's approach, which is constructed upon it, can be classified—as opposed to the Weberian reading—as normative theories. Additionally, neither approach is independent of its historical conditions. According to *The State and Revolution* Lenin never thought that socialism, a "self-governing labor democracy, commune democracy, could be easily introduced in Russia." By his estimation this was a task for a whole epoch.

In purely philosophical terms, this work was not about the subordination of society to the state. To the contrary, it "subordinates" the state to society. This is in no way altered either by what happened in Russia after October 1917 or how it is evaluated. The following observation by Jules Townshend is correct: "Clearly, Lenin did not fully address the issue of the state/civil society relation.... Both Lukács and Gramsci were inspired by the idea of Soviets as overcoming the state/civil society distinction, inscribed in liberal democracy, which separated the public from the private realm, the political from the economic."[11] The doubling of "private" and "political" is natural to bourgeois thinking; after all, its source and grounds are the market, the relations of capital. This is the problem Lenin raised in theoretical and practical terms.

The "demise of the state" as a political and theoretical problem always came up in the tradition of Marxist thought as the process of "eliminating class." Lenin identified the wartime dissolution of capital accumulation and the given, universal structure of the capitalist system with the functional failure of the *whole system*. The Great War had very different impacts on the political and intellectual development of the working class of each nation. Lenin overlooked the fact that the war also brought to the surface certain possibilities for the renewal of the capitalist system. In the short run, this strengthened a revolutionary orientation but in the long run it hindered a more complete consideration of realistic possibilities.

From this aspect, an interesting contradiction characterizes *The State and Revolution*. At the outbreak of the war, Lenin registered that in comparison with previous historical epochs, the role of the state had grown in almost every sphere of social life throughout the capitalist world-system but especially at its core. In this phase of increasing bureaucratic complexity, Lenin postulated that the proletariat could replace the bureaucratic system with its own, proactive apparatus organized from the bottom up. However, his image of the replacement of this "monster," this "colossus of a state," with the "workers' state" had such facility and ease that it must have been presumed that the crisis of power in the Russian system was typical of the whole world.

Lenin seems to have put the issue of *uneven development* that he himself had discovered in parentheses. The way he imagined the replacement of the old state apparatus with a new one, however liberatory, was too mechanistic. This becomes apparent in the article he wrote shortly before the October Revolution, "Can the Bolsheviks Retain State Power?" Setting aside the simple language demanded by the use of the material as political propaganda, the idea itself is problematic when compared with *The State and Revolution*, for there the direction of the state was defined as a task for the entire population and here it is proposed as fundamentally a political task.

In "Can the Bolsheviks Retain State Power?" Lenin states:

> We are not utopians. We know that an unskilled laborer or a cook cannot immediately get on with the job of state administration. In this we agree with the Kadets. . . . We differ, however, from these citizens in that we demand an immediate break with the prejudiced view that only the rich, or officials chosen from rich families, are capable of *administering* the state.[12]

He was absolutely clear that "a cook," as mentioned in *The State and Revolution*, cannot get on right away with the complex work of leading the state, but may nevertheless get on with its preparation. For many decades, nevertheless, critics of Lenin's book showed an attitude of derision to his proposal that "cooks" have a role in political matters. The essence of the book is certainly not encompassed by this symbolic formulation however, which he himself rescinded in the light of post-October experiences in Russia.

Anti-Utopist Utopia?

It has largely been forgotten that *The State and Revolution* came into being not only in the struggle against so-called realpolitik but also against utopia. It was common knowledge among Lenin's associates that during 1915–16 he had conflicting opinions with some of his comrades, among them Bukharin,[13] on the *abstract* denial of state and democracy.[14] In the autumn of 1915, Bukharin proposed a question to Lenin: "If our prospects lie in transforming the bourgeois democratic revolution into the socialist revolution, how will they reach, will they ever reach a declaration of the proletarian dictatorship?"[15]

In late 1916 or early 1917, in a lengthy letter addressed to Lenin, Bukharin explained his ideological stance on the structure of the coming revolution. In order to avoid accusations of any manner of anarchism, he accepted the two forward-looking slogans of revolutionary development in Russia, the "convocation of the Constituent Assembly" and establishment of the "provisional government of the revolution." There was something artificial about his approach to politics, as if the inevitable circumstances that someone invented at a desk could be foreseen in practice.

Bukharin reduced the issue of the Russian Revolution to a mere instance, a fraction, a sort of extension of the European revolution.[16] He regarded even the role of the peasant masses in their millions as an "element" of Western European influence. At the heart of the actual conflict, therefore, lay the autonomy of the Russian Revolution, a fact Bukharin was perfectly aware of. At this point in his letter he remarks: "An interesting question comes next, for which I am sure you shall scold me. The question now is *socialism in Russia.*"

A constant intent to bridge theory and practice, and to thoroughly explore the passage between them, was a particular trait of Lenin's political and theoretical thought. It was his "theoretical practice." This approach was quite alien to Bukharin however, for whom practical possibilities and objectives always appeared in a theoretical form, as exemplified by the letter cited above. In Bukharin's approach it is unimportant how local circumstances are structured, and what is their influence in shaping the situation. The focus is on the ideological extension of global tendencies in Russia, which would dictate that the days of the nation-state are over.

The following passage from Bukharin's letter is worth reviewing here, as it precedes the February Revolution by mere weeks:

> Why were we always against the Russian Revolution? Because the "objective preconditions"—agriculture based country, the overwhelming number of peasants, the diffusion of home manufacture [*remeslo*] etc.—were not prevalent. *And this was absolutely true.* But in my opinion (which I cannot positively state as yet, but am inclined increasingly toward such "anarchism"), *this state of affairs extends until we perceive Russia as an isolated state and economy.* During the 1905 Revolution there was no particular hope of a *European* revolution. The situation now is completely different. This time—if not today, then tomorrow—a pan-European, if not world-size flame is to erupt. But the social revolution, the revolution of the West will *tear down* all boundaries between nation-states. And in this context we

> *must* support this. Why would we have to keep a Russia limited by borders in existence? What for? To the contrary, we are occupied with centralizing, with soldering together . . . the whole of Europe (in the first phase). If this is the case, why would we need to preserve the "local particularities" and the bourgeoisie in power, which will be a greater *danger* (as leader = imperialism) to the West tomorrow than a rotten tsarism?

After Bukharin extrapolated the Europe-wide coalescence of capital in banking and industry, he continues: "The peasants have to be made dependent by the industrialization of the economy. They will not turn against *us*. . . . With our socialism we would throttle Russian imperialism at the roots . . . I cannot discover an ounce of 'anarchism' in this."[17] Of course, Bukharin was not capable of the anarchism he was accused of by Lenin as well as others, but he attributed great significance to the modern Western bourgeois rather than the local, backward developments and structures characteristic of the East. He underestimated historical "certainties" in contrast to the certainties of the (formal) logic of theory. In more concrete terms, he underestimated the role of the nation-state in the modern economy and the world system in general. It is no coincidence that a few years later, in 1919, when Kautsky attacked Lenin's theory of the state, Bukharin was its most active and perhaps most gifted defender on a theoretical schematic stage, though deviating toward bureaucratic centralism.[18]

The State and Revolution is historically embedded in a number of ways. It was dubbed an "utopistic work" by the moderate leftist ideologists who emerged out of the 1989 regime change in Eastern Europe.[19] They set out to use Lenin's text as a reconstruction of Marx and Engels's thought, which built its "image of the future" on a critique of the *Gotha Program*. However, in line with Marxist tradition, Lenin did not conceive this work in a utopist vein. Indeed, he raised the question:

> On the basis of what *facts*, then, can the question of the future development of future communism be dealt with? On the basis of the fact that it *has its origin* in capitalism, that it develops historically from capitalism, that it is the result of the action of a social force to which capitalism *gave birth*. There is no trace of an attempt on Marx's part to make up a utopia, to indulge in idle guesswork about what cannot be known.[20]

Lenin's exposition of this central issue, that of the "state's *demise*," was grounded in Engels's critical explanations, which were themselves censorious of "social democratic chatter." In a letter dated 28 March 1875 to Bebel, Engels suggested that the word *state* be struck and replaced by the word *community*. Lenin fell back on Marx and Engels again on this matter, when he proposed the elimination of the notion of the state in the context of socialism, and its replacement with the word *commune*.

Indeed, the word ultimately found its way into the Russian as *kommuna*.[21] It perhaps first appears in a memo by Lenin, taken at the Petrograd Party Committee meeting of 14 (1) November 1917. He deliberately avoided using the expression *soviet* (council) from the burgeoning movement of the soviets in *The State and Revolution* for political reasons, because at the time of writing he could not know whether the soviets would be capable of taking power by revolutionary means or whether they would keep to the Menshevik and Socialist-Revolutionary (S.R.) majority line.

As Lenin thought of it, even the Paris Commune was "not a state in the sense of the actual meaning of the word." The state in demise (commune), which comes into being during the period of the revolution, was presented as a fundamental institution of the *political period of transition* or *dictatorship of the proletariat.* This would, in principle, create the conditions for socialism.

In the theoretical groundwork, socialism was shown as the first phase of communism, and then communism itself was shown as the *possible* end result of a long historical course of development. All state oppression would cease to exist within the framework of socialism, but the civilized human race would only turn completely and finally into a "community of associated producers" in communism.[22] Lenin reached these conclusions after surveying the different economic fundamentals of the state and the state in demise, and the disparate producer-proprietor relations underlying them.

Criticism of this work that takes issue with Lenin's "naïveté" is not completely unfounded. Lenin recognized, or thought he recognized "primitive democratism" (Bernstein's concept), the early forms of direct democracy, as "an element of capitalism and capitalist culture." He referred not only to the high level at which the socialization of production stood, but also to the workers' old tradition of organizing their community.

Factually he was right, but it seems nevertheless that he overestimated the cultural experiences of the community already accumulated under the capitalist system. The communal tradition of the *obshchina* (Russian village communities) that he had studied in his earlier years was by then decaying. Large-scale industry, the postal service, and other institutions of capitalist organization appeared to him as perfect vehicles for "commune democracy," "soviet democracy," and "labor democracy" under the surviving hierarchical relations of the transitional phase. There's no need to dwell on how greatly the authoritarian, autocratic traditions in Russia amplified this hierarchy.

The increasingly refined mechanism of capitalist oppression and its "penetration" came up less often in Lenin's analyses; the man "created by capitalist culture" does not appear in the context of the *totality of his relations*. Rather, he appears in possession of that self-consciousness that only a small group of the truly revolutionary proletariat could boast.

On the other hand, Lenin's thought was fundamentally oriented toward a Russia whose population was largely illiterate. In spite, or perhaps on account of this, prior to the summer of 1918 he seems to have left unheeded the sociological issues stemming from the way the distribution of labor was structured. The significance and formative process of the abilities required to run the complicated economic-social structure are not really dealt with in *The State and Revolution*, nor do any signs of interest in these matters come up in his copious notes from the period.[23] Of course, this was not a fundamental task of the work; rather it was to prove the realization of the new power structure, the "semi-state" of the commune type, a realistic historical possibility. The book was written with the purpose of providing a theory of the *European revolution*, posing a certain requirement for abstraction to begin with.

As in so many fields of political strife, on the issue of socialism, Lenin's views became crystallized through the arguments he waged against old Narodism, new Bernsteinism, "legal Marxism," anarchism, and other political movements. At different historical times he tested his strength against different movements. Lenin's *theory of socialism* originated from a concrete critical stance toward the established capitalist system. A romantic perception of the future was alien to him. It was a defining characteristic of his thought process and practical-political activity that—in the name of a commitment to science—he discarded all speculative approaches in principle and methodology. He consistently aimed to denounce all utopian constructs, though not to liquidate all utopias, for in their absence all thought looking beyond the system and oriented toward the future would be eliminated.

THE STATE AND REVOLUTION: THEORETICAL BACKGROUND

The State and Revolution is an organic part and consequence of Lenin's previous theoretical work. In terms of exposition—as revealed by the first plan he wrote for the book—he thought deeply about whether to use the "historical-dogmatic, or the logical" order.[24] He finally decided to pursue a combination of the two methods, emphasizing historical chronology. His sources played a decisive role in this. Apart from Marx and Engels, Lenin utilized thematically relevant arguments and writings from Bernstein, Plekhanov, Kautsky, and Pannekoek. The field from which the book springs includes the Russian intellectual and political struggle from the 1890s to 1917. As early as his publication of *What the 'Friends of the People' Are* in 1894, Lenin made an attempt at defining the concept of *historical-social development*, which he continued in this book.

Lenin came to realize at a very early stage in his career that in Russia, especially within the framework of the Narodnik legacy, a "peasant socialism"—that is, a utopist form of socialism—had set in. It dissolved in the 1870s in such a way that it gave birth to "superficial petit bourgeois liberalism" that "dreamed of a peasant revolution." It finally awoke from the utopistic dream to find itself—in line with developments—embroiled in the wholesale expropriation of peasants.

The liberal socialism of Mikhailovsky and his followers—by then in determined opposition to Marx and the Russian Marxists—was occupied with the "defense of the economically most exposed," and the revitalization of old, antiquated communal models. Just like the "guileless petit bourgeois" whom Lenin considered representatives of a movement hopelessly stuck in the past,[25] particularly where the "social revolution" was concerned. He traced this eclecticism of the liberal Narodniks ("to borrow the 'best' from anywhere," from medieval forms of communal life to the modern enlightenment ideals of freedom and equality) to the subjective methodology of the as yet immature science of sociology, which kicked off with utopia and wound up with the most common liberal prejudices—as he put it.[26]

Mulling over the fate of the peasant communities in their day, Marx and Engels also noted that the question of socialism and revolution were intertwined in the history of Russian revolutionary thought.[27] Whereas Marx saw a faint chance for the *obshchina* to become a starting point for socialism, the first generation of Russian Marxists with Plekhanov at the helm related to the revolution as scholar theoreticians and did not perceive it as an immediate practical task. They were also convinced that the village communities were in the final state of dissolution and could not possibly fulfill any positive historical role. Their predecessors, the so-called revolutionary democrats—such as Herzen, Chernyshevsky and Dobrolyubov, not to speak of the Russian Jacobinists, Tkachov and Nechaev, or Russian Blanquism—had linked their own "peasant socialism" directly with the practical necessity of the revolution. By this they meant an idea of toppling the autocratic regime through a coup d'état that grasps the reins of power based on a minority group of revolutionaries.

In chapter three it was shown how Lenin strove to combine positive elements from both movements with his own notions for the social-democratic movement and its organizational forms. In contrast to Plekhanov, by the turn of the century he approached Russian reality from a perspective of the revolution's urgency. Unlike the "peasant socialists," however, Lenin thought exclusively in terms of the labor movement. From 1903 onward, he thought in terms of some kind of labor and poor peasant bloc in his concept of socialism. Western European circumstances were held to be the true expression of maturity.

The new prospects that had arisen for the labor movement in Russia at the turn of the century were palpable even in German social democracy (notably in the writings of Kautsky and Luxemburg). Bernstein had in part inherited Lasalle's "people's state" invented for capitalism with his proposal for the "social state." In opposition, the revolutionary Marxists did not give up the tradition, ideals, and praxis of direct democracy and community-association-collective economy.[28] In political and methodological terms, this later became a watershed in the division between the "self-governing" followers of Marx and Lenin, the social democrats, as well as the Stalinist and post-Stalinist official statist Communists,. To this day this split still exists—mutatis mutandis—in left movements around the globe.[29]

In the debates preceding the adoption of the party program at the Second RSDLP Congress in 1903, Lenin and Plekhanov were on a single platform—with regard to state and revolution—in demanding, in the terminology of the time, the "dictatorship of the proletariat." However, with the passage of years, the revolution whose "attainments the proletarian dictatorship was to defend" became increasingly insignificant for Plekhanov, and even irrelevant during the war years in particular, as he gave up the perspective of the revolutionary imperative.[30] The closer the revolution came, the further Plekhanov was removed from it. It was no different in the case of Kautsky, though the conflict with him was delayed until the outbreak of war.

In the years following 1905, there was a turn in the European labor movement that clearly placed the epicenter of the revolutionary upswing in Russia. Partly on account of Plekhanov's politically cautious theoretical influence, Lenin had come to understand—and call attention to—Russia as a possible initiator of revolution within the pan-European context.

The Experience of 1905: The Soviets

Even in his everyday political analyses during the period of the first Russian Revolution, Lenin drew a clear line between the practical problems of the revolution and socialism as a theory and prospect. In other words, he consciously dis-associated the implications of the revolutionary and post-revolutionary period.

Lenin viewed the self-organizing public bodies formed during the revolution, and especially the "professional-systemic" traits and political functions borne by the soviets as a whole, as the special element holding the revolution together. In this light the soviets were the revolution's organs of self-defense, its agents of power, whose phases of development and the tasks peculiar to each were considered separately.

After the defeat of the Moscow armed uprising of December 1905, the revolution's self-defense came into focus. Adapting to these circumstances, Lenin considered the unrealistic, quasi-concrete "promises" of popular government for the *post-revolutionary* period (future society) as utopian tendencies harmful to the movement in general. He held that they drew energy and attention away from the immediate task of defending the revolution. Nonetheless, signs of the future did come up in 1905 in that the labor organizations of self-governing and self-defense that had not been known to any period of Russian history, the soviets, came into being and undertook tasks of economic, social, and political power. In some places they even assumed military functions, from St. Petersburg to Ivanovo-Voznesensky.

In the first days of November 1905, before he even arrived in Russia, Lenin wrote the article "Our Tasks and the Soviet of Workers' Deputies."[31] He rejected the issue of "party or soviet" outright, and took the position that the soviets must be considered as the self-organization of the whole working class, even including the anti-monarchist masses of the population as a whole. They had come into being as the "professional" organs of the proletariat that no one party may appropriate. This argument held that the tasks of the labor and socialist parties differed from that of the soviets, with their social bases also differing. At this stage Lenin considered the soviets' organizations belonging expressly to the revolution and not to socialism:

> I may be wrong, but I believe (on the strength of the incomplete and only "paper" information at my disposal) that politically the Soviet of Workers' Deputies should be regarded as the embryo of a *provisional revolutionary government*.[32]

In other words, he saw this people's organization as a national political center comprising the whole of society. In the soviets he saw evidence that the social democrats wanted to leave the direction of the country firmly in the hands of the popular alliances:

> We are not trying to impose on the people any innovations thought up by us; we are merely taking the initiative in bringing about that without which

> it is impossible to live in Russia any longer. . . . We rely fully and solely on the free initiative of the working masses themselves.[33]

The Menshevik *Iskra* suggested, in support of its boycott tactics against the Duma elections, that the "revolutionary self-government" may have been a prologue to the uprising. Lenin saw the matter differently. He argued that the revolutionary uprising alone can create the circumstances suitable for self-government:

> The organization of revolutionary self-government, the election of their own deputies by the people is not the *prologue* to an uprising, but its *epilogue*. . . . It is first of all necessary to win the victory in an uprising (if only in a single city) and to establish a provisional revolutionary government, so that the latter, as the organ of the uprising and the recognized leader of the revolutionary people, should be able to get down to the organization of revolutionary self-government.[34]

As Lenin emphasized many times during the years of 1905–1906, the self-government of labor cannot exist in the framework of the old system. For those who were naïve about this, he pointed out: "While the tsar retains power, revolutionary self-government can be only a fragment of the revolution. . . . In purpose, manner of origin, and character, the organization of an armed uprising, the organization of a revolutionary army, is *quite unlike* the organization of revolutionary self-government."[35]

The State and Revolution did not come about as abruptly as it is often imagined. Lenin outlined a comprehensive examination of the experience of the Paris Commune and the first Russian Revolution in his speech "Lessons of the Commune" in 1908.[36] He gave an account of two mistakes made by the working class during the Paris Commune, which in his perception indicated that the proletariat stopped short of "expropriating the expropriators." In a Proudhonist spirit, he delivered the first mistake as the following: "led astray by dreams of establishing a higher justice . . . such institutions as the banks, for example, were not taken over." He continued, "The second mistake was excessive magnanimity on the part of the proletariat: instead of destroying its enemies it sought to exert moral influence on them; it underestimated the significance of direct military operations in civil war."[37]

If the French bourgeoisie, setting all moral considerations aside, sank into a frenzy of murder upon the defeat of the Paris Commune, it is understandable that during the reprisals of the counterrevolution Lenin reflected upon the likely and expected steps of self-defense to be taken by the future proletarian revolution. At the same time he could sense that the Russian Revolution would urge the already initiated revolution internationally: "It stirred the socialist movement throughout Europe, it demonstrated the strength of civil war, it dispelled patriotic illusions, and destroyed the naïve belief in any efforts of the bourgeoisie for common national aims. The Paris Commune taught the European proletariat to pose concretely the tasks of the socialist revolution."[38] Lenin, as was his custom, showed the inescapable necessities and historical experience of his own insight as the common experience of the proletariat, though a very significant majority of Russian laborers did not remember the Paris Commune in 1908.[39]

Recalling 1905 while reading a passage from Marx's *The Civil War in France* in 1917, in which Marx writes about the Paris Commune and presents an argument for a decrease in working hours to the effect that "*everyone* is engaged in productive work and *everyone* participates at the same time in 'governing' the state," Lenin makes the following note in the margin:

> The Russian Revolution, i.e., the proletariat applied the same procedure more weakly (timidly) than the Paris Commune on the one hand; and on a wider basis, on the other—soviets of the "worker's deputies," "railmen's deputies," "soldier's and seamen's deputies," "peasant deputies." This I add *nota bene*.[40]

It can be seen that the practical problem of keeping the political state and the possible tasks of the Commune-like state were already present in Lenin's work by 1907 and 1908.

THE PHILOSOPHY OF THE OCTOBER REVOLUTION: A CRITICAL APPRAISAL OF THE MODERN STATE AND PARLIAMENTARISM

One of the cornerstones of Lenin's theory of revolution, as with Marx, was the first phase of the social revolution, the *overthrow* and liquidation of the *political state*. The question of the state as a "central issue of every revolution" had occupied Lenin since his student years and was ingrained in pre-Marxist Russian revolutionary thought, taking a variety of historical shapes (foremost among them those proposed by the Bakuninists and other anarchists).[41] Lenin however, emphasized the *class characteristics*, as well as the *social* and universal bearings of revolution, confronting in particular the notion of "peasant" and "nationalist" utopias.

Julius Martov examined Bakunin's legacy more discriminatingly than Lenin, raising some "finer" points against anarchism. In a study from 1910, Bakunin acknowledged that many years after losing to Marx in the polemics they engaged in during the 1860s, he accepted Marx's views on economy, and the conclusion of *Capital*, "the expropriation of the expropriators." The methodological-theoretical and practical-political cul-de-sac was reached because similarly to Proudhon, Bakunin "contra-positioned the economic organization of society with its political organization": equality and justice between the people should be achieved in the field of economy, while the root cause of social inequality can be found in the field of politics—ruled, as it were, by brute force. This is why anarchism and Bakunin considered the state their foremost enemy, and saw its complete destruction as the condition of social liberation. In other words, Martov showed that cause and effect had been mixed up. This discovery laid the grounds for the conviction that Marxism must supplant anarchism in the field of revolutionary organization.[42]

No doubt, the anarchist approach to the world in general and politics in particular took root in Russia and especially the Ukraine, among certain layers of peasantry that rebutted state pressure. Thus it reflected certain regional peculiarities of historical development, but nonetheless also made some inroads where the labor movement was concerned. The main point is that their understanding of the recognized possibility and need for socialist revolution was purely that of "popular revolt," and not the Sisyphean organizational-intellectual groundwork such a revolution entailed.[43] From the end of the nineteenth century however, it became increasingly clear that Russian anarchism did not engage the new problem of *modern society*, but prepared it for other anticapitalist revolutionary movements to deal with and at the same time shook relatively wide social strata out of their lethargic state.

What interested Lenin most in the history of revolutions was how laborers gained the ability to wrest control of their lives, if only for a week or a month. He delved into the subject in a scientific manner, especially with regard to the particularities of the development of the state in Russia. Questions related to the functioning of a bourgeois state, the institutional sociology of parties and bureaucratic mechanisms, held no interest for him. The science of the bourgeois state's sociology served, in his opinion, as a defense of the state, providing a scientifically grounded justification.

Lenin investigated the modern bourgeois state as economic and intellectual exploitation of the highest order. He found that bourgeois parliamentarism is linked to the most modern forms of capitalist production, the organization of capital, and grows out of it. For historical context it must be added that the parliamentary system of the 1910s and 1920s had little in common with its current form, being marked by expressly antidemocratic traits such as the census and other limitations on voting rights, and it hardly needs reminding that women only received general suffrage in England in 1928. In Chapter Two, it was discussed that in the course of his studies, Lenin drew attention to capitalism's inevitable and continuous conflicts with democracy that extend between legal equality and social-economic inequality. The capitalist system tries to resolve this contradiction with the all-pervasive web of traits that typify "corruption" and "bribery."[44]

In Lenin's view, the basic difference between imperialism and pre-monopolist capitalism was that in the former "the power of the stock exchange increases," as the greater banks merge with the stock exchange and swallow it whole. Capital draws the sphere of politics under its supervision as if it were another item of sale, some sort of market phenomenon. Of course Lenin was aware that the prostitution and corruption of bourgeois democracy was regulated by law, and thus not unbounded. At the same time, however, he stressed that these processes of legalized corruption are rooted in wealth, because *wealth* "is fully capable of achieving domination over any democratic republic by bribery and through the stock exchange . . . that is, politically independent, republic" as well. Lenin's main thought here is that bourgeois democracy is not freedom but "the freedom of purchase." In September 1917 he formulated the problem as follows:

> The capitalists (followed, either from stupidity or from inertia, by many S.R.s and Mensheviks) call "freedom of the press" a situation in which censorship has been abolished and all parties freely publish all kinds of papers. In reality it is not freedom of the press, but freedom for the rich, for the bourgeoisie, to deceive the oppressed and exploited mass of the people.[45]

Lenin looked upon bourgeois democracy as a form of capitalist domination of the highest order. In fact, the only need (though this need makes it all the more necessary) to extol the advantages of "the easily bought and rotten parliamentarism of bourgeois society" is that the labor movement finds greater scope of development within its confines, and has more room for maneuver than in the circumstances provided by autocratic, openly dictatorial regimes. Bourgeois parliamentarism holds, in this sense, only a "historical interest" of specialized scientific bearing for Lenin, but does not have a future. The emperor has no clothes.

In the period of the revolution the specialized scientific questions in particular were far from central to his thinking. Furthermore, the experiences of the Great War only underscored how the task of politically unmasking the parliamentary democracies as the regimes responsible for the bloodshed of the war was the most important.[46] With its fundamentally future-oriented thought, *State and Revolution* does not rest on pipe-smoke–clouded dreams alone, but comprises an objective critique of parliamentarism that has not allowed the matter to be taken off the agenda since 1917.[47]

In 1917, "globalization" was not yet the subject of discussion. Rather, popular contemporary themes were *imperialism, monopolies, and the reign of finance capitalism.* As widely recognized, the state suited to this new order took up its fresh set of tasks right at the time of the First World War: it became the main organizer of, and player in, the national economy. It was the kind of "monster" that was willing to destroy anything. The last sentence of the work is important in this regard, for it presents the reasoning that led to the final call for revolution:

> The distortion and hushing up of the question of the relation of the proletarian revolution to the state could not but play an immense role at a time when states, which possess a military apparatus expanded as a consequence of imperialist rivalry, have become military monsters which are exterminating millions of people in order to settle the issue as to whether Britain or Germany—this or that finance capital—is to rule the world.[48]

Lenin took upon not only the general crisis of the capitalist system, but also the concrete areas of dysfunction in bourgeois democracy (bureaucratic, corrupt, parasitic, etc.), which in his interpretation all raised the likelihood of the revolutionary turn. His position accounted for the variety of statehoods, but the revolutionary propagandist and theoretician looked for the commonalities among them: "Bourgeois states are most varied in form, but their essence is the same: all these states, whatever their form, in the final analysis are inevitably the dictatorship of the bourgeoisie,"[49] which excludes the possibility of "reinstating" the communal form of ownership in the place of, or parallel to, capitalist exploitative private property. In his interpretation, "parliamentary rule" is only the battle of competing power cliques for the "spoils" (jobs, economic positions, etc.). The system is above calling it into question in legal and political terms. For this reason too the bourgeois democracies are also—and emphatically—dictatorships according to Lenin's theory, and therefore cannot be corrected without revolution, and the "demolition of the bureaucratic-military state machine."

Lenin reached an even more damning view of parliamentary democracy following his experiences of the war, for in them he saw only institutional expressions of the interests of finance and capital. This was a system dedicated to manipulation and deception, serving to curb the resistance of wage laborers in the interests of capitalist production of profit. This was one of the decisive arguments for the demand that the parliamentary sittings and "jabber" over the head of the people be replaced by "elected bodies of workers who can be recalled," based on the experiences of the Paris Commune: "Representative institutions remain, but there is *no* parliamentarism here as a special system, as the division of labor between the legislative and the executive, as a privileged position for the deputies."[50]

Lenin came to the conclusion that poverty and destitution make actual recourse to the legal provisions offered by democracy impossible. Not only because the poor do not have a chance to "purchase the blessings" of democracy, but because "owing to the conditions of capitalist exploitation, the modern wage slaves are so crushed by want and poverty that 'they cannot be bothered with democracy,' 'cannot be bothered with politics'; in the ordinary, peaceful course of events, the majority of the population is debarred from participation in public and political life."[51] In the revolutionary program of liquidating the state as political entity, the elimination of the "parasitical state" was an important argument as a political precondition of the "economic liberation of labor." As far as Lenin is concerned, state and freedom can be interpreted as diametrically opposed notions.

Lenin's *The State and Revolution* essentially set out, in methodological and political terms, to do away with the "opportunistic illusions" bound up with parliamentarism and with Bernsteinian revisionism, as well as the utopist anarchist approach, all at the same time. According to this argument, the parliamentarists and Bernsteinians abandoned Marx in the name of "market statism," whereas the latter "only" lost sight of their immediate prospects. The official Social Democrats of the Second International replaced the "overthrow" and "total destruction" of the bourgeois state with the democratic and compassionate "people's state." This "people's state" served as a corrective to "bourgeois democracy" (Bernstein, Kautsky, Scheidemann), a bourgeois state subject to law (*Rechtsstaat*) and led by a social democratic government.[52]

Lenin saw social democracy as the kind of plastic notion held by Engels, who noted in 1894, with regard to his articles from the 1870s, that he "used the term 'communist' instead of 'social democrat' in every article, since even the Lasalleans were calling themselves social democrats at the time." In contrast to the bourgeois conception of the state representative of the age, Lenin's approach did not treat it merely in its sociopolitical or formally legal sense. He often alluded to the fact that the apologists of the state leave the "financial," "all-capitalist," "all-landowner," that is, the economic function of the state, hidden, but no one in the revolutionary camp apart from the anarchists—not even the peasant wing of the S.R.s, for example—understood that to fight the state was in itself wholly unproductive unless its economic base was also liquidated. Accordingly, he declared that, because of its economic and class functions, the state could only be fully eliminated "after classes have been abolished by the socialist revolution, as the result of the establishment of socialism, which leads to the withering away of the state."[53]

Lenin arrived at a common position with the anarchists on the revolution as "happening," as a question of "political and theoretical necessity." Nonetheless, he called the anarchist thesis demanding the "total and final destruction" of the state the annihilation of the revolution's defenses in the subchapter dedicated to disclosing the twists in anarchist reasoning.[54] With reference to Engels he emphasized that with the disappearance of the political, state authority and subordination will not cease immediately. After all, if you "take a factory, a railway, a ship on the high seas, said Engels, is it not clear that not one of these complex technical establishments, based on the use of machinery and the systematic cooperation of many people, could function without a certain amount of subordination and, consequently, without a certain amount of authority or power?"[55]

Lenin shared Engels's difficulty with the anarchists' stated desire to "abolish the state completely overnight."[56] The Russian anarchists never understood that the "liquidation of the state" has to start with production and the economy. In general, the Russian anarchists never achieved more than a reductionist perception of Marxism. Not only were they incapable of getting a handle on his economic theory, they also apostrophized Marxist thought on relations in political history and theory as "statist theory" or simply neglected it. Alternatively, they drew a contradiction between Marx's communist end goals and his political and social theory.

Lenin's work was treated similarly by the Russian anarchists. In vain were the Bolsheviks and anarchists on a common footing in the matter of an "anti-state" end goal, or the later temporary armed compact, the heroic deeds of Makhnovist troops in combat against Denikin. As soon as the problems of a new state organization, a new bureaucratic hierarchy, and the institution of centralized production and a traditional distribution of labor were broached, the Bolsheviks appeared as "traitors" in the eyes of the anarchists, and the anarchists as "bandits" to the Bolsheviks. Their armed liquidation was related to their not accepting the authority of the state in the regions they oversaw.[57]

So Lenin outlined a sort of *tertium datur* between the reformist social democrats and the anarchists based on Marx and Engels, in the way he connected the question of revolution and state. A highly significant political understanding that Lenin came to was that the Russian bourgeoisie and the "quavering" middle class could not stabilize either the old "semi-parliamentary" system (with, or without the tsar), or the bourgeois democratic system. In his view, these attempts at stabilization opened the path to counterrevolutionary dictatorships if the revolutionary solution is set off or suffers defeat.

The fact that Lenin wrote this work after he went underground, following the order of arrest issued against him by the Provisional Government after the "July days," has symbolic significance. At the time, the bourgeois democracy had hardly taken shape and it was already in crisis. It is no surprise then that the question that preoccupied Lenin in his cottage in Razliv was which institutional system should the revolutionary class use to "replace the destroyed state apparatus" which lay in ruins across Russia. For this reason he did not bring the Russian model, the soviet, into relief, but used the Paris Commune as the "prototype" to raise the end goal of proletarian revolution in practice. The fundamental aim and subject of the new "commune-type" *self-government* as an economic and community organization was to eliminate, in the final run, economic and social inequalities.

It is not coincidental that the word *party* does not appear as a concept in *The State and Revolution*. This omission is often explained unclearly, though it is quite simple. For Lenin, classes and parties no longer exist in self-governing socialism. It is quite unscientific to state—on the grounds of the Kautsky volume, *The Dictatorship of the Proletariat* written in 1918, and various arguments raised by Martov in his later writings—that Lenin's *The State and Revolution* was criticized for introducing the one-party system in its own time. These prejudicial criticisms are directed at the realities of post-1917 Soviet Russia, drawing up arguments against it and projecting the newly formed situation back onto Lenin's earlier work, as if he had already been advocating the one-party system in 1917.[58]

Lenin's reasoning naturally evolved on numerous points in the spheres of both politics and theory over the years, but to smuggle the one-party system into *The State and Revolution* is a falsification of history or a complete misunderstanding of things as they stood. Both in principle and practice, it is a fact that the October Revolution repositioned the soviet as a practical alternative to parliamentarism, even if by 1918 the soviet, as an organ of labor self-government, had begun to infiltrate the structures of central power and the new hierarchy that gradually developed was defined by it.

Incidentally, the one-party system was never legally introduced. If an argument can be made to prove otherwise, it was done by way of the 1977 constitution under Brezhnev, which declared the Soviet system a one-party system *for the first time*. In Lenin's day, political parties were generally persecuted on an administrative basis, taking either the war or counterrevolutionary actions as their grounds, but they were not legally banned under constitutional law. What was *effectively* a fully formed one-party system by 1921 took the "official" stance—also represented by Lenin—that the *soviet dictatorship*, the "dictatorship of the majority (dictatorship of the proletariat) vis-à-vis the minority," was politically legitimated by the revolution itself. The contradictions at work here were soon to make themselves felt.

REVOLUTION AND STATE: THE FUNCTIONAL ALTERNATIVE

The State and Revolution is not an encapsulation of party philosophy or Bolshevik theory. It is the theoretical "self-definition" of an array of social-political forces organized in the framework of the soviets and other spontaneous social organizations with a largely worker-peasant support base that participated in the October Revolution. They organized with not only Russia, but the fate of all of Europe in mind.

In 1917, the Bolshevik Party of a few thousand members became an umbrella party of many hundreds of thousands. By 1919, "communism" had constituted itself as a European mass movement, a "global party" (of the Third Communist International). It is a commonplace truth that the October Revolution was the result of a much wider mass movement than Bolshevism. We can go so far as to say that the October Revolution was certainly not the *Bolshevik* revolution in terms of its driving forces—as opposed to the message the title of E. H. Carr's volume conveys. It only became "the Bolshevik revolution" in the course of political struggles, when for practical reasons Lenin and the Bolsheviks began to appropriate the ideology and organization of the revolution itself.

Their earlier allies, who had since suffered defeat and were, as a result, in the process of fragmentation, generally supported them in this. They had not been simply "ejected" from the history of the revolution by the Bolsheviks, as they themselves later clearly positioned themselves in opposition to the October Revolution. Moreover, in the eyes of the Bolsheviks' opponents—for a variety of reasons and arguments—the revolution itself was the takeoff point for all the violence.

According to a certain fashionable view frequently found in the historical literature even today—in the work of Lenin biographer Robert Service, for example—some sort of deep coherence exists between *The State and Revolution* and the bloodbath that followed the October Revolution. Service's explanation derives from the actually existing contradiction that Lenin did not perceive: how the "visions of mass initiatives on the one hand, and strict hierarchy and order on the other" were divergent courses of development in thought and action.[59] Considered in the light of this contradiction, Lenin's work appears a "strange concoction" of "the utopist expression of a utopist mind" in one instance, inclusive of the bloodbath; nevertheless, this is "perhaps not by conscious intention of the author" in the other.[60]

This reasoning is doubly unsatisfactory. Service posits in the very same place that *The State and Revolution* was an "experiment at building a great theory," not designed for Russia in the first place. By this reasoning, would not any revolutionary thought, even any revolution, be responsible for the bloodletting that takes place after its victory, on account of counterrevolutionary resistance? Are cause and effect not mixed up in this case? Does this reasoning not switch off the transitions and progression between "great theory" and the unforeseeable historical situation? This is a figurative question, of course.

Mechanical conceptualizations of this kind do not take account of the consistencies apparent in the developments of the Russian Revolution or its unforeseeable prospects. *The State and Revolution* did, however, discuss how the resistance of earlier ruling classes would be overcome as another central question related to, even a precondition of, the issue of the "demise of the state." The two goals were obviously contradictory in that even in this "ethereally sterile" work of Lenin's, the eradication of "*every form of oppression*"—inasmuch as the revolution meets with armed resistance—also comprises the issue of revolutionary violence. However, at the time no one knew, not even Lenin, that the greatest problem to be faced would be that no clear and unequivocal lines providing the boundaries and framework of "revolutionary violence" could be drawn in practice. But then every history of revolutions shows that the groups in political power, often themselves opposed, are the least competent in "gaining control" of the violence. Not to mention the problem that unexpected struggles are played out between the most unlikely forces in the course of revolutions, with unpredictable results.

The February Revolution does not have an independent history, in that developments in Russia did not branch out on a bourgeois democratic course.[61] Even so, there was an onslaught of bloodshed at its outbreak—in contrast, by the way, to the revolutionary events of October in St. Petersburg—with continuous political crisis in which the "July days," which sent the Bolshevik Party underground, provided a turning point.

But how does *The State and Revolution* enter the picture as the inciter of violence? This is simply a case—detailed above in a different context—of designs to reposition this work by Lenin from the independent-minded "libertarian interpretation" into the "authoritarian narrative."[62]

In a series of essays and lectures, Eric Hobsbawm refutes those writers who interpret the actions and consideration of Lenin and the Bolsheviks not from the given historical alternatives, but from their own political views. It is as if they derive history from the self-generated movement of ideologies. This sort of "presentism" brings the usual distortions into play, pretending as of this day that the events and crossroads of the revolution had been entirely foreseeable, and only veered off in another "wrong" direction by the will of Lenin.[63]

Another frequent approach taken to presenting *The State and Revolution* as a book based on authoritarian principles is that certain inconsistencies of Lenin's use of concepts are not taken into account. In the political fray, in the heat of battle, at times Lenin drew together specific phenomena, which he would have clearly separated elsewhere.

An example of such an inadvertent intersection of concepts in *The State and Revolution* is the use of the *transitional phase* and *socialism* in the "post office analogy." The "conflation" of these two phases saw a doubly distorted interpretation later. On the one hand, it was possible to prove during the Stalin period that socialism and rigorous state centralization presuppose one another in Lenin. On the other, it gave grounds, from the 1980s onward, for the image of Lenin as a statist thinker who accentuates state compulsions even in socialism. Actually, state centralization is a typical issue of the transitional phase; that is, the *time period immediately following the revolution*. It should be noted that the principal causes of such mistaken notions within this field of expertise is that the inner coherencies of Lenin's thought are ignored and integral sequences of thought are dissociated.

In 1917, Lenin's understanding of the inner development of the phases of the Russian Revolution underwent an evolution. His idea that the bourgeois and socialist "stages" of the revolution grow separate in the course of development did not—and could not—prove true. Even in the early spring of 1917, while the radicalization of the social masses that gave shape to the events was already in full swing, there was an unprecedented proliferation of revolutionary organizations. Lenin came to understand their practical and intrinsic significance only gradually. These would play an important role in October, such as: the factory plant committees integrating local operational powers; the reestablishment of the old labor unions; the spontaneous emergence of the soviet organ, the Military Revolutionary Committee and its wielding of power; as well as the emergence of a whole network of revolutionary committees.[64]

Since the Provisional Government had not been able to solve either the agrarian question—which was an issue of life and death for tens of millions—or exit from world war since March 1917, October saw the simultaneous uprising of a wide variety of insurgent forces making up a revolutionary camp composed of a series of stratum.

The first of these consisted of the industrial laborers in Moscow and St. Petersburg. They were functionally the product of the coexistence of modern and archaic conditions, having preserved numerous elements of their past in the village community insofar as their origins, living conditions, and ways of thinking were concerned. Their rebellion found expression in the independent functioning and internal structure of the spontaneously established soviets and workers' councils, and integration in even the most modern, well-organized social democratic workers' movement.[65]

The second stratum of the revolutionary camp was composed of the essentially conservative "past-bound" anticapitalist peasantry. These *obschinas* desired to acquire land by prohibiting the sale of land in order to put a stop to future poverty. Their rebellious aims found a voice in the famous land decrees of the October Revolution.

These two strata were further connected by the third main "stratum" of the revolution, a mass of armed soldiers numbering in the millions, who were mainly of peasant stock but had "seen the world." Historically speaking, the practical issues current in the period after the October Revolution had little in common with the theory of socialism, and more to do with all that was said in the *April Theses* and the post-October conception and practice of—to use a modern phrase—a "mixed market economy" in the beginning of 1918. Włodzimierz Brus and László Szamuely, followed by Soviet historians, established this decades ago, and became the first to theoretically ground the *transitional period* and consider it socialism under the premises of "Socialist Market Economy"—in the footsteps of Stalin.[66] The exaggeration of the "post-analogy" on ideological grounds, as a "part of socialism," also paved the way for an interpretation of this work by Lenin as an authoritarian.

Reading these *April Theses*,[67] we see that Lenin's point of view grew more differentiated under the influence of events unfolding in course of the revolution. Earlier, he had clarified that in Russia the bourgeois revolution could also only be a workers' revolution, for there existed no revolutionary, democratic bourgeoisie. Thus, the "driving force" of the laborer and poor peasant social base inevitably radicalized the bourgeois revolution, tipping it over into a phase in which the soviets might have a decisive role. Since the Provisional Government did not even broach the subject of quitting the war, and there were no signs that the participation of the soviets dominated by a Menshevik-S.R. majority could change the policies of the government "for the better," Lenin came up with a slogan, initially opposed even in his own party ranks: "No support for the Provisional Government." Lenin's position on—to paraphrase Trotsky—the "permanence" of the revolution gained theoretical foundations with his exploration of interweaving democratic and socialist "phases" in the light of the given, concrete conditions.

A new element that concerned the world war was also under consideration. The Provisional Government's demand for "revolutionary defensism" was discarded by Lenin, though in the process he outlined the concrete possibilities of the slogan as a transformation of the revolutionary process, which gained significance later during the armed interventions abroad:

> The class-conscious proletariat can give its consent to a revolutionary war, which would really justify revolutionary defensism, only on condition: (a)

> that the power pass to the proletariat and the poorest sections of the peasants aligned with the proletariat; (b) that all annexations be renounced in deed and not in word; (c) that a complete break be effected in actual fact with all capitalist interests. . . . The specific feature of the present situation in Russia is that the country is *passing* from the first stage of the revolution—which, owing to the insufficient class-consciousness and organization of the proletariat, placed power in the hands of the bourgeoisie—to its *second stage*, which must place power in the hands of the proletariat and the poorest sections of the peasants.[68]

While propelling the revolution in this direction, Lenin named the Soviet of Workers' Deputies "the *only possible* form of revolutionary government." He postulated this in thesis no. 5 of the *April Theses*, as the alternative to the bourgeois republic: "Not a parliamentary republic—to return to a parliamentary republic from the Soviets of Workers' Deputies would be a retrograde step—but a republic of Soviets of Workers,' Agricultural Labourers' and Peasants' Deputies throughout the country, from top to bottom."[69]

Any interpretation that suggests or claims that Lenin's thought and political actions in 1917 were dictated by some sort of authoritarian conceptualization of power and revolution cannot rest on documentary proof. Lenin spoke not only about the direct forms of workers' rule, as opposed to the bourgeois republic, but also distanced himself from the tradition of *state socialism*, that is, the "introduction of socialism" by means of state power. He spoke about the "commune-state," and, in thesis no. 8, about how "it is not our *immediate* task to 'introduce' socialism, but only to bring social production and the distribution of products at once under the *control* of the Soviets of Workers' Deputies." Among the main tasks of this program he mentioned the unification of all the banks "into a single national bank, and the institution of control over it by the Soviet of Workers' Deputies."[70] (The "post office analogy" fits into this context.) In order to ensure that power remained firmly in the hands of the soviets and won the support of the poor peasantry as well as the landless agrarian proletariat, he planned the confiscation of land from the landed gentry by way of immediate nationalization, so it could be redistributed under the supervision of the peasant soviets. This was put into writing by the October land decree.

The emphasis in the *April Theses* was already on cooperative agriculture.[71] This work was a turning point in Lenin's career, and signaled a turning point in the history of the revolution. It proved to be such a rare instance of foresight as to constitute a truly organic mold of theoretical analysis and political practice—a rare historical moment, which has a role in the historical context of *The State and Revolution*.

The *April Theses* defined the fundamental traits of the economic program in the supervision by laborers in industrial plants, in the soviet overseeing of trust companies, and in progressive taxation of income and property.[72] Apparently Lenin—in contrast to the commonplace statements and claims of much current historical literature—did not set out for the October Revolution with any kind of nationalizing or statist concept. The notion of *worker supervision*, borrowed from the anarchists, in itself clinches the argument where this is concerned.

A centralized postal system and the hierarchic restructuring of trusts in general must be seen as the "state capitalist" methods of the *transition* period rather than instant nationalization—which in fact did not take place until later, along with Communist military measures in the summer of 1918. This is the sense in which Lenin refers to the "planned operation" and methods of "accounting" in the economic institutions of the capitalist system as examples to be followed, as they are drawn organizationally into the scope of the workers' authority so that community interests gain prominence.[73] He could not have worked out more concrete ideas on economic policy for "indeterminable" historical-political situations at any earlier stage.

The Social Backdrop of the Revolution

Lenin and the Bolsheviks could not have taken their place at the helm of the revolutionary masses in October 1917 had they not been aware of the social backdrop of the revolution. This also explains a great deal about the immediate causes of the October turn of events. Lenin's genius is generally emphasized in his having taken the reins of power, as if he had been in possession of special abilities with regard to the "technocracy" of power. The image is one-sided, because it suggests that he "grabbed" the power he had long desired out of some sort of megalomaniacal sense of calling.

This simplistic presentation neglects the fact that Lenin theoretically worked through the difficult problem that a revolution in process cannot be halted as the political class struggle becomes increasingly radical. However, he also knew that its historical momentum unwinds the *revolutionary process*. That is, even if the Bolsheviks were wedged out, other radical political groups would take the lead with different consequences.

By the end of August 1917, Lenin had drafted the framework for the Decree on Land, adopted in October by the Second All-Russian Congress of Soviets. The decree was reminiscent of the Socialist-Revolutionary agrarian program, in that it showed that an overwhelming majority of peasants were just as opposed to capitalist ownership of land as they were to feudal large landholdings. In terms plainly understood by all, the decree aimed to unify the revolutions of the workers and peasants to contend with the old ruling classes:

> According to the summary, the peasant land demands are primarily abolition of private ownership of all types of land, including the peasants' lands, without compensation; transfer of lands on which high-standard scientific farming is practiced to the state or the communes; confiscation of all livestock and implements on the confiscated lands (peasants with little land are excluded) and their transfer to the state or the communes; a ban on wage-labor; equalized distribution of land among the working people, with periodical redistributions, and so on. In the transition period, pending the convocation of the Constituent Assembly, the peasants demand the *immediate* enactment of laws prohibiting the purchase and sale of land, abolition of laws concerning separation from the commune, farmsteads, etc. . . . You do not have to give these demands a lot of thought to see that it is absolutely impossible to realize them in alliance with the capitalists, without breaking completely with them, without waging the most determined and ruthless struggle against the capitalist class, without overthrowing its rule.[74]

This was probably the most succinct expression and practical actuation of the fact that a combination of two revolutions was unfolding: the revolution of the urban soviet and the peasant *obshchina* revolution. Lenin did not call the October Revolution a "worker-peasant revolution" by mere chance. It not only pointed to the spontaneous confiscations of land by peasants in the summer and autumn of 1917, but also to the fact that significant masses of peasants across the country had organized themselves in their own soviets as alternative seats of authority in opposition. The "revolution of peasant village communities" united with the proletarian revolution of the cities in October showed no signs of conflict, thereby strengthening the anticapitalist aspect of the revolution.

In the summer of 1917, the delegates at the first All-Russian Congress of Soviets represented over 20,300,000 persons, twenty times more than the number of party members. Of the more than 20 million people represented, nearly 6 million were workers, about 5 million were peasants, and over 9 million were soldiers (of whom two-thirds would have been peasants and land-tilling agrarian proletarians). The soviets' delegates were elected by this populace.[75] Millions were organized in what would now be called civil society organizations. People, awakened to consciousness of their freedom, gathered into groups categorized by the greatest possible variety of professions and interests. Unlike the parties, members of these civil organizations showed a wholly heterogeneous makeup, both in social and ideological terms. These organizations brought people with the most different intentions together, who later landed in quite dissimilar political camps as the revolutionary process progressed.

The party with the most members was that of the Socialist-Revolutionaries, counting 600,000 members in the summer of 1917. The Bolsheviks did not exceed 350,000 even in October 1917.[76] When Lenin expounded upon how unshakable the support base of the Bolsheviks was, he always did so in the way characteristic of the revolutionary period, by speaking of the support of the absolute majority within the *politically active* populace which then needed to draw the silent majority along with it.

In his September 1917 article "From a Publicist's Diary: The Mistakes of Our Party,"[77] he emphasized, "reference to the majority of the people decides nothing as far as the specific issues of a revolution are concerned." Laborers in large-scale industry always had a decisive role in shaping political "majority" in the revolution. Lenin used the terminology of *proletariat*, *labor*, and *workers* with three meanings: first, in the most narrow sense of the term, as the working force of large industry and plants; second, as those comprising the proletariat, inclusive of all wage workers; third, he extended the term to the "semi-proletarians," composed of agricultural laborers, servants, and the unemployed. The last of these definitions would have put the number of workers at 20 million in pre–First World War Russia.[78]

The number of those employed in large-scale industry in 1913, including rail and water transport, was 4,253,000.[79] This was no more than 10 to 12 percent of the population, even counting family members dependent on those employed. Lenin was aware of this fact. If the hundreds of thousands of laborers working in the smaller industries are also included, the number of industrial laborers (counting family) still did not exceed 7.2 million—of which 48.4 percent were women and children—in 1917. If all orders of urban laborers are taken into account, the head count of the proletariat as a whole was approximately 10.7 million persons in 1917.[80] Thus, the number of people receptive to social democratic principles, as Lenin would point out a number of times in the coming years, was a rather narrow stratum even well after the reins of revolution had been seized. But this stratum's high level of organization, as later events would prove, could not be overestimated.

The "army revolution" should be considered a special contingent of the workers' and peasants' revolution, since from February onward, millions of armed peasants and workers were on the attack against the old order in all its forms—the feudal prerogatives, the institutions of the old state, the social status and privileges of the large landholding classes, and the officers' caste. Lenin thought that the "flower of the people's forces" were in the army, and that "by October–November 1917, the armed forces were *half Bolshevik*."[81] The revolutionary fervor that swept through Russia maintained the social unity of these different revolutionary strata against the old order until the spring of 1918.[82] The takeover of the regime in Russia continued in the way it was "foreseen" because the old system suffered paralysis in almost every facet of its social life. The revolutionary forces had taken action at a psychological moment when any kind of alternative would be devastating to tens of millions of people. Yet, in spite of the obvious symptoms of a capitalist system crash, the chances of an international revolution appeared increasingly untenable in the spring of 1918.[83]

Assuming Power

The language, key terms, rhetoric, and theoretical characteristics of *The State and Revolution* cropped up in the letters Lenin wrote to the members of the Central Committee when he was in hiding. These were analyses and instructions of a political and organizational nature that encouraged implementation of an armed uprising and the seizure of power. Lenin's work was thus bound up in the practical implementation of the political revolution and was an organic part of it.

In effect, the work summed up the conceptual grounds of Lenin's thought with regard to the future, but at the same time left a deep mark on the documents and articles as well as the coherence of the instructions. The theoretical concepts of *The State and Revolution* remained an active part of Lenin's vocabulary, even much later. All this—surprisingly perhaps—did not challenge its practical and tactical flexibility.

Two basic thoughts were interwoven in Lenin's political analysis and his practical political recommendations, as reflected in his article of 16 September, "The Russian Revolution and Civil War: They Are Trying to Frighten Us with Civil War." First, he contended that *political polarization* goes on incessantly, as the revolutionary outbursts of the "July days" showed. With the Kornilov revolt "supported by the landowners and capitalists led by the Kadet Party" the civil war had "actually begun." The other thought was that the Socialist-Revolutionary and Menshevik leadership, which sought a deal with the bourgeoisie, was bound to continue vacillating. This would mean that the old state apparatus would stay, no peace would be offered, and the landed estates would not be confiscated.

Lenin speculated that the "vacillation" of the Mensheviks and the Socialist-Revolutionaries would only isolate them further from the masses, and that indignation would increase and result in "a tremendous growth of sympathy with the revolutionary proletariat, with the Bolsheviks." However, the "*peaceful development*" of the revolution, as Lenin understood it, depended on whether the "vacillating" Mensheviks and Socialist-Revolutionaries would join in taking the revolution further. Only when his hopes for such a conclusion had finally evaporated did Lenin decide upon immediately "tuning up" the revolution and seizing power, to draw in some of the vacillators as well.

> If the proletariat gains power it will have every chance of retaining it and of leading Russia until there is a victorious revolution in the West. . . . History will not forgive us if we do not assume power now. There is no apparatus? There *is* an apparatus—the soviets and the democratic organizations. The international situation *right* now, on *the eve* of the conclusion of a separate peace between the British and the Germans, is *in our favor.* To propose peace to the nations right now means *to win.* By taking power both in Moscow and in Petrograd *at once* (it doesn't matter which comes first, Moscow may possibly begin), we shall win *absolutely and unquestionably.*[84]

Lenin had a complete design for the armed uprising by the end of September, which he distinguished—distancing it from the putschist, Blanquist approach in the process—with two fundamental attributes: (1) insurrection is an art and "must rely not upon conspiracy and not upon a party, but upon the advanced class" and its spontaneous organizations, as expressed in the slogan "Power to the Soviets!"; (2) the insurrection must be executed "when the activity of the advanced ranks of the people is at its height, and when the vacillations in the ranks of the enemy and *in the ranks of the weak, half-hearted and irresolute friends of the revolution* are strongest." The revolution can then be fought successfully.[85]

Lenin's letters to the Central Committee urge the immediate start of the revolution upon his recognition of *the exceptional nature* of this historical situation:

> Together with the Left Socialist-Revolutionaries we have an *obvious* majority *in the country.* . . . The Bolsheviks have no right to wait for the Congress of Soviets, they must *take power at once.* By so doing they will save the world revolution . . . the Russian revolution (otherwise a wave of real anarchy may become stronger *than we are*). . . . The slogan is: Power to the Soviets, Land to the Peasants, Peace to the Nations, Bread to the Starving! Victory is certain, and the chances are ten to one that it will be a bloodless victory. To wait would be a crime to the revolution.[86]

These letters, which were called upon to illuminate Lenin's political genius in the old days, and are today used to serve as evidence of some sort of manic thirst for power,[87] do not in fact deal solely with the insurrection. Lenin situated the takeover of power not only in the context of current social-political realities, or the concrete political state of affairs that unseated the liberal experiments at management of power between February and October 1917, but also in a historical and theoretical dimension. The soviet forms of self-government outlined in *The State and Revolution*, the institutional system of direct democracy "recognized" by the Bolsheviks in the spontaneously organized base of power, stood ready to defend the revolution in the aftermath of a victorious conclusion of the insurrection.

The argument of the *Letters of October* was built on a recognition of the historical correlation that the structures and institutions of labor self-organization would only be able to carry out their "historical purpose" if an organizationally focused political force could shape the disparate wills represented until—as presumed—the institutional system of labor democracy was consolidated. In reality, the greater the role of the party, the less the role of the labor self-governments mattered. Lenin was sensitive to the fact that the labor organizations would be limited in the scope of their functions, and the significance of these limitations was tied to the extent to which the Russian revolutionary experiment remained alone in the international context.

Yet there seemed no turning back, as the revolution's liberal or anarchist line of development each seemed a cul-de-sac; neither would be able to defend itself and the revolution in the face of the counterrevolution. Therefore, the political proviso of success was the ability of Bolshevism to preserve its social base. Its strategy would be in vain without the support of the millions of massed workers and poor peasants. The enemy to be fought was a "militarily well-organized counterrevolution" and there was no other option for the defense of the revolution.[88]

No doubt, whatever the real political alternatives were on the day that followed the successful insurgency, it was no longer the "philosophical" main issue of *The State and Revolution* that—in essence—made it to the *functional* agenda. No debates on what the self-governing system of a future socialism *should be* ensued. The primary, practical question of the day was the military and political self-defense of the "dictatorship of the proletariat," for the restoration of "despotic capitalism" had to be averted at all costs.

It is much more likely, of course, that even in small states socialism will *not* be achieved without civil war, and for that reason the *only* program of international Social-Democracy must be recognition of civil war, though violence is, of course, alien to our ideals.

—V. I LENIN, *A CARICATURE OF MARXISM AND IMPERIALIST ECONOMISM*, LCW, VOL. 23, 69

Constitutional illusions are what we call a political error when people believe in the existence of a normal, juridical, orderly and legalized—in short, "constitutional"—system, although it does not really exist. At first glance it may appear that in Russia today, July 1917, when no constitution has yet been drafted, there can be no question of constitutional illusions arising. But it would be very wrong to think so. In reality, the essential characteristic of the present political situation in Russia is that an extremely large number of people entertain constitutional illusions.

—V. I. LENIN, *CONSTITUTIONAL ILLUSIONS*, LCW, VOL. 25, 196

6

Dictatorship and Democracy in Practice

THE DISSOLUTION OF THE ALL-RUSSIA CONSTITUENT ASSEMBLY

Democratic Illusion or Historical Actuality?

THE RSDLP AND LENIN HAD always acknowledged the necessity of convening the Constituent Assembly as a part of what would be the minimal program for a bourgeois democratic transformation. However, historical circumstances quickly bypassed the "democratic phase" in the aftermath of the February Revolution, and Lenin's political stance changed accordingly. Despite this, convening the Constituent Assembly was not expressly rejected even in *State and Revolution*, since objections were to be expected from all political parties. Nonetheless he had serious reservations about such a convention well in advance of October. As the second epigraph for this chapter demonstrates, his political evaluation of the Constituent Assembly was that a bourgeois democratic system in Russia was illusory. After February 1917, rather than thinking in terms of a bourgeois democratic regime that had degenerated into Bonapartism, Lenin had in mind a "proletarian self-government" (commune) that would follow the revolutionary period. Finally, Lenin tried to reconcile the elections of the Constituent Assembly and the declared aims of the socialist revolution on a moral and political plane.[1] Unlike a majority of Mensheviks, following the July days, Lenin considered the Constituent Assembly a sort of convent of soviets, which would in the final run embody the power of the soviets, perhaps becoming the topmost soviet. Meanwhile, he did not suppose even for a moment that the Constituent Assembly could avoid the fate of the "Frankfurt talking shop"[2] or the first Duma without a revolution. To avoid this, it must "be a Convention, it must have the courage, the capacity and the strength to strike merciless blows at the counterrevolutionaries instead of compromising with them." In his *Constitutional Illusions* article, sent to the press at the end of July while in hiding, he defined the political stances regarding the Constituent Assembly: "petit bourgeois S.R.-Menshevik," "Bolshevik proletarian," and "bourgeois," thus focusing the whole issue on concrete political class struggle:

> From the very beginning of the revolution there have been two views on the Constituent Assembly. The Socialist-Revolutionaries and Mensheviks, completely swayed by constitutional illusions, viewed the matter with the credulity of the petite bourgeoisie who will not hear of the class struggle: the Constituent Assembly has been proclaimed, there will be a Constituent Assembly and that's all there is to it! Everything else is of the devil's making. Meanwhile the Bolsheviks said: only the growing strength and authority of the Soviets can guarantee the convocation and success of the Constituent Assembly. The Mensheviks and Socialist-Revolutionaries laid emphasis on the act of law: the proclamation, the promise, the declaration to call a Constituent Assembly. The Bolsheviks laid emphasis on the class struggle: if the Soviets were to win, the Constituent Assembly would be certain to meet; if not, there would be no such certainty. That is exactly what happened. The bourgeoisie have all along been waging, both in the open and undercover, a continuous and relentless struggle against calling a Constituent Assembly.[3]

In Lenin's perspective, each subject's moral, political, and legal aspect had a different implication than had the issue as a whole. October did not change Lenin's position: soviet power required the Constituent Assembly—in principle. Only the political situation, the balance of forces in the political and class struggle, had changed. It could not have been said, even in January of 1918, that the "power of the soviets had been consolidated," and so unsurprisingly in the summer of 1917 this was the crucial question.

When the balance of forces changed in favor of the Bolsheviks at the end of August, Lenin once again presumed this to be a means for the "peaceful development" of the revolution, and declared the slogan: "All power to the soviets!" This course would still have room for the Constituent Assembly, as Lenin could still consider some sort of compromise with "petit-bourgeois democracy": "The compromise on our part is our return to the pre-July demand of all power to the Soviets and a government of S.R.s and Mensheviks responsible to the Soviets."[4]

This possibility of a compromise did not materialize, and "petit-bourgeois democracy" was not able to hold its own. In the so-called Pre-Parliament (the establishment of which Lenin termed, in free association with Marx, "sheer parliamentary cretinism") the parties categorically rejected Lenin's offer of compromise. As he wrote in a letter to Ivan Smilga, shortly before the beginning of the insurrection, with the hope of a successful takeover of power, Lenin was actually optimistic about the elections for the Constituent Assembly—inasmuch as he assumed at the time that together with the S.R.s a majority could be achieved: "Your situation is exceptionally good because you are in a position to *begin* immediately to form that bloc with the Left Socialist-Revolutionaries which alone can give us stable power in Russia and a majority in the Constituent Assembly."[5]

This is the context for Lenin's stance regarding the Constituent Assembly, even after the October insurrection. In the course of analysis it becomes clear that no radical break, no change in principle, is in evidence where his judgment of the question is concerned.

Debates and Mock-Debates, in New and Old Historiography

It must be noted that the way this subject is approached has undergone a transformation in the literature of modern historical studies. Since the collapse of the Soviet Union in 1991, a trend among ex-Soviet historians, now loyal to the West, has made a "presentist" turn by seeking to portray the history of the Constituent Assembly as a condition of (re)accession to Western parliamentarianism, the sole progressive (political) civilization.[6] The nationalist-patriotic conservative officialdom of Slavophile inspiration declaimed a return to "original Russian values," "organic nationalism," and the "organic national development of Russia." Thus the liberal historical analyses chose to exaggerate the possibility of a Western-style parliamentarianism in the period preceding the October Revolution, while the Slavophile conservatives saw the Constituent Assembly as a manifestation of the *distinguishing features of Russia*. The trend in the hard-set "national communist" camp, on the other hand, saw the dispersal of the Constituent Assembly as a means of stemming the spread of the disease of Westernization, as part of the natural path of the Russian Revolution.[7] In fact, this last interpretation represents the traditional conceptualization by Soviet historiography, which was cloaked in a particularly romantic-nationalistic, statist ideology. Perhaps the excellent Soviet historian O. N. Znamensky,[8] who recently passed away, only attributed historical interest in the Constituent Assembly in his works of 1970–1980[9] because the roots of bourgeois democracy had proved weak, unsustaining, and the revolution had only given form to these latent forces. The dispersal of the Assembly was not an action dissonant with this circumstance.

Two questions became mixed up: *why the Bolsheviks dispersed the Constituent Assembly* was conflated with *why they were able to do so* in the first place. Though the distinction of objective and subjective elements is perhaps the most difficult theoretical task of historiography, attention to this methodological requirement in the textual composition would be advisable. To cite organic historical development in the given context is pure ideological generalization. No doubt the eternal ideals of transformations in world history have many lives, and turn up in all regions of the earth where (wielded within circles of quite contrasting social forces) the real or latent possibility of their realization arises. The idea of constitutionalism had no need of introduction in Russia, as its medieval and later versions—from the zemsky sobor to the Duma—are widely known. But what were, or would have been, the means for this line of development to fit into the Western European, bourgeois concept of constitutional assembly? What organic process and linearity could be assumed of such a development? This approach simply does not take into account the fundamental differences between the social and cultural history of these two constitutional traditions. After all, the constitution-building movement within the ruling classes of Russia meant something wholly different (such as another type of monarchy) than the "modern" constituent assemblies and parliaments brought into being through general and secret ballot in the French or American revolutions, or matured by the capitalist development of England. It would be difficult to find even one social group in Russia that would have represented such a form of revolutionary constitution-building. As it has been repeatedly argued, even in the period under examination, many Russians had recognized their country's development was in a radically different position from that of France or the United States, in terms of its concrete political conditions and its sociohistorical foundations, as well as in the structure of society. This has peculiar significance today, when the social sciences are so hard pushed to satisfy the demands of universality and systems thinking[10]—which, incidentally, Lenin had a curious affinity for.

The question remains regarding what social and political system the All-Russian Constituent Assembly can be identified as a part of. The assembly's life was short and miserable: convened on the afternoon of 5 January in the Tauride Palace in Petrograd, it was dispersed by the captain of the guard, sailor Zheleznakov—on the orders of Lenin and the Bolshevik leadership—at dawn on 6 January 1918, with the explanation that the guard was tired. Its significance is not marginal from the aspect of the new order. The definition of the type of system it would be was not fully clear at the time. Not even the revolutionary leaders themselves really believed that the revolutionary grip on power, in Russia alone, could hold out for longer than a few months. When a definition was needed, they compared the system they had yet-so-far constituted with the Paris Commune. It has been the fashion in Eastern European Marxist historiography (perhaps most prominently in Hungary, East Germany, and the Soviet Union) to periodically give exact definitions to the economic and political systems, and then to engage in long-drawn-out debates about these definitions. While raging debates about the nature of the Stalinist system have become commonplace, it is not a specifically Russian trait; one need look no further than Hungary to find that historians have debated the character of the Horthy system for over four decades now, with no end in sight. Whatever the reasons, it is certain that the angles of new research are once again growing wider, due to the application of the comparative method.[11] Hungarian historiography also continues its polemics with regard to the historical precedents of current parliamentarianism in Eastern Europe, and particularly in relation to the historical character of the Horthy system.[12]

The renewal of interest in the problem of parliamentarianism cannot be disassociated from the great political transformation of 1989. This turn located the parliament, and the institution of parliamentarianism, at the center of the political system's functioning. It is therefore not surprising if now the historical role of parliamentarianism is being exaggerated in a presentist manner. This highly simplistic—and therefore popularly accepted—unscientific approach serves political-legitimist demands. It only sees two political systems as existing: parliamentarianism (democracy) and dictatorship (one-party system). A veil seems to have been drawn over the fact that both dictatorial and parliamentary systems have taken various historical forms (with a wide variety of social and political content and function), and that apart from democracies and dictatorships, other political systems have existed, especially in Eastern Europe. In other words, it is often forgotten that parliaments can operate within the frameworks of a variety of dictatorships, or may exist extraneously to a state that is neither a democracy nor a dictatorship.[13] (As seen in the pages of *State and Revolution*, Lenin was chagrined to hear of "democracy" and "dictatorship" being spoken of in general, when the terms were considered apart from their concrete political content, or concrete social-sociological and economic determining factors.)

The history of the Russian Revolution also provides an empirical example of how, with the revival of the soviets in 1905, at least for a short time a regime of direct democracy led beyond the traditional democracy-dictatorship opposition—both in principle and practice. However, it is wholly ahistorical to measure the regime of the soviets that came to power in 1917, and the actions taken by the revolutionary political forces and representatives that embodied them, against the standards set by a bourgeois constituent assembly. It would similarly be just as mistaken to believe that the people wanted Bolshevik rule.[14] For in principle the revolutionary system operated as a form of labor self-government, dealing with problems fundamental and doctrinal as well as operational, which the revolutionary democracy of the period resolutely faced. The phenomenon under examination must therefore be analyzed from a perspective resting on its own logic, framework, options, functions, concepts, and objectives. Such a critical analysis was completed as early as 1918 by Rosa Luxemburg in her famous work about the Russian Revolution, which was promptly buried by the Stalinist system (the first publication in Hungarian only appeared in the 1980s).[15] Whether right or wrong in any particular aspect, Luxemburg's analysis is interesting because its criticism is historical: she tried to evaluate and judge the revolution and the Bolsheviks in the context of their own premises and goals.

The Historical Setting

The "Judicial Council," authorized by the Provisional Government, began its work in the spring of 1917 and became known for the contributions from many famous liberal scientists, among them N. I. Lazarevsky, V. M. Gessen, V. F. Deryuzhinsky, and B. E. Nolde. This committee put into effect the legislative preparations for the Constituent Assembly, during which it became amply clear that regulation by law was considered a decisive matter by the "bourgeois-democratic powers" as a legal legitimization of their authority.[16] This was also reflected by the legal document decreeing the opening of the Constituent Assembly, which treated it as the "organizer of the highest executive body" self-evidentially, as if the Central Executive Committee of the Soviets did not exist.[17] In drafting the laws, the subdivision of the subjects also showed that all powers were to be concentrated in the hands of the Constituent Assembly, and the soviets were not even mentioned as a possible source of power. The documents only considered representative terms for the management of power and did not refer to the possibility of direct democracy. It is true, however, that they did not plan to leave land in private hands. The majority supported the S.R. concept, which regulated the distribution of land—on the recommendation of the Constituent Assembly—but did not regulate its capitalization. (The S.R. concept was also adopted by the Bolsheviks, who proceeded with its implementation.) However, an immediate exit from the war was not mentioned in the proposal, even though the highest seat of authority, the Second Congress of Soviets, had declared this in an individual decree.

Nevertheless, the elections were held normally, even if the voting masses were not clear about the power staked on their ballots. It did not bode well that Lenin came under fire from the guns of unidentified would-be assassins on 1 January 1918. Though the culprits were never apprehended, the assumption was that some members of the S.R. Party, which had a majority in the Constituent Assembly, were behind the assassination attempt. Lenin went to special lengths—justified no less by tactical considerations—to avoid any violent confrontation with the delegates. Evidence of this can be found in a dispatch he sent to the Red Guard Headquarters on 3 (16) January 1918, in which "the Council of People's Commissars orders the corps of the Red Guard Headquarters to issue thirty (30) revolvers specially for the defense of the Tauride Palace," needed also because the S.R.s were organizing a demonstration in the city. Chernov, the leader of the party, later said the demonstration was intended to morally shame the Bolsheviks[18]—not a wise decision in retrospect. The reasons for firing on the protesters heading for the Tauride Palace are contradictory, and the circumstances are unascertainable.[19] Multiple sources confirm twelve dead in the course of events. An order Lenin sent on the night of 5–6 January, as the Constituent Assembly was in session (that is, an order sent as chairman of the Council of the People's Commissariat), showed his intention to avoid further violence: "The soldier and sailor comrades on guard duty within the precincts of the Tauride Palace are instructed not to allow any violence toward the counterrevolutionary part of the Constituent Assembly and, while permitting all to freely leave the Tauride Palace, not to let anyone in without special orders."[20] A telephone message Lenin sent to the People's Commissariat of Justice on 7 January (which appeared in *Pravda* on 8 January) gives voice to Lenin's indignation at the murder of two ministers of the Provisional Government: "I have just received a report that last night sailors entered the Mariinskaya hospital and killed Shingaryov and Kokoshkin. I order you immediately: first, to begin a rigorous investigation; second, to arrest the sailors guilty of this murder."[21] It was for tactical reasons that Lenin and the Bolshevik leaders had broken up the demonstration—they were trying to prevent the spread of violence, which was connected to a number of other factors that signaled the growing breadth and intensity of the emergency situation.

During these days, Lenin was trying to solve a fundamental problem: How Petrograd could avoid famine. The Provisional Government could not address this through the "democratic" means at its disposal. The Soviet government and the Council of People's Commissars took up where the previous government had left off: governing by way of decrees, as emergency measures seemed the most effective. There was simply no time, for example, to regulate and draw up the legal terms for the distribution of firearms, and perhaps the matter was not given much importance, as armed Red Guards were required for the defense of the trains carrying wheat.[22] This sort of social backdrop not only accepted violent force, but applied it in defense of the revolution; it was always understood either as a reply to past, truly grave suffering or to counterrevolutionary violence.[23] Contrary to considerations in fashion today, the role of Lenin and the Council of People's Commissars in the explosion of violence should not be overrated; later conditions should not be projected back upon the period of 1917–18. It was the circumstance that Bolshevik leaders (and of course the leaders of the counterrevolutionary organizations) were not in possession of satisfactory information about the actual tendencies of events and processes that played a real role in the proliferation of violence.

The great national idea, the demand for the Constituent Assembly, captured almost all the significant political forces at some time or another (always during revolutionary periods, or at least periods of crisis), though they speculated on different outcomes. A significant proportion of peasants desired the creation of a constitution in the spirit of village community tradition, directly enacted by the people and circumventing the state, manifestations of which can be observed in peasant land occupations. The left wing of social democracy attributed the role of the revolutionary convention to it, as in Lenin's case, while others perceived it as an instrument of transformation, either bourgeois or of some socialist kind; the S.R.s and Mensheviks, moreover, were internally divided on the question of the assembly. So, for example, at the turn of 1917–18 the Mensheviks saw the highest form of authority in the Constituent Assembly, and Julius Martov was of the opinion that the soviets should not be hardened in their opposition to the Constituent Assembly.[24] He was also aware that the only role the Constituent Assembly could have at that moment was as a bourgeois democratic institution that had not put down strong roots in the deeper regions of social thought (and behavior). Few could understand its function—it reminded most people only of the old gentlemen of the past regime—in contrast to the soviets, which were seen as the people's organizations.

Prior to October, every important political force—with perhaps the sole exception of the Black Hundreds—demanded elections for the Constituent Assembly.[25] Each related to it differently in tactical terms, but finally an understanding was reached.[26] Curiously, the elections caused the greatest surprise among the Social Democrats. The Mensheviks suffered the biggest disappointment, receiving just 2 percent of the votes, which meant twenty of the 765 delegates. The Bolsheviks were even more disappointed, perhaps because they were not thinking in terms of sharing power. At the same time they were in an advantageous position from the point of view of holding on to power and dissolving the assembly, because they had a substantial majority in the major cities and the armed services.[27] The Bolsheviks took 24 percent (nearly 11 million) of the votes, but the S.R.s were the comfortable winners with over 19 million votes and good outlooks for coalition, for besides the Bolsheviks, no other party accepted the concept and practice of the "dictatorship of the proletariat."

In September 1917, in the interest of a peaceful development of the revolution, Lenin was still in favor of as wide a political alliance as possible in the face of the right-wing, bourgeois alternative. Fifty-two days prior to the October Revolution, Lenin made an offer to create this coalition:

> The compromise on our part is our return to the pre-July demand of all power to the Soviets and a government of S.R.s and Mensheviks responsible to the Soviets. . . . In all probability it could secure the peaceful advance of the whole Russian revolution, and provide exceptionally good chances for great strides in the world movement toward peace and the victory of socialism. In my opinion, the Bolsheviks, who are partisans of world revolution and revolutionary methods, may and should consent to this compromise only for the sake of the revolution's peaceful development—an opportunity that is extremely rare in history and extremely valuable, an opportunity that only occurs once in a while. The compromise would amount to the following: the Bolsheviks, without making any claim to participate in the government . . . would refrain from demanding the immediate transfer of power to the proletariat and the poor peasants and from employing revolutionary methods of fighting for this demand.[28]

Hardly was the article finished than Lenin admitted that his proposed compromise had lost its meaning. After reading the weekend papers, he declared his proposal belated if Kerensky stepped out of the S.R. Party and linked the petit-bourgeois democracy to the bourgeoisie. "All that remains is to send these notes to the editor with the request to have them entitled: 'Belated Thoughts.' Perhaps even belated thoughts are sometimes not without interest."[29] Nevertheless, negotiations about such an alliance—the formation of a "homogenous socialist government"—did begin later. It was soon clear that, even after October 1917, the S.R.-Menshevik camp, with the participation of the Vikzhel—the Railwaymen's Trade Union, under whose aegis the negotiations were conducted—had not accepted what was by then the revolutionary platform, composed of the fundamental decrees of soviet rule on immediate (annexation and restitution-free) peace and land, and agrarian reform.[30] By the time of the creation of the new government, the Council of People's Commissars, Lenin was unrelenting in the matter of the coalition, in spite of the protests of a number of Bolshevik leaders (among them Kamenev and Nogin). Lenin said that a revolutionary government that could not take collective steps even in the most basic questions was doomed to failure.

Only the Bolsheviks and the left-wing S.R.s admitted in the Constituent Assembly that they could not find a way out of the given situation without resorting to dictatorship. Between 1918 and 1921 there was no political force in Russia that would not have tried to stabilize the situation and its position through dictatorial measures were they to ascend to power, or do what would have been its equivalent, create the order appropriate to their different approach.[31] Whichever political force was pushed into opposition, it immediately protested vis-à-vis the dictatorship, demonstrating the objective logic of preserving power: "The circles in power introduced the state of emergency lacking any social grounds, but as a matter of a highly conscious measure to hold on to their powers."[32] It should not be forgotten that the quick polarization of political forces had begun early, in the aftermath of the revolution of February 1917, and that through the summer and autumn, almost every news source prophesied civil war and dictatorship. By April the right wing, including the Kadet Party—and, further to the right, the army officers' corps—had begun their "search for the dictator" in order to discipline the "revolutionary chaos" (in fact, starting at the beginning of April, according to Denikin's memoirs, *Ocherky russkoy smuti*). Finally, the financiers' circle settled on General Kornilov, though even then the name of Kolchak, the Siberian dictator-to-be, was in the pool of candidates.[33]

The Viewpoints of Lenin and the Bolsheviks

The 2nd All-Russia Congress of Soviets, held on 25 October 1917—and accompanied by the walkout of the Mensheviks—concentrated the highest powers in the hands of the Congress of Soviets and the Central Executive Committee it elected, which were the institutions that the new Soviet government, the Council of People's Commissars, would report and be answerable to. Right after the takeover in October, an essential attribute of direct democracy, the right to revoke delegates, was legalized;[34] this was intended to radicalize representative democracy in the preparations leading up to the elections. While they considered the issue of power decisive, this followed not only from their theoretical and moral positions, but also from the concrete historical situation, which determined the opening, proceedings, and fate of the Constituent Assembly to a major degree. These matters were expressed unequivocally in the Council of People's Commissars announcement on 28 November, which stated that "across the Urals and the Don Region, Kornilov, Kaledin and Dutov have raised the flags of civil war against the Soviets."[35] The Kadet Party, under the leadership of Miliukov, was considered—not without grounds—the main strength of the politically organized counterrevolution; the party was declared an "enemy of the people" and made illegal, on the argument that it was an emergency situation.[36] (The armed and political counterrevolution had become joined even before October, and the legal differences of their separation are not worth bringing up item-by-item, as far more important issues still could not be regulated legally.)

In light of these facts it is apparent that the dissolution of the Constituent Assembly hung in the air, foreshadowed by the resolution of the Central Executive Committee of the Soviets brought on 22 December. On the one hand it subsumed every group of the political opposition, and on the other it convened the 3rd All-Russia Congress of Soviets for practically the same date as the Constituent Assembly:

> 5 January is the date designated for the opening of the Constituent Assembly. The openly and secretively counterrevolutionary parties, the Kadets, Mensheviks, right-wing S.R.s, the Kornilovists, and saboteur chinovniks have set out, and are hoping to transform the Constituent Assembly into a fort of the rich against the poor, a bastion of the propertied classes against the power of the workers and peasants.[37]

Meanwhile, the conditions set for the Constituent Assembly were such that it could not have complied; basically they were set to account for the functions carried out by the soviets:

> The counterrevolutionary elements without exception, all line up behind the slogan of "All power to the Constituent Assembly.". . . The Constituent Assembly can only play a beneficial role in the development of the Russian Revolution if it categorically and without any compunction takes the side of the working classes in opposition to the landlords and bourgeoisie, if it affirms the power of the soviets, the decrees concerning land, labor supervision, and the nationalization of banks, and supports the foreign policy of the soviets, which seeks to arrive at democratic peace at the earliest possible date.[38]

All of the above was given voice in the *Declaration of Rights of the Working and Exploited People,* written by Lenin and adopted by the Central Executive Committee on 3 January and by the Congress of Soviets on 8 January (though the document—which was later to gain constitutional status—was originally prepared for the Constituent Assembly).[39]

Indeed, the Judicial Council appointed by the Provisional Government would foresee that the issue of power could not be skirted. In principle, they should also have been aware that the Bolsheviks were not the first to tie the hands of the Constituent Assembly; the Provisional Government had already assumed its functions in September 1917, when it declared Russia a republic.[40]

The power conflict showed itself in the opening of the Constituent Assembly.[41] When the S. R. Lordkipanidze addressed those assembled from his seat, indicating that it was four o'clock and therefore time for the oldest delegate, and fellow S.R., Sergey Petrovich Shvetsov, to open the proceedings, the left-wing delegates and Bolshevik-minded public expressed their dissatisfaction with loud noise. Hardly had Shvetsov reached the pulpit and opened the assembly than the delayed member of the Bolshevik faction, Yakov Mihaylovich Sverdlov, arrived and took the opportunity to speak first, as chairman of the Central Executive Committee of the Soviets. In his speech he expressed his hope that the assembly recognized the power of the soviets, as well as all of its decrees, and would be of assistance to the soviets in sweeping all class privileges away once and for all. He went on to list the most important decrees and aims of the revolution in five points. Only after this did he let Lordkipanidze speak, an introduction that presented an opposite stance: "There is no power other than the power of the Constituent Assembly."[42]

The fate of the Constituent Assembly was already sealed following these events. No compromise offered itself. Prior to their walkout at the Constituent Assembly, the Bolshevik faction entrusted F. Raskolnikov (and Lobov) to present the following declaration:

> The overwhelming majority of the workers' Russia—workers, peasants, soldiers—demand that the Constituent Assembly recognizes the triumphs of the Great October Revolution, that is, the decrees concerning land, peace and labor supervision and above all, the power of the soviets delegated by the workers and the soldiers.[43]

With these demands unheeded, the palace guard dissolved the assembly at the break of dawn on 6 January.[44]

The statement pronouncing the assembly dissolved reemphasized Lenin's and the Bolsheviks' principled stance, which posited that "the old bourgeois parliamentarianism had outlived its purpose, and was absolutely incompatible with the aim of achieving socialism."[45] In other words, the principles of bourgeois parliamentarianism were irreconcilable with the system that came after the revolution, reflecting an actuality of power and politics. From that moment, the instruments of bourgeois parliamentarianism always came up as the tool of counterrevolution, their "technology for power," a system that in reality would provide only them with opportunity. To give this concrete shape, Lenin, in the third item of his "Draft Decree on the Dissolution of the Constituent Assembly," wrote:

> Not national institutions, but only class institutions (such as the Soviets) were capable of overcoming the resistance of the propertied classes and of laying the foundations of socialist society. To relinquish the sovereign power of the Soviets, to relinquish the Soviet Republic won by the people, for the sake of the bourgeois parliamentary system and the Constituent Assembly, would now be a step backwards and would cause the collapse of the October workers' and peasants' revolution.[46]

The draft decree named the Constituent Assembly responsible, on the grounds that it had defended the propertied classes while not recognizing the *Declaration of Rights of the Working and Exploited People*, and thus "severed all ties with the Soviet Republic of Russia."[47] Clearly the only Constituent Assembly the Bolsheviks could have tolerated was one that conformed to the power structure of soviet rule.[48]

The Anti-Regime Character of the Labor Protests

Lenin gradually examined the experiences of the historical situation from a theoretical and socialist perspective, "from case to case." But an irresolvable contradiction emerged at the earliest possible stage, and he initially did not react to it. While the direct democracy of *State and Revolution* found expression in party documents,[49] a not insignificant segment of labor felt victimized by the centralization of power as everyday conditions deteriorated and local, self-governing organizations were disempowered by the central administration. Yet they considered the workers' and peasants' soviets their *own* organizations, right from the start, and did not take them for the "upper-class humbug" usual to politics.[50] In the Kremlin, Lenin thought that two masters could be served at once, both the self-government of the soviets and the tendencies of centralization shown by powers at the center. The obvious contradiction was also precipitated by efforts directed toward limiting the threat of famine by having grain brought to the major cities, even though at the time this centralization may have merely seemed to be the result of the interim measures required to do so.

These circumstances were the backdrop to the burgeoning demonstrations by laborers in the capital of the revolution. Lenin and the Bolshevik Party had to determine their approach to the labor demonstrations. The problem of provisioning food—which the Mensheviks and S.R.s tried to use to their own political advantage, of course—also provided the main grounds for protests against the Bolsheviks.[51] The forces aligned against the Bolshevik government and the Council of People's Commissars recognized the key role of "overseeing the distribution of grain," which rather simplified the political struggle: "whoever has the grain, has power," as the popular dictum might go.

Even the sparse displays of solidarity with the Constituent Assembly were not signs of any great devotion to bourgeois democracy. In fact, emotional manifestations of nostalgia for the monarchy were more frequent.[52] The spontaneous labor protests in the plants in major cities, especially St. Petersburg—unlike Menshevik-influenced labor union demonstrations calling for a democratic republic—did not normally repeat the slogan of the Constituent Assembly but instead demanded operational freedom for labor self-government, which was often violated in the process of the revolutionary regime's gradual concentration of power. In the spring of 1918, a number of plants in St. Petersburg became involved in the "delegate movement," which stood up to the centralizing efforts of the Bolsheviks, who had no time to spare for finding a democratic consensus with the workers.[53] Soon the workers found themselves fighting their "own state."[54]

It is no coincidence that none of the anti-regime labor unrest was directed at the soviets (instead, the Bolsheviks were the chief target), and this includes the anti-Communist Kronstadt Rebellion of March 1921. The document signed by President Petrichenko and Secretary Tukin of the Provisional Revolutionary Committee (which represented the garrison) made a plea expressly for upholding the power of the soviets,[55] and claimed that in a country drawn to the brink of crisis by the Communist Party, a political solution could be found for the soviets after a secret ballot: "Don't listen to the stupid rumors that power in Kronstadt will fall to the hands of the generals and the Whites."[56] The White Guard propaganda also took account of these events while the civil war was in progress, and directed its ideological campaign not against the soviets as workers' organizations, but mostly at the Bolshevik Party—the regime of the homeless, godless, alien, and Jew. It should be noted that even in 1921, the labor protests unfolding in the period of the NEP's introduction rarely demanded the convening of the Constituent Assembly, for that belonged in the precinct of "high politics," and the masses were instinctively distrustful regarding this.[57]

All these facts supported the developments that Rosa Luxemburg had committed to paper in the autumn of 1918 in her critical appraisal[58] that the rule of the detached institutional system, formed over the heads of the laboring masses, was solidifying. The Bolshevik Party Program of 1919—essentially composed by Lenin—perceived the detached rule of the apparatus of power over society as a catastrophic threat to both direct democracy and the prospect of socialism, which should be avoided at all costs.[59] Characteristically, Fyodor Dan, a leading figure of the Menshevik Party in St. Petersburg, actually proposed this argument when he was arrested in April 1921, after the defeat of the Kronstadt Rebellion. In his open confession of 19 April, intended for a public interested in politics, his statement on the Constituent Assembly said:

> I consider it harmful, as a practical political slogan, for due to the mood of the vast masses of peasantry, which resulted mainly from the policies of the Bolshevik government, it is invested with anti-revolutionary, anti-socialist, and anti-worker sentiments and is apt at present to mold in one, all the forces of the counterrevolution under its banner.

The alternative outlined by Dan in reply to the questions of his interrogator put forward the reinstitution of labor self-government, as no other socialist concept existed:

> In the current situation, I think that in the interests of the workers and especially the proletariat it is important to preserve the soviet system, but ensuring that this system, in accord with its theory and the constitution, is truly the self-government of the workers, and does not serve merely as the shield of party dictatorship.[60]

In the final count, therefore, even that wing of Mensheviks who had kept a socialist perspective were not able in principle to point to a future course as an alternative to the party dictatorship that had evolved, other than that which the Bolsheviks themselves had formulated theoretically (that is, in the Party Program mentioned above) and on a constitutional-legislative level. Nonetheless, Dan warned Lenin and the Bolsheviks, with good reason obviously, about the "dangers of deprivation."

Rosa Luxemburg represented a "third way" in this question, between Lenin, Trotsky, and the Bolsheviks on the one hand, and Kautsky, along with the Social Democrats and Mensheviks, on the other—although taking a stand somewhat closer to the Bolsheviks. Whereas the "dictatorship of the proletariat" was pitted against workers' democracy in the actual politics of the Bolsheviks, the whole issue of class rule was simply left out of the Kautskyite approach to democracy. Luxemburg formulated her own critical position between these two bad solutions. In her view, "The Bolsheviks . . . won for themselves the imperishable historic distinction of having for the first time proclaimed the final aim of socialism as the direct program of practical politics," and they also "did not want to entrust, nor should they have entrusted, the fate of the revolution to an assemblage which reflected the Kerenskyan Russia of yesterday, of the period of vacillations and coalition with the bourgeoisie. Hence there was nothing left to do except to convoke an assembly that would issue forth out of the renewed Russia that had advanced so far." However, Luxemburg thought that while starting out from the right principles and politics, in everyday politics the Bolsheviks had resorted to measures that went against these, especially Lenin and Trotsky, who "from the special inadequacy of the Constituent Assembly which came together in October," drew "a general conclusion concerning the inadequacy of any popular representation whatsoever which might come from universal popular elections during the revolution." And this political stance, according to Luxemburg, was "expressly contradicted by the historical experience of every revolutionary epoch. According to Trotsky's theory, every elected assembly reflects once and for all only the mental composition, political maturity and mood of its electorate just at the moment when the latter goes to the polling place."[61]

In other words, the Bolsheviks underestimated representative democracy in a period when the operation of direct democracy itself came up against practical barriers. However, it must also be noted that Luxemburg's analysis underestimated both the way in which the system of extraordinary measures (*chrezvichaishchina*) was unavoidably dictated by, and innate to, the emergency situation of the civil war period, as well as the weak democratic tradition in Russia, which was only exacerbated by the instability of the soviet governments and party dictatorship in the face of the unfolding civil war. What the Bolsheviks did might well have been necessary to uphold any form of power.

All the same, the boundaries between extraordinary measures and socialist politics were erased in the politics of the Bolsheviks, as Luxemburg pointed out through the rather apt example of how the electoral rights of the bourgeoisie and the once landed gentry were curtailed:

> But, according to the interpretation of this dictatorship which Lenin and Trotsky represent, the right to vote is granted only to those who live by their own labor and is denied to everyone else. Now it is clear that such a right to vote has meaning only in a society which is in a position to make possible for all who want to work an adequate civilized life on the basis of one's own labor. . . . Under the terrific difficulties which Russia has to contend with, cut off as she is from the world market and from her most important source of raw materials, and under circumstances involving a terrific general uprooting of economic life and a rude overturn of production relationships as a result of the transformation of property relationships in land and industry and trade—under such circumstances, it is clear

> that countless existences are quite suddenly uprooted, derailed without any objective possibility of finding any employment for their labor power within the economic mechanism. This applies not only to the capitalist and landowning masses, but to the broad layer of the middle class also, and even to the working class itself. . . . Under such circumstances, a political right of suffrage on the basis of a general obligation to labor, is a quite incomprehensible measure.[62]

Rosa Luxemburg indicated a more potent, underlying contradiction when she foresaw the problem of the NEP period. At the same time that the Bolsheviks were stripping the capitalist class of its rights, they wanted to rent out the national industries, as first conceived in the spring of 1918, to the same class—who were its prior proprietors![63] In this sense, how the Bolsheviks related to the remnants of the bourgeois class influenced the way they related to the rest of the people, in that they did not apprehend the effect of the various measures they took, and the way these contradicted each other as well as their own principles. "It is a well-known and indisputable fact," wrote Luxemburg, "that without a free and untrammeled press, without the unlimited right of association and assemblage, the rule of the broad masses of the people is entirely unthinkable." This was the context of the German revolutionary theorist's oft-quoted and aphoristic words: "Freedom is always and exclusively freedom for the one who thinks differently."[64]

Naturally, it was not the will of Lenin or Trotsky that decided events in the end, but the civil war, economic isolation, the weakness of the push for democracy, the disintegration of a working class already low in numbers (and its rise to positions in the power apparatus as well as its "militarization"), and the devotion to violent solutions both at the top and bottom. The short-lived power of the assembly suffered its final demise while overseen by Kolchak in the summer of 1918 with the outbreak of civil war, though it had sworn allegiance to an anti-Bolshevik politics.[65] The ruins of the Constituent Assembly, acting under the ideological terms of pure democracy, was finally liquidated by the martial forces of the dictatorship of the generals with the drastic tools that comport civil war.[66]

Some authors vastly magnify the role of the Constituent Assembly of 1918, and, in the romantic vein, give it a positive spin.[67] If the Bolsheviks were appraised on the basis of their programs and fundamental revolutionary principles, all humanity would have marched through the gates of "communist heaven" (equality, justice, and a non-hierarchical society free of all exploitation and oppression, standing on the basis of direct democracy, etc.).[68] The analysis is complicated by the challenge of separating objective and subjective currents, a dilemma raised by Rosa Luxemburg in 1918, when she considered how difficult it was to establish where the story of the gradual institutional independence of dictatorship begins, and where the concentration of power dictated by historical imperative ends. Let there be no mistaking that the fate of the revolution hung by a "hair's breadth," between the "moment" and the "end goal" in the eyes of the revolutionaries of the age, who would not have had the luxury to exclude the possibility of historical regression either. In March 1918, when Lenin made the proposal to change the name to the Communist Party, he also added to the agenda reshaping of the party program:

> The most accurate and comprehensive definition possible of the new type of state, the Soviet Republic. . . . The Programme must show that our Party does not reject the use even of bourgeois parliamentarianism, should the course of the struggle push us back, for a time, to this historical stage which our revolution has now passed.[69]

At the time he outlined a concept for the soviets that harmonized, in part, with views expressed in *State and Revolution*, but did not as yet take account of the fact that the driving force (tens of millions of people, both literate and cultured), which could have operated an electoral system built from the ground upward, was exhausted. Instead, people's resources were spent mainly on battling famine. To evaluate the historical reality of the situation, it must be taken into account that the political and organizational training of the tens of thousands of mostly peasant delegates elected into the rural soviets was very basic: the number of Communist Party members among them did not come to even 1 percent. An increasingly charged civil war situation did not foster a more rooted soviet democracy.[70]

The escalating civil war from the summer of 1918 onward brought with it not only significant popular support but inherently stoked the dictatorship of the Communist Party. This is the period in which Lenin's unfinished article *The Democratism and Socialist Nature of Soviet Power* was written. In repeating his well-known thoughts on the electability and revocability of delegates to the soviets, he once again reformulated the notion that:

> the Soviets concentrate in their hands not only the legislative power and supervision of law enforcement, but direct enforcement of the laws through all the members of the Soviets with a view to a gradual transition to the performance of legislative functions and state administration by the whole working population.[71]

The role of Lenin in this process, and how he "processed" the experience, also has theoretical significance. It is unequivocally clear that in terms of power and politics, the emergency situation demanded a stabilizing centralization expressing "class volition" and—in principle (!)—a thrust from the grassroots upwards. Lenin was of course sensitive to the actual problem, but he also recalled the empirical lessons of history, which taught him that democratic sharing of power in the case of the bourgeoisie only came into play after it had consolidated class domination—and then only in the central states of Europe. In the case of soviet power, however, the state as a sort of commune was built—theoretically speaking—not on the separation of the branches of power but on the people's supervision of power, integrated into the "civic" institutions of society. Autonomous "civil" initiatives continued to conflict with the political-military imperatives of centralization, in a variety of ways, thereby later becoming the barrier for bureaucratic centralization.[72]

What Form of Dictatorship?

Current political journalism and the literature in political science mainly takes the view that Lenin introduced, or at least intended to introduce, unlimited personal dictatorship. Such a hypothesis stems from a serious simplification or misunderstanding of all that happened. A detailed dissection of the relevant political history is too much a digression, but it suffices to indicate that had Lenin wanted to introduce personal dictatorship, he would still not have been able to do so, as the political conditions to do so were not present. He was better advised on this than most of the "dissident thinkers" of the time. A few documents that the censors eliminated from *Lenin's Collected Works* are of extreme importance in this regard.

In January of 1919, the famous historian Nikolay Rozhkov[73] turned to Lenin in a private letter. The two had broken off politically at the time of the first Russian Revolution. Rozhkov, who was originally a Bolshevik, joined the Mensheviks in 1908, which provided many points of difference between him and Lenin, up to 1914.[74] The letter did not travel by regular post, but was delivered to Lenin personally by, and with partial support from, Gorky.[75] It is a rare document among its kind, illuminating a great deal about the way people thought in that day, and proves that introducing dictatorship was popular even among left-wing political thinkers who were opposed to Lenin. Rozhkov found the increasingly widespread famine so tragic that he proposed the introduction of one-person dictatorship, setting aside the normal channels for the use of power; he saw martial counterrevolutionary dictatorship as the only other realistic possibility, and thought it should be avoided at all costs:

> Vladimir Ilyich, I am not writing this letter to you in the hope that it will come to your attention and make you sympathetic to its cause, but because I cannot stay silent in the situation that has come about, which seems tragic to me, and I must do everything in my power, so that we halt the disaster in the making. . . . The economic and some of the alimentary situation of Soviet Russia is on the brink, and getting worse every day. The final, terrible catastrophe is drawing near. . . . The situation here is that half the population of Petrograd is doomed to death by starvation. In such conditions you will not be able to retain power even if there were no imperialist and White Guard menace.[76]

Central to Rozhkov's argument was a factor registered accurately by every Russian historian. In periods of penury the forces of chaos and terror often wreaked havoc, leading to the dissolution of the empire, the country, and fragmenting it into lesser units; alternately, it led to the exact opposite, unbridled centralization. The historical forces of terror were at work in the Russian villages; chaos and disorganization appeared in the guise of the clash between the old way of thinking and the new set of stipulations.[77] Rozhkov conceived of the introduction of personal dictatorship combined with an immediate halt to war communism, which had just been consolidated. In other words, the forced requisitioning of grain, the state monopoly on trade, and above all the monopoly on grain would cease, and a free market would be introduced.

> Your threats of sending the requisitioning gangs are not going to help now: anarchy has taken over the country, and no one is afraid of you, no one will take heed. But were they to listen, even then the matter would not be settled, for the essence of the situation is that your whole food policy is built on the wrong premises. Who would argue with the state monopoly of basic goods, if the state would be capable of supplying the populace with them in sufficient quantities?[78]

Rozhkov gave voice to the most important demand of the New Economic Policy in that he recommended a free market for basic food articles, the organization of the all-Russian market, and shutting down the requisitioning gangs.[79] The period was rife with dictatorial ideas on both the left and right, but Rozhkov's unique contribution was to demand the reinstatement of the market economy and the introduction of the one-person dictatorship, a preventive measure to preempt a counterrevolutionary dictator seizing power:

> We have become too distanced from each other. . . . Likely, or even in all likelihood we will not understand each other. But in my opinion the situation is such that only a one-person dictatorship can get in the way of the counterrevolutionary dictator and snatch power away from him. For this counterrevolutionary dictator will not be as stupid as the generals of the Tsar and the Kadets, who took the land away from the peasant. No such intelligent dictator exists as yet. But it won't take long. . . . At this point, only you can stop this from happening; it would take authority and energy. And steps must be taken urgently, and especially in the matter of food distribution. Otherwise ruin is inevitable. But of course the changes must not be limited to this. The economic policy as a whole should be rebuilt—with socialist ends in mind. Once more, this will demand a dictatorship. Let the Congress of Soviets empower you with the extraordinary mandates necessary. . . . It is your task to decide whether there is a need for this.[80]

Though Lenin—as far as his reply to the letter is an indication—did not waver for even a moment as he read it, the document cannot be ignored either in regard to its theoretical perception of the situation or its concrete political content. And though it concerns an individual far removed from the fulcrum of political life, in fact it still carries more weight than a private initiative. Menshevik leaders such as Dan or Martov set store by the possibility of an "anti-Semitic, Black Hundreds dictatorship"—which they denounced—as an alternative to the Bolshevik seizure of power, and prohibited party members from organizing armed struggle against the Bolsheviks and soviet power—even if many Mensheviks suspected that the social base of the Bolshevik revolution included "lumpen elements" and "reactionary soldiers."[81] In this sense the rise of a White Guard dictator was not only the manic obsession of the Menshevik Rozhkov and the Bolsheviks, for indeed the figure was soon embodied by Kolchak and Denikin.

Why Lenin was averse to the idea of a one-person dictatorship is even more interesting where theory and political history are concerned. He approached this question as a completely ideology-free issue in his reply to Rozhkov.[82] The fact that Lenin replied at all (he was especially scornful of the "renegades") suggests that he found that the letter posed some essential questions of a practical nature.[83] A few weeks later, on 13 March 1919, Lenin returned to the contents of the letter in a speech he made at the People's House in Petrograd, without mentioning names, of course—this speech was also suppressed in its time.[84]

Lenin expected the historian-economist Rozhkov to take account of the social consequences of the economic policy he proposed. In other words, Lenin invited

Rozhkov to turn his attention to helping the impoverished segment of society and winning the educated circles over to this cause by supporting the spread of self-organization. The reinstatement of a market economy would only be advantageous to the rich with the depths of chaos and destitution it would create, undermining the very fundaments of the system.

> You should not be thinking about free trade—to an economist, of all people, it should be clear that free trade, given the absolute shortage of essential produce, is equivalent to frenzied, brutal speculation and the triumph of the haves over the have-nots. We should not go backward through free trade but forward through the improvement of the state monopoly, toward socialism. It is a difficult transition, but despair is impermissible and unwise. If, instead of serenading free trade, the non-party intelligentsia or the intelligentsia close to the party would form emergency groups, small groups, and unions for all-round assistance to the food supply, it would seriously help the cause and lessen hunger.[85]

Lenin did not see one-person dictatorship as a form of government that warranted serious consideration, because organizationally it would mean the destruction of the apparatus already established. It must not be forgotten that this was exactly the point of time in which the expansion of the economic method of war communism peaked. The Council of People's Commissars made a series of decisions in January–February 1919. On the same day Rozhkov's letter was dated, 11 January, they adopted the decree on the forced requisitioning of grain.

Additionally, the introduction of personal dictatorship would have meant that the soviets would have to abandon their form of power structure as an alternative to bourgeois democracy and the constituent game, that is, the perspective of another form of democracy. *Party* dictatorship, as the concrete manifestation of the dictatorship of the proletariat, may have been just defendable in the emergency situation that had evolved, but *personal* dictatorship could not be found in the political vocabulary, conceptual inventions, and theoretical traditions of Bolshevism to date. (That is why when Stalin effectively introduced personal dictatorship ten years later, he popularized his system as democracy!) In Lenin's words, written to Rozhkov:

> As for "personal dictatorship," excuse the expression, but it is utter nonsense. The apparatus has already become gigantic—in some places excessively so—and under such conditions a "personal dictatorship" is entirely unrealizable and attempts to realize it would only be harmful. A

> turning point has occurred in the intelligentsia. The civil war in Germany and the struggle precisely along the lines of soviet power against "the universal, direct, equal, and secret ballot, that is, against the counterrevolutionary Constituent assembly"—this struggle in Germany is breaking through even to the most stubborn intelligentsia minds and will succeed in breaking through. . . . At home, in Russia, they regarded this as "merely" the "savagery" of Bolshevism. But now history has shown that it is the worldwide collapse of bourgeois democracy and bourgeois parliamentarianism, that you cannot get by anywhere without a civil war. . . . The intelligentsia will have to arrive at the position of helping the workers precisely on a Soviet platform.[86]

Gorky attached a letter of his own to Rozhkov's, in which he also argued for the introduction of personal dictatorship; however, in contradiction to Rozhkov, he encouraged Lenin to introduce personal dictatorship only in the given circumstances of civil war, together with a strict ban on the private market, that is, on the basis of state monopoly on trade.[87] Lenin responded to these issues in the speech of 13 March. A piquancy of the speech, which was never published in the Soviet period, was that it pointed out the connection between the current events in the battle raging against the famine and civil war against the internal counterrevolution.

It should be obvious that the Bolsheviks were not the inventors of either forced requisitioning or state monopoly of the market. The tsar's government had introduced forced requisitioning on 29 November 1916, and the grain monopoly was given legal standing by the Provisional Government in its first days, on 25 March 1917. The latter government sent armed forces to the villages for the collection of foodstuffs in the autumn—although the efficacy of these measures is another matter. However, the steps Lenin took to alleviate the famine were not the mechanical continuation of these measures. V. Loginov—in line with research by Brus and some other Soviet historians of the 1960s and 1970s—rightly points out that in April 1918 he was thinking in terms of the peaceful possibilities of bringing grain from the villages to the cities by means of bartering produce. A few days later, in agreement with the Council of People's Commissars, a decision for a food procurement dictatorship was made. What happened was that by April–May, all of the traditional grain-growing regions had been cut off from the central region. German occupying forces had raised the hetman Pavel Petrovich Skoropadsky to power in Ukraine. The revolt of Czech prisoners of war in May cut off Siberia and a part of the Volga region, and even Moscow's contact with the North Caucasus was split by June. Needless to say, this isolation did not bode well.[88]

It is an important contributing factor to the subject under discussion here that the series of war communist measures based on curbs to democratic freedoms fundamentally affected such fields of everyday life as transport and travel. The whole chain of compulsory measures pointed toward the realization of a command economy, and this naturally did not serve as a firm basis for the construction of a stable, democratic government. The "soviet dictatorship" given political shape by the Communist Party became expedient for the pulverization of military counterrevolution and the dictatorships of White Guard generals on the fronts of the civil war.[89] Yet the increasing bureaucratization and strengthening of the state and party apparatus forced Lenin and the Bolsheviks to bring a new set of problems into view: What means were available to keep the protesting, "differently thinking" groups within their own social base? How far can oppression be validated, and when does the revolution begin turning into its opposite?

At this point, the only person attempting to give a Marxist, *internal* criticism of the Russian Revolution, at some distance (from prison in Germany, to be exact) from where events were unfolding, was Rosa Luxemburg. Unsurprisingly, the Mensheviks also saw an affirmation of their views in the critique of Bolshevism given by Luxemburg's pamphlet. Martov went so far, in a letter to S. D. Shupak from Berlin dated 23 December 1921, as to glean a validation of Kautsky from it:

> Here—the sensation you must have heard of is that Paul Levi has finally published Rosa's pamphlet (written in September 1918), which the communists kept concealed for three years. She chides them in it not only for the Treaty of Brest-Litovsk, but the dissolution of the Constituent Assembly. It matches Kautsky in the way it raises the question of dictatorship and democracy letter-for-letter, so the effect of this publication is colossal.[90]

It is clear that a document such as Rosa Luxemburg's can have many readings and interpretations. Yet the association Martov made of Luxemburg's position with Kautsky's is more than a misunderstanding. It has psychological grounds, the sources of which are rather mundane: he was merely looking for mechanical validations of his own political stance. After all, would either Kautsky or Martov in the course of the Russian Revolution ever, even for a moment, have accepted Rosa Luxemburg's oft-quoted lines, written in prison in 1918?

> Let the German Government Socialists cry that the rule of the Bolsheviks in Russia is a distorted expression of the dictatorship of the proletariat. If it was or is such, that is only because it is a product of the behavior of

> the German proletariat, in itself a distorted expression of the socialist class struggle. All of us are subject to the laws of history, and it is only internationally that the socialist order of society can be realized. The Bolsheviks have shown that they are capable of everything that a genuine revolutionary party can contribute within the limits of historical possibilities. They are not supposed to perform miracles. For a model and faultless proletarian revolution in an isolated land, exhausted by world war, strangled by imperialism, betrayed by the international proletariat, would be a miracle. . . . In this, Lenin and Trotsky and their friends were the first, those who went ahead as an example to the proletariat of the world; they are still the only ones up to now who can cry with Hutten: "I have dared!"[91]

This is the context into which the true message of Luxemburg's judgment and criticism of terror fits: "Freedom is always and exclusively freedom for the one who thinks differently." The actual, major theoretical and practical problem here, even today, is whether the possibility of any resolution to the contradiction presented existed.

VIOLENCE AND TERROR: CAUSES AND CONSEQUENCES

Since the collapse of the Soviet Union, historiographic tendencies of great diversity have aimed to force Lenin's legacy into a narrative box of terror and violence, by way of "deconstructing" the structure of the "historical account."

Lenin did not have a special theory that dealt with violence and terror, though his views and grounds for his actions can be satisfactorily reconstructed in this area. At the end of the nineteenth century and the beginning of the twentieth, revolutionaries did not normally contest the inevitability of violence in the course of revolutionary change. Lenin knew Engels's famous theoretical forays on violence in his polemics with Dühring, though even Herr Dühring admitted some role of violence in his cautious manner, thereby eliciting palpable anger from Engels:

> It is only with sighs and groans that he admits the possibility that force will perhaps be necessary for the overthrow of an economic system of exploitation—unfortunately, because all use of force demoralises the person who uses it. And this in spite of the immense moral and spiritual impetus which has been given by every victorious revolution![92]

These were the conceptual foundations Lenin inherited, which deduced the historical sources of violence from the economic contradictions, opposite interests, and class oppression of modern society. With knowledge of the history of the twentieth century, however, comes recognition of the vast difference between a theoretical approach to violence and its actual application. Decisively, in this context, the vortex of struggle for power in the Russian civil war saw irreconcilable political, socio-economic interests, theoretical and cultural traditions, and "logics" collide, which brought a variety of horrific forms of concentrated violence into existence. However, not only did the revolution not bring an end to the violence and terror, but it implemented it more widely, through a variety of forms with different aims—not to mention all of the later, at once distressing and complicated, historical developments which followed from these precedents.[93]

In his uncompleted work, *Young Lenin*, Trotsky rightly drew attention to the fact that Lenin formed his more differentiated position regarding terror over a period of years,[94] the essence of which may be summed up in the notion that terror was to be a secondary tool in political and armed struggle, for use only in the most extreme moment. Following the defeat of the 1905 uprising, Lenin viewed terror and partisan actions as an instrument of the revolutionary uprising and in relation to state tyranny. His classic work on the subject was published as "Events of the Day" in August 1906, and the title gives the essence of the writing. It dealt with terrorism as a political and combat technique based on a series of terrorist acts in Polish cities—against Stolypin, as well as S.R. revolutionary Z. V. Konoplyannikova's 13 August 1906 assassination of General G. A. Min, who had violently suppressed the armed Moscow uprising. Whether such action is politically called for depended on whether it influenced the "public mood" to be in favor or against the socialists. He posited the legitimacy of armed partisan acts against autocracy and state despotism as one possible tactic of revolutionary struggle, but rejected it as a means of "expropriating private property," because the revolutionary forces are not at war with individuals, but with the system. Therefore, Lenin noted, the Party Congress had decided correctly when it "repudiates the expropriation of private property," while "an active struggle against government terror and the violence of the Black Hundreds is inevitable" and recognizes "killing of perpetrators of violence" and that "arms and military supplies that belong to the government must be seized."[95]

One year later, having learned from the experience of the counterrevolution's rise to power, terrorist actions in answer to the terror of the regime would only have exacerbated the measure of defeat. Lenin considered the tolls of terrorism detrimental from the point of view of the revolutionary struggle and mass movement in the so-called times of peace. At the 3rd Party Conference (21–23 July 1907) in Kotka, Finland, the meeting of the Bolshevik faction closed the conference with a resolution denouncing terror, stating that it rejected terror as a method in advance. The given situation was prohibitive of terror, with "the only method suitable for the struggle at the moment is scientific propaganda and the State Duma as a forum for agitation." The faction even raised the possibility of seceding from the party if their friends of principle rejected this resolution.[96]

Spontaneity and Organization

Recent historians have mostly drawn attention to the fact that the transformative process of the Revolution of 1917 took place on various social levels, with different defining traits and means, as well as cultural and psychological persuasions. A particular cult of violence gained a foothold in significant social groups from 1914 onward.[97] Without neglecting that the Russian tradition was fertile soil for the use of violence,[98] the primary source of modern violence was the imperialist world war. It had thrown the already weakened institutions and structures of social solidarity into disarray, breaking the moral checks on murderous instincts and allowing the "*obshchina* revolution" to spread quickly, mediated by the armed peasant soldier in the ranks.[99]

In other words, in the period of civil war the Soviet government received no impulse from below—from its immediate social base and apparatus—that would *impede violence*. The organized actions of the monarchist military counterrevolution only reinforced the ties of the new regime with the use of force as a tool of survival. The counterrevolution is in fact a part of the revolution, in a historical sense. Street fights had erupted in a number of important cities in February through May 1917, followed by the days of July, the Kornilov revolt, and spontaneous peasant rebellions in the villages, and in October came the armed takeover of power in Petrograd and Moscow. The revolution then swept through the whole of Russia. Nevertheless, the psychological state of civil war did not begin with the armed conflicts of 1918, nor the interventionist strikes from abroad, but with the centuries-old tsarist system of oppression and the First World War's tide of blood. The post-October violence and terror, equipped with its own tools and institutions, grew out of this rich loam of violent oppression rather than the other way around. In other words, in terms of causality, the revolution was not the cause, but the consequence of the violence.[100] The war also played a decisive role among the causes of the revolution.

Be that as it may, Lenin based his theoretical and political approach on the view that any weakness and lack of nerve on the part of the new power apparatus would only increase the strength and chances of the old ruling classes and counterrevolutionary resistance. He thought it ridiculous that in the weeks and months following the revolution, the Bolsheviks amnestied not only a number of ministers of the Provisional Government and participants of the Junker revolt of 29 October, based on their word of honor, but also P. N. Krasnov, the most merciless Cossack general (and later an active supporter of the Nazis), who immediately joined other Junkers and continued the armed struggle against the soviets' power.

Russian realities had the potential of terror at three different levels, of which Lenin was well aware: the legacy of violence left by the First World War, the escalation of the internal class struggle, and the virus of the civil war, to be fought to mutual annihilation—a feeling which had become palpable in the Russia of 1917. In obeisance to the new reigning canon, this is now often forgotten in regard to the evolution of terror following the revolution. By January 1918 the monarchist General Kornilov had already given the order to "Take no prisoners."[101] The voice of that terror signaled the horror of what was to become commonplace during the civil war, the evolving cycle of violence.[102] The process by which violence and terror escalated was not determined by any preconceived theory, and could not have been foreseen in its singularity and almost unequalled instruments. Only the concrete circumstances in this situation could determine the "combinations" that drew together certain particular components of the Russian revolutionary tradition, such as the "Pugachovshchina," and Marxist theory, such as the "dictatorship of the proletariat."

Bakunin's approach is worth recalling, as it reappeared in some form or another in the value systems of a number of revolutionary trends, including that of Lenin. A pamphlet Mikhail Bakunin wrote from exile in Geneva in January of 1870, the year of Lenin's birth (though it seems Lenin knew the document), *To the Officers of the Russian Army*, declared that in spite of the people's immeasurable sufferings, bloodshed could be avoided in the course of a struggle for liberation if the army took up the "sacred cause of the people." There would be no bloodletting in this case, and the oppressors, the "parasites," the "idlers," would simply be "driven off the territory of Russia." Bakunin continued: "Stenka Razin who will put himself at the head of the masses during the destruction, so clearly at hand, of the Russian Empire, will no longer be an individual hero, but a collective Stenka Razin."[103] This "collective Razin" was embodied in the peasant rebellion, in Lenin and in the Red Army and Cheka of 1917. Of course, the *theory* Lenin used to justify the oppression practiced by the revolution did not reach back to Bakuninian sources. The dictatorship of the proletariat as a specific form of exercising power came about and became a "material force" under mass democracy's sphere of influence, with the purpose of breaking down the resistance of the ruling classes and establishing the regime of direct democracy. The problem was ultimately caused by the fact that oppression, as a task, came to be applied not only to the ruling classes, but against everyone contradicting the decrees of the new regime, for whatever reason. In parallel to the deepening of terror and violence, widening the scope of direct democracy was gradually taken off the agenda—it "softened" to an issue of constitutional legislation, a theoretical question. Though Lenin did not wish to sink completely into the swamp of power sustaining itself, the danger of the envisioned aims being leached out of the whole picture was very real right from the very beginning. Lenin was engaged in what one may freely call military service in the Kremlin, from the first day of the revolution. He learned the "style of military command" appropriate for the emergency situation gradually, though he was naturally fully versed in the unavoidable use and function of terror from his reading of the histories of the French Revolution and American Civil War. Two dispatches from the initial period are revealing with regard to the historical situation that had evolved:

> TELEGRAM TO KHARKOV AND MOSCOW, 13 (26) JANUARY 1918.
> ORJONIKIDZE, PEOPLE'S SECRETARIAT, ANTONOV'S STAFF, KHARKOV
> COMMANDER-IN-CHIEF MURALOV, PRESIDIUM OF THE SOVIET OF DEPUTIES, MOSCOW
>
> WE HAVE RECEIVED NEWS OF A TRAFFIC JAM BETWEEN OREL AND KURSK PREVENTING THE PASSAGE OF TRAINS WITH COAL AND GRAIN. ANY HOLD-UP THREATENS FAMINE AND STOPPAGE OF INDUSTRY. WE SUSPECT SABOTAGE BY RAILWAYMEN IN THIS LOCALITY FOR THERE HAVE BEEN SEVERAL CASES OF SABOTAGE THERE. WE URGENTLY ASK YOU TO TAKE THE MOST RUTHLESS REVOLUTIONARY MEASURES. WE ASK YOU TO SEND OUT A DETACHMENT OF ABSOLUTELY RELIABLE PERSONS. USE ALL MEANS TO ENSURE THE MOVEMENT OF TRUCKS WITH GRAIN TO PETROGRAD, OTHERWISE THERE IS A THREAT OF FAMINE. PLACE SEVERAL SAILORS OR RED GUARDS ON EACH OF THE LOCOMOTIVES. REMEMBER THAT IT DEPENDS ON YOU TO SAVE PETROGRAD FROM FAMINE. —LENIN

He repeated his "pleas" in another telegram to Antonov and Orjonikidze two days later:

> FOR GOD'S SAKE, TAKE THE MOST ENERGETIC AND REVOLUTIONARY MEASURES TO SEND GRAIN, GRAIN AND MORE GRAIN!!! OTHERWISE PETROGRAD MAY PERISH. SPECIAL TRAINS AND DETACHMENTS. GRAIN COLLECTION AND DELIVERY. HAVE THE TRAINS CONVOYED. REPORT DAILY.
> FOR GOD'S SAKE! —LENIN[104]

Elemental matters—such as the problem of control over and transportation of grain—could only be solved by utilizing the armed forces, without resorting to military force. These problems could not be "handled" in the given situation, so Lenin began to act "as required" under the pressure of wartime conditions, and unavoidably had to improvise. His decisions were shaped largely by extraneous factors such as lack of information, fear of defeat, the unmasking of true or imagined conspiracies, the formation of the armed counterrevolution, etc.[105] An array of parallel spontaneous popular institutions coexisted, such as the Military Revolutionary Committee (from which in part the Cheka was soon formed) the local soviets in close proximity with the centralizing powers, and the Council of People's Commissars at the top, which in turn reported to, and was in principle subject to, the Central Executive Committee (or the All-Russia Congress of Soviets, to be exact). However, the strong paternalist relationship survived, serving as a support for not only the central powers, but for Lenin's personal power as well. These different levels of power created a peculiar form of chaos. For example, Lenin's first decisions show he was forced to take action about situations he could hardly have imagined earlier. Among the difficulties he came up against on the first days of the revolution was that of alcoholism, which threw some of the Red Guard units into disarray. He proposed to sell what was available of quality wine and spirits abroad, so it does not "poison" and demoralize the populace locally.[106] The practice of taking hostages,[107] as well as interning the enemy in concentration camps, as a means of "temporarily isolating it from society," was developed, though it had been used in the First World War and even the earlier Boer War.

Phenomena of other kinds also signaled the wild growth of violence and terror. A row of terrorist acts against officials of soviet power whipped up emotions. Among the most spectacular was an S.R. assassin's murder of one of the leading Petrograd Bolsheviks, Volodarsky, and then an S.R.'s killing of Uritsky, the head of the Petrograd Cheka on 30 August—the same day another S.R. fanatic, Fanni Kaplan, made her well-known attempt on Lenin's life. Reacting to the "counterrevolutionary White terror," the All-Russian Central Executive Committee enacted a decree for the introduction of Red Terror on 2 September. *Pravda* published the text of the decree on 3 September, asserting that "the workers and the peasants answer the agents of the bourgeoisie with mass Red Terror." Lenin argued on both theoretical and practical levels for the *state* form of a mass terror of intimidation. At the same time he continued to reject the private form of terror rooted in personal revenge, considering it useless. The case of Mrs. Pershikova, an employee of a small town housing office, arrested in March 1919 for defacing a picture-portrait of Lenin she had torn out of a pamphlet while bored, might even be taken as a symbolic one. Lenin's attention was drawn to the liberation of the lady in question by one of the captains of the militia of Caricin, V. S. Usachev, and the Red Guard soldier Minin. Lenin's note on the document read: "Hand the whole documentation over to columnists."

> 8 March 1919, Myshkin, Chairman of the Gubernia Extraordinary Commission, Tsaritsyn. You cannot arrest people for disfiguring a portrait. Free Valentina Pershikova at once, and if she is a counterrevolutionary, keep an eye on her.[108]

A plethora of documents indicate that the leader of the revolution often took measures even at the peak of the civil war, against Chekhist or bureaucratic abuses of power. For example, one document reads:

> To the Gubernia Executive Committee of Cherepovets, 29 March 1919. Check complaint Yefrosinia Yefimova, soldier's wife of village Novoselo, Pokrovsk Volost, Belozersk Uyezd, concerning confiscation of grain for common barn, although her husband has been prisoner of war over four years and she has family of three without a farm help. Report to me results investigation and your measures.[109]

To Lenin, mass terror counted as the most extreme instrument of struggle against the enemy and was to be applied (and often demanded by him in vain), on a case-by-case basis.[110] Yet in other situations he censured the terror motivated by power-political rationales as well as social and class factors, and the use of violence. He frequently demanded curbs on the use of terror and even the elimination of concrete abuses of power, and advocated punishing Cheka employees. For instance, he protested in horror against the "evil bleakness" of some Ukrainian representatives of the Cheka:

> Kamenev says—and declares that several most prominent Cheka men confirm it—that the Chekas in the Ukraine have brought a host of evils, having been set up too early and having allowed a mass of hangers-on to get in. . . . It is necessary at all costs to discipline the Cheka men and throw out the alien elements. [111]

He knew that illiterate or semi-illiterate, politically unschooled youth were in the majority in the Cheka, including the type of "careerist people without any ideals" who showed up wherever power offered an opportunity for dominance and good living.

Thus violence was not only the product of the past, the war, and the conditions created by the civil war,[112] but an inalienable part of the new system taking root, best expressed in the fact that threats of violence seemed the only way to limit the excesses of the new bureaucracy, since the formation of a new legal order was taking years to complete. In April 1919, some peasants in certain parts of the country were going to be forced to join the collectives, rather than doing so of their own free will—a behavior categorically prohibited by Lenin in the name of the Council of People's Commissars. The peasant base formed the backbone of the Red Army, and "Compulsory measures of any kind to make the peasants pass over to the communal working of the fields are impermissible. Non-observance of this will be punished with all the severity of revolutionary law." On 10 April, Lenin and Sereda, the People's Commissar for Agriculture, published a circular letter in *Izvestia* protesting the despotism of local authorities:

> Information has reached the People's Commissariat for Agriculture that for the purpose of organizing state farms, communes and other collective associations, the land departments and state farm boards, contrary to the intent of Article 9 of the Regulations on Socialist Organization of Agriculture, are taking away from the peasants the lands of former landowners' estates which had been made over to them. The impermissibility of such practices is hereby confirmed. Lands being worked by peasants at the time of the publication of the Regulations on Socialist Organization of Agriculture, and which were put at their disposal on the basis of decisions or instructions of uyezd or gubernia land departments, may not on any account be forcibly alienated for the purpose of organizing state farms, communes or other collective associations. The alienation of lands from the peasants for the sake of the above-mentioned organizations is permissible only by voluntary consent by way of land tenure regulation. Measures of coercion to make the peasants practise joint cultivation and join communes and other types of collective farming are impermissible. The transition to collective forms is to be carried out only in strict conformity with the Regulations, without any compulsion on the part of the authorities. Non-fulfillment of the present instruction will be punished in accordance with the laws of the revolutionary period. Inform the population of the present instruction as widely as possible.[113]

Under the pressure of escalating terror, Lenin was forced—though historians like Volkogonov, Pipes, and Felshtynsky are silent on this point—to bring corrective measures against the Cheka and the courts, as they did not heed laws or regulations. During the civil war, no evidence was needed to arrest anyone—only a denunciation from the authorities. Rather than list the numerous documents that illustrate Lenin's anger at the naked inhumanity of the internal ministry and state government powers he had helped to build,[114] it is more useful to discuss the measures he took to restrict the spate of terror and the way he thought about them, which may prove instructive in theoretical terms.

With the reorganization of the Cheka in the beginning of 1922, from then on called the GPU, its basic task was defined as the defense of soviet and Communist Party power, and the deterrence, expulsion, and administrative liquidation of the political opposition.[115] The legal framework, marking out a scope for terror, was placed on the agenda, an act that can be interpreted as a form of legal summary derived from the experiences of the civil war and the new situation. As he was bringing the economic repression of war communism to an end, Lenin was looking for ways to restrain the political opposition and the new bourgeoisie, and to crop their influence. He found an unusual solution in May 1922 with new revolutionary legal norms eliminating all despotism and supporting a form of "legalized terror." He explained this in his notes to the draft law, bringing the Criminal Code of the Russian Soviet Federative Socialist Republic into force: "Put forward publicly a thesis that is correct in principle and politically (not only strictly juridical), which explains the *substance* of terror, its necessity and limits, and provides *justification* for it." It becomes clear from these comments that Lenin also arranged for a clampdown on the political opposition (especially abroad, in relation to the international bourgeoisie) with the extension of the death penalty, while at the same time making the measure of repression relative: "Add the right, by decision of the Presidium of the All-Russia Central Executive Committee, to commute the death sentence to deportation (for a term or for life)."[116] The main goal of Lenin's actions can be observed in light of these statements. His formulations show unequivocally that the broad attack upon the priesthood, churches, and bourgeois intelligentsia in 1922 was a sort of closure to the civil war, and aimed at isolating and expelling those who had supported the White Guard, the monarchist counterrevolution, and the anti-soviet camp from the hinterland during the civil war, and who still held significant positions in the intellectual-political life of Soviet society after their military defeat. The formation of that catastrophic complex of views, which could consign every form of political opposition to the counterrevolutionary camp, became apparent in the course of this process.

The main message of the Joint State Political Directorate (OGPU) report was not, as Terence Martin wrote, a "deep mistrust of the masses, and fear of their instinctive rebelliousness that characterized the Soviet leadership."[117] Rather, the documents reflect how Lenin and the other Soviet leaders wanted to meet the goals they had set for themselves, but were not able to because of the social and historical preconditions from which the revolution itself had sprung.[118]

THE 1922 WAVE OF REPRESSION: ENDING THE CIVIL WAR

It is crucial to know that as of the summer of 1918, Lenin saw foreign military intervention as the main cause of the terror. Lenin laid great emphasis on the question of terror in replying to Western criticism that portrayed the Soviet government as terrorist. From a Council of People's Commissars report to the 7th All-Russian Congress of the Soviets:

> The chief accusation made against us by the European petite bourgeoisie concerns our terrorism, our crude suppression of the intelligentsia and the petite bourgeoisie. "You and your governments have forced all that upon us," we say in reply. . . . That was real terrorism when all the powers united against a country that was one of the most backward and most weakened by war. . . . The reason for our terrorism was that we were attacked by armed forces against which we had to bend all our efforts.

On the other hand, he alluded to the fact that the petite bourgeoisie and the middle layer of society, the intelligentsia, find the trials of civil war much harder, because "they have been privileged for decades, but in the interests of the social revolution we must place that burden on their shoulders, too." Moreover, the carrying of such burdens to ensure the victory in the war requires "strict military discipline."[119]

Behind this wave of repressions was fear of the NEP's consequences, both in the context of international isolation and recent experiences of armed foreign intervention. The reinstatement of certain elements of the new bourgeoisie, the market, and capitalism in general—and the social, cultural, and ideological conflicts this involved—filled the leaders, members, and supporters of the Bolshevik Party with dread and uncertainty. This fear came to the fore in the idea that the disparate forces opposing the Soviet government could unite, partly because the NEP offered them more political opportunity, and partly because it brought into being social actors that were thought to be capable of bringing down the Soviet government.[120] It is difficult to comprehend these fears from a perspective of the present, but a historical approach may help. Further, the Bolsheviks' almost psychotic fear of losing power was sped on by new impulses in the historical moment following their victory in the civil war.[121] On the fronts of the civil war they had annihilated the White armies and the interventionists, but they still felt that the military defeat of counterrevolution did not necessarily lead to its political defeat, or if so, then in limited terms. They felt that the Eastern Orthodox Church (along with its intellectual-political influence and structure) had been the buttress of the monarchist system for a thousand years, but had been left virtually untouched. The counterrevolutionary parties had survived, and were ready to overthrow the Soviet government led by the Bolsheviks.

The most destabilizing factor contributing to the Bolsheviks' psychosis was the terrible famine of 1921–22 that affected approximately 20 million people. Some of the data available indicates 5 million dying of hunger as a result of the extreme drought, with the Volga region most affected. This development could easily delegitimize Communist Party rule and its social goals, separating the power of the soviets from their social base. This final natural catastrophe following years of famine made it obvious to the Soviet political leadership, as well as Lenin, that prolonged hunger and deprivation had transformed the psychological makeup of the people, their worldview, the way they related to power, and their intellectual abilities and temperament. A widely experienced characteristic was the degradation of personality, as brought to public attention by the world-renowned neurologist and psychologist, Professor V. M. Bechterev. The struggle with hunger, suffering, and the "common occurrence of starvation deaths" drove many to despair, and was just as conducive to crime as it was to disease, epidemics, and people's reduced capacity to work.[122]

Moreover, famine was an acute problem faced by every kind of power by 1916, which was intensified by the international conflict by 1919. The formation of the so-called Nansen Committee in the spring of 1919, under the aegis of the Red Cross, signaled that the Russian famine was a catastrophe of European proportions. Lenin welcomed the supportive approach of the polar explorer Fridtjof Nansen, but pointed out how the interventionist states wanted to turn his humanitarian goals against the Soviet government. Nansen drafted the answer of the heads of state, which made help conditional based on the suspension of all armed action. What the answer did not say, however, was that a significant part of the war operations—or it could be said a decisive measure—was "by the favor of" the allied powers. Lenin proposed that a reply be composed in such a way as to expose this hypocrisy, but gratefully accepted the international aid arranged by Nansen.[123]

The famine posed a different question in 1921. Anti-Bolshevik intellectuals founded the First-Aid Committee in July 1921, in cooperation with the Soviet authorities. As in 1919, Lenin was perfectly aware that the catastrophe could "delegitimize" the newly established government. From the perspective of power politics, once again the solution for Russia's famine was being sought by the same great powers that were at war with Soviet Russia and were financing the White generals, and so were to blame for the famine itself.[124]

Finally, in order to understand the background of the repressions, it can be said that in one sense the Russian Revolution is certainly not an exception in the history of revolutions: political battles did not cease until the influence of the social layers that upheld the old regime were eliminated. In the French, English, and American revolutions, scores were settled with those faithful to the old system in the particular circumstances offered by each nation. The situation in Russia was made additionally dire by the social power undergirding the new system; the urban labor forces became increasingly fatigued as the civil war stretched on, and this was mirrored in the fragility of the new political regime and the vulnerability of its social base.

Famine and the Expropriation of Church Treasures

A wave of repression swept across the social groups and institutions connected to the old system. Under pressure from grave circumstances and in defense of its political and ideological rule, the Communist Party wanted to get rid of the key figures of the political opposition, who the party assumed had no interest in political (and ideological) compromise, or who were not willing to engage in one. Ultimately the wave of repression was a message to both all forms of internal opposition, as well as the West, not to turn back on the road that had been taken: the Communist Party would retain its monopoly on power.[125]

The Russian Orthodox Church was seen as the most significant opposition by the Bolsheviks. Ex-Soviet scholars, such as N. N. Pokrovsky,[126] usually approach the process by which the Soviet government appropriated—"expropriated," confiscated—the church treasures, and the way the Bolsheviks in general and Lenin related to the church, in terms of a moral and legal problem. Pokrovsky admits that an act of January 1918 declared all church treasures which were not used for religious purposes to be state property. But he falls into a moral argument with the Soviet politicians of the revolutionary period, as if Lenin and the Bolsheviks had not themselves advanced a series of moral arguments in favor of the political liquidation of the Russian Orthodox Church. The documents that are available today show Lenin's progress as a politician and ideologist in regard to these questions, somewhat coloring the concepts established in previous times.

From the discussion heretofore, we have seen that all of his important political decisions were also considered in a historical perspective, and this also applies to the measures of repression. It is not widely known that the February Revolution did not divorce the state from the church. Though a deep sense of antipathy had built up against the state religion and the national church over the years, in vast swaths of Russian society it still had support, especially with older generations. The church survived the civil war as a notable opponent. The numbers of priests generally supporting the Whites and the Black Hundreds were in excess of 200,000 in 1917. The decree on freedom of conscience, which was also a declaration of freedom from the church, was enacted on 20 January 1918 and signed by Lenin. It meant that schools would no longer have Bible classes, civil marriage was introduced in place of church marriage, and the church estate was declared the "property of the people." The All-Russian Patriarch Tikhon, chosen to head the Russian Orthodox Church after the October Revolution, rejected and denounced the decree's fundamental theses. On top of this, he wrote an open letter on the first anniversary of the October Revolution, addressed to the Council of People's Commissars, in which he condemned the Bolshevik policies, the Peace Treaty of Brest-Litovsk, as well as the termination of the dominion of private property. But the Patriarch had excommunicated all those involved in the "revolutionary vigilantism" earlier, in January 1918. If so, Lenin was already among those excommunicated, though not named in the document. Alexandra Kollontai, a fighter for women's rights, was mentioned by name; Lenin noted that she, a Bolshevik revolutionary, had found rather good company with Stenka Razin and Lev Tolstoy among the excommunicated. It was also well known that Lenin had considered the Russian Orthodox Church as the tsarist autocracy's most faithful prop. However, he never identified the church with religion, or the other way round. His view on "religion having opiate characteristics" has been touched on in an earlier chapter, but it is a lesser known fact that he did not want to ban, or put into an impossible position, either the church or the practice of religion, and he even took measures against violations during the civil war.[127] On the other hand, he treated party matters differently. He was against the participation of party members in religious ceremonies on principle, and considered it intolerable for one to practice a religion. In a note to the Central Committee of 30 May 1919 he wrote: "I am for expulsion from the Party of people who take part in religious ceremonies."[128]

After the bloodbath of the First World War, Lenin wanted to relegate the church establishment, which he described as "medieval," to the peripheries of political-intellectual life. It was not just a matter of the church having taken up arms against the Soviet government, but also a question of the Bolsheviks wanting to create their own cultural hegemony in society, in opposition to the earlier ideological monopoly, the "old culture," of the Russian Orthodox Church. The first steps the Bolsheviks were determined to take were a quick elimination of illiteracy, the civilizing and uplifting of the masses through culture, and the wide "distribution of new, socialist culture."[129]

Lenin, in a spirit of "now or never," felt that the time to confront the Russian Orthodox Church and Tikhon had come in the winter–spring of 1922.[130] On Lenin's initiative, the Council of People's Commissars and the topmost Soviet organs undertook a collection in aid of the victims of the 1921–22 famine in the Volga region,[131] and ordered the confiscation of church estates and effects. In his reply on 28 February, Tikhon proclaimed open resistance, and spoke of "desecration." The requisitioning committee and the mounted police were beaten back by the faithful in Shuya. The military clashed with the demonstrators and forty individuals were injured—sixteen supporters of the church and twenty-four Red Army soldiers. This served as an occasion for Lenin to write his secret anti-church document.

Lenin's "secret letter"[132] to Molotov, and through him to the members of the Central Executive Committee, which was later suppressed by the Soviet government, outlined the GPU actions related to the political strategy indicated in the letter.[133] Publicly, and in official terms, Lenin put Mikhail Kalinin, the chairman of the soviets, in charge of the action, with Lenin as the sole source of information for the press. He entrusted its actual direction to Trotsky, letting everyone know that this had to be kept highly secret due to Trotsky's Jewish origins, which would only serve as more fuel to the anti-Semitic propaganda of the White Guard and the church.[134] (Trotsky's Jewish background had come up as an obstacle even in connection with his appointment as a people's commissar.) The document gives a number of explanations for this settling of accounts with the church. Two primary considerations prevailed over the anticipated resistance to the expropriation: thanks to Trotsky, Lenin vastly overestimated the quantity and value of the treasures,[135] and the church's defensive reflexes were underestimated. The overestimation was due to the fact that the most significant church treasures had been delivered to safe places much earlier. However, even though Lenin considered the Russian Orthodox Church the "last bastion of White Guard and Black Hundreds counterrevolution," the "expropriation of treasures" applied to all denominations and churches equally.

The military style of the Lenin letter, and his use of expressions such as "vanguard," show that he was indeed preparing for a decisive campaign. Furthermore, Lenin took into consideration that in contradiction to his original expectations, the general population was taking much longer to give its active support to the new system, and he suspected the church played a role in this. The middle peasants and the more propertied groups among the peasants had become somewhat alienated from the Bolsheviks because of the war communism and civil war regulations. The church was likely to be the ally of this particular layer. The following raw, threatening sentence of the document was primarily motivated by these factors, though a sense of revenge, though often overrated in current interpretations, may also have played a part:

> The greater the number of representatives of the reactionary clergy and the reactionary bourgeoisie that we succeed in shooting on this occasion, the better, because this "audience" must precisely now be taught a lesson in such a way that they will not dare to think about any resistance whatsoever for several decades.[136]

In reality this was a matter of converting the victories achieved in the civil war to political advantage, which could not be achieved without the application of terror. Undoubtedly, Lenin was still under the influence of the "who defeats who" psychology of civil war, which has to be taken into account to understand the repression of 1922. Reading the GPU reports gives an impression that the new apparatus of power was itself characterized by this terror psychosis.

Lenin had received a number of reports about various ways in which the church showed resistance in the larger cities that spring. In some parts of the country even the workers were demonstrating, although getting organizational commands from the church in their case would not have been easy. In his letter he had referred to a piece of information from the Russian Telegraph Agency,[137] according to which "the Black Hundreds are preparing for a show of resistance" against the decree about the confiscation of church property (23 February 1922). The Soviet leadership thought that a plan devised by the "Black Hundreds priesthood" was being realized, which the church was attempting to bring to completion at a time quite adverse to its accomplishment, thereby "falling into a strategic error." However, there are no grounds to believe that the violent events in Shuia[138] were the starting point for some sort of general resistance. In hindsight, and in light of the documents, local resistance can be presumed.

It was on account of the events that could be expected that Lenin strengthened the secret police aspect of the "campaign of confiscation."[139] The demonstration in Shuia came at an opportune moment:

> For us, on the other hand, precisely at the present moment we are presented with an exceptionally favorable, even unique, opportunity when we can in 99 out of 100 chances utterly defeat our enemy with complete success and

> guarantee for ourselves the position we require for decades. Now and only now, when people are being eaten in famine-stricken areas, and hundreds, if not thousands, of corpses lie on the roads, we can (and therefore must) pursue the removal of church property with the most frenzied and ruthless energy and not hesitate to put down the least opposition.[140]

Lenin was, it seems, certain that at this juncture the critical mass of peasants would not support the priesthood if it took up the fight against the Soviet decree. Lenin alluded to "one clever writer," Machiavelli (although not mentioned by name), to say that the people can only bear brutalities for a short time, so such things must be handled energetically and quickly.

Lenin was counting on amassing a few million gold rubles,[141] a portion of which he wanted to spend on ending the famine, with the rest to be allocated to a state fund to help finance the state and stimulate the economy. In a period of preparation for the Genoa Conference, which held the promise of reinstating Western economic relations, Lenin mistakenly considered this expropriation important from a political point of view, though his colleagues in the foreign services did not think such radical measures against the church were timely. Unlike them, Lenin thought of the campaign as a sort of demonstration of force since the greater powers only understood strength.

No doubt, Lenin underestimated the social roots of the church, inasmuch as he viewed it merely as the extended arms of the Whites and the Black Hundreds. The part it had played in the civil war did cause its social influence to narrow drastically, its moral authority to lose its footing, and its political role to be discredited. On the other hand, Lenin's ideas for the "eradication" of the church must be compared to reality. The situation would be misunderstood if it were to be construed to mean the actual physical eradication, or even an intent to achieve this goal.[142] The actions taken against the church did not lead to violent protests from broader layers of society, as per the summary report of the GPU to the higher leadership. From the point of view dictated by the logic of the power apparatus, the measures of deterrence seemed, as it were, successful.[143]

The Deportation of Intellectuals

Considered one of Lenin's political steps "knowing no moral bounds," and another manifestation of his anti-humanist, terrorist policies, in 1922 he initiated the expulsion from Soviet Russia of 228 renowned intellectuals, from Nikolay Berdyaev, through Pitirim Sorokin, to the editors of the journal the *Economist*.[144]

Banishment and exile, which was a traditional part of Russian politics, was not left out of the "tradition" Lenin established either. As in the case of the priests, Lenin did not look for any special theoretical argument or grounds of justification for the expulsion of the intellectuals, but the case does provide a window into the "secret" workings of his political mind.

Lenin's wish to bolster the Soviet government's chances of survival with dictatorial measures emerges clearly in the latest historical research. The aim was to achieve survival at the "cost of the least possible victims," which meant "expatriation rather than being shot." As the initiator and strategist of the operation, Lenin worked it out in the same detail as the attack upon the church.

Lenin discussed the possibility and concrete circumstances of the exile openly in his article of 12 March 1922, *On the Significance of Militant Materialism.*[145] The operation itself was detailed in his secret letter to Felix Dzerzhinsky written on 19 May. The Politburo of the Central Committee supported Lenin's concrete proposals unanimously at its meetings on 24 May and 8 June. The implementation of these repressive measures were planned—pointedly—to be enacted during the completion of the social revolutionaries' trial. The compilation of the final list of those to be banished was left to a three-member committee (L. B. Kamenev, D. I. Kursky, and I. S. Unshlikht).[146] The technical and organizational aspects of the operation carried out by the NKVD–GPU are irrelevant here, but the circumstances that prompted Lenin to undertake the operation must be discussed.

A close investigation stresses the overlapping nature and connections among reasons of various kinds that are found separated in both their historical chronology and location. The antipathy of the revolutionaries for a critical segment of the rebellious, resistant, or simply dissatisfied groups among the Russian intelligentsia drew upon other historical precedents. Minimally, the roots of antipathy reached back to the 1909 publication of the famous volume of *Vekhi*, and the known "Vekhist" writers (Berdyaev, Gershenzon, S. Bulgakov, Frank, Struve, and others), who gave vent to views aligned with their "anti-bolshevist–anti-socialist–anti-materialist" values even during the civil war and after the introduction of the NEP, with the famine also playing a role. Another group of intellectuals fighting the famine, the POMGOL (All-Union Public Committee for the Relief of Starving, formed in July 1921), did not cooperate with the Soviet government, but interpreted the whole situation as a sign of its incompetence and thus set about discrediting it abroad. The intention of the committee to send a delegation to the West led to a serious breakdown and conflict with the Central Executive Committee of the Soviets, culminating in arrests and the demise of the All-Union Committee on 27 August.

Cooperation with the "old" intelligentsia—"winning the experts over," an idea strongly supported by Lenin after the introduction of the NEP—came up against the resistance of a group of leading intellectuals, who did not want to lend their services to the Bolshevik government. An extensive volume, published in the 1970s, "on the involvement of the 'old' intellectuals in building socialism" that described the "operation," did not hide the fact that the most important bourgeois journals, including the *Economist*, *Economicheskoe Vozrozhdeniye*, and the *Misl*, were shut down on the basis of Article 57 of the criminal code, for "counterrevolutionary propaganda and agitation." Though inaccurate, the book did mention that "160 of the most active bourgeois ideologists (E. D. Kuskova, S. N. Prokopovich, A. S. Izgoyev and others) were exiled to the northern governorates."[147] But it did not reveal the web in which the power struggle took place, which the "banishments" followed.

Among the factors contributing to the attack upon the senior intellectuals of the old establishment was the power struggle for top offices that had erupted in the institutions of higher education. Those on the side of the Soviets had no chance of securing any serious influence within the universities or the editorial boards of the academic journals without the direct support of the regime. Moreover, by the end of 1921 and the beginning of 1922 university strikes were in full swing, and were being stopped by use of violent force.[148]

Seven members of POMGOL were exiled to the smaller towns and settlements of Russia on Lenin's suggestion. Later—in order to lessen the pain—they were given a choice of moving to any governorate capital other than Petrograd, Moscow, Kiev, Odessa, or Kharkov, or to move abroad "at their own expense."[149]

All this time the Communist intelligentsia had set about drawing up a critical appraisal of bourgeois thinking, preparing the ideological grounds for squeezing out and expelling its representatives. Lenin went so far as to suggest to members of the Politburo that they should "take 2–3 hours a week to pore through a certain amount of press materials and books, and *methodically* gather data on the time devoted by teachers and writers to political service, their work and literary achievements."[150] Well before the events of 1922, Lenin was occupied by the notion of sending the "old" intelligentsia abroad. Lincoln Steffens, an American journalist who had arrived in Russia with William Bullitt (then a diplomat who favored U.S. relations with the Soviet Union and later the first Ambassador of the United States to the Soviet Union), interviewed Lenin in April 1919. Asked about the Red Terror, Lenin said:

> Terror hurts the revolution both inside and out, and we must find out how to avoid or control or direct it. But we have to know more about psychology than we do now to steer through that madness. And it serves a purpose that has to be served.... We have to devise some way to get rid of the bourgeoisie,

> the upper classes. They won't let you make economic changes during a revolution any more than they will before one; so they must be driven out. I don't see, myself, why we can't scare them away without killing them. Of course, they are a menace outside Russia as well as in, but the émigrés are not so bad. The only solution I see is to have the threat of a Red Terror spread the fear and let them escape. . . . The absolute, instinctive opposition of the old conservatives and even of the fixed liberals has to be silenced.[151]

Trotsky's arguments to justify the terror also cemented this bias. His declarations were as open as Lenin's. Informing the international public in his interview with A. L. Strong, published in the 22 August 1922 issues of *Izvestia,* Trotksy declared that what was under discussion was a "Bolshevik manifestation of humanism."

> Those elements whom we have or will be sending into exile are politically insignificant. But they are potentially tools in the hands of our opponents. In the case of a renewed war situation . . . all of these implacable and incorrigible elements prove to be the military and political agents of the enemy. And then we shall be forced to shoot them, as required by the law of war. Therefore, in this period of respite, our preferred course of action is to deport them in advance.[152]

The operation itself revealed the unavoidable and fateful contradiction, namely, who, and on what basis, is to judge "who is friend and who is foe." This caused serious complications as early as August of 1922, when some of the 230 exiles found defenders among the best-known Bolsheviks closest to Lenin, including Lunacharsky, Krzhanovsky, Kamenev, and Voronsky, who took up the cause of the writer Y. I. Zamyatin—or the famous economist Osinsky, who defended N. D. Kondratev. They based their defenses upon the scientific, economic, and political state interests that lay at the heart of the NEP.[153] What the representatives of the Soviet government wanted from these intellectuals was not unequivocally clear. The expectation was not ideological support for the regime but recognition of the regime and conformity to it, though where the scholarly literature is concerned it does appear to be the case that Lenin and his fellows expected praise. That period was to come later, in a different era. Nonetheless, even the ejection of the "dissenting thinkers" cannot overshadow the fact that one part of the group of anti-Soviet intellectuals who were forced to emigrate was adamant on heightening the internal conflicts within Russia, especially in the intellectual field, and another part related, in a sense, positively to Soviet Russia.

A June 1922 letter from Gorky to Bukharin serves as a document of his experiences among the Russian immigrant intellectuals of Berlin:

> Some were convinced that the Soviet government is historically legitimate. . . . I have heard that the most decent emigrants say: the article pacifies the reader with regard to the Soviet government, by accepting that it is true, only Bolshevism could invigorate the peasantry. The question of brutality—this is my own question, it tortures me without respite. Everywhere I notice the meaningless brutality—notice, now, they are slandering Aleksey Tolstoy (traviat), and will probably organize a public scandal today. With what hatred they write about him in the *Rul* and *Golos*.[154]

Administrative banishment—deportation or exile without a court sentence—was not the invention of the Bolsheviks. It was used widely in the tsarist system against the representatives of the opposition. The Soviet government continued a number of the previous state administration's ways, and this practice was no exception. Besides, the Solovets Islands, along with the monastery, had been handed over to the GPU as early as 1922 for the purpose of establishing concentration camps for political prisoners. If needed, the occupants of the philosophers' ship could have been sent there, rather than Germany. Less than a year later, in a letter dated 27 March, F. E. Dzerzhinsky wrote to I. S. Unshlikht expressing his doubts about the effectiveness of mass deportations. The practice of deportations ceased at that point, and gave way to far more merciless criminal proceedings.[155]

The Message of the S.R. Trial

The plans for the so-called S.R. trial were brought to public attention in February 1922, practically at the same time the campaign against the Church was decided. The trial itself was conducted between 8 June and 7 August 1922. It was the most typical example of the liquidation of the political opposition; a component of the political closure for the civil war; and a display of the "evils" of the past and the present for the benefit of society, to convince people that anyone who turned against the Soviet government would inevitably get swept into the counterrevolutionary camp and be done away with.

A reminder is needed that the "political activity" emphasized earlier as a source of the terror had become interwoven with the role of "petit bourgeois democracy" in the revolution and the civil war from its beginning. Lenin emphasized the significance of this matter in his famous speech at the assembly of Moscow party workers on 27 November 1918. In summarizing the experiences of the civil war, he noted:

> You know that during the Czech attack, when it was at the height of its success, kulak revolts broke out all over Russia. It was only the close ties formed between the urban workers and the peasants that consolidated our rule. . . . The overwhelming majority of both the Mensheviks and the S.R.s sided with the Czechs, the Dutov and Krasnov gangs. This state of affairs forced us to make a ruthless struggle and use terrorist methods of warfare. No matter how much people may have condemned this terrorism from different points of view—and we were condemned by all the vacillating Social-Democrats—we knew perfectly well it was necessitated by the acute Civil War. It was necessary because all the petit-bourgeois democrats had turned against us. They used all kinds of methods against us—civil war, bribery and sabotage. It was these conditions that necessitated the terror. Therefore we should not repent or renounce it.[156]

His experiences up to 1922 did not soften Lenin's attitude to petit-bourgeois democracy. It is common knowledge that during these trials, S.R. leaders were sentenced for "counterrevolutionary, anti-Soviet activity." Preparation for the trials was carried on in the public eye. Earlier S.R. assaults on representatives of the Soviet government, and more recent political conspiracies against the regime, were brought into the foreground with the not overly concealed purpose of wrestling the "socialist opposition" into the pigeonhole of "anti-Soviet and counterrevolutionary intelligentsia." This was not a case of some sort of anti-intelligentsia feeling, though a certain degree of anti-intelligentsia bias was characteristic of Lenin's political disposition. It stemmed from his approach to class (the interests of intellectuals being different from that of the working class), and plainly his distrust was a product of his political experiences, according to which, due to its "individualist" traits, a significant majority of the intelligentsia would not subject itself to the "social order and discipline" of the Soviet system. The objective was the reinforcement of the Soviet political institutional system, and all the foregoing questions were subordinated to this.

The process, at any rate, permanently broke the strength of the S.R. party, which had previously been the largest. A portion of its membership had joined the Bolsheviks earlier, similarly to significant segments of other political formations (such as the Bund), which can be attributed in part to the siphoning effect of power, but also as a result of the Soviet government's victories in the civil war. If the contemporary GPU reports are to be believed, the trials—in spite of the dismissive inner opposition and the protests abroad—were met with a positive response in broad circles of society. Their wish for order proved greater even than the demand for political democracy. They did not delve into the quality and significance of the choice between a one- and a multi-party system, as apathy and disappointment meant that the development of theoretical and legal sensitivity on a social scale was left unprompted. Those on the side of the regime who did mull over this question supported Bolshevism as the "custodian of Soviet power."

Every Soviet leader, from Lunacharsky to Lenin, took a stance where the legitimacy and political significance of the trial was concerned, never denying its political nature in the slightest. They even formulated its "concept" themselves, since there was an express need, with socialists seated on the benches of the accused. The preparation of legal grounds, however, did not get too much attention wasted on it.

In the long run, the reprisals against the S.R.s and the Mensheviks came from the resolve of the regime to make the parties' leaders "voluntarily" go abroad, or to have them isolated in distant governorates in the country.[157] Published documents of the "trial of the right-wing S.R.s" show that what Lenin and the Bolshevik leaders required from the incriminated S.R. politicians—in light of their military-political resistance during the civil war—were confessions of their crimes, and pledges that they would never again oppose the Soviet government's institutions or forms of rule, either militarily or politically. They met with disappointment in these aims, even though Bolshevik leaders of the stature of Bukharin, Lunacharsky, and Pyatakov were on the prosecution's side. They had all analyzed the S.R.s theoretical and political role in the civil war, including their organization of the Constituent Assembly of Samara and their armed conflicts with the Red Army. The charge was "treason," inasmuch as the rightist S.R.s had "taken up arms against the dictatorship of the proletariat." Pyatakov posed the question, as reported by the press at the time, of how the defendants would behave if they found themselves at liberty. Would they continue their armed struggle against the Soviet government? "Comrade Pyatakov underscored that this was an important thing for the court to ascertain before it reaches its verdict."[158] Giving brave answers to the accusations, the S.R. leaders (and others such as Yelena Ivanova-Iranova), made it unequivocally clear that they held to their earlier views: "If I were to be freed I would take action as dictated to me by the hatred I have felt for you since October 1917."[159] At the end of his rather long speech, A. R. Gots—perhaps the most respectable and best-known leader of the party—offered a polemical critique of Bukharin:

> We owe you recognition for giving us the opportunity to voice our answers in full, and if fate would have it so that our confession becomes our last

> will and testament, we still believe, and will continue to believe that we are doing our duty, and doing it to the end, as revolutionaries must do. Whatever verdict is passed, we will die as revolutionaries, staring death bravely in the face. If it turns out that we are to stay alive, we will live as socialists, working in the name of socialism as we have worked till now, and as we understand socialism.[160]

Under international social democratic pressure, the death sentences were modified to prison terms. However, Lenin and the Bolshevik leaders documented that the political opposition would not make peace with the dictatorship of the Bolshevik Party. And yet what was truly at stake in the trial was a demonstrative message that the Bolsheviks would administratively liquidate "anti-Soviet political parties."[161]

Looking back, it is indisputable that disposing of political and ideological opponents this way was not just a "bad message" in terms of the future, but it also paved the way for isolating political opponents without oversight. Lenin and the Bolshevik leaders had established police checks on the free thinking of their opponents—and later any individual, political opponent or not—without creating a mechanism within the system to remove these checks on freethinking. For Lenin, the question that still trumped all others remained the one posed in October 1917: "Can the Bolsheviks retain power?"

Up to this point, the complicated way Lenin related to political oppression, violence, and terror has been approached through the logic of a given series of events. However, the exploration of this question and Lenin's cast of mind would certainly be less biased in the context of a broader process of a different nature, affecting larger masses of people. To capture the subject of violence and terror at the dawn of Soviet history and the Russian Revolution, it is fruitful to examine the fate of Jewry, a theme still out of favor with the more recent histories of the revolution.[162] Lenin's own conflict with terror and violence, anti-Semitism and racism in general, as well as the motives of his politics and thought in regard to these matters, becomes more emphatically outlined through an exploration of the "Jewish question."

LENIN AND THE POGROMS

> "Ah, you dirty Yid!" the sergeant roared in fury. "We're going to see you shot! I'll teach you to skulk in the dark corners. I'll show you! What were you doing behind those piles of timber? Spy! . . ."

> But the bloodstained man did not reply to the Cossack sergeant. Then the sergeant ran ahead, and the two men jumped aside to escape the flailing rod with its heavy, glittering brass tip. Without calculating the force of his blow the sergeant brought down the ramrod like a thunderbolt on to the man's head. Something cracked inside it and the man in black did not even groan.
>
> —MIKHAIL BULGAKOV, *THE WHITE GUARD*[163]

The Jewish Question: At the Heart of the Problem

Among Lenin's first comrades and friends, as well as those on the editorial board of *Iskra,* were a number of revolutionaries of Jewish background or origin. Martov and Trotsky could be named as the most famous among them, but later we could add Lenin's closest political pupils Kamenev and Zinovyev, the illegal party activists Taratuta and Rozalia Zemlyachka, Yakov Sverdlov and Uritsky, Litvinov, the historian Yaroslavsky, and the list stretches on.[164] At the same time a good number of his enemies were also Jews—the first that leaps to mind being the would-be assassin Fanni Kaplan. Though there were fewer Jewish revolutionaries in the Bolshevik Party than among the Mensheviks, Lenin had ample acquaintance with the Jewish revolutionary intellectuals' abilities, habits, lifestyle, and way of thinking.

Though Lenin had not undertaken any independent research in the "field of Jewish life," a composite theoretical and political stance can be outlined through his numerous reflections on the theme. He knew the literature on the Jewish people that was available to the educated classes even as a young man; this much is clear from some of his early writing. Statistical annuals were a basic source for Lenin's scientific research from the 1890s. He was most familiar with the data of the 1897 census, which pointed to some of the specifics in the development of Russian Jewry, such as the peculiar structure of labor distribution. In addition, he was apprised of the subject through the leading journals of the period, not to mention his knowledge of the significant Marxist works dedicated to the Jewish question, Kautsky's especially. Nonetheless, he did not show particular interest in Marx's writing on the subject even though it was part of the Russian social-democratic discourse, and Lunacharsky had spoken of it in superlatives.[165] Meanwhile, the Jewish philosophical and religious-messianic tradition, and its explicitly Marxist tendencies, left him completely cold.[166]

As widely acknowledged, a major component of the Jewish question in terms of a Russian historical, political, and theoretical problem was that the Jews were the only large ethnic group in pre- and post-revolution Russia that could be considered a so-called extraterritorial nationality.[167] At the turn of the century, half of the world's Jews (totaling 10–11 million) lived in the tsar's empire. A vast majority resided in the so-called Pale of Settlement on the western edge of the empire,[168] the result of numerous anti-Semitic proscriptions and regulatory restrictions.[169] For Lenin it was a serious matter that on the eve of the world war in 1914, nearly one-third (600,000 individuals) of the economically active part of the Jewish population belonged to the working class.[170]

Lenin ran into the issue of the Jews at a relatively early stage of his political career In the editorial circle of *Iskra*, Plekhanov had already taken a position opposing the Bund—the "chauvinism of the Jews"—in September 1900, and made a motion for their removal from the RSDLP. Lenin, who in principle also positioned himself in opposition to the "separatism" of the Bund, firmly rejected Plekhanov's intolerant attitude, and from an organizational point of view, his futile and insensitive approach.[171] It was in *Iskra* in February 1903 that Lenin first published an article specifically dealing with Jews, concerning the fight against anti-Semitism, and about the circumstances of the struggle against anti-Semitism in the context of the contention between the Yekaterinoslav (Governorate) Party Committee and the Bund. These pages already showed that he could only imagine an effective fight against anti-Semitism within the framework of cooperation with Russian workers and therefore rejected the separatist designs of the Bund, which styled itself the exclusive representative of Jewish workers.[172] In retrospect, Lenin may have underestimated the significance of Russian workers who had been infected by anti-Semitic prejudice, yet no really convincing argument can be brought against "Jewish" and "Christian" workers joining in a common fight against anti-Semitism, with no national subdivisions. The second time Lenin spoke up on this subject, once again in *Iskra,* was in relation to the infamous Kishinev Pogrom, at the beginning of June 1903. Based on the way in which the pogroms unfolded, "their rich history," and the course taken by the Kishinev Pogrom (6–7 April 1903), he emphasized the "prominent" role of certain groups in the Russian intelligentsia and members of the government, sensing their cooperation with the pogroms. The 1881 "pogrom epidemic" had already posed a question about collective activity of the "intelligentsia and the government in power" in the unfolding of the pogroms. Even then "educated society," a segment of the intelligentsia, had played an important part by taking upon themselves the intellectual-emotional preparation and justification of the pogroms. Kishinev gave more unequivocal evidence of the same.[173]

In these pogroms—and this is very important regarding their later history—Lenin saw an expression of the "unraveling autocracy," a disintegrating and weakening of "state order." He attributed similar tendencies to the unfolding of the "police-socialism of [police administrator] Zhubatov," which was used to manipulate the labor movement in the interest of the regime by means of secret police methods: "Without second thoughts and in full awareness of what they are doing they kindle the flames of tribal and religious war with cold calculation, aiming to draw the people's masses away from social and political protest, the path they have only recently taken."[174]

He underscored that Interior Minister Plehve, the police, and army officers deliberately based their politics on both the Kishinev Pogrom and the pogroms that followed it. They built on the "instincts" of the masses and set them against the revolutionary movement:

> They are organizing reactionary shopkeepers, clerks and shady barefoot men under a flag that reads: "Beat the Jew!," complementing naturally the organization of dark laborers that was set up with such facility under the Zhubatov regime, attended upon by priests, police, and "nationalists" arisen from society. Once past the borders of the Pale of Settlement, the militant druzhinas established to beat the Jews turn into gangs of coachmen and butchers, ready to beat "student" and labor demonstrators as in Saratov on 5 May 1902, and in Tomsk on 19 February 1903.[175]

However, Lenin repeatedly stressed that the Bund's organizational independence from the RSDLP was ultimately the wrong choice for the Jewish worker in the face of an anti-Semitic, pogromist autocracy, and Zionism was even more so, "as it draws the cultured forces of the Jewish proletariat" away from the revolutionary struggle in order to join a cause with a utopian objective. But Lenin believed that the anti-Semitic designs of the government, "calling the forces of the reaction to battle, also contributed to stirring up the forces of the revolution." This rather mechanistic position finds an exaggerated formulation:

> The class-organization of the proletariat is under far greater immediate threat from the Zionist movement than anti-Semitism, and since for us, social democrats, there exists no "chosen people" or "not chosen people," we cannot, by any means, be distracted from the "struggle with the prejudices of the Jewish masses." The Bund obviously believes that it has an exclusive monopoly on this struggle.[176]

In Lenin's view, therefore, the success of the fight against anti-Semitism and the pogroms depended on whether the "Russian proletariat" came to the defense of the "Jews in a state of panic" as a result of the pogroms. The Jewish organizers considered Lenin's position mere conjecture, rather than a composite strategy. At the same time Dimanshteyn, an early expert on the subject and later leader of the Jewish Section of the Bolshevik Party, noticed that Lenin saw a sort of competition between his party and the political forces interested in separate organization of the Jews, particularly in the Bund.[177] Unquestionably the Russian labor movement suffered from a serious deficit in cadres, and Lenin took up the fight with the Bund secondarily, with the purpose of bringing the Bundists, who had an internationalist bent, over to his side.[178]

Finally, Lenin "stumbled" across the Jewish issue in the period when the Party was founded, that is, the Second Congress, when the objective was to establish a centralized social-democratic party unfettered by questions of ethnic belonging. Contrary to this, the Jewish labor unions of Russia, Poland, and Lithuania, as well as the Bund, proposed an RSDLP with a federative party organization based on national autonomy. This proposal stood on the premise that the Jews in Russia were a "nationality" (the Fourth Congress of the Bund having already formulated this), and furthermore that the Jewish proletariat could only fully be represented by the Bund.

Though a majority at the Second Congress in the summer of 1903 rejected the separatism of the Bund—after a protracted and passionate debate in which Plekhanov, Lenin, and Martov took the lead[179]— they did not prove overly sensitive regarding the special living circumstances and life-style of the Jews. In other words, the organizational unity of the party stood above the freedom to form independent national collectives, which was why the resolution of the congress—formulated by Lenin—stated that the current situation simply meant the Bund's withdrawal from the RSDLP.[180] What seemed simple in terms of the organizational logic of a revolutionary party was considered ambiguous by the Bund, especially when seen from the presumed interests of the Jewish proletariat. It should not be forgotten that at the time of rapid increase in the pogroms a rare situation came about, pointedly expressed in a document of the Bund's Odessa chapter in April 1903. The essence of this document was that Jewry represented the most persecuted people of the empire, with accusations of murder hurled at them as an everyday part of the priesthood's propaganda.[181]

After the conclusion of the congress in London, and now aware of the experiences of the pogroms, Lenin devoted a full article to the problematic situation in Russia regarding the Bund, the RSDLP, and the Jews.[182] The sources of his theoretical thought were composed of contemporary leftist and Marxist literature, primarily from Germany, France, and Austria. He was especially struck by a trend in the Bund's argument: the "appeal to the ideal of a Jewish nation." Building on Kautsky's authority, he treated the political consequences of Jewish separatism and the aims of the anti-Semitic extreme right as virtually identical: both arrived at the same conclusion in rejecting Jewish assimilation.

> Unfortunately, however, this Zionist idea is absolutely false and essentially reactionary. "The Jews have ceased to be a nation, for a nation without a territory is unthinkable," says one of the most prominent of Marxist theoreticians, Karl Kautsky. . . .[183] All that remains for the Bundists is to develop the theory of a separate Russian-Jewish nation, whose language is Yiddish and their territory the Pale of Settlement. . . . Can we possibly attribute to chance the fact that it is the reactionary forces all over Europe, and especially in Russia, who *oppose* the assimilation of the Jews and try to perpetuate their isolation? That is precisely what the Jewish problem *amounts to*: assimilation or isolation? . . . The idea of a Jewish nationality runs counter to the interests of the Jewish proletariat, for it fosters among them, directly or indirectly, a spirit hostile to assimilation, the spirit of the "ghetto." . . . Assimilation "*is the only possible solution of the Jewish problem, and we should support everything that makes for the ending of Jewish isolation.*"[184]

A current perspective, after the Holocaust, clearly shows that Lenin—and of course Martov, Kautsky, and even Marx—had overestimated the inclination, willingness, and the "ability" of Russian (and European) society to accommodate the Jews. Unlike Lenin, Plekhanov had thought through the Zionist outlooks realistically, but found that they were even worse than that of European assimilation. He compared the foundation of a Jewish state with the creation of Liberia, pointing out that even that had not solved the problem for American Negroes. In October 1905, in an interview (*Hronika Yevreyskoy Zhizni*) that he gave to Vladimir Zhabotinsky, the leader of Russian Zionism, his opinion was:

> If you ask me, I do not believe in Zionism, but not because it is not realizable. I do not believe in Zionism as the instrument of saving the Jewish masses. . . . Let us assume that there is already a Jewish state in Palestine with a population of two-three million. Such a state would not be able to receive all of the masses of Jewish people. And it would also not be able to protect the Jewish people from anti-Semitism. . . . The full solution to the Jewish question is not possible under the conditions offered by the current social order . . . and I have repeatedly drawn the attention of the Bundists to the fact that they are the kind of Zionists who are afraid of seasickness.[185]

History soon validated Plekhanov's skeptical point of view: 1905 proved to be a decisive turn.

The 1905 Revolution and Jews in Russia

Lenin's articles during the 1905 Revolution showed the spread of anti-Semitism and the pogroms as a process organized from above, and this view was enforced when the practices of the secret police became public in the days of the revolution. The tsar's government and the authorities covered up their participation in the pogroms by presenting the phenomenon as a natural outburst of the people's anger against the "Jewish rebels" and the "Jewish revolutionaries." Lenin gave a precise description of how the pogroms were an organic constituent part of the components and control techniques of the counterrevolution. In one article, written almost on the day after the outbreak of the revolution, Lenin linked the weakening of the state to its efforts to fuel hostilities between ethnic groups. In order to achieve this it reorganized the Black Hundreds, a new extreme-right organization that aimed to preserve autocracy, for the cogs and wheels of the police machinery were worn and the armed forces no longer sufficient. To fuel ethnic tensions the Black Hundreds were being recruited "from among the politically least developed sections of the urban (*and, following that, naturally, of the rural*) petty bourgeoisie"; they would "rally to the defense of the throne all reactionary elements" within society, transforming the police's actions in defending the state into the struggle of one part of the people against the other:

> Against the people's revolution, against the class struggle the police cannot be depended on; one must have the backing of the people, too, the support of classes. . . . That is precisely what the government is now doing when it sets the Tatars against the Armenians in Baku; when it seeks to provoke new pogroms against the Jews; when it organizes Black-Hundred gangs against the Zemstvo people, students, and rebellious Gymnasium youths; and when it appeals to the loyal nobles and to the conservative elements among the peasants. Ah, well! We Social-Democrats are not surprised at these tactics of the autocracy; nor shall we be frightened by them. We know that it will no longer help the government to stir up racial animosity since the workers have begun to organise armed resistance to the pogrom-bandits.[186]

Lenin not only wrote about the "fueling of the racial hostilities," but about how it was consciously directed and carefully planned, and was finally meant to lead to the explosion of civil war, and therefore the revolution's defeat. Lenin saw a possibility of averting the victory of the counterrevolution through a "civil war" against it. As he imagined it, the "contra-civil war" (in fact, he was already discussing a preventive civil war at that stage) would give power to the millions of oppressed, putting an end to all forms of oppression, including national and racial oppression. Lenin had a surprisingly early inkling of the importance of the "Jewish question" where the scope of the revolution and counterrevolution were concerned. In his preface to the report on the Third Congress of the RSDLP, published in Yiddish, Lenin continued to call the union of workers of various ethnicities to be free of their ethnicity as a fundamental precondition of revolutionary resistance against tsarism.[187]

In accordance with this stance, Lenin almost whooped for joy upon learning that Jewish and Russian workers were taking joint steps against the pogroms. Every event in which workers themselves stood up to the pogromists was of special importance to him, as some workers had also joined the detachments of the Black Hundreds when they were set up.[188] These "errant" workers usually did not come from the industrial masses, but belonged to the backwaters of the counterrevolution. From Switzerland, Lenin had informed his readers in August that "an agreement was concluded between the Bolsheviks, the Mensheviks, and the Bund. . . . 'Joint collection of money for the purchase of arms, a joint plan of action, etc.'" to fight the pogroms.[189] True, Lenin identified the Black Hundreds, autocracy, and the government as one, and he did not reveal the forces within the government that denounced the pogroms, which was a course dictated by the practical aims of a revolutionary politician. At the same time not only Lenin, but Russian Marxists in general, were clear that an organic relationship had been forged between the Black Hundreds and the more "backward," land- and village-bound, illiterate groups of working people in many regions, including central Russia; the social-democratic workers took this experience into account when in the course of the revolutionary struggle they designed the best possible forms of battle.[190] Lenin published an innovative finding in a paper of 20 September 1905, saying that the autocracy and the counterrevolution had succeeded in making "revolutionary environs" out of the Jewry living in the Pale of Settlement, as its residents provided the revolutionary movement's main cadres. The finding is considered important by the most current historiography as well. For example, 29.1 percent of those arrested for political crimes between 1901 and 1903 were Jews (2,269 individuals), and in 1905 Jews accounted for 53 percent of the total political arrests.[191]

Lenin was among the first to realize that the oppressed Jewish masses became the supporters of the revolution by virtue of the cultural and social abilities they had developed through history. He was the first to draw attention to the "official" link between the slogan "Beat the Jew!," anti-Semitism, the pogroms, and the anti-left, anti-social democratic tendencies:

> Jewry had planted the seed of revolution in the circles of the most backward Russian workers. This was enough to make the "Jew" a symbol of the revolution in the eyes of the government. . . . In the aftermath to the Kishinev Pogroms scores of other Jewish pogroms followed; the battle against the revolution has shifted to central Russia.[192]

Lenin returned to Russia at the end of November and had the opportunity to observe how, following the suppression of the Moscow armed uprising in December 1905, the counterrevolution played the anti-Semitic and pogromist card throughout Russia—for example in Belostok, Lugansk, and Vologda. The overview that emerges from Lenin's writings is unequivocal: the pogrom is an organized phenomenon that gets its encouragement from above, while the rabble acts upon agitation and bribes. In a survey of the Belostok pogrom, Lenin relied upon a telegram of the elector of the town's civilians:

> "A *deliberately-organised* anti-Jewish pogrom has started." . . . "Vigorous agitation for the pogrom has been carried on for the past two weeks. In the streets, particularly at night, leaflets were distributed calling for the massacre, not only of Jews, but also of intellectuals. *The police simply turned a blind eye to all this*."[193]

In commenting on the old, well-known scenario, Lenin noted "leaflets are printed in government printing offices calling for a massacre of the Jews. When the pogrom begins, the police is inactive," and not only that, but:

> the troops quietly look on at the exploits of the Black Hundreds. But later these very police go through the farce of prosecution and trial of the pogromists. . . . Vile instigation, bribery, and fuddling with drink of the scum of our cursed capitalist "civilisation," the brutal massacre of unarmed by armed people.[194]

After the defeat of the revolution, anti-Semitism became rooted in an increasingly wide strata of society, especially in the Pale of Settlement and the neighboring areas.

Separatism or Assimilation?

Lenin's views related to the problematic field of the Jewish question did not change a great deal in the period from the defeat of the 1905 Revolution to the beginning of the First World War. He treated the problem ideologically and theoretically in the framework of "democratic and voluntary assimilation," though his answers normally came from conflicts that pointed toward the impossibility of assimilation. A "medieval" Russia and the "separatist Bund," which in reality "presupposed" one another, did not comply with Lenin's rational and revolutionary arguments, though in his eyes this was not a case against—but for—the revolution. He was aware, having had an excellent grounding in Russian economic and social history, that the social base of the Bund was composed of a Jewish workforce objectively in isolation, with a tradition of artisanship and possessing its own psychology.[195]

It is known that ethnic separatism was, in a sense, the "weakness" of the labor movement throughout eastern Europe. On the one hand, the national independence movements fighting the monarchies were overseen by certain groups among the old intelligentsia, the priesthood, the nobility, or the formative bourgeoisie respectively, depending upon the eastern European country concerned. Secondly, it was not easy to reconcile the values of the movements of national rebirth and the social-political aims of the labor movement, since the leadership, ideology, and social background of the national movements were starkly different from that of the labor movement, resulting in more competition than solidarity.[196]

In this sense Russian social democracy never rated the organizational and political aims of the labor movement behind those of the national movements, and, even among social democrats, Lenin was probably the most dogged about this. However, he soon recognized the peculiar role of nationalism, and thus remained devoted to the political union, independent of national belonging, of the (extraordinarily) ethnically mixed population.[197] In 1913, his attention was drawn to the emphatic difference in the way the Jewish question was "dealt with" in Russia and Western Europe, and he underscored the destructive effects of an educational system segregated along religious-ethnic lines.[198]

> The extreme expression of present-day nationalism is the scheme for the nationalisation of Jewish schools. . . . What does this nationalisation mean? It means segregating the Jews into *special* Jewish schools (secondary schools). The doors of all other educational establishments—both private and state—are to be completely closed to the Jews. This "brilliant" plan is rounded off by the proposal to limit the number of pupils in the Jewish secondary schools to the notorious "quota"! . . . The example of the advanced countries of the world—say, Switzerland in Western Europe or Finland in Eastern Europe—shows us that only consistently democratic state institutions ensure the most peaceable and human (not bestial) coexistence of various nationalities, *without* the artificial and harmful separation of education according to nationalities.

At least some of the Western European countries were models for Lenin, because in Russia "medieval" solutions typified political life:

> In Eastern Europe there exists a country where things like the Beilis case are still possible, and Jews are condemned by the Purishkeviches to a condition worse than that of the Negroes. In that country a scheme for nationalising Jewish schools was recently mooted in the Ministry. Happily, this reactionary utopia is no more likely to be realized. . . . In Austria, the idea of cultural-national autonomy has remained largely a flight of literary fancy, which the Austrian Social-Democrats themselves have not taken seriously. In Russia, however, it has been incorporated in the programs of all the Jewish bourgeois parties, and of several petit-bourgeois, opportunist elements.

It was clear that the culture of the Black Hundreds was behind the trial, and Tsar Nicholas II was a fanatic supporter of the group; his diary entries evidence a similarly fanatical anti-Semitism, having considered *The Protocols of the Elders of Zion* an excellent work until Stolypin let him know that it was a mere fabrication. Even Minister of the Interior Makarov was a supporter of the Black Hundreds' party, as was the Union of the Russian People, at the time of the Beilis Trial.[199] Lenin showed that military conflicts only deepened "ethnic separatism," not just in Russia but also beyond its borders. He built his position regarding the question of national separation on his analysis of capital relations: that though multiethnic capital can come to business agreements, it pits *labor* against those who take up labor, on the labor market and in everyday life, on national-ethnic grounds. In *Critical Remarks,* he wrote:

> What is left is capitalism's world-historical tendency to break down national barriers, obliterate national distinctions, and to *assimilate* nations—a tendency which manifests itself more and more powerfully with every passing decade, and is one of the greatest driving forces transforming capitalism into socialism.[200]

On this basis he attacked with increasing vehemence the romantic, nostalgic views cropping up behind the slogan of "national culture." He also said that Jewish tendencies of separatism reduce the revolutionary potentials hidden in Jewry to ashes—on account of its social status and culture—and wholly neglect the class perspective:

> But there are other elements in Jewish culture and in Jewish history as a whole. Of the ten and a half million Jews in the world, somewhat over a half live in Galicia and Russia, backward and semi-barbarous countries, where the Jews are *forcibly* kept in the status of a caste. The other half lives in the civilised world, and there the Jews do not live as a segregated caste. . . . Whoever, directly or indirectly, puts forward the slogan of Jewish "national culture" is (whatever his good intentions may be) an enemy of the proletariat, a supporter of all that is *outmoded* and connected with *caste* among the Jewish people; he is an accomplice of the rabbis and the bourgeoisie. On the other hand, those Jewish Marxists who mingle with the Russian, Lithuanian, Ukrainian and other workers in international Marxist organizations, and make their contribution (both in Russian and in Yiddish) towards creating the international culture of the working-class movement—those Jews, despite the separatism of the Bund, uphold the best traditions of Jewry by fighting the slogan of "national culture."[201]

However, when Lenin recalled late nineteenth-century Russia in his famous lecture on the 1905 revolution delivered on 9 (22) January 1917 at a meeting of young workers in the Zurich People's House, what must have struck him particularly in regard to this period was the immutability of autocratic rule and the change for the worse of circumstances. At the same time he sketched the outlook for Jews, in that the anti-Semitic, pogromist politics of the tsar would thrust significant masses of Jewry into the arms of the revolutionary left:

> Tsarism vented its hatred particularly upon the Jews. On the one hand, the Jews furnished a particularly high percentage (compared with the total Jewish population) of leaders of the revolutionary movement. And now, too, it should be noted to the credit of the Jews, they furnish a relatively high percentage of internationalists, compared with other nations. On the other hand, tsarism adroitly exploited the basest anti-Jewish prejudices of the most ignorant strata of the population in order to organise, if not to lead directly, *pogroms*—over 4,000 were killed and more than 10,000 mutilated in 100 towns. These atrocious massacres of peaceful Jews, their wives and children roused disgust throughout the civilised world. I have in mind, of course, the disgust of the truly democratic elements of the civilised world, and these are *exclusively* the socialist workers, the proletarians.[202]

All of these thoughts not only became timely in 1917, but also brought about a turn in world history that was in part contrary to what Lenin had hoped for.

With the world war and civil war, the revolution and the counterrevolution, a genocide of the Jewish people, on a scale unknown earlier, entered upon the stage of history.[203]

From World War to Civil War

At the helm of the freshly established revolutionary government, the Council of People's Commissars, Lenin paid serious attention to the problems related to the Jewish population from the very first days following the October Revolution. Two observations shed light upon the roots of the problem. While he knew quite well that the imperialist war had brought the mass terror against the Jews into motion, hundreds of thousands of Jews (some accounts say a million) were expatriated or evacuated because of military operations or anti-Semitic prejudice. If they were lucky enough to find work, they joined the industrial production in inner Russia's western zone: "As a result of the war, educated Jews in great numbers were relocated to Russian cities. They were the ones who brought a halt to the general sabotage, with which we were confronted immediately after the revolution, and which carried great dangers."[204] With this relocation—or "dispersal"—of the "revolutionary cadres," there was not only a marked onset of persecution of Jews and growth in anti-Semitism, but also the "preparation" of the revolutionary camp received an effective boost. History has clarified that the growing strength of anti-Semitism and the unfolding of the pogroms were the result of the policies of the highest military leadership's anti-Semitic convictions, along with the world war. The military leadership accused the whole of the Jewish population of being "traitors." This is when the Jews became the immediate scapegoat for everything that was connected with military losses and worsening living conditions—"traitors, spies, pricehitchers, speculators" etc. Any time the pogroms erupted, they served the larcenous instincts of soldiers, retreating units, and Cossacks. Years had to pass before the non-military population, specific groups of the peasantry primarily, would join these murderous anti-Semitic sprees, which only moderated temporarily in the year of the 1917 Revolution, but which exploded with much more brutal force in the course of the civil war.[205]

Lenin and the Bolsheviks took measures against anti-Semitic excesses on the first day of the revolution, when—perhaps surprisingly to them—anti-Semitism affected their own "camp." The first pogroms after the October Revolution were carried out by newly formed subdivisions of the Red Army who had not yet been trained in military discipline. As the Germans advanced in Ukraine, these Red Army units were retreating in the governorate of Chernigov in the spring of 1918.

Learning about the horrors of the Mglina pogrom, Zorin, the captain of one of the units of recruited peasants, shot two pogromists on the spot, but he himself had to flee.[206] Yet the 2nd All-Russia Congress of Soviets had, in a decree on the second day of the October Revolution (the night of 8–9 November), prescribed that all local soviets should take assertive action against all "pogroms, including those against Jews," especially since the Duma and the Provisional Government were not able to bring effective measures against this "disease."[207] With the disintegration of order, chaos led to a more deep-seated culture of pogroms; the authorities could not rein it in using normal measures.[208]

The Moscow soviet passed a separate decree on 28 April 1918, *On Anti-Semitic Pogrom Agitation in Moscow and the Moscow Region*. It emphasized that special attention must be given to the "anti-Semitic agitation of the priesthood in support of the Black Hundreds, which is a part of the counterrevolutionary work of the clergy." Strictly in keeping with a class perspective, the Soviet considered the "establishment of separate Jewish fighting detachments" unnecessary.[209] As chairman of the Council of People's Commissars, Lenin demanded further, radical measures against anti-Semitism. His efforts were rewarded with the famous decree, originally proposed by Sverdlov, that was published by the Council of People's Commissars on 27 July 1918. Lenin redrafted it regarding various points and "radicalized" the Soviet government's steps against anti-Semitism, making the "eradication of anti-Semitism" compulsory for every soviet. The document outlawed every person and organization that continued agitation for pogroms. He wrote these remarks on the document in red ink.[210]

The published decree was titled *Eradication of the Anti-Semitic Movement at its Roots*. Regarding the areas affected by the pogroms, the document noted that these were often near the front, thus emphasizing their "military aspect." The decree's signers pointed out, anti-Semitism was the most effective tool in the hands of the counterrevolution to secure a social base. As other documents also attest, this attitude also found expression in the "anti-Semitic agitation of the pro-Black Hundreds priesthood." The significance of this outlook can be seen in that it comes up in the struggle against anti-Semitism and the pogrom campaigns later, in numerous Soviet documents and articles:

> The Jewish capitalists are our enemies, but not as Jews, as the bourgeois. The Jewish worker is our brother. . . . The Council of People's Commissars declares the anti-Semitic movement and the pogroms against the Jews destructive to the cause of the peasant revolution, and calls upon the working people of socialist Russia to fight this disease with every possible means. National enmities weaken our revolutionary lines, divide the workers' front,

which is free of ethnic differences, and only plays into the hands of our enemies.[211]

The Bolsheviks were surprised that the pogroms turned into genocide across parts of Ukraine and Russia from the end of 1918 to the end of 1920. Of the hundreds of pogroms, the majority were committed by the voluntary army of General Denikin and the armed bands of Petlyurists in the name of the independent Directory of the Ukrainian People's Republic, the latter outdoing by far even the Denikinists in committing murder. The faceless pogrom campaigns led to the bestial killing of many tens of thousands of people, with some data putting the number of losses at 200,000.[212]

At the end of 1919, Lenin proposed—in a special report for the Central Committee of the Russian Communist Party regarding the situation of Jewish workers—what the Soviet government needed to accomplish among the Jewish masses. The document emphasized: "Peasants who were not enemies have come under the influence of the pogroms carried out by the bands in Ukraine, anti-Semitism has corrupted social life as a whole."[213] Anti-Semitism and the pogrom were the ideological-political cement for the White Guard officers corps dictatorship symbolized by the names of Denikin and Kolchak, and the White Guardist counterrevolution in general. The situation was similar in Petlyurist Ukraine; after the German defeat, the Polish-supported toppling of the Soviet government reinforced anti-Semitism as a common enemy—the "Jew"—was discovered. The anti-Semitic tropes that had become the norm in the first part of the First World War were significantly transformed, and the Bolsheviks needed to react quickly. The propaganda center of the Volunteer Army (*Osvag*), along with its ideological interpreters, added a new element to the traditional descriptions of Jews as "Jesus killers," "traitors," "spies," "money hoarders," and "speculators." Now, there was a new avatar of the "evil Jew"—the figure of the "Soviet communist commissar." The murder of the "venal Jew" as a "tyrant Jewish Commissar" was always accompanied by robbery and looting, which by White Guardist and Ukrainian nationalist agitation and propaganda was lifted to "new moral heights": "Hit the Jew and save Russia!" (or sometimes Ukraine), and "Beat the Jew, down with the commune!" The depth trawlers of anti-Semitism included a significant segment of the earlier liberal-conservative intelligentsia (previously concentrated in the Kadet Party), which had now dissipated to the level of White Guardist anti-Semitic propaganda. This was now evident in P. Struve's more restrained "a-Semitism" or the anti-Semitism of S. Bulgakov, a Vekhist religious philosopher who had donned the mantle of a priest, who called for pogroms. A later mode of thought contained the basic prejudice that the Russian Revolution was "sent upon Russia by alien intrigue, in the image of the Jews," which was "supplemented" with what might be called the traditional anti-Semitism of the Russian Orthodox Church.[214] While the Black Hundreds movement had ended years earlier, its ideology had permeated the thinking of broad strata of society. It was as if a major part of the society had become the Black Hundreds.

A mass of documents and research reveal clearly that the Whites tried—if only for international effect—to hide the bare facts of the pogroms behind a veil of conspiracy. The Bolsheviks did the opposite, reporting right from the start on the pogrom agitations and even the pogroms within the ranks of the Red Army.[215] Lenin and the top Bolshevik leadership knew of every occurrence in detail and were aware of the terrible facts of anti-Semitism. Dimanshteyn reported personally to Lenin on these occurrences.[216]

The reactions to the pogroms by Lenin, Trotsky, and the Soviet leadership in general was firm, committed, and well-thought-out, but also flexible, adapting to the changing situation as optimal solutions were sought. (The experiences of 1905 were useful in this regard.) Lenin and Trotsky took the position that it was not expedient to organize the army or the party on ethnic grounds, as an internationalist revolution could not poison itself with nationalism, the very ideology that united the Whites. Denikin or Wrangel, with their anti-Semitic ideology and the promise of "one, indivisible Russia," seemed simply to be reinstaters of the old tsarist system, who wanted some sort of modernized monarchy in the place of the Bolshevik system.[217] Lenin and all the Bolsheviks continuously stressed that the Whites were supported and "kept" by the West for power-political reasons, which acted to discredit the White and Western "democratic" and "national" propaganda. Lenin, on the other hand, could remain an internationalist while taking a "home defense" position against the intervention and the war—espusing a new homeland and a socially grounded "state patriotism"—but simultaneously decrying the Whites on these grounds, as representatives of "French-British-American capital."[218]

The Bolshevik leaders' attempt to subsume armed Jewish self-defense into the Red Army was related to the theoretical disposition of Lenin's politics. The 17 November 1918 decree of the Council of People's Commissars declared the "League of Jewish Soldiers closed." The merging of soldiers into a Red Army, free of ethnic separatism, was complete.

The Soviet government restricted the institutions of Jewish separatism and nationalism (Zionism) that were of explicitly bourgeois inspiration. Along with the closure of the league, the Central Office of Jewish Communities was also banned, and its property turned over to the local soviets—thus stemming the existence of an ethnically based center existing parallel to the Soviet government. As the decree of November 1918 emphasized, "The politics of these organizations was directed at dampening the class-consciousness of the Jewish working masses. . . . Taking up various government and cultural-social functions, they carried them out in an anti-proletarian spirit," and for this reason they were closed "in perpetuity." They "compensated" for the expulsion of Jewish bourgeois establishments and Zionist organizations[219] from political life by providing social support for poor Jewry, which had in part lost its means of making a living due to the economic policy of war communism. A number of decrees and practical measures were taken later, in 1920 as well, to ease the burden carried by the Jews. A leading role was played by the People's Commissariat for Nationalities, its Jewish Department, the Jewish section of the Bolshevik Party, and the Politburo.[220]

Meanwhile, for the time being at least, the operation of the Zionist socialist organizations (*Poale Zion*) were not impeded, but deliberate efforts were made at the time of the near defeat of the Soviet government in the spring–summer of 1919 to call up into the Red Army as many Jews as possible from the pogrom-hit regions. By the spring of 1919, those forces within the Central Committee of the Bund that proposed to unite with the Communist Party gained prominence.[221] They expressed their intention of doing so in a telegram sent to Moscow in April, and the Central Committee of the Bund simultaneously mobilized its members between the ages of eighteen and twenty-five to join the Red Army.[222] Such actions were especially needed because anti-Semitic agitation in the spirit of the White Guard-Black Hundreds propaganda was rife among the Red soldiers, presenting the "Jew Commissars" as the cause of all their hardships and trouble.

At the height of the campaign of pogroms by Whites and Petlyurists, a change was felt in the politics of Lenin, the Bolsheviks, and the Jewish—especially Zionist—workers' organizations. This can be traced to the 7th Congress of Soviets (December 1919), when a range of Jewish labor parties unanimously voted for the Soviet government, though they, unlike the Bolsheviks of Jewish ethnic origin, still harbored hopes of founding a Jewish socialist state in Palestine.[223] The Jewish Socialist Party and the Jewish Communist Party took a similarly determined stand on the side of the Soviet government and the Red Army.[224] The comprehensive document prepared by the Jewish Department working with the Central Committee at the end of 1919 found that the Jewish petit-bourgeois layers of society had begun seeking ways of adapting to the new political and economic conditions, rather than holding out hope for the restoration of capitalism. Therefore, in spite of the restrictions on Judaism and religion in general, or perhaps on account of them, the incorporation of an increasingly large segment of the Jewish population into the new Soviet conditions began. In 1923 5.2 percent of the party membership was Jewish,[225] and the Communist intelligentsia even more so. In 1920, the proportion of marriages of Jews with non-Jews was 34 percent, and this demonstrated, to use Lenin's frequently applied term, assimilation. Paths of life that could not have been imagined earlier were in the offing, in massive numbers.

Anti-Semitism and Political Tactics

The White Guard propaganda that probably gained the most ground in the ranks of the Red Guard was the claim that the Jews were hard to come by in the front-line trenches, but were "overrepresented" in the non-combat units. The aim of the White Guard propaganda was to position the soldier of the Red Guard in opposition to the "regime of the Jewish Commissar." Though the Jews appeared here, in the "regime," as representatives of the Soviet state, millions of Jewish civilians must have been very surprised at this. Jews were not present among the Bolsheviks, even in the highest rungs of power, in the numbers that the White propaganda claimed.[226] But another popular propaganda expression, the "Jewish Cheka," was not much closer to the truth either.[227] Lenin knew that many soldiers and officers serving either with the Whites or the Reds had fought with both armies and had made the propaganda of both sides familiar in both armies, which elicited a different, characteristic reaction from each army. People's Commissar of War Trotsky replied with a direct order to stop the anti-Semitic propaganda that had raised its head in the Red Army.[228]

A reconstruction of Lenin's politics is only possible if a clear sense of his personal attitude to the "Jewish question" is given. Lenin's political-emotional position was well reflected by an issue that came up in relation to a flyer by Maxim Gorky, *About the Jews*, in 1919, at the height of the White Guardist pogroms.[229] According to Dimanshteyn's peculiar account, he would have liked to convince the chairman of the Council of People's Commissars that Gorky had overdone it, and was "too complimentary" about the Jews; the flyer was, as one would put it today, counterproductive, and he urged its retraction. Lenin thought that it was special and fortunate for the revolution that a growing section of Jewish intelligentsia and workers were joining the Soviet side. Dimanshteyn himself emphasized in his often quoted recollections from 1924:

> It must be said that during our conversations, Lenin underscored a number of times how important in general the Jews were for the revolution, not only in Russia, but in other countries as well, as well as the importance of stopping all those wrongs that befall the Jewish working masses through the evils of the world ruled by capitalism and the religious establishments as soon as possible, for the sake of the revolution.[230]

Such were Lenin's reasons for not listening to Dimanshteyn, whose argument against Gorky was that his "overt glorification of the Jews" on the "great role they played in the revolution" would only add fuel to the fire of anti-Semitism. Though Lenin acknowledged that from a propagandistic point of view an overemphasis on positive traits may be harmful, he nevertheless agreed with what Gorky had to say, and was not willing to have his flyer retracted.[231]

Setting aside all of the "overcompensation" typical of Dimanshteyn, Lenin's response was connected to his general disposition in ethnic issues, which was that the Communists of every ethnicity should fight the nationalist and religious prejudices and ideologies of their own ethnic background. This was a case of overdoing that particular behavior, to a degree that led to a pronounced conflict between Gorky and the leadership of the "Jewish Section"—something not mentioned by Dimanshteyn. In his flyer, Gorky virtually took up the cause of those socialist Zionist parties that supported the Soviet government (at the time, these parties were not persecuted by the authorities, as opposed to the non-socialist Zionist parties). Regarding Dimanshteyn's group, however, Gorky said:

> The Jews have their own parties which are antagonistic with one another: the Jewish Zionists want to travel to Palestine . . . others stand opposed to this and are hostile to the Zionists, shutting down their schools, synagogues, forbidding that their children be taught the Jewish language.[232]

Though no documentary evidence can be found that Lenin called a halt to the persecution of bourgeois (that is, religious) Zionism, no trials against them were administered in 1919. In April 1920 the Cheka arrested approximately a hundred participants at the Moscow Conference of Zionists, although they were freed within a couple of months—on Lenin's intervention, according to some accounts. But nineteen activists of the movement were sentenced to five years in prison without trial, simply by administrative decision.[233] Lenin later met Gorky, who on a number of occasions advocated easing restrictions on Jewish cultural and political activity.[234]

Lenin considered the steps against anti-Semitism and pogroms of such great importance that he recorded by phonograph his famous speech on *Anti-Jewish Pogroms* at the end of March 1919. However, in this speech he did not emphasize the merits of the Jews, but rather attacked anti-Semitism and the pogroms from a social, political, and class point of view, and in such a way that even the simplest laborer would understand:

> When the accursed tsarist monarchy was living its last days it tried to incite ignorant workers and peasants against the Jews. . . . The landowners and

> capitalists tried to divert the hatred of the workers and peasants who were tortured by want against the Jews... in order to blind the workers, to divert their attention from the real enemy of the working people, capital. Hatred towards the Jews persists only in those countries where slavery to the landowners and capitalists has created abysmal ignorance among the workers and peasants.[235]

Obviously this speech, intended to agitate against anti-Semitism, could not capture the problem in all its shades, but the method is clear: instead of the national-ethnic and religious aspects, Lenin placed class conflict at the center of attention, indicating that he was not defending Jews themselves as an ethnic entity, but the "Jewish working masses." They were the victims of the capitalist system just as the Russian poor were:

> It is not the Jews who are the enemies of the working people. The enemies of the workers are the capitalists of all countries. Among the Jews there are working people, and they form the majority. They are our brothers, who, like us, are oppressed by capital; they are our comrades in the struggle for socialism.

At the same time he stressed:

> Among the Jews there are kulaks, exploiters and capitalists, just as there are among the Russians, and among people of all nations. The capitalists strive to sow and foment hatred between workers of different faiths, different nations and different races. . . . Rich Jews, like rich Russians, and the rich in all countries, are in alliance to oppress, crush, rob and disunite the workers. . . . Shame on those who foment hatred toward the Jews, who foment hatred towards other nations.[236]

Lenin's strict, deliberately simplified class consciousness and internationalism was corroborated by the daily events of the civil war. Jewry was a very divided community not only politically, but economically and socially: Jews participated in almost every party and served in every army, in Makhno and even Denikin's army, with some serving as officers (until they were forced out). While the Whites and the Petlyurists censored news about the pogroms, they also did not boast about how anti-Semitism was a mainstay of the dictatorships in both Kolchak's Siberia and Denikin's southern Russia. Nevertheless, the local Jewish bourgeoisie, especially the Jewish communities of Ufa and Tomsk, cooperated with Kolchak, which was probably why the bourgeois wings of Zionist organizations were not banned. Jewish capitalists financed the first "adventures" of the Volunteer Army as well. The wealthiest Jewish entrepreneurs of Rostov rescued the first, experimental drive of the White movement from collapse, and offered support to the counterrevolutionary activity of the Cossacks of Rostov, which became one of the bases of anti-Semitic horrors to come.[237]

Anti-Semitism also surfaced in the Red Army, because, after all, the soldiers were recruited from the same society. Isaac Babel's unequaled masterpiece, *Red Cavalry*, remains a literary travel guide on the subject. The chain of stories examines these problems in artistic fashion, showing how the soldiers of the 1st Cavalry Army got mixed up in the anti-Semitic pogroms of the summer and autumn of 1920, the period of the Soviet-Polish War. Lenin's political and theoretical stance in relation to these events can be relatively easily reconstructed.

The 1st Cavalry and the Pogroms

In the late summer of 1920, the defeat of the Red Army to the south of Warsaw was the last major battle of the Soviet-Polish War.[238] In the aftermath, certain tattered and demoralized units of the Red Army achieved infamy for their pogroms. When the Soviet leaders learned that the pogroms could spread to some detachments of the legendary cavalry, it became clear that even in their own lines the virus of pogrom anti-Semitism could not be restrained merely through economic and social measures, even though a *review* toward putting an end to war communism had just taken shape. The soldiers of the Polish army were also "motivated" by anti-Semitism[239]—the counterrevolution had emblazoned its flags with anti-Semitism in both Hungary and Romania. It now became clear that the fight against anti-Semitism would have to be continued.

Whole regiments were gripped in the throes of rabid anti-Semitism, looting, and a form of veiled revolt against the central regime—of which Jews were considered to be the foremost representatives—marked by the same slogan: "Beat the Jew, save Russia!" Certain retreating units of Budyonny's mounted army committed a series of horrendous crimes. The news of this reached the Kremlin at lightning speed, and an intervention by the highest powers ensured that those involved were sentenced by the revolutionary court in Yelizavetgrad by the end of October. The Soviet government and the policies of the Communist Party helped ensure that only a few of the pogroms were committed by the Red soldiers.[240]

In light of this, Richard Pipes's view of these events—according to which Lenin, as leader of the Soviet government, dealt with the horrific crimes of the pogromists with indifference, as if he had been left untouched by this degeneration of the men in the 1st Cavalry— cannot be taken seriously. Pipes tries to substantiate his view with the 18 November 1920 Report of the Central Office of the Jewish Section of the Central Committee of the Communist Party, which dealt with the pogroms committed by the demoralized cavalry on 1 October in the county of Zhitomir, on which Lenin wrote: "Archive."[241] Pipes does not take into account that a majority of the incriminated (approximately 400 individuals) had been sentenced to hard labor or executed more than three weeks earlier. In stark contrast to Pipes's representation of him, Lenin was so concerned about the investigation into the pogroms carried out by detachments of the cavalry that he met personally with the captains of the 1st Cavalry. Captain I. V. Vardin (Mgeladze), gave the meeting publicity through the official newspaper of the 1st Cavalry Army, the *Red Horseman* (*Krasny Kavallerist*), which was overseen by his office. He reported to Lenin in person on the murders and robberies committed by the 31st, 32nd, and 33rd Regiments of the 6th Army.[242] The 5 October issue of the *Red Horseman* also informed the reader of Lenin's meeting with Budyonny alone. On 10 October, that is, more than a month before the completion of the document in question, an active campaign against anti-Semitism was under way. The reports from the *Red Horseman* are worth quoting:

> Plainly the pogroms that were carried out under the slogan of "beat the Jews, and the communists" came to the attention of the topmost organs of leadership. At the muster on 2 October the Revolutionary Military Council of the 1st Cavalry Army disarmed the 31st, 32nd and 33rd Cavalry Regiments. Soldiers surrendered all the main culprits voluntarily. They were brought before the court for "attempting to bring down the worker-peasant regime and for weakening the availability of the army for action." The main criminals were given the death penalty, the rest of the participants were sentenced 5–10 years of hard labor.[243]

The following issues of the newspaper also devoted much space to the discussion of the appearance of nationalist hatred and judeophobia within the ranks, as well as to the "reaffirmation of international workers' solidarity." Vardin's instructions in the 8 November 1920 issue of the *Red Horseman* saw the notions presented in Lenin's 1919 speech reused almost word-for-word.[244] It has been said that Lenin and the Bolshevik leadership used the instruments of state terror to bring a halt to the pogroms. An example can be found in a Lenin document from late autumn 1920 that remained unpublished and secret until 1999, and dealt with the White terror.[245] It should be noted that in spite of agreements signed with Soviet Russia, the recruitment of Wrangelists and armed units for Bułak-Bałachowicz, with the intention of overthrowing the Soviet government, were continuing unhindered in the Baltic states. These units forayed into Soviet territories numerous times, robbing, looting, and terrorizing the local population. Apart from taking up other diplomatic means of protest, a register signed by L. B. Krasin was conveyed to the British government on 28 October, detailing that the Soviet state had ceased fighting the war with the reigning governments of Finland, Estonia, and Lithuania:

> But the state of war has not ended. Armed bands who have not subjected themselves to any government continue hostilities against the peaceful population of both Soviet republics Russia and Ukraine. The armed forces under the leadership of Bałachowicz and Petlyura are equipped with the arms and tools of the allies . . . which makes these states responsible for future bloodshed. . . . The governments of the Russian and Ukrainian republics will take all measures in their power to free their countries . . . liquidating and scattering the armed forces of these robbers, or forcing them to surrender.[246]

The Red Army troops liquidated the bands of Bałachowicz to the north of the Mazyr in November. The remnants crossed the border to Poland on 26 November 1920, where they were disarmed in the presence of representatives of the Soviet government.

Lenin's countermeasures were outlined in two other documents written to Sklyansky in late October or early November: "Diplomatic protest is not enough. . . . Military actions must be taken to punish Latvia and Estonia, bypassing by about a *verst* Bałachowicz's 'shoulders' to cross the border and hang about 100–1000 of their chinovniks and rich."

The lines of the other document, much quoted after the change of regimes, reads as follows: "Under cover of the 'greens' (to then later lay the blame on) we can cross about 10–20 *versts* into the territory and hang the kulaks, priests, and landlords. Premium: 100,000 rubles for each hanging."[247]

Another product of the civil war psychosis and terror, this document remains what it is, whatever the causes of its having been written, though when it comes to the interpretations given by Pipes and historians similar to him, their silence is inexplicable regarding the causes that make Lenin's proposals for measures of terror to be implemented. They did not even investigate whether these instructions were carried through, or how serious Lenin was in the first place about the numbers he used; after all, there can be no doubt that in this case, the "revenge," the state action of terror, never was realized. V. Loginov, when publishing the Lenin documents, added a remark to the effect that in spite of the signed general peace agreement, Boris Savinkov (an S.R. terrorist with a rather contorted career and who ended up in the White camp) helped Bałachowicz form significant and well-equipped detachments from the White Guard soldiers who had escaped to the Baltic states. Reminding the reader of the pogroms of the Denikinists, which had claimed the lives of tens of thousands of Jews, Loginov quoted contemporary news sources on the latest horrors committed by Bałachowicz's men:

> On 2 October Balachowicz entered Plotnitsa, where he immediately collected all the Jews and demanded money from them. After the Jews had handed over all their belongings, the most beastly murders and tortures began. Moisey Plotnik's nose was cut off and then he was hung. Puterman, whose whole family was chopped down with sabers, went mad and began to dance, then he was shot dead. Polyak's hands were cut off first, then he was skinned. Ilya Finkelshtein was burned alive. Every woman and girl, down to the age of nine, was raped. Six hundred refugees in the greatest possible extremity are now in Pinsk.[248]

Similar horrors came to pass in a number of other cities through October and November of 1920, a reminder of the bloody events of 1918–19. The virtually unimaginable atrocities of Balachowicz and his White Guard, as well as the occupying Polish forces, reverberated Europe-wide.[249] Lenin placed the merciless threats of reprisal, taking of hostages, and executions in view of those sheltering these cutthroat, robber White Guards.

Lenin and the Bolsheviks had the courage to take up the fight on theoretical, political, and military levels against the racist, anti-Semitic tide that later steeped the twentieth century in blood, which was a historical achievement on their part. One of the quoted historians must be right when he says that the pogroms were in one sense a forerunner of the Holocaust, because the Whites physically exterminated Jews en masse, without a thought for age, sex, or social status. In another sense, Lenin was perhaps the first to realize the significance of the link between anti-Semitism and anti-Communism in the ideology of the Whites and the terrorist practices of the civil war.[250]

At this most difficult moment it would be most harmful for revolutionaries to indulge in self-deception. Though Bolshevism has become an international force, though in all the civilised and advanced countries new Chartists, new Varlins, new Liebknechts have been born . . . the international bourgeoisie still remains incomparably stronger than its class enemy. This bourgeoisie, which has done everything in its power . . . to multiply tenfold the dangers and suffering attending its birth, is still in a position to condemn millions and tens of millions to torment and death through its whiteguard and imperialist wars, etc. . . . And we must skilfully adapt our tactics to this specific situation. The bourgeoisie is still able freely to torment, torture and kill. But it cannot halt the inevitable and—from the standpoint of world history—not far distant triumph of the revolutionary proletariat.

—V. I. LENIN, *ON THE TENTH ANNIVERSARY OF PRAVDA,*
2 MAY 1922, LCW, VOL. 33, 349–52

7
World Revolution: Method and Myth

THE ORIGIN OF THE PROBLEM

WHERE THE SOCIALIST WORLD REVOLUTION is understood as overthrowing capitalism on an international level, it is neither a free-standing phenomenon nor simply an organic element of Lenin's and Bolshevik political practice, but a part of the history of the Russian Revolution and the Russian civil war. Since politics cannot operate without myths, beliefs, mobilizing ideals, and ideologies, and in the end every forecast or calculation of the future is wholly subject to unpredictable factors, the "scientific prediction" also constitutes a part of the struggle to determine political alternatives. All of this applies where the Marxist and Leninist traditions of world revolution are concerned.

Some of the common ideological perceptions are that Lenin's theoretical views of world revolution derived from Marx alone, or on the contrary refuted them on the basis of Marx's theories. Looked at from the general position of the Soviet period, he brilliantly developed Marx's views on revolution by tying the beginning of world revolution to Russian revolutionary practice. From the point of view of the Mensheviks and their successors, Lenin's "catastrophic revision" of Marx was the product of a break with Marxian thought, as Marx nowhere mentions any sort of autochthonic Russian socialist revolution. Either interpretation leaves the misleading impression that the question could be settled with a mere definition of ideology or concept. The "unity" and "difference" of Marx and Lenin is not only a theoretical, but also a historical, issue. The difference between the periods in which these two thinkers and revolutionaries lived was manifested in their different historical "missions": their political and theoretical tasks differ from each other objectively, and not in a "teleological" sense (although there are continuities both in the questions they posed as well as their comprehensive anticapitalist orientation). An examination of Lenin's publications and documents makes more nuanced hypotheses possible today than previously.

To begin with, there was never a question of any form of autochthonous Russian socialist revolution. From the start what differentiated his ideas from any preceding revolutionary movement was that he placed the prospect of the Russian Revolution in the context of a potential European (and international) revolutionary upswing, the international workers' movement, as did Marx. Both were aware—confirmed historically by the 1848 wave of European revolutions—that due to the trans-regional nature of modern capitalist development great social changes were bound to unfold on a European scale.[1] Marx discussed this universal tendency of capitalist development (globalization) in many ways in his works, drawing his own anticapitalist conclusions—also accepted by Lenin and the Bolsheviks—as we can see in his *Grundrisse*:

> Thus, while capital must on one side strive to tear down every spatial barrier to intercourse, i.e. to exchange, and conquer the whole earth for its market, it strives on the other side to annihilate this space with time, i.e. to reduce to a minimum the time spent in motion from one place to another. The more developed the capital, therefore, the more extensive the market over which it circulates, which forms the spatial orbit of its circulation, the more does it strive simultaneously for an even greater extension of the market and for greater annihilation of space by time.[2]

Marx's analysis had already shown that it was not revolution alone that holds the possibility of a violent overthrow of the universal capitalist system, but the crises of the capitalist system accompanied by violence. During such periods, progress "suspends the self-realization of capital." During these critical times

> the material and mental conditions of the negation of wage labour and of capital, themselves already the negation of earlier forms of unfree social production, are themselves results of its production process. The growing incompatibility between the productive development of society and its hitherto existing relations of production expresses itself in bitter contradictions, crises, spasms. The violent destruction of capital, not by relations external to it, but rather as a condition of its self-preservation, is the most striking form in which advice is given it to be gone and to give room to a higher state of social production.

Lenin often referred to this set of problems because he recognized that these crises were partly to blame for the inescapability of the world war as the "begetter" of revolution. Marx, in a similar vein, remarks:

> These contradictions, of course, lead to explosions, crises, in which momentary suspension of all labour and annihilation of a great part of the capital violently lead it back to the point where it is enabled to go on fully employing its productive powers without committing suicide. Yet these regularly recurring catastrophes lead to their repetition on a higher scale, and finally to its violent overthrow.[3]

With the outbreak of the First World War, Lenin could feel the universality of the catastrophe in the Marxist sense of the word, from which it followed that the famous idea in *The German Ideology* stating that "communism is only possible as the act of the dominant peoples 'all at once' and simultaneously"[4] could be set aside for good. By 1905, Lenin had already formulated the "spark," the political concept of the Russian Revolution, and 1905 and 1917 convinced him the idea was correct. The spread of the revolution from China to Latin America, and from Germany to Hungary did indeed give an impression of confirming both Lenin and Marx. Lenin stripped the concept of world revolution of its simultaneity, that is, he structured it. His starting idea however remained rooted in the global nature of capitalism. What his theory added, however, was that due to uneven development, world revolution develops in different ways at different times and places.

Lenin returned to this array of issues just a few days before the October Revolution. In his *Revision of the Party Program,* published during October 1917, he again pointed out, while reflecting on debate about the crisis of imperialism and capitalism, the universally conjoined development of the system of capital and the revolution. He assumed that the capitalist system was in an imminent and potentially permanent crisis in an easily determined region of the world. An organic interrelation and a radical contradiction could be observed between technical progress and the relative decrease of labor force demand; and that a crisis of overproduction is related to the circumstance that the conditions of accumulation are in conflict with the conditions of realization. At the same time, besides portraying the "self-evident" characteristics of the crisis of the system, Lenin underlined that modern capitalism in general cannot be described by the term "anarchistic" (even though this feature constitutes an essential part of the crisis and the system). On the contrary, "Trusts produce commodities not anarchically but according to a plan." Though their role in preventing crises had not yet developed in that era (which is also reflected in Lenin's stance), he had still arrived at the issue and come to raise it. "Every joint-stock company with a membership of capitalists from various countries is an internationally organised association of capitalists." Here the emphasis is on the concept of being organized, a new quality emerging in the age of imperialism: "The economic partitioning of the world among international trusts, the partitioning of countries, *by agreement* into market areas."[5]

Yet the problem lies here: the international organization of capital cannot be contested or broken down on the national level, on the divergent tracks of the national workers' movements—a realization Marx and Lenin had in common. In 1922, Lenin perceived the results of the "national solution" in Italian fascism. Lenin could never give up the hypothesis that the revolution had an international character, which is how the world war would signify the beginning of world revolution. This formed one of the reasons for his 1914 accusation of nationalist "treachery" against the 2nd International. It gave up this internationality in order to support the war, which in the long run led to the proletariat's aversion to the revolution and the relative restabilization of capitalism. Such an outcome was not yet evident to Lenin (and the entire European internationalist left) in 1917, so he was still convinced that there were only two practical alternatives: either the barbarities of the war or socialism. The well-known lines[6] of the Hungarian poet, Endre Ady, and Lenin's summary of the substance of the war[7] anticipated liberation from barbarity through the international compass of the revolution. Just as the revolution, subject to its law of uneven development of time and place, did indeed conquer the most important regions of Europe from October 1917 onward, it also overtook central Europe in its role as intermediary between the Russian revolution and developments in Western Europe.[8] This way Russia, the weakest link of imperialism, remained the failed spark of world revolution; and even though it failed, it became an integral part of Marxism, theoretically, philosophically, politically, and in terms of the movement. This is understandable if we consider that Lenin and the international revolutionary left were not alone in recognizing the potential of world revolution, just as John Maynard Keynes—who belonged to the bourgeois camp and later became the economist-ideologist of the welfare state—regarded Bolshevism as a universal challenge for the capitalist system in his famous work *The Economic Consequences of the Peace,* published in 1919.

Whether the concept of world revolution was properly grounded economically, theoretically, and in terms of the movement may be open to debate, it is certain that Lenin's much-debated thesis of "turning the imperialist world war into a civil war" became a justified element of his strategic position after the February revolution. This way he could directly relate progression in the Russian Revolution to the prospect of German revolution as a natural historical sequel of European development. Lenin would repeat these ideas when he returned home, in his analytical note *Farewell Letter to the Swiss Workers*:

> The objective circumstances of the imperialist war make it certain that the revolution will not be limited to the first stage of the Russian revolution, that the revolution will not be limited to Russia. The German proletariat is the most trustworthy, the most reliable ally of the Russian and the world proletarian revolution. When, in November 1914, our Party put forward the slogan: "Turn the imperialist war into a civil war" of the oppressed against the oppressors for the attainment of socialism, the social-patriots met this slogan with hatred and malicious ridicule, and the Social-Democratic "Centre" with incredulous, skeptical, meek and expectant silence.... Now, after March 1917, only the blind can fail to see that it is a correct slogan. Transformation of the imperialist war into civil war is becoming a fact. Long live the proletarian revolution that is *beginning* in Europe![9]

Lenin sustained this point of view even more vigorously after October 1917, and was so meticulous in doing so as not to accept the invitation of the "traditional" social democratic conference. Not all political factions had been invited and he was not willing to organize the councils of the various wings of the European workers' movements by the rules of the fighting parties.[10] His objective was clear: to unite the social democrats and other revolutionary forces committed to the revolution in a Europe-wide front.

Lenin later began to describe Western revolution as having been "delayed," a kind of phenomenon that can and should be accelerated, but could not be unleashed artificially. The establishment of the Communist International was part of this strategy. Lenin regarded the Comintern as the "General Staff of the World Revolution," but Moscow was not Rome, even though it temporarily appeared at the center of the Communist world party. Berlin remained the natural center. This determination was reflected first by the Founding Congress of the Comintern, then by its 2nd Congress, which defined the twenty-one conditions for belonging to the Comintern. These constituted the "military" and "disciplinary" foundations of the "world party." Sectarian seclusion is not the most important issue here as is often stressed by historiographers, but the fact that the communist parties themselves also came from two different directions. As Hobsbawm put it: "Each Communist Party was the child of the marriage of two ill-assorted partners, a national left and the October Revolution." Those who shared the Moscow concept did not regard the role of the local idiosyncrasies as important. The horizons of those who were nationalist-minded were defined by the eastern European lowlands and mountain ranges. It is true that researchers usually see the classic symptoms of sectarianism in the strict conditions for joining, and indeed the severe, almost military centralization carried the danger of insularity, especially if the joining party operated illegally. What is most important however is that their aim was to strengthen cohesion within the Comintern. Of course the organizational hierarchy and military order that communist parties maintained in those times met the requirements of their own "world revolutionary" political trends.[11] Lenin's conditions were in fact to become the real embodiment of sectarianism under the changed historical circumstances of a later time, but that is a different epoch.

Thus the idea of world revolution and overestimating the processes of its realization were an organic part of the revolution itself, and without this awareness and belief, the history of the October revolution and the whole European revolutionary wave would be unthinkable. While this expectation preoccupied the revolutionary masses in Russia, it was less so in Western Europe. In all its naïveté, it still served as inspiration to unsophisticated communist peasants in the 1930s, among them a literary figure in one of Solokhov's novels, Nagulnov, the party secretary of a kolkhoz who perpetuates this feeling for posterity. At the same time, the political self-definition of the notable groups among Western intellectuals may also be subject to reflection on this count. *World revolution* was also the idea and the *abstract* practice that attracted a whole generation to gather under the banner of communism (and the Soviet Union), as so beautifully related by Eric Hobsbawm in writing about both his life and the lives of others.[12]

THE PEACE TREATY OF BREST-LITOVSK AND PATRIOTISM

In the minds of many central Europeans, the demands coming from the social revolution, such as the elimination of the disparity between the rich and poor, as well as social and ethnic/national oppression, were closely bound up with the demands of national independence. A sense of patriotism of some type is convincingly documented, for example, by the army letters published (and analytically presented) by Péter Hanák.[13] Almost everywhere the middle classes, officers' class, and better-off peasantry "sacrificed" the social demands, popular among the masses, at the altar of national demands—with Russia being perhaps the only exception. In the final round, with the help of nationalism (and then fascism), the ruling elites of nations large and small crushed the social movements from Romania to Italy, from Hungary to Germany and the Balkans. Yet this was a conscious and politically coordinated response to the rise of revolutionary social movements and organization in all of the defeated countries: the labor committees, the labor councils, and the short-lived Soviet republics (Hungary, Slovakia, Germany, and Italy).[14] Lenin and Bolshevism faced up to this tide of nationalism at the time of the Brest-Litovsk Treaty, when it became apparent that the revolution had ended along with the Soviet government's "victory parade." For ninety years after the ratification of the treaty, not a single serious historian would argue Soviet Russia's military forces could have withstood the German troops. Thus, among the political and class power relations, internationally and internally, no other realistic alternative of a peace treaty offered itself.[15]

Though theoretically Lenin upheld worldwide—or at least international—revolution as a strategy, until the autumn of 1920, as a *practical* prospect he was measuring the Soviet government's chances of the survival, and was paving the way to this end. His stance at the Brest-Litovsk Treaty talks and ratification (which demanded unheard-of energy on his part, but was worth it) can only be understood as a model of revolutionary realpolitik and political compromise with imperialism—primarily in the matter of war and peace, but also of patriotism and internationalism. In reality, these phenomena did not split apart from each other. After all, the well-known arguments within the Central Committee of the Bolshevik Party on the question of signing an armistice with imperial Germany raised quite a dilemma: Is any sort of peace treaty with an imperialist country possible? Does this not mean the betrayal of the European, and especially the German proletariat? Can the reformulated slogan of *defend the country* and the actual political actions that it covers be reconciled with Marxist internationalism? What is more important in the eyes of the socialists: To hold on to the positions they had achieved in terms of the realpolitik, or to uncompromisingly "export" the world revolution at all costs?

The fundamental theoretical lessons of the Brest-Litovsk Treaty's consequences, as formulated by Lenin, can be grouped around two big issues: *patriotism*, the way "petit-bourgeois democracy" relates to the revolution; and the way Soviet realpolitik deals with the "concretization" of internationalism. The "Tilsit peace," as Lenin called the treaty, threw even his closest friends and comrades into despair, even though they would have marched up to Berlin with him under the banner of world revolution. Unlike Lenin, many driven by the spirit of abstract internationalism, such as Bukharin, Dzerzhinsky, and Radek, rejected positive answers to the questions raised above. The events that unfolded are now part of history. Trotsky, who as the People's Commissar for Foreign Affairs headed the Soviet delegation at the treaty talks that had begun at the end of December 1917, did not wish to sign or reject the peace treaty, citing the slogan of "neither war, nor peace." The German Army's answer to this was to occupy vast tracts of Ukrainian territory, leaving Chicherin, the new People's Commissar for Foreign Affairs, a peace treaty with far worse conditions to sign (even though Trotsky's abstention gained it more support on the Central Committee). In the face of the *revolutionary* war demanded by the abstract internationalists and the nationalist-patriotic phantasmagoria of the S.R. defenders of the nation, Lenin was only able to push the treaty through by a hair's breadth. During the debate of the Central Committee members, Stalin gave evidence of a fantastic "sense of realism": he denied even the slightest signs of a European revolution.[16] Though Lenin distanced himself from such a "pessimistic" position, it nevertheless indicates that some in his circle were out-and-out skeptics regarding the chances of an international revolution.

Having secured a moment of respite, it was nevertheless apparent that Lenin would have much tacking to do between the two sorts of behavior emerging in the party. One of them remained devoted to world revolution, and gave precedence to a revolutionary politics of offense, especially where the German developments were concerned. The other interpreted and evaluated European processes from the unilateral perspective of Soviet-Russian interests in the arena of international power distribution. While continuing to uphold the "scientifically predictable" international revolution, Lenin discarded all conjecture that was not based on the strict accounting of facts. For him, the revolution had not been simplified to any one or another surge, or to the repetition of abstract principles: he dealt with international politics in concrete measures. For example, when the Kaiser was toppled in November 1918 and the German revolution unfolded, Lenin's first idea was to contact the German military units stationed in Russia. His telegram (sent in his capacity as the chairman of the Council of People's Commissars), to the Orel and Kursk Gubernia Executive Committees and Gubernia Party Committees, though exaggerating the proletarian revolutionary aspect of the events, reflected the practical positioning in its virtually paradigmatic form:

> A radio message has just been received from Kiel, addressed to the international proletariat and stating that power in Germany has passed into the hands of the workers and soldiers. This radio message is signed by the Council of Sailors' Deputies of Kiel. In addition, German soldiers at the front have arrested a peace delegation from Wilhelm, and have themselves begun negotiations for peace directly with the French soldiers. Wilhelm has abdicated. It is essential to make every effort to communicate this as soon as possible to the German soldiers in the Ukraine, and to advise them to attack the troops of Krasnov, because then we shall together win tens of millions of poods of grain for the German workers, and beat off an invasion by the British, whose squadron is now approaching Novorossiisk.[17]

And though the German revolution confirmed Lenin's expectation that the peace of Brest-Litovsk was not to last, he nevertheless did not give up the Brest-Litovsk tactic. His stance did not change that, until a general European revolution unfolded, the most important position was to defend the gains of the Russian Revolution.[18] This was seen as a sort of patriotic turn by certain social strata in Russia (especially by the leftist communists who rejected this position), whereas others (especially the S.R.s) had the opposite view, seeing it as an act of unpatriotic self-sacrifice and national capitulation. Regarding the accusations of allowances made to patriotism, by the beginning of January Lenin had written to his Muscovite critics that they "have not even taken into consideration the fact that we Bolsheviks have now all become defensists."[19]

As seen previously, Lenin, though indicating that various forms of war were possible from a political and class point of view, considered the "defense of the fatherland" nothing more than a justification for taking part in the war. As he put it, "to generalize this, to make it a 'general principle,' is ridiculous, supremely unscientific."[20] However, the passionate, almost unappeasable, debates surrounding the Brest-Litovsk Treaty showed that the changed political situation put the question of patriotism in a much more complex light.[21] Even in the heat of the argument Lenin correctly analyzed the essential point regarding patriotism. Marxism, when pitted against the wartime patriotism of the tsar and the landlords, stood on a political and ideological platform of "anti-patriotism"; but following the October Revolution the notion of "fatherland" had gained a new meaning, as the Brest-Litovsk peace debates showed. In an article published in the 11 March issue of *Izvestia*, Lenin quoted the following lines by Nekrasov in defense of the "Tilsit" peace and against the two "one-sidednesses" described above: "Thou art wretched, thou art abundant, / Thou art mighty, thou art impotent—Mother Russia!"[22] Yet this had changed on 25 October, and this was why the new notion of *motherland*, which took territorial-social-cultural factors as its basis, could no longer bear any kind of nationalistic, ethnic, or religious content. The White Guard ideology of a "single and undividable Russia" had fallen into its grave, along with the empire and the old ruling classes. In "temporary lieu" of world revolution, however, the new notion of fatherland and of *defensism* gained in place of the old ethnic-national content, in that it applied to the territory where the Soviet government was at any given time victorious, thereby carrying anti-racist ideological implications for multiethnic territories. It also molded social and universal matters to itself, and this revealed the provisional nature of the new political establishment, for the country did not even have an official name for a long time, and its size and expanse were hardly clear or definite. Lenin summed up the essence of this turn:

> Since October 25, 1917, we have been defencists. We are for "defence of the fatherland"; but that patriotic war towards which we are moving is a war for a socialist fatherland, for socialism as a fatherland, for the Soviet Republic as a contingent of the world army of socialism. "Hate the Germans, kill the Germans"—such was, and is, the slogan of common, i.e., bourgeois, patriotism. But we will say "Hate the imperialist plunderers, hate capitalism, death to capitalism" and at the same time "Learn from the Germans! Remain true to the brotherly alliance with the German workers."[23]

Another aspect regarding the issue of patriotism reflects upon the way the regime related to the intelligentsia, the petit-bourgeois, and the middle and peasant strata of society; and its reverse, the way these strata related to Soviet Russia. The ever-widening front of foreign intervention on Soviet territory elicited a "positive shift" among the patriotic layers of society, as national-patriotic feeling now tilted in favor of the Soviet government. This had extraordinary significance, in spite of the "attic-clearing" reformist nature of war communism. Later, in the spring of 1919, Lenin returned to the question at the 8th Party Congress, where he shed light on the very deep roots of national feeling and patriotic sentiment, saying they were "bound up with the economic conditions of life of precisely the small proprietors." Drawing lessons from the period of the Brest-Litovsk Treaty, Lenin underscored the change in relations between the party and the "middle strata" of society. They had first turned against the Bolsheviks because of the territorial concessions, but under attack from interventionist troops, patriotism had brought millions into the Bolshevik fold.[24] In a sociological sense, Lenin understood "patriotism" as the middle layer of society's emotional-ideological expression of their interests. It is no coincidence that Lenin also drew the attention of the Hungarian Soviet Republic's leadership to this strata's political significance, for they are especially adept allies in a war of defense, and in Hungary—noting the expected territorial losses and the foreign military presence—they were already watching the events from the stance of defending the motherland: "The difficulty of our position was that we had to give birth to Soviet power in opposition to patriotism." In the final run, the bourgeoisie always joins the forces where it senses greater power, which is the position from which it can better defend its "national interests."[25] It is interesting that—in contrast to the later Polish-Soviet War—Lenin was quite aware then about how the nationalism of these social layers may distance them from the revolution. Gripped by a thirst for revenge after the military defeat, with a choice of *nationalism* and *revolution*, many drifted toward choosing the first, whereas significant segments of the labor masses in victorious countries favored the patriotic choice under the spell of the "national successes" of the ruling classes.

The third "layer" of patriotism, which Lenin later excavated and interpreted after the introduction of the New Economic Policy (NEP), was rooted in the famous politics of concessions, discussed in the next chapter. In the conclusion to his speech about concessions at the 8th Soviet Congress in December 1920, he pointed out that the rural protests against the concessionary policies did not reflect an "unhealthy mood," but rather were a phenomenon expressing positive patriotic sentiments. He referred here to peasant patriotism—"without which we could not hold out for three years"—the type of patriotism which leads a peasant to accept hunger for years "rather than hand over Russia to foreigners. ... This is the finest revolutionary patriotism." Giving this form of patriotism concrete shape in social and political terms as the sensibility of the "non-party middle peasant," even differentiating it from the sensibilities of the "kulaks" (the peasants with means), he suggests: "As for the kulaks being prepared to go hungry for three years to keep out the foreign capitalists, from whom they have something to gain—that is untrue."[26] These socially defined forms of patriotic feeling, its alternate image, and the rather varied faces it showed in changing situations were all an integral part of the politics of alliance—*smichka*, the "worker-peasant alliance" and the relationship with the intelligentsia—carried on by the Bolshevik Party. Lenin's speeches and actions intimate that he tried to capture the increasingly complicated "mediations" and contradictions between world revolution and the local interests of the Russian Revolution.

His theoretical views on patriotism—expressing the concrete political and class power relations behind the political *compromises*—can be summarized as an unwillingness to risk the positions already secured by the revolution for any European (or Asian) revolutionary offensive whose outcome was not clearly foreseeable. In his critique of Bukharin's approach, which ruled out accepting any compromise with the imperialists, he aimed his barbs at an abstract image of world revolution which was oblivious to the concrete balance of forces. Lenin was not willing to make a dogmatic issue of what he believed to be most relevant to the interests of the revolution, and was therefore willing to purchase food from any foreign enemy right from the start, not basing his actions on the typically lefty-intellectual valuation of "capitulation to imperialism."[27]

In the course of the year 1919, Lenin tried to avoid (at least as a matter of principle) the contraposition of the European perspectives of revolutionary development with the "local" interests and military defense of the Russian Revolution—despite the contradictions coming to light, as demonstrated unequivocally in the aftermath of the Brest-Litovsk Treaty and the socialist turn in Hungary. Lenin always made his decisions after making a concrete analysis, gauging which interests were more important and which could be better defended in the given situation. Nonetheless he continued to voice his opinion that the fate of the Soviet government, in the long run, hung in the balance of the development and victory of the European revolution. With the passing of the revolutionary upsurge of the spring of 1919, to put it euphemistically[28]—that is, of the Hungarian Soviet republic, the short-lived Slovakian, and the proclamation of the Bavarian Soviet Republic on 7 April—the balance of forces did not shift in favor of the Soviet government. This also played an important part with respect to Lenin's evaluation of relations with the Hungarian Soviet Republic. He wanted to support the revolution's taking root in Hungary at all costs, but the internal power-relations developed disadvantageously. In April 1919 he sent the following instruction to commander Vatsetis:

> The advance into part of Galicia and Bukovina is essential for contact with Soviet Hungary. This task must be achieved more quickly and surely, but beyond this task no occupation of Galicia and Bukovina is needed, for the Ukrainian army must on no account be distracted from its two main objectives: the first, the most important and most urgent, is to help the Donets Basin. . . . The second objective is to establish a secure link by rail with Soviet Hungary.[29]

This order of importance was dictated by the catastrophic turn in the balance of military forces, and not any other factors the leader of the Hungarian revolution Béla Kun came to believe regarding this (he frequently appraised the revolutionary developments in a state of complete delirium).[30] Regarding Béla Kun's demand of 11 July—that certain units of the Red Army should attack Galicia—the Ukrainian Council of People's Commissars turned to Commissioner of Foreign Affairs Chicherin and Lenin on 14 July. Lenin's note to Sklyansky, the immediate colleague of Trotsky, and who was both the People's Commissar for War and the Vice-Chairman of the Revolutionary-Military Council of the Republic, jotted the text of this telegram: "To Sklyansky! Wouldn't it be possible to organize a demonstrative effect, make a noise and fool them?"[31] However, not even the "noise" came off, and the Hungarian Soviet Republic was put down; Lenin, along with the Bolsheviks, tasted defeat in this and other such events. This is also why the unrealistic series of demands and personal attacks emanating from Béla Kun, and his delirious panic attacks,[32] left Lenin wondering seriously about the wisdom of the leader of the Hungarian revolution.[33]

At this stage, in the summer of 1919, the armed counterrevolution grew stronger within Russia; Denikin was hatching his plans for the occupation of Moscow, the Baltic and Finnish soviet governments had been defeated, and White terror was widespread. This situation spawned a politically inorganic, but nevertheless typical (and now-famous) Trotsky document (5 August 1919) that expressed a sense of political improvisation—setting a mirror to the dimming hopes for the future of European revolution. Trotsky recommended to the members of the Central Committee a reorienting of Soviet politics, from the West to the East:

> The arena of uprisings in the vicinity may be Asia. . . . We have lost Riga, Vilna, and under duress we are risking the loss of Odessa and Petrograd. We have taken back Perm, Yekaterinburg, Zlatoust and Chelyabinsk. This change in circumstances necessitates a change of direction. In the coming period it would be timely to take on the preparation of components for an "Asian" reorientation, and partly prepare for a military attack against India, in support of the Indian revolution.[34]

However, with the defeat of Denikin and Kolchak, the question once again came to be rephrased in "Eurocentric'" form. Following the "peace settlement" of Versailles, it became clear that Soviet Russia was being hedged around with a *cordon sanitaire* to protect the "capitalist environment." Numerous deliberate falsifications have been published in recent years that describe Lenin's "concept of world revolution" as a realistic "Russian military threat" with a drive to conquer Europe. In reality, the concrete political manifestations of this concept only belonged to the revolutionary wave's rearguard actions, whose purpose would have been to inspire and support local outbreaks of the expected revolutions. All philosophical and geopolitical concepts aside, Soviet Russia—mired deep in chaos and civil war—could not have posed any danger to Europe, either in economic or military terms. The reality was quite the opposite: the principled insistence on world revolution incorporated the belief in a chance of survival, which later became intertwined with the conflicts of interest between the Great Powers, after the Soviet Union grew to become a great power at the end of 1922. "Soviet patriotism," or in fact state patriotism, which was to fill the role of national ideology until the breakup of the Soviet Union, was the ideological expression of this entire historical development.

The Polish-Soviet War was the embodiment of the "volatile state of the world," which in its denouement offered perhaps the last chance for Lenin and his generals to tie—through Poland—the fate of the Russian Revolution with that of the European revolution, or, in other words, was the last possibility to prevent the isolation of the revolution from Western Europe, and most importantly, Germany. In the summer of 1920 Lenin, counting on the truly promising perspectives of an international revolution, did take risks; on the one hand he gave way to the pressure from the "left," and on the other followed his own analysis. In a sense, the siren song of the world revolution once again became a force shaping history. Lenin chose the more cautious approach in the spring of 1919, but the Soviet government could take a more self-assured stand in the spring of 1920, after it had put Kolchak down. Though the international balance of forces did not change favorably in terms of European revolutionary progress, the successes on the civil war front seemed decisive.

THE POLISH-SOVIET WAR

There is an extensive literature that deals with the Polish-Soviet War and Soviet historiography's point of view on it,[35] but a number of Lenin documents that surfaced in the 1990s are also important.[36] They make it amply clear that Lenin gave international revolution a central place of importance in the end goals of the Russian Revolution, because he was concerned above all with Russian socialism becoming isolated from its European background. After all, in 1920 he looked at the Polish-Soviet conflict (which began with an unprovoked attack on Soviet Russia) from this angle. Even the year before, Polish forces controlled the western territories of Belorussia, despite the fact that by December 1917, in advance of any peace treaty, Lenin and the Soviet government had recognized the independence of Poland.

The various levels on which the civil war in Russia was conducted (social, political, national-ethnic, between superpowers, and in economic trade) are known. When Piłsudski—following agreements with the Ukrainian nationalist politician Petlyura—took Kiev, it was clear to Lenin that the war had a special significance in terms of *all* of these different aspects.[37] The interventionist troops of the Entente fought (and wrought destruction) on Soviet territory in "defense" of their capitalist economic interests in Russia, while the interventionist countries competed with one another for power and economic positions. There were a number of fields within Soviet Russia in which the German-English-French-Turkish-Japanese-American interests clashed or intersected. (This battle of interests manifested itself in ways ranging from open pillage to the disposition of economic interests.) Therefore Lenin looked upon Piłsudski's advance, begun at the end of April, in the light of this pan-European context, and appraised it accordingly. Poland was an extension to the arm of the Entente, which had already once suffered defeat in Russia, and an aggressive embodiment of the peace regime of Versailles. This was not to say that Lenin did not understand the significance of Polish empire-building fantasies; nonetheless, he could not attribute too much weight to them.

Any position which sees the Polish-Soviet War as a one-dimensional "border conflict" is too simplistic. Piłsudski and the Polish propaganda did indeed begin the attack in the throes of the dream of national reunion and a nationalist stupor of Greater Poland, but it would hardly have set out on the risky military campaign without the support of both France and Petlyura, the "counterrevolutionary" leader of Ukraine. In the spring of 1920, new hopes for Europe awoke in Bolshevik circles: The Kapp putsch was brought down in Germany with the help of the workers, definite sympathies with the Comintern and the Soviets were expressed on the left wing of European social democracy, and the international communist general staff saw new revolutionary perspectives in the near future. Lenin was for a more cautious approach in the spring, orienting himself in the direction of preparation, rather than "direct attack." In March 1920, Béla Kun raised this point in a letter, saying that Lenin's circumspect comments were used by the "opportunists within the communist parties" to their advantage. For this reason, Kun wrote, "Do not prevent the Russian Bolshevik method from being used, citing your authority, in Western Europe."[38]

Kun's attitude was not an isolated phenomenon, and a sense of optimism gradually overtook the whole leadership of the Comintern, Lenin included. In July–August 1920, at the time of the 2nd Congress of the Comintern, they were already confident of the success of a counteroffensive. This euphoria is conveyed by the coded telegram Lenin sent to Stalin, who was stationed in Kharkov on 23 July 1920 (the day Tukhachevsky received the command to cross the Bug River and occupy Warsaw):

> The situation in the Comintern is splendid. Zinovyev, Bukharin, and I, too, think that revolution in Italy should be spurred on immediately. My personal opinion is that to this end, Hungary should be sovietized, and also perhaps Czechia and Romania. We have to think it over carefully. Communicate your detailed conclusion. German Communists think that Germany is capable of mustering three hundred thousand troops from the lumpen against us.[39]

This was also the point when the Bolshevik leadership came to the decision that preparations must be made for the sovietization of Armenia and Georgia, to "spur on the world revolution," a demand that had been heard from the Caucasus office of the party since the beginning of August. A document still exists—a telegram to Smilga—proving that, at this point, Lenin had still not given up hope of sovietizing Lithuania.[40] Even though Trotsky, the People's Commissar for War, took a highly skeptical stance regarding a large Soviet military advance on Warsaw following the spent Polish attack, the supporters of an immediate counterattack won the day under the influence of the high morale.

As Piłsudski's advance petered out and the Soviets counterattacked quickly, British foreign minister Curzon, in a memo of 11 July, gave a warning to the Red troops about respecting the Curzon line,[41] though this no longer had any moral ground. (It is a different matter to judge whether it was worthwhile for the Red Army to cross the border.) Lenin was not impressed with this sudden wish for peace. His reaction to the Polish attack on Soviet Russia was that they would "probe whether the Polish proletariat was ready to support the world revolution," or at least the sovietization of Poland, "with the point of a bayonet." A base of power and organization was found in a "provisional Polish revolutionary committee" composed of Bolshevik leaders of Polish nationality, and led by the famous revolutionary Marchlewski, with essentially the same program presented by the Bolsheviks in 1917.

In the aftermath of the grave defeat south of Warsaw suffered by the Soviets in August, Lenin admitted at the 9th Congress of the RCP(B) in September 1920 that as a consequence of erroneous diplomatic, military, and political estimations a "catastrophic defeat" had occurred, and that he personally wished to "learn" from this experience. At the same time he did not remove from the agenda his theoretical-strategic considerations and basic appraisal of the situation: *that a counterattack was a possible reply to Polish aggression; in principle he still argued for the legitimacy of the course of world revolution.*[42] Full knowledge of the documents previously suppressed or truncated is especially important in this regard, because Lenin's horizons, both as a revolutionary theoretician and practitioner of foreign policy, can be seen in a new light by a speech of September 1922, which gave a complete account of the reasoning behind the concept of broadening the war with Poland. The speech (which was not intended for the public, and was never edited in its written form), contains, in a nutshell, Lenin's political and theoretical fundamentals on the links and interconnections between world progress and the international revolutionary transformation.

General Piłsudski attacked Soviet Russia despite the Russian peace proposals and border demarcations which were highly advantageous to Poland, or to be precise, to the Polish ruling classes.[43] Lenin perceived the initiative as coming from the whole Versailles regime, the Entente, and the French, rather than being an independent move on Poland's part. Lenin said Warsaw was situated in close proximity to the "center of the whole current international imperialist system," and the city's defeat would affect the defeat of the whole imperialist system. Lenin appended this obviously exaggerated deduction with the seemingly geopolitical, but more far-reaching, factor that "Poland is a buffer state between Germany and

1. Lenin plays chess with Bogdanov in Italy, as a guest of Gorky. Island of Capri, after 19 April 1908.

2. Vladimir Ilyich Lenin. Paris, 1910.

3. Lenin after having been freed from Austrian prison. Zakopane (Poland), after 19 August 1914.

4. Demonstration in July 1917. Petrograd, 1917.

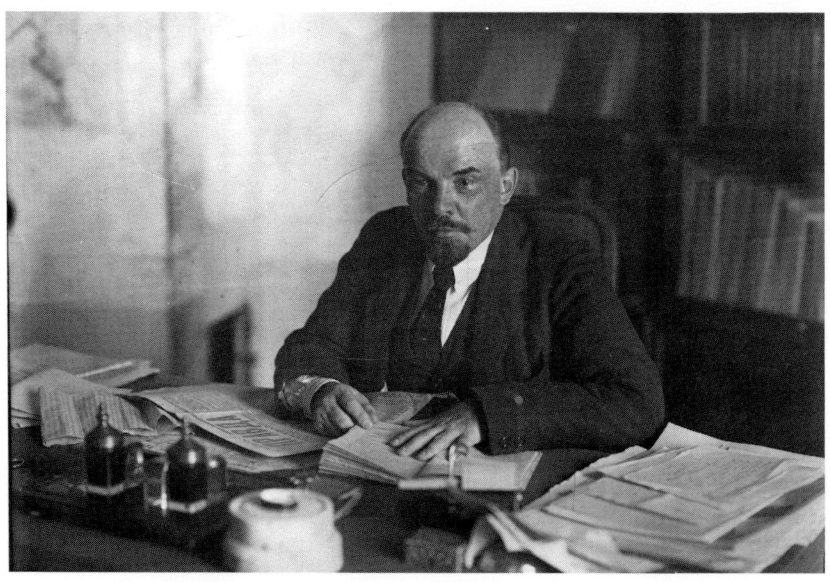

5. Lenin in his office. Moscow, Kremlin, 16 October 1918.

6. Lenin in Red Square, speaking at the inauguration of the Stepan Razin Memorial. Moscow, 1 May 1919.

7. N. K. Krupskaya. (1918–1919, probably Moscow.)

8. Lenin in "camouflage." The photo was prepared for an illegal identification card. Razliv, 8–16 August 1917.

9. The "Leninian agitprop corner" in the summer camp of one of the sections of the Red Army. 1927.

10. Lenin and Kamenev. Gorki, 1922. Between 1 August and 13 September.

11. Lenin at the wall of Red Square on the first of May demonstration.
Moscow, 1 May 1919.

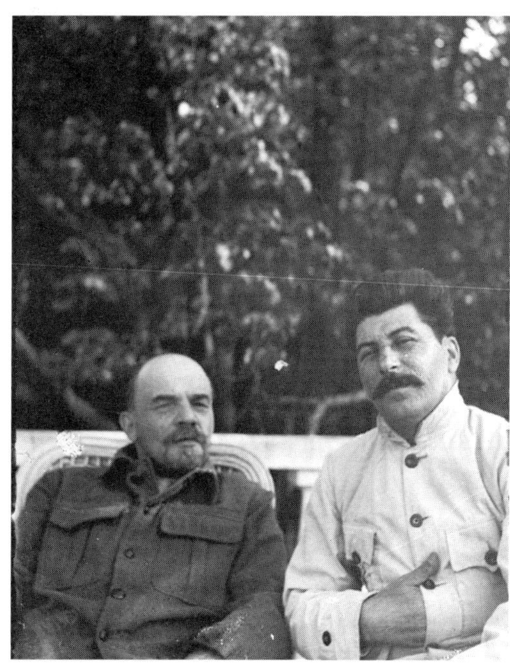

12. Lenin and Stalin.
Gorki, August 1922.

13. J. V. Stalin sketched by
N. I. Bukharin. 20 February 1928.

14. J. V. Stalin sketched by
N. I. Bukharin. April 1929.

15. N. K. Krupskaya sketched by
V. I. Mezhlauk. 1 June 1933.

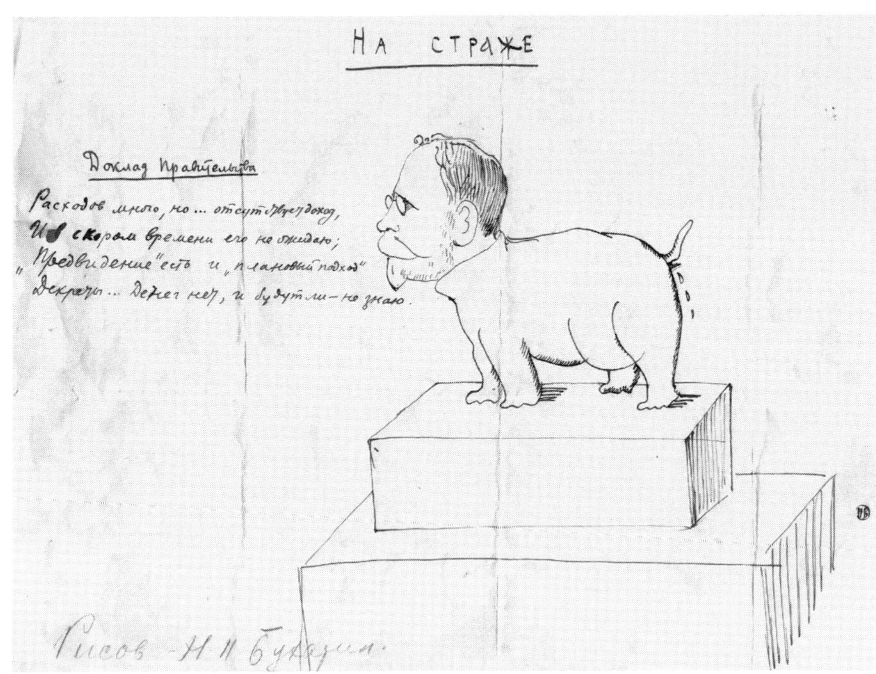

16. L. B. Kamenev sketched by N. I. Bukharin. 25 June 1923.

17. L. D. Trotsky sketched by V. I. Mezhlauk. Undated.

18. G. Y. Zinoviev sketched by
N. I. Bukharin. 3 March 1926.

19. N. I. Bukharin, self-portrait.
17 February 1927.

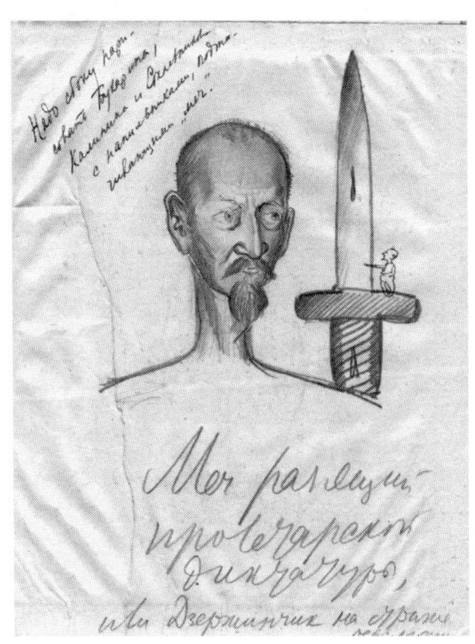

20. F. E. Dzerzhinsky sketched by
N. I. Bukharin. 30 June 1925.

21. G. K. Ordzhonikidze sketched by
N. I. Bukharin. 17 February 1927.

22. I. T. Smilga, G. Y. Zinoviev, L. B. Kamenev, L. D. Trotsky, and J. V. Stalin sketched by G. M. Krzhizhanovsky (?).

23. M. M. Kaganovich sketched by V. I. Mezhlauk. 20 February 1934.

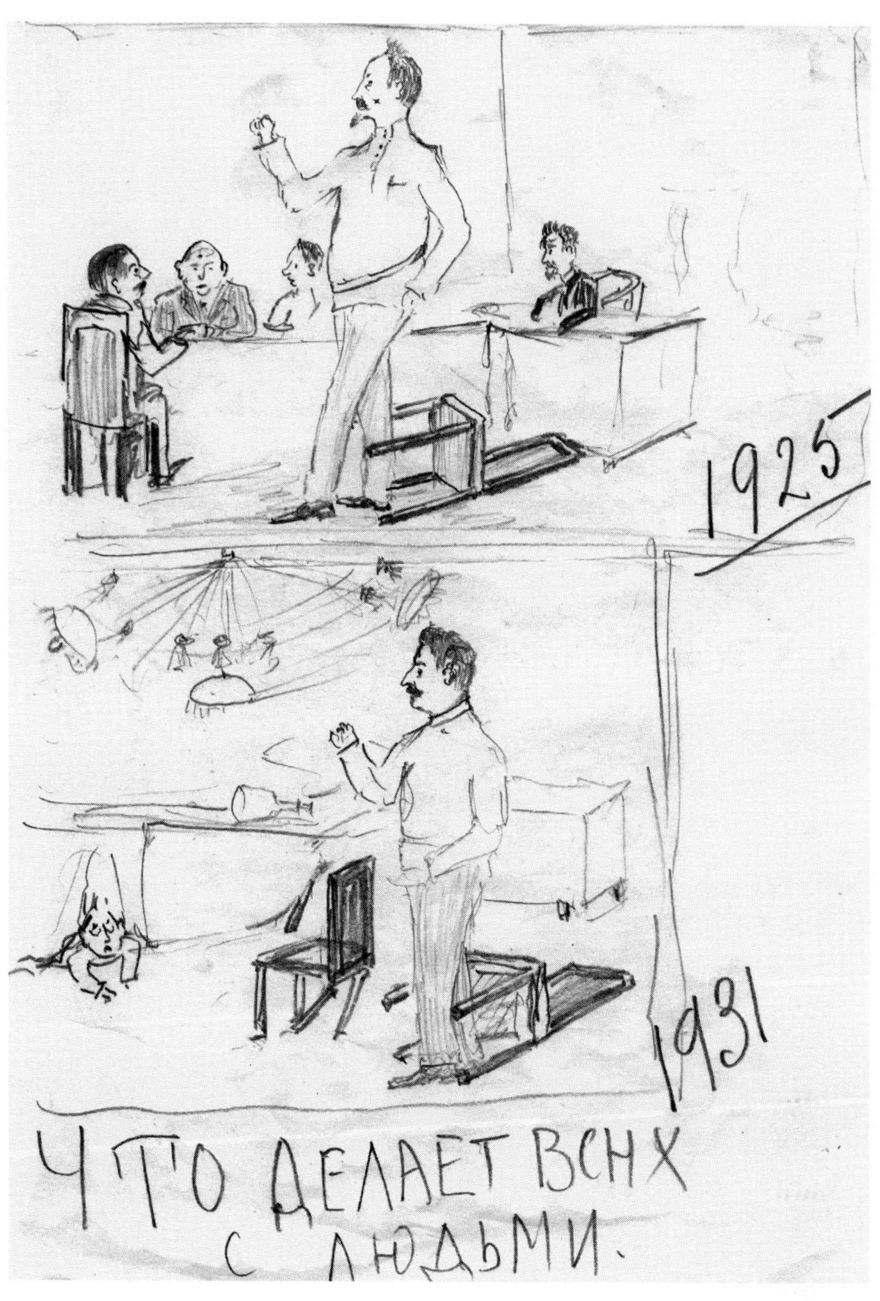

24. F. E. Dzerzhinsky and G. K. Ordzhonikidze sketched by V. I. Mezhlauk. (1931?)

25. Vladimir Ilyich Lenin sketched by N. I. Bukharin. 31 March 1927.

26. Vladimir Ilyich Lenin sketched by N. I. Bukharin. 15 June 1927.

27. Vladimir Ilyich Lenin. Author unknown. Undated.

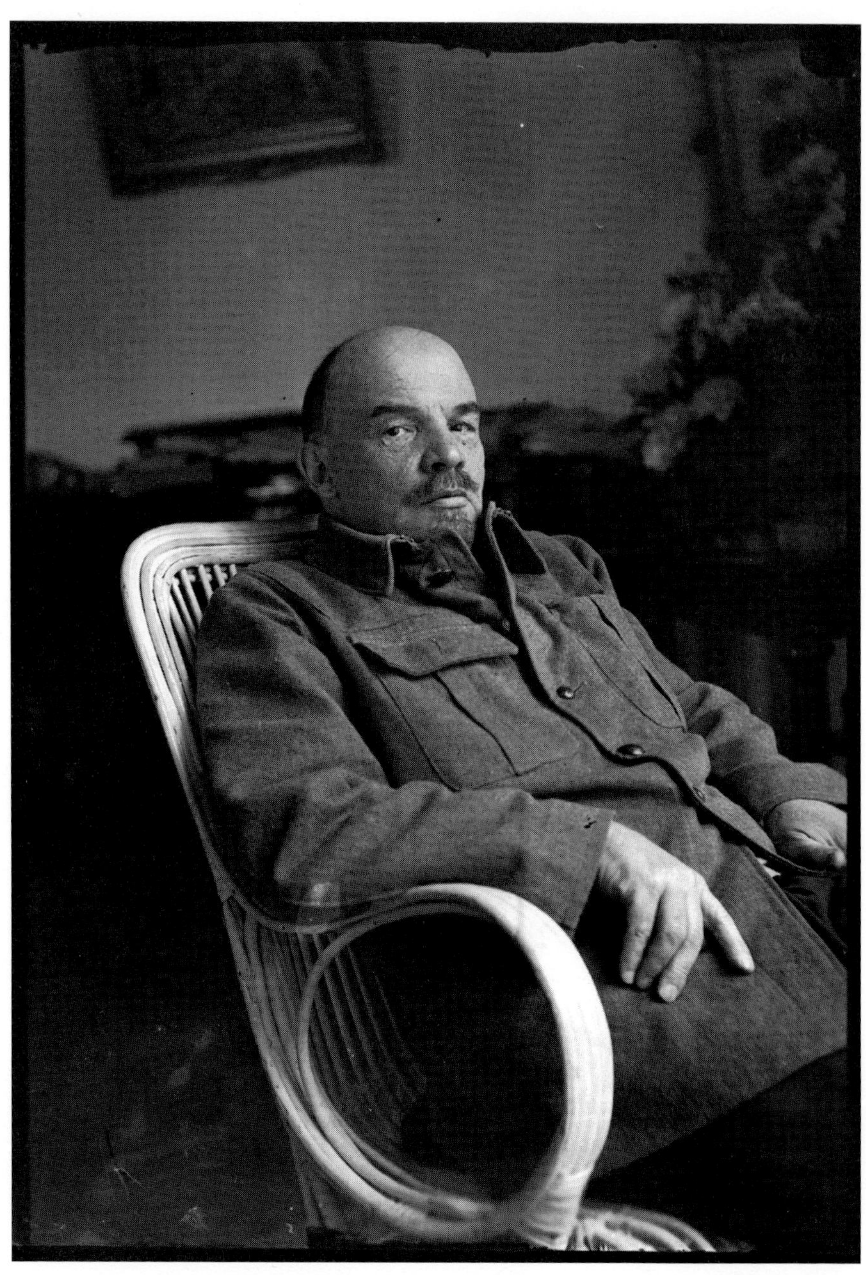

28. Lenin in Gorki. The photograph was taken between the beginning of August and 24 September 1922.

Russia," and the last state in that system's hands opposing Russia. In this sense, as Lenin exaggerated, "Warsaw was the bastion of the whole Versailles system." But in his strategic thinking the isolation of revolutionary Russia could only be imagined by revolutionary means, and the value of combinations between the great powers also grows during this process; in other words, he had the fate of the whole peace regime hanging by Warsaw. Russia would have come into direct connection, an organic union, with revolutionary eastern-prussia,[44] which would have an explosive effect on the Entente states. As a revolutionary strategist, Lenin learned to speak the language of the great powers—the language of force—and thus the two types of speech, that of the *revolutionary strategist* and the *politician in power,* became interwoven.

Lenin also saw France and England's cooperation as an attempt to subject Russia to the great powers.[45] Just as the Entente, and especially the "English-French axis," had stood behind Denikin and Kolchak, so Piłsudski was a representative of the new "imperialist world order" of Versailles, ready to participate in the reallocation of Russia. From a power-politics point of view, one of Lenin's aims in the campaign against Warsaw was to demonstrate the strength of the new Soviet Russian state, which the Entente could not humiliate. Lenin had a sense of the Entente's powers being on the wane; they were not able to provide a cohesive background to the Russian counterrevolution. The Entente was not able to gather its financial powers either, primarily because interests collided where the robbing and dismantling of Russia were concerned.

Of course, Lenin was convinced as of 1918 that the immediate objective of the Entente was the military isolation of Soviet Russia, with the small and medium-size countries becoming tools to this ploy. He made reference to a 1919 international conference where he pronounced that without the Entente, neither Denikin nor Kolchak could have held their own, and the neighboring countries would not have become military bases for their attacks on Soviet Russia:

> It was *not* we who torpedoed the Princes Islands, but the *monarchists* and *anti-Jew pogromists*, the restorers of *the landowners' estates*. Explain, develop, *prove* these three points, that Denikin and Kolchak 1) are monarchists; 2) pogromist thugs; 3) are restoring the estates of the landowners and introducing redemption payments for the peasants. We agreed to a truce *for negotiations* about peace, of course, with those who are *really* to blame for the war, i.e., with Great Britain, France, America, and not with pawns. Explain in detail that it is *they* who are waging war, with *their* ships, their *guns*, their cartridges, *their* officers.

Lenin unmasked the hypocrisy and unabashed lies of the Great Powers of the West when he later pointed out that "their renunciation of intervention" was a lie, if they "*support* (even instigate) the Estonians, the Finns, the Poles." In his speech of 15 October 1920, however, alluding to differences that had arisen between the French and the British, he indicated that they could not unite on the issue of the Poles, the smaller Baltic countries, and Wrangel, because "Britain ... was not interested in the restoration of tsarist or whiteguard or even bourgeois Russia; she even stood to lose from it."[46]

From another angle, Lenin saw the Polish attack as both a possible model for other surrounding states that had risen out of the Russian Empire, and springboard for the great powers of Europe against Soviet Russia. This logic drove Lenin's thesis that the time had become ripe for the anti-imperialist "defensive war against the Entente be turned into a war of offense."

Lenin interpreted the whole war on the basis of this concept; his words testified that he could not wholly reevaluate this strategic position, even after the Warsaw defeat:

> And so, in sum, our conviction ripened that the Entente's military offensive against us was over, that the defensive war with imperialism had ended, and that we had won it. The stake was Poland. And Poland thought that as a great power with imperialist traditions, she was capable of changing the nature of the war. This meant that the assessment was as follows: the period of defensive war was finished. (Please take fewer notes. This should not get into the press.) On the other hand, the offensive showed us that because the Entente was powerless to crush us militarily, powerless to utilize its troops, it could only push various small countries against us, countries that have no military worth and that maintain a landowner-bourgeois system only at the cost of such violence and terror as the Entente provides them with. There is no doubt that the Menshevik democratic capitalism that still maintains itself in all the countries bordering on Russia, formed out of the previous territories of the former Russian Empire, starting with Estonia, Georgia, etc., maintains itself with the help of what England delivers. She provides cannons, soldiers, uniforms, and money to keep the workers in subjection. We faced a new task. The defensive period of the war with worldwide imperialism was over, and we could have, and had the obligation to exploit, the military situation and launch an offensive war. We had defeated them when they advanced against us; we would now try to advance against them in order to assist the sovietization of Poland. We will help to sovietize Lithuania and Poland, as was said in our resolution.[47]

The notion of "offensive war" expressed the intention of sovietizing the territories which had earlier belonged to the Empire, and this demonstrates the gradual and unavoidable intertwining of "world revolutionary internationalism" and being a great power. The mixing of the two disparate terms was characterized by the political-military setting and political reflexes that had developed in the civil war, phrased by the Soviet leaders in terms of Soviet Russia fighting a life-and-death battle in the "capitalist environment," surrounded by the "ring of imperialist, capitalist countries."

In the cases of Georgia and Armenia, a decision against a military solution had been accepted earlier, but this brought a spate of dissatisfaction from these countries' communists:

> They made speeches against us full of bitterness, asking how we could conclude peace with the White Guard Latvian henchmen who subjected to torture and hanged on the gallows the best Latvian comrades, who had shed their blood for Soviet Russia. We heard similar speeches from the Georgians as well, but we did not assist the sovietization of Georgia and Latvia. But we cannot do this now either—we have other things to attend to.... We charted this policy with regard to Poland. We decided to use our military forces to assist the sovietization of Poland.... We formulated it not in an official resolution recorded in the minutes of the Central Committee and representing the law for the party and the new congress, but we said among ourselves that we must probe with bayonets whether the social revolution of the proletariat in Poland had ripened.[48]

In late autumn of 1920, Lenin, even though he was aware of the Warsaw defeat, did not hesitate to perform "the revolutionary duty with military support"[49] for the sovietization of the Caucasian republics. So irrespective of his argument, in this case revolutionary internationalism was already linked to the superpower politics of the new, potential great power, the hegemonic interests of Soviet Russia. Later, in the Stalinist period, and in a changed historical situation, these world power interests would essentially become the only basis of decisions. Therefore, Lenin's motivations indicate that he acted within the scope of the world revolution's ideal, but brought his day-to-day decisions under the primary influence of the realpolitik of a dominant power.

After Warsaw, Lenin practiced rigorous self-criticism on certain questions. Many participants of the 9th Party Conference said that the party and military leadership had overestimated the opposition of the Polish labor force and peasantry to the system, their hatred for the ruling classes, and their anti-feudal and anticapitalist position; and conversely had underestimated the strength of peasant patriotism, national feeling, nationalism, and sense of dedication to the new Polish nation-state. Lenin admitted these aspects were the most important empirical lessons of the experience. Yet the leading Soviet figures of the Polish revolutionary government had earlier underscored the negative consequences of leaving local specificities out of consideration; for example, just trying to gain acceptance from the local populace for officials of Jewish origin was, to put it mildly, not free of problems. The Bolshevik leader Felix Kon, who knew local circumstances well, wrote that there were too many Russians and Jews in the local governments, and the Soviet leaders had left growing local anti-Semitism ignored—a problem which, as pointed out in the previous chapter, also raised its head in the Red Army. Thus the Poles were not only fighting the communists, but also traditional Russian oppression and its "Jewish supporters"; in other words, Soviet power appeared in the guise of Russian oppression.[50] In the eyes of the nationalists, the Jews had always seemed to be the representatives of central power and "traitors" to local interests. In Piłsudski, Lenin mainly saw a representative of the Entente; he did not sense the mass influence the Polish leader had acquired. Piłsudski was an embodiment of the grandiose ambitions and the narrow, merciless, Russophobic traits of the nationalism of the Polish nobility and peasantry that were so typical in other regions of eastern Europe, and whose causes must be explored primarily in the oppressive role of the tsarist autocracy.

At the same time the issue that revealed the weakest point in Lenin's pragmatic political concept was also raised: Has the demand for a "world revolutionary turn" matured in the minds of Polish and Western workers? Have they recognized the possibility as their own interest? Lenin could only confront this issue in very narrow confines at the party conference. One question regarded the patriotism of the Polish laborers and peasants; it had turned against the Soviet government and the Red Army, even though Lenin himself recognized this trait in the Brest-Litovsk period. Lenin also mentions another defining trait—that a majority of the Western workers were not ready to seize power. However, he only sensed that they were subjectively ill-prepared for it, and he neither analyzed the causes nor sought the origins of this phenomenon. He understood that revolutionary Bolshevism could not penetrate the cultural traditions of the Western working masses, but he lacked a well-differentiated sociological analysis of the reasons for the inner stratifications of Western labor (not to mention its Polish equivalent). Perhaps this is why he did not understand the British workers' political behavior; the following comment caught his incomprehension in a picturesque and typical manner:

> When an English workers' delegation visited me 26 May 1920, and I told them that every decent English worker should desire the defeat of the English government, they understood nothing. They made faces that I think even the best photograph could not capture. They simply could not get into their heads the truth that in the interests of world revolution, workers must wish the defeat of their government.[51]

Typically, Lenin did not perceive that an understanding of his thesis—"the defeat of one's own government"—does not depend solely on the presence of subjective-intellectual conditions, but that the very *existential conditions* of revolutionary self-consciousness were lacking in England, in the sense in which he himself approached it theoretically. In England, as in most Western bourgeois systems, the conflict between the working class and capital evolved quite differently from the way it did in Russia. And not only were a chain of completely different mediations at question here, but also a mentality leaning more toward compromise, which their history had forged. Lenin had acquainted himself with it in the years of his emigration, even trying to describe the phenomenon along with its causes, but without developing a deeper empathy or affinity for it. What he certainly was aware of was that the "development of the revolution" is "more complex," and "runs on divergent tracks." The real intricacy of the problem was shown by the fact that he himself criticized *leftism*, on the grounds that it does not take account of the regional and national specificities of development. Finally, all of these questions are not simple at the dawn of a new age, as even historians are sometimes prone to admit. Lenin had been critical of the left communists at the time of the Brest-Litovsk Treaty, and it was precisely during the year 1920 that he dedicated his most lively consideration to the problem of "Left-Wing Communism: An Infantile Disorder." But at the time perhaps he himself did not realize in its complete actuality the historical significance of the chasm separating "the theoretical consciousness and the practical consciousness of the proletariat." Thus Lenin did not draw far-reaching conclusions from his experience with the workers' delegation from England, and he certainly did not apply it to the Polish situation, though it was clear from the autumn of 1920 onward that nationalism proved stronger than socialism throughout all of Europe, even if the forms this nationalism took differed.

In a spirit of self-criticism and disappointment at the party conference, Lenin questioned his earlier conviction that "in Poland the proletarian population is well matured and the rural proletariat is better educated which tells us: you must help them sovietize." A number of times he cited with emphasis, "a great national surge of petit-bourgeois elements who, as we got closer to Warsaw, were terrified for their national existence" as the cause of the "enormous defeat." Lenin stressed that the regions with the industrial proletariat started even farther away than Warsaw, which they did not come close to occupying,[52] and thus could not secure any palpable experience of their readiness for revolution. (As if the absence of revolutionary behavior of most of the Polish industrial labor until then had not been sufficient "palpable experience"!)

In reexamining the errors that had been made, the chairman of the Council of the People's Commissars concluded that it had been a mistake to reject the offer made in the Curzon note of 12 June, but he nevertheless upheld the necessity of the strategic shift ("counterattack"):

> Given the international situation we must limit ourselves to a defensive posture with regard to the Entente, but despite the complete failure in the first instance, our first defeat, we will keep shifting from a defensive to an offensive policy over and over again until we finish all of them off for good.[53]

In the meantime Lenin was looking for opportunities to cooperate more closely with the West in economic terms. He still had not clarified his own position on the question of what form, and in what degree, the revolution was "exportable." As for capitalism, its normal form of "export" was the migration of capital—the "free flow of capital"—along with the military defense of the capital interests and markets acquired.

Karl Radek showed the contradictions in Lenin's argument and the political strategy of the Central Committee. He raised the issue from the angle of whether it was expedient to "probe" the readiness of a country—in the present case, Poland. Radek pointed out the weakest points of Lenin's argument when he said it was not enough to reject this probe as a replacement for serious analysis: "I get the sense that if comrades Lenin and Trotsky probe somewhere, there is something amiss." Alluding to Lenin's discussion with the British workers' delegation, he declared, "Neither in Germany, nor France, nor England are we so immediately close upon the eve of revolution that were we to capture Poland, Germany would break out in revolution."[54]

Here was the main point: the theoretical compass remaining a constant was the real problem, and not that Lenin acted under the spell of an ambition for some sort of "political superpower." It was a challenge to comprehend the possibilities offered by the new period for him, and he did wrack his brains on it, though never getting a chance to set it down in ordered writing and systematize the characteristic traits of the new international situation, the new developments of the worldwide system following the world war. It could not have been the least bit consoling that in this field, no one in Europe or America outpaced him at the time; after all, it was only a matter of a new epoch *being born.*

Radek, who spoke numerous languages and knew Western Europe well, also underscored that the party and the leadership of the Comintern were vastly overestimating "how ripe for revolution" Central Europe was. He repeated in the conclusion of his speech: "We must reject the method of 'probing' the international situation 'with bayonets.'" Meanwhile, Lenin did not desire a public debate of the issue of "probing." In a two-line note of 6 October regarding a writing of Radek's that followed up the conference, Lenin reacted, "I oppose a discussion of the (possible) future assistance we may provide the Germans through Poland; it must be struck out."[55]

Criticism came in from a rather disparate range of positions. Some of the important ones were formulated on moral grounds by known intellectuals such as Korolenko, Gorky, and even Kropotkin, but the policy of "expansion by force" also received criticism at the 9th Party Conference. On a different tack, critical comments were also voiced by representatives of the German Communist Movement in the *Die Rote Fahne* circle, which Lenin dealt with at the conference: "*Rote Fahne* and many others cannot tolerate even the thought that we will assist the sovietization of Poland with our own hands. These people consider themselves communists, but some of them remain nationalists and pacifists."[56]

Lenin's closest associates had, in the main, a more dogmatic approach to the wide field of questions around world revolution. For example, during the period of the party conference (14 October), G. Zinovyev, the chairman of the Comintern, was at the Halle Conference of the German Independent Social Democratic Party. There he was trying to convince an audience of German workers that the basic task was "the preparation of the working masses for world revolution," even though this—not only from the present perspective, but compared to the German politics of the time—proved to be an escape from reality:

> There needs to be a methodic declaration and preparations made for world revolution, for which all the preconditions are present. These are not the phrases of the romantics of revolution. The backward strata among laborers and peasants must be educated, they must be told that the hour of world revolution has struck—this is what is needed (lively acclamation throughout the room).

Against those who brought up an absence of preconditions, Zinovyev argued that the labor parties had two choices regarding a capitalism that had self-destructed or been destroyed in the course of the world war. "Would you," he said, and turned to the audience, "want to first rebuild capitalism, so that you can then overthrow it? This is a basic confusion of international reformism."[57]

Though this was also Lenin's dilemma, he approached it differently, turning it into a more thorough theoretical and political criticism of leftism, thereby opening a new course for the party leaders and the Comintern. The euphoric atmosphere had been crushed by the Warsaw defeat, and in its place in the Soviet political leadership there was a growing influence of the new realpolitik. This was a way of thinking that the Western statesmen could understand, and since it paralleled the buildup of power in Soviet Russia, they gradually began to accept it. Though Lenin continued to uphold an international revolutionary outlook to his death, as a practicing revolutionary from 1921 onward he did not count on this theoretical premise. Memoirists recount how vehemently he argued with those who excused their lack of solutions in concrete situations by falling back upon the "world revolutionary outlooks," giving him cause to proclaim reforms to replace the revolutionary methods not only in internal policy but also in foreign policy.[58] In other words, the Soviet republic began to "integrate" into the new world order in the sphere of foreign policy. When Lenin was no longer there to toe the line, the call to spread world revolution was being replaced by an increasing pragmatism of world powers, a bureaucratic combination of revolutionary internationalism and superpower politics. After Lenin's death, Stalin openly proclaimed this in December 1924 with the slogan "Socialism in One Country." The history of the Polish-Soviet War certainly had an important role in this turn of events.

MESSIANIC LEFTISM

Lenin's pamphlet *Left-Wing Communism: An Infantile Disorder* and his Polish "error" did not spring from the same motives in terms of methodology, theory, or politics. Lenin interpreted the Polish situation mistakenly at first, underestimating the blaze of national emotion and the depth of hatred for Russia, as well as its counterrevolutionary trend.

The main problem with leftism as a phenomenon was how it related to political compromise. It clarified how the overall rejection of compromises, stemming from a misunderstanding of the new historical situation, came from an inability to adapt to the new balance of class forces. The leftist movement was stuck in the pre-revolutionary point of view. To throw some light on this, Lenin wrote his famous political polemic in April 1920, just in time for the 2nd Congress of the Communist International.[59]

Lenin demonstrated the typical characteristics of this phenomenon with countless examples from the Netherlands, Germany, England, and even Hungary. Leftist communism represented a revolutionary stance in matters that did not prove manageable even with direct political actions. The political content of Lenin's criticism can be adequately understood in the process by which the Third International was established and consolidated politically and institutionally. Without dwelling too long on the labyrinthine and perhaps dry history of the day-to-day political relationships, it is plain that Lenin made his argument to prepare a historical turn. In the final conclusion to the pamphlet, he wrote:

> The Communists must exert every effort to direct the working-class movement and social development in general along the straightest and quickest road. . . . That is an incontestable truth. But it is enough to take one little step further—a step that might seem to be in the same direction—and truth becomes error. We have only to say, as the German and British Left Communists say, that we recognized only one road, only the direct road, that we will not permit tacking, maneuvering, compromising—and it will be a mistake which may cause, and in part has already caused, and is causing, very serious harm to Communism.[60]

A break with the doctrinaire politics of leftism only came about after serious political conflicts at the Third Congress of the Comintern, in the spring of 1921. Under the aegis of the Comintern, the more flexible politics, evasion of sectarianism, and broadening of the worldwide ebb in revolutionary activity all led to the more mature "political tactic of the united workers' front."[61] Earlier, in August 1919, Lenin had already written to the anti-parliamentarian representative of the leftist movement, Sylvia Pankhurst, to say that one of the main traits of leftism was sectarianism (as manifested in anti-parliamentarism), which was a cul-de-sac in both methodological and political terms.[62] Georg Lukács had a lifelong trust in the accuracy of Lenin's censure in regard to his "anti-parliamentarism,"[63] whereas Lenin's argument with Béla Kun seemed almost to become permanent, because Kun spoke the language of revolutionary slogans even in situations that were decidedly not revolutionary. At the time of the Treaty of Brest-Litovsk, leftism was recognized as not only manifesting itself in the "secondary" issue of parliamentarism, but in forming a whole system of views and actions.[64] The phenomenon came into its full "classical" international form in the spring of 1920, marked by Lenin's pamphlet, which was a reaction to these developments. Its truth was finally vindicated by the sad German experiences in the spring of 1921, with the defeat of the German worker's revolt, the so-called *Märzaktion*.

A number of groups within the young communist movement were still under the spell of world revolution in the spring of 1921, even though the Third Congress of the Comintern had—not just in principle and institutionally, but also in tactical and theoretical terms—rejected the leftist movements. The philosophically grounded messianic sectarianism, as Lukács later called his own movement (whose most proficient ideologue was himself), made itself noticeable in a no-longer-revolutionary situation with its dedication to finality both in regard to parliamentarianism, as well as the revolution's general development. As a theoretician of offensive tactics, the Hungarian philosopher approached the unfolding events from a perspective of the coming German revolution of March 1921, though he was slowly coming around to accepting the tactic of the "united labor front," which Lenin proposed, prioritizing the politics of mass movement and labor unions over the direct struggle for revolution. Béla Kun, on the other hand, supported the Italian and German amendments to the *Russian Theses* proposed by Radek, which had been sharply denounced by Lenin as "sectarian."[65] In Lenin's strategic thought, emphasis was placed on the "lack of theory" as the peculiarity of this period, in which all the alternatives, however disadvantageous they might be, are apparent, and the main tasks lay in practical orientation among them.

Lenin found the theoretical incursion of the "messianic leftwing" an unexpected and unwelcome phenomenon. Unexpected, because he could not have known its nature in the party of the Second International, and from the theoretical books that, like a skipping record, identified it with anarchism. This was not a wholly mistaken idea, for the origin of the messianic leftwing can be traced back—as István Hermann pointed out many decades ago—to Georges Sorel, a socialist but not a Marxist. He was the embodiment of the practical trend of "French praxis orientation," as opposed to abstract theory, who:

> turned to Nietzsche, and Bergson, so as to give philosophical props to his own general political philosophy based on strikes, becoming highly influential not only in France, but also Italy, some parts of Germany and Hungary also. The way in which Ervin Szabó or members of the Sunday Group, Lukács or Korsch, connected to this messianic perception of the world is not a task of the present writing to unfold, but it is certain nevertheless that the problem of *revolutionary praxis* took roots as a fundamental question in the thought of intellectual groups who, though of Marxist outlook, were opposed to the Second International.[66]

Who might be considered representatives of the "prehistory" of these trends in Russia is a matter of debate, but no doubt Bogdanov, discussed in an earlier chapter, would be among those elected.

Lenin, however, considered these philosophical approaches to practice either lacking in practical solutions or too unworldly altogether. This was demonstrated during the Kapp-putsch in the *Rote Fahne* of 20 March, which was a deadly threat to the Weimar democracy: "The proletariat will not lift a finger to save the democratic republic." This sectarian disposition—*in statu nascendi*—found full political expression a year later, in the March action. It was apparent in Paul Levi's removal as German communist leader who was the antisectarian representative of "united labor front" tactics; as well as in the fact that Béla Kun, who opposed those tactics, and was for the "theory of the offensive," supported the politics leading to this action on behalf of the Comintern, even if not directly involved in them.[67] The experiment of the German revolutionary forces in March 1921, a joint action of the left-wing German communists and a number of leading figures in the Comintern, became—not the launch of the proletarian revolution—but the final event of its demise. The aim of the armed revolt in central Germany (22 March–1 April 1921) was to "overthrow the government" and to "make an alliance with Soviet Russia," according to the 17 March plenary resolution of the Central Committee meeting of the United German Communist Party. This armed uprising broke out when Prussian authorities in Saxony used force to crush the protests by workers and "reinstate order." The uprising was soon cut off and defeated, at the cost of 145 lives, according to some accounts, and approximately 35,000 arrests.[68]

This sectarian trend did not only originate in messianic sources, but also in a peculiar bureaucratic root within the movement itself, a "revolutionary voluntarism" and the tyranny of power, a belief that practical problems of the greatest significance can be solved through administrative-forceful means. Lukács later referred to this tendency as "bureaucratic sectarianism," and no doubt it was reinforced in Russia by the concentration of power. The revolutionary experiment of 21 March coincided with the armed defeat of the Kronstadt anticommunist sailors' rebellion, and the rise of the labor opposition. Yet the wings of "proletarian messianism" within the party (labor opposition, etc.) carved an idol out of the proletariat, making them the most self-aware of all revolutionaries. This predisposition was immediately confuted by both the rebellion and its suppression. The armed repression of the rebellion was, on Lenin's part, arguably compulsory; others simply accounted for it on "philosophical" and emotional grounds, in that they perceived every "revolt" as a manifestation of the counterrevolution.

These two forms of sectarianism came to meet in the German action of March, when they confronted each other in Russia. At this time Lenin was engaged in political conflict with a third kind of messianism at the 10th Party Congress, a manifestation of "proletarian messianism" in the form of labor opposition—which, as we shall later discuss, perceived the historical situation from a perspective of the immediate realization of socialism. This form of messianism was a quite different phenomenon from that of bureaucratic redemption, represented by, for example, Béla Kun. Lenin considered the sectarianism of the Hungarian leader highly damaging, though valuing and respecting Kun's dedication. To him Kun seemed an embodiment of "political narrow-mindedness and lack of vision," of "idiotic ineptitude," "insensitivity to the masses," "sectarianism," and the "phraseology of revolution."[69] As a point of reference, Lenin's position came to be defined as the third movement, between "opportunism" and "leftism." He emphasized that "the bourgeoisie sees practically only one aspect of Bolshevism—insurrection, violence, and terror; it therefore strives to prepare itself for resistance and opposition primarily in *this* field." In this context he referred to the mass murders of the Finnish and Hungarians in the White Terror. Lenin saw his own country as a fortress besieged, in which the Mensheviks, the social democrats in general, and the S.R.s were apparently unable to make a break with the old world, theoretically and politically. Meanwhile "leftism," as if it were some sort of punishment for the right-wing degeneration of social democracy, walks in the same boots, in that leftism, or "left-wing doctrinairism," could also not adapt to the new set of conditions and new "challenges," and "persists in the unconditional repudiation of certain old forms, failing to see that the new content is forcing its way through all and sundry forms."[70] Thus Lenin's little pamphlet on "leftism" aimed at achieving political results and attempted to give form to the methodological and political preconditions for understanding the new historical situation. It is no coincidence that interest in the piece peaked in the Khrushchev period, when Stalinism was interpreted from the framework of "leftism," "leftist excess," and the conceptual framework of sectarian doctrinairism. Thus a row of divergent, fundamentally opposed trends were brought under the same umbrella, from the Stalinists to the communists of the Soviet republics. Lenin and Stalin were similarly merged as the "recapitalizers" and representatives of the "new class of intelligentsia" in the service of quite different aims, but using the same methods. At the end of the 1930s, Karl Korsch reformulated this critique of Lenin, continuing Pannekoek's line.[71] The direct political insinuation of this "amalgamation" only burst into bloom later, with the change of regimes in Eastern Europe, belonging to its ideological context.

This work by Lenin finally demonstrated that he had broken for good with all political and theoretical approaches and traditions that suggest or urge revolutionary action in nonrevolutionary situations. He recognized and emphasized the need for a flexible politics suitable to the reigning political situation, that is, a politics that appreciates the significance of compromise. "Representation of the politics of the working class" does not always, and in most cases moreover expressly does not, mean solutions of the most "revolutionary" or "radical kind," but entails an overview of the concrete historical-political opportunities in the context of "the tactic-strategy-theory." And so in the spirit of "concrete situation-concrete analysis," he declared war on the new sectarianism and dogmatism, which had put down roots in the first phase of the communist movement despite his efforts to prevent it. The battle of these various types of sectarian trends gained separate significance in later times, and burdened the whole history of the international communist movement, the study of which could be the subject of another line of research.

Bourgeois professors attempted to use the concept of equality as grounds for accusing us of wanting all men to be alike. . . . But in their ignorance they did not know that the socialists—and precisely the founders of modern scientific socialism, Marx and Engels—had said: equality is an empty phrase if it does not imply the abolition of classes. . . . A society in which the class distinction between workers and peasants still exists is neither a communist society nor a socialist society.

—V. I. LENIN, *CONSTITUTIONAL ILLUSIONS, FIRST ALL-RUSSIA CONGRESS ON ADULT EDUCATION,* LCW, VOL. 29, 358-99

8
The Theory of Socialism: Possibility or Utopia?

IN OCTOBER 1917 LENIN SURELY must have believed that history had confirmed his political and theoretical convictions, plans, and prophecies to a surprising degree. But *after* October he would observe that not a single one of his prognoses had been validated, or if they were—as in the case of the civil war—their form and course was accompanied by unforeseen catastrophes. All of this weighed heavily on the development of his theory of socialism. To begin with, a majority of the Mensheviks interpreted the October Revolution as a form of bourgeois revolution (with numerous movements to follow in their footsteps), a factor that came to mark the perimeters of the debate around this issue.[1]

If the theoretical deductions of Lenin's work and his perspectives on socialism are viewed from the angle of his last writings, from 1922 to 1923, a reconstruction of the formative history of his intellect is unavoidable.[2] Foremost, though, his theory illustrates a neatly presentable framework and conception. To reach intellectual maturity it had to come under the influence of five phases of development, clearly defined in terms of political history. The first phase covers the period prior to the 1905 Russian Revolution, and the second period stretches to the October Revolution, whose results were summarized in the work *State and Revolution*. But after 1917, the statesman Lenin was no longer in a position to write a theoretical prospectus and not simply due to a lack of time. Developments were not yet susceptible to classical analysis. But the three phases following the October Revolution—the "market economy" that characterized the period until spring 1918, the war communism of 1918–20, and the "state capitalism" of the New Economic Policy (NEP) from March 1921 onward—left substantive and easily outlined theoretical traces in Lenin's thought.

THE CONCEPTUAL ORIGINS OF SOCIALISM

Even in the first stages of his career as a thinker, Lenin had tried to define the idea of socialism conceptually. In the approach to this task he did not have much literature at his disposal other than the works of Marx and Engels,[3] for he was not only unmoved by the views of premodern Russian peasant socialism or the phantasms of utopian socialism, but rejected them outright as intellectual requisites belonging to the romantic past that could not comprehend the relations of a capitalist market economy. This by no means belittles the great respect he held for the work of all those thinkers who examined the possibilities of establishing a noncapitalist community. One of them was certainly Kropotkin (who felt very positive about the October Revolution). In 1919, Lenin actually proposed the publication of the great anarchist writer's works in four volumes.[4]

In the first half of the 1890s Lenin, contradicting Mikhailovsky in his *What the "Friends of the People" Are*, rejected all somnolent images of what the future and vision of socialism might be. He made it clear that

> Marx's work never painted any prospects for the future as such: it confined itself to analysing the present bourgeois regime, to studying the trends of development of the capitalist social organisation, and that is all. "We do not say to the world," Marx wrote as far back as 1843, and he fulfilled this programme to the letter, "we do not say to the world: Cease struggling—your whole struggle is senseless. All we do is to provide it with a true slogan of struggle. We only show the world what it is actually struggling for, and consciousness is a thing which the world must acquire, whether it likes it or not." Everybody knows that Capital, for instance . . . restricts itself to the most general allusions to the future and merely traces those already existing elements from which the future system grows.[5]

All of these thoughts inevitably bring to mind a comment of Lenin's twenty years hence about the "icon painters daubing,"[6] so often quoted from the 1960s onward. But in addition to the switch from peasant socialism to labor socialism, there is a critical momentum of reliable constancy in Lenin. The fundamental question of socialism, independent of capital and state, is the *community*, cooperative, or commune of producers and consumers, which had already come to his attention in his study of Kautsky's *On the Agrarian Question*, as well as in other books on agrarian history and theory in the late 1890s.[7]

As discussed in chapter 2, in the course of his debates with the Narodniks in the 1890s Lenin came to reject the myth of "Russian exceptionality" and originality (*samobitnosty*). He approached a critical appraisal of capitalism from a perspective of the "communist revolution" which presupposed socialism. Following Marx's dialectical method, he described social-historical development in terms of a movement from the simpler leading to the more complex, in which modern society and its state of property relations is reached imperatively. Its origin and postcapitalist future organically is connected according to the law of "negation of negation," referring to the well-known debate between Engels and Dühring. He outlined the whole problem of socialism through the historical development of *property*, according to which the new communal society appears in modern history after the dissolution of the ancient communities. It was a higher form of communal ownership, the manifestation of new "individual property":

> The abolition of "individual property," which since the sixteenth century has been effected in the way indicated above, is the first negation. It will be followed by a second, which bears the character of a negation of the negation, and hence of a restoration of "individual property," but in a higher form, based on common ownership of land and of the instruments of labour. Herr Marx calls this new "individual property" also "social property," and in this there appears the Hegelian higher unity, in which the contradiction is supposed to be sublated (*aufgehoben*—a specific Hegelian term).

Therefore socialism as a philosophical and historical possibility has its inception with the beginning of modern capitalist society in the original capital accumulation. Lenin quoted Marx at length on individual property coming into existence again, which now meant the shared ownership of the tools of production. That is, the "labour-power of all the different individuals is consciously applied as the combined labour-power of the community" on a socialist basis, as a "community of free individuals":

> Capital becomes a fetter upon the mode of production, which has sprung up and nourished along with, and under it. Concentration of the means of production and socialisation of labour at last reach a point where they become incompatible with their capitalist integument. This integument is burst asunder. The knell of capitalist private property sounds. The expropriators are expropriated.[8]

The Marxist idea captured the imagination of a whole generation at the start of the twentieth century with Lenin's mediation from Berdyaev to Bulgakov. The utopian kind of peasant socialism had been entrenched in Russia—due in part to the rudimentary stage of capitalist development—and fallen apart in the 1870s, as Lenin noted early on. This gave birth to "superficial petit-bourgeois liberalism" which dreamt of a peasant revolution and came to find, as progress dictated, that the mass expropriation of the peasants was under way. Mikhailovsky's liberal socialism and its followers, having become determined opponents of Marx and the Russian Marxists, were engaged like "guileless petit bourgeois" in the "protection of the weakest in society" and were breathing new life into old, antiquated social forms. Lenin considered this a movement hopelessly stuck in the past as seen from the perspective of "social revolution."[9] The liberal Narodniks reached back to the moralizing and subjective method of sociology for their eclecticism of "'borrowing' the best of everything," from the medieval social forms to the modern, bourgeois enlightenment ideals of freedom and equality. They began with a utopia and ending up with the most ordinary liberal prejudices.[10]

At the same time, Lenin was (and is) accused by the left of exaggerating the "progressiveness" of the "central countries" and the historical development of bourgeois democracy in general, understandable in ideological terms. If imperialist monopoly capitalism is the "reception room" of socialism and is mature enough for revolution, there is no logical way to avoid introducing a normative concept of "stage of development" into the analysis with an obviously practical, political purpose. It must be added, however, that alongside the idea that capitalism had entered into a destructive phase that ripened during the years of the world war, he exaggerated the system's level of decomposition and underestimated capitalism's ability to adapt, thus closing the history book on capitalism. On the other hand, in quasi self-contradiction, he also seemed to overestimate capitalism's "reserves" of progress. In this regard it seems that Lenin's thought continued the Marxist notion that had been formulated in *The Communist Manifesto* about capitalism sweeping away the old feudal fetters, while with modernity, a global modern society would prepare the free development of the labor movement precisely through the spread of democracy and "prepare the ground for socialism." Despite the fact that the First World War fundamentally affected Lenin's views on capitalism, he recognized the capitalist ability for innovation, its aptitude for technical renewal, and watched for the prospects of socialism with some devotion, perhaps in order to bring it "closer to home." This occurred with other socialist thinkers of the time who spent their exile years in Western Europe or America where they had an opportunity to compare the levels of freedom in the West and in the East. The difference was so apparent that Axelrod and Plekhanov were convinced, in the aftermath of 1907, that Russia must complete the full course of Western bourgeois development.

Lenin examined theoretical principles in relation to how capitalism organized technical matters and labor, including transformations in the distribution of labor. By studying the automation of production and the Taylor system prior to the war, he became convinced that this new organizational facility of large industrial production made it possible for labor organizations to easily seize the reins of production. At the beginning of the twentieth century the steps capital took in order to rationalize and apply common sense to its processes were built into the arguments supporting the possibility of socialism. After all, the economic use of human resources and work time would lead to more humane results in a social system that is not constrained by the detached, hierarchically regimented structures of capitalism or regulated by subsequent market mediations. Lenin reached an important conclusion in this regard:

> The Taylor system—without its initiators knowing or wishing it—is preparing for the time when the proletariat will take over all social production and appoint its own workers' committees for the purpose of properly distributing and rationalizing all social labor. Large-scale production, machinery, railways, telephone—all provide thousands of opportunities to cut by three-fourths the working time of the organised workers and make them four times better off than they are today. And these workers' committees, assisted by the workers' unions, will be able to apply these principles of rational distribution of social labor when the latter is freed from its enslavement by capital.[11]

When Lenin posited his own "three-step" concept in his *State and Revolution*—in which socialism, as the "lower phase" of communism, is preceded by a "transitional period"—he could not have known that the Russian Revolution would be left on its own. As a result, theoretical socialism as a practical issue would be put off in perpetuity and history would actuate the possibility of socialism in peculiarly Russian form, something he would very much have wanted to avoid.

FROM MARKET ECONOMY TO WAR COMMUNISM

Central to Lenin's thinking after October 1917 was how to preserve the hard-won strength: the power of the soviets. In practice this was never separate from the power of his party, which saw it as the political condition upon which continuing soviet power depended. He surveyed the practical possibility of communal-socialist proletarian ends from this point of view. The contradiction, which strained the tortuous daily battles for survival and the end objectives, increasingly set the discrete problems of the so-called transitional period in the forefront.

Such was the mass of problems he confronted at the first congress following October. There, he drew attention to the particularity of their revolution:

> The difference between a socialist revolution and a bourgeois revolution is that in the latter case there are ready-made forms of capitalist relationships; Soviet power—the proletarian power—does not inherit such ready-made relationships, if we leave out of account the most developed forms of capitalism.[12]

He emphasized the significance of labor's control of large enterprises and the creation of a single huge economic organism, the "organization of accounting." But the soviet as the sole form of state power was in principle to be "centralized from below." Yet this was precisely the task that could not be accomplished in practice, for the revolutionary proletariat consisted of such a small segment of the population that it could not provide the necessary dynamic for the soviet—in a self-governing mode—either on a national scale or for a prolonged period. In the meantime, in early 1918 the "traditional" forms of control against the dispersal of small property and the chaotic proliferation of market networks were quickly resumed in the name of state efficiency, and given a sense of virtually unremarked normality or reaffirmed by the Red Guard assault on capital that followed in October.

To a certain extent Lenin had reckoned on such a contingency of power concentration even at the stage preceding October. He had prepared for a civil war in abstract terms, but naturally he did not have an economic policy worked out for any of the possible political scenarios. He did nevertheless have important matters to consider in addition to the program presented in the *April Theses*. In the first section of his September 1917 brochure, *The Impending Catastrophe and How to Combat It*,[13] to which he gave the title "The Famine Is Approaching," he called attention to the impending threat of a famine of incalculable proportions. He located the other cause of the catastrophe in the context of the then-unprecedented mass unemployment. As he put it, in six months "absolutely *nothing* of any importance has actually been done to avert catastrophe, to avert famine" by the "democrats," the S.R.s and the Mensheviks.

Lenin summarized the necessary measures as: state control; state supervision; state accounting; proper distribution of labor-power in the production and distribution of goods; husbanding of the people's forces by the state; the nationalization of the largest monopoly associations and the banks; and forced mergers of the biggest ventures into syndicates. These should have been the tasks of the revolutionary democratic government but he saw the failure to address these issues as rooted in the fact that "their realization would affect the fabulous profits of a handful of landowners and capitalists." The government feared encroaching on "the supremacy of the landowners and capitalists, on their immense, fantastic and scandalous profits, profits derived from high prices and war contracts." And "these Mensheviks and Socialist-Revolutionaries, with the serious mien of statesmen, now prate (I am writing this on the very eve of the Democratic Conference of September 12) that matters can be furthered by replacing the coalition with the Kadets by a coalition with commercial and industrial Kit Kityches,[14] the Ryabushinskys, Bublikovs, Tereshchenkos and Co." Lenin pointed out that the democratic parties wanted to solve these problems in alliance with the same political forces that had opposed interests. "Are we to regard them as political babes in the wood who in their extreme foolishness and naïveté do not realize what they are doing and err in good faith? Or does the abundance of posts they occupy as ministers, deputy ministers, governors-general, commissars and the like have the property of engendering a special kind of 'political' blindness?"[15] Though the key to the solution was a takeover of power, the problems and the predicament remained.

It is clear that Lenin was hardly as naïve as he is sometimes portrayed. He did not plan on the liquidation of the market and in fact rejected in no uncertain terms this accusation. Moreover, in the spring of 1918 it seemed as if markets were to be preserved as the most fundamental and indispensable "appendage" of production. He opposed the introduction of socialism because his thinking suggested that a social form cannot simply be "introduced." In the passage quoted above, written in September, he "unmasked" those leaders whose scare tactics about the "introduction" of socialism figured as one of their arguments against taking the revolution further:

> Those leaders deceive themselves and the people by saying that "Russia is not yet ripe for the introduction of socialism." Why must we treat such assertions as deception? Because, through such assertions, the situation is misrepresented to make believe that it is a question of unprecedentedly complicated and difficult changes, such as are bound to break up the normal way of life of millions of people. The situation is misrepresented to make believe that some want to "introduce" socialism in Russia by decree, without considering the existing technical level, the great number of small undertakings, or the habits and wishes of the majority of the population.

> That is a lie from beginning to end. Nobody has ever proposed anything of the kind. No party or individual has had any intention of "introducing socialism" by decree. It is, and has been, a question solely of measures which, like the public duty imposed on the rich in Yekaterinburg, have the full approval of the mass of the poor, i.e., the majority of the population, measures which are perfectly ripe, technically and culturally, and will bring immediate relief to the poor and make it possible to ease the hardships of the war and distribute them more evenly.[16]

In his pamphlet, *The Immediate Tasks of the Soviet Government*, published as a *Pravda* insert on 28 April 1918, Lenin once again raised these same questions, and gradually formed his own position in light of the new situation. The reason he attributed such grave importance to the difficulties caused by the "chaotic" situation was that "the military party, tempted by Russia's momentary weakness . . . may gain the upper hand at any moment"[17] in the West. He intended to establish a concrete economic alternative to market-dominated production in an "anarchically built capitalist society" and the "spontaneously growing and expanding national and international market" system,[18] but which had not yet overstepped the limitations of the existing "mixed market economy." True, he had already advocated "the strictest and universal accounting and control of the production and distribution of goods." Since he spoke about "setting up an extremely intricate and delicate system of new organisational relationships," whose realization was not merely a technical matter, it is natural that he did not envisage a complete and immediate termination of all market relations as "time is needed" to "convince the people" and "deepen the consciousness." Nevertheless, just such a termination would shortly be implemented under civil war conditions. As the organization of the new method of production and distribution was not proceeding at the required pace and with the expected reach, Lenin concluded that the capitalist sector would have to remain standing. He said, "If we decided to continue to expropriate capital at the same rate at which we have been doing up to now, we should certainly suffer defeat," and elsewhere that "the expropriation of the expropriators" is easier than introducing a new system. He believed that the Red Guard attacks on capital had drawn to a close and the period of "utilising bourgeois specialists by the proletarian state power" had begun.[19] He even strayed from every theoretical premise and declared unequivocally that these specialists must be engaged in the service of the new regime with "high remuneration." Lenin described this "winning over the 'stars' of the intelligentsia" as a "step back" and a "partial retreat"[20] when compared with socialist equality. In the same breath—and with great prescience—he spoke of a certain and inevitable corruption of this system, the weakening of its moral fiber as a sort of natural concomitant of "market economy." "The corrupting influence of high salaries—both upon the Soviet authorities (especially since the revolution occurred so rapidly that it was impossible to prevent a certain number of adventurers and rogues from getting into positions of authority . . .) and upon the mass of the workers—is indisputable." Yet he never found a convincing solution to this contradiction, always thinking in terms of "socialist" and "proletarian" consciousness and its persuasion, because they had not been able to establish "comprehensive control and accounting," and had "fallen behind with the socialist reforms." "We have introduced workers' control as a law, but this law . . . is only just beginning to penetrate the minds of broad sections of the proletariat."[21] Essentially, the expansion of state regulation to capitalist production and turnover of goods (to the cooperatives as well) may become a fundamental question regarding financial and market conditions in the "transition leading to socialism."[22]

A virtually unnoticed shift took place within this political framework toward war-communist restrictions of the market economy. Originally instrumental in defending against foreign capital and establishing independence internally, the state monopoly on grain (introduced by the Provisional Government's law of 25 March 1917) was followed by plans for both a state monopoly on foreign trade and a property tax, as a way of "supplementing" the budget.[23] At the same time, in *The Impending Catastrophe*, he drew a clear line between state control of the bourgeoisie and the expropriation of private property that applied to the bourgeoisie, even arguing against expropriation in this specific case:

> If nationalisation of the banks is so often confused with the confiscation of private property, it is the bourgeois press which has an interest in deceiving the public. . . . Whoever owned fifteen rubles on a savings account would continue to be the owner of fifteen rubles after the nationalisation of the banks; and whoever had fifteen million rubles would continue after the nationalisation of the banks to have fifteen million rubles in the form of shares, bonds, bills, commercial certificates and so on.[24]

The purpose of nationalization was to oversee the financial and economic processes, the actual collection of personal income taxes, etc. Lenin contrasted reactionary-bourgeois regulation to revolutionary democratic regulation, with bottom-up control, with whose limitations he soon came face-to-face. He had already stipulated that the construction of the most modern heavy industry would require state-of-the-art technical-technological progress, to apply "much of what is scientific and progressive in the Taylor system; we must make wages correspond to the total amount of goods turned out, or to the amount of work done by the railways, the water transport system, etc., etc." Lenin thought that the feasibility of socialism depended on the successes that could be achieved in the field of "combining the Soviet power and the Soviet organisation of administration with the up-to-date achievements of capitalism."[25] Apart from the cooperation and competition of economic sectors and modes of production, Lenin also spoke about the "competition of communes," and etched out its moral driving forces more clearly than its material and economic bases. In contrast to the "allowances" made to market and financial conditions and the "bourgeois cooperatives," the "socialist state can arise only as a network of producers' and consumers' communes, which conscientiously keep account of their production and consumption, economise on labour, and steadily raise the productivity of labour, thus making it possible to reduce the working day to seven, six and even fewer hours." Lenin also thought it would be possible to "ensure that *every* toiler . . . shall perform state duties *without pay*," after regular work hours. (He obviously overestimated the opportunities, in terms of developing Soviet democracy, that could be realized in the "moment of respite" offered by the Treaty of Brest-Litovsk.) So Lenin presumed that a kind of peaceful competition between capitalism and socialism could evolve under the supervision of the Soviet state. Soon it became clear that the political prerequisites for the envisioned mixed market economy were, to put it mildly, not favorable. The basic problem, predicted by the Russian bourgeoisie in the summer and autumn of 1917, soon became apparent: the "skeletal hand" of hunger would strangle the Soviet Republic. Lenin had taken note of this, and by the spring of 1918, famine ravaged the cities.

It had now taken six months for Lenin to pose the same questions to himself that he had earlier addressed to the Provisional Government. On his initiative, the Council of People's Commissars introduced the "dictatorship of state subsistence," the formation of the poor peasant committees that swept out the attics. Many writers tend to wax theoretical about these spontaneous measures, as if Lenin had ventured upon these in line with a concept he had invented earlier; on some theoretical basis; or even with the assumption that some sort of special socialism or theoretical model could be erected on the basis of these actions. In fact, a political turn was outlined in May 1918, leading from a state-supervised mixed market economy to a dictatorship of state subsistence that swept spontaneously toward war communism. The latter, in the beginning, was determined and validated by the internal armed counterrevolution and interventionist military attacks. The civil war broke out on an increasingly wide front in the summer of 1918. What chances could there have been of establishing "the special forms of recall and other means of control from below,"[26] when the main focus was setting up a war of defense with the help of the centralization of state power? The theoretical justification for war communism only came later.

Lenin drew up the substance of this political turn in his *On the Famine: Letter to Workers of Petrograd*, composed after a conversation with A. V. Ivanov. One of the workers in the Putilov factory, Ivanov had been asked to deliver the decree granting A. D. Tsyurupa, the People's Commissar for Food, special powers to battle famine. At the same time, in support of Tsyurupa's initiative, Petrograd workers were called to form armed brigades to combat "the rural bourgeoisie" and the "concealing of grain stocks"—the expropriation committees in embryonic form.[27] The *Letter* argued that the main problem was that the well-to-do peasants, "the rural rich, the kulaks, are thwarting the grain monopoly." Lenin justified the authoritarian measure by saying: "He who does not work, neither shall he eat." This was easily understandable ideological "message," which sought to abolish of all forms of "private trade in grain." Further concentration of power—not planned in advance—became the primary instrument to surmount famine, which was the fundamental political objective.

> One has only to reflect ever so slightly on these conditions for coping with the famine to see the abysmal stupidity of the contemptible anarchist windbags, who deny the necessity of a state power . . . for the transition from capitalism to communism and for the ridding of the working people of all forms of oppression and exploitation. . . . Our state grain monopoly exists in law, but in practice it is being thwarted at every step by the bourgeoisie . . . [who] throw the blame for the famine on Soviet power.[28]

The gradual introduction of the dictatorship of state subsistence was grounded in the ungoverned shifts in the market economy, producing a shortage of grain and heating fuel. This resulted in the consolidation of these resources by military means.[29]

The May 1918 decrees empowered the People's Commissariat for Food to determine norms of production and collection, product barter, and distribution throughout the territory of the Soviet Republic. In this way, trade policy was turned into food policy. Finally, on 1 June, the Council of People's Commissars introduced the compulsory appropriation of grain, practically outlawing private trade.[30] The series of war-communist measures gained breadth alongside the mopping up of financial and market conditions in the autumn of 1918. The decree of 21 November 1918, regulating the feeding of the general populace, made the state's role dominant in virtually every branch, in addition to nationalizing banks, transport, etc. Bolshevik ideologists made virtue out of necessity when the militarization of labor and the war economy—a product of the civil war—was suddenly described as the realization of socialism. Lenin, too, became a proponent of this switch.

Yet in the spring of 1918 he described the effort to use Soviet state supervision of trusts and company management to combat chaotic relations in "capitalist small-scale production" as "state capitalism." On the other hand the conditions of war communism brought the notions of "transitional period" and "socialism" too close to each other in theoretical terms. Bukharin and Preobrazhensky's *The ABC of Communism* gave a theoretical basis to the conflation of war communism (as a relatively integrated sequence of economic policy measures) and the realization of socialism as such. The work was a curious mixture of the mutually exclusive ideas of Soviet labor self-government and state socialism. These two famous Bolshevik writers attempted to "translate" the Marxist conception of socialism into the reality of war communism. It was as if the first stage of communism, the realization of socialism, was coming into a state of full development, and was able to transcend commodity and finance relations thanks to both unprecedented inflation and the forced measures of war communism:

> But it is perfectly plain that we cannot believe State capitalism to be possible unless we also believe in the possibility of the socialist organization of economic life. The only difference between the two systems lies in this, that in one case industry is organized by the bourgeois State, and that in the other case it is organized by the proletarian State.[31]

Left unexplained was that the matter does not simply rest on state power, for in war communism the state as a military force of authority, as a "deterrent to class enemies through dictatorial" power, acted as the mainspring of the economy. This had no roots in any form of Marxist theoretical tradition from Marx's own time, and even contradicted his period's idea of socialism. The "dictatorship of the proletariat" was whittled down to a single function.

No doubt Lenin made concessions to the socialist concept of war communism in the period of 1919–20, identifying nationalization and the administrative liquidation of market conditions with possibilities for the immediate realization of socialism. However, he was perfectly aware of the distinction between *nationalization* and *socialization* earlier on, and he later drew a clear distinction. Nationalization played a role in the "period of political transition," and of course socialization was part of socialism, even though it was conceived during the transitional period. Lenin was not so naïve as to identify war communism with "complete socialism," for he continued to believe that "as long as workers and peasants remain, socialism has not been achieved."[32] Moreover, he never deduced the concept of equality theoretically from the reality of war communism, using it only to refer to eliminating social class in economic terms, a final and indispensable requirement of the liberation from capital and achieving freedom. Lenin's real theoretical mistake in 1919–20 was that he overestimated the possibilities of socialization, of social supervision within the framework of nationalization, and underestimated the inveteracy of the market and money in a regulating role, a fact he later recognized. The "atmosphere" of the epoch, the romantic attitude of the civil war, was also expressed in war communism's compulsory egalitarianism. The roots of this "primitive" egalitarianism ran deep in Red Army units and partisan brigades engaged in life-and-death combat with the Whites—a phenomenon picked up by innumerable literary works and films.

War communism also influenced theory, which interpreted the "system" as socialism, despite that being suggestive of an anachronism—especially in light of the famous thesis of the "semi-state" in *State and Revolution* (which can be traced back to Marx). There, Lenin was already engaged in a polemical attack on what was a conceptual muddle. He used Engels' critique of the draft program of Erfurt, which he had handed over to Kautsky in 1891, who published it a decade later in the *Neue Zeit*. This is interesting because the "opportunist wing" of the social democrats had already suggested that the state, in itself, might in itself be able to consolidate socialism.

This line of thought incorporated the increased role of the state in modern capitalism. Lenin mentions the concept of "state socialism," opposed to the revolution and revolutionary socialism, inasmuch as the role of socialism is defined in opposition to the state:

> The latter capitalism must be emphasized because the erroneous bourgeois reformist assertion that monopoly capitalism or state-monopoly capitalism is no longer capitalism, but can now be called "state socialism" and so on, is very common.[33]

In Engels's and Lenin's thinking, the socialist economy is organized from below. Lenin wrote after October: "We recognise only one road—changes from below; we wanted the workers themselves, from below, to draw up the new, basic economic principles."[34] This approach, however, quickly lost its currency. War communism's focus was on the consolidation of the new military-power hierarchy under civil war conditions, even though it simultaneously exacerbated the economic situation. Meanwhile, Lenin held that socialism, as a system that had reached completion, would only be composed of voluntary associations of economic-productive communities organized from below. It was still a *state*, though, for "there remains for a time not only bourgeois law, but even the bourgeois state, without the bourgeoisie" in order to defend the "equality of labor" and public property.[35] Lenin differentiated between state and social property even at its inception; before the introduction of war communism, he believed that the productive classes would themselves have to create socialist conditions. War communism was, however, a consistent system of compulsory state-military measures; according to some writers it carried certain traits of the state economic policy of "German war socialism." Lenin kept the formation theory in sight even while making his most propagandistic political speeches, indicating that until his last day he continued to view the history of the revolution through the lens of Marxist theory (as reconstructed by him).[36] Until March 1919, Lenin did not even use the term war communism, and did so afterward mostly in quotation marks. This means that, not just had Lenin not planned "war communism" in either theory or practical political terms, but also that the war communist measures only "coalesced" into a system much later, by the summer of 1919. The "naturalization" of production and distribution, along with the introduction of the ration system and the persecution of private trade, were not a priori economic measures, but sprang from immediate political and social needs.

When arguing with Kautsky and Vandervelde in the autumn of 1918, Lenin claimed that the revolution and the dictatorship of the proletariat was not only to be recognized in general, but also under the "concrete conditions of the class struggle," together with the grain monopoly and the dictatorship of distribution. In his opinion, these were required for the survival of the Soviet government. Calling upon democracy and the free market were pleasant-sounding phrases, but in practice they meant surrendering the revolution. The alternative had boiled down to something quite simple: *tertium non datur*. If the revolution was perceived, as in Kautsky's and Vandervelde's case, as a *bourgeois revolution*, there was no justification for Lenin's Bolshevik measures. On the other hand, if it were a socialist or workers' revolution—inclusive of equalizing agrarian land distribution and other peasant (petit-bourgeois) demands—then Lenin thought that the nationalization of the factories and the land, the ban on "speculation" in the form of private trade, state grain monopoly, rationing, and the introduction of the whole "dictatorship of distribution" as instruments of saving the regime, could not be avoided.[37] Lenin, generalizing the issue in principle, formulated it as: "The Soviet Constitution was not drawn up according to some 'plan'; it was not drawn up in a study, and was not foisted on the working people by bourgeois lawyers. No, this Constitution *grew up* in the course of the development of *the class struggle* in proportion as *class antagonisms* matured."[38]

He drew the same parallel between the political and power aspects of war communism later. In his speech of 19 May 1919, the "Deception of the People With Slogans of Freedom and Equality," he justified the ban on free trade because of the chaotic conditions created by the civil war and political weakness of the regime—

incidentally, with reference to Marx and Kautsky—but did not present them as actions which lead to socialism:

> in the midst of a proletarian revolution against the bourgeoisie, at a time when landowner and capitalist property is being abolished, when the country that has been ruined by four years of imperialist war is starving, freedom to trade in grain would mean freedom for the capitalists, freedom to restore the rule of capital. This is Kolchak's economic program, for Kolchak does not rest on air.[39]

NEP VS. WAR COMMUNISM—IRRECONCILABLE CONTRADICTIONS

Just as war communism was not the application of a theory, neither was the NEP the experiment or exercise of one. The Soviet government implemented both war communism and the NEP under the pressure of concrete circumstances, requirements, and needs—without foreseeing its internal or international effects. In both cases their ideologies—the theoretical justification of the "systems"—were developed either parallel to their introduction, or as a follow-up (though war communism incorporated a number of elements from German war economic policy, and the NEP included elements from the "market economy" of the winter and spring of 1918). The NEP meant substituting militarized production—including the ration system, strict state distribution, and the compulsory appropriation of grain—with money and market conditions, reinstituting free trade and introducing taxes in kind.

Often forgotten is that, at the same time, the partial reinstatement of capitalist conditions entailed a general social transformation, a restructuring of social classes and groups, and a change in their relationships. The development of production from a natural economy to a market economy brought about a differentiation between layers of village populations. It resulted in a quick improvement in the living conditions of a significant segment of the rural populace, as compared to those of the working class. In addition, earlier unknown (or differently known) social groups came to the fore in villages and cities alike. The private ventures and the partial freedom of private intermediary commerce created a new bourgeoisie. Trade in grain and other agricultural goods not only created a new peasant bourgeoisie, but also a social group of merchant dealers, equally urban and rural, often called "NEPmen." They were able to accumulate capital, and replaced the (old and banned) "speculating money-bags." This "bourgeois" transformation also incrementally incorporated the possibility of full-blown wage labor, which served as the source of new social conflicts. A complete, epochal change was under way.

The introduction of the NEP in March 1921, along with how Lenin appraised it and determined its outlook, is interesting both theoretically and historically. The Central Committee rejected a February 1920 proposal, from the People's Commissar for War Trotsky, to switch from compulsory grain appropriation to a tax in kind. This gave war communism a new impetus, but it faced increasing social resistance. Between the autumn of 1920 and the spring of 1921, peasant resistance and workers' protests made it clear that war communism was no longer tenable.

In these changed circumstances Lenin at last understood that buying and selling, the conditions of "free commerce," were so deeply rooted in human behavior and heritage that war communism was not going to bring about their "elimination." He recognized that not only was war communism not leading to socialism, but because it faced such resistance, it actually threatened the collapse of the Soviet system—in spite of the victory in the civil war. The war economy had prepared for the transition to a "peace economy," which would lead, in Lenin's words, to "the partial reinstatement of capitalism"—that is, a goods and market economy. All of this was presented as part of the NEP, and declared at the 10th Party Congress in March 1921, when a tax in kind was introduced in place of compulsory appropriation. The widely supported Petrograd and Moscow workers' movements of discontent, alongside the Kronstadt revolt, all unfolded parallel to the introduction of the NEP.

The defeat of the Kronstadt revolt actually became part of the NEP itself, inasmuch as—using the language of the period—"the concessions made to capitalism could not be allowed to undermine the political and social foundations of the Soviet government." The Kronstadters had demanded the introduction of free commerce and the market system in order to combat famine, and wanted to direct the "new regime" through the instruments of direct democracy (as discussed in chapter 6). Only one extant document from Kronstadt deals with the economy, dated 1 March 1921. It shows a curious combination of war communism and the emergent NEP, built in contradictory fashion on the freedom of peasant commerce and a ban on wage labor: "an immediate disbanding of the food brigades . . . complete freedom for the peasantry, to be allowed to do with the land and the produce as he pleases . . . permission for small industries on the basis of his own labor, no wage labor."[40] This bastion of the October Revolution wound up with the slogan "Soviet power without the communists." The leaders of the Soviet government had to confront this development. When the president of the Soviet state, M. I. Kalinin, gave a speech to a crowd of approximately

16,000 who gathered on the Yakornaya Square in Kronstadt on 1 March 1921, he was not able to convince the seamen and local populace of the futility of this anticommunist turn.[41] The revolt had the effect of speeding up the process of introducing the market economy.

The NEP did not appear on the agenda of the 10th Party Congress without preparation; it was not a result of coincidences, though it was overdue. The Soviet leaders sensed that war communism was stalling soon after Kolchak's defeat. This was reflected in Trotksy's rejected proposal in February 1920. This idea had gained ground in S.R. and Menshevik circles as well—it is enough to remember the argument between Lenin and Rozhkov in January 1919. Through 1919 and 1920, the reinstatement of free commerce came up frequently in the Menshevik Party, and not a few Mensheviks later claimed that Lenin stole the concept of the NEP from them. Most curious was that, alongside their demands for the reinstatement of free commerce and market conditions, their documents show that at the height of war communism and the civil war (at the turn of 1918–19), they upbraided the Bolsheviks for "not having realized labor self-government"—an unusually naïve idea, as the two systems excluded each other. A year later, another group of Mensheviks was trying to convince Lenin and the Bolshevik leadership to give up the NEP, alluding to its consequences of creating inequalities and giving up on realizing socialism. Their position seemed mainly to have integrated the final conclusions of the *labor opposition*, led by Shlyapnikov, which rejected the NEP at the party congress that introduced it.[42]

The introduction of a market economy and direct democracy—broadening "workers' democracy"—also proved to be a contradiction that could not be bridged. Significant segments of the laboring masses became tired of the sacrifices they were called upon to make and were demanding a "loosening of the bolts," but very few were in possession of the skills required for direct democracy. Lenin later expressed the necessity of the NEP, neatly and self-critically summarizing it at the 11th Party Congress in the spring of 1922: "We must organise things in such a way as to make possible the customary operation of capitalist economy and capitalist exchange, because this is essential for the people."[43]

One of the main trends of the current historical literature[44] emphasizes the capitalist market characteristic of the NEP, but also that—with its well-known measures permitting rural wage labor from 1922 onward—the Soviet state integrated social conflicts into the as yet not fully formed "web" of Soviet society, which later threatened instability and inner combustion, and finally had a major role in the later defeat of the NEP. Nevertheless, it is commonly acknowledged that, in lieu of external economic resources, the state's only "solution" was in "overseeing" the villages and grain. Lenin's efforts to give concessions to a segment of Soviet industry or to exploit natural resources failed, because of the Western powers' political stipulations. From 1922 on, economic relations with the West basically meant relations with Germany. For Soviet Russia, this was a period of establishing diplomatic contact. Meanwhile Lenin was extremely wary of growing resistance in the bourgeois-intellectual and NEPman-peasant quarters. Lenin was not planning to give up political terror.[45] It is a separate matter, meanwhile, that in Soviet Russia—an isolated territory on the "semi-periphery" of the world economy—an operating market economy was not possible even *with* a bourgeois democratic institutional system and its tools. (Russia was no exception, however, and this was also true in other parts of the semi-periphery, where no communist revolution had taken place. Latin America and Southern Europe were shining examples, but major regions of eastern Europe were also not excluded from this.)

After the year 2000, a lately departed Soviet historian who had switched to the "new" ideological paradigm, even though he had been one of the most significant commentators of the period, looked at the NEP. By projecting the latest developments in a presentist fashion, he concluded that the NEP could have been the political instrument for a development of liberal capitalism.[46] It could not have been, for what was special about the NEP was exactly that it was conceived as a market economy managed by a state regime that was "special."[47]

THE NATURE OF POWER AND PARTY DICTATORSHIP

Historiographers have shown that international isolation helped create the circumstances that compelled Lenin to give a radical critique of war-communist "socialism." He realized that "political socialism," the grip on power in itself, would not help in eliminating rural Russia's backwardness. He had taken unduly long to turn against war communism, which had become woven into the ideology of socialism. His new proposition was directed at taking a general, civilizational-cultural, "bourgeois" turn, in which concepts such as organization, technology, culture, and education played a role in "preparing" the ground for "real socialism." A formulation of the new contradictions could not be avoided, for the *multisector economy* shaped by the NEP was not in the interest of a *direct democracy* and the completion of a "commune-like state." This was because historical development had swiftly shifted in the direction of excluding alternatives, which became apparent in an unprecedented expansion of the role of the state in economic production and distribution (although this was not peculiar to Russia).

Lenin defined the "survival of socialism as a possibility" as a question of a "proletarian" Soviet government overseeing and regulating the reinstated capitalist conditions. However, an impartial analysis leads to the discovery of the most significant contradiction of Lenin's entire theoretical and political work after the revolution. His term for the realization of the Soviet government was "the power of the proletariat"—despite contradicting his own critical considerations at an earlier juncture, formulated during the so-called trade union debate.[48] These theoretically well-founded critical theses, which he held for the rest of his life, dealt with the "not so proletarian character traits" of the power apparatus. The debate about the role of the trade unions exploded in the totalitarian context of war communism in the autumn of 1920.[49] This history was uncovered in the Soviet Union under *perestroika*; for unknown reasons, the sources had been inaccessible to Soviet researchers.[50] In his writings and speeches, Lenin constantly drew attention to the dissipating weight of the proletariat—weak in numbers—and the "sea of petit bourgeoisie." This suggests that the "dictatorship of the proletariat" had not even been established, though he had spoken about it at the 1920 Congress of the Comintern with such assurance.

Regarding the trade unions, which had become instruments of the militarization of labor, Lenin outlined the traits particular to the war communist regime in a new manner. As he saw it, the trade unions (in which membership was often compulsory) were playing a mediating role between the Communist Party and the state apparatus. His argument made it clear that it was the party, and not the proletariat, that would realize the "dictatorship of the proletariat":

> What happens is that the Party, shall we say, absorbs the vanguard of the proletariat, and this vanguard exercises the dictatorship of the proletariat. The dictatorship cannot be exercised or the functions of government performed without a foundation such as the trade unions.[51]

Therefore the basic task of the trade unions was to "create the link" between the party (dictatorship) and the working masses. Lenin staked his claim for the party dictatorship not only on the "grounds" of the scarcity of proletarians, but also that as "in all capitalist countries (and not only over here, in one of the most backward) the proletariat is still so divided, so degraded, and so corrupted in parts (by imperialism in some countries) that an organization taking in the whole proletariat cannot directly exercise proletarian dictatorship." Lenin described the trade unions, situated between the Soviet apparatus and the party, as parts of a general power structure forming "an arrangement of cogwheels." In the course of appraising and transforming the "labor regime" managed by the party dictatorship, Lenin faced two types of opposition.[52] One of the opposition groups, led by People's Commissar for War Trotsky, rejected all functions of trade unions in the power structure, looking upon them solely as compulsory organizations for the militarization of labor. The other was the so-called labor opposition, which, in contrast, was seeking to broaden the social base of the dictatorship by considering the trade unions as organs of "economic democracy" in production and plants. Lenin stressed the need for *labor self-defense* against Trotsky's argument. In the latter case, Lenin argued there could be no labor state in the period of *transition*, even if it was not a bourgeois state either. The Soviet state, as he wrote in his January 1921 polemic against Bukharin, *The Party Crisis*, was not a pure workers' state:

> A workers' state is an abstraction. What we actually have is a workers' state with this peculiarity: firstly, that it is not the working class but the peasant population that predominates in the country, and, secondly, that it is a workers' state with bureaucratic distortions.[53]

The fact that trade unions would have had to function as the organizations of labor self-defense followed from the distinctive sociological and political features Lenin cites above.

> We now have a state under which it is the business of the massively organised proletariat to protect itself, while we, for our part, must use these workers' organisations to protect the workers from their state, and to get them to protect our state.[54]

Lenin saw the separation of democracy in politics from democracy in production as a step backwards, and one that raised the fear of an end to Soviet power. He recognized that the Russian Revolution in itself could not eliminate the established structure of labor distribution in manufacturing, nor could it remove compulsion from production (in the form of one-person management, military requirements, performance-based compensation, etc.) without risking total collapse. The political system, and the bureaucratic mode of operation at the level of state government, could not easily challenge these restrictions. The concept of *community*, the essence of which was the "commune," was rounded out with a higher state and party leadership, an external and often unobserved external hierarchy. If economics and politics did not "unite," the parallel existence of the two spheres would inevitably bring about their own "detached apparatus," cementing the privileged circles of both spheres.

Lenin's stance had a number of weaknesses. It was a mistake to think that the workers could defend themselves against their own state without democracy. It was therefore theoretically untenable to speak of the "power of the proletariat" in regard to the realized Soviet state. This does not mean that wide groups of the proletariat and peasantry were unintegrated within the power structure, or that the Soviet government did not represent their main interests. However, the formulation was not wholly true, and put ironically, "a bureaucratic state with proletarian offshoots" would have been a better definition. Lenin was aware of this problem, and in the theses he put forward in January 1922, he spoke of protecting the economic interests of the working classes from the renters and management as state companies transformed to commercial-capitalist operational grounds. The reinstitution of capitalism under the NEP incorporated a significant number of state companies recalibrated to what was called independent cost accounting, entailing the legal involvement of economic special interests on the part of "renters" and the management in general.

In the course of the debate on trade unions Lenin developed the idea that, apart from cultural and human factors, state regulation of capitalism on a Soviet basis depended too much upon the Soviet system handling the contradiction of capital and labor. As he put it: "Even if this regulation is completely successful, the antagonism of class interests between labour and capital will certainly remain." Lenin's theses, seeking "to protect in every way the class interests of the proletariat," were even questioned by his well-known supporters, who claimed that he was mistaken because the opposition between the management and workers of the factory was not a class issue.[55] Of course, Lenin's reasoning was sound, since no great change had been brought about in the division of labor in factories, as compared with the way the division of labor was typically structured in capitalist companies. The soviets had for the most part rather speedily changed into regular bureaucracies. The dependence of the management on (private) capital was, moreover, an insurmountable factor from the point of view of both profit yield and apportioning surplus.

Democracy was curtailed even within the party when the 10th Congress "temporarily" banned all factious behavior. This was based on Lenin's proposal to limit critical-opposition platforms, and he was able to find numerous reasons for this measure. The "leftist" opposition groups, unable to reconcile themselves to the partial reinstatement of capitalism and a market economy, had brought up abstract arguments aiming to realize socialism immediately. For example, they demanded the eradication of the division of labor in plants inherited from capitalism and the introduction of democracy in production, which were patently unrealistic suggestions under the circumstances.

In support of Lenin, Trotsky (in his own critique of Kautsky) rejected every "abstract criticism" for not offering a viable solution for the existing situation. Trotsky was obviously right both philosophically and politically in claiming that the "normative perception of values," with its own abstraction, will at times only bolster the bourgeois line of argument, and may thrust political developments in the direction of a prerevolution state. He marked out the apologetic methodological foundations of the liberal approach to democracy in the "metaphysics of democracy," which—following Kant's reasoning—is not based on "vital history," as in "what is," but "eternal and unchanging standards of law," in which the "categorical imperative of the theory of natural law replaces the theory of scientific socialism." Trotsky, just like Lenin, portrayed the "democratic" turn of their earlier teachers, Kautsky and Plekhanov, as a conservative return to a pre-Marxist theoretical tradition.[56] In the course of "reestablishing party unity," torn asunder by critical platforms, the critique of a *normative approach* came up in relation to the labor opposition. They accused the "leftist" formations of not basing their explanations of the difficulties among laborers on "objective economic dissatisfaction" (hunger, unemployment, normative wages, wage arrears, etc.), but on a lack of democracy instead—an obvious confusion of cause and effect. This could have been a valid counterargument, but it did not pierce the most serious error in the operation of the political system, namely an understanding that the soviets had been unable to fulfill the political tasks given to them by the Party Program of 1919. An objective that seemed especially utopian was that no socially detached apparatus, with independence in ruling over the productive classes, should be allowed to come about.

Robert Mayer pointed out Lenin's fundamental methodological and political limitations accurately. These cannot be explained through simple subjective mistakes alone, but only in contradictions that followed from concrete historical sets of relations that could not be transcended at the time. No one, Lenin included, could come up with "dialectical solutions" in those days. It is nevertheless fair to ask whether the "dictatorship of the party is consistent with a dialectical sensibility." This question is especially important because, as Mayer writes, "Like Aristotle Lenin believed there was always one correct tactic for any given situation." And if this is the case, then only one right solution for the contradiction between democracy and dictatorship can be presumed from Lenin's perspective.[57] It might even follow from this that, in a changed situation, Lenin might have reinstituted a multiparty system if it did not threaten a return to the reign of private property. It is not a coincidence that political parties were not legally banned. The election of the soviets by a direct democratic process, and the right to the immediate revocation of delegates, in principle remained intact. The real problem was not that the bourgeoisie, relatively small in numbers, had been stripped of its electoral rights (though this is not necessarily a self-evident restriction), but rather that for Lenin, in *principle*, the sense and validity of democracy was only meaningful as a tool for the emancipation of the proletariat. In *practice*, however, the party, the "avant-garde," took the place of the proletariat after October. It repressed growing dissent within the proletariat, and this is very difficult to justify from a dialectical standpoint, in that "paternalistic practices can be emancipatory, at most stringent conditions must be met in order to make such arguments plausible." The problem with Lenin's "dictatorship" was that "instead of admitting that his regime was oppressive and then showing how that oppression served emancipatory purposes," Lenin "denied that Soviet workers were oppressed in any way."[58]

First, Lenin was very much aware of and reacted to the contradiction, trying to ensure that the workers could defend themselves against the "distorted workers' state." Second, in his theses Lenin put up a determined defense of the right of the trade unions to "protect the workers by all means at their disposal" in their "struggle against capital." These were the bases of his demands for the establishment or replenishment of the "strike funds." This is a yet more interesting move when seen in the context of Soviet labor's powerful and frequent use of the strike as a weapon in the fight for its rights. It is also not a negligible matter that workers' protests in the NEP period were not generally directed at the Soviet government, but were for better provisioning and of improvement of material conditions, and against rising work expectations, management, the bureaucratic apparatus, and capital. It was typical of the self-awareness of the workers—and this reaffirmed Lenin's stance—that, of those employed at factories and plants, great numbers participated in making decisions on questions that decided the fundamental policies of the party. The party debates of 1923 may be the first such case, when the workers supported the Central Committee line in a majority of the cases against the Left Opposition that had formed under the leadership of Trotsky. For example, on 29 December 1923, 630 main organizations of the party supported the position of the majority in the Central Committee, while 178 supported the opposition. Significant groups of workers who were not members of the party also took part in the debate, though in those lean years, they were obviously more interested in the economic and social issues.[59] Lenin calculated well in supporting the labor strikes that served the interests of the workers, as this was a sort of balance to the "dictatorship of the party," helping to protect the interests of the laborers on the social level. However, developments did not show a tendency toward the realization of worker democracy.

Thus the real difficulty was that Lenin could not point to the instruments of self-defense on a practical level, and even in his final writings he could only come up with an office, the Workers' and Peasants' Inspectorate, to oversee the bureaucracy. The other weakness of Lenin that had a long-lasting effect was that he was not able to grasp the institutionalization of opposition activity. It was characteristic of him to categorize every criticism of oppression that did not come from either himself or the Communists as the machinations of "petit bourgeois" or "bourgeois" class enemies. As he was obliged to argue that the dictatorship of the proletariat was only possible through the dictatorship of the Communist Party, he found himself in a "non-dialectical situation" from the start. State oppression was justified to preserve party dictatorship. Lenin's real mistake was not showing how the character of the dictatorship could be authentically "proletarian," even as the party suppressed dissident thinkers and restricted electoral freedom. As Mayer noted, Lenin did not bring dialectics on a par with the "injunction [to] seek and speak the truth." In this sense he "betrayed" dialectics, to which he had been faithful most of his life. He never felt the pangs of conscience, however, always justifying the "hiatus" with the power already won and the need to preserve the achievements of the revolution. Rosa Luxemburg did not accept this argument, although her practical proposals were limited to "rescuing" the Constituent Assembly. Lenin had a basic counterargument, which—as it later turned out—lacked actual guarantees. Central to Lenin's "theory of the state" from 1917 onward was the question of the Soviet state in a multisector economy (with small private property, large capital venture, state-community, and cooperative sectors). The state had to defend and support the sectors and circumstances aimed toward socialism, because capital was not able (or willing) to restrain itself.

What was the likelihood, however, that a "still semi-bourgeois state" could resist all social pressure, and that its self-interest would become stronger than even those of its society? Although it is better to not get ahead of the analytical argument at this juncture, a note should be added that Lenin—unlike his wise critics in posterity—certainly observed one fact quite clearly: the narrowing and closure of the "vast historical outlooks of socialism" did not support theoretical thinking in the least. The revolution gave expression to everything Lenin and his revolutionary associates already knew, and the task became simpler in October: short-term political and power objectives came into the foreground, in order to *keep the hope of socialism alive*. Virtually every line he wrote was permeated with the notion that all political restrictions, even the "dictatorship of the proletariat, through party dictatorship," was a historically demanded stage of development, which must in the *future* be replaced by the regime of *direct democracy of the workers*. This alone could justify *party dictatorship*. His "last papers," in 1922–23, were an exposition of the historical and Soviet roots of Soviet bureaucracy and bureaucratization. Their significance can be appreciated in the light that no theoretical criticism of the system, other than what Lenin himself had outlined in a few of his writings, was possible in Russia for decades to come.[60] And these writings were only a consequence of his serious ailments that prevented actual political activity; before his death Lenin had little time left to create a theoretical analysis of some of the important implications of things as they stood.

THE PERIOD OF TRANSITION— "STATE CAPITALISM"

With the ascent of the NEP, the question of socialism in Lenin's thinking was broadened by new elements and hypotheses. He made it clear that he was unwilling to become subject to his own party's propaganda, and he differentiated conceptually between the NEP period and socialism. The NEP came to be defined as an unpremeditated "transitional phase" within the transitional period. Lenin consciously took precautions not to make the same mistake, made during war communism, of attempting to give the conditions of the "war economy" legitimacy in socialist theory.[61] A sort of "restoration" in terms of theoretical and ideological thought took place after the introduction of the NEP, and the concept of the transitional period once again gained status, replacing socialism. In theoretical terms, socialism was removed one step further from being attained as well.

Bukharin's new book, intended as a rectification of the earlier volume, no longer discussed communism, even in its title. *The Economy of the Transitional Period* sought to lay the foundations of the new period's ideology, that of *transition*. Yet he brought the two periods, the two stages, far too close together. Bukharin practically identified socialism with "organized society"—which theoretically belonged to the "period of transition" and took the place of the capitalist society of commodity production—qualifying political economy's categories as "invalid" for the NEP. He did not comprehend that the transitional period was still a commodity-producing, market-oriented society.[62]

This "misunderstanding" was not the only reason Lenin disliked the book, although Bukharin had made an earnest effort to take the "teacher's" viewpoint into account: for example, he used Lenin's basic concept with respect to the transitional period, "state capitalism." But Bukharin constructed a purely political terminology that underscored the difference between the concepts of capitalism and socialism. Lenin had indeed made state capitalism central as part of the transition after the spring of 1918, but in a structured manner. The concept had an immediate political meaning. The Soviet state gave preferential treatment to organized large-scale capital and market-oriented state property rather than anarchic private property, the uncontrollably chaotic economy of the petit bourgeois (25 million small estates in the place of a single large one!). The grounds for this were that "a capitalism overseen by the state" was the only solution for an "ordered retreat," and only state capitalism could replace bureaucratic war-communist centralism, which had also begot chaos. Of course Lenin called this a "retreat" compared with theoretical socialism; in concrete terms, he spoke about a step forward from the practice of economic policy under war communism. Just as he had described the transitional period's state as a "bourgeois state" without a bourgeoisie, he spoke about a state capitalism without a bourgeoisie coming into being as a consequence of the NEP, as long as (and along with other developments) "the state enterprises will to a large extent be put on a commercial, capitalist basis."[63] This was a real "retreat" from theoretical socialism, as a *needs-based orientation* was replaced by profitability as a central concern. Politically, however, it was a step forward, since the social basis of the regime, the *smichka* (worker-peasant alliance), had been stabilized.

In November 1922, in contradiction to the groups linked with the left-communist tradition of the party, Lenin stated in his last public speech that the realization of socialism was not on history's agenda yet. Now was the time of the transitional period, of creating the historical-cultural *preconditions* for socialism, in light of which the "socialism" of war communism was viewed as a "mistake," a dead end. In other words, while in 1919 Lenin tried to make a virtue out of the necessity for war communism, by 1921 he looked upon it as a "necessity," and, as Kronstadt and the peasant revolts (notably, the *antonovshchina*) showed, an overdone one at that. This was how the "pure form of state capitalism," which the Soviet government needed to function, came to be considered the opposite of war communism. Lenin marked out the purpose of the NEP in one of his last writings: "to lease out concessions. In the prevailing circumstances, concessions in our country would unquestionably have been a pure type of state capitalism."[64] For Lenin, as he himself stressed, "the practical objectives were always of primary importance," and so he could only experiment with a theory that also reinforced the practical objective. Now what was essential to him was precisely that a special type of capitalism had come into being in Russia, one previously unknown to history:

> It was important for me to show the continuity between ordinary state capitalism and the unusual, even very unusual, state capitalism to which I referred in introducing the reader to the New Economic Policy.

The concept of state capitalism is used in two senses here: on the one hand as a *sector* of a mixed market economy. On the other it is a term from *formation theory* denoting the economic *method* and *arrangement* for the transitional period and seen as a phase of it. It is a type of "state capitalism," in quotes, that cannot be found in "any textbooks," "nor in the writings of Marx and Engels":

> On the question of state capitalism . . . our press and our Party make the mistake of dropping into intellectualism, into liberalism; we philosophise about how state capitalism is to be interpreted, and look into old books. But . . . not a single book has been written about state capitalism under communism.[65]

The word *communism* here is identical to the concept of "political socialism" ("raw communism," in Marx's words), which describes the phase when socialism becomes a state objective and task that represents the interests of the working class, but is not yet economically feasible. One of Lenin's greatest admissions was that the Soviet government—the "workers' state," that is, political socialism—was not in itself sufficient for a changeover to socialism in an economic sense. This is the context in which his following remark can be better appreciated:

> State capitalism would be for us, and for Russia, a more favourable form than the existing one. . . . We did not overrate either the rudiments or the principles of socialist economy, although we had already accomplished the social revolution. On the contrary, at that time in 1918 we already realised to a certain extent that it would be better if we first arrived at state capitalism and only after that at socialism.[66]

As indicated, "Soviet state capitalism"—the way Lenin thought of it, and the party congress declared it—was intended to establish the political and cultural preconditions of socialism. This was a matter of serious contention between Lenin and the Mensheviks, Western social democrats, liberals, and others, who doubted the "reasonability of the Bolshevik experiment" while remaining insensitive to its uniqueness. Lenin saw himself as the representative of a historical alternative, in circumstances in which no other *reality* had materialized on the left. He repeatedly said the originality of the Russian Revolution was that the prerequisites of socialism came into existence not before it—but after.

> If a definite level of culture is required for the building of socialism . . . why cannot we began by first achieving the prerequisites for that definite level of culture in a revolutionary way, and then, with the aid of the workers' and peasants' government and Soviet system, proceed to overtake the other nations?[67]

Even earlier, his reasoning about the international isolation of the revolution and "remaining alone" was that "if, owing to the backwardness with which we came to the revolution, we have not reached the industrial development we need, are we going to give up?"[68] But if "giving up" was unacceptable (after all, this finding was "sanctified" by the victory in the civil war), what remained except to fight for "survival"?

BUREAUCRATIC CENTRALISM AND THE THERMIDORIAN ALTERNATIVE

It was amply clear, even during Stalinism, that the fight against bureaucracy factored decisively in the "Lenin legacy."[69] This "perspective" was taken to such limits that it became a determining factor in the terror that unfolded in the 1930s, chastening the bureaucracy. Where Lenin was concerned, this was not supposed to apply to "class enemies" or "pen pushers," but was connected to the quality of the new state. The character of the new system, and system-specific traits, represented both a formative problem of the new type of society and a social and cultural problem (an issue that remained unexplored through the whole Soviet period). The theoretical and political significance of the problem of bureaucracy came up in two important contexts: The first was the polemical exchange about the NEP between Lenin and the Bolsheviks on the one side, and Kolchak's onetime propaganda chief Nikolay Ustryalov and his intelligentsia followers on the other. The second was in the internal struggles during the creation of the Soviet Union and Lenin's fight against the consolidation of a privileged stratum, detached from society.

Ustryalov and the national Bolshevism he inspired, in the form of the intelligentsia's Smena Vekhist movement, intuited the inextricable historical situation of the Soviets. They wanted a deal with the Soviet government and the Red Army, which defended the imperial interests of Russia. Ustryalov's willingness to "wed" a decommunized Soviet government was not only a service to an imperial nationalism. This fraction of the Russian intelligentsia appraised the evolution of Bolshevism and the NEP as the "degeneration of communism," and encouraged emigrés to make peace with the Bolsheviks in the interests of deepening this "evolution":

> The tactical "degeneration of Bolshevism," which we foresaw one and a half years ago, is being played out in front of our eyes. Out of a realistic program, communism gradually turns into a peculiar "regulative principle," less and less reflected in the concrete organism of the country.[70]

Ustryalov, following the analogy the French Revolution's progress from Jacobin dictatorship to Napoleon's ascent, thought communism "liquidates itself."

The program Ustryalov drafted is related to several White concepts of "modernization": the liquidation of communism and the stabilization of the well-to-do village peasantry; "making peace" with the great powers while preserving the "national greatness" of Russia; drawing in foreign capital under strict state supervision; a strong dictatorial regime supported by the army and the "active agents" in the country (understood as a merger of the apparatus with the new propertied classes); a total rejection of monarchist restoration; and a "friendly alliance with the revolution." In the place of an "irreconcilable liberal counterrevolution," this program suggested Thermidorian restoration, a form of bourgeois degradation of the revolution, on the basis of a new type of autocratic regime.[71] These were the outlines of a counterrevolutionary concept for *national capitalism*, which Lenin took seriously enough to cite and digress upon in a number of his writings and speeches as a form that the restoration of capitalism could take, but did not share the simplifying critical notions of Ustryalovism, which surfaced in the Soviet press. Lenin himself was well aware that the Bolsheviks were themselves risking the reinstatement of capitalism ("self-Thermidorianization"), while others, looking to the myth of war communism, described the NEP as the economic policy of Brest-Litovsk. At the 11th Congress Lenin challenged those Communists who underestimated the analytical insights of Ustryalov and the Smena Vekh—the "Thermidorian alternative." Watching "capitalism without a bourgeoisie" take root in Russia, Lenin was keenly interested in what social relations and strata were strengthened and what their influence on political power was. Ustryalov had the same approach, and in fact Lenin was primarily concerned that Ustryalov's hope for an alliance between the strata of state officials and the reborn bourgeoisie would be successful. In March 1922, Lenin posed the matter at the 11th Party Congress:

> In this connection, I should like to deal with the question: what is the Bolsheviks' New Economic Policy—evolution or tactics? This question has been raised by the Smena Vekh people. . . . "What sort of state is the Soviet government building? The Communists say they are building a communist state and assure us that the new policy is a matter of tactics: the Bolsheviks are making use of the private capitalists in a difficult situation, but later they will get the upper hand. The Bolsheviks can say what they like; as a matter of fact it is not tactics but evolution, internal regeneration; they will arrive at the ordinary bourgeois state, and we must support them. . . ." I think that by being straightforward like this, Ustryalov is rendering us a great service. . . . We must welcome this frank utterance of the Smena

> Vekh people. The enemy is speaking the class truth and is pointing to the danger that confronts us.... Smena Vekh adherents express the sentiments of thousands and tens of thousands of bourgeois, or of Soviet employees whose function it is to operate our New Economic Policy. This is the real and main danger.... The fight against capitalist society has become a hundred times more fierce and perilous, because we are not always able to tell enemies from friends.[72]

Soon after Lenin's death, Bukharin, the other main theorist and a party favorite, demonstrated that Ustryalov's autocratic solution was not a traditional approach. Instead, Ustryalov was very much in tune with the spirit of the age, and sensed in his epoch the "heart throbs of Caesarism." Only dictatorial forms of capitalist restoration could be considered in Russia, and a Thermidorian degeneration, as in the French Revolution, certainly meant (or would have meant) this in the final run. At the time of this debate, in 1922, the unprecedented famine was still continuing. But this afflicted reality only strengthened the need for order—not only in the way those in power thought, but also among simple people whose passion could be fueled by nationalism. Bukharin reflected on this in his pamphlet *Caesarism in a Revolutionary Mask*, where he dissected the Ustryalovist challenge.[73] In Ustryalov he saw a threat that could scare off party members from the NEP; they might turn back from the more "liberal" line to the earlier "war communist tools." Following Lenin's reasoning, Bukharin did not yet suspect that the real danger was not coming from the direction of a Ustryalovist prefiguration of a "capitalist dictatorship." It had not been decided at the time which social-political forces would have control over the villages and their complex contradictions serving state accumulation, nor of what form it would take. Bukharin formulated the theory of and essence of Ustryalovism as such:

> The theory, strategy and tactics of Russian fascist Caesarism ... its "national Bolshevism" (some German fascists have called themselves precisely that), its anti-parliamentarism of the heavily military top-brass and *reichswer* kind, its cult of Mussolini, unabashed Caesarist ideals, "national imperialist" daydreams, the cult of power's sex appeal, (for the moment, cautious) struggle with socialism, and its peculiarity of building on the "simple" capitalist bourgeoisie trailed by the tough *muzhik*. It sets its hopes on all these elements coming to maturity in more than their own instance, so that the great "messiah" can be born, to really straighten out the "riff-raff."[74]

Ruminating over the social base of a Thermidorian Caesarist restoration, Bukharin came across its roots in the NEP:

> As a matter of fact, strange as it is, Mr. Ustryalov is defending a *post-reform autocracy*, a new type of autocracy. After all the Caesarism of the fascist kind is nothing more than the slick, knowingly villainous form of autocracy, where instead of the old coat of arms of the nobility, only the coat of arms of embezzlers, speculators, and shady "businessmen" are to be seen, and leans on a "mass" of a new order of servants, kulaks, "black marketeers," and a crowd of recruits from déclassé, corrupt and co-opted elements.[75]

Bukharin had taken Lenin's analysis to its conclusion and even refined it; however, he lost sight of the fact that dictatorship, whose foundations were to be the newly established bureaucracy itself, was no longer a threat from the right. Analyzing the Soviet form of "Caesarism" may not have served the purposes of those holding power at the time, but it touched upon the issue using the term "Bonapartism" amid the power-position struggles that were escalating during Lenin's illness. It is widely known that Trotsky, the People's Commissar for War, had also been accused of Bonapartism in 1922–23, in the heat of his power struggle with Stalin. On the other hand, the historical fundamentals of "Caesarist autocracy" were far more stable than many Bolshevik theoreticians imagined. Though Lenin was not among them, he had long been occupied with the specificities of Russian autocracy. He recognized that the Soviet bureaucracy incorporated virtually every significant trait of the old historical Russia (corruption; merciless falls from grace; eager, flexible ambitions; etc.), but he did everything in his power to preclude a return to the capitalist setup. The glimmer of optimism for him was that socially the resources of the new bureaucracy were the laborers and peasants.

Lenin looked for ways to "humanize" the Soviet bureaucracy, for example by "public inspections," curbs on privileges, and elevating Communist worker cadres. These passionate causes were also apparent in the party debates surrounding the creation of the Soviet Union. His views gained clarity especially in the process of establishing the Soviet Union, when he confronted Stalin's concept of "autonomization." (Stalin conceived of all the Russian republics as autonomous republics of the Russian federation.) Lenin's image as founder of the state also took its final shape at this time. Seriously ill, he dealt with the significance of the national question, particularly in relation to the formations of the Soviet Union in an important work, referenced below. The chastisement of bureaucratic solutions for this matter was an important factor in the search for "democratic options."[76] What was really at stake[77] in this battle was whether *bureaucratic centralism*—as a peculiar manifestation of state oppression, forming a constellation of relationships with deep historical roots—could be restrained. Lenin considered the curbs on bureaucratic centralism a matter of principle on three correlated grounds. From the perspective of bringing the Soviet Union into existence, since the so-called Georgian conflict in 1922, he had seen that the small peoples of Russia were defenseless in the face of greater Russian chauvinism. It was an overbearing, centralized, merciless, and Russian bureaucracy, inherited in large part from the tsarist system. For the small peoples, resistance to their oppression found expression in nationalism and the rejection of the central power of the soviet. On the other hand, Lenin also saw how the nationalism both of the "hegemonic" and the "oppressed" peoples developed, and saw bureaucratic centralism as one of its sources.

Examining the way in which these two types of nationalism related to each other—in a show of sensitivity unparalleled in his party and his time—he warned in his last writings that the nationalism of the larger people, the "chauvinism of Greater Russia," always carried more danger. The small people had borne so many centuries of oppression that it would be impossible for them to immediately let go of their nationalist reflexes of "self-defense," and so the "communists of Greater Russia" had to make allowances for this. Mortally ill, Lenin was probably not very optimistic on the day when Stalin—instead of Lenin—declared the formation of the Soviet Union at the 10th All Russian Congress of Soviets. On 30 December, Lenin wrote these famous lines about nationalism:

> A distinction must necessarily be made between the nationalism of an oppressor nation and that of an oppressed nation, the nationalism of a big nation and that of a small nation. In respect to the second kind of nationalism we, nationals of a big nation, have nearly always been guilty, in historic practice, of an infinite number of cases of violence; furthermore, we commit violence and insult an infinite number of times without noticing it. . . . That is why internationalism on the part of oppressors or "great" nations, as they are called (though they are great only in their violence, only great as bullies), must consist not only in the observance of the formal equality of nations but even in an inequality of the oppressor nation, the great nation, that must make up for the inequality which obtains in actual practice. Anybody who does not understand this has not grasped the real proletarian attitude to the national question, he is still essentially petit bourgeois in his point of view and is, therefore, sure to descend to the bourgeois point of view.[78]

Lenin criticized the nationalism of the onetime oppressors in this spirit, in *The Question of Nationalities or "Autonomisation,"* making his case for the greater independence of the national republics within the Soviet federation, with the aim of creating as strong a league of nations as possible.

Lenin connected this whole field of issues to the problems with the new apparatus. When Stalin rejected his proposal for the Soviet republics to join the Russian Soviet Socialist Republic (proposing instead that every republic join the Soviet federation with equal rights), what he had in mind was avoiding giving more power to the bureaucratic centralism of state domination over the nations. Instead Lenin sought to reinforce the federal state structure (of course, in implementation it could only be called a federation with strong reservations), so as to ensure greater freedom for the development of national frameworks and heritages (language, culture). From the way Stalin, Ordzhonikidze, Dzerzhinsky, and the infamous "bureaucratic centralists" stamped out the wing of the Georgian Communist Party's leadership that was oriented toward federal solutions, it was clear that the construction of the state, its institutional system, and the basic issues of the transitional period were inseparable.

Another important remark of Lenin's pointed out that at times Communists of other ethnicities, perhaps on account of their inferiority complex, played at being "greater Russian henchmen"—alluding here to Stalin's "impatient" political attitude to the smaller nations. This "compensating" behavior—"to be more Russian than the Russians"—affirmed a chauvinistic tradition in the bureaucracy with deep roots in tsarist Russia. Lenin also referred to the fight against nationalism (which must inevitably be followed through in every local apparatus) as only truly efficient when members of both the large and small nations first took steps against their own nation's nationalism.[79] But what should be done if no steps are taken? This rather obvious question did not receive an answer. The assumption was that, in lieu of other social forces, this would be another task the Communist Party would have to shoulder.

In a dictated text dated a few days later, on 4 January 1923, Lenin discussed how a "lack of culture" is the true quagmire of bureaucracy. A bureaucracy, which is a detached apparatus, has its own interests, and is kept by society as an army of leaders with their own peculiar "traditions," which become the main obstacle to the realization of socialism. According to the statistics he cites—not counting Central Asia (where illiteracy stood at 90 percent even in 1923)—an average of 223 people among 1,000 could read and write at the time of the 1897 census, and twenty-three years later, in 1920, only 319 out of 1,000 were literate. "We must bear in mind the semi-Asiatic ignorance from which we have not yet extricated ourselves, and from which we cannot extricate ourselves without strenuous effort—although we have every opportunity to do so, because nowhere are the masses of the people so interested in real culture as they are in our country."[80] This social setting was shaped by the scarcity of truly grounded revolutionary workers, who were few in number to begin with, having been practically liquidated (dying on the front or in epidemics, rising into the power apparatus, or fleeing the famine by escaping to the villages). The setting was also affected because the drill of "Soviet ideology" and culture, the initiatives given for self-activation in rural regions, came up against unheard-of difficulties among the illiterate peasant population.

A more authentic picture was painted by the now-classic Soviet literature of the 1920s. The liberal-bourgeois civilization of Western origins, and the socialist culture that had been imagined, could not be built directly onto the "sociocultural fundament" that was so captivatingly and deeply portrayed by Soviet writers such as Babel and Vesyoliy, Pilnyak and Mayakovsky, Ilf-Petrov and Zoshchenko, Solokhov and Bulgakov, and Ivanov and Shishkov. Lenin did not take Bukharin and others on for a fight and say that they should not be fantasizing about the creation of a "proletarian culture" on the basis of a vulgar perception of class, but should elevate general cultural standards to a "bourgeois" level. For an overview of the cultural preconditions of socialism, it is worth remembering Shishkov's Red soldier,[81] Pilnyak's *The Naked Year*, or Babel's *Red Cavalry*, to understand the particularities of this "social bed" upon which Lenin's late theoretical streams of thought reflected.

Better Fewer, But Better was one of the last articles Lenin lived to see published, appearing in *Pravda* on 4 March 1923. He asked the question that had occupied him even in his interpretation of the Thermidor alternative: In what way does the system of relations under "state capitalism" corrupt an administration of historically Asiatic descent, and how will the party be able to mobilize this apparatus for its social aims and interests? He would have wholeheartedly liked to overcome the old bureaucratic traditions, and scolded the dreamy intellectuals fantasizing about a "proletarian culture" in regard to this matter: "For a start, we should be satisfied with real bourgeois culture; for a start we should be glad to dispense with the cruder types of pre-bourgeois culture, i.e., bureaucratic culture or serf culture, etc."[82] An apparatus that would "deserve the name of Soviet socialist" has not yet come into being, but he saw the chance of this in the popular interest in, and dedication to, culture. In his closing, he seems to say these words to himself, and his call for patience in the elimination of cultural backwardness seems prophetic: "Nothing will be achieved in this by doing things in a rush, by assault."[83]

In spite of this, he hated copying others and did not believe in it. He even dedicated a separate article to those who copied the West (*Our Revolution*, 17 January 1923), reacting to the Menshevik Sukhanov's "notes," who criticized Lenin's "revisionist" stance from an orthodox Marxist (or, as Lenin put it, "pedantic Marxist") point of view— which seemed deeply conservative and antirevolutionary in 1923. As "orthodox Marxists," the Mensheviks had not comprehended what Antonio Gramsci would formulate a few years later—that the October Revolution had been carried out *against* Marx's *Capital.* Criticizing the "petit-bourgeois democrats" and "heroes of the 2nd International," Lenin wrote:

> Even the best of them fortified themselves with reservations—apart from this characteristic, which is common to all petit-bourgeois Democrats and has been abundantly manifested by them throughout the revolution, what strikes one is their slavish imitation of the past.[84]

The First World War, out of which the revolution had sprung, was unprecedented in world history, and even the richest states had not yet been able to restore "normal bourgeois conditions." Similarly, Russia's historical development served as the grounds from which the *particular* traits of its revolution could be deduced. "Russia stands on the borderline," as he put it, "between civilized countries and the countries which this war has for the first time definitely brought into the orbit of civilization—all the Oriental, non-European countries."[85] The "Oriental particularities" provided him the ground on which he could pose questions about "pedantic Marxism":

> You say that civilization is necessary for the building of socialism. Very good. But why could we not first create such prerequisites of civilization in our country by the expulsion of the landowners and the Russian capitalists, and then start moving toward socialism? Where, in what books, have you read that such variations of the customary historical sequence of events are impermissible or impossible?

A tinge of uncertainty seemed to permeate the question of why the peoples of Russia were allowed to take another route from that of the most "developed" bourgeois states: "Why cannot we . . . with the aid of the . . . Soviet system, proceed to overtake the other nations?"[86] Nor is it coincidental that he composed his thoughts in the form of questions. Since October 1917, Lenin had known precisely that the possibility of defeat was built into the fact of isolation. He tried to find a way through the *particular* revolution to the *general* one—over which, however, he did not, and could not, have supervision.

THE THEORY OF SOCIALISM AND ITS SYSTEMIC COHERENCIES

This reconstruction has shown that after the introduction of the NEP, Lenin thought in terms of a mixed market economy overseen by the Soviet state, in which the most important sector (next to the "state capitalist" and "state socialist" sectors) would be the privately owned peasant economy, subjected to state taxation.[87] In principle, voluntary cooperatives, self-governing cooperative ventures, and working in communes were all to have had an important role, especially in agriculture. These forms of production would have formed "islands of socialism" prefiguring the voluntary associations of a future socialist society, and its economic-administrative, production, and consumer-communal units.

In terms of accumulation, the industrial and banking entities formed the most important sectors. Having come under the ownership and supervision of the Soviet state, they provided the most significant part of its budget. The importance of the "state socialist" sector in Lenin's eyes was well demonstrated in one of his last debates, in which he struck out for preserving the state monopoly on international trade. He considered this an essential component of capital accumulation and continued a prolonged battle for its preservation, even while he fought his health problems. He put forward his concept in a letter addressed to Stalin and the Plenary Meeting of the Central Committee dated 22 December 1922, arguing in this instance with Bukharin and Pyatakov who, in the name of private trade and market interests, were against upholding a state monopoly.[88] On the question of forming mixed companies and capital accumulation itself, he believed—contradicting Bukharin, but supporting Krasin—the problem as a whole had economic, social, and political dimensions. It had to be understood from the perspective of the whole system, the actual balance of political and class forces, "the formation of mixed companies as a means, firstly, of mobilizing the peasants' stocks of goods, and secondly, of obtaining for our Exchequer no less than half the profits accruing from this mobilisation." Lenin's opinion was that Bukharin had missed the essence of the question by not understanding that the "mobilization of the peasant's stocks of goods" would lead to the entire profit landing in the pockets of the NEPmen. In regard to the class impact of surrendering the monopoly on foreign trade, quoting Krasin, he remarked that without a monopoly "the most pernicious exploiter, the merchant, profiteer, the agent of foreign capital, operating with dollars, pounds and Swedish crowns, will be artificially introduced into the rural districts."[89] Here Lenin, because of his political goal, did not mention that the state could assume the role of the "exploiter." But he argued persuasively, and prevailed on his comrades, by emphasizing the global economic aspect. The material-economic difference between rich and poor countries could only be reduced if they employed the powers of their state, since in the given circumstances of grim economic competition they had no other recourse.[90] It became clear to many people that Russia was not capable of rebuilding its industry without defenses such as a monopoly on foreign trade, as customs policy was simply not enough. This was because, as Lenin noted, a rich state "pays a premium on the foreign sale" for the export of those goods, on which Russia demands a levy. (Finally, in the spring of 1923, the 12th Congress took a definitive position in support of the state's monopoly on foreign trade.)

Unregulated market competition and the crises that attended it—such as the curtailing of inflation, the financial reform, and the so-called agrarian-industrial price-scissors experienced in 1923[91]—all pressed for state intervention. At the same time, Lenin considered this intervention an indispensable precondition to the bare possibility of socialism, placing emphasis on a close examination of the differences between the various forms of state ownership. The issue was starkest in commerce, for agricultural trade was in decisive measure held by private owners in 1920–21. In spite of a grain monopoly, the urban populace secured nearly two-thirds of its grain products from those that were called in the terminology of the day "hucksters" or "speculators," and the NEP only strengthened this. The other major source of private capital accumulation was illegal alcohol, with the new bourgeoisie also profiting from city-manufactured goods sold in rural areas.[92] "State capitalism," the "purest form" of ownership, did not represent a strong force. According to data from 1925, the thirty-one concessions granted in Russian industrial production did not exceed 0.6 percent. State lease was another, more widely used form, of state capitalism, but the most numerous of these forms in the early 1920s was mediation in private commerce and by commission.[93] As the most significant form of ownership in the industrial sector, "state socialism" meant a direct source for accumulation, although a mixture of "state capitalist" and "state socialist" forms was not rare. However, rather than eliminating the differences and conflicts between particular classes, sectors, or forms of ownership, it only exacerbated them.[94] A "state capitalist" company (overseen by the Soviet state) preserved the logic of capitalism and economic self-accounting, while "state socialist" companies also functioned according to the NEP's market laws (although state property was, in *principle*, legally inalienable from the working class). Within the internal system of labor distribution, the institutions of "worker supervision"—such as the labor unions or plant committees—could, in principle (!) influence the company directorate, in the interest of the workers—but the state had final control over the profit.

Therefore Lenin thought that it was impossible to eliminate competition, since NEP's reinstatement of capitalism relied on it, and he also had a realistic understanding of international economic relations. He knew the state would have to compensate for the inequalities generated by the ongoing competition in the global and national economies, using social-political measures, for example. In his speech at the 11th Party Congress he stressed in particular that during the NEP period Russia would develop in the framework of a multisectoral mixed economy, in which the various forms of economy compete, and mobilize different social forces: "When I spoke about communist competition, what I had in mind were not communist sympathies but the development of economic forms and social systems."[95]

These various forms—small proprietors, the state capitalist, state socialist, and self-governing cooperative sectors—brought about a system of market economy, which meant that the realization of socialism was taken off the practical-political agenda. On a theoretical plane, Lenin looked at this development in terms of formation theory, seeing the concept of state capitalism as a phase within the transitional period. In other words, everything stood to help socialism survive as a *sector*. (Seen from a current perspective, of course, only the "state socialist" sector had a realistic "chance" of survival, being an "overweight" sector.)

Lenin's theory of socialism fit this coherent structure, in which each sector was composed of further subsectors and organizational forms. The special characteristic of direct communal ownership and production was realized either in the form of voluntary associations or by way of state mediation, though only in a small fraction of agricultural and industrial units or fields.[96] (The story of their demise was an aspect of the "Great Breakthrough.") Lenin focused much of his attention at the end of his life on "self-governing" and "cooperative socialism"—the historical possibilities of an economic system *built on direct democracy*—which he called "islands of socialism."[97] The significance of the experiments with cooperatives[98] was of immense importance to Lenin, because "this political power owns all the means of production, the only task, indeed, that remains for us is to organize the population in cooperative societies. . . . Socialism . . . will achieve its aim automatically."[99] Though the NEP had been "made to last," theoretical socialism was never struck off Lenin's agenda, even under the everyday circumstances of market restoration. As he explained it: "Formerly the stumbling block for very many socialists" was how to first subordinate the "concession to the peasant as a trader, or to the principle of private trade," "for the sake of common interests" only to come around once again in the process to the cooperative as a solution. Though he knew that thinkers and politicians who had been nursed by the market and state looked down upon cooperatives, even "from the standpoint of transition to the new system by means that are the *simplest, easiest and most acceptable to the peasant*." He knew that incorporating the whole population in voluntary cooperatives of production and consumption would take an epoch to realize—precisely on account of the absence of the cultural-civilizatorial preconditions—and yet he insisted on posing this problem.[100]

The precise relationship between cooperatives and socialism that Lenin had in mind becomes clear in the light of his whole approach, the complete coherency of his thoughts. The cooperatives, as he wrote, are the products of capitalism; they are "collective capitalist institutions" in which the future of socialism can be glimpsed. Producers have the opportunity to shape the cooperatives in their own image in the course of a revolutionary reform of state power, similarly to how in the NEP, "when we combine private capitalist enterprises . . . with enterprises of the consistently socialist type . . . the question arises about a third type of enterprise, the cooperatives, which were not formally regarded as an independent type differing fundamentally from the others." He spoke about the possibility of coexisting *state socialist* and *cooperative socialist* enterprises, though a differentiation between the two forms of cooperative, state and self-governed, would come due.[101] By the mid-1920s, nearly 10 million people had been pooled into state-organized and state-subsidized consumer cooperatives. Lenin marked out explicitly that a shift must be made from the interpretation of socialism previously reached (war communist, state powered, and politicized) to the position of "cooperative socialism":

> Now we are entitled to say that for us the mere growth of cooperation . . . is identical with the growth of socialism, and at the same time we have to admit that there has been a radical modification in our whole outlook on socialism. The radical modification is this; formerly we placed, and had to place, the main emphasis on the political struggle, on revolution, on winning political power, etc. Now the emphasis is changing and shifting to peaceful, organizational, "cultural" work. I should say that emphasis is shifting to educational work, were it not for our international relations, were it not for the fact that we have to fight for our position on a world scale.[102]

Of course he treated the outlook for real socialism very cautiously on account of the "ridiculously inadequate elements of knowledge, education and training." It is interesting that Trotsky came to a very similar theoretical conclusion, rejecting a purely economic critique of war communism, and thus differentiating between the political and economic definition of socialism: "The economic imperative does not always coincide with the political imperative."[103] Trotsky also believed that on power-political grounds the "old (market) form of economic control had been eliminated, as a consequence of the civil war, before we had a chance to create new ones," and so he also delayed the realization of socialism to a future date, defining "completed socialism" as "planned social economy," with its "initial stages necessarily played out in a capitalist shell." Other Bolshevik theoreticians, most importantly Preobrazhensky and Bukharin, also ditched the purely normative approach to socialism for a historical and economic one, with their discussion of an "Asiatic form of socialism" under Russian conditions.[104]

Lenin's point of reference, even during war communism, was that work had to be measured according to the time put into it, with differing categories of "hardship," "importance," and "significance." He had four categories in the earlier period of war communism: hard physical labor was at the top of the list, and administrative and office work in the lowest category. Of course, the means of measurement could be different in voluntary associations, as they would be dependent on internal agreement. The sphere of the cooperatives and agricultural cooperatives could relate to the other market and state sectors after the introduction of the NEP. Therefore, the producers (while directly ensuring for their own needs) could also put products on the market, even though profit was not a determining factor. A direct replenishment of needs had the advantage of presenting internal needs and "potential output" that could be calculated in advance, without employing an office to do such work.[105] The most comprehensive modern theory of socialism has been published by István Mészáros, who ties his work on capital to the theoretical fundamentals of Marx and Lenin, and links his concept of socialism, not to the concepts of market production, but both looks for and defines these concepts beyond the market and the state—"beyond capital," in short.[106]

The first generation of Soviet ideologues, including Lenin, defined the difference between the state capitalisms under the reign of capital and the dictatorship of the proletariat in that they wielded power in the name of a different class. They consolidated different modes of distribution and ownership, with a preference for different cultural values, marking out different political goals for society. Lenin limited the direct socialist exchange of goods (following war communism) to the state-socialist sector, its fate hanging by the market competition that connected to the capitalist sectors of the NEP and the "state-regulated buying and selling, to the money system."[107] Contrary to Lenin, Bukharin often defined this "state economy" as socialism, in both the *ABC* he wrote with Preobrazhensky, and in his *Transitional Economy*. This definition of socialism as *state socialism* transitioned directly—leaving Lenin out—to the ideological medium of the Stalinist period.

Lenin outlines four potential courses of development during the "state capitalist" phase of the transitional period, which also explains why such a wide variety of movements, both inside and outside of Russia, refer to his ideas. Three of these possibilities remained aligned with the conceptions of socialism (the fourth being the Ustryalov scenario). In the course of time, the three basic trends could be observed not only in political thought and factional struggles, but also in historiography:

1. Intellectual groups, politicians, and thinkers who considered the multisector economy (defined by a state-regulated market and the state overseen by society) of the NEP as socialism—later identified as the "market socialists"—and took their inspiration from the late work of Bukharin, although he never actually called a market economy "socialism" (despite counting on the market economy continuing for a long time, even if differently from Lenin).[108]
2. Stalin and his followers were called, in this sense, "state socialists"—although it was Lenin who was proclaimed the progenitor of the market reforms to socialism in 1951. In the 1980s, this trend finally merged with the market socialists,[109] who had earlier been designated "revisionists." István Mészáros gives a generous summary of the characteristics of market socialism's nature. Most importantly he unmasks the common motives of social democratic thinking and the Stalinist tradition in their similar "superstitious" way of relating to state and market. Both camps positioned themselves rigidly in opposition to the conversion of state property into communal property. Both the traditional forms of labor division and the power of disposing with the surplus value remained within the scope of the detached apparatus. Every experiment that tried to reform this was undermined by the leaders of that party, even though Lenin had founded it with exactly the opposite aim. Though the later forms of market socialism were advertised as reformed state socialism, the first (market socialism) proved to be an evolved state of the second (state socialism), which in the end led to capitalism.[110]
3. The conception of socialism founded on autodynamic—self-generating—and needs-based production, direct democracy, cooperative ventures, and the "cooperative system" of producer and consumer collectives, traces back to Lenin's way of thinking and has a rather extensive historiography to its credit.[111]

Therefore, on various grounds, the market socialists, the state socialists, and the "self-governors" all could be traced back to Lenin, whose theoretical stance on socialism was founded on the Marxian concept of social self-government. Let us not forget that the *Leninian approach to socialism* was validated as the ideology of state socialism during the Stalinist period. The 1936 constitution declared Stalinist state socialism to be complete socialism; under Khrushchev, Lenin's conception of socialism was defined as the theory of social self-government in the theoretical program of the 22nd Congress (1961); and eventually this interpretation was pushed aside in the period of Gorbachev's perestroika. Lenin's theory of socialism justified the existing reality (*perestroika*) as a "market socialism" of sorts, leading to and concluding with the collapse of the Soviet Union.[112] The interpretation provided by mainstream historiographers has gone beyond all of the above. According to their views the "natural" evolution of the NEP and the "normal" unfolding of capitalism were thwarted by Lenin and the Bolsheviks, which is a logically and historically perfect fit for the Thermidorian-Ustryalovist "paradigm."[113]

The key to Lenin's approach to socialism is therefore provided by his "cooperative socialism," which can be traced back to theoretical roots before October 1917.

Currently, the Ustryalovist, Thermidorian school of interpretation can in fact consider itself in the most powerful seat, as "national" capitalism, restored under the rule of the "new class," is apparently stable in the new world order. From its standpoint, the history of "socialism" only crops up as a utopian cul-de-sac. Whether it can be held against Lenin's theory that the twentieth century saw "socialism" crushed between the big wheels of "marketization" and "nationalization," does not predict the future, though it is advertised with incredible vehemence by various ideologues proclaiming "the end of history" and has the support of competing market beliefs. Moreover, it is the study of the Leninian legacy that is particularly persuasive about how history can never be taken as absolute evidence. Perhaps *socialism* never seemed more of a "utopia" than today, and yet there is still no other historically and theoretically grounded alternative to the established world order than *socialism*.

The original concept . . . became the tool of a kind of socialist-bureaucratic manipulation of the "citoyen characteristic," unifying in a formal socialist manner, and thereby compromising from the current perspective of its practice, the ways—discovered by Marx and given concrete form by Lenin—to fight bourgeois dualism. If we want to revitalize this practice, we must apprehend where Lenin had failed.

—GEORG LUKÁCS, *A TÁRSADALMI LÉT ONTOLÓGIÁJÁRÓL [THE ONTOLOGY OF SOCIAL BEING]*

Summary Comments in Place of a Postscript

I MENTIONED BOTH AT THE BEGINNING of this book and elsewhere that certain authors have deliberately eliminated from Lenin's legacy the essential philosophical tenets and methodology that made him who he was. For one thing, they neglect his most important practical discovery, namely his precise theoretical interpretation of Marxist *dialectics*, its reconstruction, and his practical application of those dialectics.[1] Lenin understood, even on the basis of its Hegelian roots, that *dialectical materialism* (and epistemology) incorporates the *self-movement* in things, phenomena, processes, as well as the *conscious human activity to transform society*. Thus it is not a matter of the historical dialectic of ideas, but rather the self-movement and self-creation of history through social classes and individuals. For Lenin, epistemology was not simply a matter of getting to know reality. It did not exist for its own sake. He aimed instead to seek out the truth, the solution to contradictions within things, and the struggles that resulted. He wanted to see a radical transformation of the world so that humanity could rid itself, by its own will, of the dominant powers. Lenin gave Marx's eleventh Feuerbach thesis a new urgency: "The philosophers have only interpreted the world, in various ways; the point is to change it."[2] In other words, history was not an abstract whole, an object of study for him, but a tool through which the elements and tendencies to be continued or transformed could be located in the midst of "collapse."[3]

Though the starting point in his theoretical practice was to gain knowledge of the general laws of the world and of ideas, his objective nevertheless was to be mindful of ideas and action while not getting bogged down in details, in barren particularism. This was an endeavor particularly pronounced in his struggles against scholasticism, relativism, and mysticism. He had a passion for seeking the truth since childhood, as manifested in his rejection of all forms of oppression and exploitation. This was also at the root of his struggle against institutions and ideologies dominating humankind—for example, the radical rejection of clericalism. He reached a perception of totality, according to which the *whole* is composed of a variety of contradictions that must be laid bare in order to discern the continuous and discontinuous elements and processes of a changing history.[4] The "social revolution," that is, the conceptualization's "qualitative leap," is an organic and inalienable part of the history of modern society, and Lenin understood this as one of the most important discoveries of Marxism.

A historically adequate interpretation of Lenin's Marxism—in Marxist terms—must begin with the recognition that Lenin's legacy is essentially a specific, practical application of Marx's *theory of social formation*, and how he took it further theoretically, in light of historical circumstances and experiences of an easily circumscribed epoch and region (primarily the development of capitalism in Russia, the Russian Revolution of 1905, the crisis of Marxism in 1914, the evolution of imperialism, the Revolution of October 1917, war communism, and the New Economic Policy). Lenin's basic awareness that humankind stood at the gates of the *possibility* of a social revolution and socialism (or to be exact, a *transition* leading to it) was the most fundamental conclusion he drew from the experiences of his political practice during these years.

Because of this, Lenin's political and theoretical legacy, as a historical variant of Marxism, is unique and unrepeatable. On the other hand, it is an original experience and methodology of revolutionary theory and action, which played an inarguably colossal role in twentieth-century history.. The circumstances by which, even today, Lenin remains at the center of furious political and theoretical skirmishes that engage almost every political and intellectual trend, including various tendencies of Marxism itself, amply demonstrates this.

In our own time, under less than promising circumstances, there are attempts to "refurbish" Lenin's Marxism for the anti-globalization movement.[5] The main reason for this is that the Leninist tradition of Marxism is the only one that has offered, at least for a time, an alternative to capitalism. It alone made a breach in the walls of capitalism, even if today that breach seems mended.[6] The world situation since the 1990s demonstrates that the global dominance of capital has engendered new forms of discontent. These have not obviated the need for Marxism (whatever name it may be given!) as a theory and a movement. Indeed, they could not. Instead, in a search for alternatives, the discontented keep running into "Lenin's Marxism" at every turn. This tradition constitutes points of reference, arguments, and practical conventions of the movement to confront that form of progress that flows into capitalism. Marxist writers such as Lukács in the 1920s or Gramsci in the 1930s as well as movements sometimes polemically engaged with each other and opposing political and theoretical trends within the Communist movement, have found their source in Lenin. Thus, if we talk of Marxism, the stakes are higher than we may think, for the legacy of the primacy of Lenin's Marxism is not a thing of the past.

Concept and Systemization

Though Lenin knew everything there was to know at that time about Marx and Engels, he did not simply excavate Marxist theory from beneath layers of European social democracy and anarchism. He applied it—in his own way—to Russian circumstances, *by tying theory and revolutionary-organizational practice together*. In the process he contributed many original ideas to the theoretical reconstruction of revolutionary action and movement in opposition to reformist social democratic tendencies.[7]

The systemization of Lenin's legacy began in his lifetime as part of the struggle over the inheritance of his mantle and concurrent legitimization of that struggle.[8] What was characteristic of these deconstructions was not merely that Marxism was identified with Lenin's legacy, nor that Marxism was "russified"[9] as a result of that struggle. Rather, Lenin's Marxism was interpreted exclusively as the theory and practice of revolution and class struggle, omitting the stages and method of development that made the phenomenon what it was. This reductionist approach simplified Lenin's Marxism to the ideology of political class struggle and, above all, an ideology that justified the Bolsheviks' preservation of power. The subsequent Stalinist period came to see Leninism only as party ideology, the main and almost exclusive vehicle of Marxism, with the Communist Party, then its general staff and eventually its leader, alone functioning as its sole guardian. The soviets, the labor unions, and other forms of social self-organization, all of which Lenin thought to be central elements in the transition to socialism, were increasingly omitted in the reproduction of theory and ideology: everything became nationalized. *Marxism-Leninism* became the new ideological legitimation for the preservation of the system. Only with the collapse of the Soviet Union did the "emperor with no clothes" become plainly apparent, when the legitimizing ideology of Leninism sank into the pits of history along with the system itself. The result is that it is impossible to excavate the legacy of Lenin without steady determination and strict analysis.

The still powerful elements of pre-Stalinist Marxism were analyzed in the 1960s by Lukács and his anti-Stalinist followers (just as they had been earlier by

Gramsci). The resulting "Lenin renaissance" permitted under Khrushchev rose to a high philosophical level. By the 1970s many European and anti-Soviet Marxist Communist writers—from Rudolph Bahro to the Italian Gerratana, or Ferenc Tőkei for that matter; or for a different aspect, from Bence-Kis to reconstructions of a self-governing society—attempted to mobilize these views as a criticism of state socialism, constituting an authentic socialist alternative. Such writers made it clear that the historical, political, and theoretical/scientific power of Lenin's Marxism could not be reduced exclusively to power management or to the "welfare state" as the Soviet ideologues and their bourgeois adversaries (with an opposite purpose) had tried to do for the past several decades.

These efforts formed part of a worldwide attempt to sketch a new critical framework for Marxism. Marxists from a wide range of perspectives sought during these decades to forge a kind of "third way" between the preservation of state socialism and the restoration of capitalism, a way back to a Marxist politics that could lead to authentic socialism. *Existentialist Marxism* gathered strength in opposition to Marxism inspired by *epistemology*, in parallel with the *ontological-anthropological* interpretation of Marxism, and numerous other interpretations of *auto-directed* Marxism (*communism of the soviets*, spreading in waves such as those of *structuralist* and *humanist* Marxism). In contrast to these attempts for systematization—which may be considered philosophical expressions of individual and collective freedom, or participatory democracy—the arguments of the anti-Leninists, almost regardless of ideology, all derive from folding Lenin's heritage back into Stalinism. To this day they form vital elements of the discourse of anti-Leninist anticapitalism.

The reservations voiced with regard to Lenin's Marxism are understandable, as it only became widely apparent after the collapse of the Soviet Union that this historically specific intellectual and practical achievement, which no longer serves state legitimation, wholly resists—be it in theoretical, political, or methodological terms—all liberal and nationalist justifications of the system, as well as any religious or speculative appendages and interpretations. At the same time, the internal logic of Lenin's Marxism can only be resuscitated by combining Marx's theory of social formations with revolutionary anticapitalist practice.

Yet another subjective ground for the rejection of Lenin's Marxism by leftist experts in academia is that Lenin's ideas philosophically resist fragmentation or segmentation by discipline, as the experience of many decades has shown. All its constituent elements point toward the *totality*, the indivisible process. Following Marx, Lenin knocked down the walls separating science from philosophy, theory from practice. Lenin's theoretical work cannot possibly be separated from the movement to go beyond the capitalist system. In this sense his Marxism is linked indissolubly to industrial workers in the twentieth century and their movement, though at the same time it is a surprisingly adept methodological tool for the apprehension of processes within different frameworks. Marx's philosophical and economic achievements may continue to exist apart from any revolutionary workers' movement—but not Lenin's. Until 1917 all his theoretical and political arguments were aimed at the workers' movement and revolution. After 1917, as the founder of a Soviet state in the grips of the acute contradictions between holding on to power and the announced aims of the revolution, between tactics and strategy, Lenin tended to vacillate, becoming increasingly aware that the objectives of the revolution had to be postponed for the foreseeable future.[10]

The Origins of Lenin's Marxism

Lenin's Marxism derives from different sources, each representing in its time an opportunity for changing society in a revolutionary way. These include the French Enlightenment and revolutionary Jacobinism as the inheritance of the revolutionary bourgeoisie, without which it would not be possible to transcend traditional (Asiatic, feudal, etc.) society. Then there was the Paris Commune as the apex of French socialism. Among Lenin's Russian roots we find Chernyshevsky and the Russian westerners (Herzen, Bielinski, and others), reinforcing and complementing one another, as well as the revolutionary Narodniks, the mainstay of the Russian Jacobin tradition. Lenin synthesized them all on the basis of Marx and Engels, absorbing a lot, particularly the interpretation of philosophical materialism, from the earlier generation of Russian Marxists, chiefly Plekhanov. He also absorbed the ideology and practice of modern workers' movement organization from German social democracy, chiefly Kautsky. These are the sources of his thought in terms of the movement and in terms of politics.

All of the sources of Lenin's Marxism were combined in the articulation of theory with practice, of the class approach to culture and politics. And yet Lenin resisted the vulgar ideology of class, the populist perception of class struggle, and the appeal to its negative counterpoint, the teleological abstraction of reality. In Lenin's theoretical practice the basic issue is always the relation between action and theory, the transitions, and the elaboration of the contacts between the two. The sources of his Marxism evolved into an anti-messianic and anti-utopian approach. Lenin's interest in long-range objectives was deeply pragmatic. Finally, the issues he raised and the solutions he advocated always incorporated the objections or conclusions of his comrades in debate. In this sense, Lenin's comrades in the Second International also belong to the array of sources for his Marxism:

in addition to Plekhanov and Kautsky, there was Bernstein and the young Struve, Berdyaev with the ethical socialism of his younger years, Maslow and Trotsky, Bogdanov and Pannekoek, Bakunin and Sorel, Rosa Luxemburg and Bukharin. These were in addition to the "leftist" tendencies with which he had to contend in the aftermath of the revolution, tendencies that postulated a permanent revolution at a time when the counterrevolution was already under way. Lenin transcended these tendencies—albeit with grave contradictions. Nevertheless, his responses to their queries reflected a narrowing of alternatives, even in the particular political context of his office.

Lenin was an independent thinker, but he did not create an independent theoretical system, an *ism* within Marxism, although many modern thinkers systematizing Lenin speak of *Leninism*.[11] What he did was rediscover, reenergize, and deepen elements of the Marxist tradition that mainstream European social democracy was intent on burying. Certainly, his Marxism was a Marxism and not the theory of a "conspiratorial party." To steer clear of another misinterpretation, it is important to stress that Lenin's Marxism, focused on the movement and on political action, was not the theory of a "conspiratorial party" determined by its "Russian sources." •

The Issue of Organization

Lenin's notion of a centralized, vanguard underground party—"the party of professional revolutionaries"—is usually ascribed to Russian origins and, indeed, this has some factual basis. In effect, the historical experience of building an underground party was important to Lenin's Marxism, and his "party theory" was a product of this. What remains important is Lenin's promotion of a social counter-power (*not oppositional!*), a political and cultural leader of a network of civil society organizations, the "workers' party"—which never exclusively signified the party of "manual" laborers. In this context, the party becomes a network promoting understanding and an articulation of interests, the "organizational form of proletarian class consciousness" (Lukács). This party was the demiurge of a broad, horizontally and vertically segmented social resistance, the "moving force of which is the proletariat." In Lenin's concept and practice, the cadres of the "counter-society" were trained by the underground and centralized revolutionary party. Thus in Lenin's theory the historical role of the party (social democratic, later communist) was not simply to "import class consciousness into the proletariat from the outside" (this was already understood by Kautsky, from whom Lenin "inherited" the idea), but rather that the party, as part of the social class's "most revolutionary part," becomes an independent actor with a vested interest in the conscious, revolutionary transformation of society. Lenin raised the issue in April 1917 when he argued that the existence of the party is justified only as long as the class of wage-earners has not created the economic and political conditions for its own liquidation. He had no ready-made theory that the party should become the embodiment of the missing components of socialism—whether in organization, in theory, or in sociology. One cause and consequence of the one-party system that eventually emerged in the USSR was that the party itself took on the functions of the proletariat. But even the communist parties that came into existence elsewhere in Europe included only the most revolutionary strata of the working class. Lenin was aware that in this situation the evolution of the party was impacted by the combination of bureaucratic pragmatism and revolutionary messianism. Proletarian class consciousness was increasingly embodied in the Russian Bolshevik Party as a kind of substitute: the organizational issue was thus raised to the level of the general issue of the application of state power. Looking at it from the point of view of the 1930s, the "state-ization" of the party became inevitable with the defeat of European revolution.

Lenin never adequately explained the failure of the revolutionary breakout in Western Europe. The young Lukács, analyzing the causes of the surprising ideological crisis of the proletariat in his magisterial work *History and Class Consciousness*, came to the conclusion that the "Menshevism" and "economism" of the working class, or the emphasis on the role of the workers' aristocracy and on their bourgeoisification, probably did not affect the "*totality* of the issue, that is, its *essence*." In recognizing the "limits of revolutionary spontaneity," Lukács found that it was not enough merely to enlighten the masses with propaganda that endowed them with consciousness sufficient to overcome the impasse. The party must hold "the entire proletariat" through its direct immediate interests. According to this argument: "The experiences of the revolutionary struggles have failed to yield any conclusive evidence that the proletariat's revolutionary fervor and will to fight corresponds in any straightforward manner to the economic level of its various parts."[12] Thus, on the basis of his analysis of the German situation in particular, Lukács came to the decisive role of "forcing decisions" by increasing the role of the people in organizations.

The older Lukács—in polemics with his younger self some fifty years later—discovered the weak points of Lenin's analysis regarding the party and proletarian class consciousness in his book *The Ontology of Social Being*.[13] The elder Lukács was no longer seeking the resolution of the basic problem in the "ideological backwardness of the proletariat." Neither the mechanistic theory of spontaneity nor the superficial understanding of the importation of class consciousness from the outside could "adequately" explain the crisis in the anticapitalist consciousness of the proletariat. In his critique of Lenin he drew attention away from the ideological aspect toward the economic aspect, to the changes in the nature of the capitalist economy, and to the subjective consequences of these changes:

> Lenin's general thinking—contrasting Marx's concept in a revolutionary way with the reality of the present—placed too much emphasis on revolutionizing the ideology. Hence he did not direct this ideology specifically on the object to be revolutionized, the capitalist economy.[14]

Lenin was unable to identify the economic features of the "latest" stage of capitalist development, the transformation of the workers' movements in the "developed countries." Thus, according to the late Lukács, economic interest as a social motive was not at the center of Lenin's thought in the years following the revolution. Although Lenin's Marxism did consider many of the new features of capitalism—as, for instance, in his analysis of the Taylor system—he did not attribute sufficient significance, as Lukács put it, to the fact that "when the relative surplus values became dominant the mode of exploitation of the workers changed."[15] Indeed, Lukács notes:

> There is no reference, in all of Lenin's writings, to the most important distinction to be made between the unionist perspective and political class consciousness: whether this came about as a result of changes in the essence of capitalism, or whether it applies to every stage in the development of capitalism. He simply refers to the conflict between two behaviors from an ideological standpoint.[16]

Lenin provided a means to break out from the notion of apologetics found in realpolitik, only to become the theoretician of a new version of the same. The party itself became the organization embodying this new realpolitik, eventually becoming the party-state, the objective of which was no longer to locate the rights to power in the working class but to preserve the power of an isolated elite.

Uneven Development and the Hierarchy of the World System—Is Revolution still Possible?

Lenin started with the contemporary analysis of capitalism. The point of departure was his understanding that the development of capitalism in the Russian context toward the end of the nineteenth century was both a general and a specific manifestation of capitalism. He analyzed Russian capitalism's peculiarities with a scientific approach to its history, taking Marx's theoretical and methodological concepts as his point of departure. He was aware of the social-political consequences of the coexistence and constriction of various social formations (and not only in regard to Russian history!) and their penetration by the overwhelmingly dominant capitalist form. Even before 1905, Lenin revealed this particular development, namely that Russia became embedded in the world system through a process that today we might describe as "semiperipheral integration," whereby precapitalist forms are preserved under capitalism in order to reinforce subordination to Western capitalist interests. Capitalism integrated precapitalist forms within its own functioning. Lenin was able to tie the mixing of precapitalist and capitalist forms to the concept of internal colonialism under the tsarist regime. He also defined the existence of a center-periphery relation inside Russia in light of this internal colonialism. He was aware (long before Wallerstein)[17] not only of the triple structural hierarchy and basically unequal relations of capitalism, but also of a hierarchy within regions and nation-states.

Learning the lessons of the Great War, Lenin offered a theory regarding the hierarchical constitution of the capitalist world system, outlining the so-called law of uneven development of capitalism in the age of imperialism. Within this framework he regarded dynamics at the colonial periphery as the by-product and manifestation of international capitalist competition and capital accumulation. Parallel to this was the contradictory alliance between anticapitalist "proletarian resistance" and the struggles for national independence (or development) of third world capitalism—a struggle that ties in with the anti-regime struggle of the semiperiphery with the center (primarily in Russia). He brought to light the variety of forms in which the national struggles for independence existed, their different social and class makeup, and the possible historical connection between the "proletarian class struggle and the national, anti-imperialist struggles for independence."

Lenin's break with a Eurocentric worldview in the summer of 1914 entailed a total theoretical, political, and organizational break with revisionist social democracy. That was when the official nuclei of social democracy in Europe decided to support the imperialist governments of their respective countries. In the process of Lenin's examinations, he was able to outline not only the historical forms of nationalism, but also nationalism in its manipulations, its quasi-religious function within ruling-class policies and propaganda. The collapse of social democracy in 1914 made Lenin acutely aware that it represented primarily the interests of the upper echelon, of the "bourgeois-inclined" stratum of the proletariat: that it was revisionist social democracy, the political expression of those who had surrendered the concept and praxis of the universal revolution and class struggle as theorized by Marx.

Although Lenin wrote no original works in sociology or philosophy,[18] he clearly defined the practical-organizational and theoretical requirements necessary for the overthrow of capitalism. Nevertheless he did not fully envision the political, sociological, psychological, and organizational *configuration* that arose as a consequence of the very *uneven development* of global capitalism, which he himself had discovered. In other words, he did not fully deduce (or could not recognize at the time) the consequences of the fact that the contradiction between "uneven development" and "even development" within a national community or the world system did not match; the relative nature of the contradiction between these two has only become apparent in the present.[19] As we know, history can never provide decisive proofs on theoretical issues. And the developments after 1945 certainly did not validate the expectations of Lenin (or of Marx). Rather than the capitalism of the center growing ripe for socialist revolution, the center nations stabilized capitalism in the form of the welfare state. Acknowledging this is not to excuse the historical role of social democracy. On the contrary, since the "end of history" did not occur in 1989, one need not be a prophet to foresee that the need for the revolutionary salvation of the world will arise again.

Method and Philosophy of Revolution

The Great War signaled the arrival of a new period, one that promised the fulfillment of the conditions for the revolution. At the same time, a turn took place in Lenin's revolutionary tactics inspired by his study of Hegel, which was an integrated conception of theory, politics, and organization. From the beginning of the war his revolutionary strategy was based on the premise that there could be no compromise with any pro-war attitude or with pacifist half-solutions, as the war must engender a potentially revolutionary situation within Russia (and in Europe). He addressed the masses that had no interest in pursuing the war *directly*, because he counted on the evolution of the *subjective* conditions of a revolutionary situation. Hence he broke with the centrists and called for a new International. Authors who argue that Lenin's Marxism elicited a radical reinterpretation of subjectivism, mainly as a result of his reading of Hegel, are right. Lenin became aware of the historical circumstances that caused the awakening of the consciousness of the individual and of the masses. He understood that this could provide a "foundation" for revolutionary politics. That is, the objective relations of forces can be reconfigured, since even ten may suffice to confront the war: under the new set of circumstances, millions may join them. Lenin knew this already at the time the recruits were marching to the front, singing in high spirits. In contrast to the elitist and speculative "mass philosophies" and the utopian, "prophetic" socialists, Lenin, on the basis of his study of Hegel and Marx, emphasized the ideas and practice of revolutionary change. It was partly this challenge that motivated his philosophical studies and debates, as well as the notion that the revisionism of official social democracy was striving to "save" the collapsed world order. Their empiricism or neo-Kantian "messages" sought to lull workers with the promise of the pacification of the capitalist order.

The opinion of some experts that at the turn of the century Lenin considered revisionism merely an ideological or political "aberration" would suggest to us that the Bernsteinian "turn" (reconciliation of capitalism and the workers' movement) has been validated in light of recent decades. Ultimately, they argue, social reforms, rather than social revolution, found their justification.[20] Of course, this apology for revisionism does not stand up to analysis, because it continues to reflect only the Eurocentric view of the center countries. The global capitalist system did not overcome the starvation affecting hundreds of millions, the crises, the wars, the dictatorships, the unemployment, not to mention the social and cultural alienation affecting the lives of many more millions. Lenin's Marxism strove for *totality* in its manner of contemplation. That is, in contrast to his previous contemplative materialism, he moved in the direction of an "activist dialectical practical philosophy."[21] With the Great War, the time had come when the proletariat could take its fate into its own hands worldwide. In contrast with Western social democracy and the partial solutions it had offered since the turn of the century, Lenin took the position of considering the whole. He restored the Hegelian Marxist theoretical and methodological awareness, based on "totality," to its rightful place, including, first of all, the qualitative leap of *revolutionary change*, the dialectical dismissal of the old civilization. In accord with his basic objective Lenin's Marxism had arrived at the *theory and practice of social transformation* in the historical moment when it did indeed prove possible to break through the surface of the capitalist world order, at least for a time.

In Lenin's social theory history provides multiple potentialities. Hence the art of revolutionary politics is contained in recognizing and finding a way among alternatives. This does not necessarily signify "from the perspective of the proletariat" a choice of the most radical revolutionary action. The starting point can only be what is *specifically possible*. In Lenin's thought, the prerequisite for determining what is and what is not *possible* resides in the historical, concrete analysis of political relations and the respective power of the classes, a selection of the direction of change and of strategy for securing lasting allies for the working class.

Lenin's theoretical and political theses, grounded in historical and economic fact, held that the tsarist autocracy could only be dislodged by revolution. This was accompanied by his recognition that the Russian bourgeoisie could play "no leading role" in the revolution. For Plekhanov, such an assessment of the Russian bourgeoisie was disagreeable. Lenin, by contrast, grasped the Russian "national revolution" or "bourgeois revolution" as a joint venture of the urban workers and the landless peasantry. This is precisely what the events of 1905 demonstrated. This naturally led to the well-known thesis that "the bourgeois revolution cannot be separated from the proletarian revolution by a Chinese wall." With capitalist globalization reaching a higher level by the time of the Great War, this view was vindicated globally as the movement of the disgruntled masses of armed workers and peasants, as well as the movements of the nationalities, gained momentum and intimated the possibility of another revolution, namely the revolution of the workers, soldiers, and peasants, premised on land reform and an exit from the war. Though Lenin called this simply "proletarian revolution," he was perfectly aware that a purely proletarian revolution was impossible in Russia. His well-known intermittent debates with Trotsky reflect how complex was the actual relationship of policy making and theory.

Yet Lenin had to modify the notion, inherited from Marx, regarding the world revolution and the law of uneven development—"the weakest link in the chain of imperialism." He argued that *world revolution*, as a long-range historical process, *may indeed begin* in Russia. The Russian Revolution might well become the spark of world revolution. Although Lenin knew well that this was merely a historical possibility, he also knew that nothing could be worse than the war itself (even if capitalist civilization was nowhere near its end). Lenin drew his political conclusions from these facts. Other leaders of European Marxism, such as Rosa Luxemburg and Karl Liebknecht, agreed.

The real analytical difficulties arose from 1917, for history took a different course than had been presumed by Marxism up to that point (including Lenin). Political revolution was formulated as a part of the *social revolution* in Lenin's theory, in reflection of the universality and depth of the whole revolutionary transformation, but the tangential development of history bred serious contradictions. That is, the Russian Revolution came under well-known world historical constraints, on the basis of which Lenin came to the conclusion that the historical mission of the "semi-peripheral" Russian Revolution was *to establish the cultural-civilization and economic-psychological preconditions of socialism locally*, until global developments wrenched Russian history out of the shackles of conventions engrained over a thousand years to become integrated into the new European socialist civilization. Numerous extant comments and analyses after 1917 by

Lenin deal with this matter, including his last writing in particular. The historical constraints—rather neatly in accord with historical dialectics, incidentally—only allowed a distorted and one-sided proposition of socialism as practice. In place of realizing a communal society, the path of authentic socialism led to the *bureaucratic* system of *state governed* community.

Right from the beginning, the problem of *revolution* was linked to the question how the *state and society* are related in Lenin's theory. As discussed, his concepts of "counter-publicity," "counter-power" (social democratic press, debating clubs, self-training circles, the party of proletarians), and a network of social self-organizations (soviets, trade unions, and other social structures for the protection of interests) were soon buried under the power demands of the system he himself had helped to create, and finally the one-party system. In principle, the revolution would have cleared the way for a system based on self-organization in society as a whole. A self-governing social order built from the bottom up could have come into existence in such a society, whereas a dissociated bureaucratic institutional system could not have established itself.[22] The feasibility of the "historical cause" presupposed the support of an international revolution.

To the degree that history confirmed Lenin's Marxism where the Russian Revolution was concerned, it did not confirm his idea and aspirations for developments *after the revolution*. One of the cornerstones of his political concept prior to 1917, the question of democracy, fixed the stages of transition on the path to revolution. Not only did he underpin his critique of *bourgeois democracy* and bourgeois approaches to democracy with the economic and social dimensions of democracy—demonstrating the oppressive functions of the bourgeois system aligned with his critique of capitalism—but he also outlined a set of political-organizational stipulations: bourgeois democracy in turn becomes plebeian democracy and then a *workers' democracy* (semi-state), presupposing a transformation within the power structure of the social-economic change of regimes as a whole.

Without social forces to support an upswing, the *workers' democracy,* which is in both theory and practice a dictatorship—i.e., the dictatorship of the proletariat—against defenders of the old system, soon descended into "party dictatorship" (Lenin), a concept that came to take precedence in Lenin's theoretical work. The answer to the given situation Lenin bequeathed within his own reading of Marxism, and outlined theoretically, was that not only could socialism not be introduced, but numerous stages of *transition* would be required— "transitions within the transitions." However, theoretically and politically, the dimensions of transcending "party dictatorship" dimmed and became convoluted, and finally sank irrevocably under the demands of the regime's self-preservation.

The Socialist Perspective: The Unresolved Contradiction

Because of the limits imposed by historical circumstances and individual mortality, Lenin was able to provide only a limited Marxist answer to the issue of having to resort to a dictatorship even against its own social base for the sake of preserving Soviet power. On the one hand, he tried to compensate for political oppression by proclaiming, in opposition to the remaining and ever stronger state power, that "the working class must defend itself against its own state." He left unexplained how it could do so with the support of that very state. In other words, the workers must confront the state, yet defend the state and all its institutions at the same time. There was no dialectical solution for such a contradiction. Moreover, there was another contradiction without resolution: Lenin reserved to the party and the state the capacity for extra-economic compulsion, which was proportional to the lack of conditions for realizing socialism. Even Peter the Great had to resort "to barbarian methods to sweep away the barbarian conditions." The earlier theory and practice of social self-defense in Lenin's ideas not only grew faint, but were eventually completely displaced by the Stalinist turn, which later obviously contributed to the fall of state socialism.

The dead end of war communism, the removal of ideology from military measures accompanying a specific kind of state socialism, the realization that the change of social forms can be carried out only partially, were formulated in Lenin's thinking. The New Economic Policy entailed the recognition that neither direct workers' democracy nor cooperative economics built on social self-government could be established. He identified this stage as one of "transitions within the transitions," as "*state capitalism*" overseen by the Soviet state.[23] Unlike the majority of the Bolsheviks, Lenin stressed at this point that the new society could not be introduced by political means, by a revolutionary assault. Increasing development or reforms could not be confused with the revolutionary leap if we take into account the human, subjective boundaries of development and the significance of step-by-step progress. Yet Lenin never turned into a Bernsteinian, as some authors have suggested.[24] He never dissolved the Marxist heritage into methodological and scientific parts. Rather, he accepted the contradiction, and he conceived of it as a relative whole or as a system that could not be complemented or "pluralized"—a concept that could not be deconstructed at will. As opposed to anarchist and dogmatic thinking, which treats totality as an absolute and stresses the universality of gradualness, segmentation, the partial tasks, and against the particularism of revisionism (and of liberalism), Lenin emphasized a totalizing approach to the totality of the goals of socialism.

Lenin's key discovery after the revolution was precisely that Russia had to assimilate the basic achievements of Western technology and cultural civilization at the same time that it attempted to create a new mixed economy. In such circumstances, the Soviet state was called upon to back the competing social community sectors as "islands of socialism." The chief imperative was that this "modernization" must advance the state and the social-community sectors, because the free market and the uninhibited domination of capital are the foundation of human oppression. The autonomy of the individual and of personality as the communal society's main context of unfolding was missing not only from Lenin's legacy but from the legacy of the entire period, which insisted on other dimensions of development. In other words, the task of Lenin's Marxism did not lie in playing the nineteenth-century role of Western European liberalism but in combining the economic, cultural, and other sectors that supported each other. Yet objective historical circumstances brought about an irreconcilable contradiction between a political philosophy bent on preserving power and social-economic theory (communist theory). This concept of theoretical socialism, originally broached in *State and Revolution,* activated certain, almost forgotten, views of Marx: socialism was the outcome of a protracted historical process, the first phase of communism. It inaugurated a possibly universal evolution toward a future of the "community of associated producers," the global freedom of civilized humanity.

The lifework of Lenin reflects that Marxism as both a theory and political praxis deals directly in the project of *going beyond capitalism.* For him Marxism was not a sort of abstract discipline valuable for its own sake. Certainly, it was no abstract philosophizing about the meaning of life. Science and philosophy are merely tools to achieve human emancipation. The starting point for Lenin's Marxism is, therefore, the correct mapping of its own historical background. At the center of his thought and all his activities we find the exploration of opportunities for the proletarian revolution in Russia and the world at large, and their inherent potential for practical realization.

The specific historical form of the revolutionary trajectory examined here—from an aspect of its end goal of social equality, that is, the end of social classes and the achievement of freedom—was stranded in historical circumstances and human limitations. But at the same time the methodology of world community transformation survived the failure of the practical experiment. This is the contradiction that modern Marxist tendencies live through day in and day out. The conclusions are still being drawn. The modern triumph of revisionism has revived the ideological hypothesis confuted by the bloodstained history of the twentieth century, the hypothesis that capitalism can be rendered globally civilized, can have a human face. Revisionism's main discovery was that capitalism can be civilized and can espouse civilization at the "center" of the capitalist system. What Lenin understood was the meaning of the system itself, namely that if it can be improved in some way (and we must strive for such improvement locally and internationally), this can be achieved only at the expense of the welfare of peripheral populations. Thus to genuinely improve the system for all requires overcoming the system. To this day, the issue is: can capitalist civilization be conquered by means of social emancipation?

Any attempt at answering this question cannot overlook Lenin's theoretical and political contributions. His political adversary, Nikolai Ustrialov, in a writing dedicated to Lenin, looked at the Bolshevik leader's achievements from the point of view of the "greatness of the Russian nation" and opined that Lenin was deeply rooted in Russian history, that his place was clearly among the "great Russian national heroes," embodying Peter the Great and Napoleon, Mirabeau and Danton, Pugachev and Robespierre, all at the same time.[25]

Slavoj Žižek has summarized the problem on a Marxian footing: "To repeat Lenin does not mean that we must repeat what he achieved, but rather what he was not able to achieve." Even Václav Havel admits, as Žižek notes, that bourgeois democracy has exhausted its own resources and is incapable of resolving the world's basic problems, "but if a Leninist makes this claim, then he is immediately accused of totalitarianism." Lenin's topicality resides in the fact that he transformed his own historical experiences into a set of theoretical concepts that undermine and destroy any justifications for bourgeois society and, in spite of the contradictions involved, he provides tools for those who still think of the possibility of another, more humane world.[26]

Chronology of Russian History 1917–1924

1917

JANUARY-FEBRUARY: Food and fuel shortages in the capital. Continuous strikes and protests against the war and autocracy to improve living conditions.

23 FEBRUARY (8 MARCH): Thousands march on the streets of Petrograd: hunger strike on International Women's Day; the march turns into a general strike. The second Russian revolution begins: the monarchy will be overthrown; the soviets will be formed again.

27 FEBRUARY (12 MARCH): Tsar Nikolay II dissolves the Duma and orders disturbances suppressed. Duma stays together. In Taurian Palace the Petrograd Soviet of Workers is formed under Menshevik and SR influence; its leader is the Menshevik Nikolay Cheidze, deputies are Trudovik Aleksandr Kerensky and the Menshevik Matvey Skobelev.

28 FEBRUARY (13 MARCH): The Provisional Committee of Duma announces that it will take power. The ministers of the tsarist government are discharged.

2 MARCH (15 MARCH): In his special train at the Pskov railway station Tsar Nikolay II receives the deputies of the Duma: the Octobrist Aleksandr Guchkov and the monarchist Vasily Shulgin. At their request he abdicates in favor of the Grand Duke Mikhail. The Provisional Government is formed; it is led by the Kadet Prince Georgy Lvov, who will also take the post of Minister of Interior—among the members are the Kadet Pavel Miliukov as Minister of Foreign Affairs, the Octobrist Aleksandr Guchkov, Minister of War, the Trudovik Aleksandr Kerensky as Minister of War, etc. This event is the beginning of the "double power" of the bourgeois government and the Socialist Petrograd Soviet (with a Menshevik–SR majority). The Grand Duke Mikhail abdicates the same day.

4 MARCH (17 MARCH): In Kiev the separatist Ukrainian Central Rada (national assembly) is formed. Members are Ukrainian social democrats, SRs, and petit-bourgeois parties. Its head is the SR Mikhail Grushevsky, a historian; his deputy is Volodimir Vinnichenko, a writer.

8 MARCH (21 MARCH): On the soviets' demand Nikolay Romanov (Mikhail

II) is held under house arrest while the Provisional Government is preparing for the tsar's emigration to England.

9 MARCH (22 MARCH): The Provisional Government forms the Special Committee in Tiflis (Tbilisi) in order to govern the Transcaucasian territories. The committee works until 15 (28) November 1917.

17 MARCH (30 MARCH): The government recognizes the separation of Poland.

4 APRIL (17 APRIL): Lenin arrives in Petrograd from Swiss exile. He immediately takes part in controlling the revolutionary processes. He outlines the possibilities and tasks of the proletarian revolution in the *April Theses*.

14 APRIL (27 APRIL): Vladimir Lvov, the new chief procurator for the Holy Synod, discharges the clerical dignitaries who gained ranks with Rasputin's support, and he also replaces the members of the Synod. Fourteen bishops are dismissed because of their close relationship of interest with the starets.

18 APRIL (1 MAY): Foreign minister Miliukov sends a note to the allies promising war to victory on the old terms.

24-29 APRIL (7-12 MAY): Beginning of All-Russia Conference of the Bolshevik Party in Petrograd. The meeting deals with the questions of the relationship with the soviets, the party program, the agricultural and organizational problems, the peace conference, and the character of the revolutionary process. Lenin declares that the bourgeois revolution is finished. Kamenev and Stalin refuse to accept this viewpoint.

3 MAY (16 MAY): The government falls because of its warfare foreign politics. Pavel Miliukov and Aleksandr Guchkov resign.

4-28 MAY (17 MAY-10 JUNE): The First All-Russia Congress of Peasant Deputies opens in Petrograd. They ask for "sovietization" (equal distribution) of land and elect an SR leadership.

8 MAY (19 MAY): First coalition cabinet of Provisional Government formed including six "socialist" ministers.

18 JUNE (1 JULY): Kerensky as Minister of War orders the army to start an offensive in Galicia. After a successful start the offensive soon collapses.

END OF JUNE: The Provisional Government recognizes the General Secretariat, elected by the Ukrainian Central Rada, as the provisional government of the Ukraine. The Rada declares Ukrainian autonomy on 10 (23) June.

3-4 JULY (16-17 JULY): The failure of the Kerensky offensive prompts thousands to take to the streets in protest. The mass meetings in Petrograd organized by the soviets turn into pro-Bolshevik demonstrations, but the Bolshevik leadership finds a revolution premature. The government prohibits the Bolshevik Party; its leaders are either arrested or decleared illegal. On 7 (20) July an arrest warrant against Lenin is issued with the signature of Andrey Vishinsky, a right-wing Menshevik. On 5 (18) July *Pravda* is banned. The democratic period of revolutionary development ends.

24 JULY (6 AUGUST): Kerensky forms a new coalition government. Most of the ministers are either Menshevik or SR members.

26 JULY-3 AUGUST (8-16 AUGUST): Sixth (illegal) Congress of the Russian Social Democratic Labor (Bolshevik) Party in Petrograd. The congress adopts the plans of an armed insurrection and the achievement of a proletarian revolution, with the nationalization of land. Lev Trotsky and the so-called Mezhraiontsy—Anatoly Lunacharsky, Adolf Yoffe, David Ryazanov, Moisey Uritsky, and Konstantin Yurenev—join the Bolshevik Party.

2 AUGUST (15 AUGUST): The government declares that the elements threatening the inner security of the state must be prosecuted without judicial procedure.

12-15 AUGUST (25-28 AUGUST): Kadets demand that the Provisional Government hold a state conference in Moscow. The conference has 2,500 participants out of which 488 represent the Duma, 129 are peasant deputies, 100 are worker and soldier deputies, 147 represent the municipal dumas, 117 are deputies of the army and the fleet, 313 represent cooperatives, 150 represent industrial and bank capital, 176 are deputies of the trade unions, 118 are deputies of the zemstvos, 83 represent the intellectuals, 24 represent the church, and 58 deputies represent the nationalities. Generals Kornilov and Kaledin, Miliukov, and Shulgin all ask for the elimination of the social control over the soviets and the army.

25-30 AUGUST (7-12 SEPTEMBER): The monarchist general Lavr Kornilov, Supreme Commander-in Chief of the Provisional Government's armed forces, demands that the Kerensky government resign, but his forces advancing against Petrograd are stopped by workers. Kornilov is arrested in Mogilov.

31 AUGUST (13 SEPTEMBER): The Petrograd Soviet adopts a resolution on power. Its chairman is Leon Trotsky.

1 SEPTEMBER (14 SEPTEMBER): The Provisional Government falls apart as Kadet ministers support the general during the Kornilov revolt. The newly formed directory, with five members headed by Kerensky, declares Russia a "republic."

5 SEPTEMBER (18 SEPTEMBER): The majority of the Moscow Soviet is now Bolshevik.

14-22 SEPTEMBER (27 SEPTEMBER-5 OCTOBER): In Petrograd the All-Russia Democratic Conference meets and elects a "pre-parliament' in order to control the future Provisional Government.

25 SEPTEMBER (8 OCTOBER): The third coalition Provisional Government is formed, led by Kerensky, who is also the Supreme Commander-in-Chief.

7 OCTOBER (20 OCTOBER): Opening of the pre-parliament (the Provisional Council of the Russian Republic) in the Maria Palace, Petrograd. Out of its 550 members 135 are SRs, 92 Mensheviks, 75 Kadets, 58 Bolsheviks, and 30 are people's socialists. The remaining 165 delegates are representatives of different capitalist and landowner groups, as well as SRs, Mensheviks, and Bundists, etc. The Bolshevik delegates refuse to participate on the first day. The pre-parliament operates until 25 October (7 November) when the Bolsheviks disband it.

9 OCTOBER (22 OCTOBER): At the meeting of the Petrograd Soviet a resolution is adopted to form the Petrograd Military Revolutionary Committee, which will lead the armed insurrection.

10 OCTOBER (23 OCTOBER): Having gained a majority in the Petrograd and Moscow Soviets, the Bolshevik Central Committee votes 10–2 in favor of Lenin's demand to seize power (he is present, in disguise).

18 OCTOBER (31 OCTOBER): The Bolshevik Central Committee members Lev Kamenev and Grigory Zinoviev announce the Bolshevik plan for revolution in Gorky's newspaper, *Novaya zhizny*, and also express their differences of opinion.

24 OCTOBER (6 NOVEMBER): The Provisional Government attempts to close the current underground Bolshevik newspaper, *Rabotchy Puty,* which since July has moved its office and changed its name. It was published under this title between 3 (16) September and 26 October (8 November). At the same time, an offensive is launched against Smolny to arrest the Bolshevik leaders. In a letter, Lenin, still undercover, claims the Central Committee should immediately start the armed insurrection. At night, the soldiers of the Red Army occupy key buildings of the capital.

25 OCTOBER (7 NOVEMBER): During the early morning hours, units linked to the Military Revolutionary Committee occupy key points, including post offices, telegraph offices, train stations, and the state bank.

At 10:25, the Military Revolutionary Committee led by Lev Trotsky proclaims that they have overthrown the Provisional Government. At 13:00 soldiers of the Red Guard occupy the naval port and the headquarters of the navy. At 21:40 the sign given by the *Aurora* indicates the beginning of the siege of the Winter Palace, seat of the Provisional Government, which has refused to surrender.

Midmorning: Kerensky leaves Petrograd by car to seek loyal forces at the front. Forces of the Military Revolutionary Committee close preparliament at noon. At 22:40 the Second All-Russia Congress of Soviets of Workers' and Soldiers' Deputies convenes in Smolny. Lenin announces that soviets have taken governmental power into their own hands. The Menshevik and the SR representatives walk out of the Bolshevik majority congress.

In Moscow, revolutionary forces encounter stiff opposition from Colonel Ryabtsev. At the local Duma in the evening, Kadets, right-wing Mensheviks, and SRs form the Committee for Social Security, a counterrevolutionary organization which is guarded by local kadets wearing armbands. They call themselves Whites or White Guards in order to distinguish themselves from soldiers of the Red Army.

26 OCTOBER (8 NOVEMBER): At 2:10 the revolutionaries occupy the Winter Palace. Vladimir Antonov-Ovseenko arrests members of the Provisional Government except for Aleksandr Kerensky, who has fled. The Congress of the Soviets passes decrees on peace and land reform. The first Soviet government is created: the Council of People's Commissars (CPC). The chairman is Vladimir Ulianov—Lenin. The commissars elected to the council are: V. P. Miliukov, commissar of agriculture; V. A. Ovseyenko, N. V. Krylenko, and P. V. Dybenko, commissars of army and navy; V. P Nogin, commissar of commerce and industry; A. V. Lunacharsky, commissar of education; A. I. Rykov, commissar of food; I.A. Teodorich; L. D. Trotsky, commissar of foreign affairs; A. I. Rykov, commissar of interior; G. I. Oppokov, commissar of justice; A. G. Shlyapnikov, commissar of labor; I. V. Dzhugashvili (Stalin), commissar of nationality affairs; N. P. Avilov, commissar of post and telegraghs; and I. I. Skvortsov-Stepanov, commissar of treasury.

1 NOVEMBER (14 NOVEMBER): In Gatchina, the Bolsheviks arrest Piotr Krasnov, one of the main figures organizing the counterrevolutionary military. In the Ukraine, the separatist bourgeois government takes power. Colonel Aleksandr Dutov, ataman of the Orenburg Cossacks, wages war against the Soviet government.

2 NOVEMBER (15 NOVEMBER): Aleksey Kaledin, a Don Cossack White general, revolts against the Soviet government. Lenin proclaims the *Declaration of Rights of the People of Russia*, giving equal rights and sovereignty to the nationalities of Russia and permitting them to break away and have full independence.

3 NOVEMBER (16 NOVEMBER): The bloody battle in the streets of Moscow starting on 25 October (7 November) ends with the victory of the soviets.

5 NOVEMBER (18 NOVEMBER): The Synod of the All-Russia Orthodox Church selects Tikhon, Metropolitan of Moscow, for the position of Patriarch of the Russian Orthodox Church.

7 NOVEMBER (20 NOVEMBER): The Central Rada declares the Ukrainian People's Republic but does not report the breakaway from the Russian Empire. It starts negotiations with the Council of People's Commissars.

11 NOVEMBER (24 NOVEMBER): In a decree the CPC abolishes feudal rights (classes and civil ranks). The property of trading and bourgeois firms is transferred to local governments, but the implementation of the decree is in the hands of the newly formed local soviets. In Yekaterinodar (Krasnodar), the Rada of the Kuban Cossacks forms a government and declares the independence of the Kuban region.

15 NOVEMBER (28 NOVEMBER): After the Special Committee set up by the Provisional Government in Tiflis (Tbilisi) is dissolved, the Transcaucasian Commissariat is formed with Georgian, Armenian, and Azeri Menshevik-SR politicians participating. The body does not recognize the soviets power. Its chair, the Georgian Menshevik lawyer Yevgeny Gegechkori, is looking for relations with the White ataman of the Kuban Rada and the Cossacks in Terek and Dagestan.

18 NOVEMBER (1 DECEMBER): Vladivostok is controlled by the local soviets.

19–28 NOVEMBER (2–11 DECEMBER): The left wing of the SR Party (Maria Spridonova, Boris Kamkov, Mark Natanson), who were expelled for cooperating with the Bolsheviks, forms an independent party, 20 November (3 December). Commander-in-Chief General Nikolay Dukhonin is arrested because he refuses to execute the CPC's command to seek an immediate armistice with the Germans. The angry crowd beats him to death at Mogilyov railway station because he has freed the officers arrested after the Kornilov revolt.

23 NOVEMBER (6 DECEMBER): Finland announces its independence from Russia.

26–29 NOVEMBER (9–12 DECEMBER): In Kokand Uzbek, Kazakh, Kirghiz, and Tajik Muslim leaders form a government that strives to free Turkestan from Soviet Russia.

28 NOVEMBER (11 DECEMBER): The decree of the CPC declares the Kadet Party the enemy of the people and bans it. Patriarch Tikhon excommunicates the Soviet power and calls believers to fight against the Bolsheviks. In November in Tashkent, the congress of the Soviets of Turkestan Workers' Peasants' and Soldiers' Deputies gathers. All the members of the government elected by the Congress are Russian. Out of the fourteen leaders of the Turkestan government, only four are members of the Bolshevik Party. The forces of the Tashkent government crush the counter-government in Kokand, led by Mustafa Chokay.

NOVEMBER-DECEMBER: Results from the elections to the Constituent Assembly are tallied, with mixed results for the Bolsheviks. The elections take place in only 65 of the 76 constituencies; instead of 90 million votes, only 45 million are cast. 40.4 percent go to the Socialist Revolutionaries; 28.3 percent to the Russian and national bourgeois parties; 24 percent to the Bolsheviks; 4.7 percent to the Kadets; and 2.6 percent to the Mensheviks. At the beginning of December six left SRs become members of the Council of People's Commissars.

2 DECEMBER (15 DECEMBER): In Brest-Litovsk, an armistice is signed between Russia and the Central Powers.

3 DECEMBER (16 DECEMBER): The CPC's proclamation recognizes the Ukrainian people's right to sovereignty but regards the Central Rada counterrevolutionary.

7 DECEMBER (20 DECEMBER): The Cheka (All-Russian Emergency Commission) is created by the CPC; Feliks Dzerzhinsky is appointed as chairman. The main task of the Cheka is to repress counterrevolutionary and sabotage actions.

9 DECEMBER (22 DECEMBER): Peace talks with the Central Powers begin in Brest-Litovsk. Germany demands that 150,000 square kilometers of territory be evacuated.

11-12 DECEMBER (24-25 DECEMBER): In Kharkov, the First All-Ukraine Congress of Soviets declares Ukraine a Soviet Socialist Republic, still independent from Russia, and disavows the Central Rada. (Kharkov remains the capital until 1934.)

15 DECEMBER (28 DECEMBER): Under the leadership of the Belarus Rada (formed by Mensheviks, SRs, Bundists, and nationalists in July 1917), the All-Belarus Congress opens in Minsk. It does not recognize Soviet power.

16 DECEMBER (29 DECEMBER): The CPC's decree on the democratization of the army is that all power should be handed to the soldiers' committees. Officers are elected and political commissars appointed to control tsarist officers.

18 DECEMBER (31 DECEMBER): The CPC issues a decree on the state independence of Finland.

23 DECEMBER (5 JANUARY 1918): Lloyd George and Clemenceau make a secret agreement to intervene against Russia.

26 DECEMBER (8 JANUARY 1918): The revolutionary forces start an offensive against the Rada in Ukraine to establish Soviet power.

1918

JANUARY: Romania occupies Bessarabia. Within the Bolshevik Party a left-Communist faction forms against the Leninist wing. Its leaders are Nikolay Bukharin and Yevgeny Preobrazhensky, Karl Radek (Sobelsohn), Georgy (Yury) Pyatakov, and Valerian Osinsky (Obolensky). They oppose the Brest-Litovsk peace talks on the basis of refusing to make any compromise with imperialism.

5-6 JANUARY (18-19 JANUARY): The Constitutional Assembly holds session in Petrograd. The Bolsheviks close the meeting.

10-18 JANUARY (23-31 JANUARY): The Third All-Russia (United) Congress of Soviets of Workers', Soldiers', and Peasants' Deputies convenes. It elects the All-Russia Central Executive Committee with Yakov Sverdlov as chairman (among its members are 160 Bolsheviks, 125 left SRs, 7 maximalist SRs, 7 right SRs, 2 Mensheviks, 3 Anarchists, and 3 Menshevik-Internationalists).

11 JANUARY (24 JANUARY): Central Rada proclaims Ukrainian independence. Fearing the Red Army's pushes forward, the Rada relocates to Volonyn and on 27 January (9 February) asks Germany and the Austrian Monarchy for military help. The Central Committee of the Bolshevik Party splits into three factions on the question of the Brest-Litovsk peace talks: supporters of the forced separate treaty (Vladimir Lenin, Grigory Zinoviey, Grigory Sokolnikov (Briliant), Yosif Stalin); supporters of the revolutionary war (Nikolay Bukharin, Yevgeny Preobrazhensky); and unilateral disarmament, but refusing to sign the treaty—"Neither war, nor peace" (Lev Trotsky, Adolf Yoffe, Nikolay Krestyinsky).

15 JANUARY (28 JANUARY): Council of People's Commissars decree is formulated on establishing the Workers' and Peasants' Red Army.

21 JANUARY (3 FEBRUARY): According to a CPC decree, a Jewish Commissariat headed by S. Dimanstein will work side-by-side with the Commissariat of Nationalities.

21 JANUARY (3 FEBRUARY): The Central Executive Committee passes a resolution to repudiate all foreign debts.

31 JANUARY (13 FEBRUARY): The CPC appoints Stepan Shaumyan (Surent), a Bolshevik from Baku, as its Commissar Extraordinary for the Caucasus. Turkish troops begin occupying East Armenia while German and Turkish troops extend their influence over southern Georgia.

10 FEBRUARY: Lev Trotsky, Commissar for Foreign Affairs, breaks off peace talks with the Germans in protest over annexation claims.

11 FEBRUARY: Decree establishes the Red Fleet.

16 FEBRUARY: Lithuania proclaims independence.

18 FEBRUARY: A small number of German troops begins offensive against Petrograd.

21 FEBRUARY: The CPC's decree, "The Socialist Fatherland in Danger," gives the Cheka license to use "special measures" that allow them to execute ordinary criminals under summary procedure until 5 September 1918.

23 FEBRUARY: In Tiflis, the Transcaucasian Seim is formed, deputies to the Constituent Assembly are elected. German troops get close to Pskov and Narva. "The Socialist Fatherland in Danger" flyer is circulated in the army and in the cities publicizing the CPC's decree of 21 February.

24 FEBRUARY: Estonia proclaims independence.

3 MARCH: George Chicherin, deputy Commissar of Foreign Affairs, signs the Brest Treaty since Lev Trotsky was called back. Soviet Russia loses a million square kilometers of territory, i.e. most of the Ukraine. In a meeting at the beginning of March, the delegates of the workers' councils of 56 Petrograd factories protest against the termination of workers' control in the workplaces. They accuse the CPC of arbitrariness, ask for a new election of the soviets, and refuse the Brest treaty. It is the beginning of the movement of the trustees (*dvizhenie upolnomochennih*), which lasts until the beginning of July 1918.

6-8 MARCH: The Seventh (Extraordinary) Congress of the Bolshevik Party discusses two major items on the agenda. It approves the Brest-Litovsk Treaty and discusses the preparations of a new party program. The party adopts a new name: Russian Communist (Bolshevik) Party, RCP(b).

9 MARCH: English troops land in Murmansk, beginning foreign intervention. In April and August respectively, Japanese and American troops land in Vladivostok; in May, British and German troops enter the Caucasus.

11 MARCH: The Bolshevik government transfers to Moscow because the front is nearing Petrograd. On 12 March, Moscow becomes the capital.

14-16 MARCH: Extraordinary Fourth All-Russia Congress of Soviets is held in Moscow to ratify the Brest-Litovsk Treaty. As a protest against ratification, the Left SR Party announces its withdrawal from the Council of People's Commissars.

24 MARCH: The Hungarian Group (Béla Kun, Tibor Szamuely, Ernő Pór, etc.) of the Russian Communist Party is founded at the Hotel Dresden in Moscow. In Minsk, the government of Belarus People's Republic proclaims independence; it is formed from the Belarus Rada and is backed by Polish, and later German, military forces.

1 APRIL: By decree the flag of the Russian Republic deletes the white-blue-red tricolor from the state symbol.

22 APRIL: The Tiflis Seim proclaims the Transcaucasian Democratic Federative Republic consisting of the Transcaucasion territories. The head of the new government is Akaki Chkhenkeli, a Georgian Menshevik.

25 APRIL: The Baku Commune is established. In Baku as early as 31 October (13 November) 1917, victory of the Soviet power was proclaimed but it is only in April 1918 that the Musavatists (the Muslim Democratic Party since 1911) are ousted from the local soviet, whose revolt on 30 March 1918 had been suppressed by Bolsheviks, Left SRs, and Left Mensheviks. The commune exists for 97 days.

28 APRIL: General Hermann von Eickhorn, the commander of the occupying German forces in Ukraine, dissolves the Central Rada. Under German pressure, the power is given to General Pavlo Skoropadsky, a monarchist and Tsar Nicholay II's former Fliegel-adjutant; he is formally elected Hetman of Ukraine on 29 April at the "Congress of the Peasants."

30 APRIL: In Tashkent, the Turkestan Autonomous Soviet Socialist Republic is proclaimed. During the civil war some smaller khanates and emirates circumvent its control. In April, the Cheka liquidates the Petrograd anarchist organizations. In the Red Army, military commissars are introduced to head military units.

3 MAY: After provisional Red power (January–March), the Don region returns to the White forces and the government of the "Great Don Army" headed by Ataman Pyotr Krasnov is elected. The independence of the Don region is proclaimed.

25 MAY: Along the Trans-Siberian Railway the Czech prisoners of war who support the White forces start a revolt.

26 MAY: The Transcaucasian Seim declares itself dissolved. Under the pressure of German and Turkish occupational forces, the Seim, rent by contradictions between the nationalist parties, disintegrates into separate bourgeois republics. In Georgia the Mensheviks, in Armenia the Dashnahks (a national party since 1890), and in Azerbaijan the Musavatists all form governments. The Mensehviks proclaim the independent the Georgian Republic.

27 MAY: In Tiflis, the Azerbaijan Republic is proclaimed. The government of Musavatists relocates to Gandzha (Kirovobad); and in order to liquidate the Baku Commune asks for the help of the Turkish Army that has invaded Armenia.

28 MAY: The Armenian Republic is formed. The Dashnahk government is at war with the Turkish army that occupies the eastern region of the country.

30 MAY: After the Brest-Litovsk Peace Treaty is signed, Trotsky, who has advocated a different position, resigns. Georgy Chicherin is appointed Commissar of Foreign Affairs. Trotsky is appointed People's Commissar of the Army and Navy and the chairman of the Supreme Military Council of the republic. Also in May, the Eighth Party Council of the Party of Socialist Revolutionaries decides to start an armed attack on Bolsheviks. The German Army occupies parts of the Northen Caucasus and Transcaucasus. As a result of a serious food and grain shortage, the People's Commissariat for Food gains more power to collect and distribute food. The "food dictature" starts and armed brigades of workers are organized to confiscate food throughout the countryside.

4 JUNE: In Batumi, Georgia and Armenia sign a peace treaty with Turkey, thus legalizing the Turkish-German occupation of both countries. The Armenian territory remaining under Dashnahk control is reduced to 12,000 square kilometers.

11 JUNE: A decree is issued by the poor peasants' committees of the villages to confiscate surplus grain from the kulaks.

14 JUNE: The Executive Committe of RCP(b) excludes right SRs and Mensheviks from its body and from local soviets. The reasons are extraordinary conditions, inner counterrevolutionary activity, connections with the enemy at a time of internationalist imperialist aggression, and destruction of the Soviet power from inside.

16 JUNE: Reelection of the Petrograd Soviet; though the Bolsheviks lose several seats, they still retain majority.

2 JULY: The first great political strike in Petrograd since the October Revolution is triggered by famine and hardship. The mass strike organized by the workers' trustees is fruitless, and the Bolshevik-led soviets put down the movement.

4-10 JULY: The Fifth All-Russia Congress of Soviets in Moscow adopts the first soviet constitution and renames the country the Russian Soviet Federative Socialist Republic with Yakov Sverdlov as *de jure* head of state. The constitution claims that the congresses of the soviets and their executive committees have the right to nullify decisions of local soviets. It orders local soviets to establish administrative apparatus (council departments).

6-8 JULY: Uprising of the Left SRs. Count Wilhelm von Mirbach, German ambassador, is assassinated. After the uprising is put down by Bolsheviks, the activities of the Left SR Party are suspended.

17 JULY: Tsar Nicholay II, six members of his family, and his servants are executed by the Yekaterinburg (Sverdlovsk) soviet.

20 JULY: Moisey Volodarsky (Goldstein), the Commissar for Press and Agitation, is assassinated by an SR.

27 JULY: The CPC issues a decree on combating anti-Semitism.

29 JULY: In Baku, the SR-Menshevik group of the local soviet calls in British forces stationed in northern Iran to help them keep their power and fight against the Musavatists and the approaching Turkish army.

31 JULY: The Baku Commune fails; the commissars flee from the town.

7 AUGUST: In Kazan, White Czechs seize the gold reserves of the RSFSR and hand it over to Kolchak. The counterrevolutionary uprisings of the Whites against the Soviet power broaden into civil war. The church offers full support to the Whites. At the end of August, the Cheka unveils the so-called conspiracy of the ambassadors. The conspiracy is disclosed and British diplomat Robert Lockhard is arrested in Moscow .

30 AUGUST: Moisey Uritsky, chairman of the Petrograd Cheka, is assassinated by a student. Workers hold a rally at the Michelson factory in Moscow region at which Lenin speaks to workers; he is seriously wounded by three shots.

5 SEPTEMBER: In a decree the Council of the People's Commissars—as a consequence of the murderous attacks against Bolshevik leaders—announces the "Red terror," that is, Cheka gets a free hand to liquidate or deport White Guardist conspirators and rioters to camps. (In September more than 6,000 people are killed, a number far greater than the 4,141 people killed in August, or the 824 killed in twenty-two gubernias of the RSFSR in July.)

15 SEPTEMBER: The Turkish army that supports the Musavatists and is an ally of the Central Forces besieges Baku. The British and the Menshevik-SR local magistrates flee. The Musavatists take power in Baku.

20 SEPTEMBER: The evacuating British troops take twenty-six commissars from Baku and later execute everyone, including Stepan Shaumian.

29 OCTOBER-4 NOVEMBER: At the first Congress of All-Russia Communist Union of Youth, Komsomol is formed.

BEGINNING OF NOVEMBER: The West Ukrainian People's Republic is proclaimed in Lemberg (Lvov). Its government supports war against the Bolsheviks.

3 NOVEMBER: The Commissar for Education orders that national schools must be established wherever at least twenty-five children of the same age live.

6 NOVEMBER: In Cracow the independence of Poland is proclaimed.

13 NOVEMBER: On news of the German capitulation and the revolution in Berlin, the CPC annuls the Brest-Litovsk Treaty. In Belaya Tserkov, the Ukrainian Directory is formed in order to take power in Ukraine after the German withdrawal.

18 NOVEMBER: Latvia proclaims independence. Admiral Kolchak sets up his own dictatorship in Siberia after having overthrown the SR-Menshevik government. The SR and Menshevik members of the Constituent Assembly are arrested and executed in Omsk.

30 NOVEMBER: The Central Executive Committee recognizes the Russian Social Democratic Labor Party (Menshevik) after the latter recognizes Soviet power and the CEC withdraws its 14 June decision on Mensheviks being excluded from the soviets.

NOVEMBER: As a consequence of the defeat of the Central Powers and the armistice negotiations, Turkey withdraws its army from the occupied Armenian, Azeri, and Georgian territories. The Turkish are followed by British and American troops. The Germans evacuate the Ukraine. On 20 November in Moscow, the Provisional Workers' and Peasants' Government of Ukraine is announced.

8 DECEMBER: The CPC recognizes the independence of the Estonian Workers Commune.

14 DECEMBER: Hetman Pavlo Skoropadsky flees to Germany. Power goes to the Ukrainian Directory representing the national union and is supported by the well-to-do land-owning peasantry. Its chairman is Volodimir Vinnichenko; the military commander is Simon Petliura.

15 DECEMBER: The newspaper *Zhizn natsionalnostey* publishes the CEC's instructions ordering the creation of "national sections" side by side with the executive committees of local soviets.

22 DECEMBER: The People's Commissariat recognizes the independence of the Latvian and Lituanian Soviet Republics.

END OF YEAR: A wave of pogroms sweeps the Ukraine and is still at its peak in the spring of 1919. The bloodshed imposed by Petliura's "free troops" and the White Guards leaves 500,000 victims; the number of those killed is about 200,000.

1919

3 JANUARY: The Bolshevik Ukrainian Government arrives in Kharkov with the Red Army. Its purpose is to overthrow the counterrevolutionary Ukrainian Directory, which is an ardent enemy of Soviet power.

11 JANUARY: The People's Commissariat decrees the surplus appropriation system that authorizes the confiscation of grain from the peasantry for a nominal fixed price. It also introduces rationing and the general obligation to work.

16 JANUARY: The Ukrainian Directory wages war on Soviet Russia and asks the Entente for help.

6 FEBRUARY: The Red Army occupies Kiev. The Directory flees; its chairman, Volodimir Vinnichenko, transfers all power to Simon Petliura (10 February) who makes an alliance with the Lvov (Lemberg) government of the Western Ukrainian People's Republic to fight against the Bolsheviks.

2-6 MARCH: The First (founding) Congress of the Communist International (Comintern) is held in Moscow. It creates the world Communist Party by uniting the international left socialist party groups. Its chairman is Grigory Zinoviev, its deputy chairman is Nikolay Bukharin.

10 MARCH: The Third All-Ukrainian Congress of Soviets adopts the first constitution of Soviet Ukraine. (The final version is adopted on 14

March.) Grigory Petrovsky is elected chairman.

16 MARCH: Yakov Sverdlov dies and Mikhail Kalinin replaces him as president of the All-Russia Central Executive Committee. The titular head of state of Soviet Russia, Stalin, is appointed head of People's Commissariat for State Control.

18–23 MARCH: The 8th Congress of the Russian Communist (Bolshevik) Party in Moscow convenes. It decides about the extension of war communism and adopts a new party program to replace the first program of 1903. At the congress, the so-called Military Opposition (Vladimir Smirnov, Kliment Vorosilov, Timofey Sapronov, and Semion Budonny, with Stalin in the background) introduces itself. They protest against the employment of military experts; tsarist officers in favor of people's militias; partisan war; and the eligibility of military leaders. They oppose Trotsky, Commissar of War, who wants a skilled regular army. The majority of the congress, headed by Lenin, supports Trotsky's ideas.

END OF MARCH: The RCP(b) adopts a resolution on the war against SRs, Anarchists, and Mensheviks. Their newspapers are banned and their leaders are arrested. Aleksandr Kolchak occupies Ufa and wants to unite his army with Anton Denikin's troops, which control the Donets basin, in order to jointly march against Moscow. The Russian Soviet Federative Socialist Republic, consisting of autonomous territories and a federation of republics, signs bilateral military-political treaties with the independent Soviet republics (the Ukraine, Belarus) that have formed in the place of the tsarist empire.

4 APRIL: With the support of Entente forces, Kolchak starts a decisive attack on the eastern front, the first campaign of the Entente.

15 APRIL: The All-Russia Central Executive Committee orders the creation of forced labor camps. (In a resolution of 17 May, it orders the establishment of a labor camp of at least 300 persons close to capitals of each gubernia.)

APRIL: The *Bund* mobilizes its members between the ages of 18 and 25 to enter the Red Army. In order to facilitate operations in the Central Committee, organizational measures are taken by the Secretariat, Organizational Bureau.

9 JULY: The Central Committee's call: *Everyone to fight against Denikin!*

25 JULY: The Council of People's Commissariat renounces all extraterritorial rights claimed by the tsarist government in China.

JULY: The Central Committee of the Menshevik Russian Social Democratic Labor Party issues a proclamation and calls for the elimination of war communism and also takes a stand against Denikin and Kolchak.

24 AUGUST: Lenin declares victory over the main forces of Kolchak.

AUGUST: The British army starts evacuating the territories it has occupied. General Anton Denikin invades Kiev. The Ukraine comes under control of the White and Cossack forces.

25 SEPTEMBER: Underground anarchists bomb the Moscow Committee of the RCP(b). Of the 150 participants, twelve are killed, including the local secretary, V. Zagorsky, and 55 are injured, including Bukharin, Olminsky, and Yaroslavsky.

SEPTEMBER: Anton Denikin's cavalry

comes within 150 kilometers of Moscow.

8 OCTOBER: Patriarch Tikhon issues a message to the Russian Pravoslav clergy and asks them not to get involved in political struggles.

13 OCTOBER: White Guards occupy Oriol and prepare to attack Moscow.

OCTOBER: Entente groups are withdrawn from the north. Extraordinary revolutionary tribunals are set up with juridical authority.

NOVEMBER: Under Semion Budonny's command, the First Red Cavalry is organized, which will become famous during fights against Denikin, Wrangel, and the Poles. The Red Army beats off Anton Denikin and forces Nikolay Yudenichy to retreat after he tries to attack Petrograd.

2-4 DECEMBER: The 8th All-Russia Conference of the RCP(b) institutes party control over state and social institutions.

5-9 DECEMBER: The 7th All-Russia Congress of Soviets resolves the further consolidation of soviets and government bodies and gives an exact formulation of their rights and duties in the center and in the provinces. The latter are in double dependence: local apparatuses are subordinated to both the local elected body and the upper-level sectorial units. These steps reinforce the centralized character of Soviet government. The congress protests against the White terror in Hungary.

12 DECEMBER: The Red Army marches into Kharkov, and on 16 December, into Kiev. The Reds completely sweep Denikin's White Guards from the Ukraine, lasting until February 1920.

1920

7 JANUARY: The Red Army occupies Krasnoiarsk. This marks the end of Kolchak's rule in Siberia.

17 JANUARY: In accordance with Lenin's instruction after the victory over Denikin, the death penalty imposed by revolutionary tribunals and extraordinary committees on those convicted for political crimes is canceled.

1 FEBRUARY: Soviet troops occupy Khiva after a week of siege. Revolutionary committee takes power.

7 FEBRUARY: Aleksandr Kolchak is executed in Irkutsk.

19 FEBRUARY: A general obligation to work is introduced. Denikin's scattered troops are reorganized by General Wrangel in the Crimea.

29 MARCH-5 APRIL: The 9th Congress of RCP(b) enlarges the secretariat, which is formally subordinated to the Central Committee, though in practice it still controls the party apparatus. It organizes the meetings of the Politburo, deals with individual matters, and liaises with lower party organizations. The Central Committee consists of about 600 people; nationwide there are about 15,000 party workers.

8 APRIL: In Moscow the Caucasian Bureau (Kavburo) is formed. It is a regional body authorized to represent the Central Committee of the RCP(b) in the Caucasus. Its main task is to prepare the attacks on the independent Azeri, Armenian, and Georgian states, and to organize local rebellions. The body's head is Grigory (Sergo) Ordzhonikidze.

21 APRIL: The Treaty of Warsaw is signed sealing the alliance between the second Polish Republic, represented by Josef Pilsudski, and the Ukrainian Directory, represented by Simon Petliura, against Bolshevik Russia. The "independent Ukraine" gives territorial concessions to Poland in return for its help.

25 APRIL: Poland attacks Soviet Russia. Polish troops occupying Zhitomir mark the beginning of the Polish-Soviet war. Josef Pilsudski is supported by Piotr Wrangel's forces that start an offensive from the Crimea, and also by Petliura's army.

28 APRIL: Red Army occupies Baku. Soviet power is declared.

2 MAY: A Red Army campaign gives support to a Communist uprising in Georgia.

7 MAY: The independence of Georgia is recognized by Russia and concludes a nonaggression pact. The treaty *de jure* establishes the existing borders between the two nations and obliges Georgia to surrender all third-party elements considered hostile by Moscow. Georgia also promises to legalize the local Bolshevik Party and to withdraw British troops from Georgia. Polish troops invade Kiev.

14 MAY: In a treaty with Japan, Soviet Russia recognizes the Far Eastern Republic, a buffer state between RSFSR and the territories occupied by Japan.

MAY: In Aleksandropol (Leninakan) in Armenia, a Bolshevik revolt breaks out as a result of the Red Army's approach. The revolt is suppressed by the Entente-supported Dashnak government. (On 10 August Armenia also signs a peace treaty with the RSFSR on the model of the peace conditions for Georgia.)

11 JULY: Lord George Curzon, British Foreign Secretary, makes a proposal to determine the Polish-Russian armistice line on the basis of the demarcation border suggested on 8 December 1919.

19 JULY-17 AUGUST: The Second Congress of Comintern is held in Petrograd and Moscow. Grigory Zinoviev is elected chairman of the Executive Committee; his deputy is Nikolay Bukharin. The congress elaborates twenty-one conditions as prerequisites for any group wanting to become affiliated to the Third International. The conditions call for the demarcation between Communist parties and other socialist groups, democratic centralism, recognition of dictatorship of the proletariat, and use of both legal and illegal operational methods, etc. The congress condemns leftist impatience in forcing an unprepared revolution. It makes important decisions on national and colonial questions.

AUGUST: At the time of the Comintern Congress, the International Provisional Bureau of Proletkult is also organized. Lenin, stimulated by Aleksandr Bogdanov's theoretical and public activity, initiates a new edition of *Materialism and Empirio-Criticism*.

16-17 AUGUST: Red troops under the command of Mihail Tukhachevsky are defeated near Warsaw.

28 AUGUST: In Chardzhou (Türkmenabat), a small town close to Bukhara, a Bolshevik revolt breaks out. The rebels asks for the Red Army's help. At the same time, Mihail Frunze's troops overthrow the Bukhara emirate.

1-7 SEPTEMBER: At the Congress of the Peoples in the East in Baku, a call goes out for a joint anti-imperialist struggle.

5 SEPTEMBER: The Cheka orders search for the deserters from the "labor armies."

13 SEPTEMBER: The RSFSR and Khorezmi People's Republic sign an agreement of alliance.

22-25 SEPTEMBER: Ninth All-Russia Conference of RCP(b).

SEPTEMBER: The delegation of the Second International headed by Karl Kautsky makes an official visit to the Georgian Republic.

12 OCTOBER: Preliminary peace talks in Riga terminate the Polish-Soviet war.

28 OCTOBER: The Red Army commanded by Frunze leads a decisive attack on the southern front.

16 NOVEMBER: After subduing Piotr Wrangel, the Red Army occupies Sevastopol. The liberation of Crimea marks the end of the civil war in European Russia.

20 NOVEMBER: In Warsaw Simon Petliura announces that the Ukrainian Directory fighting for independence will cease its activities.

25 NOVEMBER: According to Frunze's instructions, liquidation begins of the anarchist peasant troops fighting against both Reds and Whites since the end of 1918 in left-bank Ukraine.

29 NOVEMBER: In Delizhan and the Kazakh territories of Armenia, a Bolshevik revolution breaks out; its members request help from the Red Army residing in neighboring Azerbaijan. The Soviet commissioner in Yerevan presents an ultimatum to the Dashnak government to resign in favor of the Bolshevik counter-government formed in Baku.

NOVEMBER-DECEMBER: At different party forums a debate starts on the role of the trade unions (the debate is closed by the 10th Congress of the RCP(b) in 1921). The three main trends are: the "militarists" (Lev Trotsky, Nikolay Bukharin, Yevgeniy Preobrazhensky), the "workers' opposition" (Aleksandr Shlapnikov, Sergey Medvedev, Aleksandra Kollontay), and the "democratic centralists" (Andrey Bubnov, Valerian Osinsky, Timofey Sapronov).

2 DECEMBER: The Armenian government hastily signs a peace agreement with Turkey in which it gives up all territorial claims, but this does not prevent its breakdown.

6 DECEMBER: The Red Army occupies Yerevan.

20 DECEMBER: Feliks Dzerzhinsky's decree orders that political prisoners must be held separately from ordinary prisoners, under circumstances that make intellectual activity possible.

22-29 DECEMBER: 8th All-Russia Soviet Congress draws up a balance sheet of the civil war, adopts the plans for reconstruction and the electrification of Russia (GOELRO).

1921

14 JANUARY: *Pravda* publishes the so-called Rudzhutak-theses, *The Tasks of the Trade Unions in Production*. The "Platform of 10"—Yan Rudzutak, Mihail Tomsky (Yefremov), Grigory Zinoviev, Lev Kamenev, Yosif Stalin, etc.—is supported by Lenin in the debates.

12 FEBRUARY: At the border area between Georgia and Armenia, a Georgian revolutionary committee calls for a revolt and asks the Red Army for military help.

13 FEBRUARY: The death of Piotr Kropotkin (age 79), "father of Russian anarchism." The imprisoned anarchists are allowed to attend the funeral if they promise to return to prison after the event. They do so.

25 FEBRUARY: After a week of siege the

Red Army occupies Tbilisi and overthrows the Menshevik government. Soviet power is declared in Georgia.

28 FEBRUARY-18 MARCH: In Kronstadt, a rebellion breaks out among sailors over dissatisfaction with war communism. The rebels' main slogan is "Soviets without Communists."

MARCH: The 13th Extraordinary Conference of the Jewish Bund, adopting the conditions of the Communist International, issues a resolution on joining the RCP(b).

8-16 MARCH: The 10th Congress of RCP(b). The New Economic Policy (NEP) is decided. The debate on trade unions—in view of the new situation—is concluded with the adoption of Rudzutak Platform. The 300 members of the congress help suppress the Kronstadt rebellion. In order to achieve party unity, a Provisional Government order bans internal factions.

18 MARCH: In Riga, Poland and Soviet Russia sign a peace agreement that relocates the new borderline east of the Curzon line, roughly following the ethnic borders (Grodno–Brest-Litovsk).

21 MARCH: The presidium of the All-Russia Central Executive Committee decrees the replacement of the surplus appropriation system with the food tax.

APRIL: Cooperatives get the right to sell their surplus products on the market.

13 APRIL: In Tashkent, the Turkestan Autonomous Soviet Republic is proclaimed.

17 MAY: Decree on nationalization of small-scale industry is withdrawn.

21 MAY: Soviet Georgia and the RSFSR sign an Agreement of Federation.

26-28 MAY: The Tenth All-Russia Conference of RCP(b) analyzes the problems arising at the introduction of the NEP.

22 JUNE-12 JULY: The Third Congress of Comintern is held in Moscow. The policy of "workers' united front" is announced.

JUNE: The Cheka is restrained: it cannot inflict an imprisonment longer than two years.

3-19 JULY: The founding Congress of the Red International of Labor Unions is held in Moscow. The general secretary of the new council is Aleksandr Lozovsky (Solomon Dridzo).

JULY: The labor armies are dissolved.

JULY: Leasing of properties belonging to the Supreme Soviet of the National Economy is regulated. But a termination of nationalization rarely occurs; the presidium of the Soviet returns 76 firms to former owners.

JULY-AUGUST: In the state sector wages are paid in cash again.

6 AUGUST: A severe famine sweeps through the country. Lenin asks for help from the proletariat of the world, stating that in some Russian gubernias the food situation is worse than it was at the time of the 1890 famine. In 1890 the number of those starving was 964,620; their number in 1921 can only be expressed in millions. Twenty percent of the country's city population and 25 percent of the rural population is starving.

8 AUGUST: Patriarch Tikhon turns to believers to raise funds to feed famine victims. A collection begins in the church.

16 AUGUST: Government makes decrees on individual accounting (*hozraschot*) in state-owned industry and commerce. The criteria of the state-owned trusts' efficiency are their profitability and avoidance of losses.

AUGUST: The Red Army in Mongolia liquidates the remnants of the Russian White Guards. The White commander, Baron Unger von Sternberg, is executed on 15 September.

SEPTEMBER: Workers International Relief is formed in Berlin to channel relief from international working-class organizations and Communist parties to famine-stricken Soviet Russia. Among the founders are Albert Einstein, Martin Andersen-Nexö, Romain Rolland, and Anatole France. Fridtjof Nansen sets up a committee for famine relief with the support of the League of Nations.

13 OCTOBER: Turkey and Georgia, Armenia, and Azerbaijan sign a peace treaty. Turkey gives up the protectorate in Nakhichevan, withdraws from southern Georgia (Ahaltsih and Ahalkala regions) and the Armenian Aleksandropolis (Leninakan), but keeps the regions of Kars, Argadon, Artvin, and Sarikamish populated with Armenians.

14 OCTOBER: The All-Ukrainian Sobor (Synod) is called in Kiev and declares the Ukrainian Autocephalous Orthodox Church independent from the Moscow Patriarchate. Patriarch Tikhon does not recognize it.

18 OCTOBER: A common decree of the All-Russia Central Executive Committee and the People's Commissariat declares the Crimean Autonomous Socialist Soviet Republic within the borders of the RSFSR.

1 NOVEMBER: The new Mongol state signs a peace agreement with Soviet Russia.

DECEMBER: Lenin proposes tightening the area of Cheka activities, and a decree is issued on the personal juridical responsibility of those reporting false information on others.

19-22 DECEMBER: The 11th All-Russia Conference of the RCP(b). The main points on the agenda are commodity and financial conditions, restoring the market (NEP). The conference also discusses the results of "Party purges."

23-28 DECEMBER: The 9th All-Russia Congress of the Soviets orders the reorganization of the Cheka and consolidation of legality. The congress expresses "warm appreciation to the workers of all countries who came to the assistance of the famine-stricken gubernias of Soviet Russia."

1922

JANUARY: A philosophical and socioeconomic monthly journal, *Pod znamenem marksizma,* is published for the first time.

END OF JANUARY-EARLY FEBRUARY: The Society of Old Bolsheviks is formed. To apply, at least eighteen years of party membership is required; in the first year it consists of 64 members.

6 FEBRUARY: The decree of the All-Russia Central Executive Committee liquidates the Cheka; the State Political Directorate (GPU) takes over its role. The first chief is the Cheka's former chairman, Feliks Dzerzhinsky. Unlike its predecessor, the GPU is subordinated to the People's Commissariat for Internal Affairs and becomes one of its departments. The GPU inherits its headquarters and organization from the Cheka. Until 1930 the GPU will act with more restraint than the Cheka: it does not have the right to arrest or shoot suspects, and has no juridical authority.

23 FEBRUARY: The All-Russia Central

Executive Committee issues a decree ordering the church to turn over jeweled objects and other valuables that can be exchanged for hard currency, which will be used to make purchases of food abroad.

28 FEBRUARY: Patriarch Tikhon resists and condemns the confiscation of the property of the church.

FEBRUARY: The First Congress of the Communist Organizations of Transcaucasia elects a Transcaucasian Regional Committee of the RCP(b), which takes over the role of the Kavbiuro.

MARCH: The first issue of *Novaya Rossiya*, a Smena Vekhist journal, appears.

12 MARCH: Georgia, Armenia, and Azerbaijan, which are formally independent of RSFSR but in close alliance with it, form the Transcaucasian Federation.

27 MARCH–2 APRIL: The 11th Congress of the RCP(b) reorganizes the secretariat that coordinates the work of the Central Committee and the Central Control Commission, and introduces a new party function: General Secretary of the Politburo. The party's conditions of admission of new members are rendered more severe. This is the last party congress in which Lenin participates.

3 APRIL: The beginning of the Plenum of the Central Committee. In Lenin's absence, the presiding Kamenev recommends Stalin as general secretary.

10 APRIL–19 MAY: A Soviet Russian delegation takes part in the international economic conference in Genoa.

16 APRIL: In Rapallo, Germany and the RSFSR sign an agreement in which Germany accords Soviet Russia *de jure* recognition. The two signatories mutually cancel all prewar debts and renounce war claims. Particularly advantageous for Germany is the inclusion of the most-favored-nation clause and extensive trade agreements.

BEGINNING OF MAY: Patriarch Tikhon is interrogated by the court as a witness, later as an accused. He is confined in Donskoy monastery.

12 MAY: The leaders of the Renovated Church (Vvedensky, Kalinovsky, Belkov), a reform movement supported by the Soviet government, secede from Patriarch Tikhon's church and restore a Holy Synod to power. Patriarch Tikhon, under house arrest, agrees to step down from the patriarchal throne and hand authority to Metropolitan Agafangel of Yaroslavl, whom Tikhon has chosen as his successor.

19 MAY: In a letter to Feliks Dzerzhinsky, Lenin proposes preparing for the expulsion from Russia of the intellectuals who are dissatisfied with Soviet power. He does not see it timely to ban *Novaya Rossiya*.

19 MAY: At the All-Russia Conference of the Komsomol, a resolution is adopted on the organization of the first Pioneer groups.

22 MAY: The All-Russia Central Executive Committee decrees the conditions of leasing land.

29 MAY: In Moscow the group consisting of priests named "Living Church" is formed—political parties serving as a model—and sharply attacks the Orthodox Church loyal to the Patriarch.

6 JUNE: The People's Commissariat decrees the forming of Glavlit (Main Directory for Literary and Publishing Affairs) as the main authority for censorship of press and literature.

JULY: Authorities introduce a new currency, called chervonets, which is fully convertible and backed by the gold standard. (In the second half of 1922 and most of 1923 the new currency exists side-by-side with the banknote rubles, while the chervonet continuously loses value. In October 1922 a kopek of 1913 equals 100,000 rubles. The yearly budget is calculated in prewar rubles.)

4-7 AUGUST: The Twelfth All-Russia Conference of the RCP(b) calls attention to the danger of bourgeois political forces, and condemns the Smena Vekhist trend. It modifies party rules to limit admission of new members coming from non-proletarian classes.

11 AUGUST: The Politburo forms a committee to elaborate the principles of unifying the Soviet republics, with Valerian Kuybishev as president. Members are Grigory Sokolnikov, Christian Rakovsky, and the representatives of the republics. The committee insists on Stalin's autonomization project, which does not consider the new Soviet state as a federation of republics with equal rights, and if necessary would make the republics enter the Russian federation by force.

SUMMER: Thirty-four SR leaders are publicly tried for high crimes against the Soviet state. In their defense, the Second International intervenes. Émile Vandervelde and Theodor Liebknecht arrive in Moscow for the trial. In the end, these efforts lead to the commutation of the death penalty.

26 SEPTEMBER: The ill Lenin sends a letter to the Politburo criticizing Stalin's ideas, suggesting that the principle of the organization of the Soviet Union should be a voluntary and equal unity of the republics instead of the forceful autonomization.

6 OCTOBER: Lenin's proposals are accepted by the plenum of the Central Committee. In accordance with the changes, the resolution is revised by the Preparatory Commission. With Lenin's consent it suggests a federation for the Transcaucasian territories.

19 OCTOBER: In Tiflis (Tbilisi) at the plenum of the Transcaucasian Borderland Committee some members of the Central Committee of the Georgian CP—Kote Tsintsadze, Sergey Kavtadze, Filip Maharadze, and M. Okudzhava—announce their support for Budu Mdivani's motion: Georgia should enter the Soviet federation independently, not as a member of a Caucasian confederation. Grigory (Sergo) Ordzhonikidze, head of the CC of RCP(b)'s Transcaucasian Borderland Bureau, denounces it as chauvinism and relieves Okudzhava from his office for violation of party discipline.

25 OCTOBER: The Red Army liberates Vladivostok from the reign of the Japanese interventionist forces, and the last American interventionist troops set sail.

OCTOBER: The Party Congress of the Menshevik RSDLP demands political freedom and a democratic republic.

5 NOVEMBER-5 DECEMBER: The Fourth Congress of the Comintern is held.

15 NOVEMBER: The Far Eastern Republic unites with the RSFSR.

NOVEMBER: Ordzhonikidze, a representative of the party center (in Tbilisi), punches Akaky Kobakhidze in the course of a fierce debate on the question of the Transcaucasian federation. Kobakhidze complains about Ordzhonikidze at the Central Control Commission.

25 NOVEMBER-12 DECEMBER: To investigate the "Georgian affair," the

Politburo dispatches a committee to Tbilisi with three members, headed by the Cheka chief, Dzerzhinsky. The Committee stands by Ordzhonikidze and condemns the Georgian Central Committee.

1 DECEMBER: The Land Code is put into effect; it confirms the nationalization of land, prohibits trading of land, rejects cutting up farms, and at the same time allows leasing of land and the use of wage labor.

2-12 DECEMBER: A conference on reduction of armaments is held in Moscow in which the representatives of Latvia, Poland, Estonia, Finland, and the RSFSR take part. The Soviet state's offers on serious reductions of armies of the countries is rejected by the participants. In spite of this, the People's Commissariat reduces the Soviet-Russian army by 50 percent.

13 DECEMBER: In Baku, the Transcaucasian Socialist Federative Soviet Republic is formed, uniting Georgia, Azerbaijan, and Armenia. (Later it is incorporated into the Soviet state.)

18 DECEMBER: The plenum of the Central Committee makes Stalin personally responsible for the medical regimen prescribed for Lenin by his doctors.

22 DECEMBER: Stalin uses offensive language against Krupskaya, who turns to Kamenev for protection.

23-27 DECEMBER: The Tenth All-Russian Congress of Soviets adopts a resolution to unify two national (Ukrainian SSR and Belarus SSR) and two federal (RSFSR and Transcaucasian SFSR) republics into a single union state: the Union of Soviet Socialist Republics (USSR).

30 DECEMBER: The First Congress of Soviets of the USSR proclaims the creation of the Soviet Union, elects members of the Central Executive Committee (CEC) and head of state, Mihail Kalinin.

DURING 1922: The number of people living on wage and salary drops to six and a half million by 1921–22, which means a ca. 50 percent reduction compared to 1912. Real income is 9.47 rubles calculated at constant prices. The real wage level in 1913 at constant prices is 25 rubles. In mid-1922, 50 percent of wages are still paid in goods and services. A new labor code is introduced that guarantees an 8-hour workday—in case of hard physical labor, shorter workdays—two weeks of paid holidays, and social security for the workers. For young men extraordinary rights are provided, for example, a six-hour workday. Wages and working conditions are regulated by collective contracts made between trade unions and management. In order to provide industry with the necessary loans, Prombank (Industrial Bank) is established. According to official statistics, an estimated five million people died as a result of the famine of 1921–22.

1923

JANUARY: The number of registered unemployed is 461,000. *Suhoy zakhon*, the prohibition on alcoholic drinks introduced at the outbreak of the First World War, is lifted. The most important reason for implementing the state monopoly on selling vodka is to increase state income. The main argument of those opposed to its repeal is alcoholism and its destructive effects on the people, a consequence not compatible with the principles of socialism. As a compromise, a new kind of vodka is produced that has half the usual alcoholic content (20 percent). This "weakened" vodka is named *rykovka,* after Aleksey Rykov, Deputy Chairman of the Council of the People's Commissars, who signed the decree.

4 JANUARY: Lenin, now seriously ill, makes an addition to his *Letter to the Congress* to say that Stalin should be removed from the post of Secretary General.

25 JANUARY: Lenin's article, *How We Should Reorganize the Workers' and Peasants' Inspection,* is published in *Pravda.* It emphasizes the importance of democratizing the leadership.

21 FEBRUARY: A plenary session of the Central Committee of the RCP(b) discusses Stalin's draft thesis on the national question for the Twelfth Party Congress. It is basically accepted, but at Lenin's suggestion some corrections are also made.

5 MARCH: In a letter Lenin asks Trotsky to represent his standpoint at the Twelfth Congress on the "Georgian affair" in a debate on national policy. Trotsky declines to confront Stalin on the issue.

14 MARCH: An official medical report on Lenin's state of health is issued. Stalin's article *Concerning the Question of the Strategy and Tactics of the Russian Communists* is published in *Pravda* and a more detailed version in *Petrogradskaya Pravda.*

17-25 APRIL: At the Twelfth Congress of RCP(b), Lev Trotsky does not dare to take Lenin's position on right-wing nationalism. Still, with Nikolay Bukharin's lead the congress condemns "the remnants of Great-Russian chauvinism." At the congress Stalin announces the so-called policy of *Korenizatsiya* (establishing), in which the goal is to grow national cadres for every nationality. Thus the party line can be pursued everywhere by representatives of the local nationality and the national proletariat will rise against its exploiters. Networks of schools, theaters, libraries, journals, publishing houses, and associations disseminating the state ideology are created, all using the vernacular.

29 APRIL-2 MAY: The Renovationist, Second All-Russia Synod condemns capitalism as an anti-Christian social formation and welcomes socialist revolution. It puts Patriarch Tikhon on ecclesiastical trial *in absentia* (he is under house arrest) for his opposition to Communism and strips him of his episcopacy, priesthood, and monastic status. It withdraws his pastoral circular letter that anathematizes the Soviet power.

16 JUNE: Patriarch Tikhon sends an open letter to the Supreme Court of RSFSR to "admit" his guilt but he does not officially get back his title before his death in 1925. The letter is published in the newspaper *Bezbozhnik.*

JULY: Within the borders of Azerbaijan, the Mountain-Karabakh Autonomous Region, with a majority Armenian population, is formed.

1 JULY: Labor camps on Solovki Island and in the Petsora Valley start to function (they are open until 1939).

4 JULY: In the gazette of the Central Executive Committee, Tikhon announces that the Orthodox Church refrains from engaging in politics.

15 JULY: Tikhon publishes his free decision to return as head of the church and does not recognize the decisions of the 1923 synod, which brings about a schism within the clergy. The minority (Renovationists) conform to the decisions concerning the changes in the canonical rules of ordinations and other reforms, and the majority supports Tikhon and the moderate reforms he has already accepted.

8 OCTOBER: Lev Trotsky sends a letter condemning the secretariat to the Central Committee, after which the Left Opposition movement unfolds (Yevgeny Preobrazhensky, Georgy Piatakov, Valerian Osinsky, Vladimir Antonov-Ovseenko). Its economic program is based on "primitive socialist accumulation of capital," with the accumulation, serving rapid industrialization, based upon unequal exchange.

15 OCTOBER: The Declaration of the 46, the platform of the left oppositon, repeats the concerns of Lev Trotsky's letter: the restoration of party and workers' democracy, though forced industrialization will not serve to widen workers' democracy.

15 NOVEMBER: The Central Executive Committee reorganizes the State Political Directorate (GPU) and transfers it to the All-Union Joint State Political Directorate (OGPU).

9 DECEMBER: Under circumstances that are still unclear, an assault is made upon Patriarch Tikhon.

11 DECEMBER: *Pravda* publishes Lev Trotsky's article *New Course* in which he demands that the party give grassroots organizations greater democratic rights in internal party life.

DURING 1923: In Moscow the SR Party announces its dissolution. The passport system used in the tsarist era is canceled. (Free movement needed special permission.) Instead a personal certificate (*udostovereniye*) is issued to those who claim it.

In the first quarter of the year, the proportion of paying in kind is still 20 percent. In 1922–23 the terms of trade between town and country begin to diverge in favor of the state-run industrial economy and at the expense of rural consumers: the "Scissors Crisis" reaches its peak in October 1923. Industrial prices are then 276 percent of 1913 levels, while agricultural prices are only 89 percent. According to a trade census of 1923, NEPmen control 15 percent of wholesale trade and 83 percent of retail trade. The state sector controls 77 percent of wholesale trade and 7 percent of retail trade, and the cooperative sector dominates 8 percent of wholesale trade and 10 percent of retail trade.

1924

16-18 JANUARY: The 13th Conference of the RCP(b) starts a counterattack on the opposition. In order to discredit members of the opposition, Stalin publicly reveals for the first time the provisions of the Tenth Congress, the 1921 resolution on party unity relating to disciplinary procedures against Central Committee members. One of Lev Trotsky's main supporters, Vladimir Antonov-Ovseenko, is dismissed after he, as director of the Political Administration of the Republic Revolutionary War Council, sends out a circular to army party cells demanding democracy. Grigory Zinoviev and Lev Kamenev want Trotsky to be expelled from the party but Stalin opposes it for tactical reasons.

21 JANUARY: In Gorky, Lenin, the head of the People's Commissariat, dies at the age of fifty-four. Lenin's body is embalmed and exhibited in a temporary wooden mausoleum on 27 January in Red Square.

26 JANUARY-2 FEBRUARY: Second All-Union Congress of Soviets. On the eve of Lenin's funeral, Stalin—in the name of the Bolshevik Party—takes a solemn vow to hold sacred and fulfill the behests of Lenin. To perpetuate the memory of Lenin, the congress adopts a decision to change the name of Petrograd to Leningrad. The congress adopts the first constitution of the Soviet Union and elects members of the two chambers of the Central Executive Committee: the Soviet of the Union and the Soviet of Nationalities. Aleksey Rykov is elected head of the People's Commissars.

29-31 JANUARY: The plenum of the RCP(b) proclaims the "Lenin enrollment." Until 15 May, more than 240,000 new members, of whom 90 percent are workers, are enrolled in the party. The social composition of the party improves: the proportion of workers rises from 44 to 60 percent. These steps help isolate the opposition.

1 FEBRUARY: The United Kingdom recognizes the USSR.

7 FEBRUARY: Italy recognizes the Soviet Union.

11 FEBRUARY: Efraim Skliansky, Trotsky's close companion and deputy of the Commissariat for War, is dismissed, and Mikhail Frunze, the hero of the war against Wrangel, is appointed in his position.

21 MARCH: The resolution of the CEC terminates legal procedures against Patriarch Tikhon.

18 MAY: Nadezhda Krupskaya hands ver Lenin's *Letter to the Congress*, which he originally wrote to the Central Committee during the Twelfth Congress.

24 MAY: The meeting of the Central Committee introduces a resolution that Lenin's letter cannot be publicly read or printed; it will be read to each delegation separately in executive sessions. Stalin pledges to mend his ways.

23-31 MAY: The Thirteenth Congress of the RCP(b) reelects Stalin General Secretary of the Central Committee of the RCP(b). The Political Committee (Zinoviev, Kamenev, Bukharin, Rykov, Kalinin, and Stalin), the Central Committee, and the majority of the congress delegates condemn the ideas of the left opposition led by Trotsky.

17 JUNE-8 JULY: The Fifth Congress of the Comintern diagnoses a partial and temporary stabilization of capitalism. A decision is made distorting the earlier correct slogan of the United Workers' Front, saying it will only take permissions from "below," which makes cooperation with non-Communists impossible. Its new slogans are: "Out among the masses!" and "Let's make the Communist parties Bolshevik."

19 SEPTEMBER: In Bukhara the Kurultai of Soviets adopts a resolution that liquidates the independent state. Uzbek and Turkmen SSR and the Tadjik Autonomous SSR are formed.

SEPTEMBER: Stalin calls social democracy a variant of fascism.

AUTUMN: Trotsky, in his *Lessons of October,* revives the thesis of permanent revolution that he elaborated in 1905–1907, and analyzes the importance and main processes of the October Revolution. The analysis becomes the subject of factional struggles.

OCTOBER: Before the parliamentary elections in England, the Foreign Office publishes the so-called Zinoviev letter calling for intensified Communist agitation in Britain. The letter, an obvious forgery, helps ensure the fall of the

Labour government in the October elections.

18 NOVEMBER: At the plenum of the Moscow Party Committee, Lev Kamenev classifies Trotskyism as an independent trend that has always been opposed to official party ideology.

DECEMBER: Stalin puts forth his theory of socialism in one country against Trotsky's theory of permanent revolution. Stalin's theory stresses that the Soviet Union, being isolated internationally, should fully industrialize before embarking on a policy of spreading communism to the world, and that socialism can be built in Russia without the victory of the working class in developed countries. The theory is published as *The October Revolution and the Tactics of the Russian Communists*.

Based on Tamás Krausz, Ákos Szilágyi, Zoltán Sz. Bíró, eds., Oroszország és a Szovjetunió XX, századi képes krónikája *(Budapest: Akadémiai Kiadó, 1992).*
Translated by Katalin Baráth.

Biographical Sketches

Adler, Victor (1852–1918) was an Austrian social democratic politician. He founded the Marxist journals *Gleicheit* (1886) and *Arbeiter-Zeitung* (1889). He was the founder and first leader of the Austrian Social Democratic Party. In October 1918 he became minister of foreign affairs in the Austrian government.

Agursky, Samuel (Samuel Khaimovich) (1884–1947) was a communist, politician, and historian of the revolutionary movement. In 1902 he joined the *Bund*. In 1906 and 1907 he emigrated first to Great Britain and later to the United States. He joined the RCP(b) in 1918 and worked for the People's Commissariat for National Affairs. In the 1920s he traveled to the United States to collect donations for Soviet Russia. He authored several scholarly works on the history of the October Revolution. In 1938 he was arrested on fabricated charges and was sentenced to five years of exile in Soviet Central Asia, Kazakhstan. In 1947 he returned to the prohibited city of Moscow to look after his affairs but was forced by the authorities to return to Pavlodar. He died there shortly thereafter. He was posthumously rehabilitated in 1956.

Akhmatova (Gorenko), Anna Andreyevna (1889–1966) was a Russian and Soviet poet. Her famous cycle, *Requiem,* documents her personal experiences and was published in 1987. She belonged to the Akhmeist school led by Mandelstam. In 1962 she was nominated for the Nobel Prize in Literature.

Akimov, Vladimir PetrovicH (1875–1921) was one of the spokesmen for the economists in the Russian Social Democratic Party. He took part in the activities of the Union for the Struggle for the Liberation of the Working Class. He was arrested, then emigrated. Later he joined the emigrant Russian Social Democrates and became the leader of its right wing. He returned to Russia in 1905 but no longer participated in politics.

Akselrod, Pavel Borisovich (1850–1928) was a social democratic revolutionary, a leading Menshevik politician, and publicist. He was a member of the Liberation of Labor group and the founding editor of *Iskra*. He was one of the leaders of the group called Liquidators. In 1912 he participated in the August Bloc. During the October Revolution he was head of the Central Committee of the Russian Social Democratic Labor Party (Menshevik). He opposed the revolution, and emigrated.

Aleksander II (1818–1881) was a Russian tsar (1855–1881). He proclaimed the reforms of 1861.

Aleksander III (1845–1894) was a Russian tsar (1881–1894).

Aleksandrov, Mikhail Stepanovich; see Olminsky (Aleksandrov), Mikhail Stepanovich.

Aleksinsky, Grigory Alekseyevich (1879–1967?) was a Bolshevik, representative of the Second State Duma. A popular orator of the Bolshevik faction of RSDLP, he emigrated after the dissolution of the Duma. In 1909 he—with Bogdanov—was a member of the *Vperyod* group. After the February Revolution he returned to Russia, joined the Plekhanovist Unity group, and adopted an anti-Bolshevik stance. He charged Lenin with being a German spy. In 1918 he was arrested; he emigrated upon his release.

Antonov, Dmitry Ivanovich (1896–?) was a Bolshevik revolutionary, and a member of the Russian Communist Party (Bolshevik) from 1918. He served in the Red Army (1918–22) and fought in the civil war. He worked for the party after 1922. Between 1935 and 1938 he was the head of the Central Committee's Industrial department. Between 1938 and 1940 he was the first secretary of the RCP(b) in the Chelyabinsk district.

Aralov, Semyon Ivanovich (1880–1969) was a revolutionary, Soviet politician, and a military officer. He was the first head of the Soviet Red Army Intelligence Directorate. In 1921 he began a career in diplomacy. He volunteered for service in the Second World War, then retired.

Armand, Inessa (1874–1920) was born in Paris and from the age of five was brought up in Moscow. She joined the RSDLP in 1904. She was in close contact with Lenin, then living in foreign exile. After arriving in Russia in April 1917 she kept working as an organizer. She joined the left over the question of Brest-Livovsk. In 1920 she participated in the Second Congress of the Comintern. She died of cholera and is buried in the Kremlin Wall Necropolis in Moscow.

Arshinov, Piotr Andreyevich (1886–1938) was a Bolshevik, later an anarchist. He was Nestor Makhno's secretary as of 1919. In 1923 he wrote *The History of the Makhnovist Movement*. In 1938 he was arrested and died in prison.

Babel, Isaac Emanuilovich (1894–1940) was a writer who became a literary sensation. In 1920 he was assigned to Field Marshal Semyon Budyonny's First Cavalry Army. Between 1921 and 1925 he wrote at least fifty short stories, which were published as a collection titled *Red Cavalry* in 1926. In 1931 he published *Odessa Tales*. He visited Paris several times. In May 1939 he was arrested on fabricated charges and was executed on 27 January 1940. He was rehabilitated on 18 December 1954.

Babushkin, Ivan Vasilyevich (1873–1906) was a worker and Bolshevik revolutionary. He studied in the workers' Marxist circle under the guidance of Lenin in Petersburg in 1894; he was arrested several times. He was one of the first correspondents for Lenin's *Iskra*. He participated actively in the 1905 Revolution. He was a member of the committee of the RSDLP in Irkutsk. In 1905 he went to Chita to collect weapons; upon his return he was taken captive by General A. N. Meller-Zakomelsky's troops and executed.

Badayev, Aleksey Yegorovich (1883–1951) was a Bolshevik politician and member of the RSDLP beginning in 1904. In 1912 he was elected a member of the Bolshevik faction in the 4th

Duma; he was arrested in 1914 and exiled to Siberia. Between 1912 and 1913 he was the official publisher of *Pravda*. He held a number of positions connected to food procurement in various Soviet organizations in Petrograd and the northern territory. From 1930 he was chairman of the Central Union of Consumers Societies. In 1938 and 1939 he was the People's Commissar for the food processing industry of the Russian SFSR. Between 1938 and 1943 he was chairman of the RSFSR Supreme Soviet and the deputy chairman of the presidium of the Supreme Soviet of the USSR.

Bakunin, Mikhail Aleksandrovich (1814–1876) was a revolutionary and theorist of anarchism. In 1848 and 1849 he was one of the leaders of the riots in Prague and Dresden. In 1851 he was turned over to Russia where he was imprisoned. He escaped to Japan, then travelled to the United States, and ended up in London. He joined the First International, which was dominated by a struggle between Marx and a faction around Bakunin. Finally Bakunin was expelled from the International. He died in Switzerland. His main works are *Confession* and *Statism and Anarchy*.

Balabanova, Angelica Isaakovna (1877–1965) was an activist in the Italian workers' movement. She left Russia in 1897, joined the Union of Russian Social Democrats Abroad, and settled in Italy. After the Second Congress of the RSDLP she was a Menshevik. Between 1912 and 1916 she was a member of the Italian Socialist Party. She was one of the editors of the party newspaper, *Avanti*. In 1917 she joined the Bolshevik Party and participated in the First Congress of the Comintern where she worked alongside Lenin. In 1922 she left Soviet Russia. In 1924 she was expelled from the RCP(b).

Bauer, Otto (1881–1938) was an Austrian social democratic politician. He was an early inspirer of the New Left movement and Eurocommunism. His first book, *Social Democracy and the Nationalities Question*, was published in 1906. He was the founder of *Der Kampf*, a theoretical journal. During the First World War he spent three years as a prisoner of war in Russia. From 1918, after Victor Adler's death, he was the leader of the Austrian Social Democratic Party. For a short time he was a minister of foreign affairs. After the 1934 Schutzbund uprising he was forced into exile in Czechoslovakia and France.

Bazarov, Vladimir Aleksandrovich (1874–1939) was a philosopher, economist, and Social Democrat. Between 1904 and 1907 he was a Bolshevik, and from 1905 a member of the editorial board of *Partiynie izvestiya*. From 1917 to 1919 he was a Menshevik. In 1921 he joined the staff of the State Planning Commission as a member of the presidium.

Bebel, August (1840–1913) was a German social democratic politician. First a leftist liberal, he became a revolutionary Marxist under Wilhelm Liebknecht's influence. From 1867 on he was the president of the Union of German Workers' Association, one of the founders of the Social Democratic Workers' Party of Germany, and between 1875 and 1913 the cochairman of the party. His main works are *Our Aim* and *Women and Socialism*.

Beiliss, Menahil-Mendel (1873–1934) was arrested and accused of ritual murder of a Christian boy in Kiev in 1911. The blood libel sparked fierce debates in Russian political life. After his release he left for Palestine and later emigrated to the United States with his family.

Belinsky, Vissarion Grigoryevich (1811–1848) was a literary critic, philosopher, and publicist. Between 1828 and 1832 he studied at Moscow University; he was expelled for political activity. In 1830 he wrote a play, *Dmitry Kalinin*. From 1839 on he lived in St. Petersburg. In 1839–46 he worked for *Otechestvennye zapiski*, and in 1846 for *Sovremennik*. He belonged to the circle of N. V. Stankevich and M. A. Bakunin.

Berdyaev, Nikolay Aleksandrovich (1874–1948) was a philosopher influenced by Marxism, a *legal Marxist*. Later he departed from radical Marxism to focus his attention on Christian existentialism and personalism. He took part in the publishing of *Vekhi* (1909) which sharply rejected revolution. In Paris he published *Puty*, a "Russian religious organ," as he called it. His popular works deal with the problems of the Russian Revolution and Soviet development. He was exiled in 1922.

Bernstein, Eduard (1850–1932) was a German Social Democratic political theorist and politician. He was concerned with refuting Marx's predictions about the inevitable demise of capitalism. He is considered to be the "father of revisionism" and opportunism. His ideas are still much debated.

Berzin, Yan Karlovich (1889–1938) was a revolutionary and Soviet politician of Latvian origin. He was a member of the RSDLP beginning in 1905. He was a participant in the Russian Revolution of 1905–1907. In 1907 he was arrested and charged with political murder, and was sentenced to eight years' imprisonment, which later was reduced to two years. In 1911 he was arrested again for revolutionary activities but managed to escape. He was drafted into military service but did not join. He actively took part in the 1917 Revolution. He was one of the founders of Soviet military intelligence, commander of Lenin's guard. In 1936 and 1937 he was a deputy commander in the Spanish Civil War. After his return to the Soviet Union he was arrested and executed. He was posthumously rehabilitated in 1956.

Bialik, Haim Nahman (1873–1934) was a Jewish poet. He lived in Russia until 1920 when he emigrated to Palestine. He published a collection of poetry, *In the City of Slaughter* (1904).

Blanqui, Louis Auguste (1805–1881) was a French socialist and political activist. A representative of utopian socialism, he thought that revolution should be carried out by a small group that would establish a temporary dictatorship by force. In 1830 he took part in an armed uprising. He was arrested several times. In 1840 he was sentenced to death but this was later commuted to life imprisonment. In 1848 he was released by the revolutionary partisans. He again took part in the uprising and was sentenced to ten years' imprisonment. He was granted amnesty in 1859. He lived in London, Paris, and Brussels. In 1871 he was a member of the Paris Commune. After its fall he was again imprisoned and he died in Paris.

Bogdanov (Malinovsky), Aleksandr Aleksandrovich (1873–1928) was a revolutionary, party politician, philosopher, economist, and physician. After the split of the RSDLP (1903) he was a member of the Bolshevik faction. In 1907 he emigrated with Lenin. He was the editor of the Bolshevik newspapers *Proletary* and *Novaya Zhizny*, and leader of the *Otzovists*. In Capri, together with Gorky and Lunacharsky, he started a school for Bolshevik rank-and-file party members. He was a member of the *Vperyod* group but later left it, and took a stand against the Bolsheviks. After the faction struggles in 1911 he abandoned political activities and dealt with sciences. During the First World War he served as a doctor. He was an ideologist of Proletkult. He was the founder of a systems analysis called tectology. In 1926 he founded the Institute of Hematology and Blood Transfusion, the first institution of its type in the world. A transfusion cost him his life.

Bonch-Bruyevich, Vladimir Dmitrievich (1873–1955) was a Bolshevik politician. He worked for *Iskra*. He participated in the 1905 Revolution. In February 1917 he was a member of the Executive Committee of the Petrograd Soviet. In October he was a commander of the Smolny–Tavrichesky district and a fellow worker of Lenin. Later he turned to social science, and dealt with history of religion. He was one of the founders of the Central Committee's Archives and wrote several books about Vladimir Lenin.

Bosh (Bosch), Yevgeniya Bogdanovna (1879–1925) was a Bolshevik revolutionary and a member of the RSDLP beginning in 1901. With Pyatakov, in 1914, she managed to escape from exile to Japan and then to the United States. Later she took part in the Bern Conference. She opposed Lenin's position on nationalities. She actively participated in the 1917 Revolution. She served as the chairwoman of the People's Secretariat of the Ukrainian SSR.

Bryukhanov, Nikolay Pavlovich (1878–1938) was a revolutionary and Bolshevik politician. He was a member of the RSDLP beginning in 1902. He moved to Ufa where he worked for the party's local newspaper. In February 1918 he was made a member of the collegium of the People's Commissariat of Supplies, and during the civil war he worked as the head of the Main Supplies Directorate of the Red Army. He was the first head of the People's Commissariat of Supplies of the new federation (1923), and later was made Deputy People's Commissar of Finance. In 1938 he was arrested and sentenced to death; in 1956 he was rehabilitated.

Bublikov, Aleksandr Aleksandrovich (1875–1941) was an engineer in transportation. He was a representative in the Fourth State Duma. He was commissar, later minister of the Ministry of Transportation in the Provisional Government. He took part in the arrest of Tsar Nikholay II on 8 March 1917. After the October Revolution he emigrated.

Budyonny, Semion Mihailovich (1883–1973) was a Soviet military commander, Marshal of the Soviet Union (in 1938). In 1904 and 1905 he fought in the Russo-Japanese war, then in the First World War. He became a member of the RSDLP in 1918. He participated in the civil war, was the commander of the First Cavalry, and a firm supporter of Stalin. In 1937 he was made a member of the Supreme Council, in 1938 a member of the Presidium, in 1940 Deputy Minister of War. He fought in the Second World War. After his death he was buried in the Kremlin Wall Necropolis.

Bukharin, Nikolay Ivanovich (1888–1938) was a Bolshevik revolutionary, politician, and theoretician. From 1924 to 1929 he was a member of the Political Committee of RCP(b), and from 1919 to 1929 a member of the Executive Committee of the Comintern. Between 1918 and 1929 he was the chief editor of *Pravda*, between 1934 and 1937 the chief editor of *Izvestiya*. He was the principal framer of the 1936 constitution. In 1937 he was excluded from the party. He was arrested on charges of conspiring to overthrow the Soviet state. On 13 March 1938 the Military College of the Supreme Court of the Soviet Union found him guilty and he was executed two days later. He was posthumously reinstated as a party member by the Supreme Court on 8 February 1988, and by the Central Committee of SCP on 21 June 1988.

Bulakh-Balachowicz (Bei-Bulakh Balakhovich), Stanislaw Nikodimovich (1883–1940) was a counterrevolutionary general. In 1920 he fought against the Reds on the Polish side. With the SR Savinkov and Petliurist troops he marched into Belarus and organized mass pogroms. After the Soviet troops occupied the territories he fled to Poland. He was assasinated in Warsaw.

Bulgakov, Mikhail Afanasievich (1891–1940) was a physician by education, and a writer and dramaturge. His first work was published in 1919. His best known book, *The Master and Margarita*, was not published during his lifetime. Although Stalin was known to have liked his play *Days of the Turbins* and his novel *The White Guard* (upon which the play was based), Bulgakov's plays were banned.

Bulgakov, Sergey Nikolaievich (1871–1944) was a philosopher and economist. He taught political economy at the Moscow University between 1906 and 1918. In 1906 he was elected representative of the Second State Duma. During the civil war he actively sided with the Whites. He was forced to emigrate in 1923. His articles were published in the journal *Puty* whose editor-in-chief was Berdyaev.

Bulygin, Aleksandr Grigorevich (1851–1919) was a tsarist politician. In 1905 he was Minister of Internal Affairs. He was executed by the Cheka.

Bunin, Ivan Alekseievich (1870-1953) was a writer and poet. He started publishing in 1891, and published works in *Znaniye*, a journal edited by Gorky. He visited Western Europe and the Near East. From 1918 to 1920 he lived in Odessa; he later emigrated. He won the Nobel Prize for Literature in 1933.

Chapaev, Vasily Ivanovich (1887–1919) was a celebrated partisan commander during the civil war. In 1919 he fought against Kolchak. The White Army forces ambushed and executed him.

Chernyshevsky, Nikolay Gavrilovich (1828–1889) was a Russian revolutionary, philosopher, literary critic, and writer. In 1854 he became the chief editor of *Sovremennik* in which he published his main literary reviews and essays on philosophy. He was an emblematic figure in his fight against autocracy. In 1862 he was arrested and in 1863 he wrote his famous novel, *What Is To Be Done?* in prison. It was an inspiration to many later Russian revolutionaries, including Lenin. Later he was exiled to Siberia and returned in 1883. He died in Saratov.

Chernov, Viktor Mihailovich (1873–1952) was the leader of the SR Party. He was the editor of the newspaper *Revolutsionnaya Rossiya*. In 1905 he took part in the revolution and in 1908 he emigrated. After the 1917 February Revolution he returned to Russia. He was Minister for Agriculture in the Provisional Government. In 1918 he was the chairman of the Constituent Assembly. After the assembly was dissolved he went to Samara and presided at the meeting of members of the assembly.

After Kolchak's takeover he opposed him and was arrested. He was freed by the Czechs, then emigrated in 1920. In 1940 he moved to the United States.

Chicherin, Georgy Vasilievich (1872–1936) was a revolutionary, politician, and diplomat. He became a member of the RSDLP in 1905. A wealthy man, he financially supported revolutionary activities. After the October Revolution he was People's Commissar of Foreign Affairs. He was one of the advocates of the Brest-Litovsk Treaty.

Cornelissen, Chistiaan Gerardus (1864–1942) was a Dutch syndicalist writer, economist, and trade union activist. Living in France, he actively supported the 1914–1918 war.

Dalin (Levin), David Yulyevich (1889–1962) was a Menshevik publicist and politician. He participated in the student movement in Petrograd. He was arrested for a short time, then emigrated and got a doctoral degree at Heidelberg University. In 1917 he returned to Russia where he joined the Mensheviks. He condemned the October Revolution, and in 1921 he left the country. In 1940 he settled in the United States.

Dan (Gurvich), Fyodor Ilyich (1871–1947) was one of the leaders of the Menshevik Party and a physician. He was arrested and exiled several times. In exile he became friends with Lenin and Martov and later led the Menshevik faction in the Fourth State Duma. He did not participate in the October Revolution. He criticized the revolution, the Brest-Litovsk Treaty, and Bolshevik policy in general. In 1921 he was arrested and sent into exile in Berlin; after Hitler came to power he lived in Paris and then New York City.

Danielson (Nikolay-on), Nikolay Frantsevich (1844–1918) was a Russian economist. He was one of the first theoreticians of the Narodnik movement. He corresponded with Marx and in 1872 made the first translation of *Das Kapital* into Russian. He wrote several books on economics.

Denikin, Anton Ivanovich (1872–1947) was one of the foremost generals of the White Guard movement in the Russian civil war. He emigrated in 1920.

Dimanshtein, Semyon Markovich (1886–1939) was a revolutionary. In February 1918 he was appointed a head of Yevsektsia and the commissar for the Jewish matters at the People's Comissariat for Nationalities. In 1919 he was People's Commissar for Labor in the Lithuanian-Belarus SSR. In 1920 he worked as the People's Commissar of Nationalities of the Turkmenian Republic. Later in Moscow he headed different propaganda departments. In 1939 he was arrested and executed. He was rehabilitated in 1955.

Dubrovinsky, Yosif Fyodovich (1877–1913) was a revolutionary and Bolshevik. He participated in the 1905 Revolution. He was arrested several times and after his release he emigrated. At the Fifth Congress of the RSDLP he was elected to the Central Committee. In 1910 he returned to Russia where he was arrested again and sent into exile. He committed suicide because of his debilitating tuberculosis.

Dunayevskaya, Raya (1910–1987) was an American Marxist revolutionary of Ukrainian origin. In her childhood she emigrated to the United States with her parents. She was a member of the American Communist Party but was expelled at the age of eighteen with the charge of Trotskyism. In 1929 she joined the group of American Trotskyists in Boston. In 1937 and 1938 she worked as Trotsky's Russian-language secretary in Mexico. She broke with Trotsky after the Molotov-Ribbentrop Pact. Later she was a member of different communist organizations in the United States and published several theoretical Marxist books.

Durnovo, Piotr Nikolayevich (1843–1915) was a graduate of the Imperial Naval Law Academy. In 1884 he was appointed director of police. In 1900 he was appointed Assistant Minister of the Interior, in 1905 he became Minister of the Interior of the Tsarist Empire.

Dutov, Aleksandr Ilyich (1872–1921) was an ataman, general, and Cossack leader. He fought against the Bolsheviks as head of the All-Russia Cossack Army Union. In 1920 he emigrated to China where he was assassinated by a Bolshevik agent.

Dzerzhinsky, Feliks Edmundovich (1877–1926) was a revolutionary, Bolshevik, and Soviet politician. He was one of the founders of the Social Democracy of the Kingdom of Poland and Lithuania. He was involved in the 1905 Revolution and was arrested several times. He spent many years in prison and in exile. After the October Revolution he was a member of the Petrograd Military Revolutionary Committee, the director of the Cheka (GPU, OGPU). From 1919 to 1923 he was People's Commissar of Internal Affairs; in 1921 he was also People's Commissar for Transport. In 1924 he was chairman of the Supreme Soviet of National Economy.

Ehrenburg, Ilya Grigorievich (1891–1967) was a Soviet writer, publicist, war correspondent, and twice the winner of the Stalin Prize. He joined the Bolsheviks in 1905. He was arrested, freed, and later emigrated to France where he lived from 1921 to 1930. He was a correspondent for *Izvestiya*, and during the Spanish Civil War a correspondent in Spain. During the Second World War he wrote roughly 3,000 articles and reports. After the war he supported the work of the Jewish Anti-Fascist Committee. In 1950 he was elected deputy president of the World Peace Council. His novel *Thaw* (1954–56) became well known internationally.

Essen, Mariya Moiseevna (1872–1956) was a Social Democratic politician. She was a member of the Union for the Struggle for the Liberation of the Working Class. She became a member of the RCP(b) in 1920. She was active in Georgia as a party worker (1921–25), then lived in Moscow. She retired in 1955.

Fedoseyev, Nikolay Yevgrafovich (1869–1898) was one of the first Russian Marxist theoreticians. In 1888 he began to organize Marxist study groups in the Volga region. He died in exile.

Fotiyeva, Lidiya Aleksandrovna (1881–1975) was a Bolshevik politician. She became a member of the RSDLP(b) in 1904. In 1905 she emigrated to Geneva and Paris. She actively took part in three revolutions. Between 1918 and 1931 she became the secretary of the Council of People's Commissars and was simultaneously Lenin's secretary from 1918 to 1924. In 1938 she worked at the Central Lenin Museum, and from 1941 to 1945 worked for the International Red Aid (MOPR).

Frank, Semion Lyudvigovich (1877–1950) was a philosopher, religious thinker, and psychologist. He took part in publishing *Problemi idealizma* (1902), *Vekhi* (1909), and *Iz glubini* (1918). He supported the autocracy against the revolution. He wanted to synthesize rational thinking and religious faith on the basis of Christian Platonism.

Frunze, Mihail Vasilevich (1885–1925) was an army officer and Bolshevik revolutionary. He joined the RSDLP in 1904. In 1918 he was the military commissar of the Yaroslav Military Province. In 1919 he was appointed head of the Southern Army Group. From 1920 to 1922 he fought in Ukraine and Crimea as commander of the southern front. In 1925 he was appointed chairman of the Revolutionary Military Council, People's Commissar of War and Navy. He died during surgery and was buried in the Kremlin Wall Necropolis.

Ganetsky, Yakob Stanislavovich (1879–1937) was a revolutionary and Bolshevik politician. He studied at Berlin, Heidelberg, and Zurich universities. He became a member of the RSDLP in 1896. From 1903 to 1909 he was a member of the main administration of Social Democracy of the Kingdom of Poland and Lithuania. He took part in the revolution in Poland (1905–1907). He was one of the financial wizards of the Bolshevik Party. In 1917 he was active in the revolution; later he worked in different positions for the People's Commissariat for Finance and Foreign Affairs. In 1935 he was director of the Museum of the Revolution of the USSR. In 1937 he was arrested and executed during the great purges and was rehabilitated posthumously.

Gentile, Giovanni (1875–1944) was an Italian neo-Hegelian philosopher. He described himself as the "Philosopher of Fascism." His main work is *A Doctrine of Fascism* (1932). He was executed by partisans in 1944.

Gershenzon, Mihail (Meylekh) Osipovich (1869–1925) was a Russian literary specialist, philosopher, publicist, and translator. He was the editor of the famous essay collection *Vekhi* (1909) and wrote its preface. He was the Chair of the All-Russian Writers' Union, 1920–21.

Gessen, Vladimir Matveyevich (1868–1920) was a lawyer, jurist, and prominent leader of the Kadet Party. After the October Revolution he was head of the emigrant Kadet Party's right wing. He was editor of the White Guard journal *Rul*, published in Berlin.

Gippius, Zinaida Nikolayeva (1869–1945) was a poet, writer, and literary critic. She denounced the October Revolution. In 1920 she emigrated to France with her husband, the writer Mereshkovsky.

Glyasser, Mariya Ingateva (1890–1951) was a Bolshevik. She became a member of the RCP(b) in 1917. She worked at the secretariat of the Council of People's Commissars (1918–24), then for the Marx-Engels-Lenin Institute of the CC of the RCP(b).

Gorbunov, Nikolay Petrovich (1892–1937) was a Bolshevik politician and academician in chemistry. He became a member of RCP(b) in 1917 and was elected head of the Information Bureau of the All-Russia Central Executive Committee. In November 1917 he became secretary of the Council of People's Commissars and personal secretary to Lenin. In 1919 and 1920 he was assigned to political work in the Red Army serving as a member of the Revolutionary Military Council. Between 1923 and 1929 he was rector of the Moscow Higher Technical School. In 1935 he became permanent secretary of the Academy of Sciences of the USSR. On 19 February 1937 he was arrested and on 7 September, sentenced to death, and executed. He was rehabilitated in 1954.

Gorky (Peshkov), Aleksey Maksimovich (1869–1936) was a Soviet writer and playwright. He participated in the 1905 Revolution. From 1905 to 1917 he was a member of the RSDLP(b). From 1906 to 1913 he lived in emigration in the United States, and later in Capri, Italy, from which he wrote for *Zvezda* and *Pravda*. He published *Letopis*, a journal of his own. In 1917 he was critical of the Bolsheviks and the revolution, but a year later became sympathetic. From 1921 to 1931 he lived abroad, but after his return home he became a celebrated writer and president of the Soviet Writers Union. He died of tuberculosis in 1936.

Gramsci, Antonio (1891–1937) was an Italian Marxist theoretician. He was a founder of the Communist Party of Italy (CPI). In 1922 and 1923 he lived in Soviet Russia; in 1923 and 1924 was the leader of the CPI. In 1926 he was arrested and sentenced to twenty years in prison. He was released in 1937 and died soon after.

Gringmut, Vladimir Andreyevich (1851–1907) was in 1905 a founder of the organization Black Hundreds, the Russian monarchist union. In 1880 he published *Moskovskye vedomosty* (Moscow News) and edited it until his death.

Guchkov, Aleksandr Ivanovich (1862–1936) was a capitalist, the leader of the conservative Octobrist Party. In 1910 he was chairman of the Third State Duma. From 1907 to 1915 he was head of the Military-Industrial Committee. In 1917 he held the office of war and navy minister in the Provisional Government. He supported Kornilov's coup d'état. In 1920 he emigrated.

Guesde, Jules Basile (1845–1922) was a French socialist journalist and politician.

Gumilev, Nikolay Stepanovich (1886–1921) was a Russian poet and playwright. He was Anna Akhmatova's husband. Between 1918 and 1921 he was an outstanding figure in Petrograd literary life. On 3 August 1921 the Cheka arrested and executed him.

Herzen, Aleksandr Ivanovich (1812–1870) was a Russian philosopher. He was a member of the first generation of the Russian revolutionary democrats and founder of the Narodnik movement. Herzen, together with Chernysevsky and Ogaryov, created the secret revolutionary movement, *Liberty and Land*. From 1852 to 1864 he lived in exile in England. He was the editor of *Kolokol*.

Hobson, John Atkinson (1858–1940) was an British economist. He published several books on the crisis of modern capitalism and liberalism. In 1902 he published *Imperialism*, which had a great impact on many, including Lenin. In 1919 he joined the Independent Labour Party. He was a notable critic of the Labour government of 1929.

Hourwich, Isaac Aaronovich (1860–1924) was an American economist, statistician, and socialist activist. He supported the Russian Revolution. He taught statistics at the University of Chicago, and then was a professor at Columbia University. His main works are *The Economics of the Russian Village* (1892) and *Immigration and Labour* (1912).

Khrustalyev-Nosar, Georgy Stepanovich (1879–1918) was a working-class politician. He was in 1905 head of the St. Petersburg Soviet of Workers' Delegates. In 1906 he was exiled and lived in France. In 1914 he returned to Russia where he was arrested again. He supported the rightist Ukrainian nationalists Skoropadsky and Petliura and persecuted communists. He was executed in 1918.

Ilf-Petrov was the pen name of two Soviet prose authors: **Petrov, Yevgeny Petrovich (Katayev)** (1903–1942) and **Ilf, Ilya Arnoldovich (Faynzilberg)** (1897–1937). In 1928 they wrote the famous satirical novel *The Twelve Chairs*, a satire of the NEP period.

Ivanov, Andrey Vasilyevich (1888–1927) was a Bolshevik politician. He joined the RSDLP in 1906. In 1918 and 1919 he was the People's Commissar for Interior Affairs of the Ukrainian SSR. From 1920 to 1925 he was head of the Central Executive Committee of the Ukrainian SSR. From 1925 to 1927 he was the secretary of the Central Executive Committee of the Soviet Union, and a member of its presidium.

Ivanov, Vsevolod Vyacheslavovich (1895–1963) was a notable Soviet writer and playwright. His literary career was supported by Maxim Gorky. In 1947 he published his recollections, *Meetings with Maksim Gorky*.

Ivanova-Iranova, Yelena Aleksandrovna (1883–1937) was an SR revolutionary and terrorist. She was a member of the Central Committee of the SR Party. In 1918 she took part in a terrorist attack against Lenin. In 1937 she was arrested on fabricated charges and executed. She was rehabilitated in 1989.

Izgoyev (Lande), Aleksandr (Aron) Solomonovich (1872–1935) was a Kadet politician. He was among the authors of *Vekhi* (1909). From 1906 to 1918 he was a member of the Central Committee of the Kadet Party. He wrote the first biography of Stolypin. At the 8th Congress of the Kadet Party he attacked the government but supported Miliukov's foreign policy. After the October Revolution he was arrested several times. In 1922 he was deported to Germany with several famous writers. He lived in Estonia in his later years.

Kaledin, Aleksey Maksimovich (1861–1918) was a White general. He was ataman of the counterrevolutionary Don Cossack Army. After his army's situation had become hopeless, he resigned from his post and committed suicide.

Kalinin, Mikhail Ivanovich (1875–1946) was a Bolshevik revolutionary and Soviet politician who joined the RSDLP in 1898. He was one of the founders of *Pravda*, and was arrested several times. He took an active part in the February Revolution. From 1919 to 1938 he was the chairman of the All-Russia Central Executive Committee and simultaneously the chairman of the Central Executive Committee of the Soviet Union. From 1938 to 1946 he was a member of the presidium of the Supreme Council. He is buried in the Kremlin Wall Necropolis.

Kamenev (Rosenfeld), Lev Borisovich (1883–1936) was a Bolshevik revolutionary, Soviet politician, one of the leaders of the Bolshevik Party, and one of Lenin's political disciples. He studied at the Law Faculty of Moscow University and was expelled for his Social Democratic activities. He went to Paris, where he met Lenin and Trotsky's sister, Olga, whom he married. After returning to Russia he was arrested several times. In 1905 he became a member of the Central Committee. With Zinoviev and Lenin he edited *Proletary*, a Bolshevik newspaper. In 1918 he was member of the presidium of the All-Russia Central Executive Committee, in 1922 the deputy chairman of the Council of the People's Commissariat. In 1922 Lenin handed over his archival materials to him, and this became the basis of the Lenin Institute. From 1923 to 1926 he was the head of the institute. In 1925 Kamenev allied with Zinoviev, Krupskaya, and Grigory Sokolnikov; the alliance was known as the Leningrad Opposition. In 1927 he was expelled from the party but a year later was readmitted. In 1932 he was expelled again and sent to exile in Minusinsk. On 24 August 1936 he was sentenced to death and executed. He was rehabilitated on 13 June 1988 by the Supreme Court.

Kamo (Ter-Petrosyan), Simon Arshakovich (1882–1922) was one of the chief organizers of illegal revolutionary activities. From 1918 to 1920 he was the organizer of the illegal party in the Caucasus and southern Russia. He died in a road accident.

Kaplan, Fanni (Dora) Yefimova (1890–1918) joined the anarchists in 1905. She was known as Dora in revolutionary circles. In 1906 she was sentenced to death, which was later changed to life imprisonment and forced labor. During her years in prison she became closer to SR ideas. In 1917 she was released and sent to a sanatorium in Crimea because of poor health. On 30 August 1918 she attempted to assassinate Lenin. She was arrested, and on 3 September she was executed.

Karamzin, Nikolay Mikhailovich (1766–1826) was an historian and writer.

Kautsky, Karl (1854–1938) was one of the main figures of German Social Democracy, a theoretician, and emblematic figure of the so-called Centrist faction in the Second International. In 1883 he founded *Die Neue Zeit*, the theoretical journal of German Social Democracy, and worked for it until 1917. From 1885 to 1890 he was a close friend of Engels, and from 1905 he opposed the standpoint of the radical Marxists, for example, Rosa Luxemburg. At first he supported the First World War but later opposed it. He was an outspoken critic of the October Revolution.

Kerensky, Aleksandr Fyodorovich (1881–1970) was a Russian lawyer and politician. He was a member of the SR Party beginning in 1917. He worked as the Minister of Justice in the Provisional Government, and later as Minister of War and Navy. Between 8 July and 25 October 1917 he was prime minister, and at the same time, from 30 August, the general-in-chief of the army.

Klasson, Robert Eduardovich (1868–1926) was a Soviet electrical engineer and inventor. He helped to draft the plan for GOELRO (the State Commission for the Electrification of Russia). He died under mysterious circumstances.

Klyuchevsky, Vasily Osipovich (1841–1911) was an historian and academician.

Kokoshkin, Fyodor Fyodorovich (1871–1918) was a jurist and a founder and leader of the Kadet Party. He was professor of Political Law at Moscow University. On 28 November 1917 he was arrested; he was murdered by anarchist sailors on 7 January 1918.

Kolchak, Aleksandr Vasilyevich (1871–1920) was an admiral in the tsar's navy, oceanographer, and hydrologist. He took part in two Arctic expeditions (1900–03 and 1908–11). He fought in the Russo-Japanese War. In the First World War he was commander of the Black Sea fleet. During the civil war he was one of the leaders of the White Guard movement. He created a military dictatorship in Siberia. In the winter of 1918 and the summer of 1919 he started an offensive against Moscow to overthrow the Soviet power. He was defeated and executed in Irkutsk.

Kollontai, Aleksandra Mihaylovna (1872–1952) was a Bolshevik revolutionary and diplomat. She emigrated to Western Europe, and lived in Berlin, Paris, Copenhagen, and Stockholm. She was arrested several times. In 1915 she moved to Norway and later to New York City. She worked for the secretary of International Socialist Women. She took part in preparing the Zimmerwald international socialist conference. Returning to Russia in 1917 and 1918 she was People's Commissar for Social Welfare. In 1920 she became the head of the women's department of the RCP(b). She joined the Left Opposition faction; later she was one of the members of Workers' Opposition. In 1923 she was appointed Soviet ambassador to Norway, in 1926 to Mexico, and in 1927 she was accredited to Norway. From 1930 to 1945 she was ambassador to Sweden.

Kon, Feliks Yakovlevich (1884–1941) was a Polish Bolshevik activist. He joined the revolutionary movement in 1882. He was one of the leaders of the left faction in the Polish Socialist Party. He was arrested and in 1914 emigrated. In 1918 he helped create the Ukrainian Communist Party. He joined the RCP(b) in 1918. He had several state and party functions and in 1920 he was put on the Polish Provisional Revolutionary Committee during the Polish–Soviet war. In 1922 and 1923 he was secretary of the Executive Committee of the Comintern. Between 1927 and 1935 he was deputy head of the International Executive Committee of the Comintern.

Kondratyev, Nikolay Dmitrievich (1892–1938) was an economist. In 1905 he joined the SR Party. In 1905 he took part in the strike movement and was arrested. Later he studied law at Moscow University. He was active in the February Revolution, and in fall 1917 he published an article on the agrarian question and broke with the SR program: land could not be the property of anyone; the liberation of society would be the result of the nationalization of land. After the October Revolution he worked for some state and economic institutions. He elaborated the theory of fifty-year business cycles, also known as Kondratyev waves. In 1930 he was arrested on fabricated charges and sentenced to eight years in prison. On 17 September 1938 he was executed; he was rehabilitated in 1987.

Konoplyannikova, Zinaida Vasilyevna (1879–1906) was a revolutionary. She joined the SR Party in 1902 and was arrested several times. On 13 August 1906 she assassinated Major General G. A. Min. On 26 August the Court of the Petrograd Military District sentenced her to death.

Kornilov, Lavr Georgievich (1870–1918) was a tsarist general, and leader of the White forces. He fought in the Russo–Japanese War, then in the First World War. At the time of the revolution he was commander of the Petrograd Military District. He was one of the organizers of the White Volunteer Army. In August 1917 he started an unsuccessful endeavor ("Kornilov coup d'état"). On 31 March 1918 he was killed by a Soviet shell.

Korolenko, Vladimir Galaktionovich (1853–1921) was a writer. While studying in college, he was expelled for participating in revolutionary activities with the Narodnik movement. He was imprisoned and sentenced to exile. In 1896 he and N. K. Mikhaylovsky edited *Ruskoye Bogatstvo*, the Narodnik periodical. He was a member of the Russian Academy of Sciences but resigned in 1902 when Maxim Gorky was expelled as a member because of revolutionary activities. After the 1905 Revolution he protested against police atrocities in his writing. After the October Revolution he considered himself an independent socialist, and rejected both proletarian dictatorship and counterrevolution.

Kossovsky, Vladimir (1867–1941) was a Jewish politician. He was one of the founders and ideologists of *Bund*. From 1930 he lived in Warsaw, then emigrated to New York in 1939.

Krasin, Leonid Borisovich (1870–1926) was a revolutionary and Bolshevik politician. He joined the Social Democratic movement in 1890; in 1903 he was a member of the RSDLP. He was one of the editors of *Vperyod*. In 1912 he withdrew from political activities for many years. After the October Revolution he returned to the RCP(b). He was a member of the presidium of the Supreme Soviet of the People's Economy, the People's Commissar for Trade, Industry and Transport, and in 1921 the People's Commissar for Foreign Trade. He was envoy of the Soviet Union in London, 1920–23 and 1925–26.

Krasnov, Piotr Nikolayevich (1869–1947) was a writer, Cossack ataman, and White general. He was rewarded for bravery in the First World War several times. He took part in Kornilov's coup d'état. After the October Revolution he was arrested but later released. He fought in the Don region during the civil war, and after the White Army's defeat he emigrated to Germany. During the Second World War he collaborated with Nazi Germany, and in 1945 surrendered to British forces in Austria. He was handed over to the Soviets and was sentenced to death by the Military Collegium of the Supreme Court of the USSR.

Krilov, Ivan Andreyevich (1769–1844) was a poet and writer. His stories were translated into several languages.

Kropotkin, Piotr Alekseyevich (1842–1921) was a revolutionary, anarchist theoretician, and scientist. In the 1860s he took part in several expeditions to the Far East and eastern Siberia. He studied at the Faculty of Physics and Mathematics in St. Petersburg. In 1870 he was elected secretary of the Russian Geographical Society; later he worked for the Ministry of the Interior. He went to Sweden where he joined the First International. After returning to Russia he proclaimed his anarchist program. He was arrested, and after fleeing from the prison hospital, emigrated. With Bakunin's death he became the leading anarchist theoretician. In 1917, after forty years abroad, he returned to Russia. He did not oppose the October Revolution but criticized the terror. His main work is *Mutual Aid: A Factor of Evolution*.

Krupskaya, Nadezhda Konstantinovna (1869–1939) was a revolutionary and Bolshevik. She joined in the activities of Marxist circles in 1890. From 1891 to 1896 she was an instructor at a workers' school, and dealt with propaganda. Together with Lenin she took part in founding the Union for the Struggle for the Liberation of the Working Class. She was arrested but later allowed to join Lenin in Siberia, where they married. In 1902 she emigrated. From 1905 to 1907 she remained in Russia, then emigrated again. In April 1917 she and Lenin returned to Russia. From 1920 she organized the educational system, working for the People's Commissariat for Culture. In 1924 she was elected member of the Central Control Commission. At the 14th Congress she sided with the Zinoviev-Kamenev opposition, but later she voted for the exclusion of Trotsky, Zinoviev, and Kamenev from the party.

Kugelmann, Louis (Ludwig) (1828–1902) was a German physicist, Social Democratic theoretician, and activist. He was a close friend of Marx and Engels.

Kun, Béla (1886–1938) was a Hungarian communist politician. He founded the Hungarian Communist Party on 24 March 1918 during which time he built personal relations with Lenin and other Bolshevik leaders. In 1919 he was People's Commissar for Foreign Affairs, later People's Commissar for War of the Hungarian Soviet Republic. From 1920 he mostly lived in the Soviet Union. Between 1921 and 1936 he was a member of the Executive Committee of the Comintern. In 1938 he was arrested on fabricated charges, and on 29 August 1938 he was executed. He was rehabilitated in 1956.

Kursky, Dmitry Ivanovich (1874–1932) was a Bolshevik statesman and politician. He joined the RSDLP in 1904. He took an active part in the revolutions of 1905–07. From 1918 to 1928 he was People's Commissar for Justice of the RSFSR and the USSR. He was the first Soviet attorney general. In 1928 he was the Soviet Union's envoy to Italy.

Kuskova, Yekaterina Dmitriyevna (1869–1958) was a journalist. While involved in the radical activities of the mid-1890s she wrote the *Credo*, a manifesto of the revisionist Bernsteinian school. She took part in the 1905 Revolution. In 1917 her second husband, Prokopovich, was a member of the Provisional Government. After the October Revolution she lived in Moscow, and did not join any of the struggling parties; she made her living as a journalist. In 1922 she was forced to emigrate; she lived first in Prague, later in Geneva.

Kzhizhanovskiy, Gleb Maksimilianovich (1872–1959) was a revolutionary, Soviet politician, and academician. He took part in the activities of Marxist circles beginning in 1891. He was one of the leaders of the Union for the Struggle for the Liberation of the Working Class in Petrograd and a close friend of Lenin. He was active in the 1905 Revolution. After the 1917 revolutions he worked for the Supreme Soviet of the People's Economy, and from 1920 he worked for the GOELRO committee. From 1929 to 1939 he was the president of the Academy of Sciences of the Soviet Union. From 1937 to 1946 he was a representative of the Supreme Soviet.

Labriola, Antonio (1843–1904) was an Italian philosopher and Marxist theoretician. He was an activist in the Italian workers' movement.

Lafargue, Laura (1845–1911) was a French Socialist and activist in the workers' movement. She was a daughter of Karl Marx.

Lafargue, Paul (1842–1911) was a French Marxist, husband of Laura Marx, and close friend of Marx. He actively participated in the Paris Commune, then he emigrated to Spain. He returned to France and played a central role in the development of French socialism.

Lalayants, Issak Hristoforovich (1870–1933) was a revolutionary and Bolshevik. He was one of the founders of the Union for the Struggle for the Liberation of the Working Class. He was arrested several times. From 1914 to 1917 he worked as a statistician in Irkutsk. In 1922 he was head of the

Political Enlightenment Division of the RSFSR. In 1929 he retired.

Landau, Grigory Adolfovich (1877–1941) was a Russian philosopher, critic, publicist, and politician. He was a member of the Central Committee of the Kadet Party. He was a leader of the Jewish democratic group. In 1919 he moved to Germany, and from 1922 to 1931 was deputy editor of the journal *Rul* in Berlin. In 1933 he moved to Estonia and worked for the journal *Segodnya*. He was arrested in 1940 and died in a labor camp.

Larin, Yury (1882–1932) was a Social Democratic politician. He took part in the revolutionary movement beginning in 1900 and joined the Mensheviks. In February 1917 he was a leader of the group of Menshevik Internationalists; later he joined the Bolshevik Party. In 1918 he was a member of the Supreme Soviet of National Economy, and in practice was the head of the presidium. He had an active role in reconstructing and managing the economy, and also in collectivization. He was a founder of the Public Planning Institute. His daughter Anna was Bukharin's wife. He is buried in the Kremlin Wall Necropolis.

Latsis, Martin Ivanovich (Yan Fridrihovich Sudrabs) (1888–1938) was a Bolshevik revolutionary. He joined the party in 1905. In 1917 he was a member of the Petrograd Military Revolutionary Committee. He was one of the leaders of the Cheka. He was arrested on fabricated charges and executed in 1938, rehabilitated in 1956.

Lefebvre, Henri (1901–1991) was a French sociologist and Marxist philosopher.

Lengnik, Fridrikh Vilgelmovich (1873–1936) was a revolutionary and a Soviet politician. He took part in the revolutionary movement beginning in 1893; he was a member of the Union for the Struggle for the Liberation of the Working Class. He was a member of the RSDLP from the beginning. He was arrested and sent into exile. From 1905 to 1917 he worked as a party activist. He participated in the October Revolution, then worked in different party posts.

Lepeshinsky, Panteleymon Nikolayevich (1868–1944) was a revolutionary, Bolshevik politician, and historian. He was a member of the RSDLP from 1898. He took an active part in the activities of the Union for the Struggle for the Liberation of the Working Class. He was sentenced to exile in Yenisey Province with V. I. Lenin. He emigrated, later returned to Russia and participated in the 1905 Revolution. From 1918 to 1920 he worked in the People's Commissariat of Education. He was founder of the International Red Aid (MOPR), and in 1925 was also its chairman. From 1927 he was director of the Historical Museum, and director of the Museum of the Revolution (1935–36).

Levi, Paul (1883–1930) was a German communist politician and lawyer. He joined the German Social Democratic Party in 1906. He was a lawyer for Rosa Luxemburg and her comrades several times. He was leader of the Spartacus League. After the Spartacist revolt he was the general secretary of the German Communist Party. In 1920 he headed the German delegation to the Second World Congress of the Communist International in Moscow. Following the failure of the uprising in March 1921, Levi was expelled from the Communist Party for publicly criticizing party policies. He soon formed the Communist Working Collective, and later reentered the Social Democratic Party. He died in 1930 after he fell from his window and succumbed to injuries.

Liebknecht, Karl (1871–1919) was a German Social Democratic politician and lawyer. He joined the German Social Democratic Party in 1900. He was the first Social Democratic member of the Reichstag to openly oppose the war. Imprisoned in 1916, he was cofounder with Rosa Luxemburg and other left Social Democrats of the Spartacus League, transformed in 1918 into the Communist Party of Germany. In January 1919, during the Spartacist uprising, he was captured and murdered by officers of the White Freilcorps.

Liebknecht, Wilhelm (1826–1900) was a German Social Democratic politician and close friend of Karl Marx. He was one of the founders of the German Social Democratic Party. He was Karl Liebknecht's father.

Litvinov, Maksim Maksimovich (1876–1951) was a member of the RSDLP from 1898. In 1918 he was a member of the Collegium of the People's Commissariat for Foreign Affairs. In 1921 he was elected deputy People's Commissar of Foreign Affairs. In 1930 he was People's Commissar for Foreign Affairs. In 1934 and in 1939 he was elected member of the Central Committee. From 1934 to 1938 he was the representative of the Soviet Union in the League of Nations. He was a deputy Commissar for Foreign Affairs (1944–47) and took part in the peace treaty negotiations.

Lobov, Semion Semionovich (1888–1937) was a member of the Bolshevik Party beginning in 1913. In 1924 he was elected member of the Central Committee. From 1926 to 1930 he was a member of the Supreme Soviet of the National Economy and commissar of the forestry industry of the USSR from 1932 to 1936. In 1937 he was arrested and executed.

Lordkipanidze, Grigol (1881–1937) was a Georgian politician and author. In 1917 he was active in the struggles for Georgian independence. He was minister of education and minister of war in the independent Georgian Menshevik government. As a result, he was arrested in 1921 and deported to Suzhdal. He was released in 1928. In 1929 he was arrested again and sentenced to exile. He was executed in 1937.

Lukács, György (1885–1971) was a philosopher, aesthetician, professor, and one of the main figures of twentieth-century Marxist thinking. He was a founding member of the Sunday Circle (*Vasárnapi Kör*) and Galilei Circle (*Galilei Kör*). He published his writings in *Nyugat, Huszadik Század,* etc. In 1910 he published his first book, *Soul and Form (Lélek és a formák)*. He lived in Berlin until 1911, and in Heidelberg from 1912 to 1917. In 1918 he joined the Communist Party of Hungary. In 1919, during the Hungarian Soviet Republic, he was deputy minister of culture; from 3 April he was People's Commissar; and in May and June he was Commissar of the Fifth Division of the Hungarian Red Army. After the fall of the Hungarian Soviet Republic he fled to Vienna where he became a member of the Provisional Central Committee of the Communist Party of Hungary. He and Jenő Landler were in a faction against Béla Kun. In 1921 he took part in the Third Congress of the Comintern in Moscow. He settled in Moscow. He worked for the Marx-Engels-Lenin Institute. On 29 June 1941 he was arrested by the NKVD and held for some weeks. After the war, in August 1945, he returned to Budapest. He was a member of the Hungarian Academy of Sciences from 1948. In 1949–50 the so-called Lukács Debate took place. On 26 October 1956 he was appointed minister of public education. In 1956 he was arrested by Soviet authorities and deported to Romania. On 11 April 1957 he was allowed to return home. He lived in inner emigration and published his works only in Western Europe. In 1967 he joined the Hungarian Socialist Workers' Party. He was awarded the Kossuth Prize (1948, 1955).

Lunacharsky, Anatoly Vasilyevich (1875–1933) was a Bolshevik politician of education, aesthetician, art critic, writer, and translator. In 1892, as a student of the Kiev Gymnasium he joined the workers' movement. From 1895 to 1898 he lived in Zurich where he met Plekhanov and Akselrod. In 1898 he returned to Moscow, where he was arrested for disseminating illegal propaganda and was imprisoned. He was released in 1904, and moved to Western Europe. He published in *Vperyod* and *Proletary*. He was active in the 1905 Revolution, and was arrested. In the summer of 1907 he emigrated again and joined Bogdanov; later he joined the *Vperyod* group (1909). For a while he was the ideologist of the so-called God-builders. He represented the Bolsheviks at the Stuttgart (1907) and Copenhagen (1910) congresses of the Second International. In August 1917 he joined the Bolshevik Party. After the October Revolution he served as People's Commissar for Education (1917–1929), then appointed ambassador to Spain.

Luxemburg, Rosa (1871–1919) was an internationalist revolutionary, Marxist theoretician, economist, and Social Democratic politician and propagandist. In 1893 she played a key role in creating the Social Democracy of the Kingdom of Poland and Lithuania. In 1898 she joined the Social Democratic Party of Germany and became a leader of the left wing of German socialism. She was imprisoned for her opposition to the war in 1915. She cofounded the Spartacus League with Karl Liebknecht, which became the Communist Party of Germany in 1918. She was one of the leaders of the Spartacist uprising, and in January 1919 she and Karl Liebknecht were murdered by counterrevolutionary army officers.

Lyadov, Martin Nikolayevich (Mandelstam) (1872–1947) became a member of the Bolshevik Party in 1903. In 1909 he joined the Mensheviks, and in 1920 returned to the Bolsheviks. He was head of the GLAVTOP and the oil industry in Baku. From 1923 to 1929 he was rector of the Sverdlov Communist University. In 1930 he was appointed director of the Archives of the October Revolution. He published works on party history.

Makhno, Nestor Ivanovich (1889–1934) was a Ukrainian anarchist revolutionary and partisan commander. He joined the anarchists during the Revolution of 1905. In 1908 he was sentenced to death by hanging, which was commuted to life imprisonment. He was released after the February Revolution in 1917. When he returned home he organized peasants' movements to distribute land among the peasants. He organized peasant guerilla bands, the core of the Makhnovshcsina being Taganrog and the neighboring region. In 1918 he went to Moscow where he met Lenin. He fought against both White and Red forces. He emigrated and died abroad.

Malinovsky, Roman Vasilievich (1876–1918) joined the RSDLP in 1906. He was an agent for the Okhrana from 1911. In 1912 he was a member of the Central Committee, and the Bolshevik representative of the Fourth State Duma. Suspected of being a spy, he was expelled from the party. He fled Russia in 1914 and was deported to an internment camp in Germany. In 1918 he returned to Russia. After a trial he was sentenced to death and executed.

Malov, Piotr Pavlovich (1867–1946) was a Social Democrat, economist, and Menshevik politician. He wrote several books on the agrarian question. After the October Revolution he gave up politics and studied agrarian history, economic development, and education.

Manuilsky, Dmitry Zaharovich (1883–1959) was a politician and a military official. He emigrated in 1907, and was member of the *Vperyod* group. In 1919 he was People's Commissar of Land in the Ukraine. In 1921 he was first secretary of the Ukraine. From 1928 to 1943 he was secretary of the Executive Committee of the Comintern. From 1942 to 1944 he worked at the General Political Department of the Soviet Army. He was a member of the Supreme Soviet of the USSR (1947–54).

Marhlevsky, Julian-Baltazar Yozefovich (1866–1925) was a Polish Bolshevik revolutionary and close associate of Rosa Luxemburg. He was among the founders of the Comintern. In 1920 he was a member of the Polish Bolshevik Provisional Government.

Martinov-Piker, Aleksandr Samoylovich (1865–1935) was a member of the Narodnik movement in the 1880s. During his university years in Petrograd he was arrested several times; later he was sentenced to exile in Odessa and Kolominsk until 1899. He joined the RSDLP in 1900. From 1905 to 1907 he played an active part in the revolutions. As a Menshevik leader he opposed the Bolsheviks in 1917. From 1918 to 1922 he worked as a teacher and abandoned politics. In 1922 he joined the Bolshevik Party. He was professor of the Marx-Engels Academy; later he edited the newpaper *Krasnaya Nov*. In 1933 he worked for the Comintern.

Martov, Yuliy (Yuly Osipovich Zederbaum) (1873–1923) was a Marxist Social Democratic revolutionary, politician, and publicist, the leading figure of the Menshevik faction of the Russian Social Democratic Labor Party. He became close to the revolutionary movement in Vilna (Vilnius) as a member of the *Bund*. From the beginning he was a close colleague of Vladimir Lenin. The two politicians founded the Union for the Struggle for the Liberation of the Working Class, and for this he was exiled in 1898. He was one of the founding members of *Iskra*, but his political connections with Lenin were practically broken at the Second Congress. During the First World War he was the leader of the left faction of the Menshevik Party. After October 1917 he opposed the Bolshevik power, though during the civil war he supported the Red Army against the Whites. He emigrated to Germany where he organized *Sotsialistichesky Vestnik*, a journal of Menshevik thought.

Mayakovsky, Vladimir Vladimirovich (1893–1930) was a revolutionary and poet. He was 15 years old when he joined the RSDLP. He became in the 1920s the leading literary figure of the Soviet Union. On 14 April 1930 he committed suicide in his home in Moscow.

Mehring, Franz (1846–1919) was a German Social Democratic Party politician. He joined the SDP in 1890, and became well known as a Marxist theoretician. Later he was a leader of the Spartacus League, then a founding member of the Communist Party of Germany.

Menzhinsky, Vyacheslav Rudolfovich (1874–1934) joined the RSDLP in 1902; he was a Bolshevik. He took part in the 1905 Revolution. In 1907 he emigrated and returned to Russia after the February Revolution in 1917. He was active in the October Revolution. In 1918–19 he was consul general in Berlin. In 1919 he became a member of the presidium of the Cheka. After Feliks Dzerzhinsky's death he became chairman of the OGPU.

Mgeladze, Illarion Vissarionovich ("Vardin") (1890–1941) was a member of the RSDLP from 1906. He was one of the leaders of the Saratov party organization, and editor of the *Social-Demokrat*. In 1919 he published his writings in *Pravda* and *Izvestiya*. During the civil war he was the head of the political division of the First Red Cavalry. In 1925 he was chairman of RAPP, the Union of Proletarian Writers. He was member of the Left Opposition. In 1927 he was expelled from the party as a member of the Trotskyist opposition. In 1929 he rejoined the party. In 1935 he was arrested and in 1941 he was executed.

Mikhaylovsky, Nikolay Konstantinovich (1842–1904) was a Russian literary critic and journalist, one of the ideologues of the Narodnik movement. He came from an impoverished gentry family and studied at the Mining Institute in Petrograd. He started working as a journalist in 1860. From 1868 to 1884 he published in the popular Petersburg literary magazine *Otechestvenniye Zapiski*. He became editor of the journal *Ruskaya Ekonimka* in 1892.

Miliukov, Pavel Nikolayevich (1859–1943) was a Russian liberal historian and politician. He was one of the founders and leaders of the Kadet Party. He was a member of the Third and Fourth State Duma. Between March and November 1917 he was minister of Foreign Affairs in Prince Lvov's Provisional Government. After the October Revolution he supported Kornilov. In 1919 he emigrated to Paris.

Minin, Nikita (Nikon) (1605–1681) was a Russian patriarch. He unsuccessfully tried to subordinate the Russian state to the Orthodox Church. His reforms based on Greek models resulted in the great schism known as *Raskol* in the Russian Orthodox Church.

Mirbach-Harff, Wilhelm Graf von (1871–1918) was the leader of the German delegation at the Brest-Litovsk peace negotiations. In 1918 he was ambassador in Moscow where he fell victim to a terrorist attack in July 1918.

Molotov, Vyacheslav Mikhaylovich (Skryabin) (1890–1986) was a party member from 1906, and a Bolshevik. In 1917 he was the head of the Press Bureau of the Central Committee. In 1920–21 he was the secretary of the Ukrainian Central Committee. In 1921 he became a member of the Soviet Central Committee. Between 1926 and 1957 he was a member of the Politburo. He was a close coworker of Stalin. From 1930 to 1941 he was chairman of Council of People's Commissars. He was People's Commissar (later Minister) of Foreign Affairs (1939–49). Between 1946 and 1953 he was deputy premier. From 1953 to 1956 he was minister of foreign affairs again. In 1961 he was removed from all his positions and expelled from the party.

Muralov, Nikolay Ivanovich (1877–1937) was a military leader and a revolutionary. He joined the RSDLP in 1903 as a Bolshevik. In 1905 he took part in the revolution. In 1917 he was one of the founders of the Military Section of the Moscow soviet, and the military leader of the Moscow armed uprising. In 1917 he was commander of the Moscow district; in 1924 he was commander of the northern Caucasian district. He became member of the Central Committee in 1925. In 1927 he was expelled from the CC. As a former member of the Trotskyist Left Opposition he was sentenced to death on fabricated charges and executed in 1937.

Muranov, Matvey Konstantinovich (1873–1959) was a member of the Bolshevik Party from 1904. In 1912 he was a member of the Duma. He was arrested and exiled because of revolutionary activities. In 1917 he was a member of the editorial board of *Pravda*. He took part in the October Revolution. In 1917 he was elected deputy commissar of the interior. From 1919 to 1924 he was a member of the Central Committee. In 1923 he became a member of the Supreme Court. He retired in 1939.

Nadson, Semyon Yakovlevich (1862–1887) was a popular Russian poet.

Nechayev, Sergey Gennadiyevich (1847–1882) was a Russian revolutionary. He set forth the creation and operation of a secret revolutionary organization. In 1868–69 he participated in the revolutionary student movement in St. Petersburg. He died in prison.

Nekrasov, Nikolay Alekseyevich (1821–1878) was a Russian Narodnik poet and journalist.

Nikholay I (1796–1855) was the Russian tsar between 1825 and 1855. He was one of the most reactionary of the Russian monarchs. He suppressed the revolutions of 1848–49 on the European continent.

Nogin, Viktor Pavlovich (1878–1926) was a correspondent for *Iskra* in 1901. He joined the Bolshevik Party in 1903. He was active in the revolutions of both 1905 and 1917. Later he worked in several leading posts.

Nolde, Boris Emmanuilovich (1876–1948) was a politician, jurist, diplomat, historian, and literary critic. After graduating from the Law Faculty of Moscow University he worked in the Ministry of Foreign Affairs. He taught law at different institutions. He was a colleague of the Minister of Foreign Affairs in the Provisional Government. In the summer of 1919 he emigrated. At the Sorbonne, Paris, he organized the Russian Department and was the dean of Law Faculty of the Institute for Slavic Studies. He was head of the Directorate General of the Russian Red Cross in Paris. In 1947 he was chairman of the International Institute of Law.

Noskov, V. A. (Boris Nikolayevich Glebov) (1878–1913) was a revolutionary. He was a member of the Union for the Struggle for the Liberation of the Working Class. He took part in the preparations for the Second Congress of the RSDLP.

Noulens, Joseph (1864–1939) was French ambassador to Russia in 1917.

Okudzhava, Bulat (1924–1997) was a Soviet poet, writer, and singer.

Olminsky (Aleksandrov), Mikhail Stepanovich (1863–1933) was a revolutionary, politician, and historian, one of the leaders of the *narodovolets* organization. He participated in the revolutionary movement in the 1880s. He joined the RSDLP in 1898. He was on the editorial board of *Vperjod* and *Proletary*, and took part in the activities of *Zvezda* and *Pravda*. He played an active role in the October Revolution. He was head of Istpart (Department of History) in the party, and the founder of the newspaper *Proletarskaya Revolutsiya*. He was a member of the directorate of Lenin University. From 1920 to 1924 he was director of the Institute of Party History, and the chairman of the Society of Old Bolsheviks.

Ordzhonikidze, Grigory Konstantinovich (Sergo) (1886–1937) was a Bolshevik politician. He joined the party in 1903. He was military commissar, plenipotentiary of the Transcaucasian Republic (1918–20). In 1926 he became a member of the Central Control Committee, and People's Commissar for Supervision of Workers and Peasants. In 1930 he was elected to the Politburo. In 1932 he was appointed People's Commissar for heavy industry. He committed suicide after Pyatakov's arrest.

Osinsky, N. (Valerian Valerianovich Obolensky) (1887–1938) was a communist revolutionary, a "leftist" communist. From March 1918 he worked for the Supreme Soviet of the National Economy. He was on the editorial board of *Pravda*. In 1920–21 he was one of the leading figures of "democratic centralism," a party faction. He was chairman of the Supreme Soviet of the National Economy, and from 1923 he had several important party and state posts. He was executed on fabricated charges.

Pannekoek, Anton (1873–1960) was a Dutch astronomer, astrophysicist, and socialist politician. He was the main theorist of the so-called Council on Communism. He joined the Social Democratic Workers' Party of the Netherlands in 1901. He founded *Tribune* in 1907. In 1909 he left the party. From 1906 to 1914 he was an active member of the Social Democratic Party of Germany. He worked for *Die Neue Zeit*. In 1914 he became a member of the ISD (International Socialists of Germany), which later reorganized as IKD (International Communists of Germany). During the war he was the founder of *Vorbote*, the journal of the Zimmerwald socialists. From 1918 to 1921 he was a member of the Communist Workers' Party of the Netherlands; in 1921 he left the party. In 1925 he was appointed professor at the University of Amsterdam and became a member of the Academy of Sciences. He is the author of *Lenin as Philosopher* (1938).

Parvus (Aleksandr Izrail Lazarevich Gelfand) (1867–1924) was a German socialist and theoretician of Russian origin. He developed the concept of permanent revolution that Trotsky further expanded. He went to Turkey and was an advisor to the leaders of the "Young Turks." As a result of his military trade manipulations Lenin broke connections with him.

Pasternak, Boris Leonidovich (1890–1960) was a Russian-Soviet poet and writer. He worked for *Lef*, Mayakovsky's avant-garde journal. In 1958 he was awarded the Nobel Prize for Literature for his novel, *Doctor Zhivago,* which he wrote between 1948 and 1955. The book was first published in Italian in 1957 followed by a Russian language edition financed by the CIA. Under pressure from Soviet authorities he refused to accept the prize.

Perovskaya, Sofia Lvovna (1853–1881) was a revolutionary and a member of *Narodna Volya*. In 1870 she joined anarchist groups in the Samara and Tver provinces. In 1873 she returned to St. Petersburg and maintained conspiracy apartments for secret anti-tsarist meetings. In 1874 she was arrested and put on house arrest. In 1877 she was arrested again but then went into hiding. She took part in the unsuccessful attempts against the tsar in 1879 and 1880. She reorganized her group, and managed to assassinate Tsar Alexander II in 1881. She was sentenced to death by hanging.

Peters, Yakob Hristoforovich (1886–1938) joined the Latvian Bolshevik Party in 1904. He participated in the 1905 Revolution. He emigrated to England, in 1917 he returned to Russia and was active in the 1917 Revolution. In 1917 he was elected a leading member of the Cheka. In 1918 he was Dzherzhinsky's deputy. He took part in the struggles against the Interventionist armies. In 1925 he was inspector general of the frontier guard armies. Between 1930 and 1934 he was a member of the Central Control Commission. In 1938 he was arrested and executed on fabricated charges.

Petliura, Simon Vasilyevich (1879–1926) was a founding a member of the Ukrainian Social Democratic Labor Party (1905). Before the First World War he edited and published two socialist weeklies. In 1914 he served as an officer in the tsarist army. In 1917 he was a member of the Central Rada, the ataman of the army of the Ukrainian People's Republic, in 1918 the head of the directorate. He cooperated with the German forces to fight against the Bolsheviks. During his term as head of state (1919–20) pogroms continued to be perpetrated on Ukrainian territory. In 1920 he signed an alliance with the Warsaw government to overthrow the Bolshevik regime. He emigrated to Western Europe, and was assassinated in Paris.

Petrovsky, Grigory Ivanovich (1878–1958) was a Bolshevik revolutionary, politician, and statesman. He joined the party in 1897. In 1914 he was arrested since he was a member of the Bolshevik faction of the State Duma, and was sentenced to exile in Turuhansk in 1915. Between 1919 and 1938 he served as chairman of the All-Ukrainian Central Executive Committee. In 1940 he was made deputy director of the Museum of the Revolution and never returned to politics.

Pilnyak, Boris (Boris Andreyevich Vogau) (1894–1937) was a Soviet symbolist author, short story writer, and one of the influential figures of Soviet literature in the 1920s. His main works are *Naked Year* and *Spilled Time*. He was arrested on fabricated charges and executed.

Pilsudski, Jozef (Klemens) (1867–1935) was a Polish nationalist military leader, politician, and statesman. He was the first head of state for the new independent Poland (1918–22). He started his political career as a member of the Polish Socialist Party and ended up as an authoritarian dictator of Poland (1926–35). In the spring of 1920 he attacked Soviet Russia.

Platten, Fritz (1883–1944) was a Swiss communist politician. He took part in the 1905 Revolution. He returned to Switzerland, where in 1912 he was the secretary of the Swiss Social Democratic Party. During the First World War he pursued antiwar politics. He helped Lenin's return to Russia in 1917 by making use of his political connections. In 1918 he shielded Lenin with his own body when their car came under fire in Petrograd. He was a member of the presidium of the Communist International in 1919 and later of the Comintern. In 1921 he founded the Swiss Communist Party and became general secretary. In 1923 he settled in the Soviet Union and taught at universities. In 1938 he was arrested and moved to prison camp, and in 1944 he was shot.

Plehve (Pleve), Vyacheslav Konstantinovich (1846–1904) was an extremely conservative Russian politician. From 1879 he served in different posts at the state administration, in 1899 he was Actual Privy Counsellor. In 1902 he was appointed Minister of the Interior and chief of the Gendarmes.

Plekhanov, Georgy Valentinovich (1856–1918) was a theoretician, a philosopher, the "Father of Russian Marxism." He was born into the family of a small-scale landlord. In 1873 he studied at the Konstantinov Military Academy in Voronezh, then enrolled at the Metallurgical Institute in St. Petersburg. He soon abandoned his studies and turned to the Narodnik revolutionary movement. In 1880 he emigrated to Western Europe. In 1883 he founded the first Russian Marxist group. He also took part in the creation of RSDLP and the newspaper *Iskra*. He was one of the leading figures of the Menshevik faction. He opposed the October Revolution.

Pokrovsky, Mikhail Nikolayevich (1868–1932) was a historian, one of the founders of Soviet Marxist historiography. He joined the party in 1905 as a Bolshevik. After the 1905 Revolution he emigrated and was affiliated with the *Vpered* group. He opposed the war, and edited Lenin's *Imperialism* for publication. He became one of the leaders of the October Revolution in Moscow. From 1918 to 1932 he was vice commissar for education. In 1922 he was appointed director of the Central Archives. He is buried by the Kremlin Wall.

Pospelov, Piotr Nikolayevich (1898–1979) was a Bolshevik Party ideologist. He joined the RSDLP in 1916. During the civil war he worked underground in the Urals. In 1924 he worked for the Central Committee. In 1931 he became an editor of *Bolshevik* and *Pravda*. He was elected a member of the Central Committee and was editor of *Pravda* from 1940 to 1949. From 1953 to 1960 he was secretary of the CC. He was director of the Marx-Engels-Lenin Institute. From 1967 to 1979 he was a member of the presidium of the USSR Academy of Sciences.

Potresov, Aleksandr Nikolayevich (1869–1934) was a Russian Social Democratic revolutionary. He was one of the leaders of the Mensheviks before October 1917. In the 1890s he joined the Marxists. He was one of the founders of the Union for the Struggle for the Liberation of the Working Class. In 1900 he took part in editing *Iskra*. In 1917 he was a supporter of the Provisional Government; he condemned the October Revolution and went into exile. In 1919 he was arrested; in 1925 he was allowed to move abroad.

Preobrazhensky, Yevgeniy Alekseyevich (1886–1937) was a Bolshevik revolutionary, economist, and theoretician. He joined the party in 1903. In 1918 he was chairman of the presidium of the Ural Regional Committee. He was elected a member of the CC in 1920, as an expert on economic financial questions. In 1923 he joined the Left Opposition led by Trotsky. He was expelled from the party first in 1927, and again in 1933 after he had been restored. In 1936 he was arrested, sentenced to death, and shot in 1937.

Prokopovich, Sergey Nikolayevich (1871–1955) was an economist and politician. First he was a Social Democrat; later, in 1905, he joined the Kadet Party, but he soon left it. In 1917 he was Minister of Industry and Trade in the Provisional Government. From 1918 he pursued anti-Bolshevik politics and as a consequence was arrested in 1922 and sent into exile.

Proudhon, Pierre-Joseph (1809–1865) was a French socialist writer and journalist, considered among the most influential theorists and organizers of anarchism. In 1840 he published *What Is Property?*, in 1846 *The System of Economic Contradictions or the Philosophy of Poverty*. In 1847 he became a Freemason. He took part in the 1848 French revolution, and later worked for newspapers. He was an anti-Semite and misogynist.

Pugachev, Yemelyan Ivanovich (ca. 1742–1775) was an illiterate Don Cossack and leader of the greatest Cossack and peasant insurrection. He fought in the Russian Army in the last battles of the Seven Years' War (1756–63), later in the campaign in Poland in 1764, and in the Russian-Turkish war (1768–74). During the siege of Bender (1769–70) he was wounded and returned home. In 1772 he was arrested as a fugitive and sentenced to exile in Siberia. He managed to flee. In June 1773 he claimed to be the dead Tsar Peter IV and sought to overthrow Tsarina Catherine II. He gathered his army consisting of peasants, Old Believers, and mineworkers from the Ural-Volga region. He proclaimed to free the serfs, to overthrow Catherina II, and to form a Cossack-peasant state. In 1775 he was beheaded in Moscow.

Purishkevich, Vladimir Mitrofanovich (1870–1920) was a Bessarabian Russian nobleman and politician noted for his extreme right-wing and anti-Semitic views. He was one of the founders of the reactionary organizations Black Hundreds and the Union of the Russian People Party (1905). Before 1917 these organizations were known for their violent attacks against leftists, Social Democrats, and Jews. He was elected as a deputy for the First, Second and Fourth State Duma. During the 1917 Revolution he was arrested by the Red Guard and under unknown circumstances escaped from the Peter and Paul Fortress and went to southern Russia, which was controlled by the White Army. He tried to reorganize the Black Hundreds movement. He died from typhus in Novorossiysk.

Pyatakov, Georgiy (Yuriy) Leonidovich (1890–1937) was a Bolshevik, a member of the party from 1910, and one of the "leftist" communists. In 1912 he joined the Bolsheviks. He was the leader of the Kiev Bolsheviks. After 1917 he took part in the organization of the Red Army in the Ukraine. In 1918 he was head of the State Bank. From 1923 to 1927 he was a member of the Central Committee. In 1927 he was forced to resign from all his posts and was expelled from the party. After revising his opinion (as a party member again) he was again head of the State Bank in 1929. In 1930 he was deputy People's Commissar for heavy industry, one of the organizers of industrialization. In 1934 he was elected a member of the Central Committee. In 1936 he was arrested, sentenced to death, and executed.

Radchenko, Stepan Ivanovich (1869–1911) was a Russian revolutionary and engineer. He was a member of the revolutionary group led by Brusnev from 1890. He was one of the founders of the Union for the Struggle for the Liberation of the Working Class. In 1906 he withdrew from political life.

Radek, Karl Berngardovich (Karl Sobelsohn) (1885–1941?) was a highly intelligent journalist, Bolshevik Party leader, and one of the main figures of the Comintern. He joined the Social Democracy of the Kingdom of Poland and Lithuania in 1904 and took part in the 1905 Revolution in Warsaw. He moved to Germany and joined the Social Democratic Party of Germany in 1907, and became a leading journalist in SPD papers. From 1918 to 1919 he was a vice commisar for Foreign Affairs. From 1920 he was a member of the Executive Committee of the Comintern and of the Central Committee. As part of the Left Opposition he was removed from the Central Committee in 1924 and in 1927 was expelled from the party. After signing a document capitulating to Stalin he became head of the International Information Bureau of the Central Committee and an editor of *Izvestiya,* and again a party member. In 1937 he was arrested and sentenced in the second great political trial. He died in a labor camp.

Radzutak, Yan Ernestovich (1887–1938) was a revolutionary and a communist politician. He became a member of the arty in 1905. Between 1920 and 1937 he was a member of the Central Committee. In 1926 he was elected to the Politburo, and made deputy chairman of the People's Commissariat. From 1924 to 1930 he was People's Commissar for Transport. From 1931 to 1934 he was chairman of the Central Control Commission, and a member of the Workers' and Peasants' Inspection. In 1938 he was arrested, sentenced to death, and executed.

Rahya, Ivan Abramovich (1887–1920) was a Bolshevik politician. He joined the RSDLP in 1902. He took part in the 1905 Revolution. He was active in the February Revolution in 1917. In 1918 he was one of the founders of the Communist Party of Finland. He was murdered in Petrograd by White Guardists.

Rakovsky, Christian Georgevich (1873–1941) was a Bulgarian Bolshevik revolutionary, statesman, and physician. He was active in Bulgarian, Romanian, and Russian revolutionary politics, and in 1917 he became a leading figure in the Bolshevik faction of RSDLP as head of the Ukrainian People's Commissariat. He was Soviet ambassador to France from 1925 to 1927. He was a member of the Left Opposition; he was arrested in 1938 and sentenced to imprisonment. In 1941 he was executed.

Rasputin, Grigory Yemifovich (Grigory Yefimovich Novikh) (1872?–1916) was a Russian Orthodox Christian, mystic, and swindler of Siberian peasant origin. He became a monk and was said to possess the ability to heal through prayer, and to give some relief to Tsarevich Aleksey Nikholayevich, who suffered from hemophilia. He soon became an influential favorite of Nikholay II and Tsarina Aleksandra. He was accused by many eminent persons of various misdeeds ranging from sexual debauchery to undue political domination over the royal family. In 1911 and 1914 there were attempts to kill him, but both failed. He was murdered in 1916.

Razin, Stenka (Stepan Timofeyevich Razin) (1630?–1671) was a Cossack leader who led a major uprising against the nobility and the tsar's bureaucracy in south Russia in 1670–71. He was born into a wealthy Don Cossack family. In 1660 he was Cossack ataman. In 1662 he was commander of the Cossack army in a campaign against the Crimea Khanate and the Ottoman Empire. His relationship with the Russian Empire deteriorated because of the execution of his brother, Ivan, in 1662. In 1667 he started a successful campaign against Persia and the southern region of the Volga when he closed down commercial roads. In 1670 he incited an uprising among the Cossacks and peasants and occupied several towns. In 1671 he was captured by the tsarist forces and executed that year in Moscow.

Rikov, Aleksey Ivanovich (1881–1938) was a revolutionary and a statesman. He joined the Bolshevik Party in 1899. He was elected a member of the Central Committee and the People's Commissariat. In 1918 he became chairman of the Supreme Soviet of the National Economy. In 1921 he was elected deputy chairman of the Council of People's Commissars and, after Lenin's death, he became chairman. In 1924 he was a member of the Executive Committee of the Comintern. In 1926 he was elected chairman of the Soviet Council of Labor and Defense. As a member of the Right Opposition he lost all his posts between 1929 and 1930. In 1933 he was People's Commissar of Posts and Telegraph. In 1937 he was expelled from the party, and arrested. He was executed on 15 March 1938.

Rozhkov, Nikolay Aleksandrovich (1868–1927) was a historian and a Social Democratic revolutionary. In 1898 he was appointed Privatdozent at Moscow University. He joined the RSDLP in 1905. He participated in the 1905 Revolution, and he went underground in 1906. After 1907 he adopted the Menshevik point of view. In 1908 he was arrested, and in 1910 sentenced to exile in Irkutsk province. In 1917 he was deputy chairman of the revolutionary soviet in Novonikolayevsk. He was Deputy Minister of Posts and Telegraph in the Provisional Government. In 1917 he joined the Menshevik Party. He opposed the October Revolution but did not resist the events. In 1921 he was arrested. In 1922 he broke with the Mensheviks, condemning their political line. Also in 1922 he became a professor and later gave lectures in several universities of the Soviet Union. In 1926, he was appointed director of the State Historical Museum.

Ryabushinsky, Pavel Pavlovich (1871–1924) was a Russian entrepreneur, banker, and owner of a textile factory. In 1906 he was a leader of the Moscow Stock Exchange; in 1915 he became its chairman. One of the leading figures of the Kadet Party, he was a deputy of the Duma. In 1915 he was head of the Military-Industrial Committee. After the fall of his supporter Kornilov, he emigrated to France in 1920.

Ryazanov, David Borisovich (1870–1938) was a Marxist scholar and archivist. In 1885 he joined the Narodnik movement and was sentenced to five years in prison. In 1891 he was sentenced to four years' exile in Siberia for disseminating Marxist propaganda. He took part in the 1905 Revolution and again was sentenced to exile in Siberia but escaped to the West. Working in the archives of the German Social Democratic Party and the British Museum, he published a collection of the journalism of Marx and Engels and a history of the First International. In 1917 he participated in the February and October revolutions. In 1921 he took part in the foundation of the Marx-Engels-Lenin Institute and became its director. He initiated the project of publishing the collected works of Marx and Engels. In 1931 he was arrested as a Menshevik, expelled from the party and sent to Saratov. Beween 1931 and 1936 he worked at the Saratov University Library. In 1937 he was arrested again, charged with rightist, Trotskyist conspiracy, and executed on 21 January 1938.

Saltykov-Shchedrin, Mikhail Yevgrafovich (Saltikov or N. Schedrin) (1826–1889) was a writer with radical views and one of the best satirists of Russian literature. From 1841 he published his works in different literary journals and also worked in the tsarist bureaucracy. In 1848 he was sentenced to exile in Vyatka for his radical political views. In 1855 he received permission to leave Vyatka. In 1858 he was appointed vice governor of Ryazan; in 1860 he held the same post in Tver, and later worked in many leading administrative posts in different towns. He worked for the Russian magazine *Otyechestvenniye Zapisky* (Patriotic Notes) until 1884.

Samoilov, Fyodor Nikitich (1882–1952) was a revolutionary and party official. He joined the RSDLP in 1903 as a Bolshevik and took part in the 1905 Revolution. In 1914 he was arrested and sent into exile. In 1917 and 1918 he was one of the leaders of the Ivano-Voznesensk Soviet. From 1937 to 1941 he was director of the Museum of the Revolution. In 1940 he published his memoir *On the Traces of the Past.*

Savinkov, Boris Viktorovich (1879–1925) was a terrorist-revolutionary who later supported the First World War and the Whites in the Russian civil war. In 1903 he joined the SR Party and became the leader of the Fighting Organization, a terrorist group. He organized the assassination of Grand Duke Sergei and V. K. Plehve. During the First World War he served in the French Army. He was Deputy Minister of War in Kerensky's Provisional Government. In 1924 he was sentenced to death for terrorist attacks against the Soviet Union, but the sentence was commuted to ten years of imprisonment. He committed suicide in 1925. He wrote several novels.

Scheidemann, Philipp (1865–1939) was a German Social Democratic politician. He joined the Social Democratic Party in 1883. As a journalist and a parliamentary representative of the Social Democratic Party (from 1903) he supported Germany's role in the First World War. On 9 November 1918 he proclaimed the republic from a balcony in the Reichstag building. Later he became the first chancellor of the republic. After the Nazi takeover in 1933 he went into exile in Denmark.

Semashko, Nikolay Aleksandrovich (1874–1949) was a physician and Bolshevik revolutionary. In 1893 he was a member of a Marxist circle. In 1895 he was arrested and sentenced to exile in the Livonia district. From 1901 he worked as a physician, and in 1905 he took part in the revolution. In 1906 he emigrated to Switzerland, and in 1908 moved to Paris. In 1913 he participated in the antiwar movements of the Serbian and Bulgarian Social Democrats and interned at the start of the World War I. In 1917 he returned to Russia. After the October Revolution he was People's Commissar for Public Health (1918–36). He was editor-in-chief of the *Great Medical Encyclopedia* (1927–35). From

1930–36 he was a member of the All-Russian Central Executive Committee. After the war he took leading posts in the field of medical education.

Shaginyan, Marietta Sergeyevna (1888–1982) was a Soviet journalist and poet. From 1915 to 1918 she taught in Rostov and wrote for several newspapers. During the Second World War she was the correspondent of *Pravda* in the Urals. She was awarded the Stalin Prize in 1951 and the Lenin Prize in 1972.

Shagov, N. R. (1882–1918) was a textile worker and member of the party since 1900. He was deputy of Kostroma province in the Fourth State Duma. Because of his antiwar activity he was arrested in 1914 and sentenced to exile in Siberia.

Shaumyan, Stepan Georgievich (1878–1918) was a Bolshevik revolutionary from Baku. During the time of his studies, in 1900, he joined the RSDLP. He became a Bolshevik in 1903. He was arrested many times and sentenced to exile. He emigrated to Germany. He took part in 1905 Revolution. He was sentenced to prison for organizing the great Baku strike in 1914. After the 1917 February Revolution he was leader of the Baku soviet. He took part in the October Revolution, and was elected a member of the Central Committee. He was appointed Extraordinary Commissar for the Caucasus. In 1918 there was a Muslim uprising in Baku. He and twenty-five other Baku commissars fled but were arrested by troops under British command and executed.

Shingaryov, Andrey Ivanovich (1869–1918) was a physician and a member of the Kadet Party. He was the leader of the Kadet faction in the Second, Third, and Fourth State Dumas. In 1917 he was Minister of Economy in the Provisional Government. At the time of the October Revolution he was arrested. He was murdered in prison by a group of sailors.

Shishkov, Vyacheslav Yakovlevich (1873–1945) was an author and architect. In the 1900s he worked for the Tomsk district's Department of Waterways. He published several short stories and novels on his experiences. In the 1910s he worked in St. Petersburg and met Gorky. He was a member of the Union of Writers from 1928. During the Second World War he played an active part in the Red Army's propaganda work. His main works are *Vataga* (1925), *Grim River* (1933), and *Yemelian Pugachev* (1943).

Shklovsky, Viktor Borisovich (1893–1984) was a critic, writer, and theoretician. He was a leading figure of the "Formalist School," which made a deep impression on literary thought in the 1920s. He studied at St. Petersburg University. He took part in the creation of the Society for the Study of Poetic Language (OPOYAZ). His main works are *Matvey Komarov, Resident of the City of Moscow* (1928) and *Lev Tolstoy* (1968).

Shlyapnikov, Aleksandr Gavrilovich (1885–1937) was a worker and revolutionary. He became a member of the RSDLP in 1901. In 1903 he became a Bolshevik, and was imprisoned from 1904 to 1907. In 1908 he left Russia, worked in English, French, and German factories. In 1914 he worked in Petrograd but had to go into exile. Returning to Petrograd in 1915 and 1916, he was a primary link between the Bolsheviks in Russia and those in exile. He took part in the February Revolution, then was a founder of the All-Russia Metal Workers' Union. He supported the Bolshevik takeover. In 1917–18 he was chairman of the Revolutionary Military Council of the Caspian Caucasian Front. In 1920 he was one of the leaders of the Workers' Opposition in the party, and rejected the NEP. In 1924–25 he was on diplomatic mission in Paris. At the end of the 1920s he was the head of Metalloimport. He published his memoirs in 1917. In 1933 he was expelled from the party for alleged factionalism. In 1934 he was deported to Karelia. In 1935 he was sentenced to exile in Astrakhan for participating in the Workers' Opposition. In 1936 he was arrested again and sentenced to death. He was rehabilitated in 1988.

Shmidt, Nikolay Pavlovich (1883–1907) was a Bolshevik revolutionary. Nephew of a rich textile magnate, and owner of a furniture factory, he took part in the 1905 Revolution. He was a member of the RSDLP. He was executed in Butirka prison. His funeral turned into a political protest demonstration.

Shotman, A. V. (1880–1937) was a Bolshevik revolutionary. He took part in revolutionary activities from 1899 as well as the first Russian Revolution. In 1911–12 he was a member of the Helsingfors Committee of the Finnish Social Democratic Party. In June 1917 he became a member of the Petrograd district committee of the RSDLP(B). It was he who organized Lenin's move from Razliv to Finland. After the 1917 Revolution he worked in several important posts in economy, in the soviets, and in the party.

Shub, David Natanovich (1887–1973) was a journalist and a Menshevik. He became close to Russian social democracy in the 1900s. In 1905 he took part in the revolution and in 1907 emigrated to the United States. From 1910 he worked as a journalist in New York City and after 1923 wrote for the *Vorwärts* newspaper. He published his book on Lenin in 1928 in Yiddish and in 1948 in English.

Shvetsov, Sergey Porfirevich (1858–1930) was an ethnographer and revolutionary. He was active in the Narodnik revolutionary movement. In 1878 he was arrested and sentenced to exile in Siberia, where he conducted ethnographical research. In the 1900s he was a member of the SR Party. He took part in the 1905 Revolution. In 1918 he abandoned political activity to do scientific work.

Sklyansky, Efraim Markovich (1892–1925) was a member of the RSDLP in Kiev. In 1916 he was drafted into the army where he served as a doctor. In October 1917 he was a member of the Revolutionary Military Committee. In 1918 he became a member of the Supreme Military Council. From 1918–24 he was deputy chairman of the Revolutionary Military Council and a member of the Defense Council. He was a close comrade of Trotsky. He died in a boating accident while touring the United States to acquire technical information.

Sklyarenko, Aleksander Pavlovich (1869/1870–1916) was a revolutionary. In 1886 he took part in the Narodnik movement. In 1887 he was arrested and imprisoned in St. Petersburg. In 1894 he was arrested for disseminating Marxist propaganda and was sentenced to exile in Arkhangelsk province. From 1903 he worked as a party activist in Petrograd and Samara, where he was one of the leaders of the RSDLP. In 1907 he was arrested and exiled to the far north. In 1911 he returned to St. Petersburg and participated in editing some newspapers, among them *Pravda*.

Smilga, Ivar Tenisovich (1892–1938) was chairman of the Regional Committee of the Soviets in Finland in 1917. During the October Revolution he was chairman of the Central Committee of the Baltic Fleet. In 1917 he was a member of the Central Committee and later a member of the Revolutionary Military Council. He led the Seventh Army along with Tukhachevsky in the 1920 Polish-Soviet War. From 1914 to 1926 he was deputy chairman of GOSPLAN. As an active Trotskyist he was arrested and sentenced to exile in Siberia. In 1929 he revised his political views. Between 1930 and 1934 he was again a member of the Supreme Soviet Council of the National Economy. After Kirov's assassination he was arrested, and in 1938 executed on fabricated charges.

Smirnov, Vladimir Mikhaylovich (1887–1937) was a Bolshevik revolutionary. He was active in the 1905 Revolution. He joined the Bolshevik fraction of the RSDLP in 1907. He was among the editors of *Nashe puty*, *Spartak*, and *Social-Demokrat*. In 1917 he was a member of the Military Revolutionary Committee during the October Revolution in Moscow. He was one of the leading figures of the so-called Democratic Centralist Opposition, which protested the concentration of power in the party and state institutions. The faction was formed in 1919–20 when the central party and state organizations took stronger measures on controlling the local soviets and party organizations during the civil war. He was an oppositionist in the 1923–1927 period and was expelled from the party in 1928 and sentenced to prison in the Ural region and then sent to the Suzdal prison. After Kirov's assassination he was arrested again, and sentenced to three years. In 1937 he was executed on fabricated charges.

Sorel, Georges (-Eugene) (1847–1922) was a French socialist thinker, the theoretician of the revolutionary syndicalist movement. He developed an original and provocative theory on the positive, even creative, role of myth and violence in the historical process. He came from a middle-class family and trained as a civil engineer. He opposed World War I.

Sorokin, Pitirim Aleksandrovich (1889–1968) was a sociologist. In 1906 he was a member of the SR Party and was arrested the same year and imprisoned for three months. In 1917 he became a leader of the right SRs. In 1922 he was sentenced to foreign exile for his oppositional activity. From 1924 to 1930 he was a professor at the University of Minnesota. From 1930 to 1959 he taught at Harvard University and was one of the founders of its sociology department.

Spencer, Herbert (1820–1903) was an British sociologist and philosopher, an early theorist of evolution, which he saw as the progressive development of the physical world, biological organisms, the human mind, and human culture and societies. His work is the source of "social Darwinism."

Steffens, Lincoln (1866–1936) was an American journalist and political analyst, and one of the leading figures of muckraking journalism.

Stolypin, Pyotr Arkegyievich (1862–1911) was a conservative Russian statesman. After the 1905 Revolution he introduced land reforms in order to resolve peasant grievances and quell dissent, and tried to improve the lives of urban laborers. His reforms would serve the economic and political consolidation of the autocracy. He was governor of Grodno (1902), later of

Saratov (1903). From 1906 to 1911 he was prime minister and minister of the interior of Russia. In 1911 he was assassinated in the Kiev Opera House.

Strong, Anne Louise (1885–1970) was an American journalist and author. In 1921 she visited Poland and the Soviet Union; in 1925 she went to China. In 1930 she founded *Moscow News* (the first English-language newspaper in the city). She actively supported the foreign policy of the USSR. In 1937 she sent reports about the republican army in Spain. During 1937 and 1938 she was back in China. In 1944 she reported from the Soviet eastern front. In 1946 she interviewed Mao Tse-tung. In 1949 Stalin expelled her from the Soviet Union as an American spy. Later, she settled in China.

Struve, Pyotr Berngardovich (1870–1944) was a liberal economist, publicist, and politician. He started out as a Marxist and later became a liberal. After the Bolshevik Revolution he joined the White movement. He studied economic theory and history at St. Petersburg University. He wrote the Manifesto of the Russian Social Democratic Labor Party in 1898. In 1901 he lived in exile. From 1905 to 1916 he was a member of the Kadet Party, and became one of the party's leaders. In 1909 he was one of the authors of *Vekhy*. In 1913 he worked as a university professor. In 1918 he joined the Volunteer Army council. After the White army was defeated, he emigrated to Sofia, Prague, Berlin, and finally settled in Paris.

Sukhanov, Nikolay Nikolayevich (1882–1940) was a revolutionary, economist, and journalist. He joined the SR Party in 1903. In 1904 he was arrested and sentenced to one and a half years in prison. He took part in the 1905 Revolution, and after its fall he emigrated to Switzerland. In 1907 he broke with the SRs and joined the Social Democrats. In 1910 he was arrested and sentenced to three years of exile. In 1913 he returned and worked illegally. In 1917 he was one of the editors of the first issues of *Izvestya* and joined the Menshevik Party. In 1921 he broke with the Mensheviks and after revising his views joined the Communist Party of Germany. He was not allowed to join the Bolshevik Party. In the 1920s he studied economic problems concerning the Soviet Union. In 1930 he was arrested and sentenced to ten years of imprisonment. In 1935, at his request, his trial was reviewed. He then worked as a teacher in Tobolsk. In 1937 he was arrested again and sentenced to death on fabricated charges.

Sverdlov, Yakov Mihaylovich (1885–1919) was a revolutionary, one of the leaders and organizers of the RCP(b) in Russia. He joined the RSDLP in 1902. At the time of the party schism he joined the Bolshevik faction. In 1905 he was the leader of the Ural party organization. On 10 June 1906 he was arrested in Perm. He was in prison until 1909. From 1910 to 1912 he was sentenced to exile, twice in Narim and once in Maksimkin Yar on the Arctic Circle. In 1912 he was elected a member of the Central Committee at the Prague Conference. In 1912 he fled exile and returned to Petrograd. He worked on *Pravda* until he was betrayed by the double agent Roman Malinovsky and from 1913 to 1917 was exiled in Turukhansk, Siberia (for a while, together with Stalin in Kureyka). In April 1917 he was a member of the CC and the Revolutionary Military Committee of the Petrograd soviet. He helped organize the October Revolution.

On 8 November 1917 he was elected chairman of the All-Russian Central Executive Committee. In 1918 he was the second-most important leader of the country. He died of tuberculosis in Oryol.

Taratuta, Olga G. (Leonid) (1879–1938) was a Bolshevik and an active revolutionary in Ukraine. She was a member of the RSDLP from 1897 and worked for the newspapers *Iskra*. In 1904 she left the party and joined the anarchists; she was a member of the Buntar group, and in 1907 the group's messenger. In 1908 she was arrested and sentenced to prison for twenty-one years. She was released in March 1917. After the October Revolution she edited and published works of Bakunin, Kropotkin, and other anarchists. In 1937 she was arrested and, in 1938, executed on fabricated charges.

Tikhon (Vasily Ivanovich Belavin) (1865–1925) was the Patriarch of the Russian Orthodox Church between 1917 and 1925. From 1898 to 1907 he was Bishop of the Aleutians and Alaska. By order of the Synod he moved the center of the bishopric to New York from San Francisco in 1905 (at which time the St. Nikolay church was built). From 1907 to 1913 he was Bishop of Yaroslav. During the war he lived in Moscow. After the 1917 Bolshevik Revolution he was elected Patriarch of the Russian Orthodox Church. He condemned Bolshevik attacks on the church. In 1920 he granted autonomy to the parishes outside of Russia. In 1922 he was put under house arrest in Danskoy Monastery. In 1923, after he had revised his views, he was released.

Tkachov, Pyotr Nikitich (1844–1885) was a revolutionary, the ideologist and main representative of Russian Jacobinism. In the 1860s he actively participated in student protests. He was arrested several times. His writings in *Ruskoye Slovo* and *Delo* were censored. In 1869 he was arrested, and in 1871 he was sentenced to exile in the Pskov province. In 1873 he escaped and emigrated. He worked for the journals *Vperyod* and *Nabat*.

Tolstoy, Aleksey Nikolayevich (1883–1945) was a writer. In spite of his father's noble origins (he was a distant relative of Lev Tolstoy) and his White emigrant past, he became a main supporter of the Soviet system, and later returned to the USSR. His main works are *Nikita's Childhood* (1921), *Peter I* (1929–45), and *The Road to Calvary* trilogy (1921–40). He was awarded the Stalin Prize three times. In 1936 he was elected chairman of the Writers' Union.

Trotsky, Lev Davidovich (Bronshtein) (1897–1940) was an internationalist revolutionary, politician, statesman, journalist, and party theoretician. In 1903 he was a Menshevik, and later an independent member. After the 6th Congress in August 1917 he was a Bolshevik Party member. From 1898 on he was arrested many times for his revolutionary activities, and was sentenced to exile. In 1905 he was chairman of the Petrograd soviet. After the demise of the revolution he fled from Siberian exile and emigrated, settling in Vienna. In the course of the debates between the party factions he had many conflicts with Lenin. From 1908 to 1913 he was editor of the workers' newspaper, *Pravda* (not to be confused with Lenin's *Pravda*). He returned to Russia in May 1917. After the victory of the October Revolution he became People's Commissar of Foreign Affairs. In March 1918 he became commissar for war and built the victorious Red Army. During the struggle for power after Lenin's death he gradually lost to Stalin. In the fall of 1923 he was leader of the Left Opposition, a faction within the party. In 1928 he was sentenced to exile in Alma-Ata. In 1929 he was expelled from the Soviet Union. He settled in Mexico. He was assassinated in a plot inspired by Stalin.

Tsereteli, Irakli Georgevich (1881–1959) was a Menshevik leader and politician. He was a member of the Second State Duma. He was exiled to Siberia. After the February Revolution he returned to Petrograd. He was a member of the Executive Committee of the Petrograd Soviet and the Minister of Posts and Telegraphs in the Provisional Government. He was a fiery opponent of the October Revolution. In 1923 he emigrated to France, and in 1940 he moved to the United States.

Tsvetaeva, Marina Ivanovna (1892–1941) was a Russian and Soviet poet. In 1922 she was exiled; she returned to Moscow in 1939. She committed suicide in 1941.

Tsyurupa, Aleksandr Dmitrievich (1870–1928) was a Bolshevik revolutionary, statistician, agronomist, and politician. He became a member of the RSDLP in 1898. In 1918 he was Deputy People's Commissar of Food. During the civil war he was responsible for supplying the Red Army and directed the operations of the Food Requisitioning Army. In 1925 he became People's Commissar for Foreign and Internal Trade. He is buried in Red Square by the wall of the Kremlin.

Tugan-Baranovsky, Mikhail Ivanovich (1865–1919) was an economist. First he was a Social Democrat and belonged to the so-called legal Marxist faction. He began a new way of thinking about business cycles. He attempted a synthesis between Marxist political economy and subjective value theory. His works are *The Russian Factory in Past and Present* (1898), *Sketches from the Latest History of Political Economy and Socialism* (1903), *Foundations of Political Economy* (1917), and *Socialism as a Way of Learning* (1918). He was a member of the Kadet Party, but after the 1917 Revolution was associated with the German-sponsored Ukrainian regime.

Tukhachevsky, Mikhail Nikolayevich (1887–1936) was a revolutionary, Marshal of the Soviet Union, statesman, and one of the most prominent figures in the Soviet military leadership. He started his career as a tsarist officer. He joined the Bolshevik Party in 1918; in 1919 and 1920 he was one of the commanders of the Red army. In 1920 he commanded the Red army in Poland during the Soviet-Polish war. In March 1921 he was the commander of the Seventh Army during the suppression of the Kronstadt rebellion. From 1925 to 1928 he was chief-of-staff of the Red Army. In 1928 he was commander of the Leningrad Military District. In 1934 he was a member of the Central Committee and in 1935 became Marshal. In 1936 he was arrested and charged with conspiring with Germany. He was found guilty and executed.

Unshlikht, Yosif Stanislavovich (1879–1938) was a Bolshevik Party official and one of the founders of the police organization. He joined the RSDLP in 1906. He was arrested many times. In October 1917 he was a member of the Revolutionary Military Committee. In 1917 he was elected member of the collegium of the Cheka. In 1918 he fought against the German interventionist forces in Pskov. In 1918 and 1919 he was leader of the supervision of prisoners of war. From 1919 to 1921 he was a member of the Revolutionary Military Committee on the Western front. In 1921 he was Deputy Minister of the Interior and organized the reconnaissance department. In 1924 he was a member of the Central Revolutionary Council. From 1925 to 1930 he was deputy commissar of the Soviet armed forces, and commander of the civil fleet from 1933 to 1935. He was arrested in 1937, and in 1938 sentenced to death.

Uritsky, Moisey Solomonovich (1873–1918) was a revolutionary and politician. He began his revolutionary activity in the 1890s. After the Second Congress he was a Menshevik. In 1906 he was arrested and sentenced to exile. In 1914 he emigrated to France. In February 1917 he returned to Russia as a Bolshevik and in October became a member of the Petrograd Revolutionary Military Committee. In 1918 he was deputy for Dzherzhinsky. He was a member of the Petrograd Revolutionary-Defense Committee and a temporary Commissar of Foreign and Internal Affairs. In 1918 he was head of the Petrograd Cheka. He was assassinated.

Uspensky, Gleb Ivanovich (1843–1902) was a Russian writer who presented a realistic picture of peasants' lives.

Ustryalov, Nikolay Vasilyevich (1890–1937) was a political journalist and politician. He taught at Moscow University between 1916 and 1918. As a member of the Kadet Party he was a supporter of the Whites in the civil war. He became the judicial consultant under Kolchak's government. In 1921 he emigrated to France, and later moved to China. He was the founding ideologist of Smenovekhist political thought or National Bolshevism. From 1926 to 1935 he was adviser to the Chinese Eastern Railways. He returned to the Soviet Union in 1935. In 1937 he was arrested as a counterrevolutionary spy and sentenced to death.

Vandervelde, Émile (1866–1938) was a Belgian statesman and one of the main figures of the Second International. From 1914 to 1937 he was a member of the coalition government in Belgium. He played an influential part in the peace negotiations after the First World War. In 1889 he joined the Belgian Labor Party and later became one of its leaders. In 1894 he was elected a member of parliament as a Socialist. From 1918 to 1921 he was Minister of Justice. In 1922 he went to the Soviet Union as an attorney for the SRs on trial. He was Minister of Foreign Affairs from 1925 to 1927, and Minister of Health in 1936 and 1937.

Vaneyev, Anatoly Aleksandrovich (1872–1899) was a revolutionary and one of the founding members of the Union for the Struggle for the Liberation of the Working Class. He took part in the technical preparations of publishing the newspaper *Rabochaya Delo*. In 1895 he was arrested and sentenced to exile in Siberia.

Vatsetis, Yoakim Yoakimovich (1873–1938) was a Soviet military leader of Latvian origin. In 1891 he studied at the Riga Military School of Non-Commissioned Officers. He was made an officer in 1897 and fought in the First World War and became a colonel. In 1918 he joined the Bolsheviks and fought on the eastern front. In 1918–19 he was the first commander-in-chief of the Red Army. In 1919 he was a member of the Revolutionary Military Council. Later he taught at the RKKA Military Academy. In 1937 he was arrested on fabricated charges; he was executed in 1938.

Vesalyi, Artem (Kochkurov, Nikolay Ivanovich) (1899–1939) was a writer and poet. He joined the RSDLP in 1917. He took part in the October Revolution and the civil war as a volunteer, sailor, and later as a Chekist. He was a member of the Russian Association of Proletarian Writers (Russian acronym is RAPP) from 1929 on. In 1937 he was arrested on fabricated charges and died 2 December 1939. His main work is *Russia, Washed Clean by Blood* (1932).

Vodovozov, Vasily Vasilevich (1864–1933) took part in the Narodnik movement. In 1887 he was arrested and sentenced to exile in the Arkhangelsk district. In 1904 he was sentenced to one year of fortress prison in Petrograd. He was active in the 1905 Revolution, and was a leading member of the Trudovik group in the 1906 Duma. He opposed the October Revolution. He emigrated to Western Europe in 1926.

Volodarsky, V. (Goldshtein, Moysey Markovich) (1891–1918) was a revolutionary. In 1905 he joined *Bund*. He took part in the 1905 Revolution. In 1911 he was sentenced to exile in the Arkhangelsk district. In 1913 he was released and emigrated to the United States and worked with Trotsky and Bukharin on the journal *Novy Mir*. After the February Revolution in 1917 he returned to Russia. He was active in the October Revolution. In 1918 he was commissar for the press and information. He was assassinated by an SR terrorist.

Volsky, Nikolay Vladislavovich (Valentinov N.) (1879–1964) was a revolutionary, journalist, and economist. He was a Bolshevik until 1904 but later turned to Menshevik ideas; in exile in the West he was a bourgeois liberal. He opposed war communism but supported the NEP. In 1928 he emigrated to France. In 1956 he published his main work, *The NEP and Party Crisis after the Death of Lenin*, a book on the economy of the Soviet Union.

Vorontsov, Vasily Pavlovich (V. V.) (1847–1918) was a Russian economist, sociologist, and writer. His main works are *The Fate of Capitalism in Russia* (1882), *Description of the Theoretic Economy* (1895), *On the History of Community in Russia* (1902), *The Fate of the Capitalist Russia* (1907), *From the '70s to the '90s* (1907), and *Production and Consumption in the Capitalist Society* (1907).

Webb, Beatrice (1858–1943) was an English sociologist. During the 1890s she was a member and leader of the Fabian Society.

Webb, Sidney James (1859–1947) was an English socialist historian and economist. He was among the first to join the Fabian Society and played a crucial role in the foundation of the London School of Economics and Political Science.

Witte (Vitte), Sergey Yulyevich Count (1849–1915) was a Russian politician in the Russian Empire. From 1892–1903 he was minister of finance and imposed a reform on tariffs in 1897. In 1905–6, as prime minister, he tried to bring about the modernization of Russia through authoritarian methods. He retired in 1906.

Wrangel, Pyotr Nikolayevich (1878–1928) was commanding general of the anti-Bolshevik White Army in Southern Russia in the later stages of the Russian civil war. Of Baltic German origin, he served in the tsarist guard. In the First World War he was assigned command of a cavalry squadron. He remained in the army after the February 1917 Revolution.

In 1920 he was commander-in-chief of the White forces in the South. After the defeat in the Crimea, he emigrated to Turkey and then Yugoslavia. In 1924 he formed the All-Russia Military Union, an organization established to fight for the preservation and unity of all White forces living abroad. He settled in Brussels in 1927 and died of illness in 1928.

Yanuskhevich, Nikolay Nikolayevich (1868–1918) was a Russian general. He served as Chief of Staff of the General Headquarters at the tsar's request in 1914. After the February Revolution he was retired from active service. At the beginning of 1918 he was arrested in Mogilev and sent to Petrograd but was killed by his guards en route.

Yaroslavsky, Yemelyan Mikhaylovich (1878–1943) was a Bolshevik revolutionary and historian of the party. He joined the RSDLP in 1898. In 1917 he was the military commissar of the Kremlin and the Moscow region. In 1921–22 he was secretary of the Central Committee. He was an academician from 1939 on. He was awarded the Stalin Prize (1943). He is buried in the Kremlin Wall Necropolis.

Yelizarov, Mark Timofeyevich (1863–1919) was a Russian revolutionary and Soviet politician. He joined the RSDLP in 1893. He married Anna Ilyinichna, Lenin's sister. In 1919 he was People's Commissar of Transportation. He contracted typhus and died.

Yemelyanov, Stepan Fyodorovich (1902–1970) was chief of the security agencies in Azerbaijan from 1939 to 1953. In 1927 he joined the RCP(b). From 1939–41 he was the People's Commissar for Internal Affairs in the Azerbaijan SSR (ASSR). From 1941–43 he was People's Commissar for State Security in the ASSR. In 1956 he was sentenced to twenty-five years of imprisonment, and was released in 1970.

Yesenin, Sergey Aleksandrovich (1895–1925) was a Russian lyrical poet, known for his image both as a religious, puritan poet and a reckless, blasphemous exhibitionist. He had four wives and many childern. *Pugatsov*, an epic poem, reflects his faith in revolution. In 1925 he committed suicide.

Zamyatin, Yevgeny Yvanovich (1884–1937) was a writer of novels and plays. A satirist and writer of science fiction, he was one of the best authors of the post-revolutionary period. He was a father of the twentieth-century dystopian genre. He emigrated to Paris in 1931.

Zasulich, Vera Ivanovna (1849–1919) was a Russian revolutionary, first a Narodnik, then a social democrat. She joined the revolutionaries in 1868. In 1878 she wounded Fyodor F. Trepov, the governor of St. Petersburg, with a revolver, but at the widely publicized trial the sympathetic jury found her not guilty. She spent the following years in exile. In 1880 she worked with Plekhanov in Switzerland. In 1885 she was cofounder of the Union for the Struggle for the Liberation of the Working Class. She was co-editor of *Iskra*. In 1903 she became a Menshevik. In 1905 she returned to Russia. In 1917 she opposed the October Revolution.

Zemlyachka, Rozalia Samoylova (born Zalkind; party pseudonyms: Demon, Osipov) (1876–1947) was a Bolshevik revolutionary and a Soviet politician. In the 1890s she was active in the revolutionary movement. She joined the RSDLP in 1896. In 1901 she was a representative of the newspaper *Iskra* in Odessa. She was an active participant in the Central Committee. After 1905 she was arrested many times. She took part in the events of the revolution and the civil war. From 1922–43 she was a member of several state and party control organizations. From 1939 to 1943 she was deputy chairman of the Council of People's Commissars of the USSR.

Zetkin, Clara (born Eissner) (1857–1933) was a German politician, feminist, socialist, and communist leader. After the First World War she played an active part in the Communist Party of Germany and the Comintern (the Third International). She was an active member of the Social Democratic Party of Germany until 1917, then joined the Independent Social Democratic Party of Germany. She subsequently joined the Spartacus League, later transformed into the Communist Party of Germany, which she represented in the Reichstag during the Weimar Republic of 1920–33. In August 1932, as the chairwoman of the Reichstag by seniority, she called for people to fight National Socialism. In 1933 she emigrated to the Soviet Union.

Zhabotinsky, Vladimir Yevgenyevich (1880–1940) was an essayist, translator, and journalist. A leading figure of rightist Zionism, he was the founder of the revisionist Zionist movement and *Betar*, the organizer of the Jewish Legion. In Odessa he founded the Jewish Self-Defense Organization. After the First World War he emigrated to Palestine. He wanted to create the Jewish state on both sides of the Jordan with the help of the British Empire.

Zheleznyakov, Anatoly Grigoryevich (1895–1919) was a sailor and anarchist. In 1915 he served with the Baltic Fleet. In 1916 he deserted and went into hiding on trading vessels. In October 1917 he took part in the revolution and fought with the Bolsheviks in the civil war and was mortally wounded in battle.

Zhelyabov, Andrey Ivanovich (1851–1881) was a Russian revolutionary, one of the leaders of the Narodnik movement. He studied law in Odessa but was expelled for his participation in student unrest in October 1871. He was active in Kiev and Odessa revolutionary circles and was arrested but released on bail. He was a member of the *Zemlya i volya* group from 1879. He was one of the chief organizers of the successful attempt to assassinate Alexander II on 1 March 1881. He was preparing for another terrorist attack, but was arrested two days before the assassination and was tried together with the 1 March case and hanged.

Zinoviev (Radomilsky), Grigory Yevseyevich (1883–1936) was a Bolshevik revolutionary, politician, and agitator. He joined the party in 1901 and was a close friend to Lenin in exile. From 1917–19 he was the chairman of the Petrograd soviet and a founding member of the Executive Committee of the Comintern in 1919. In 1917 he was elected a member of the Central Committee and, in 1919, a member of the Politburo. As he gradually turned against Stalin, he lost all his posts in 1926 and '27 and was expelled from the party. In 1928 he publicly acknowledged his mistakes, but in 1933 he was expelled again and arrested in 1934. In 1936, as one of the accused at the first Moscow show trial, he was sentenced to death and executed.

Zoshchenko, Mikhail Mikhaylovich (1895–1958) was a writer and satirist. His short stories and sketches belong to the most humorous writings of the Soviet period. He attended the Faculty of Law but in 1915 served in the army as a field officer. Between 1917 and 1920 he traveled throughout the country and worked at several jobs. After October 1917 he sided with the Bolsheviks, and volunteered in the civil war. From 1920 on, he was on the editorial board of the satirical magazine *Krokodil*. During the Great Patriotic War he was evacuated to Alma-Ata. Zoshchenko's and Akhmatova's apolitical literary works published in *Zvezda* and *Leningrad* elicited anger from the authorities. From 1946–53 he was expelled from the Union of Writers. In 1953 he was readmitted and worked for *Krokodil* and *Ogonok*.

List of Photographs and Illustrations

The publisher would like to thank the Russian State Archive of Socio-Political History (RGASPI) and the Russian State Documentary Film and Photo Archive at Krasnogorsk (RGAKFD) for their kind permission to reproduce the images in this book.

1. Lenin plays chess with Bogdanov in Italy, as a guest of Gorky. Island of Capri, after 19 April 1908. Photo by Yu. A. Zhelyabuzhsky. RGASPI - f. 393, op. 1, d. 13.
2. Vladimir Ilyich Lenin. Paris, 1910. Photo by E. Vallois. RGASPI - f. 393, op. 1, d. 17.
3. Lenin after having been freed from Austrian prison. Zakopane (Poland), after 19 August 1914. Photo by B. D. Vigilyov. RGASPI - f. 393, op. 1, d. 18.
4. Demonstration in July 1917. Petrograd, 1917. Photo by Petr Ocup. RGAKFD - 431993.
5. Lenin in his office. Moscow, Kremlin, 16 October 1918. Photo by: Petr Ocup. RGASPI - f. 393, op. 1, d. 43.
6. Lenin in Red Square, speaking at the inauguration of the Stepan Razin Memorial. Moscow, 1 May 1919. Photo by N. P. Agapof. RGASPI - f. 393, op. 1, d. 134.
7. N. K. Krupskaya. (1918–1919, probably Moscow.) Photographer unknown. RGASPI - f. 395, op. 2, d. 24.
8. Lenin in "camouflage." The photograph was prepared for an illegal identification card. Razliv, between 8–16 August 1917. Photo by D. Letsenko. RGASPI - f. 393, op. 1, d. 24.
9. The "Leninian agitprop corner" in the summer camp of one of the sections of the Red Army. 1927. Photo by Petr Ocup. RGAKFD - 40.
10. Lenin and Kamenev. Gorki, 1922. Between beginning of August and 13 September. Photo by Maria Ilyinichna Ulyanova. RGASPI - f. 393, op. 1, d. 352.
11. Lenin at the wall of Red Square on the first of May demonstration. Moscow, 1 May 1919. Photo by Goskino. RGASPI - f. 393, op. 1, d. 143.
12. Lenin and Stalin. Gorki, August 1922. Photo by Maria Ilyinichna Ulyanova. RGASPI - f. 393, op. 1, d. 323.
13. J. V. Stalin sketched by N. I. Bukharin. 20 February 1928. Black and blue pencil. RGASPI - f. 74, op. 2, d. 169, l. 11.
14. J. V. Stalin sketched by N. I. Bukharin. April 1929. Pencil. RGASPI - f. 74, op. 2, d. 169, l. 44.
15. N. K. Krupskaya sketched by V. I. Mezhlauk. 1 June 1933. Black and red pencil. RGASPI - f. 74, op. 2, d. 169, l. 179.
16. L. B. Kamenev sketched by N. I. Bukharin. 25 June 1923. Black ink. RGASPI - f. 74, op. 2, d. 168, l. 1.
17. L. D. Trotsky sketched by V. I. Mezhlauk. Pencil; undated. RGASPI - f. 74, op. 2, d. 170, l. 15.
18. G. Y. Zinoviev sketched by N. I. Bukharin. 3 March 1926. Black ink. RGASPI - f. 74, op. 2, d. 168, l. 66.
19. N. I. Bukharin, self-portrait. 17 February 1927. Black ink. RGASPI - f. 74, op. 2, d. 168, l. 105.
20. F. E. Dzerzhinsky sketched by N. I.

Bukharin. 30 June 1925. Pencil. RGASPI – f. 76, op. 2, d. 35, l. 4.

21. G. K. Ordzhonikidze sketched by N. I. Bukharin. 17 February 1927. Black ink. RGASPI – f. 74, op. 2, d. 168, l. 106.
22. I. T. Smilga, G. Y. Zinoviev, L. B. Kamenev, L. D. Trotsky and J. V. Stalin sketched by G. M. Krzhizhanovsky (?). Black ink. RGASPI – f. 669, op. 1, d. 14, l. 172.
23. M. M. Kaganovich sketched by V. I. Mezhlauk. 20 February 1934. Pencil. RGASPI – f. 74, op. 2, d. 170, l. 7.
24. F. E. Dzerzhinsky and G. K. Ordzhonikidze sketched by V. I. Mezhlauk. (1931?) Pencil. RGASPI – f. 74, op. 2, d. 169, l. 142.
25. Vladimir Ilyich Lenin sketched by N. I. Bukharin. 31 March 1927. Black ink. RGASPI – f. 74, op. 2, d. 168, l. 125.
26. Vladimir Ilyich Lenin sketched by N. I. Bukharin. 15 June 1927. Pencil. RGASPI – f. 74, op. 2, d. 168, l. 132.
27. Vladimir Ilyich Lenin. Author unknown. Pencil; undated. RGASPI – f. 74, op. 2, d. 168, l. 160.
28. Lenin in Gorki. The photograph was taken between beginning of August 1922 and 24 September. Photo by V. V. Loboda. RGASPI – f. 393, op. 1, d. 349.

Bibliography

ARCHIVAL SOURCES

Hoover Institution, Archives, Boris Nicolaevsky Collection, Box 1, nos. 6, 7, 9, 16, 17, 119

RGASPI, Rossijszkiy Gosudarstvenniy Arhiv Sotzialno-politicheskoy Isztorii (Russian State Archive of Social and Political History). Earlier known as CPA IML, Centralnij Partijniy Arhiv Instyitut Marksizma-Leninizma (Central Party Archive Institute of Marxism-Leninism) Fond 2. op. 1–5.

RGANI, Rosszijskiy Gosudarstvenniy Arhiv Novejsey Istoriy (Russian State Archive of Modern History) Fond 2. 5. op.

NEWSPAPERS AND JOURNALS

Bolshevik
Izvestiia
Kommunisticheszkiy Internacional
Krasnaya Nov
Krasniy Kavaleriszt
Pod Znamenem Marksizma
Pravda
Smena veh
Vestnik Kommunisticseskoy Akademii
Zhizny Natzionalnostyey

OTHER SOURCES, DOCUMENTS

Agursky, M. "Gorky i yevreyskiye pisateli" (Gorky and Jewish writers), *Minuvsee. Istoricheskiy almanakh,* no. 10. Moscow and Leningrad: SPb, 1992.

Akimov, V. P. *K voprosu o rabotah Vtorogo Syezda RSDRP.* Geneva, 1904.

Aleksandrov, M. *Absolyutism, gosudarstvo i byurokratiya.* Moscow, 1910.

Alekseev, V. A. Shver. *Sem'ia Ul'ianovykh v Simbirske (1869–1887)*, ed. A. Ulyanova Elizarova, Institut Lenina pri TS K.R.K.P. Moscow and Leningrad: Gosudarstvennoe izd-vo, 1925. Zaporozhee, Gyikoje Pole, 1995, l.

Bakunin, Mikhail. "K ofitseram Russkoy armii" (To the officers of the Russian army), in *Revolyutsionniy radikalizm v Rossii: Vek devyatnadsadtiy.* Moscow: 1997. Excerpts in English: *The Hague Congress of the First International September 2–7, 1872.* Moscow: Progress Publishers, 1976.

Berdyaev, Nikolay. *Istoki i smisl russkogo kommunizma.* Moscow, 1990.

Biblioteka V. I. Lenina v Kremle: katalog (Library of V. I. Lenin in the Kremlin: Catalogue), ed. N. N. Kucharkov et al. Moscow: Izdatel·vo Vsesojuznoj Knožnoj Palaty, 1961.

Bogdanov, A. *Desyatiletiye otlucheniya ot marksizma: Jubileyniy sbornik (1904– 1914),* vol. 3, comp. N. S. Antonova. Moscow: AIRO-XX, 1995.

Bolshevistskoye rukovodstvo, Perepiska, 1912–1927 (Bolshevik leadership, correspondence). Moscow: ROSSPEN, 1996.

Bubnov, A. *Osnovniye voprosi istorii RKP.* Moscow, Giz: Sbornik statyey, 1925.

———. "Razvitiye roli Lenina v istorii russkovo marxizma," in *Osnovniye voprosi istorii RKP.*

Bukharin, Nikolai. "Tsezarizm pod maskoy revolyutsii" (Caesarism in a revolutionary mask), *Izd. "gazeti Pravda."* Moscow: 1925.

——. *Ekonomika perehodnogo perioda.* Moscow: Gos. izdat, 1920; in English, "The Economics of the Transition Period," in *The Politics and Economics of the Transition Period*, ed. and with an introduction by Kenneth J. Tarbuck, trans. Oliver Field. London and Boston: Routledge & Kegan Paul, 1979.

——."On the Tactics of Offence." Orginally published in *Kommunistichesky Internatsional*, 15 December 1920.

——."Teoriya proletarskoy diktaturi" (Theory of the dictatorship of the proletariat), *Ataka.* Moscow: Gosizdat, 1924.

——. *Teoriya istoricheskogo materializma.* Moscow: 1921.

Bukharin, Nikolai, and Evgeniy Preobrazhensky. *The ABC of Communism*, trans. Eden and Cedar Paul. Harmondsworth, Middlesex: Penguin Books, 1969; in Russian, Bukharin and Yevgeni Preobrazhenskiy. *Azbuka kommunizma.* St. Petersburg: Gosizdat Peterburg, 1920.

"Call of the Provisional Revolutionary Committee to the Peasants, Workers and Red Guard Soldiers," in *Kronstadt, 1921: Dokumenti o sobitiyah v Kronstatye vesnoy 1921 goda* (Kronstadt, 1921: Documents of the spring events in 1921), ed. Vladimir Pavlovich Naumov, Aleksandr Albertovich Kosakovsky. Moscow: Demokratiya, 1997.

Chuyev, F. *Stosorok besed s Molotovim.* Moscow: Terra, 1991.

Vtoroy syezd RSDRP. Iyul–avgust 1903 goda. Moscow: Protokoli, 1959. 2. Congress of RSDWP (Russian Social Democratic Workers´ Party).

Dalin, David. *Posle voyn i revolyutsii.* Berlin: Grani, 1922. (After the wars and revolutions).

Dekreti sovyetskoy vlasti, vol. 7. Moscow: 1975. (The decrees of the Soviet power).

Dnevniki imperatora Nyikolaya II. Moscow: Orbita, 1991. (Diaries of Imperator II. Nicholas).

Dukelskiy, Sz. "Cheka na Ukraine," in *VCHK-GPU: Dokumenti i materiali,* ed. Ju. G Felshtinszky. Moscow: Gumanitarnoy Literaturi, 1995.

Engels, Friedrich. *Az erőszak szerepe a történelemben* (The role of violence in history). Budapest, Kossuth, 1970.

Iz literaturnogo naslediya: Gorky i yevreyskiy vopros (From the literary legacy: Gorky and the Jewish question), ed. M. Agurskiy and M. Shklovskaya. Jerusalem, 1986.

Izveshcheniye o konferencii organizacii RSDRP. Organizacionnogo Komiteta, September 3, 1912.

Kamenev, Lev. "Plodi prosveshcheniya," *Pravda,* 14 June 1917.

Kamenev, L. B. *Mezhdu dvumya revolyutsiami.* Moscow: Sbornik Statyei Izd. 2-oye, 1923.

Kautsky, Karl. *Die Agrarfrage: Eine Übersicht über die Tendenzen der modernen Landwirtschaft und die Agrarpolitik der Sozialdemokraten.* Stuttgart: 1899.

——. *Die historische Leistung von Karl Marx.* Berlin: Singer, 1919, http://www.archive.org/details/diehistorischele00kaut; in Hungarian, *Marx Károly történelmi jelentősége*, trans, Ernő Garami. Budapest: 1919.

——. *Neue Zeit*, 22/4 1903.

——. *Kautskys russisches dossier: Deutsche Sozialdemokraten als Treuhänder des russischen Parteivermögens 1910-1915,* Quellen und Studien zur Sozialgeschichte, vol. 2, ed. Dietrich Geyer. Frankfurt am Main and New York: Campus Verlag, 1981.

Kniga pogromov: Pogromi na Ukrainye, v Belorussii i yevropeyskoy chastyi Rossii v period Grazhdanskoy voyni 1918–1922, ed. L. B. Milyakova. Moscow: ROSSPEN, 2007.

Kropotkin, P. *Mutual Aid: A Factor of Evolution*, ed. with an Introduction by Paul Avrich. New York: New York University Press, 1972.

Krupskaya, Nadezhda Konstantinovna. *Izbrannye proizvedeniia: k 120-letiiu so dnia rozhdeniia N.K. Krupskoi.* Moscow: Politizdat, 1988.

Lenin, Vladimir Ilyich. *Biograficheskaya Chronika,* vols.1–12, ed. G. N. Golikov. Moscow: Izdatelstvo politicheskoy literature, 1985.

——. *Vladimir Ilyich Lenin; A biography,* ed. P. N. Pospelov. Moscow: Progress Publishers, 1965.

——. *Lenin i kniga.* Moscow: Izd. Pol. Lit, 1964.

Lenin (N.): *O evreiskom voprose v Rossii* (Tel Aviv: Aticot, 1970); previously published in *Vvedenie S. Dimanshteyna*, Introduction by P. Lepesinszkij. Zaporozhye: Kommunar, Kooperativnoe Izdat, Proletary, 1924.

——. *V. I. Lenin: Neizvestnye dokumenty, 1891–1922* (V. I. Lenin: The Unknown Documents), ed. Yuriy Nikolaevich Amiantov, Yuriy Aleksandrovich Akhapkin and Vladlen Nikolaevich Stepanov, V. T. Loginov. Moscow: ROSSPEN, 1999.

Leninskii Sbornik (Lenin miscellany), vol. 9. Moscow: SOTSEGIZ, 1931.

Leninskii Sbornik, vol. 22. Moscow: Party Publishing House, 1933.

Leninskii Sbornik, vol. 19. Konspekt knigi K. Kautskogo "Agrarniy vopros." 1932.

Leninskii Sbornik, vol. 14. Moscow–Leningrad: Gos. Izd., 1930.

Leniniana, ed. Lev Kamenev. Moscow–Leningrad: Gos. Izd., 1926.

Lubyanka: Stalin i VCHK-GPU-OGPU-NKVD, Yanvar 1922–dekabr 1936, ed. A. N. Yakovlev. Moscow: ROSSPEN, 2003.

Luxemburg, Rosa. *The Essential Rosa Luxemburg.* Chicago: Haymarket, 2008.

——. *Gesammelte Werke.* Berlin: 1970.

Makhno, Nestor. "My Interview with Lenin," in *My Visit to the Kremlin.* Berkeley, CA: Kate Sharply Library, 1993.

Martov, Julius. *Obshchestvennye i umstvennye techeniia v Rossii 1870–1905.* Leningrad–Moscow: Kniga, 1924.

Martov, Julius. *Zapiski sotsial-demokrata.* Berlin–St. Petersburg–Moscow: Izd-vo Z.I. Grzhebina, 1922.

Marx, Karl, and F. Engels, "Theses on Feuerbach," *Marx/Engels Selected Works,* vol. 1, trans. W. Lough. Moscow: Progress Publishers, 1969.

Mensheviki v Bolshevistkoy Rossii 1918–1924 (Mensheviks in Bolshevik Russia). Moscow: ROSSPEN, 1999.

Mensheviki v 1921–1922. Moscow: ROSSPEN, 2002.

Neizvestnaya Rossia XX vek. (The unknown twentieth century), ed. V. A. Kozlov. Moscow: Obyedyineniye "Mosgorarchiv," 1993.

Neizvestny Bogdanov, vol. 2: *A. A. Bogdanov i gruppa RSDRP "Vperyod" 1908–1914*, ed. Gennadiy Arkadevic Bordugov. Moscow: AIRO-XX, 1995.

Ochistim Rossiiu nadolgo: Lenin (Ulianov) Repressii protiv inakomysliashchikh Konets 1921–1923, ed. A. N. Artizov. Moscow: ROSSPEN, 2008.

Obshchestvo i vlasty: Rossiyskaya provintsiya, vol. 1: *1917-seredina 30-h godov* (Moscow: Nizhniy Novgorod, Paris, 2002).

Parvus (I. L. Gelfand). *Rossija is Revoljucija.* St. Petersburg: Glagolev, 1908.

Perepiska sekretariata CK RKP(b) s mestnimi partijnimi organyizacijami (janvar–mart 1919 g.) Moscow: Sbornik materialov, 1971.

Piletskii, I. A. *Dve teorii imperializma: Marksistskaia legenda i Vozvrat k Marksu.* Kharkiv: Kooperativnoe izd-vo Proletarii, 1924.

Plekhanov, G. V. "Our Differences," *Selected Philosophical Works,* vol. 1, trans. R. Dixon. Moscow: Foreign Languages Publishing House, 1961; and London: Lawrence & Wishart, 1961.

——. "K agrarnomu voprosu v Rossii" (On the Agrarian Question in Russia), in *Sochineniya* (Works), vol. 15. St. Petersburg-Leningrad: Gosudarstvennoe izdatelstvo, 1923–1927.

——. *Sochineniya: V 24-h tomakh,* vol. 20. Moscow: 1925.

Preobrazhensky, J. "Sotsialisticheskiye i kommunisticheskie predstavleniya o sotsializme," *Vestnik Kommunisticheskoy Akademii* (1925): 12.

Russian Provisional Government, 1917: Documents, ed. Robert Paul Browder, Aleksandr Fyodorovich Kerensky. Stanford, CA: Stanford University Press, 1961; in Russian: *Revolyucitsia i nacionalniy vopros: Dokumenti i matyeriali po istorii natsionalnogo voprosa v Rossii i SSSR v XX veke,* vol. 3, ed. S. M. Dimanshteyn. Moscow: 1917.

Ryazanov, David. *Anglo-Russkoye otnosheniya v ocenke Marxa (Istoriko-lkriticheskiy etyud).* St. Petersburg: Petrogradskovo Sovyeta i Krestyanskih Deputatov, 1918.

——. *Razbitie illyuzii: K voprosu o prichinah krizisha v nasey partyii.* Geneva: 1904.

Sedmoy vserossiyskiy syezd sovetov rabochih, krestyanskih i kozachyih deputatov. Moscow: Stenograficheskiy otchot, 1919.

Szedmaya (Aprelskaya) Vserossiyskaya konferenciya RSDRP (bolshevikov): Protokoli. Moscow: 1958.

Az SZKP kongresszusainak, konferenciáinak és központi bizottsági plénumainak határozatai 1898–1954 (Resolutions of the congresses, conferences, and central committee plenary meetings of the Communist Party of the Soviet Union Part 1), vol. 1: 1898–1924. Budapest: Szikra, 1954.

Slepkov, A. "K tretyey godovshchine kronstadtskogo myatezha," *Bolshevik* (1924): 1.

"Smena Vekh, 12 November 1921, 3/1," in *V borbe za Rossiyu*, Harbin: 1920.

"Sovershenno sekretno": Lubianka—Stalinu o polozhenii v strane (1922-1934 gg.) ("Top secret": Lubyanka to Stalin on the state of the nation (1922–1934)), vol. 1. Lewiston, NY: Edwin Mellen Press for the Institute of Russian History, 2000.

Stalin, J. V. *Kratki Kurs* (The short course). Moscow: 1938.

Struve, P. "Moi vstrechi i stolknovenija s Leninim," *Novii Mir* 4 (1991).

———. "Velikaya Rossiya," in *Patriotica: Politika, kultura, religija, sotsialism—Sbornik statey za pyat let (1905–1910)*. St. Petersburg: 1911.

Sudebniy process nad sotsialistami-revolyutsionerami ijuny-avgust 1922 Dokumentov, ed. S. A. Krasilnikov, K. N. Morozov, I. V. Chubikin. Moscow: ROSSPEN, 2002.

Traynin, I. P. *SZSZSZR i natsionalnaya problema. Po natsionalnim respublikam i oblastyam Sovetskogo Soyuza*. Moscow: 1924.

Trotsky, L. D. *Nashi polityicheskiye zadachi*. Geneva: 1904; in English, L. D. Trotsky, *Our Political Tasks*. London: New Park Publications, 1980.

———. *1905*. Moscow: 1922.

———. *Dnevniki i pisma*, ed. Yuriy Felshtinsky. Cambridge, MA: Houghton Library, Heritage, 1986.

———. *The Trotsky Papers*. Hague–Paris; 1971.

Uchreditelnoye sobraniye: Rossiya 1918 (Constituent Assembly: Russia 1918). Moscow: Nedra, 1991.

Ulyanova, A. I. *Detszkie i skolnie godi Il'icsa*, "Detszkaja Literatura." Moscow: 1983.

Ulyanova-Jelizarova, A. I. *Vospominaniya ob Alekszandre Iljicse Uljanove*. Moscow: 1930.

Ulyanova, M. *Otets Vladimira Ilyicha Lenina, Ilya Nikolayevich Ulyanov (1831–1886)* (The father of Vladimir Ilyich Lenin, Ilya Nikolayevich Ulyanov). Moscow–Leningrad: 1931.

The Unknown Lenin: From the Secret Archive, ed. Richard Pipes. New Haven and London: Yale University Press, 1996.

Ustryalov, Nikolai. *Nacional-Bolshevizm*. Moscow: Algoritm, 2003.

———. *V borbe za Rossiyu*. Harbin: 1920.

Valentinov, Nikolay (N. V. Volsky). *Encounters with Lenin*. trans. Paul Rosta and Brian Pearce, with a Foreword by Leonard Schapiro. London: Oxford University Press, 1968.

Valentinov N. *NEP i krizis partyi: Vospominaniya* New York: Stanford University Press and Teleks, 1991. A facsimile of the original publication of 1971.

———. *Maloznakomyj Lenin*. Moscow: Na boyevom postu, 1992.

Vardin, I. "A zsidó ellen—a cárért" (Against the Jew—for the Tsar!), *Pravda*, 14 May 1918.

VCHK-GPU: Dokumenti i materiali, ed. Yu. G. Felshtyinskij: Moscow: Gumanitarnoy Lityeraturi, 1995.

Vekhi. Sbornik statey o russkoy intelligentsii N. A. Berdyayeva, S. N. Bulgakova, M. O. Gershenzona, A. S. Izgoyeva, B. A. Kistyakovskago, P. B. Struve, S. L. Franka. Moscow, 1990.

Visilka vmesto rasstrela: Deportaciya intelligencii v dokumentah VCHK-GPU 1921–1923. Moscow, Ruszszkij put', 2005.

Vodovozov, V. *Moyo znakomstvo s Leninim: Na chuzhoy storonye* 12. Prague: 1925.

V-iy (londonszkiy) szjezd, RSDRP. Moscow: Protokoli, 1961.

Vtoroj szyezd RSDRP Iyul–avgust 1903 goda. Moscow: Protokoli, 1959.

Yevreinov, N. *Istoriya telesnih nakazaniy v Rossii* (The history of physical disciplining in Russia). Moscow: 1911.

Zinoviev, G. *Leninizm: Vvedeniye v izucsenyie lenyinyizma* Leningrad: Gos. Izdat, 1925.

Zinoviev, G. *Sochineniya*, vol. 3. Leningrad: Gos. Izdat, 1924.

———. "Borba za bolshevizm iz epokhi *Zvezdi i Pravdi* (1913–1914)," *Sochineniya,* vol. 4. Leningrad: Gos. Izdat, 1926.

BIBLIOGRAPHY

1917 god revolyucionnaya Rossiya: Sbornik obsorov i referatov. Moscow: INION Press, 2007.

1917 god v sudbah Rossii i mira: Fevralskaya revolyutsiya: Ot novih istochnyikov ko novomu osmislenyiyu, ed. P. V. Volobuyev: Moscow: RAN, 1997.

Adibekov, G. M., Z. I. Shahnazarova, and K. K. Shirinya. *Organizatsionnaya struktura Kominterna 1919–1943* (The organizational structure of the Comintern 1919–1943). Moscow: ROSSPEN, 1997.

Ágh, Attila. *A politika világa* (The world of politics). Budapest: Kossuth, 1984.

———. "Társadalmi önszerveződés és szocializmus" (Social self-organization and socialism), in *Válaszúton* (Crossroads), ed. Tamás Krausz and László Tütő. Budapest: ELTE ÁJTK, 1988. 49–61.

Agursky, M. *Yevreyskiy rabochiy v kommunistyicheskom dvizhenii.* Minsk: Gos. Izdat, 1926.

Államszocializmus: Értelmezések— viták—tanulságok (State socialism: Interpretations—debates—lessons), ed. Tamás Krausz and Péter Szigeti. Budapest: L' Harmattan- Eszmélet Alapítvány, 2007

Anderson, Kevin. *Lenin, Hegel and Western Marxism: A Critical Study.* Urbana : University of Illinois Press, 1995.

Andor, László. "Dilemmák és ellentmondások" (Dilemmas and contradictions), *Eszmélet* 74 (2007): 135–44.

Arsinov, Petr. *The History of the Makhnovist Movement: 1918–1921,* London: Freedom Press, 1987. 7–24.

Avreh, A. Ya. *Tsarism nakanunye sverzheniya.* Moscow: Nauka, 1989.

Balabanoff, Angelica. *Impressions of Lenin.* Ann Arbor: University of Michigan Press, 1964.

Batkis, Grigoriy. *Szeksualnaya revoljuciya v Szovjetskom Soyuze.* Moscow: 1925.

Bayer, József. *A politikai gondolkodás története* (The history of political thought). Budapest: Osiris, 1998.

Bebesi, György. *A feketeszázak* (The Black Hundreds). Budapest: MRI, 1999.

Béládi, László. "A bolsevik párt kongresszusai a számok tükrében 1917–1939" (The Congresses of the Bolshevik party seen through the figures), *Világtörténet* 3 (1983) 86–89.

Béládi, László, and Tamás Krausz. *Életrajzok a bolsevizmus történetéből* (Biographies from the history of Bolshevism). Budapest: ELTE, ÁJTK, 1988.

Belov, Sergei Vladimirovich. *Istoria odnoi "druzhby": V. I. Lenin i P. B. Struve.* St. Petersburg: SPbGU, 2005.

Berdyaev, Nikolay. *Istoki i smisl russkogo kommunizma.* Moscow: 1990.

Bettelheim, Charles. *Class Struggles in the USSR: Second Period 1923–1930.* Sussex: Harvester Press, 1978.

Biggart, John. "Antileninist Bolshevism. The Forward Group of the RSDRP," *Canadian Slavonic Papers* 2 (1981).

———. "Introduction: 'Antileninsky bolshevizm': gruppa RSZDRP 'Vperyod,'" in *Neizvestny Bogdanov,* vol. 2: *A. A. Bogdanov i gruppa RSDRP "Vperyod" 1908–1914,* ed. Gennadiy Arkadevic Bordugov. Moscow: "AIRO-XX," 1995.

Bihari, Ottó. *A szocialista államszervezet alkotmányos modelljei* (The constitutional models of socialist state structure). Budapest: Közgazdasági és Jogi Könyvkiadó, 1969.

Bilder der Russischen Revolution. Berlin–Frankfurt/M, Wien.

Blackledge, Paul. "'Anti-Leninist' Anti-Capitalism: A Critique," *Contemporary Politics,* 11/2–3 (June–Sept. 2005): 99–116.

———. "Learning from Defeat: Reform, Revolution and the Problem of Organisation in the First New Left," *Contemporary Politics* 10/1 (March 2004): 21–36.

Bonch-Bruyevich, V. "Ob antisemitizme," in *Protiv antisemitizma.* Leningrad:1930.

Borsányi, György. *Kun Béla.* Budapest: Kossuth, 1979.

Bratka, László, ed. *A négylábú tyúk: Mai szovjet szatírák* (The four legged hen: Contemporary Soviet satires). Budapest: Szépirodalmi Könyvkiadó, 1984.

Brus, Włodzimierz. *The General Problems of the Functioning of the Socialist Economy.* London: Oxford, 1961.

Budgen, S., St. Kouvalekis, Žižek, S., eds. *Lenin Reloaded: Toward a Politics of Truth*. Durham, NC; London: Duke University Press, 2007

Budnitsky, O. V. *Rossiyskie yevrei mezhdu krasnimi i belimi (1917–1920)*. Moscow: ROSSPEN, 2005.

———. "Jews, Pogroms and the White Movement: A Historiographical Critique," *Kritika: Explorations in Russian and Eurasian History* 2/4 (Fall 2001): 752–53.

Buharayev, Vladimir. "1917—Az obscsina-forradalom pirruszi győzelme" (1917—The Pyrrhic victory of the Obshchina Revolution), in *1917 és ami utána következett*, ed. Tamás Krausz. Budapest: Magyar Ruszisztikai Intézet, 1998.

Bukharin, Nikolai, and Evgeniy Preobrazhensky. *The ABC of Communism*, trans. Eden and Cedar Paul. Harmondsworth, Middlesex: Penguin Books, 1969. In Russian, Nikolai Bukharin and Yevgeni Preobrazhenskiy. *Azbuka kommunizma*. St. Petersburg: Gosizdat Peterburg, 1920.

Buharin-tanulmányok: Demokrácia, cezarizmus, szocializmus (Essays on Bukharin: Democracy, tyranny, socialism) Budapest: ELTE ÁJTK, 1988.

Buldakov, Vladimir P. "Istoki i posledsztviya soldatskogo bunta: k voprosu o psihologii cheloveka s ruzhyom," in *1917 god v sudbah Rossii i mira. Fevralskaya revolyutsiya: Ot novih istochnyikov ko novomu osmisleniyu*, ed. P. V. Volobuyev. Moscow: RAN, 1997.

———. *Krasnaya smuta* (Red time of troubles), Moscow: ROSSPEN, 1997.

Bulgakov, Mikhail A. *Sárba taposva: Naplók, levelek 1917–1940* (Stamped into the mud: Diaries, letters 1917–1940). Budapest: Magvető, 2004.

———. *The White Guard*, trans. Michael Glenny. New York: McGraw-Hill, 1971.

Burtin, Yu. *Drugoy sotsializm: "Krasniye holmi."* Moscow: 1999.

Bustelo, Joaquin. "Critical Comments on 'Democratic Centralism,'" Atlanta: 2005. See www.marxmail.org/DemocraticCentralism.pdf.

Caffentzis, G. "Lenin on the Production of Revolution," in *What Is to Be Done? Leninism, Anti-Leninism and the Question of Revolution Today*, ed. W. Bonefeld and S. Tischler. Aldershot: Ashgate, 2002.

Carr, Edward Hallett. *The Bolshevik Revolution, 1917–1923*, vol. 1. London: Macmillan, 1960.

Clark, Ronald W. *Lenin: Behind the Mask*. London: Faber and Faber, 1988.

Cliff, Tony. *Lenin: Building the Party 1893–1914*. London: Bookmarks, 1986.

Cohen, S. F. *Bukharin and the Bolshevik Revolution: A Political Biography 1888–1938*. New York: Oxford University Press, 1973.

Coletti, L. *Il Marxismo e Hegel*. Bari: Laterza, 1976.

Corney, F. C. *Telling October: Memory and Making of the Bolshevik Revolution*. Ithaca: Cornell University Press, 2004.

Churakov, Dmitry. "A munkásönkormányzatok közösségi aspektusai az 1917-es orosz forradalomban" (Community in the laborers' local governments of the Russian Revolution of 1917), in *1917 és ami utána következett* (1917 and what followed), 53–67.

———. "Protestnoye dvizheniye rabochih v period skladivaniya sovyetskogo gosudarstva" (Workers' protest movements in the period of soviet state formation), *Alternativi* 2 (1999): 98–101.

Davies, N. *White Eagle, Red Star: The Polish-Soviet War, 1919–1920*. London: Random House, 1972.

Dmitrenko, V. P. *Sovyetskaya ekonomicheskaya politika v pervie godi proletarskoy diktaturi* (Soviet economic policy in the first years of the dictatorship of the proletariat). Moscow: Nauka, 1986.

Dolmányos, István. *A nemzetiségi politika története a Szovjetunióban* (The history of the politics of ethnic minorities in the Soviet Union). Budapest: Kossuth, 1964.

———.*Ragyogó Október: A nagy oroszországi szocialista forradalom története* (Radiant October: The history of the Great Russian Revolution), Budapest: Kossuth, 1979.

———. *A Szovjetunió története* (The history of the Soviet Union). Budapest: 1971.

Donáth, Péter. "A csak politikailag releváns Kanonizált Nagy Elbeszéléstől a tanulságos kis történetekig" (From the politically relevant, canonized great narratives to the little stories with morals), in *1917 és ami utána következett.*

———. *Elmélet és gyakorlat: A "baloldaliság" korai történetéhez: Gorkij, Lunacsarszkij, Bogdanov* (Theory and practice: Toward an early history of "leftism": Gorky, Lunacharsky, Bogdanov). Budapest: Budapesti Tanítóképző Főiskola, 1990.

Drama rossiskoy Istorii: Bolsheviki i revolyuciya, ed. O. V. Volobuyev et al. Moscow: Novij Hronograf, 2002.

Dumova, N. G. *Kadetskaya partiya v period pervoy mirovoy voyni i Fevralskoy revolyutsii.* Moscow: Nauka, 1988.

Dutschke, Rudi. *Versuch, Lenin auf Die Füsse zu stellen: Über den halbasiatischen und den west-europäischen Weg zum Sozialismus. Lenin, Lukács und die Dritte Internationale.* Berlin: Verlag Klaus Wagenbach, 1974.

El a kezekkel Szovjet-Oroszországtól (Hands off Soviet Russia). Budapest: Kossuth, 1979.

Életünk Kelet-Európa: Tanulmányok Niederhauser Emil 80 Születésnapjára (Our life is Eastern Europe: Essays for the 80th birthday of Emil Niederhauser), ed. Tamás Krausz and Gyula Szvák. Budapest, Pannonica, 2003.

Elwood, Ralph Carter. *Inessa Armand: Revolutionary and Feminist.* Cambridge: Cambridge University Press, 1992.

Farkas, Péter. *A globalizáció és fenyegetései: A világgazdaság és a gazdaságelméletek zavarai* (Globalization and its dangers: Disturbances in global economy and economic theory). Budapest: Aula Kiadó, 2002.

Fedukin, S. A. *Velikiy Oktyabr i intelligentsiya: Iz istorii vovlecheniya staroy intelligentsii v stroiteltstvo sotsializma.* Moscow: Nauka, 1972.

Felshtinsky, Yuriya. "O terrore i amninstiyah pervih revolyutsionnikh let" (On terror and amnesty in the first years of the revolution), in *VCHK—GPU: Dokumenti i materiali,* ed. Yu. G. Felshtinsky. Moscow: Gumanitarnoy Leteraturi, 1995.

Fischer, Louis. *The Life of Lenin.* New York-Evenston-London: Harper and Row Publisher, 1964.

———. *Zhizn' Lenina,* trans. Omry Ronena. London: Overseas Publications, 1970.

Froyanova, Ya. *Oktyabr semnadkatogo (Glyadya iz nastoyashchego)* (October 1917, From a current perspective). St. Petersburg: S P. Univesiteta, 1997.

Furet, François. *The Passing of an Illusion: The Idea of Communism in the Twentieth Century,* trans. Deborah Furet. Chicago: University of Illinois Press, 1999.

Fülöp, Mihály, and Péter Sipos. *Magyarország külpolitikája a XX. században* (Hungarian foreign policy in the twentieth century). Budapest: Aula, 1998.

Ganyelin, R. S., and M. F. Florinskiy. "Rossiyskaya gosudarstvennosty i pervaya mirovaya voyna" (Russian statehood and World War One), in *1917 god v sudbah Rossii i mira Fevralskaya revoluciy: Ot novikh istochnikov k novomu osmisleniyu* (The year 1917 in Russian and world history: The February Revolution, from the new sources to a new interpretation), ed. P. V. Volobuyev. Moscow: Instyitut Rossiyskoy Istorii RAN, 1997.

Gaponenko, L. S. *Rabochii Klass Rossii v 1917.* Moscow: 1970.

Garaudy, Roger. *Lenin.* Paris: PUF, 1968.

Gessen, Yu. I. *Istoriya yevreyskogo naroda v Rossii.* Leningrad: 1925; repr. Moscow and Jerusalem: 1993.

Getzler, Israel. *Martov: A Political Biography of a Russian Social Democrat.* Cambridge: Cambridge University Press and Melbourne University Press, 1967.

Gimpelson, E. G. *Novaya ekonomicheskaya politika Lenina-Stalina: Problemi i uroki (20-e godi XX v.)* (The NEP of Lenin and Stalin: Problems and lessons). Moscow: Sobranie, 2004.

Gimpelson, E. G. *Sovyetskiy rabochiy klass 1918–1920.* Moscow: 1974.

———. *Sovyeti v godi interventsii i grazhdanskoy voyni* (The Soviets in the years of intervention and civil war). Moscow: Nauka, 1968.

———. *Voyenniy kommunism: Politika, praktika, ideologiya.* Moscow: 1973.

Globalizáció, tőkekoncentráció, térszerkezet (Globalization, capital concentration and space structure), ed, Ágnes Bernek and Péter Farkas. Budapest: MTA Világgazdasági Kutatóintézet, 2006.

Göncöl, György. "Rosa Luxemburg helye a marxizmus fejlődéstörténetében" (Rosa Luxemburg's place in the evolutionary history of Marxism), Afterword in Rosa Luxemburg, *A tőkefelhalmozás* (*The Accumulation of Capital*). Budapest: Kossuth, 1979.

Gorodetsky, E. N. *Rozhdeniye sovetskogo gosudarstva 1917–1918*. Moscow: Nauka, 1987.

Gramsci, Antonio. *Selections from the Prison Notebooks*, trans. Quintin Hoare and Geoffrey Nowell Smith. London: ElecBook, 1999.

The Gramsci Reader: Selected Writings 1916-1935, ed. David Forgacs. New York: NYU Press, 2000.

GULAG: A szovjet táborrenmdszer története: Tanulmányok és dokumentumok (GULAG: The history of the Soviet camp system: Studies and documents), ed. Tamás Krausz. Budapest: Pannonica, 2001.

Gyáni, Gábor. *Posztmodern kánon* (The postmodern canon). Budapest: Nemzeti Tankönyvkiadó, 2003.

Dakin, V. S. *Bil li shans u Stolipina?* Moscow: LISS, 2002.

Hajdu, Tibor. *Közép-Európa forradalma 1917–1921* (The revolution of Central Europe 1917–1921). Budapest: Gondolat, 1989.

Hajdu, Tibor. "A szocialista állam elméletének történetéhez" (On the history of the socialist state), *Magyar Filozófiai Szemle* (Hungarian Philosophical Review) 2 (1970): 205–33.

Halász, Iván. *A tábornokok diktatúrái—a diktatúrák tábornokai: Fehérgárdista rezsimek az oroszországi polgárháborúban 1917–1920* (The dictatorships of the generals—the generals of the dictatorships: The White Guard regimes during the Russian civil war 1917–1920). Budapest: Magyar Ruszisztikai Intézet, 2005.

Hanák, Péter. "The Garden and the Workshop: Reflections on Fin-de-Siècle Culture in Vienna and Budapest," in *The Garden and the Workshop: Essays on the Cultural History of Vienna and Budapest*. Princeton: Princeton University Press, 1999. In German: "Die Volksmeinung wahrend des letzten Kriegsjahres in Österreich-Ungarn," in *Die Auflösung des Habsburgerreiches: Zusammenbruch und Neuorientierung im Donauraum,* vol. 3. Vienna: 1970), 58–66. And in Hungarian: "Népi levelek az I. világháborúból," in *A kert és a műhely*. Budapest: Gondolat, 1988.

Harding, Neil. *Lenin's Political Thought*, Vol. 2. New York: St. Martin´s Press,1981.

———. *Leninism*. Durham, NC: Duke University Press, 1996

Harman, Chris. *Party and Class*, ed, T. Cliff. London: Pluto Press, 1996.

Harsányi, Iván. "A spanyol liberalizmus történeti útja" (The historical road of the Spanish liberalism), *Múltunk* 3–4 (1998).

Hermann, István. "Az elméleti vita feltételei. A messianisztikus marxizmus avagy az úgynevezett nyugati marxizmus" (The conditions of a theoretical debate. Messianic Marxism or, so-called Western Marxism). *Világosság* 4 (1984): 214–15.

———. "Marxizmus és totalitás" (Marxism and totality), in *A gondolat hatalma* (The power of thought). Budapest: Szépirodalmi, 1978.

Hilferding, Rudolf. *Finance Capital: A Study of the Latest Phase of Capitalist Development*, ed. Tom Bottomore. London: Routledge & Kegan Paul, 1981.

Hobsbawm, E. J. *The Age of Extremes: The Short Twentieth Century, 1914–1991.* New York: Pantheon Books, 1994.

———. *Interesting Times: A Twentieth-Century Life*. London: Abacus, 2005.

———. *Nations and Nationalism since 1780: Programme, Myth, Reality*. Cambridge: Cambridge University Press, 1990.

———. *The Age of Capital, 1848–1875*. London: Abacus, 1975.

———. *On History*. New York: New Press, 1997.

Holquist, Peter. *Making War, Forging Revolution: Russia's Continuum of Crisis 1914–1921.* Cambridge, MA: Harvard University Press, 2002.

Horváth, Gizella. "A fasizmus és a kommunizmus összefüggéséről: François Furet titkai" (On the correlation between fascism and communism: The secrets of François Furet). *Eszmélet* 47: 33–44.

Illeritskaya, N. V. "Razrabotka Yemelyanom: Yaroslavskim biografii V. I. Lenina," *Istoriskaya is istoriki*. Moscow: Nauka, 1981.

Ilinichna-Elizarova, Anna et al. *Reminiscences of Lenin by His Relatives.* Moscow: Foreign Languages Publishing House, 1956.

Ilyuhov, A. *Zhizny v epohu peremen: Materialnoye polozheniye gorodskih zhitelev v godi revolyutsii i grazhdanskoy voyni* (Life in the period of change: The material situation of urban dwellers in the period of revolution and civil war). Moscow: ROSSPEN, 2007.

Ivanov, Yu. M. *Chuzhoy sredi svoih: Posledniye godi zhizni Lenina.* Moscow: 2002.

Joffe, G. Z. *Beloye Delo: General Kornilov* (White matter: General Kornilov). St. Petersburg: 1989.

Joffe, G. Z. *Kolchakovskaya avantyura i yeyo krakh* (Kolchak adventure and its collapse). Moscow: Misl, 1983.

Jukes, Geoffrey et al. *The First World War: The Eastern Front 1914–1918,* vol. 1. Oxford: Osprey Publishing, 2002.

Kelet-Európa: történelem és sorsközösség, Palotás Emil 70. születésnapjára (Eastern Europe: History and a common lot, Commemorating the 70th birthday of Emil Palotás), ed. Tamás Krausz. Budapest: ELTE Kelet-Európa Története Tanszék, 2007.

Kelner, V. "Russkaya intelligentsiya i 'yevreyskiy vopros' v nachale XX veka," in *Russko-yevreyskiy i istoriko-yevreyskiy literaturniy i bibliograficheskiy almanakh* 4–5 (2004)..

Klier, J. *Imperial Russia's Jewish Question, 1855–1881.* Cambridge: Cambridge University Press, 1995.

Knei-Paz, Baruch. *The Social and Political Thought of Leon Trotsky.* Oxford: Clarendon Press, 1978.

Koenker, D.P., Rosenberg, W.G. and Suny, R.G., eds. *Party, State and Society in the Russian Civil War: Explorations in Social History.* Bloomington: Indiana University Press, 1992.

Kolesov, Dimitri Vasilyevich. *V.I. Lenin: Lichnost i sudba.* Moscow: Izd. "Flinta," 1999.

Kolganov, Andrey. *Puty k sotsializmu: Tragediya i podvig.* Moscow: Ekonomika, 1990.

Komintern i ideya mirovoy revolyutsii. Moscow: Nauka, 1998.

Kornai, János. *The Socialist System. The Political Economy of Communism.* Princeton: Princeton University Press, and Oxford: Oxford University Press, 1992.

——. *By Force of Thought: Irregular Memoirs of an Intellectual Journey.* Cambridge, MA; London: MIT Press, 2007.

Kostirchenko, G. V. *Taynaya politika Stalina: Vlasty i antisemitizm.* Moscow: M. O, 2003.

Kotelenec, Elena. *V. I. Lenin kak predmet istoricheskogo issledovania.* Moscow: Izdatel'stvo Rossijskogo universiteta družby narodov, 1999.

Kotkin, St. "1991 and the Russian Revolution: Sources, Conceptual Categories, Analytical Frameworks," *Journal of Modern History* 70/3 (1998): 384–425.

Krasuski, Jerzy. *Tragiczna niepodległosc: Polityka zagraniczna Polski w latach 1919–1945* (Tragic independence: Polish foreign policy 1919–1945). Poznań: 2000.

Krausz, Tamás. "Szocializmus-képek a húszas években: Átmeneti korszak és szocializmus" (Images of socialism in the twenties: A transitional period in socialism). *Világosság* 4 (1984): 202–10.

——. *The Soviet and Hungarian Holocausts: A Comparative Essay*, Hungarian Authors Series no. 4, trans. Thomas J. DeKornfeld and Helen D. Hiltabidle (Boulder, CO: Social Science Monographs; Wayne, NJ: Center for Hungarian Studies and Publications; New York: Columbia University Press, 2006), 13–14. Hungarian original: *Antiszemitizmus—holokauszt—államszocializmus* (Anti-Semitism—Holocaust—state socialism). Budapest: Nemzeti Tankönyvkiadó, 2004.

——. "Bolsevizmus és nemzeti kérdés" (Bolshevism and the national question). *Világosság* 1 (1980): 681–88.

——. "Az első orosz forradalom és az oroszországi szociáldemokrácia 'második' szakadása" (The "second split" of the first Russian revolution and Russian social democracy). *Századok*4 (1983).

——. "A jelCINIZMUS" (What is yelTSINICISM), in *Jelcin és a Jelcinizmus* (Yeltsin and Yeltsinism), ed. Tamás Krausz, Ákos Szilágyi. Budapest: Magyar Russzisztikai Intézet, 1993, 67–92; and *Konyec Jelcinscsini.*

Budapest: Magyar Russzisztikai Intézet, 1999.

——. "Kutatás közben: Megjegyzések a Lenin-tematikához az 'új' dokumentumok fényében" (In the course of research: Comments regarding the Lenin topic in light of the "new" documents), in *Lenintől Putyinig* (From Lenin to Putin). Budapest: La Ventana, 2003, 15–27.

——. "Lenin és a lengyel-szovjet háború" (Lenin and the Polish-Soviet war), in Életünk Kelet-Európa, 120–26.

——. "Lenin marxizmusa" (Lenin's Marxism), *Eszmélet* 76 (Winter 1997).

——. "Az Összorszországi Alkotmányozó Gyűlés és a bolsevikok" (The All-Russia Constituent Assembly and the Bolsheviks), in *Dél-Európa vonzásában: Tanulmányok Harsányi Iván 70: Születésnapjára*. Pécs: Special edition, 2000, 1–15.

——. *Pártviták és történettudomány: Viták "az orosz történelmi fejlődés sajátosságairól", különös tekintettel a 20-as évekre* (In-party conflicts and historical science: Debates about the "specificities of Russian historical development," especially in the 20s). Budapest: Akadémiai Kiadó, 1991.

——. "Perestroika and the Redistribution of Property in the Soviet Union: Political Perspectives and Historical Evidence," *Contemporary Politics* 13/1 (March 2007). In Hungarian, "A peresztrojka és tulajdonváltás. Politikai koncepciók és történelmi valóság," in *Peresztrojka és tulajdonáthelyezés. Tanulmányok és dokumentumok a rendszerváltás történetéből a Szovjetunióban (1985–1991)*, ed. Tamás Krausz and Zoltán Sz. Bíró. Budapest: MRI, 2003, 52–102.

——. "A 'Rövid tanfolyam' és a történelem" (The "short course" and course of history), *Világosság* 3 (1989): 174–79.

——. "'Stalin's Socialism'—Today's Debates on Socialism: Theory, History, Politics," *Contemporary Politics* 11/4 (2005): 235–38.

——. "A szakszervezeti kérdés az OK(b)P X. kongresszusán (1921)" (The trade union issue at the Tenth Congress of the RCP(b) 1921), in *A nemzetközi munkásmozgalom történetéből*. Évkönyv 1981 (Toward a history of the international workers' movement. Annuary 1981). Budapest: Kossuth, 1980, 156–66.

——. *A Szovjetunió története* (The history of the Soviet Union). Budapest: Kossuth, 2008.

——. *Szovjet thermidor: A sztálini fordulat szellemi előzményei 1917–1928* (Soviet Thermidor: The intellectual roots of the Stalinist turn). Budapest: Napvilág, 1996.

——. "Ahistorical Political Economics," *Social Scientist* 24/1–3 (January–March 1996): 111–39.

Krausz, Tamás, and Miklós Mesterházi. *Mű és történelem: Viták Lukács György műveiről a húszas években* (The written word and history: Controversies about Lukács's work in the 1920s). Budapest: Gondolat, 1985.

Kropotkin, P. *Mutual Aid: A Factor of Evolution*, ed. with an Introduction by Paul Avrich. New York: New York University Press, 1972.

Krupskaya, N. K. "Kak Lenin rabotal nad Marksom?," in *Lenin i kniga*. Moscow: Izd. Pol. Lit, 1964.

——. "How Lenin Approached the Study of Marx," *Lenin and Books*, trans. and comp. A. Z. Okorokov. Moscow: Progress Publishers, 1971.

Kun Béláról: Tanulmányok (On Béla Kun: Essays), ed. György Milei. Budapest: Kossuth, 1988.

Laqueur, W. *Chornaya sotnya*. Moscow: Tekst, 1994.

Latishev, A. G. *Rassekrechionniy Lenin*. Moscow: MART, 1996.

——. "Lenin és Inessza," *Eszmélet* 42 (1999): 67–95.

Lefebvre, Henri. "La pensée de Lénine," first published in 1957, repr. in *Lenin Reloaded*.

Lengyel, István. *A breszt-litovszki béketárgyalások* (The peace talks of Brest-Litovsk). Budapest: Kossuth, 1975.

Lenin, Vladimir Ilyich: A Biography, ed. P. N. Pospelov. Moscow: Progress Publishers, 1965.

Lenin i Simbirsk. Saratov, 1968.

Lenin műveinek Magyar bibliográfiája 1960-1969 (A Hungarian bibliography of Lenin's works, 1960–1969). Budapest: MSZMP KB Párttörténeti Intézete, 1970.

Le Blanc, Paul. *Lenin and the Revolution-*

ary Party, with an introduction by Ernest Mandel. Atlantic Highlands, NJ: Humanities Press, 1990.

Lezhava, O., and N. Nelidov. *M. S. Olminsky: Zhizn i deyatelnosty*. Moscow: Politizdat, 1973.

Liebman, Marcel. *Leninism under Lenin*, trans. Brian Pearce. London: Jonathan Cape, 1975. Originally published in French as *Le léninisme sous Lénine*. Paris: Édition du Seuil, 1973.

Lih, Lars T. *Lenin Rediscovered:* What Is To Be Done? *In Context*. Chicago: Haymarket Books, 2008.

Loginov, Vladlen. *Vladimir Lenin: Vybor puti*. Moscow: Respublika, 2005.

Lopuhin, Yuriy Mikhaylovic. *Bolezny, smerty i balzamirovanie V. I. Lenina*. Moscow: Respublika, 1997.

Losskiy, B. N. "O deportatsii ljudej mishleniya." (On the 'Deportation of the Men of Thought' in 1922), *Stupeni: Filosofsky zhurnal* 1/4 (1992).

Löwy, Michael. *Redemption and Utopia—Jewish Libertarian Thought in Central Europe: A Study in Elective Affinity*. Stanford, CA: Stanford University Press, 1992.

Lukács, Georg. *Lenin: A Study on the Unity of His Thought*. New York: Verso Books, 2009.

———. *A társadalmi lét ontológiájáról* (The ontology of social being), vol. 3: *Prolegomena*. Budapest: Magvető könyvkiadó, 1976.

———. *History and Class Consciousness*, trans. Rodney Livingstone. Cambridge, MA: MIT Press, 1971; and Budapest: Magveto, 1971.

Lunacharsky, A. V. *Ob antisemitizme*. Moscow and Leningrad: 1929.

———. "Lenin i literaturovedenie," *Literaturnaya Entsiklopediya*, vol. 11. Moscow: 1932.

Lyandres, Semion. *The Bolsheviks' "German Gold" Revisited: An Inquiry into the 1917 Accusations*, Carl Beck papers in Russian and East European Studies, no. 1106. Pittsburgh: Center for Russian and East European Studies, University of Pittsburgh, 1995.

Majoros, István. "A lengyel-szovjet háború: Wrangel és a francia külpolitika 1920-ban" (The Polish-Soviet War: Wrangel and the French foreign policy of 1920), *Századok* 3 (2001): 533-67.

Maysuryan, Aleksandr A. *Drugoj Lenin* (A different Lenin). Moscow: Vagrius, 2006.

Makarov, V. G., and V. S. Hristoforov. "Predislovie," in *Visilka vmesto rasstrela: Deportatsiya intelligentsii v dokumentah VCSK-GPU 1921-1923*. Moscow: Russkiy puty, 2005.

Maksimova, V. A. *Leninskaya* Iskra *i lityeratura*. Moscow: Nauka, *Iskra*, 1975.

Mandel, Ernest. "Trotsky's Marxism: A Rejoinder," *New Left Review* 56 (1969): 69-96.

Marie, Jean-Jacques. *Lénine, 1870-1924, Biographie*. Paris: Editions Balland, 2004.

Marx, Karl. *Die Geschichte der Geheimdiplomatie des 18 Jahrhunderts*. West Berlin: Verlag Olle und Wolter, 1977.

———. *Grundrisse*, trans. Martin Nicolaus. New York: Random House, 1973.

———. *Capital*, vol. 1, trans. Samuel Moore and Edward Aveling.

Mayer, Robert. "Lenin and the Practice of Dialectical Thinking," *Science and Society* 63/1 (Spring 1999): 40-62.

Melnichenko, Vladimir. *Lichnai'a zhizn' Lenina*. Moscow: Voskresen'e, 1998.

———. *Fenomen i Fantom Lenina. (350 miniatur)* (The Lenin phenomenon and phantom. 350 miniatures). Moscow: Lenin Museum, 1993.

Menyhárt, Lajos. *Az orosz társadalmi-politikai gondolkodás a századfordulón (1895-1906)* (Russian sociopolitical thought at the turn of the century, 1895-1906). Budapest: Akadémiai Kiadó, 1985.

Mészáros, István. *Beyond Capital*. London: Merlin Press, 1995.

Mihutina, I. B. "Nekotorie problemi istorii polsko-sovetskoy voyni 1919-1920" (Some of the problems of the history of the Polish-Soviet War), in *Versaly i novaya Vostochnaya Yevropa*. Moscow: 1996, 159-76.

Miliukov, P. N. *Ocherki po istorii russkoy kulturi*, vol. 1. Paris: 1937.

Miller, Viktor I. "Revolyutsiya v Rossii 1917-1918" (Revolution in Russia 1917-1918), lecture based on the author's PhD diss., in *Ostorozhno: istoriya!* (Watch out: History!). Moscow: ETC, 1997.

——. "Grazhdanskaya voyna: Istoricheskiye paralleli" (The civil war: Historical parallels), in *Ostorozhno: istoriya!*

Mironov, Boris N. *The Social History of Imperial Russia 1700–1917*, vol. 1. Boulder, CO: Westview Press, 2000.

"Dissemination and reception of the *Grundrisse* in the world. Introduction," in *Karl Marx's Grundrisse*, London–New York: Routledge 2008, pp. 177–188.

Musto, Marcello. "The Rediscovery of Karl Marx," *International Review of Social History* 52 (2007) 477–98.

Nedava, Joseph. *Trotsky and the Jews*. Philadelphia: Jewish Publication Society of America, 1971.

A NEP tapasztalatai a Szovjetunióban (The empirical evidences of the NEP in the Soviet Union). Budapest: Kossuth, 1975.

Niederhauser, Emil. "Lenin és a nemzeti kérdés" (Lenin and the national question), in *Nemzet és kisebbség* (Nation and minority). Budapest: Lucidus, 2001, 65–83.

——. *Nemzet és kisebbségek: Válogatott tanulmányok* (Nation and national minorities: Selected essays). Budapest, Lucidus, 2001

——. *A nemzeti megújulási mozgalmak Kelet-Európában* (The movements for national renewal in Eastern Europe). Budapest: Akadémiai Kiadó, 1977.

——. "On the Slavophile Approach to History," *Acta Universitatis Debreciensis de L. K. nominatae*, Series Historica. Debrecen: 1966.

Nove, Alec. "Lenin as Economist," in *Lenin: The Man, the Theorist, the Leader*, ed. Leonard Schapiro and Peter Reddaway. New York: Praeger, 1967.

Obshchestvennoye dvizheniye v nachale XX veka, vol. 1. St. Petersburg: 1909.

Oyzerman, T. I. *Opravdanyije revizionyizma*. Moscow: Kanon, 2005.

Omelyanchuk, I. V. "Sotsialniy sostav chernosotyennih partiy v nachale XX veka" (The Black Hundreds Party and its social composition at the beginning of the twentieth century), *Otechestvennaya istoriya* 2 (2004).

Önkormányzás vagy az elitek uralma (Self-government or the reign of the elites), ed. Tamás Krausz and László Tütő. Budapest: Liberter Kiadó, 1995.

Ostrovsky, V. *P. A. Stolipin i ego vremya*. Novosibirsk: Nauka, 1992.

Palotás, Emil. *A Balkán-kérdés az osztrák-magyar és az orosz diplomáciában* (The issue of the Balkan in the Austro-Hungarian and Russian diplomacy). Budapest: Akadémiai Kiadó, 1972.

Pannekoek, Anton. *Lenin as Philosopher: A Critical Examination of the Philosophical Basis of Leninism*. New York: New Essays, 1948.

——. *Living Marxism* 4/5 (November 1938), available at http://www.marxists.org/archive/pannekoek/1938/lenin/app-korsch.htm.

Pantin, I. K. *Socialisticheskaya misl v Rosszii: perehod ot utopii k nauke*. Moscow: Polit. Izdat, 1973

——. "Istoricheskiye sudbi marxizma," *Vestniik Rossiyskoy, Akademii Nauk*8 (2006).

Pastor, Peter. "Hungary between Wilson and Lenin: The Hungarian Revolution of 1918–1919 and the Big Three," East European Monographs 20, Boulder, Colorado:*East European Quarterly 1976.* (1976).

Pavlyuchenkov, S. P. "Yevreyskiy vopros v revolyutsii, ili o prichinah porozheniya bolshevikov na Ukrainye v 1919 godu," in *Voyenniy kommunizm: Vlasty i massi.* Moscow: 1997.

Pinkus, Benjamin. *The Jews of the Soviet Union: The History of a National Minority*. Cambridge, New York, and Sidney: Cambridge University Press, 1989.

Pipes, Richard. *Social Democracy and St. Petersburg's Labor Movement 1885–1897*. Cambridge, MA: Harvard University Press, 1963.

——. *Struve, Liberal on the Left, 1870–1905*. Cambridge, MA: Harvard University Press, 1970.

——. *Struve, Liberal on the Right, 1905–1944*. Cambridge, MA: Harvard University Press, 1980.

Platten, Fritz. *Lenin iz emigracii v Rossiju*. Moscow: Moskovsky rabochy, 1990.

Pokrovsky, N. N. *Politburo i tserkov 1922–1925* (The Politburo and the Church). Moscow: ROSSPEN, 1997.

———. "Istochnikovedeniye sovetskogo perioda: Dokumenti Politburo pervoy polovini 1920-h godov" (Archival research in the Soviet period), in *Arheograficheszky Yezhegodnik za 1994.* Moscow: 1996.

Polan, A. J. *Lenin and the End of Politics.* London: Methuen, 1984.

Poselov, P.N., ed. *Lenin, Vladimir Ilyich: A Biography,* Moscow: Progress Publishers, 1965.

Protasov, L. G. *Vserossiyskoye uchreditelnoye sobraniye, istoriya, rozhdeniya i gibeli* (The All-Russia Constituent Assembly: Its history, formation and demise). Moscow: ROSSPEN, 1997.

Regelson, L. *Tragediya Russkoy Tserkvi, 1917–1945.* Paris: 1977.

Réti, László. *Lenin és a magyar munkásmozgalom* (Lenin and the Hungarian labor movement). Budapest: Kossuth, 1970.

Ripp, Géza. *Imperializmus és reformizmus* (Imperialism and reformism). Budapest: Kossuth, 1982.

Sakharov, Andrei Nikolaevich et al. *Rossiia v nachale XX veka.* Moscow: Novyĭ khronograf, 2002.

Sakharov, V. A. *"Politicheskoe zaveshchaniye" Lenina. Realnosty istorii i mifi politiki.* Moscow: Moskovskogo Universiteta, 2003.

Schapiro, Leonard and Reddaway, Peter, eds. *Lenin: The Man, the Theorist, the Leader,* New York, Praeger, 1967.

Scherrer, Jutta. "The Relationship between the Intelligentsia and Workers: The Case of Party Schools in Capri and Bologna," in *Workers and Intelligentsia in Late Imperial Russia: Realities, Representations, Reflections,* ed. Reginald E. Zelnik. Berkeley: Regents of the University of California, 1998, http://escholarship.org/uc/item/27p076zk.

———. "Culture prolétarienne et religion socialiste entre deux revolutions: Les Bolsheviks de gauche," *Europa* 2/2 (1979): 69–70.

Service, Rober. *Lenin: A Political Life,* 3 vols. London: Macmillan, 1985–1995.

Setinov, Yu. A. "Melkoburzhoaznie partyi v Kronshtadtskom myatyezhe 1921 goda" (The petit-bourgeois parties in the Kronstadt revolt of 1921), *Vestnik Moskovskogo Universiteta* 3 (1974): 28.

Shtein, M. *Ulyanovy i Leniny: Tainy rodoslovnoi i psevdonima.* St. Petersburg: VIRD, 1997.

Shub, David. *Lenin: A Biography.* Baltimore: Penguin, 1967.

Sikman, A. P. *Deyateli otechesztvennoj isztorii: Biograficheskiy spravochnik.* Moscow: 1997.

Sipos, Péter. "A Nemzetközi Szakszervezeti Szövetség és az 1920 évi lengyel-szovjet háború" (The International Association of Labor Unions and the Polish-Soviet War of 1920), in *El a kezekkel Szovjet-Oroszországtól* (Hands off Soviet Russia). Budapest: Kossuth, 1979.

Somogyi, Erika. "Magyarország részvételi kísérlete az 1920-as lengyel–szovjet háborúban" (The Hungarian effort to participate in the Polish-Soviet War of 1920), *Történelmi Szemle* 2 (1986).

Steffens, Lincoln. *The Autobiography of Lincoln Steffens.* New York: Harcourt, Brace, 1931.

Swain, Geoffrey. *The Origins of the Russian Civil War.* Essex: Longman, 1996.

Szabó, András György. "Marx és az államszocializmus" (Marx and state-socialism), *Eszmélet* 4 (March 1990): 103–14.

———. *A proletárforradalom világnézete: A filozófia bírálata* (The proletarian revolution's worldview: A critique of its philosophy). Budapest: Magvető, 1977.

Szabó, Márton. *Politikai idegen* (The political stranger). Budapest: L'Harmattan, 2006.

Szakszervezetek és államhatalom: Dokumentumok a szovjet-oroszországi szakszervezetek történetéből 1917–1923 (Trade unions and state power: Documents from the history of trade unions in Soviet Russia, 1917–1923), ed. Béládi László. Budapest: ELTE ÁJTK, 1985.

Szamuely, László. *Az első szocialista gazdasági mechanizmusok* (The first socialist economic mechanisms). Budapest: Közgazdasági és Jogi Könyvkiadó, 1971.

Székely, Gábor. "Kun Béla a Kommunista Internacionáléban" (Béla Kun in the Communist International), in *Kun Béláról: Tanulmányok* (On Béla Kun: Essays), ed. György Milei. Budapest: Kossuth, 1988.

Szekfű, Gyula. *Lenin.* Budapest: Magyar-Szovjet Művelődési Társaság, 1948.

Szigeti, Péter. *Világrendszernézőben: Globális "szabad verseny"—a világkapitalizmus jelenlegi stádiuma* (Survey of world orders: Global "free competition"—the current stage of world capitalism). Budapest: Napvilág, 2005.

Sziklai, László. "A materializmus és empiriokriticizmus történelmi tanulságai" (The historical lessons of materialism and empiriocriticism), in *Történelmi lecke haladóknak* (Advanced lessons of history). Budapest: Magvető, 1977.

Szilágyi, Ákos."Totális temetés" (Total funeral), *2000* 5 (1993).

Silvin, Michail Aleksandrovich. *Lenin v period zarozhdeniya partii vospominaniya*. Leningrad: Lenizdat, 1958.

Struve, Petr. "Lenin kak chelovek," repr. in *Novoe Russkoe Slovo,* 25 January 1976, 2–28.

Tarle, E. V. "Germanskaya orientaciya i P. N. Durnovo," *Biloe* 19 (1922):161–62.

Therborn, Goran. "After Dialectics. Radical Social Theory in a Post-Communist World," *New Left Review* 43 (2007).

Trudovie konflikti v Szovetszkoj Roszszii 1918–1929. Moscow, Editorial URSZSZ, 1998

Tütő, László. "Gramsci és a gazdasági demokrácia kérdése" (Gramsci and the question of economic democracy), in *Tanulmányok Gramsciról* (Studies on Gramsci), ed. József Banyár. Budapest: MKKE Társadalomelméleti Kollégium, 1987, 85–111.

Tütő, László, and Tamás Krausz. "Lenin a szocializmusba való politikai átmenet időszakáról" (Lenin on the period of transition to socialism), *Társadalmi Szemle* 6–7 (1984): 108–16.

Tucker, Robert C. "Lenin's Bolshevism as a Culture in the Making," in *Bolshevik Culture: Experiment and Order in the Russian Revolution*, ed. Abbott Gleason, Peter Kenez, and Richard Stittes. Bloomington: Indiana University Press, 1985.

Tumarkin, Nina. *Lenin Lives! The Lenin Cult in Soviet Russia.* Cambridge, MA/London: Harvard University Press, 1983.

Tyrkova-Williams, Ariadna. *Na putiakh k svobode* (On the road to freedom). New York: Chekhov Publishing House, 1952.

Tyutyukin S. V.. *Pervaya rossiyskaya revolyutsia i G. V. Plekhanov.* Moscow: Nauka, 1981.

Ulyanova, Olga Dmitrievna. *Rodnoy Lenin.* Moscow: ITRK, 2002.

Urilov, Kh. *Martov—polityk i historic* (Martov—politician and historian). Moscow: Nauka, 1997.

Válaszúton (Crossways), in the series *Politikatudományi Füzetek* no. 7, ed. Tamás Krausz and László Tütő. Budapest: ELTE ÁJTK, 1988.

Varga, Lajos. "Az Oroszországi Szociáldemokrata Munkáspárt első, 1903-as agrárprogramja" (The first agrarian program of the Russian social democratic labor party from 1903), *Párttörténeti Közlemények* (Party historical publications) no. 3. 1978.

Velikanova, Olga. "Lenin alakja a 20-as évek tömegtudatában" (The figure of Lenin in the mass consciousness of the '20s), *Eszmélet* 20 (December 1993).

Volkogonov, Dmitriy. A. *Lenin: istoricheszkij portret. T. 1–2.* Moscow: Novosztyi, 1994.

Volkov, F. D. *Velikij Lenin i pigmei istorii.* Moscow: MID RF, 1996.

Volkova, G. "Istoricheskiy vibor" (Historical choice), in *Leninskaya kontseptsiya sotsializma.* Moscow: Polityicheskoy literature, 1990.

Wade, Rex A. *Revolutionary Russia: New Approaches.* London: Routledge, 2004.

What Is to Be Done? Leninism, Anti-Leninism and the Question of Revolution Today, ed. W. Bonefeld and S. Tischler. Aldershot: Ashgate, 2002.

Williams, Robert. *The Other Bolsheviks: Lenin and His Critics 1904–1914.* Bloomington: Indiana University Press, 1986.

Wirth, Ádám. *Lenin a filozófus* (Lenin the philosopher). Budapest: Kossuth, 1971.

Yakovlev, A. N. *Rossiya nepovskaya.* Moscow: Noviy hronograf, 2002.

Yakovlev, Egor. *The Beginning: The Story about the Ulyanov Family, Lenin's Childhood and Youth*, trans. Catherine Judelson. Moscow: Progress Publishers, 1988.

Yazhborovskaya, I. S., and V. S. Parsadanova, *Rossiya i Polsa: Sindrom voyni 1920* (Russia and Poland: The syndrome of the war of 1920). Moscow: 2005.

Zalezhskiy, K. A. *Imperiya Stalina. Biograficheskiy entziklopedicheskiy slovar.* Moscow, Veche, 2000.

Zetkin, Clara. *Reminiscences of Lenin.* London: Modern Books, 1929.

Zilbershtein, I. S. *Molodoy Lenin v zhiznyi I z rabotoy: Po vospominaniyam sovremennikov I dokumentam epochi.* Moscow: 1929.

Žižek, S. "Afterwords: Lenin's Choice," in *Revolution at the Gates,* ed. S. Žižek. London: Verso, 2002.

——. *13 opitov o Lenine.* Moscow: Izdatelstvo Ad Marginem, 2003.

Zsidókérdés Kelet- és Közép-Európában (The Jewish question in Eastern and Central Europe). Budapest, ELTE ÁJTK TSZ, 1985.

Notes

PREFACE

1. Karl Marx, *Capital*, vol. 1, translated by Samuel Moore and Edward Aveling (Moscow: Progress Publishers, 1887), 536.
2. If not the figure of Lenin itself, then at least the history and interpretation of the Russian Revolution has naturally remained a central theme in Russian studies. A succinct account of the coexisting different approaches in historiography—from postmodern to the old conservative and new cultural explanations—can be found in: *1917 god revolyucionnaya Rossiya. Sbornik obsorov i referatov* (Moscow: INION Press, 2007).
3. Georg Lukács, *Lenin: A Study on the Unity of His Thought* (New York: Verso Books, 2009).
4. In the early 1970s, Rudi Dutschke discovered the importance of this Lukács study in the history of Lenin's reception, and thereon made a serious effort to reconstruct Lenin's theoretical achievement, to "put Lenin on his feet." See *Versuch, Lenin auf Die Füsse zu stellen. Über den halbasiatischen und den west-europäischen Weg zum Sozialismus. Lenin, Lukács und die Dritte Internationale* (Berlin: Verlag Klaus Wagenbach, 1974).
5. Gyula Szekfű, *Lenin* (Budapest: Magyar-Szovjet Művelődési Társaság, 1948).
6. *Lenin műveinek Magyar bibliográfiája 1960-1969* [A Hungarian bibliography of Lenin's works, 1960–1969], (Budapest: MSZMP KB Párttörténeti Intézete, 1970). The volume was published "with the objective to support the increase of general and scientific interest on the occasion of the Lenin Centenary." Another publication befitting the times, which appeared for the centenary published by Kossuth Kiadó, was *Lenin és a magyar munkásmozgalom* [Lenin and the Hungarian labor movement] by László Réti, a truly exhaustive treatment of the subject.
7. The last such extensive Soviet Lenin biography to appear in Hungarian came out in 1980, *Lenin. Életrajz* [Lenin. Biography], edited by P. N. Pospelov, 3rd edition (Budapest: Kossuth Kiadó, 1980).
8. See Tamás Krausz, "Kutatás közben. Megjegyzések a Lenin-tematikához az 'új' dokumentumok fényében" [In the course of research. Notes on the Lenin theme in light of the "new" documents], *Történeti Tanulmányok IX.* (Debrecen: Debrecen University, 2001), 83–84, 97.
9. Louis Fischer, *The Life of Lenin* (New York, Evanston, London: Harper and Row Publisher, 1964).
10. Louis Fischer, *Zhizn' Lenina*, translated by Omry Ronena (London: Overseas Publications Limited, 1970).
11. The historiographic exploration of research dealing with Lenin's biography in the 1920s had already begun. See N. V. Illeritskaya, "Razrabotka Yem. Yaroslavskim biografii V. I. Lenina," *Istoriskaya is istoriki* (Moscow: Nauka, 1981), 165–184. Usually only the "Leninisms" of Stalin, Zinoviev, Kamenev or Bukharin are mentioned when speaking about the 1920s, while the *Leniniana* (Moscow–Leningrad: Gos. Izd., 1926), edited by Kamenev, published two volumes of literature on Lenin. In Hungary, progressive literature on contemporary

Soviet history of the period and Lenin's role within it was published from 1980 onwards in *A nemzetközi munkásmozgalom történetéből. Évkönyv* [On the history of the international workers' movement. Annual], ed. by Iván Harsányi, János Jemnitz, and Gábor Székely.

12. This enormous, multiauthored project elaborated the scientific framework and historical content of Marxism-Leninism over thousands of pages, but the work finally remained truncated as the change of regimes discontinued the series. *Istoriya marksizma-leninizma* (Moscow: Politicheskoy Literaturi, 1986, 1990), Vols. 1-2.
13. E. Hobsbawm, *Interesting Times. A Twentieth Century Life* (London: Abacus, 2005), 328.
14. Ibid., 137.
15. Ibid, 137.
16. A. G. Latishev, *Rassekrechionniy Lenin* (Moscow: MART, 1996).
17. Possibly the best specialist historical outline of the new period is given by the writers' collective led by Volobuyev (A. A. Kosakovskiy, V. I. Startsev, A. I. Stepanov, S. V. Ustinkin, A. I. Utkin), O. V. Volobuyev, *Drama rossiskoy Istorii: Bolsheviki i revolyuciya* (Moscow: Novij Hronograf, 2002).
18. Ibid., introduction.
19. In the course of his political deployment of the new documents that emerged from the archives, Richard Pipes published a selection of the "new" Lenin documents without even undertaking a proper source analysis. For the results of this tendentious selection process, see the 120 Lenin documents in Richard Pipes, *The Unknown Lenin: From the Secret Archive. Annals of Communism* (New Haven: Yale University Press, 1996).
20. The best conceptual experiment born of this intellectual "subversion" is Robert Service's extensive, three-volume work whose first volume—of the 1980s—was written in the knowledge of Lenin's "greatness," the two following volumes of the 1990s are essentially about the "disjointedness" of Lenin's thought, the argument mostly going no further than to put forward an apologia of the "narrative" of the terror and dictatorship, along with the "decontextualization," "deconstruction," and "disassembly" of the Leninian texts. See Robert Service, *Lenin: A Political Life*, Vols. I–III (London: Macmillan, 1985–1995).
21. *V. I. Lenin: Neizvestnye dokumenty. 1891–1922* [V. I. Lenin: The Unknown Documents], edited by Yuriy Nikolaevich Amiantov, Yuriy Aleksandrovich Akhapkin, Vladlen Nikolaevich Stepanov, and V. T. Loginov (Moscow: ROSSPEN, 1999).
22. V. I. Lenin, *Neizvestnya dokumenty, posleslovie*, op. cit., 581.
23. Vladimir Melnichenko, *Lichnai'a zhizn' Lenina* (Moscow: Voskresen'e, 1998), 113.
24. Nonetheless, the last director of the Lenin Museum (from 1991–1993), tasked with its "liquidation," engages in research in this field with the aim of gaining respect for the facts in Vladimir Melnichenko, *Fenomen i Fantom Lenina. (350 miniatur)* [The Lenin phenomenon and phantom. 350 miniatures] (Moscow: Lenin Museum, 1993).
25. Elena Kotelenec, *V. I. Lenin kak predmet istoricheskogo issledovania* (Moscow: Izdatel'stvo Rossijskogo universiteta družby narodov, 1999), 9–10. He counted as the most popular by far in 1989, as 68 percent of those surveyed thought him the most outstanding historical figure, above Marx and Peter the Great.
26. There was a district where the workers demanded the execution of participants and organizers of the imagined assassination of Lenin. The secret police reports that in the regency of Tambov "Lenin's death has depressed the workers. With 1,000 participants the Rail Worker's Club brought a unanimous decision to have all imprisoned Esers [Socialist Revolutionaries] shot without delay [a reference to the fact that an Eser assassin, Dora Kaplan, wounded Lenin in August 1918], their being implicated in Lenin's death." *Neizvestnaya Rossia XX vek. IV.* [The unknown twentieth century], edited by V. A. Kozlov (Moscow: Obyedyineniye "Mosgorarchiv," 1993), 13.

27. An analysis of the documents is in Olga Velikanova, "Lenin alakja a 20-as évek tömegtudatában" [The figure of Lenin in the mass consciousness of the 20s], *Eszmélet* 20 (December 1993), 190–202. The problem is made even more explicit by the various secret GPU reports for the upper echelons of power, which registered the "people's mood" about Lenin's sickness. Compare with *"Sovershenno sekretno": Lubianka—Stalinu o polozhenii v strane (1922–1934 gg.)* ["Top secret": Lubianka to Stalin on the state of the nation (1922–1934)], Vol. 1, chap. 2 (Lewiston, NY: Edwin Mellen Press for the Institute of Russian History, 2000), especially 825–826, 838, 880.
28. See on this subject, Ákos Szilágyi, "Totális temetés" [Total funeral], *2000* (1993/5).
29. For example, the secret police reports: "a strong interest and desire on the part of workers in the Zamoskvorecki district to participate in taking leave of Ilyich's body in as great numbers as possible has been observed, and it has been difficult to talk the workers into selecting a delegation . . ." *Neizvesnaya Rossiya XX vek.* IV, 12. These occasional songs are analyzed by O. Velikanova in comparison with Eastern legends and Russian folk stories, such as, for example, this Uzbek song: "So has Lenin died? No, only his body. He himself could not have died. Prophets do not die. Unscathed till today. Anyone else's body would have turned to dust by now. He sleeps, and sometimes opens his eyes, and it burns with joy. Because he can see: he has worthy heirs in the form of Rikov and Kalinin. He can see: They have left no room for discord, They have realized his every command. Let him sleep in peace. He can rest assured: not a word of his will be falsified." Ibid., 194.
30. Vera Panova, *Sentimentalniy roman* (1958).
31. S. Budgen, St. Kouvalekis, S. Žižek, eds., *Lenin Reloaded. Toward a Politics of Truth* (Durham and London: Duke University Press, 2007); S. Žižek, "Afterwords: Lenin's Choice," in S. Žižek, ed., *Revolution at the Gates* (London: Verso, 2002). But other Marxist movements, among them the Trotskyists in Western Europe especially, cultivate the Lenin tradition in their own way. Take for example Jean-Jacques Marie, *Lénine. 1870–1924. Biographie* (Paris: Editions Balland, 2004); Tony Cliff, *Lenin: Building the Party 1893–1914* (London: Bookmarks, 1986). Perhaps the most significant Lenin reconstruction of the last period was published in the United States: Lars T. Lih, *Lenin Rediscovered:* What Is To Be Done? *In Context* (Chicago: Haymarket Books, 2008).
32. Goran Therborn, "After Dialectics. Radical Social Theory in a Post-Communist World," *New Left Review*. no. 43, (2007): 106.
33. Charles Bettelheim had called attention to the methodological mistake, which was rooted in an attempt to derive (Soviet) history from the principles. C. Bettelheim, *Class Struggles in the USSR. Second period 1923–1930* (Sussex: The Harvester Press, 1978), 11–12. (http://www.marx2mao.com/Other/CSSUi76NB.html). An approach to socialism of this kind, modern "idealist" in its nature, is represented by János Kornai, *The Socialist System. The Political Economy of Communism* (Princeton: Princeton University Press; Oxford: Oxford University Press, 1992), critically reviewed by the author in regard to this historical approach. See Tamás Krausz, "Ahistorical Political Economics," *Social Scientist* Vol. 24, no. 1–3 (New Delhi: January–March 1996): 111–139. János Kornai honored the review by responding to the criticism as a "leftist" perspective, but did not reflect on the methodological problem. See János Kornai, *By Force of Thought. Irregular Memoirs of an Intellectual Journey* (Cambridge, Massachusetts;London: The MIT Press, 2007). For a review of the book see László Andor, "Dilemmák és ellentmondások" [Dilemmas and contradictions], in *Eszmélet* 74 (2007): 135–144.
34. On this subject see St. Kotkin, "1991 and the Russian Revolution: Sources, Conceptual Categories, Analytical Frameworks," *Journal of Modern History* Vol. 70, no. 3 (Chicago, 1998): 384–425.
35. For a highly illustrative work in this vein by a Hungarian historian, see István Dolmányos,

Ragyogó október [Radiant October] (Budapest: Kossuth, 1979), the likes of which are rarely so written anywhere these days. For a more recent publication with a similar approach, see F. D. Volkov, *Velikij Lenin i pigmei istorii* (Moscow: MID RF, 1996). For an objective overview of post-regime-change literature on Lenin, see Jelena Anatoljevna Kotelenec, *V. I. Lenin kak predmet istoricheskogo issledovania*, op. cit.

36. The enlightened *A Szovjetunió története* [History of the Soviet Union] (Budapest: Kossuth, 1971), written by Dolmányos in the 1960s, made its way onto the list of banned books soon after the death of Khrushchev. This circumstance had a decisive role in the later change of his approach as writer, expressing the need for a conservative, pathetic manner of portrayal that was the norm in the Brezhnev era.

37. For a documentation of the various schools of interpretation see Rex A. Wade, *Revolutionary Russia: New Approaches* (London: Routledge, 2004).

38. An ironic statement from Goran Therborn with regard to this state of affairs: "Class, formerly among the most important concepts in left discourse, has been displaced in recent years; in part, ironically, through the latter's own defeat in capitalist class struggle. . . . Class persists, but without a secure abode, and with its philosophical right to existence contested. Its social appearance has become almost unrecognizable after being dropped into an acid of pure politics, as in the political philosophy of discursive hegemony developed by Ernesto Laclau and Chantal Mouffe's *Hegemony and Socialist Strategy* (1985), arguably the most intellectually powerful contribution of post-Marxist political theory . . . Europe provided the origins of class theory as well as of explicit class mobilization and politics; its working-class movements became models for the rest of the world . . . Nevertheless, in terms of analysis and social theory, class is wintering better in North America. The work of Erik Olin Wright has played a central role in securing a legitimate location for Marxist class analysis within academic sociology." Therborn, op. cit., 87, 89.

39. For a "narrative" from this point of view, substantiated with great erudition and thorough research, see F. C. Corney, *Telling October: Memory and Making of the Bolshevik Revolution* (Ithaca: Cornell University Press, 2004), especially 1–7.

40. Gábor Gyáni's *Posztmodern kánon* [The postmodern canon] (Budapest: Nemzeti Tankönyvkiadó, 2003) seeks to provide the legitimizing ideology of the new "post-socialist" system with the use of the *postmodern*, while weakening the positions of "traditional" historiography, and primarily (but not exclusively!) opposed to the movements with a Marxist approach. His conceptualization throws the gate open to history as an interpretation of the *history of memory*—inevitably transforming historiography into a sort of political endeavor.

41. A detailed analysis of the subject is offered in Gérard Noiriel, *Sur la "crise" de l'histoire* (Paris: Belin, 1996); also published in Hungarian: *A történetírás válsága* (Budapest: Napvilág Kiadó, 2001), especially 116–135, 150–168.

42. These intellectual and political struggles with power and legitimacy as their aim were examined in their own historical factuality many years ago in a book coauthored by the author and Miklós Mesterházi, *Mű és történelem. Viták Lukács György műveriről a húszas években* [Work of art and history. Debates on the works of George Lukács in the twenties] (Budapest: Gondolat, 1985), 101–130. An analysis, rich in history, of this process of legitimization is given by the already mentioned work of Corney, especially on pages 155–198.

43. It would be difficult to ascertain who used the term *Leninism* first; whether it was Parvus or Miliukov is after all not important, but the indicator did not originally cover definitions of a theoretical nature, but simply referred to Lenin's "conspirative" approach to the party. See Parvus (originally I. L. Gelfand), "Posle vojni," *Rossija is Revoljucija* (St. Petersburg: Glagolev, 1908), 188.

44. It has to be admitted in all honesty that even Robert Service's trilogy represents these points

of view throughout. His constant judgments allow the reader to think that he is "wiser," "more moral," and "better prepared" than Lenin. The author steps out of the role of the analytical historian on more than one occasion, and teaches his protagonist the basics of how to make politics from the pulpit of the final arbiter. See Robert Service, *Lenin: A Political Life,* Vol. III, xiv–xv.

45. Even the eminent historian Robert Service was aware of the problem when he wrote that while he assembled the trilogy, he had the feeling that perhaps "Lenin's influence at political conjunctures such as the decisions to seize power in October 1917, to sign the Brest-Litovsk treaty in 1918, to establish a Communist International in 1919 and to initiate the New Economic Policy in 1921 had been exaggerated." Ibid., Vol. III, xvi.

CHAPTER 1—WHO WAS LENIN?

1. Biographers usually mention that Lenin noted "I do not know" in the box for his paternal grandfather's profession when filling out the detailed questionnaire for the 1922 party survey. See Vladlen Loginov, *Vladimir Lenin. Vybor puti* (Moscow: Respublika, 2005), 11. It is no coincidence that historians in Russia (and elsewhere) were ready (and able) to do an extensive study of the genealogy when interest arose under the ideological effect of the legitimization of the new system.
2. Alekseev, V., A. Shver, *Sem'ia Ul'ianovykh v Simbirske (1869–1887)*, edited and prepared for publication by A. Ulyanova Elizarova, Institut Lenina pri TS K.R.K.P (Moscow–Leningrad: Gosudarstvennoe izd-vo, 1925), 6–7.
3. Loginov, *Vladimir Lenin. Vybor puti*, 30; Service, *Lenin: A Biography*, 13–16.
4. Fischer, Louis, *The Life of Lenin*, 8–9; *Lenin i Simbirsk* (Saratov: 1968).
5. *Vladimir Ilyich Lenin: Biograficheskaya Chronika. 1891–1922*, edited by G. N. Golikov (Moscow: Izdatelstvo politicheskoy literature, 1970). For the father's life in more detail, see M. Ulyanova, *Otets Vladimira Ilyicha Lenina, Ilya Nikolayevich Ulyanov (1831–1886)* [The father of Vladimir Ilyich Lenin, Ilya Nikolayevich Ulyanov] (Moscow–Leningrad: 1931).
6. Document no. I, "Zapis o ceil priyezda v Skt. Petersburgi," 29 March–1 April 1891, *V. I. Lenin, Neizvestnye dokumenty. 1891–1922*, 15. "Registered in the Simbirsk Government records of family trees of nobles, and given to Vladimir Ilyich Ulyanov, the son of the acting councilor, as proof of his rights, the title of hereditary nobility." Ilya Nikolayevich could have gained the title of noble earlier, having received the order of knight of Saint Vladimir, 3rd grade, as well as being one of those persons who had reached the required position on the scale of rank to acquire the noble title, but he did not wish to partake of these opportunities. Only after his death, did M. A. Ulyanova make the necessary arrangements for her and her children's accession to the ranks of nobles.
7. Loginov, *Vladimir Lenin. Vybor puti*, 12–13.
8. Anna Ilinichna-Elizarova, "Lenin," in Anna Ilinichna-Elizarova et al., *Reminiscences of Lenin by his relatives* (Moscow: Foreign Languages Pub. House, 1956). Anna Iljinyicsna-Jelizarova: "Lenin" in *Életrajzok a bolsevizmus történetéből* [Biographies from the history of Bolshevism], edited by László Béládi, Tamás Krausz (Budapest: ELTE, ÁJTK, 1988), 9–10.
9. See Service, Robert, *Lenin: A Biography*, 21; and Loginov, *Vladimir Lenin. Vybor puti*, 28.
10. Ilya Nikolayevich Ulyanov received the order of St. Vladimir 3rd grade, along with the right to a noble title, for his prolonged and fruitful work. Golikov, *Biograficheskaya Chronika*, Vol. 1, 11.
11. Anna Ilinichna-Elizarova, "Lenin," in *Reminiscences of Lenin by his relatives*, 10; on young Lenin also see Egor Yakovlev, *The beginning: the story about the Ulyanov family, Lenin's childhood and youth*, translated from the Russian by Catherine Judelson (Moscow: Progress Publishers, 1988); I. S. Zilbershtein, *Molodoy Lenin v zhiznyi I z rabotoy. Po vospominaniyam sovremennikov I dokumentam epochi* (Moscow: 1929); *Lenin i Simbirsk.*

12. See Loginov, *Vladimir Lenin. Vybor puti*, 34.
13. On this, see Fischer, *The Life of Lenin*, 3–4. It is strange, for this reason as well, that Lenin's younger brother's daughter, Olga Dimitriyevna Ulyanova, while taking up a battle of international scale against the degradation of Lenin memorials in the '90s, in opposition either to the rules ingrained or the nationalist spirit of the times, was willing to acknowledge only the Russian, German, and Swedish roots of the family in her little book aimed at "putting everything in place." Olga Dimitriyevna Ulyanova, *Rodnoy Lenin* (Moscow: ITRK, 2002), 15–20.
14. M. Shtein, *Ulyanovy i Leniny: tainy rodoslovnoi i psevdonima* (St. Petersburg: VIRD, 1997), 57–60.
15. Ibid.; and Loginov, *Vladimir Lenin. Vybor puti*, 14. Also see *Otechestvenniye archivi* (1992), 4: 78–81.
16. The case of Marietta Saginyan and other scholars distinctly demonstrates this development. On the subject, see Shtein, *Ulyanovy i Leniny*, 3–37, 136–143. Even the official *Khrushchevist* Lenin biography of 1963, prepared under the leadership of P. N. Pospelov, does not mention the ethnicity of his grandfather, all it states is that he was a doctor. P. N. Pospelov, ed., *Vladimir Ilyich Lenin; A Biography* (Moscow: Progress Publishers, 1965), 2. The subject essentially remained a taboo until the times of Gorbachev.
17. See Shtein, *Ulyanovy i Leniny*, 43; and Loginov, *Vladimir Lenin. Vybor puti*, 17–18.
18. Zilbershtein, *Molodoy Lenin*, 41.
19. Later, on 7 November 1888, he also saw Gounod's *Faust*, with his sister Olga. Golikov, *Biograficheskaya Chronika*, Vol. 1, 39.
20. See Fischer, *The Life of Lenin*, 6–7.
21. Golikov, *Biograficheskaya Chronika*, Vol. 1, 5. Dates throughout the text refer to the Julian Calendar, which was used in Russia until February 1918. When the Gregorian Calendar—long the international standard—was adopted by the Bolsheviks, 1 February became 14 February. Where a date is indicated parenthetically, it refers to the Gregorian Calendar.
22. Service, *Lenin: A Biography*, 52.
23. The role of this aspect is emphasized by Ronald W. Clark in *Lenin. Behind the Mask* (London: Faber and Faber, 1988), 9.
24. Elizarova, "Lenin," in *Reminiscences of Lenin by his relatives*, 10.
25. Golikov, *Biograficheskaya Chronika*, Vol. 7, 9.
26. This became a commonplace assumption in the literature based on the memoirs. Alexander reportedly once told a friend: "It is an absurd, and even immoral thing if a person does not have a knowledge of medicine, but wants to cure people. It is even more absurd and immoral if someone wants to heal social diseases without understanding their causes." David Shub, *Lenin: A Biography* (Baltimore: Penguin, 1967), 13–14; and Loginov, *Vladimir Lenin. Vybor puti*, 69.
27. Alekseev, Shver, *Sem'ia Ul'ianovykh*, 42.
28. Fischer, *The Life of Lenin*, 11.
29. In his letter to Maria Ilyinichna (Manyachka) written from St. Petersburg to Moscow on 13 December 1894, Vladimir Ilyich asks her to get hold of the third volume of *Capital*. See *LCW*, vol. 37, *Letters to Relatives 1893–1922* (Moscow: Progress Publishers, 1977), 68–69.
30. N. K. Krupskaya, "Kak Lenin rabotal nad Marksom?" in *Lenin i kniga* (Moscow: Izd. Pol. Lit., 1964), 299; or in English see Krupskaya, "How Lenin Approached the Study of Marx," *Lenin and Books*, translated from the Russian and compiled by A. Z. Okorokov (Moscow: Progress Publishers, 1971) 139.
31. See the reminiscences of Maria Essen, in *Lenin i kniga*, 299; or *Lenin and Books*, 251.
32. Valentinov, Nikolay [N. V. Volsky], *Encounters with Lenin*. Translated from the Russian

by Paul Rosta and Brian Pearce, with a Foreword by Leonard Schapiro (London: Oxford University Press, 1968), 133–134. The late reminiscences have to be addressed with due skepticism, of course, as the Chernyshevskyan approach to dialectics was far from the sort Lenin reconstructed and applied in the 1910s.

33. See Golikov, *Biograficheskaya Chronika*, Vol. 1, 39. Ulyanov could not have met Chernyshevsky, because the great revolutionary died the following year.
34. Aleksandr A. Majsurjan, *Drugoj Lenin* [A different Lenin] (Moscow: Vagrius, 2006), 23, 27–31.
35. Golikov, *Biograficheskaya Chronika*, Vol. 1, 16.
36. Perhaps the first adept discussion of the subject is in Anatoly Vasilievich Lunacharsky, "Lenin i literaturovedenie," *Literaturnaya Entsiklopediya* Vol. 11 (Moscow: 1932), 194–260, esp. 226–247.
37. Golikov, *Biograficheskaya Chronika*, Vol. 1, 17; *Krupsykaja Leninről*, 1965, 35–36; Majsurjan, *Drugoj Lenin*, 435.
38. Golikov, *Biograficheskaya Chronika*, Vol. 1, 23; see also Alekseev, Shver, *Sem'ia Ul'ianovykh*, 30, 33; and Ulyanova-Elizarova, *Vospominanniya ob Alexander Ilyich Ulyanov* (Moscow: Molodaya Gvardiya, 1930).
39. Golikov, *Biograficheskaya Chronika*, Vol. 1, 25–26, 29.
40. His attachment to his elder brother in his memory remained very strong. Much later, in a letter written in emigration after his exile, from London to Samara on 14 September 1902, he thanked his mother for photographs of Alexander. In a letter of September 1906 he asked a comrade to forward these "relics" to him from Geneva to St. Petersburg. All these communications also refute the statements claiming that his relationship with his brother was disturbed by any motives rooted in human or character flaws. See LCW, Vol. 37, 348; and LCW, Vol. 43, 173.
41. On this subject see Majsurjan, *Drugoj Lenin*, 15.
42. Golikov, *Biograficheskaya Chronika*, Vol. 1, 29.
43. It is a fashion of our times to label Lenin a moral nihilist. Dimitri Vasilyevich Kolesov's book in the "popular journalistic" vein, *V.I. Lenin: Lichnost i sudba* (Moscow: Izd. "Flinta," 1999). According to Kolesov's trendy psychologizing interpretation, Alexander was a man of traditional morals, inflexible, with the primacy of morals in the interest of justice, whilst Vladimir appears in the form of an amoral pragmatist.
44. Golikov, *Biograficheskaya Chronika*, Vol. 1, 31–32.
45. Police reports clearly reflect that Vladimir Ilyich Lenin, as the younger brother of the would-be "Tsar assassin," was kept on record as a potentially dangerous revolutionary. Nonetheless, in an effort to defend the boy after his participation in the student demonstrations, the principal of the high school, F. M. Kerenskiy, wrote to the chief inspector of the educational district as follows: "Vladimir Ulyanov has become emotionally overheated in the aftermath of the fateful catastrophe [his brother's execution], which has shaken the unfortunate family and, probably, had a devastating effect on the sensitive young man." Golikov, *Biograficheskaya Chronika*, Vol. 1, 37.
46. LCW, Vol. 33, 452–3.
47. Golikov, *Biograficheskaya Chronika*, Vol. 1, 41.
48. Ibid., 45–46, 48.
49. On this historiographic tradition see Tamás Krausz, *Pártviták és történettudomány. Viták "az orosz történelmi fejlődés sajátosságairól", különös tekintettel a 20-as évekre* [In-party conflicts and historical science. Debates about the "specificities of Russian historical development," especially in the 20s], (Budapest: Akadémiai Kiadó, 1991), 101–5, 112–13.
50. See for example Sergei Vladimirovich Belov, *Istoria odnoi "druzhby": V.I. Lenin i P.B. Struve* (St. Petersburg : SPbGU, 2005), especially 17.

51. Service, *Lenin: A Biography*, 53–57; Golikov, *Biograficheskaya Chronika*, Vol. 1, 70–1, 73–5.
52. V. Vodovozov was a relation of N. V. Vodovozov (1870–1896), the publisher who had died at a young age, and whose wife first published Lenin's book, *The Development of Capitalism in Russia*.
53. Belov, *Istoria odnoi "druzhby."* The author compares Lenin's achievements with those of Pyotr Struve, with the latter becoming an embodiment of the revolutionary intellectual in possession of "moral foundations."
54. Belov, *Istoria odnoi "druzhby,"* 16–7; V. Vodovozov, *Moyo znakomstvo s Leninim. Na chuzhoy storonye* No. 12 (Prague: 1925), 89.
55. Loginov, *Vladimir Lenin. Vybor puti*, 124–5.
56. LCW, Vol. 4, p. 247.
57. Loginov, *Vladimir Lenin. Vybor puti*, 128–35.
58. P. N. Durnovo, the infamous director of the police department, made a note on M. Ulyanova's petition, which said "unlikely as it is that anything could be brought up in Ulyanov's defense." Golikov, *Biograficheskaya Chronika*, Vol. 1, 37.
59. Ibid., 51, 54–5.
60. Ibid., 59–61.
61. Golikov, *Biograficheskaya Chronika*, Vol. 1, 67; and Majsurjan, *Drugoj Lenin*, 20–21.
62. *V. I. Lenin, Neizvestnye dokumenty*, 18.
63. The matter was reported by N. Valentinov in his reminiscences, Valentinov, *Encounters with Lenin*, 5–11.
64. For a background on financial matters see *V. I. Lenin, Neizvestnye dokumenty*, 18.
65. Service, *Lenin: A Biography*, 66.
66. Vladimir Ilyich's letter to his mother dated 5 October 1893, written after he had moved to St. Petersburg. LCW, Vol. 37, 65–6.
67. Ulyanova-Elizarova, "Vospominanniya ob Alexander Ilyich Ulyanov," in *Lenin i Kniga*, 319.
68. Michail Aleksandrovich Silvin, *Lenin v period zarozhdeniya partii vospominaniya* (Leningrad: Lenizdat, 1958); Gleb M. Krzhizhanovsky, *Velikiy Lenin* (Moscow: 1968).
69. Golikov, *Biograficheskaya Chronika*, Vol. 1, 84.
70. Their first meeting has often been described, and Krupskaya herself serves as the "main source," but Western literature in the field has also dealt with the event in detail, as for example in Ronald W. Clark, *Lenin. Behind the Mask*.
71. For more on the history of this debate see Richard Pipes, *Struve, Liberal on the Left, 1870–1905* (Cambridge, MA: Harvard University Press, 1970) and *Struve, liberal on the right, 1905–1944* (Cambridge, MA: Harvard University Press, 1980). The latest work on the subject, Belov's approach is no longer simply a conservative take, like Pipes's angle, but remains consistent in presenting an overview of the relationship between Lenin and Struve from a Russian monarchist point of view.
72. One version of Struve's reminiscences that appeared in the pages of the fourth issue of *Novi mir* in 1991, under the title "Moyi vstrechi i stolknoveniya s Leninim," had originally been published in the *Russkaya Misl* right after Lenin's death, titled "Podlinniy smisl i neobhodimiy konec bolshevistskogo kommunizma." In English, Petr Berngardovich Struve, *My contacts and conflicts with Lenin* (Indianapolis: Bobbs-Merrill, 1934).
73. Struve also supported Lenin's research in exile with books acquired at the bookshop owned by Mihaylovna Kalmykova, with immediate results of this work published in the book *The Development of Capitalism in Russia*. In February 1889, Petr Struve, after his father's passing, moved in with his friend from college and son to Senator D. A. Kalmykov. He spent seven years with the family, and his Marxist approach took shape here. Kalmykova taught at the famous St. Petersburg Sunday school, where Krupskaya was also a teacher. See also

Valentinov, *Encounters with Lenin*, 14–16. Struve's later reminiscences of his first meeting with Lenin were colored by the sensibilities typically felt by the loser toward his victorious opponent. Petr Struve, "Lenin kak chelovek," reprinted in *Novoe Russkoe Slovo* (25 January 1976), 2–28.

74. Richard Pipes had taken Russian historiography to task over exaggerating Lenin's role in establishing the organization and suppressing the real role of his "rivals" as early as 1963. Meanwhile, however, current historiography does not deny Lenin's outstanding role in the organization's coming into being either. See Richard Pipes, *Social Democracy and St. Petersburg's Labor Movement 1885–1897* (Cambridge, MA: Harvard University Press, 1963).

75. Belov, *Istoria odnoi "druzhby,"* 13, 41–43. Ariadna Tyrkova-Williams—author of *Na putiakh k svobode* [On the road to freedom] (New York: Chekhov Publishing House, 1952), reprinted in Moscow, by Moskovskaya shk. politicheskih issled in 2007—describing the Lenin–Struve relationship from the aspect of their "girlfriends," gave an account in her memoir of how one of the three best friends from high school, teaching at the Sunday school, Krupskaya became Lenin's wife, the second Struve's, while the third lady married Tugan-Baranovsky.

76. In one of his letters to his sister, Anna Ilyinichna, from 11 November 1898, Lenin documents all of the above. Ulyanov acknowledged the help he was afforded by Struve and his wife with singular gratitude. LCW, Vol. 37, 194–5; as well as Valentinov, *Encounters with Lenin*, 14-16.

77. Belov, *Istoria odnoi "druzhby,"* 37. Martov candidly explains that while Struve was a well-read person, he reminded one of a German social democrat, being a desultory speaker, etc. Lenin, on the other hand, showed leadership qualities from the beginning, especially in the renewal of revolutionary agitation. Julius Martov, *Zapiski sotsial-demokrata* (Berlin–St. Petersburg–Moscow: Izd-vo Z.I. Grzhebina, 1922), 94–95.

78. Letter to Maria Ilyinichna, from St. Petersburg to Moscow. Lenin refers to the fact that Klyuchevsky's speech, "In Memory of the Late Emperor Alexander III, May He Rest in Peace," was published as a brochure. Students of the Moscow University bought up a few hundred copies of the publication and, appending copies of D. I. Fonvizin's fable about the scheming fox, resold it as an "improved and extended edition." A copy was ceremoniously handed over to Kluchevsky himself at one of his lectures, and then he was whistled and hissed out of class. Arrests followed. LCW, Vol. 37, 68–69 and notes.

79. Letter to his mother, 29 August 1895, from Berlin to Moscow. Ibid., 78–79.

80. Golikov, *Biograficheskaya Chronika*, Vol. 1, 104–105.

81. Ibid., 112–113.

82. A. Ulyanova-Yelizarova, "Apropos of Lenin's Letters to Relatives," LCW Vol. 37, 46–63, especially 47.

83. His most superlative praise and gratitude were reserved for the occasional important reading experience, especially if it led to reviews, articles, or critical papers: "*Merci* for Bogdanov. I have read half of it. Very interesting and to the point. I am thinking of writing a review." LCW, Vol. 37, 152. He did indeed complete his book review of A. Bogdanov's *A Short Course of Economic Science*, published in April 1898 in the magazine *Mir Bozhy*, No. 4, LCW, Vol. 4, 46–54. Or a letter to his mother of 14 February in the same year, once more mentions the book by the later Bolshevik, and then trenchant opponent Bogdanov, as well as the work of Bulgakov, who was then still drawn by Marxism. "I liked it [Bogdanov's book] very much and have written a review. Bulgakov's book is not too bad, either, but I do not like the chapter on turnover and his formulation of the question of the foreign market is not quite correct. I was, of course, very pleased to receive it." LCW, Vol. 37, 155.

84. For prison, exile, and emigration, "the involuntary seclusion and the lack of contact with the life of the outside world" which were his fate, was "a condition that makes even the most

restrained people turn to letter-writing. . . . in these letters he stands out, if one may put it so, in clearest relief as a person." LCW, Vol. 37, 48.

85. Concerned especially about their health, he gave advice, worried about them, and tried to care for them even from a distance. He felt a tender love for his mother who, when "several of us were arrested at the same time and she, though advanced in years, had to go again and again to prisons to visit her family and take things to them, to sit for hours in the waiting-rooms of the gendarmerie and the secret police." Ibid., 40.

86. Vladimir Ilyich was always displeased with unpunctuality, with delays in work, in carrying out instructions or in answering letters. In his letters sent from exile he inveighs against Struve for his "slackness in answering," Anna Ilyinichna writes. Ibid., 60.

87. Majsurjan, *Drugoj Lenin*, 79.

88. LCW, Vol. 37, 85.

89. See Vladimir Efimovich Melnichenko, *Lichnaia zhizn Lenina* (Moscow: Voskresenie, 1998), 37.

90. Valentinov, *Encounters with Lenin*, 131–132; Majsurjan, *Drugoj Lenin*, 49, 59; Melnichenko, *Lichnaia zhizn Lenina*, 9, 23. A similar portrait is etched by A. Balabanoff, who left Russia in 1922, after breaking off with Lenin and the Bolsheviks, and who had perhaps the closest understanding of him, and drew up the most detailed analysis of his character. Angelica Balabanoff, *Impressions of Lenin* (Ann Arbor: University of Michigan Press, 1964).

91. Balabanoff, *Impressions of Lenin*, 4–5, 122–123.

92. It is typical in this relation as well that later he would be able to laugh at and test his vitriolic humor on the wrongs of the Soviet system. On an occasion when the delegates of the eastern peoples were invited to a meeting of the Political Committee in October of 1920, "The Kalmyk delegate, M. A. Amur-Sanana, pronounced some words of greeting and then Vladimir Ilyich asked the Kalmyk delegation how the Kalmyk people relate to the Soviet government. The delegation, quite unabashed, said that in the view of the Kalmyks 'there had been the great plague, but it passed; that there was cholera, but it passed as well; now the Bolsheviks are here, but they are not going to leave.' Lenin laughed even louder than all the others." See Melnichenko, *Lichnaya zhizn*, 39.

93. "[O]ne notices the simplicity and the natural manner of Vladimir Ilyich, his great modesty, the complete absence not only of conceit and boastfulness but of any attempt to play up the services he had rendered or to show off; and this was in his youth, when some sort of showing off is natural in a talented person. For a long time he would not agree to call his big, fundamental monograph *The Development of Capitalism in Russia*, which, he said, 'is too bold, too broad and promises too much . . . and should be more modest' (February 13, 1899)." LCW Vol. 37, 59–60.

94. Ibid., 58–59.

95. Just to pick one example, he mentioned Martov on one occasion to his mother with some concern, having received news to the effect that "Yuly is freezing in Turukhansk (2° below zero in his room in the mornings) and is anxiously awaiting a transfer." Ibid., 205. Or "Yuly writes from Turukhansk that he is living tolerably well—not the kind of fellow to lose heart, fortunately." Ibid., 165.

96. For a more recent overview of Martov's career, see I. Kh. Urilov, *Martov—polityk i historic* [Martov: politician and historian] (Moscow: Nauka, 1997).

97. Nadezhda Konstantinovna Krupskaya, *Reminiscences of Lenin*, translated by Bernard Isaacs (New York: International Publishers, 1970)..

98. LCW, Vol. 37, 150–1. From the letter Lenin wrote his sister Manyachka from Munich on 19 May 1901, delivered to her in the Moscow prison—with the prosecutor's permission—he tried to impress upon both Mark Yelizarov and Manyachka the importance of gymnastics

and a good rubdown in prison. "In solitary confinement this is absolutely essential." Ibid., 327.

99. Letter to his mother from Krasnoyarsk to Moscow, dated 5 April 1897: "I am very pleased with my place of exile . . . because Minusinsk and its district are the best in these parts both on account of the excellent climate and the low cost of living." He notes also, "I have seen *Novoye Slovo* and read it with great pleasure." LCW, Vol. 37, 99–100.
100. He also informed Maria Alexandrovna of his old comrade friends in exile who, among them G. M. Krzhizhanovsky, V. Starkov, Y. O. Martov (Tsederbaum), and A. Vaneyev, traveled on state expense—unlike him—but also listed the "contacts in Krasnoyarsk": p. Krasikov, V. A. Bukshnis, N. A. Merkhalev, A. A. Filippov, V. A. Karaulov, and V. N. Kuryashev. Letter dated 15 March 1897, from Krasnoyarsk to Moscow. Ibid., 95.
101. Ibid., 91.
102. Letter of 10 March 1897, from Krasnoyarsk to Moscow. Ibid., 94.
103. Letter of 17 April 1897, to his mother and Yelizarova (A. I.), from Krasnoyarsk to Moscow. Ibid., 102.
104. Ibid., 135–6.
105. V. I. Lenin, *Gems of Narodnik Project-Mongering*, LCW, Vol. 2, pg. 459.
106. LCW Volume 37, pages 106–110.
107. Ibid., 135–7, 141–2. For an authentic account of the exile period see N. Krupskaya, *Reminiscences of Lenin*, 29–49.
108. LCW, Vol. 37, 171–172. A reference to his friends—who counted as old exiles.
109. Ibid., 175.
110. As early as 20 May 1895, he had written to his mother, from Switzerland to Moscow, to say "It seems that servants are very expensive here—25 to 30 francs a month, all found—and they have to be fed well." Ibid., 73; or in another letter to his mother from Paris, dated 8 June 1895: "Lodgings here are very cheap; for instance, 30 to 35 francs a month for two rooms and a kitchen," Ibid., 74. In a letter from Shusha to Podolsk, addressed to his mother and brother Dmitry, on 28 November 1898 he commented on their recreations as follows: "We now have a new attraction, a skating rink that takes me away from shooting quite a lot." Ibid., 204.
111. Letter to his mother from Shusha to Moscow, dated 12 October 1897, ibid., 130. At another point he remarks in jest: "P.S. I have a gun dog again, a setter. . . . It has one disadvantage—it is of the female estate. . . ." Ibid., 145.
112. Ibid., 212–7.
113. The letter is dated 24 January 1898. Ibid., 148–9. For more on the slander of N. YA. Fedoseyev, see note 78 to the letter.
114. Ibid., 178.
115. Letter from Shushenskoye to Podolsk, dated 16 August 1898. Ibid., 184–5, 205.
116. Ibid., 564; Melnichenko, *Lichnaia zhizn Lenina*, 180.
117. *V. I. Lenin, Neizvestnye dokumenty*, Proshcheniye direktoru departamenta policii 10 (23) March 1900. LCW, Vol. 37, 89–90. In a letter to his mother from Pskov to Podolsk, dated 6 April 1900, he wishes to visit his wife in the spring, because she has to convalesce in bed due to gynecological problems, and he is sending her money, "because her treatment will entail considerable expense." Ibid., 290.
118. He wrote to his mother in February 1901, in a letter sent from Munich to Moscow: "I was at the opera a few days ago and heard La Juive with the greatest pleasure; I heard it once in Kazan (when Zakrzhevsky sang)—that must be thirteen years ago, and some of the tunes have remained in my memory. The music and singing were good. I have also been to theaters (German) on a few occasions and sometimes understood something, the general idea, at any

rate. Do you go to the Moscow theaters? . . . What is this new play of Chekhov's, Three Sisters? Have you seen it and do you like it?" LCW, Vol. 37, 317–20.

119. Krupskaya simply names *Iskra* Lenin's child, in the publication of which he had invested incredible effort. Between December 1900 and 22 October 1903, 51 issues appeared with Lenin as chief editor, the Mensheviks taking control only after that. Lenin had Herzen's journal called *Kolokol*—also published abroad between 1857 and 1867—in mind, for its great influence upon Russian intellectuals in general. See Nadezhda Konstantinovna Krupskaya, *Izbrannye proizvedeniia: k 120-letiiu so dnia rozhdeniia N.K. Krupskoi* (Moscow: Politizdat, 1988), 201.
120. LCW, Vol. 5, 33.
121. Shtein, *Ulyanovy i Leniny*, 176–7.
122. See, for example, LCW 37, 356. Letter to his mother dated 22 February 1903, from London to Samara. Lenin was invited to Paris in February of 1903 for his expertise on this subject, giving a lecture series at the Russian Academy of Social Sciences.
123. He wrote to his mother from London to Samara in order to prepare the summer holidays together on the beaches of northern France, and to save her any unnecessary trouble. In the summer of 1902, Lenin spent his summer holidays, which lasted from the beginning of June to 25 July, together with his mother and sister Anyuta in Loguivy, by the sea. The letter began with a note to the effect that he had received Manyachka's card with a view of the Volga. The Volga is mentioned once again in the next letter of 7 June. "Manya's tale of her boat trip made me very envious. . . . How I should like to be on the Volga in summer!" LCW, Vol. 37, 346.
124. The attitude described here is reflected in another letter written on 4 February 1903, to his mother in Samara from London: "Nadya and I are both well and are jogging along as usual. We recently went to our first concert this winter and were very pleased with it—especially with Chaikovsky's latest symphony (*Symphonie pathétique*). Are there any good concerts in Samara? We went once to a German theater but what we should like would be to visit the Russian Art Theater and see *The Lower Depths*." Ibid., 355. His interest in music cannot be narrowed down to Beethoven and Tchaikovsky. His wife wrote about it after his death: "his musical memory was good" and "he loved the violin best." "The piano too." "He liked Wagner greatly. But he usually left, almost ill, after the first act." See Krupskaya, *Reminiscences*, 514.
125. Letter to Anyuta from Saratov to Paris, dated 24 March 1912. LCW, Vol. 37, 359, 474.
126. Melnichenko, *Lichnaia zhizn Lenina*, 33.
127. Ibid., 24.
128. See Petr Struve, "Lenin kak chelovek."
129. In *Istoria odnoi "druzhby"*, 50, Belov quotes Valentinov, but even Lenin's biographers today quote Potresov. See Majsurjan, *Drugoj Lenin*, 59. Valentinov gets caught up in an unsolvable contradiction on this subject as well. On the one hand, he states that Lenin "approached people with the deepest possible suspicion," but "undoubtedly possessed a secret charisma." No further explanation. See Valentinov, *Encounters with Lenin*, 92.
130. See Clara Zetkin, *Reminiscences of Lenin* (London: Modern Books Ltd., 1929), 7.
131. Krupskaya also stresses this dedication in her *Reminiscences* written after his death: "He never set himself in opposition to Plekhanov." Krupskaya, *Izbrannye proizvedeniia*, 122.
132. Majsurjan argues very convincingly on this account as well, in *Drugoj Lenin*, 153–8, 163–6. It should be noted that he turned to Plekhanov after the outbreak of revolution, in October 1905, in a letter, to forward the cause of a unified social democracy: he invited him to take up a role in *Novaya Zhizny*, and also invited him for a personal meeting. See Golikov, *Biograficheskaya Chronika* Vol. 2 (Moscow: Izdatelstvo politicheskoy literature, 1971), 192. The following sentence is also to be found in the letter referred to above: "That we Bolsheviks earnestly

desire to work together with you is something I need hardly repeat to you. I have written to St. Petersburg asking all the editors of the new newspaper (at present there are seven of them: Bogdanov, Rumyantsev, Bazarov, Lunacharsky, Orlovsky, Olminsky and myself) to send you a joint and official request to join the editorial board." LCW, Vol. 34, 363.

133. N. Valentinov suspects some financial motives underlying the relationship of Lenin and Gorky, in that the writer may be able to secure some funds for the Bolsheviks through his fame. He himself contradicts this later when he writes about how the relationship with the writer was extended, and that importunate demands and disputes—especially on Lenin's initiative—were typical. Gorky did not reply even to Lenin's letter of apology for years after it was sent, in 1913, though even so, the relationship did last. Valentinov, *Encounters with Lenin*, 72–75.
134. Golikov, *Biograficheskaya Chronika,* Vol. 2, 31–87.
135. Ibid., 202.
136. Ibid., 198.
137. Ibid., 218–19.
138 An account of this performance can be found in Majsurjan, *Drugoj Lenin*, 175; and Golikov, *Biograficheskaya Chronika* Vol. 2, 251.
139. Melnichenko, *Lichnaia zhizn Lenina*, 19; Majsurjan, *Drugoj Lenin*, 104, 109.
140. Golikov, *Biograficheskaya Chronika* Vol. 2, 266–280.
141. Ibid., 320–3.
142. Ibid., 349.
143 Ibid., 360, 364, 370.
144. Ibid., 371, 373.
145. Anna Ilyinichna Ulyanova, "Lenin," in *Reminiscences of Lenin by His Relatives*, 18–19.
146. Inessa was already a mother of four when she came to know Vladimir Ilyich. The lady was of French descent on the paternal side, and of Scottish or English descent on the maternal side. Her husband was a successful businessman, who, it is said, helped *Pravda* "find money" at one point. See Ralph Carter Elwood, *Inessa Armand. Revolutionary and Feminist* (Cambridge: Cambridge University Press, 1992), 91.
147. Krupskaya, "O Vladimir Ilyiche," in *Izbrannie*, 123.
148. "Perepiska L. D. Trotskogo, L. B. Kameneva i V. I. Lenina" [Correspondence of Trotsky, Kamenev and Lenin], in *V. I. Lenin, Neizvestnye dokumenty. 1891–1922*, 34.
149. Letter of 14 January 1908, to M. I. Ulyanova in St. Petersburg. LCW, Vol. 37, 372.
150. Letter of 8 January 1904, from Geneva to his Mother. Ibid., 359. Four years later, in his letter to his mother written on 22 January 1908, he commented on recent events as follows: "We are now settling down here and our arrangements, of course, will not be worse than before. The only unpleasant thing was the actual moving, which was a change for the worse. That, however, was inevitable. About Capri—as soon as I arrived I found a letter from Gorky, who very insistently invites me there. Nadya and I have made up our minds to accept that invitation." Ibid., 374.
151. In a letter to his mother, sent from Geneva to Moscow on 17 November 1908, he indicates that he wants to move to Paris: "we are tired of staying in this provincial backwater. It is true, of course, that Paris is more expensive." Ibid., 396.
152. See letter to his mother written on 10 December 1908, and sent from Geneva to Moscow. Ibid., 400. In his first letter from Paris, sent to Anyuta (on 19 December) he had still expressed favorable impressions in regard to the expensive but quiet apartment far from the city center. Ibid. 402.
153. Ibid., 451.
154. Letter to Anyuta, sent on 2 May 1910 to Saratov. Ibid., 459. Also see on this subject Lenin's letter to Gorky. LCW, Vol. 34, 419–22.

155. "In general we have made good use of the holidays—we have been to museums, the theater and the *Musée Grévin*, which gave us much pleasure. This evening I intend to go to an estaminet to listen to a '*goguette révolutionnaire*' by 'songsters' [an unhappy translation of *chansonniers*]." Letter to Manyasha, dated 2 January 1910. LCW, Vol. 37, 445.
156. Letter to Manyasha, early January 1910, from Paris to Moscow. Ibid., 447.
157. Ibid., 436, and Melnichenko, *Lichnaia zhizn Lenina*, 135; as well as LCW, Vol. 37, 449.
158. Letter of 12 January 1910 to Manyachka. LCW, Vol. 37, 448.
159. He informed his mother in a letter dated 1 June 1910 that he had arrived from Marseilles to Naples by ship: "It was like travelling on the Volga. I am going to Capri from here for a brief visit." Ibid., 462.
160. Ibid., 41.
161. By the autumn, Lenin and company were already taking respite in Dunajec, a town close to Poronino, and in October they held the Central Committee meeting in the latter place, in Lenin's rented flat. For a period the Zinoviev family also stayed here, and Kamanev also visited, and of course Inessa—often on her way to Russia. Elwood, *Inessa Armand*, 96–97.
162. LCW, Vol. 37, 507–8. It is apparent in Lenin's correspondence that he felt much more comfortable here, because he was closer to Russia and intrigues and backbiting were fewer, as emphasized by his sister Maria, in her commentary of the letters. Ibid., 56–57.
163. Melnichenko, *Lichnaia zhizn Lenina*, 158; Majsurjan, *Drugoj Lenin*, 74–75.
164. Lenin, "Lev Tolstoi and His Epoch" (*Zvezda*, No. 6, January 22, 1911), LCW, Vol. 17, 49–53.
165. Lenin, "L. N. Tolstoy," in *Sotsial-Demokrat* No. 18 (November 16 (29), 1910). *LCW*, Vol. 16, (Moscow: Progress Publishers, 1974), 323–327.
166. LCW, Vol. 17, 323–5.
167. Armand, herself, in a letter written later to Lenin, described the feelings she first harbored for Lenin: "During that time I was terribly scared of you. I wanted to see you, but I would have preferred to die on the spot than to have approached you, and when for some reason you came into N.K.'s room, I at once became flustered and behaved like a fool. . . . It was only in Longjumeau and the following autumn in connection with the translations, etc., that I got used to you a little." Latishev, *Rassekrechionniy Lenin*, 289.
168. Krupskaya, *Reminiscences*, 213.
169. The documents on this subject that became newly available after the change of regimes were processed first by A. Latishev in *Rassekrechionniy Lenin*, 284–327. Readers who respect source criticism will have strong reservations with regard to some of the more frivolous deductions Latishev permits himself. See in Hungarian, "Lenin és Inessa," 1999) 42, 67–95.
170. In a letter to his mother sent from Paris to Saratov, Lenin acknowledged the sad news of his two sisters' arrest. "Does anybody visit you? Sudden loneliness is the worst thing that can happen at such times." LCW. Vol. 37, 476. It is with great enthusiasm that he first reports to his mother in his letter of 1 July, 1912: "This summer we have moved a long way from Paris—to Krakow. Almost in Russia! Even the Jews are like Russians and the Russian frontier is 8 versts away . . . , the women go barefoot and wear brightly-coloured clothes, exactly as in Russia." Ibid., 479.
171. Some sources are confident that it can be assumed that her arrest was "arranged" by R. Malinovsky, the agent of the Okhrana himself. See Elwood, *Inessa Armand*, 95.
172. Krupskaya, *Reminiscences*, 261. Though Krupskaya was not as beguiled by the Polish countryside as Lenin, the good air of the mountains was prescribed for her by her doctor, as an antidote for her Bazedow's disease. See Lenin's letters to Manyasha, from Poronino to Vologda dated 12 or 13 May 1913, LCW, Vol. 37, 495–6; and 22 April 1914. LCW, Vol. 37, 518. "In a fortnight or so we are again going to Poronin—there are mountains there and I hope

that Nadya's thyroid trouble will pass—mountain air is good for people suffering from this disease. The weather here is wonderful and I frequently go cycling."

173. Quoted from: "Lenin as a Man" in *Communist Morality*, edited by N. Bychkova, R. Lavrov and V. Lubisheva (Moscow: Progress Publishers, 1962). LCW, Vol. 35, 146; see also Melnichenko, *Lichnaia zhizn Lenina*, 199.
174. LCW, Vol. 35, 146.
175. Latishev quotes Inessa's confessions of love at length, though unable to quote Lenin himself, as Vladimir Ilyich had asked Inessa to return his letters on the summer of 1914, which was the occasion of their "breaking off" their relationship, though never quite breaking up. "Well, my dear," Inessa wrote to Lenin, "that's enough for today—I want to send this off. There was no letter from you yesterday! I'm rather afraid my letters are not reaching you! . . . I get the most unlikely ideas thinking about it. . . . I send you a big kiss, Your Inessa." Further along she also quotes Lenin on the basis of Volkogonov: "Oh, how I would like to kiss you a thousand times even, to greet you and wish great success! I am absolutely certain that you will achieve an all round success. Sincerely Yours. V.L." (See CPA IML (GASHPRI), f 2, op. 1, delo 3327) Latishev, *Rassekrechionniy Lenin*, 286–7. The author is also convincing in arguing that if Lenin had so wished, Krupsakaya would have stepped aside. While he did not wish it, he remained in love with Inessa Armand all his life. This is documented by the reminiscences of those women (N. Krupskaya, A. Balabanova, A. Kollontay) who recalled Lenin's breakdown at Inessa's funeral, after she had died of cholera. Inessa was buried by the Kremlin wall on the Red Square, on 24 September 1920.
176. Finally they left Bern and settled in Zurich: "Nadya and I," he wrote to his sister on 20 February 1916, "are very pleased with Zurich; there are good libraries here." He wrote then wrote a "situation report" to his mother on 12 March. LCW, Vol. 37, 529.
177. Petr Nikolaevich Pospelov, *Vladimir Ilyich Lenin: A Biography* (Moscow: Progress Publishers, 1965), 285.
178. On this subject see Latishev, *Rassekrechionniy Lenin*, 304–316. What Latishev speculates is not of interest in and of itself, but the quoted documents are important for understanding the story of their love.
179. LCW, Vol. 35, 180–1.
180. Ibid., 182–4.
181. Latishev, *Rassekrechionniy Lenin*, 102–3.
182. LCW, Vol 43, 552–3.
183. It is a point of controversy, made up in great part for the debate, whether the return of the Bolsheviks, which led, so to say, to the overthrow of the Provisional Government, was organized by the German secret service, the German military command, and "German gold," the "German millions." Where "German money" is concerned, no data that can be taken seriously exist; this is real regime-change humbug. What can be proven is that the Swiss social democrat, Karl Moor (who was later revealed to have been an agent of the German government), handed over 35,079 dollars to Ganetsky, Radek, and Vorovsky, which they returned in 1925 and 1927. This amount serves A. G. Latishev as evidence on which to build his impossible accusations. See Latishev, *Rassekrechionniy Lenin*, 102–3. Other suspicions of fraud emerged in regard to this within the business-oriented segment of historiographers. The whole field of questions was reassuringly unraveled by Semion Lyandres, proving that prior to their gaining hold of power the Bolsheviks never received any money from the German government or German foundations. The Provisional Government's document accusing Lenin and the Bolsheviks of the above would not stand up to a critical examination by current legal practice, or that of the day, either in terms of its documentation or its legal argument. See Semion Lyandres, *The Bolsheviks' "German Gold" Revisited: An Inquiry into the 1917*

Accusations, Carl Beck papers in Russian and East European studies, no. 1106 (Pittsburgh: Center for Russian & East European Studies, University of Pittsburgh, 1995), especially 93–104, and for a historiographic critique of the subject, mainly Volkogonov's false presentation, 166.

184. See Zinoviev's recollection in Fritz Platten, *Lenin iz emigracii v Rossiju* (Moscow: Moskovsky rabochy, 1990), 121–4.
185. Reminiscences detail the great mood in which (a part of) the revolutionary general staff returned on the "sealed train," with Lenin also singing some of his favorite revolutionary songs, at times nevertheless sending his friends out of his cabin, as he continued to work intensely on what would later become the famed *April Theses*. Platten, *Lenin iz emigracii*; see for example the recollections of E. Usiyevich, ibid., 149–51.
186. Pospelov, *Vladimir Ilyich Lenin: A Biography*, 370–1.
187. In Hungarian, perhaps one of the works that allows a glimpse into the unfolding of events is István Dolmányos's "neo-Baroque" book, *Ragyogó Október. A nagy oroszországi szocialista forradalom története* (Budapest: Kossuth, 1979), 269–290.
188. The first steps taken from above in the direction of a personality cult may have been in July 1923, in the period when the Central Executive Committee of the Soviets elected the ailing Lenin Chairman of the Council of the People's Commissars. Two days later the Lenin Institute was established in Moscow, for the purpose of collecting Lenin's biographical data, and then, on 18 July, the so-called Council of the Smaller People's Commissariat voted for a resolution to nationalize the family home of the Ulyanovs in Simbirsk, to house the Lenin Museum to be established there. Golikov, *Biograficheskaya Chronika*, Vol. 12, 618–19.
189. See N. Meshcheryakov, *Literaturnaya Entsiklopedia* Vol. 11, 192.
190. Melnichenko, *Lichnaia zhizn Lenina*, 91.
191. An enormous store of documents is available to show what overwhelming significance Lenin attributed to books, and to the public library from the point of view of mass culture, even after October. See *Lenin and Books*.
192. See LCW, Vol. 17, 304.
193. On 22 December 1922 Lenin dictated the following note: "Do not forget to take all steps [...] if paralysis also sets in to stop my speech, out of humane feeling let me be given cyanide, as also taken by the Lafargues." Stalin himself wrote this up in a secret memo to the Politburo, on 17 March 1923. See, F. Chuyev, *Stosorok besed s Molotovim* (Moscow: Terra, 1991); Majsurjan, *Drugoj Lenin*, 128–9; Melnichenko, *Lichnaia zhizn Lenina*, 251–2.
194. Golikov, *Biograficheskaya Chronika*, Vol. 5, 170–1.
195. Golikov, *Biograficheskaya Chronika*, Vol. 6, 112–114; Majsurjan, *Drugoj Lenin*, 120–3.
196. Golikov, *Biograficheskaya Chronika*, Vol. 6, 445; Majsurjan, *Drugoj Lenin*, 125–7. The automobile and the criminals were later found.
197. N. N. Kucharkov, et al., *Biblioteka V. I. Lenina v Kremle: katalog* [Library of V. I. Lenin in the Kremlin, Catalogue, Moscow] (Moscow: Izdatel·vo Vsesojuznoj Knožnoj Palaty, 1961). The catalogue describes 8,450 texts.
198. Golikov, *Biograficheskaya Chronika*, Vol. 12, 1571–4, 638.
199. Majsurjan, *Drugoj Lenin*, 342–5. In 1925, Grigory Batkis wrote in his book titled *Seksualnaya revolyutsia v Sovietskom Soyuze*: "Soviet law proclaims the absolute non-interference of the state in any matters relating to the sexes, until no one suffers damages, and no one's rights are infringed."
200. Kolesov, *V.I. Lenin: Lichnost i sudba*, 8, 101.
201. A favorite subject of postmodern Leninology is that Lenin died of syphilis, but not a single book that could prove this has been written, not that this could have any significance with regard to his lifework, but the sources are rather unequivocal on this matter. Yuriy

Mikhaylovic Lopuhin, *Bolezny, smerty i balzamirovanie V. I. Lenina* (Moscow: Respublika, 1997).

202. See an objective account in, for example, Clark, *Lenin. Behind the Mask*, 463–6.
203. Note to LCW Vol. 45, 607.
204. In his recommendations and evaluations of the famous Letter to the Congress, the characterization of some Bolshevik leaders took a place of prominence. As dictated by Lenin on 24–25 December 1922. LCW, Vol. 36, 594–6.
205. About Trotsky: "He is personally perhaps the most capable man in the present C.C., but he has displayed excessive self-assurance and shown excessive preoccupation with the purely administrative side of the work." He had not forgiven Kamenev and Zinoviev the October episode. He declared Bukharin (along with Pyatakov) the most talented among the younger members of the party, as a "favorite of the whole party, but his theoretical views can be classified as fully Marxist only with great reserve, for there is something scholastic about him (he has never made a study of the dialectics, and, I think, never fully understood it)." LCW, Vol. 36, 595.
206. "Dear Comrade Stalin: You have been so rude as to summon my wife to the telephone and use bad language. Although she had told you that she was prepared to forget this, the fact nevertheless became known through her to Zinoviev and Kamenev. I have no intention of forgetting so easily what has been done against me, and it goes without saying that what has been done against my wife I consider having been done against me as well. I ask you, therefore, to think it over whether you are prepared to withdraw what you have said and to make your apologies, or whether you prefer that relations between us should be broken off." LCW, Vol. 45, 607.
207. LCW, Vol. 45, 608.
208. Golikov, *Biograficheskaya Chronika*, Vol. 12, 662.
209. Ibid., 664.
210. Ibid., 665.
211. Though everyone would still have had in mind that the cloyingly opulent festivities arranged for his fiftieth birthday had repelled the man being celebrated. ". . . avoided anything that even seemed like a cult of his personality." Balabanoff, *Impressions of Lenin*, 5. When his wife, Nadezhda Konstantinovna, in an article of July 1924, added the oft-quoted sentence in connection with her study of his lifework that "Lenin need not be made into an icon," it was in fact already too late. See N. Krupskaya, "Podgotovka leninca," in *Izbrannye proizvedeniia*, 125. For one of the earliest investigations of the Lenin cult see Nina Tumarkin, *Lenin Lives! The Lenin Cult in Soviet Russia* (Cambridge, London: Harvard University Press, 1983).

CHAPTER 2—RUSSIAN CAPITALISM AND THE REVOLUTION

1. Andrei Nikolaevich Sakharov et al., *Rossiia v nachale XX veka* (Moscow: Novyĭ khronograf, 2002), 20–22.
2. Attempting to compile a comprehensive list is impossible, so only a few controversial publications are offered here for further attention. Sakharov et al., *Rossiia v nachale XX veka*; V. S. Dakin, *Bil li shans u Stolipina?* (Moscow: LISS, 2002); A. Ya. Avreh, *tsarism nakanunye sverzheniya* (Moscow: Nauka, 1989); I. V. Ostrovsky, *P. A. Stolipin i ego vremya* (Novosibirsk: Nauka, 1992).
3. In his well-known brochure about imperialism, written twenty years later, he still brought this "impersonality" of the system into prominence when discussing the issue of war violence: "The capitalists divide the world, not out of any particular malice, but because the degree of concentration which has been reached forces them to adopt this method in order to obtain profits." LCW, Vol. 22, 253.

4. LCW, Vol. 1. The first four works by Lenin can be found in this volume. The first piece he wrote was a review: *New Economic Developments in Peasant Life* (On V. Y. Postnikov's *Peasant Farming in South Russia*, 1891). Lenin put his observation down on paper in the spring of 1893; the article first appeared in 1923.
5. LCW, Vol. 1, 129–332. It was written in the spring and summer of 1894 and was published the same year, while it had been in preparation since the summer of 1892–93, when he gave a lecture on the subject in Marxist circles in Samara. In the autumn of 1894 he gave readings of his book in the Marxist circle of St. Petersburg. For further information on the distribution and fate of the book see ibid.
6. Even economic historians and economists of the highest standing, such as Alec Nove, held Lenin's book in high regard, though naturally he was not considered an economist. Nove indicated at the same time that Lenin's interest in economics was "one-sided." While Lenin had an outstanding interpretation of Marx, and knew Adam Smith and the classical economic theories well, he did not deal with microeconomics at all, as he did not have the time, as a politician, to delve into this. See Alec Nove, "Lenin as Economist," in *Lenin: The Man, the Theorist, the Leader*, edited by Leonard Schapiro and Peter Reddaway (New York: Praeger, 1967), 187–210.
7. The subject does indeed have a serious tradition in theoretical thought, as for example in some of Attila Ágh's explorations prior to 1989, in which he tried to outline the theoretical significance of Lenin in relation to this very book, *The Development of Capitalism in Russia*. See Attila Ágh, *A politika világa* [The world of politics] (Budapest: Kossuth, 1984), 190. But another work may also be cited here, Ferenc Tőkei, *A szocializmus dialektikájáról* [On the dialectics of socialism] (Budapest: Kossuth, 1974).
8. A letter to his mother from Krasnoyarsk, dated 26 March 1896, in which he requested literature on economic history: *Yezhegodnik Ministerstva finansov* [The annual report of the ministry of finance] (St. Petersburg: 1869); *Statistichesky vremennik Rossiiskoi imperii* [The statistical annual of the Russian Empire], published by the Central Statistical Committee of the Ministry of the Interior; *Materialy dlya statistiki fabrichno-zavodskoi promyshlennosti v Yevropeiskoi Rossii za 1868 god.* [Material for the annual industrial statistics of European Russia for the year 1868], edited by I. Bock (St. Petersburg: 1872); etc. LCW, Vol. 37, 98.
9. LCW, Vol. 1, 12–13.
10. Ibid., 69–70. In relation to this subject he was studying Engels's *The Origin of the Family, Private Property and the State* at the same time, the spring of 1874, Golikov, *Biograficheskaya Chronika*, Vol. 1, 87.
11. Meanwhile Lenin could not have known a number of rather important works by Marx, such as the *Grundrisse*, which was discovered by David Ryazanov, the director of the Marx-Engels Institute in Moscow working on the first edition of the collected works of Marx and Engels, in 1923. The famous *Introduction* was found by Kautsky. See Marcello Musto, *Dissemination and Reception of the* Grundrisse *in the World. A Contribution to the History of Marxism*, manuscript.
12. Julius Martov, *Obshchestvennye i umstvennye techeniia v Rossii 1870–1905* (Leningrad–Moscow: Kniga, 1924), 1.
13. Ibid.
14. "It is obvious that Marx's basic idea that the development of the social-economic formations is a process of natural history cuts at the very root of this childish morality which lays claim to the title of sociology." LCW, Vol. 1, 136–141.
15. "The analysis of material social relations (i.e., of those that take shape without passing through man's consciousness: when exchanging products men enter into production relations without even realizing that there is a social relation of production here)—the analysis of material social

relations at once made it possible to observe recurrence and regularity and to generalize the systems of the various countries in the single fundamental concept: *social formation*." Ibid., 140.

16. LCW, Vol. 1, 195.
17. "In Russia," wrote Lenin ironically upon Mikhailovsky's doubts as to the very existence of a proletariat, "—the only country where such a hopeless poverty of the masses and such shameless exploitation of the working people can be found; which has been compared (and legitimately so) to England as regards the condition of the poor; and where the starvation of millions of people is a permanent thing existing side by side, for instance, with a steady increase in the export of grain—in Russia there is no proletariat!!" LCW, Vol. 1, 195–196.
18. Ibid., 63–64, 72.
19. Ibid., 73.
20. Before writing this study, he presented it at a self-training debate (related to G. B. Krasin's lecture on *The Market Question*). Lenin expressed his views as a follow up to Krasin's lecture. Lenin wrote the study in the autumn of 1893, and it was first published in 1937. See Golikov, *Biograficheskaya Chronika*, Vol. 1, 80–1; LCW, Vol. 1, 75–128.
21. "The development of capitalism certainly needs an extensive home market; but the ruin of the peasantry undermines this market, threatens to close it altogether and make the organization of the capitalist order impossible. True, it is said that, by transforming the natural economy of our direct producers into a commodity economy, capitalism is creating a market for itself; but is it conceivable that the miserable remnants of the natural economy of indigent peasants can form the basis for the development in our country of the mighty capitalist production that we see in the West?" LCW, Vol. 1, 79.
22. Ibid., 91–2.
23. See *The Development of Capitalism in Russia*, LCW, Vol. 3, 25–6, and 193–198.
24. "With all the endless variety of forms . . . , the economic organization of contemporary landlord farming amounts to two main systems, in the most varied combinations—the *labor-service* system and the *capitalist* system. The first . . . is a direct survival of Corvée economy . . ." Ibid., 194.
25. In his decidedly anti-Bernsteinian article (reviewing Karl Kautsky's book, *Bernstein und das Sozialdemokratische Program*) written at the end of 1899, he outlined the liberal, "Bernsteinian" tendencies of "legal Marxism." LCW, Vol. 4, 193–204.
26. LCW, Vol. 1, especially 400–508, in his review of Struve's *Kriticheskie zametki k voprosu ob ekonomicheskom razvitii Rossii* (St. Petersburg: 1894), *The Economic Content of Narodism and the Criticism of It in Mr. Struve's Book—The Reflection of Marxism in Bourgeois Literature*. This is the first important theoretical document in this respect. The time of the study's writing is late 1894–early 1895. It first appeared with the title *Material for a Characterization of Our Economic Development* authored under the alias of K. Tulin in 1895.
27. Lenin, *Book Review: J. A. Hobson. The Evolution of Modern Capitalism*, LCW, Vol. 4, 100–4. His interest in Hobson also found expression later. On 28 August 1904, he wrote from Geneva to his mother in Sablino (near St. Petersburg): "I have now received Hobson's book on imperialism and have begun translating it." LCW, Vol. 37, 365.
28. LCW, Vol. 37, 290. Even in 1900, in a letter to his mother (6 April), Lenin wrote: "I do not intend to answer P. Struve (I sent a short note against him to be inserted into my reply to Skvortsov)." Yet the subject was Struve's article, "The Fundamental Antinomy of Labor Value Theory," *Zhizn* (1899), No. 10, and the insertion was added to the article titled *Uncritical Criticism*, LCW, Vol. 3, 632.
29. For more on the activities of this circle and Struve's role in them see Lajos Menyhárt, *Az orosz társadalmi-politikai gondolkodás a századfordulón (1895–1906)* [Russian sociopolitical thought at the turn of the century (1895–1906)] (Budapest: Akadémiai Kiadó, 1985).

30. Lenin had already come to suspect the "intimacy" between certain Marxists and liberals when he received Yekaterina Kuskova's *Credo* in July 1899. This was essentially identical with Struve's intellectual transformation, but in a liberal social democratic cloak, That is, it recommended a "gradual, democratic transformation of society" instead of the revolution. See Belov, *Istoria odnoi "druzhby"*, 73–5, 83–5. Even in 1902, Lenin was rather restrained in criticizing Struve in a preface (Geneva: December 1902) to the second edition of his pamphlet, *The Tasks of the Russian Social-Democrats*, only "unmasking" him once in the quite extensive text, stating that one should be grateful to the "Zemstvo constitutional party" of "the liberal land-owning gentry" "for removing Mr. Struve from Russian Social-Democracy, and with this completing his metamorphosis from a quasi-Marxist into a liberal, helping us by a living example demonstrate to one and all the real meaning of Bernsteinism in general and of Russian Bernsteinism in particular." LCW, Vol. 6, 212–1 3.
31. LCW, Vol. 1, 349–54.
32. V. I. Lenin, "Konspekt i kriticheskiye zamechaniya na knigu S. Bulgakova" [Konspectus drafts and critical notes to the book by S. Bulgakov] *Leninskii Sbornik* [Lenin miscellany], (Moscow: Party Publishing House, 1933), esp. 119. Notes to this volume amply document the depth of Lenin's knowledge of the international literature as well. In the course of his studies on agrarian capitalism Lenin analyzed the works of Kautsky, David, Hertz, S. Bulgakov, and others, fitting them into his design for the universal development of capitalism.
33. Karl Kautsky, *Die Agrarfrage. Eine Übersicht über die Tendenzen der modernen Landwirtschaft und die Agrarpolitik der Sozialdemokraten* (Stuttgart: Dietz, 1899). This volume prompted Lenin to make perhaps the most extensive notes, forty-nine handwritten, notebook-size pages. See "Konspekt knigi K. Kautskogo 'Agrarnii vopros,'" in *Leninskii Sbornik*, Vol. 19, 27–83.
34. The German "academic socialists" in the second half of the nineteenth century—such as Luya Brentano and Werner Sombart—formulated theories of the "peaceful transition" from capitalism to socialism, in contradiction to the revolutionary trends of the labor movement.
35. On this question see S. V. Tyutyukin, *Pervaya rossiiskaya revolyutsiya i G.V. Plekhanov* (Moscow: Nauka, 1981), 134–136.
36. LCW Vol. 1, 493–5.
37. Ibid., 495.
38. After the 1905 Revolution, taking measure of the intellectual distance covered and the fight against Narodism, as well as the performances of Struve, Bulgakov, Tugan-Baranovsky, Berdaev, and others in retrospect, Lenin wrote: "They were bourgeois democrats for whom the break with Narodism signified transition from petit-bourgeois (or peasant) socialism to bourgeois liberalism, and not to proletarian socialism as was the case with us." LCW, Vol. 13, 97.
39. As an example he cited French history, in line with Marx. LCW, Vol. 1, 419.
40. "The Narodnik-like Bourgeoisie and Distraught Narodism," *Iskra* 54 (1 December 1903). See LCW, Vol. 7, 105.
41. This last question is dealt with in more detail in chapters 3 and 8.
42. Looking back from 1907, in his "Preface" to the collection *Twelve Years*, Lenin defined the political stake of the arguments that had taken place in the mid-1890s as follows: in Struve's opinion the Russian peasant suffers not under the reign of capitalism and capitalist exploitation, but the "unsatisfactory productivity" of his own labor, that is, the lack of integration into the system of capital, underdeveloped capitalism. "[T]he old, and in many respects outdated, polemic with Struve is important as an instructive example, one that shows the practical and political value of irreconcilable theoretical polemics." LCW, Vol. 13, 97.
43. On this, see Ágh, *A politika világa*.
44. LCW, Vol. 3, 258.

45. See György Göncöl, "Rosa Luxemburg helye a marxizmus fejlődéstörténetében" [Rosa Luxemburg's place in the evolutionary history of Marxism], "Afterword" in Rosa Luxemburg, *A tőkefelhalmozás* [The accumulation of capital] (Budapest: Kossuth, 1979), 510–1.
46. György Göncöl, "Rosa Luxemburg helye," in Luxemburg, *A tőkefelhalmozás*; and LCW, Vol. 4, 91. Göncöl gave an accurate account of the development of Lenin's views in other terms as well, when he pointed out that in Lenin's earlier quoted text on the "market question" he shared Adam Smith's thesis on the causal and linear connection between labor distribution and the market and explains capital's tendency for growth basically with technological advance alone, while in his later study (*Once More on the Theory of Realization*) he writes about the "horizontal" and "vertical" tendencies involved in the spread of capitalism, as well as its universal and local bearings "in the creation of colonies, drawing wild tribes into the whirlpool of world capitalism." Ibid., 77–78.
47. *Leninskii Sbornik* XXII [Lenin miscellany] (Moscow: Party Publishing House, 1933), 343–390, translated for the *Lenin Internet Archive* (2010) by Steve Palmer [http://www.marxists.org/archive/lenin/works/1913/apr/rl-acc-capital-notes.htm]. A different translation is also available by James Lawler and annotated to the English edition of Luxemburg by Paul Zarembka as "Marginal Notes on Luxemburg's Accumulation of Capital," in *Research in Political Economy*, Volume 18 (Elsevier Science, New York, 2000), 225–235. These annotations make it clear that Lenin was highly skeptical of whether Rosa Luxemburg interprets the Marxist theory dealing with processes of recapitalization correctly. His chief issue with Luxemburg's theory of capital accumulation was that in his opinion, as widely known, there is no need necessarily for noncapitalist "sectors" and regions for there to be capital accumulation or realization of value.
48. Göncöl, "Rosa Luxemburg helye," in Luxemburg, *A tőkefelhalmozás* [The accumulation of capital], 513.
49. The speed of falling in debt "in the case of backward regions surpasses the tempo of growth as a mathematical rule." See Göncöl, ibid.; and more current literature in Hungarian, *Globalizáció, tőkekoncentráció, térszerkezet* [Globalization, capital concentration and space structure], edited by Ágnes Bernek and Péter Farkas (Budapest: MTA Világgazdasági Kutatóintézet, 2006); Péter Farkas, *A globalizáció és fenyegetései. A világgazdaság és a gazdaságelméletek zavarai* [Globalization and its dangers. Disturbances in global economy and economic theory] (Budapest: Aula Kiadó, 2002).
50. After Lenin's death, as soon as February 1924, Lukács was the first to pose the problem indicated here in its full magnitude, in the already cited study on Lenin, which he wrote in Vienna, *Lenin: A Study on the Unity of His Thought*, 41–43. Though at the time Lukács was not too far advanced in matters of economics, he believed that the economic part of Lenin's later analysis, his imperialism theory, was not as deep as Rosa Luxemburg's (theory of accumulation, colonial markets, the origins of war, etc.); but he nevertheless speaks of Lenin's "theoretical superiority" in one decisive aspect: that of "evaluating the process as a whole," that is, when it comes to actually judging a concrete world situation, he was able to take into account the mediations between theoretical analysis and practice. See Lukács, *Lenin: A Study on the Unity of His Thought*, 89–93. (The debate surrounding the accumulation of capital is discussed again later in a different context.)
51. LCW Vol. 3, 329.
52. For more on the history of these scientific and political-theoretical debates and struggles see Krausz, *Pártviták és történettudomány*. An array of important contiguities with this debate will be addressed in greater detail later.
53. For a historical background to this see Tamás Krausz, *A Szovjetúnió története* [The history of

the Soviet Union] (Budapest: Kossuth, 2008), I. fejezet: A "gyenge láncszem [Chapter 1. The weak link].

54. LCW, Vol. 1, 277, 320–1.
55. LCW, Vol. 1, 233–236.
56. "When its advanced representatives have mastered the ideas of scientific socialism, the idea of the historical role of the Russian worker, when these ideas become widespread, and when stable organizations are formed among the workers to transform the workers' present sporadic economic war into conscious class struggle—then the Russian WORKER rising at the head of all the democratic elements, will overthrow absolutism and lead the RUSSIAN PROLETARIAT (side by side with the proletariat of ALL COUNTRIES along the straight road of open political struggle to THE VICTORIOUS COMMUNIST REVOLUTION." Ibid., 300.
57. In his preface to the second edition of *The Development of Capitalism in Russia,* composed in July of 1907, he clearly suggests that the final balance of the revolution cannot yet be drawn, "[h]ence, the time has not yet come . . . for a thorough revision of this essay," though he complains that subjectively speaking he would still not have time for this, as "the immediate Party duties of a participant in the working-class movement leave no leisure." LCW, Vol. 3, 34.
58. See Krausz, *Pártviták és történettudomány*, esp. 60–2.
59. LCW, Vol. 3, 27.
60. Current mainstream literature in (economic) history reaches a conclusion not far removed from that of Lenin's, with regard to the basic structure of Russian capitalism, but does not take a class-conscious view of armed revolutionary uprising; it speaks not of "the conflict between the seat of power and society," but views it in terms of "the opposition between power and the extremist leftist social movements." See A. N. Sakharov, "Introduction" in *Rossiya v nachale*, 52–53. The viewpoint of economic history is also shifting, as reflected in the final balance drawn under the pre–First World War decade of economic development drawn by Iu. A. Petrov in the quoted book: "At the beginning of the twentieth century Russia remained a country with a backward economy by the standards of the developed nations, but entered the sphere of healthy economic growth within the framework of the market model." "Rossiyskaya economica v nachale XX veka," in *Rossiya v nachale*, 219.
61. In the literature of history, a fact that is often not properly considered is that, in writing his pamphlet on imperialism, Lenin used an incredible force of scientific studies and statistical work. Just his notes and research cards filled two whole volumes, which came to fill 400 and 500 pages respectively in print. See *Leninsky Sbornik* Vol. XXII (1933), and Vol. XXVII (1934), 489, with the name index in the volume in print alone coming to 470 items, whose majority comprises economists, historians, philosophers, sociologists, statisticians, and of course, politicians. From Carnegie to Sombar, R. Hoeniger to E. Théry, and J. Lescure to the Japanese Hishida, or J. Patouillet to Riesser, the works of these annotated authors and the related data or commentary lines these sheets. See LCW, Vol. 39.
62. LCW Vol. 20, 152–4. The article appeared in the 13 March 1914 edition of the journal *Puty Pravdi*. The manuscript of the article in question, which was confiscated by the Okhrana—the Political Department—as evidence of the antigovernment activity of *Pravda*, remained hidden in the archives for many a decade.
63. As generally acknowledged, apart from Hobson, Hilferding had the most influence on Lenin's theory of imperialism, but it would be a mistake to overestimate their role. Alec Nove, the first serious Western analyst of this work of Lenin, did not question its significance even purely in economic terms, though critical of many of its claims. See Nove, "Lenin as Economist," in *Lenin: The Man, the Theorist, the Leader*, 198–203. Lenin, in a sense, underestimated the technical ability the system of capital had for renewal, and the consequences this would have

in the center countries in terms of manipulating consciousness. At the same time, it is also obvious that imperialism did not prove to be the "death rattle" of capitalism. It is another matter, and Nove did not digress on this, what cost to humanity the "endurance" of capitalism entails. Lenin, however, did give an effective answer to this question, according to his own political system of thought. The title of this work bears the words "highest stage" of capitalism, though some writers contend that the words *visshaya stadiya* would translate more accurately as "higher stage." Were it not so, theoretically this would still be more exact.

64. The oppositely oriented, brutal simplifications of the theory of imperialism honed in the Stalinist period spring to life even in some of the professionally mature works of our times. See Volobuyev, *Drama rossiskoy Istorii*, 154–9.
65. *Imperialism, the Highest Stage of Capitalism*, LCW, Vol. 22, 278.
66. LCW Vol. 22, 299. "Private property based on the labor of the small proprietor, free competition, democracy, all the catchwords with which the capitalists and their press deceive the workers and the peasants are things of the distant past. Capitalism has grown into a world system of colonial oppression and of the financial strangulation of the overwhelming majority of the population of the world by a handful of 'advanced' countries . . . who are drawing the whole world into their war over the division of their booty." Ibid., 191.
67. "But when nine-tenths of Africa had been seized (by 1900), when the whole world had been divided up, there was inevitably ushered in the era of monopoly possession of colonies and, consequently, of particularly intense struggle for the division and the redivision of the world." Ibid., 299–300. Here Lenin did not dwell on the by now evident fact that this "division" could be of a permanent nature.
68. Lenin waxed polemical on the "*state socialists*" who had "fallen in love" with monopolist organization. "It is time our state socialists, who allow themselves to be blinded by a beautiful principle, understood, at last, that in Germany the monopolies have never pursued the aim, nor have they had the result, of benefiting the consumer, or even of handing over to the state part of the promoter's profits; they have served only to facilitate, at the expense of the state, the recovery of private industries which were on the verge of bankruptcy. [...] We see plainly here how private and state monopolies are interwoven in the epoch of finance capital; how both are but separate links in the imperialist struggle between the big monopolists for the division of the world." LCW, Vol. 22, 250–51. Lenin's theoretical limitations are brought into focus by Péter Szigeti in *Világrendszernézőben. Globális "szabad verseny"—a világkapitalizmus jelenlegi stádiuma* [Survey of world orders. Global "free competition"—the current stage of world capitalism] (Budapest: Napvilág, 2005), 37. Undoubtedly Lenin did not foresee either the possibility of a later creation of "welfare capitalism" (or even later developmental stages of capitalism) and its consequences, but note that no one among his contemporaries theoretically anticipated these developments at the time. Or if someone did, partially, that was Bernstein, who was mulling over the possibilities of a "good capitalism" without seeing any of its concrete forms in advance. In this sense Lenin considered the efforts of Bernstein an expression of the ideology of the workers' aristocracy. Perhaps only Keynes emphasized (*The Economic Consequences of the Peace*, 1919), based on the immediate experience of the Bolshevik-Communist revolution specifically, that the world of capital must give an adequate social and economic answer to the challenge thrown up by the economic and social challenge of Bolshevism, and that it may be capable of doing so.
69. LCW, Vol. 22, 240.
70. LCW, Vol. 19, 454. He examined the question of emigration in the light of very detailed data, indicating that "[t]he advanced nations seize, as it were, the best paid occupations for themselves and leave the, semi-barbarian countries the worst paid occupations" while "[t]he bourgeoisie incites the workers of one nation against those of another." This fact should perhaps in itself

have led Lenin to think over once again the conclusion of his article that said "the workers of Russia . . . are uniting with the workers of all countries into a single international force for emancipation." Ibid., 456–7.

71. LCW, Vol. 22, 17.
72. LCW, Vol. 22, 337–8.
73. It is no coincidence that when after his exile he finally met Plekhanov, their first disagreement of a political nature came about in the process of defining their relationship with the Russian bourgeoisie, at first as a mere shift of emphasis, in a political-strategic sense. (For a highly nuanced analysis of the acquaintance and first contacts between Lenin and Plekhanov see Loginov, *Vladimir Lenin. Vybor puti*, 356–428.)
74. The debate of the political questions was carried through at the London Party Congress of 1907, in the course of which the Bolsheviks and Mensheviks split irreparably as regarded the outcomes of the revolution. The Mensheviks continued to see the future of revolutionary development in cooperation with the bourgeoisie, while the Bolsheviks were with the poor peasantry. For more detail on this see Krausz, *Pártviták és történettudomány*, 30–37, 49–51; also Tamás Krausz, "Az első orosz forradalom és az oroszországi szociáldemokrácia 'második' szakadása" [The "second split" of the first Russian revolution and Russian social democracy], *Századok* [Centuries] (1983/4), 840–870.
75. In preparing for his Paris lecture of early 1903 (*Marxist Views on the Agrarian Question in Europe and in Russia*, 23–26 February 1903, Paris), he made a number of drafts that are important sources in regard to this field. See *Leninskii Sbornik*, Vol. XIX (1932), 225–95. In English, LCW, Vol. 40, 40–52.
76. LCW, Vol. 13, 319. On the development of Lenin's views on the agrarian question see in Hungarian, Lajos Varga, "Az Oroszországi Szociáldemokrata Munkáspárt első, 1903-as agrárprogramja" [The first agrarian program of the Russian social democratic labor party from 1903], *Párttörténeti Közlemények* [Party historical publications], (1978)3.
77. It was published as an independent book in St. Petersburg in 1908 by Zerno, but confiscated; only a single copy remained extant as Lenin's own comment informs, on the basis of which it was republished in 1917. LCW, Vol. 13, 217–428.
78. Ibid., 225.
79. Ibid., 229.
80. For his argument with M. Shanin, see ibid., 287–93. And here Lenin, actually in self-criticism, mentions that the program for the Second RSDLP Congress exaggerated the level of Russian agriculture's capitalization, offering in fact a sort of critique of his own historical work (*The Development of Capitalism in Russia*), though he was right that this exaggeration coincided with the main trend of the historical trend.
81. LCW, Vol. 13, 323.
82. Ibid., 237.
83. Ibid., 239.
84. LCW, Vol. 9, 59.
85. LCW, Vol. 9, 85.
86. LCW, Vol. 13, 117–18. See also *Two Tactics of Social-Democracy in the Democratic Revolution*, LCW, Vol. 9, 106–7.
87. See Lenin's article on the subject, "Russia's Finances," from the period of the 1905 Revolution, written after 1 (14) October 1905. First published *Leninskiy Sbornik*, Vol. XVI, 1931. "We have repeatedly pointed out that the autocratic government is more and more confused over its financial affairs (tricks would be a more apt word, I think). It is increasingly obvious that a financial collapse is inevitable." LCW, Vol. 41, 176.
88. LCW, Vol. 23, 250–1.

89. LCW, Vol. 23, 47.
90. The extensive literature dealing with this subject makes any further explication of the matter unnecessary. The author has himself dealt with the literature elsewhere (*Pártviták és történettudomány*). Apart from the work by Béla Kirchner cited above, see on the subject Baruch Knei Paz, *The Social and Political Thought of Leon Trotsky* (Oxford: Clarendon Press, 1978).
91. LCW, Vol. 23, 252. "The Russian revolution engendered a movement throughout the whole of Asia." He referred to the revolutionary fervor that caught on in Turkey, Persia, and China. "One must not forget that news of the tsar's constitutional manifesto, on reaching Vienna on October 30, 1905, played a decisive part in the final victory of universal suffrage in Austria." (Huge street demonstrations began in Vienna.)
92. LCW, Vol. 23, 236-7.
93. On this, see Amil Niederhauser, "On the Slavophile approach to history," *Acta Universitatis Debreciensis de L. K. nominatae*, Series Historica (Debrecen: 1966), esp. 27–41.
94. Hegel, Marx, and Engels commented on the peculiarities of Russian historical development numerous times; see for example G. W. F. Hegel, *Előadások a világtörténet fifilozófiájár* (Budapest: Akadémiai Kiadó, 1966), 189–190; K. Marx, *Die Geschichte der Geheimdiplomatie des 18 Jahrhunderts* (West Berlin: Verlag Olle und Wolter, 1977); F. Engels, *Az emigráns irodalom című ciklus*. MEM, Vol. 18, 493–554, 651–661.
95. For a pre- and post-history of the wide-ranging argument, see Krausz, *Pártviták és történettudomány*.
96. See *IV-y Obyedinitelny syezd R.S.D.R.P. Aprel (aprel-mai) 1906 goda. Protokoly* [Proceedings of the Fourth Unity Congress. April (April–May) 1906] (Moscow: 1959); and G. V. Plekhanov, "K agrarnomu voprosu v Rossii" [On the Agrarian Question in Russia], in *Sochineniia* Vol. 15 [Works] (St. Petersburg-Leningrad: Gosudarstvennoe izdatelstvo, 1923–1927), first published in *Dnevnik Sotsialdemokrata* (1906): 5.
97. G. Plekhanov, "Our Differences," *Selected Philosophical Works* Vol. 1, translated by R. Dixon (Moscow: Foreign Languages. Publishing House, 1961), also (London: Lawrence & Wishart, 1961), 218.
98. LCW, Vol. 10, 331–333.
99. For more on this, see Krausz, *Szovjet Thermidor*, 83–91.
100. See Sruve's much quoted text from 1908, "Velikaya Rossiya," in *Patriotica. Politika, kultura, religija, sotsialism. Sbornik statey za pyat let (1905–1910)* (St. Petersburg: 1911), 78.
101. L. B. Kamenev's analysis of the subject is interesting; see his "Vekhisti. O teni Bismarcka," in *Mezhdu dvumya revolyutsiami* Sbiornik Statyei Izd. 2-oye (Moscow: 1923), 291–316.
102. See for further details, Krausz, *Pártviták és történettudomány*, 40–57.
103. Lev Trotsky, *1905* (Moscow: 1922), 15, 19–22. (Especially the chapter "Sotsialnoye razvitiye i tsarism" [Social development and tsarism].
104. The Menshevik social democrats compiled their own historical analyses in a separate volume. See especially *Obshchestvennoye dvizheniye v nachale XX veka,* Vol. 1 (St. Petersburg: 1909). In this volume also, P. P. Maslov's study, "Razvitiye narodnogo hozyaytsva i yev vliyaniye na borbu klassov v 19 veke," ibid., 643–62, especially 649–57.
105. Find an overview of Olminsky's life in O. Lezhava and N. Nelidov, *M. S. Olminsky. Zhizn i deyatelnosty* (Moscow: Politizdat, 1973). M. Olminsky belonged to Lenin's closest circle already in 1904, and participated in the Council of 22 Bolsheviks convened at the end of July, beginning of August, in 1904. This is when the decision to establish a periodical party organ was taken, giving the green light to the later famous *Vperyod*, the first issue of which appeared on December 22 of the same year. See ibid., 90.
106. See M. Aleksandrov, *Absolyutism, gosudarstvo i byurokratiya* (Moscow: 1910).

107. The well-known historian Pyotr Miliukov, who became one of the founders of the liberal Kadet party, then its leader, and finally the foreign minister of the Provisional Government, had already pointed out the "demiurgic" role of the state in Russian history, and though he undoubtedly overamplified the independence of the bureaucratic state machinery from the ruling classes, he nonetheless formulated important historical questions in his time, in particular about the development of the state. Following in V. O. Klyuchevsky's tracks, he raised the problem of the way Western influence comes to bear on Russian development. L. P. N. Miliukov, *Ocherki po istorii russkoy kulturi,* Vol. 1 (Paris: 1937), a Jubilee publication. Miliukov developed his approach to history under the influence of Comte's positivist and Spencer's "synthetic" philosophies. The theory of "sociological lines" provided for the "organic" and "stadial" perception of historical "cultures." On these grounds he battled the "one-sidednesses" of Marxism.
108. M. Aleksnadrov, *Absolyutism*, 65–67.
109. See David Ryazanov, *Anglo-Russkoye otnosheniya v ocenke Marxa (Istoriko-lkriticheskiy etyud)* (St. Petersburg: Petrogradskovo Sovyeta i Krestyanskih Deputatov, 1918), 36, 47–48; see a more detailed discussion of this set of issues in Krausz, *Pártviták és történettudomány*, 52–59.
110. LCW, Vol. 17, 362–3.
111. LCW, Vol. 15, 321.
112. Ibid., 271.
113. Ibid., 271–72.
114. LCW, Vol. 17, 389–90.
115. Ibid., 90.
116. See Lenin's views concerning the subject in LCW, Vol. 6, *A Letter to the Zemstvoists* and *The Draft of a New Law on Strikes*, and Vol. 34, 437–440.
117. LCW, Vol. 19, 195–6; LCW, Vol. 34, 407–8; LCW, Vol. 21, 246–7, 424, 430–1; LCW, Vol. 22, 81, 146–147.
118. See Plekhanov's philosophical-historical fundamentals on Russia, in which he describes the characteristics of the swing between *Western and Asian development*, in his famous *Introduction* in Georgi Valentinovich Plekhanov, *Sochineniya. V 24-h tomakh* Vol. 20 (Moscow: 1925), 11–22.
119. See on this the investigations of one of the outstanding figures of the first generation of Soviet party historians in the 1920s, A. Bubnov, in "Razvitiye roli Lenina v istorii russkovo marxizma," in Uő., *Osnovniye voprosi istorii RKP* (Moscow: Sbornik statyey, 1925), 113–133.
120. See Krausz, *Pártviták és történettudomány,* 76–77. The comparative analysis of Lenin and Plekhanov's conceptual approach to revolution was completed by Tyutyukov in the Soviet period, taking Lenin's perspective on the unfolding events, of course, but framed generally in objective analyses, in *Pervaya rossiyskaya revolyutsia i G. V. Plekhanov* (Moscow: Nauka, 1981).
121. A controversial debate stretching from the 1960s to this day surrounds this question in the field of Russian historiography, with a late branching off more recently in 1990, in the form of a decades-long polemic between V. S. Dyakin and A. Ya. Avreh. See V. S. Dyakin, *Bil li shans u Stolipina?* The book was published posthumously. See especially "Proyekt otveta V. S. Dyakina na kriticheskie zamechanyiya A. Ya. Avreha," 352–357, as well as A. Ya. Avreh, *tsarism nakanunye sverzheniya.*
122. LCW, Vol. 17, 410.
123. Recent historiography offers plenty of social and cultural data in particular, where this "bourgeois transformation" is concerned. See, for example, Boris N. Mironov, *The Social History of Imperial Russia 1700–1917,* Vol. 1 (Boulder, CO: Westview Press, 2000). Though Mironov is capable of going into superlatives as regards the tsarist monarchy, which would

have made not only Lenin, but any Menshevik or S.R. very uncomfortable ibid., 227. The writer at another point speaks, with no intention of humor, about "constitutional monarchy" following 1906, though the Duma did not have legislative powers, or a "state rule of law" (ibid., 159), and at the same time the center countries serve as the sole "standard of measure" for any form of progress. From a professional angle the book fortunately refutes its own basic ideology, that is, the utopia of "good autocracy" with its regrettably raw apologetics, through the store of valuable data that it brings to light.

124. LCW, Vol. 17, 466.

CHAPTER 3—ORGANIZATION AND REVOLUTION

1. The international literature—with mainly Marxist leanings—that deals with the theme of the "organizational question" as posed by Lenin reflects, at the beginning of the twenty-first century, that under radically different circumstances the polemics of the twentieth century still remain. See, for example, Paul Blackledge, "Learning from defeat: reform, revolution and the problem of organisation in the first New Left," *Contemporary Politics* Vol. 10, no. 1 (March 2004): 21–36; and by the same author, "'Anti-Leninist' anti-capitalism: a critique," *Contemporary Politics*, Vol. 11, No. 2–3 (June–Sept. 2005): 99–116. See also Neil Harding, *Leninism* (Basingstoke: Macmillan, 1996); Chris Harman, *Party and Class*, edited by T. Cliff (London: Pluto Press, 1996); Paul Le Blanc, *Lenin and the Revolutionary Party*, with an introduction by Ernest Mandel (Atlantic Highlands, NJ: Humanities Press, 1990); Tony Cliff, *Building the Party. Lenin 1893–1914* (London,Chicago,Melbourne: Bookmarks, 1986); Lih, *Lenin Rediscovered.*
2. Golikov, *Biograficheskaya Chronika*, Vol. 1, 241, 259–61. Lenin's intellectual input to *Iskra* has been analyzed a number of times. One book typical of this trend came out in the 1970s: see V. A Maksimova, *Leninskaya* Iskra *i lityeratura* (Moscow: Izdat. "Nauka", Iskra, 1975).
3. On the role of "Lenin's" *Iskra* in the social democratization of Russian workers see A. I. Sereda, *Leninskaya* Iskra *i stanovlenyie mestnih organyizacii RSZDRP* (Moscow: "Misl", 1983).
4. See the documents of the congress in *Vtoroy syezd RSDRP Iyul–avgust 1903 goda, Protokoli* [Minutes Second Congress of the RSDLP July–Aug 1903] (Moscow: Gos. izd-vo polit. lit-r, 1959).
5. See Loginov, *Vladimir Lenin. Vybor puti*, 230–9.
6. Ibid., 235.
7. In Bustelo's interpretation, the pamphlet is bereft of any kind of "secret," which revolutionaries and scholars have been trying so intensively to uncover in it over the decades. Joaquin Bustelo, "Critical Comments on 'Democratic Centralism'" [www.marxmail.org/DemocraticCentralism.pdf] (Atlanta: 2005).
8. Service, *Lenin: A Biography*, 138–40. Service overstates the intellectual influence of Narodism in *What Is To Be Done?* Quite the opposite, it is the polemics taken up with Narodism that is the more important moving force of the work.
9. See Lih's extensive work, which deals comprehensively with the subject both on historical and theoretical levels. Lars Lih, *Lenin Rediscovered.*
10. Lars Lih, "Lenin and the Great Awakening," in *Lenin Reloaded*, 283–296.
11. The *Credo*, which originally appeared without the knowledge of its authors (Kuskova and Prokopovich) in *A Protest by Russian Social-Democrats* in 1899, reflected the views of the Kiev Committee of the RSDLP. Lenin reacted fast and very critically in his article "Apropos of the *Profession de Foi.*" He was especially damning of the separation of the workers' economic struggles from the political class struggle. He cited the appropriate conclusions of the *Communist Manifesto*, where the *Credo* represented a break with the fundamental principles, abandoning Marx for Bernstein. LCW, Vol. 4, 286–96.

12. Lenin, *What Is To Be Done?* "Preface," LCW, Vol. 5.
13. On this, see András György Szabó, "Marx és az államszocializmus" [Marx and state socialism], *Eszmélet* 4 (March) 1990, 103–114.
14. LCW, Vol. 5, 352–4. Loginov reconstructs Lenin's path to holding these views and the early dispute with Bernsteinism in the second half of the 1890s with great understanding in Loginov, *Vladimir Lenin. Vybor puti*, 331–55.
15. "Second, the Social-Democratic movement is in its very essence an international movement. This means, not only that we must combat national chauvinism, but that an incipient movement in a young country can be successful only if it makes use of the experiences of other countries. In order to make use of these experiences it is not enough . . . simply to copy out the latest resolutions. What is required is the ability to treat these experiences critically and to test them independently." LCW, Vol. 5, 370.
16. LCW, Vol. 7, 263.
17. LCW, Vol. 6, 241–2.
18. George Caffentzis calls this Lenin's "communication theory of revolution" and claims that its relevance today is as great as it was in 1902: activists organizing demonstrations on the internet, though not considering themselves "Leninists," use the communications model of the revolutionary organization that was originally postulated by Lenin. Quoted by Paul Blackledge, "'Anti-Leninist' anti-capitalism: a critique," *Contemporary Politics*, Volume 11, Number 2–3 (June–September 2005): 105.
19. See, for example, "From Lenin's movement 'dream' of 1902 to his post-revolutionary dream of a society in party-led movement toward socialism and communism there was a straight line of continuity," Robert C. Tucker, "Lenin's Bolshevism as a Culture in the Making," in *Bolshevik Culture. Experiment and Order in the Russian Revolution*, edited by Abbott Gleason, Peter Kenez, and Richard Stittes (Bloomington: Indiana University Press, 1985), 37.
20. In his 1924 study on Lenin, Lukács insisted that the Communist Party is "the tangible embodiment of proletarian class-consciousness," a formulation that had not yet taken stock of the role of alienated "structures" and "organizational mediations." See Lukács, *Lenin*, 27.
21. LCW Vol. 5, 375–6.
22. Antonio Gramsci was the first to recognize for its very own philosophical significance how deeply Lenin, over time, had grasped—in contrast to Trotsky in particular—the difference between Russian ("the gelatinous character of bourgeois society") and Western development ("the fortifications of bourgeois society"), and the serious consequences thereof. See Antonio Gramsci, "Political Struggle and Military War," in *Selections from the Prison Notebooks*, translated by Quintin Hoare and Geoffrey Nowell Smith (New York: International Publishers, 1971), 237–8.
23. LCW, Vol. 5, 450–3.
24. LCW, Vol. 5, 327–8. *Anarchism and Socialism (1901)*, published first in 1936, presumably in connection with the situation in Spain.
25. LCW, Vol. 5, 417–20.
26. "The consciousness of the working masses cannot be genuine class-consciousness, unless the workers learn, from concrete, and above all from topical, political facts and events to observe *every* other social class in *all* the manifestations of its intellectual, ethical, and political life . . . In order to become a Social-Democrat, the worker must have a clear picture in his mind of the economic nature and the social and political features of the landlord and the priest, the high state official and the peasant, the student and the vagabond; he must know their strong and weak points; he must grasp the meaning of all the catchwords and sophisms by which each class and each stratum *camouflages* its selfish strivings and its real 'inner workings'; he must understand what interests are reflected by certain institutions and certain laws and how they are reflected." LCW, Vol. 5, 412–13.

27. LCW, Vol. 5, 452.
28. LCW, Vol. 5, 475–6.
29. The defense of "professionalism" took shape in many formulations: "demagogy as cannot be explained solely by naïveté or by primitiveness of political views," LCW, Vol. 5, 495; "and demagogues are the worst enemies of the working class," LCW, Vol. 5, 463; "leave pedagogics to the pedagogues, and not to politicians and organizers!" LCW, Vol. 5, 471; "the worker-revolutionary must likewise become a professional revolutionary," LCW, Vol. 5, 472.
30. Ibid., 475.
31. Ibid., 510.
32. Ibid., 515–6. This was confirmed not only by December 1905, but even more so by October 1917.
33. Ibid., 516.
34. Bustelo, "Critical Comments on 'Democratic Centralism.'"
35. LCW, Vol. 7, 208–9.
36. Commenting on the 1903 party split and *What Is To Be Done?* he wrote: "Essentially there were no political trends even, only differences in the tendencies of political thought. It is only possible to speak of Leninism in terms of how Lenin, in his *What Is To Be Done?* and the resolutions of the Second Congress . . . gave the most biting expression to the clearly defined system of his political and organizational ideals . . . this, as Starover put it at some point . . . distances the organization from the working masses. This is a wholly different conspiracy" (from the Narodnaya Volya). See Parvus (Izrael Lazarevics Helfand), "Posle voyni," in *Rossiya i revolyutsiya*, 188–189.
37. Parvus, "Posle voyni," 190–1.
38. Parvus, "C chom mi rashodimsya?" in *Rossiya i revolyuciya*, 167.
39. Parvus, "Pismo N. Leninu," in *Rossiya i revolyuciya*, 177–81.
40. In order that these experiences were taken into account, Lenin called for a close study of the *Minutes of the Second Regular Congress of the RSDLP*: "If the writer of these lines only succeeds in stimulating the reader to make a broad and independent study of the minutes of the Party Congress, he will feel that his work was not done in vain." LCW, Vol. 7, 205–6.
41. He posed the question with regard to the congress in his pamphlet as follows: "What, then, was the substance of the matter in dispute? I already said at the congress, and have since repeated it time and again, that I by no means consider our difference [over Paragraph 1] so vital as to be a matter of life or death to the Party. We shall certainly not perish because of an unfortunate clause in the Rules!" [LCW Vol. 6, 501] "Taken by itself, this difference, although it did reveal shades of principle, could never have called forth that divergence (actually, to speak unreservedly, that split) which took place after the congress. But every *little* difference may become a big one if it is insisted on, if it is put into the foreground, if people *set about* searching for all the roots and branches of the difference. Every *little* difference may assume *tremendous* importance if it serves as the starting-point for a *swing* toward definite mistaken views. . . ." Therefore the first paragraph gained such importance, because in the course of the election of the Central Committee and the overseeing bodies in general, Lenin's followers overpowered Martov's in numbers due to the distribution of forces, which were only half by chance, as Lenin admitted, for it was by no means chance that it was the economists who supported Martov, who quit the congress. See LCW Vol. 7, 253–4.
42. Marcel Liebman stressed that the revolution made a democratic mass party out of the earlier "elite party," but he is not right in describing the Bolshevik-Menshevik argument at the Second Congress as a dispute around the question of support or opposition for centralism. See Marcel Liebman, *Leninism under Lenin*, translated by Brian Pearce (London: Jonathan Cape, 1975). Originally published in French as *Le léninisme sous Lénine* (Paris: Éditions du Seuil, 1973), 38–45.

43. See on this the 31st meeting of the congress, held on the morning of 7 (20) August 1903, at which thirty-six delegates with forty-four mandates could vote. *Vtoroy Syezd*, 369–85.
44. LCW, Vol. 7, 341–2.
45. See V. P. Akimov, *K voprosu o rabotah Vtorogo Syezda RSDRP* (Geneva: 1904); N. Ryazanov, *Razbitie illyuzii. K voprosu o prichinah krizisha v nasey partyii* (Geneva: 1904).
46. Akimov, *K voprosu o rabotah*, 8–9, 14–5, 27, 77; exploration of these issues of detail were completed by the author in cooperation with Péter Donáth during the 1980s. With the resulting paper unpublished, the material is put to use here with his permission.
47. LCW, Vol. 7, 322. See the cited Kautsky in *Neue Zeit*, XXII. I, 1903 no. 4, 99–101.
48. LCW, Vol. 7, 323.
49. L. D. Trotsky, *Nashi polityicheskiye zadachi* (Geneva: 1904); in English, L. D. Trotsky, *Our Political Tasks* (London: New Park Publications, 1980).
50. Ibid., 9–12, 131–6, 140–2, 155–8, 176. The last of these issues was a matter of serious debate among the Trotskyists themselves. See, for example, the polemics between N. Krasso and E. Mandel in Ernest Mandel, "Trotsky's Marxism: a rejoinder," *New Left Review* 56 (1969): 69–96, and for the precursors of the debate, see *New Left Review* 44, 47, and 48.
51. Trotsky, *Nashi polityicheskie*, 90–107, 140–2, 181–208, and for the following quotation, 102. "In order to prepare the working class for political power, it is necessary to develop and exercise in it the spirit of initiative and the habit of constant and active control over the entire executive personnel of the revolution[....] But for the 'social democrat Jacobins,' for the fearless representatives of the system of organizational substitutionalism, the immense social and political task, the preparation of the class for the government of the country, is supplanted by an organizational technical task, the preparation of the apparatus of power." (Translation by the Comintern.) These seem to be important thoughts from the point of view of later developments (when Trotsky himself stood on very different grounds, and himself became a "Jacobin").
52. See *Preface to the Collection Twelve Years*, LCW, Vol. 13, 94–113.
53. LCW, Vol. 13, 112.
54. This "compromise" soon found expression in an ideological-philosophical document: *Vekhi. Sbornik statey o russkoy intelligentsii N. A. Berdyayeva, S. N. Bulgakova, M. O. Gershenzona, A. S. Izgoyeva, B. A. Kistyakovskago, P. B. Struve, S. L. Franka* (Moscow: 1909).
55. After the downfall of the revolution, evaluating the historical role of Russian liberalism Martov, for example, reached a conclusion very similar to that of Lenin, as he examined Struve's Vekhist formation. "Liberalism tries to review its own past, break those ties that traditionally bound it to revolutionary and socialist ideologies and constitutes an ideological system which is adequate for the *ruling* class.... Liberalism seeks in principle to form monarchist, nationalist and antidemocratic political concepts of its own, is in principle counterrevolutionary in its legal views, strictly individualistic in the economic sphere, deeply nationalist in its relation to the state and the church." Martov, *Obshchestvennie i umstvennie tyechenyiya*, 118–119.
56. "[I]f the anarchists, while rejecting the political struggle, apply for representation in an institution which is conducting such a struggle, this crying inconsistency merely goes to show once again how utterly unstable are the philosophy and tactics of the anarchists. But, of course, instability is no reason for excluding anyone from a 'parliament,' or an 'organ of self-government.' . . . The Soviet of Workers' Deputies is not a labor parliament and not an organ of proletarian self-government, nor an organ of self-government at all, but a fighting organization for the achievement of definite aims. . . . The exclusion of anarchists from the fighting alliance which is carrying out, as it were, our democratic revolution, is quite necessary from the point of view of this revolution and is in its interests. There can be a place in a fighting alliance only for those who fight for the aim of that alliance." LCW, Vol. 10, 72–3.

57. Lenin, *The Dissolution of the Duma and the Tasks of the Proletariat*, published in pamphlet form in August 1906 by the *Novaya Volna* Publishers, Moscow. LCW, Vol. 11, 125.
58. According to a report for the international social democratic congress of 1914, to be held in Vienna, prepared by a Russian (St. Petersburg) "liquidator" party organ, the growing distance between the labor movement and social democracy was represented in the data of 1 September 1907, which showed 9,494 members of the metalworkers' union had paid their fees, whereas a decrease of almost two-thirds was evidenced by the figures of June 1911, while the fee-paying membership of the union of workers in the oil industry in Baku fell from 9,000 to 500 in the same period. See Hoover Institution, Archives, Boris Nicolaevsky Collection, No. 9. *Otchot k predpologavshemusja mezhdunarodnomu social. dem. kongressu v Vene.* 1914. 1–30, especially 13–26.
59. The literature has revealed for some time that this was not a case of Lenin's peculiar "sectarian struggles" either, but a typical post-revolution organizational fragmentation. 1905 "made" the Bolsheviks, and the Russian social democrats in general, into a party with a popular base—a mass movement out of an elite party. The revolution widened, forcing the case for the development of democracy within the party organization. See Liebman, *Leninism*, 45.
60. Karl Kautsky, *Die historische Leistung von Karl Marx* (Berlin: Singer, 1919), http://www.archive.org/details/diehistorischele00kaut. *Marx Károly történelmi jelentősége.* (Ford.: Garami Ernő.) Budapest, 1919.
61. Kautsky, *Die historische Leistung von Karl Marx*, 45–46.
62. Ibid., 51.
63. Péter Donáth wrote on the subject in Hungarian, in *Elmélet és gyakorlat. A "baloldaliság" korai történetéhez: Gorkij, Lunacsarszkij, Bogdanov* [Theory and practice. Toward an early history of "leftism": Gorky, Lunacharsky, Bogdanov] (Budapest: Budapesti Tanítóképző Főiskola, 1990).
64. For details see Donáth, *Elmélet és gyakorlat*, 15–70.
65. For the details of these events see John Biggart, "Antileninist Bolshevism. The Forward group of the RSDRP," *Canadian Slavonic Papers* No. 2 (1981): 141; and Robert Williams, *The Other Bolsheviks: Lenin and his critics 1904–1914* (Bloomington: Indiana University Press, 1986).
66. See V. Ilyin [Lenin], *Materialism and Empirio-criticism. Critical Comments on a Reactionary Philosophy* (Moscow: Zveno, 1909).
67. Lenin, *On Bolshevism*, LCW, Vol. 18, 486.
68. John Biggart, "Introduction. 'Antileninsky bolshevizm': gruppa RSZDRP 'Vperyod,'" in *Neizvestny Bogdanov* Vol. 2, *A. A. Bogdanov i gruppa RSDRP "Vperyod" 1908–1914*, edited by Gennadiy Arkadevic Bordugov (Moscow: "AIRO-XX", 1995), 6–7. At the Third National Congress of the RSDLP one of the fundamental theses Lenin formulated was: "to explain to the masses that the boycott of the Duma is not by itself capable of raising the working-class movement and the revolutionary struggle to a higher level, and that the tactics of boycott could be appropriate only provided our efforts to convert the trade-union upswing into a revolutionary assault were successful." LCW, Vol. 13, 61.
69. A hard to resolve complication of inheritance was behind the matter. The owner of the furniture factory of Presna, Nikolay Pavlovich Schmidt—who had participated in the revolutionary events of 1905, and died in the prison of Butirk on 13 (26) February 1907—left a significant bequest to the Bolsheviks. Ekaterina and Elizaveta were entrusted with their brother's will. The first lady handed over a part of the inheritance to the Bolshevik center in 1908–09; the second did so in 1909–11. The funds became a part of complicated factional infighting, the Bolsheviks finally, after the January 1910 plenary of the Central Committee, handed over most of the sum to the so-called *dyerzhatel*s ("treasurers" Kautsky, C. Zetkin, Bebel) for safekeep-

ing. The sum of approximately 300,000 rubles—which was left after various subtractions, for example, costs entailed by the carrier of the amount, Elizaveta—belonged to the Bolshevik center, that is, the extended editorial board of the *Proletary*. See the following documents for more on this: Doc. 13. *Raspiski Lenina, Zinovieva i V. L. Shantseva v hozyaystvennuyu komissiyu bolshevistskogo centra o poluchenii deneg*, 4 (17) November 1908–2 (15) October 1909; Doc. 14. *Protokol peredachi bolshevistskomu centru chastyi nasledstva N. P. Schmidta*, 8 (21) February 1909. Protokol (Paris); "Doc. 17. Postanovlenie ispolnitelnoy komissii bolshevistskogo centra o rashchotye s Yel. P. Schmidt," in *V. I. Lenin. Neizvestnye dokumenti. 1891–1922*, 29–32, 37–39.

70. The *Proletary* was discontinued on the basis of the decision of the plenum in January 1910. On this, see *Neizvestnye dokumenti*, Doc. 31. *Pismo zagranichnomu Byuro CK RSDRP*. 18 (31) January 1911, 61–62. A letter, bearing the marks of Lenin's hand, signed by G. Zinoviev by the mandate of Lenin and L. Kamenev, initiating the convention of a new plenary meeting, which followed, in any case, from the decisions of the January plenary. Since, in the opinion of the Bolsheviks, the Mensheviks had not fulfilled the condition by the end of 1910, the demand of a return of the money was in place. Lenin, Kamenev, and Zinoviev turned to the Foreign Office of the Central Committee on 5 December 1910, on their own and I. P. Goldenberg's (Meshkovsky's) behalf, for the plenary to be convened urgently, on the issue of the funds being returned. They later turned to Kautsky with this issue, but a decision was never made. For more on the historical background, see Dietrich Geyer, ed., *Kautskys russisches dossier. Deutsche Sozialdemokraten als Treuhänder des russischen Parteivermögens 1910-1915* (Quellen und Studien zur Sozialgeschichte, Vol. 2) (Frankfurt am Main and New York: Campus Verlag, 1981).

71. Biggart, "Introduction. 'Antileninsky bolshevizm': gruppa RSZDRP 'Vperyod,'" 9. For the same story in another light, see Péter Donáth, "A csak politikailag releváns Kanonizált Nagy Elbeszéléstől a tanulságos kis történetekig," [From the politically relevant, canonized great narratives to the little stories with morals], in *1917 és ami utána következett: Előadások és tanulmányok az orosz forradalom történetéből* [1917 and what followed thereafter: lectures and studies on the history of the Russian revolution] (Ruszisztikai Könyvek Vol. III), edited by Tamás Krausz and Erzsébet Schiller (Budapest: Magyar Ruszisztikai Intézet, 1998), 80–84.

72. The history of the party schools was researched by Jutta Scherrer from the 1970s onwards in Jutta Scherrer, "The Relationship between the Intelligentsia and Workers: the case of Party schools in Capri and Bologna," in *Workers and Intelligentsia in Late Imperial Russia: Realities, Representations, Reflections*, edited by Reginald E. Zelnik (Berkeley: Regents of the University of California, 1998). http://escholarship.org/uc/item/27p076zk (22 October 2011).

73. Péter Donáth, "A csak politikailag releváns." The philosophical and theoretical background to this problem is tackled in a way that has not lost its validity to this day by the "complementary" studies of two Hungarian authors. See András György Szabó, *A proletárforradalom világnézete. A filozófia bírálata* [The proletarian revolution's worldview. A critique of its philosophy] (Budapest: Magvető, 1977), chap. 2, "A leninizmus világnézeti nóvuma" [The novelty of Leninism's worldview], 74–181; and László Sziklai, "A materializmus és empiriokriticizmus történelmi tanulságai" [The historical lessons of materialism and empirio-criticism], in *Történelmi lecke haladóknak* [Advanced lessons of history] (Budapest: Magvető, 1977), 197–224. When Lenin met Bogdanov (and A. M. Ignatev, who was involved both in the Kamo exploit as well as the Schmidt deal) on Capri in April 1908 (between 10 and 17 April), Biggart believes, he was already certain that he would receive 200 thousand rubles. He could allow himself, partly on these grounds, to break with the Bogdanov group, and come closer to the Plekhanov circle. This may of course have influenced these relations, but could hardly have

touched on the fundamental trends, for Lenin's interest in Plekhanov was a problem of earlier beginnings. Lenin always wanted to reinstate better relations with Plekhanov!

74. Biggart, "Introduction. 'Antileninsky bolshevizm,'" 9. Shantser took Bogdanov's place on the editorial board. After the December conference, the "anti-boycott" core pushed back "left Bolshevik" influence by means of financial pressure as well. In February 1909, relinquishing its "philosophical neutrality," the *Proletary* published an article attacking Lunacharsky, written by Lev Kamenev, "Ne po doroge," in his *Mezhdu dvumya revolyutsiyani*. See also Donáth, "A csak politikailag releváns."
75. See the document dated 28 December 1909 in Bordugov, *Neizvestny Bogdanov,* Vol. 2, 36.
76. Lenin's letter to Gorky dated 25 November 1908. LCW, Vol. 13, 454.
77. The same letter, ibid., 448.
78. "When we worked together, Plekhanov and I often discussed Bogdanov. Plekhanov explained the fallacy of Bogdanov's views to me, but he did not think the deviation a terribly serious one. I remember perfectly well that in the summer of 1903 Plekhanov and I, as representatives of the *Zarya* editorial board, bad a conversation in Geneva [...] Plekhanov made it *a condition* of his collaboration that he would write against Mach [...]. Plekhanov at that time regarded Bogdanov as an ally in the fight against revisionism, but an ally who erred in following Ostwald and, later on, Mach." Ibid., 449.
79. László Sziklai is accurate in his interpretation when he writes that the answer Lenin gave to the "fundamental question of philosophy" in his *Materialism and Empirio-Criticism* was rooted in the new developments of the age itself. It was not just a question of the religious principles coming to the fore, but that "in those philosophical schools and ideological trends, in which the bed for their theoretical deductions is laid by qualms about the traditional, physical perception of the world" "escape" into a surrender of the "old materialism." The weighted emphasis on the matter-consciousness relationship and the epistemological side of the issue was elicited by the indicated ideological task. See Sziklai, "A materializmus és empiriokriticizmus történelmi tanulságai," 218–19.
80. Lenin noted, with regard to the collection of writings published at the time under the title *Studies in the Philosophy of Marxism, in the above-quoted letter to Gorky:* "I have read all the articles except Suvorov's (I am reading it now), and every article made me furiously indignant. No, no, this is not Marxism! [...] To try to persuade the reader that 'belief' in the reality of the external world is 'mysticism' (Bazarov); to confuse in the most disgraceful manner materialism with Kantianism (Bazarov and Bogdanov); to preach a variety of agnosticism (empirio-criticism) and idealism (empirio-monism); to teach the workers 'religious atheism' [and] 'worship' of the higher human potentialities (Lunacharsky)," LCW, Vol. 13, 450.
81. See Szabó, "Marx és az államszocializmus," 22–6.
82. Marcello Musto was right in referring to Gramsci, in whose critical opinion Bukharin returned to this "non-dialectical concept" in his book published in 1921, *Historical Materialism—A System of Sociology*, which was already opposed by Lenin. Bukharin gave Marxist philosophy a "sociological twist," and replaced dialectics with "vulgar evolutionism" and the "law of causality." See Marcello Musto, "The Rediscovery of Karl Marx," *International Review of Social History* (2007), 52: 477–498; and Antonio Gramsci, *Selections from the Prison Notebooks*, 415–7, 434, 437.
83. Antonio Gramsci, *Selections from the Prison Notebooks*, 465–6. Anton Pannekoek's critique from a Marxist point of view, written in 1938, *Lenin as Philosopher, A Critical Examination of the Philosophical Basis of Leninism* (New York: New Essays, 1948)—on which the field of study is divided, to say the least, in its judgment—defined Lenin's interpretation of religion by way of a peculiar "sociological angle" as "middle class materialism" (?) through an overly limited, "systemizing" way of thought.

84. Lenin's political-ideological passions are encapsulated well in one of his comments on censorship in a letter to Anyuta, written on 8 November 1908: "Incidentally, if the censor turns out to be *very* strict the word '*popovshchina*' can everywhere be changed to 'fideism' with a footnote to explain it [...] it is to *explain* the nature of the concessions I am making." LCW, Vol. 37, 395. Or in a letter to Gorky (7 February 1908), he cried out against the Bogdanov group: "and they drive me to give *all* my sympathy *to Plekhanov*! It takes physical strength to keep oneself from being carried away by the mood, as Plekhanov does! His tactics are the height of ineptitude, and baseness. In philosophy, however, he upholds the right cause. I am for materialism against 'empirio-' etc." LCW, Vol. 34, 381. In another letter to Anna he wrote as follows: "P.S. Please do not tone down the places against Bogdanov and against Lunacharsky's *popovshchina*. We have *completely broken off* relations with them. There is no reason for toning them down, it is not worth the trouble." LCW, Vol. 37, 416. In his next letter to her, he basically repeats the same. He spoke about the publication of the book with great satisfaction: "I have received the book and find that it has been nicely published.... Everyone complains of the price [2 rubles 60 kopeks]—and rightly so." LCW, Vol. 37, 430.
85. Donáth, "A csak politikailag releváns," 81–3. Bogdanov later wrote a whole book on the "story of his excommunication," which shall be discussed.
86. Donáth, *Elmélet és gyakorlat*, 174–84, and 187–93; Jutta Scherrer, "Culture prolétarienne et religion socialiste entre deux revolutions: Les Bolsheviks de gauche," *Europa* (1979) 2/2: 69–70.
87. LCW, Vol. 10, 83.
88. Ibid., 87.
89. Lenin's letter to Gorky, written on 13 or 14 November 1913. LCW, Vol. 35, 122.
90. "A million *physical* sins, dirty tricks, acts of violence and infections are much more easily discovered by the crowd, and therefore are much less dangerous, than the *nubile*, spiritual idea of God, dressed up in the most attractive 'ideological' costumes. The Catholic priest corrupting young girls (about, whom I have just read by chance in a German newspaper) is *much less* dangerous, precisely to 'democracy,' than a priest without his robes [...] [f]or it is *easy* to expose, condemn and expel the first priest," ibid.
91. Ibid., 127–9.
92. Ibid., 127.
93. Ibid., 127–9.
94. Ibid., 129.
95. A. A. Bogdanov, *Desyatiletiye otlucheniya ot marksizma. Jubileyniy sbornik (1904– 1914),* Vol. 3, compiled by N. S. Antonova (Moscow: AIRO-XX, 1995), especially 66–86.
96. To cite only the end of the story in this regard, Lenin himself, as a conclusion to the whole dispute and battle as it were, in an article that appeared in the Bolshevik paper *Puty Pravdi*, dated 25 February 1914, reacted to the protest of 13 "left Bolsheviks" who opposed Bogdanov's removal from the editorial board. Lenin explained Bogdanov's "banishment" from the Bolshevik paper purely on grounds of philosophical nature and as a principle. See *Concerning A. Bogdanov*, LCW, Vol. 20, 121–4.
97. Bordugov, "Letter to the extended editorial board of the *Proletary*, 11 April 1909," *Neizvestny Bogdanov*, 159.
98. At the same time a number of "left Bolsheviks"—though not wholly without tensions—worked as permanent contributors to *Pravda*, established by Lenin in 1912, among them: Aleksinsky, Volsky, Lyado, only later joined by Lunacharsky and Manuilsky. Bogdanov wrote a series of articles on the Taylor system for the same journal from the beginning of 1913. It is quite another matter that Lenin, following events from Cracow and Poronino, tried to edge Bogdanov out of the editorial board, with success rewarding his efforts at the end of 1913. Biggart, "Introduction. 'Antileninsky bolshevizm': gruppa RSZDRP 'Vperyod,'" 18–19.

99. Bordugov, *Neizvestny Bogdanov* Vol. 2, 23.
100. Ibid., 16–17.
101. Ibid., 175.
102. Ibid., 21. Doc. *Report to the Bolshevik Comrades on behalf of the Expelled Members of the expanded editorial board of the* Proletary (3 July 1909), 177–90. From the perspective at which they had arrived by 1909, participation in the Duma elections was already conceivable, but they rejected this as the main line of battle. "At the July 1907 Conference, of 10 Bolshevik leaders only Lenin took a position in favor of participation in the Duma." In opposition to the boycott of the Third Duma Lenin published an extensive study at the end of July 1907, *Against Boycott. Notes of a Social-Democratic Publicist*, LCW, Vol. 13, 15–49.
103. Bordugov, *Neizvestny Bogdanov,* Vol. 2, 218–20.
104. Ibid., 223–4, Doc. 42, *Letter* (1 December 1912).
105. Ibid., 225.
106. Ibid., 231–2.
107. Ibid., 231–3.
108. When the Bolsheviks, led by Manuilsky, split with the Mensheviks in the Duma (this independence of action was exactly what Lenin had aimed for), Martov's group appealed to the International about the split, in order for it to unify them with the Bolsheviks again. See Israel Getzler, *Martov. A Political Biography of a Russian Social Democrat* (Cambridge: Cambridge University Press and Melbourne University Press, 1967), 137.
109. For more detail see Getzler, *Martov*, 134–5.
110. Through the articles he published in *Novaya Zhizny* in the course of January 1918, Bogdanov's evaluation of the October Revolution is clearly outlined, wherein it is posited that it should have been the Constituent Assembly and not the soviets that realized the creation of Russia's political institutions. See Biggart, "Introduction, 'Antileninsky bolshevizm': gruppa RSZDRP 'Vperyod,'" 24.
111. Trotsky, who, much to Lenin's disappointment, joined the Mensheviks to begin with, was "accused" as early as 1904 of wanting to appease the contentious groups—at which Lev Davidovich was offended as recorded in a letter to Martov—and, further, placed under suspicion of wanting to bring about a third party. See Hoover Institution, Archives, Boris Nicolaevsky Collection (Box 1) No. 17, 51–9, item 3–4.
112. *Pravda*, 3 (16) October 1908, 1, 1.
113. *Pravda*, 17 (30) December 1908, 2, 10.
114. See, for example, G. Zinoviev, "Borba za bolshevizm iz epokhi 'Zvezdi' i 'Pravdi' (1913–1914)," *Sochineniya,* Vol. 4 (Leningrad: Gosizdat, 1926); and Zinoviev, *Sochineniya,* Vol. 3 (Leningrad: Gosizdat, 1924).
115. See Hoover Institution, Archives, *Boris Nicolaevsky Collection* (Box 1) No. 17. The council of the "pro-party" faction (Plekhanovists) among the Mensheviks and the Vperyodists, in December 1911, turned to the Viennese editorial board of *Pravda*, led by Trotsky, to debate the proposal that all party blocs and trends unite. A. Joffe, the secretary of the *Pravda* office under Trotsky, welcomed the proposal as a great cause. Later the *Vperyod* group, supported the Organizational Committee formed by the Mensheviks, the Latvian Social Democratic Party's Central Committee, Trotsky's *Pravda*, and representative s of the Bund, formed, but finally only sent one representative to the Conference, G. Aleksinsky, and him only with the right to council, because Trotsky's performance was unchecked. Not a single central group from Russia sent delegates. Even Aleksinsky could not accept that a "Conference of the RSDLP" had been convened, and actually left the conference in August prior to its completion, for he did not wish to take political responsibility for the event. Biggart, "Introduction. 'Antileninsky bolshevizm': gruppa RSZDRP 'Vperyod,'" 256.

116. It is a typical affair in this context that Trotsky's effort toward unification, the so-called August Block of 1912, was rejected even by the manic party unifiers, with the attitude that it went against the (conceived) *party unity*. Besides, "Mark" (Lyubimov), the August Conference invitee and representative of the paper called *Za Partiyu* [For the party], which supported the conference, wrote to S. Semkovsky in a letter dated 31 August 1912, which already captured the essence of the problem: "Under such conditions [for example, all the wings were not represented in the organizational body] your conference is at bottom not a party conference, even less an all-party conference, only a further step organizationally down the path of the split initiated by Lenin, whatever the length of the organizational committee's speech about its wishes to unify the party. The editorial board of *Za Partiyu* does not wish to take part in any experiment that breaks the party apart." Hoover Institution, Archives, *Boris Nicolaevsky Collection*, No. 119.
117. *Pravda*, 14 (27) March 1912, 24, 1.
118. *Izveshcheniye o konferentsii organizacii RSDRP*, Organizatsionnogo Komitetyeta, 3 September 1912, 16.
119. Italics in original.
120. Georg Lukács, *History and Class Consciousness*, translated by Rodney Livingstone (Cambridge, MA: MIT Press, 1971), 284–5.
121. See Georg Lukács, *A társadalmi lét ontológiájáról*, Vol. 3, *Prolegomena* [The Ontology of Social Being] (Budapest: Magvető, 1976), 270.
122. Italics in original. Ibid.

CHAPTER 4—THE WAR AND THE NATIONAL QUESTION

1. Rosa Luxemburg, *The Essential Rosa Luxemburg* (Chicago: Haymarket, 2008), 49. In German: *Gesammelte Werke*, vol. 1 (Berlin: Dietz Verlag, 1970), 380. See also on the subject Géza Ripp's analysis from much earlier, *Imperializmus és reformizmus* [Imperialism and reformism] (Budapest: Kossuth, 1982), 46–56.
2. "I am very pleased to see that on the main point you come to the same conclusion as I did in the polemic with Tugan-Baranovsky and *Volkstümler* [the Narodniks] 14 years ago, namely, that the realisation of surplus-value is possible also in a 'purely capitalist' society." LCW, Vol. 43, 332–33.
3. See contemporary debates in, for example, Ia. A. Piletskii, *Dve teorii imperializma; Marksistskaia legenda i Vozvrat k Marksu* (Kharkov: Kooperativnoe izd-vo Proletarii, 1924); also P. Aleksandrov's review of this work in *Bolshevik* (1924), 15–16.
4. In this sense the emphasis is not even on "overthrowing," but rather on overtaking; as many forms of overthrow can be imagined as there are historically specific forms of national-regional development. Later Antonio Gramsci gave the problem a concrete form. See Antonio Gramsci, *Selections from the Prison Notebooks*, 185–86.
5. András György Szabó came to the following conclusions with regard to Luxemburg's theory, on the basis of Lenin: "The actual action of the revolutionary theory and organization is at the end brought to a head by the spontaneous automatism of capitalist development in this case, and the act of becoming conscious enters the scene as a *deus ex machina* to transform the economic necessities latent in the spontaneous relations into the freedom of conscious action… the proletariat… should not expect the revolutionary moment *only* to emerge from the crises of the capitalist system, for the revolutionary moment postulates not only that those 'above' can't live as they have done before, but also that those below don't *want to*." András György Szabó, *A proletárforradalom világnézete*, 173, 316–17.
6. Neil Harding, *Leninism* (London: Macmillan, 1996), 51. As one of the interpreters of Lenin's theoretical legacy noted: "Until 1917 he made no real impact upon the general disposition of

European socialism. His was the voice of an outmoded doctrinaire. His Marxism was bookish and academic and, precisely *because* it derived from a thorough reading of the classic texts, it harked back to times and themes that had been largely forgotten by European socialists."

7. The most "successful" works of current historiography also confirm that the world war had a decisive significance with regard to the outbreak of the revolution. This seemingly evidential truth is documented on the basis of events in the Don region by Peter Holquist, in *Making War, Forging Revolution: Russia's Continuum of Crisis 1914–1921* (Cambridge, MA: Harvard University Press, 2002).
8. Though the Soviet Marxist-Leninist canon held the fact that the "unity of theory and practice" was realized in Lenin's lifework as evidence, an actual examination of the matter was never undertaken. The basic reason for this "hiatus" in the scholarship on this subject (apart from the significant materials missing from the archival sources) was that Lenin was portrayed as a solitary historical hero, who shaped history and its interpretation alone, as it were, in his "infallibility."
9. Lenin's text, *Konspekt knigi Gegelya: Nauka Logiki* (1914). First complete publication in *Leninsky Sbornik,* vol. 9 (Moscow: SOTSEGIZ, 1931), 300. This is when he reread many of Aristotle's, Kant's, Clausewitz's and Plekhanov's works.
10. Even Neil Harding's exciting work sets overly rigid intellectual confines when structuring Lenin's lifework, though he is certainly right in stating that Lenin was the first to introduce Marx's methodology to socialist thought and action. See Harding, *Leninism*, 14. This is moreover documented by Lenin's often cited article on Marx for the *Granat Encyclopedia*. This study, written between July and November 1914, attributes a fundamental importance to the whole issue of the dialectical method. LCW, Vol. 21, 43–91. This subject has also been explored seriously in recent scholarship, such as in Kevin B. Anderson, "The Rediscovery and Persistence of the Dialectic in Philosophy and in World Politics"; and Stathis Kouvelakis, "Lenin as Reader of Hegel: Hypotheses for a Reading of Lenin's Notebooks on Hegel's *The Science of Logic*," in *Lenin Reloaded*, 120–204.
11. See on this, Tibor Hajdu, *Közép-Európa forradalma 1917–1921* (Budapest: Gondolat, 1989); and Service, *Lenin,* Vol. 2, 219–20.
12. For the latest conspectus of this "discovery" by one of its old representatives, see Kevin B. Anderson, "The Rediscovery," in *Lenin Reloaded*, 120–47. The concept of "discovery" perhaps first appeared in Henry Lefebvre's study *La Pensée de Lénine,* published in 1957; see page 138. The Bolsheviks were already disputing the significance of dialectics in Lenin's lifework following his death. For more on this see Tamás Krausz and Miklós Mesterházi, *Mű és történelem: Viták Lukács György műveiről a húszas években* [The written word and history: Controversies about Lukács's work in the 1920s] (Budapest: Gondolat, 1985), especially the chapter "A lenini hagyatékról" [About the Lenin legacy], 101–29.
13. Lenin fully recognized the neo-Kantian philosophical roots of this new development and the motto, "back to Kant," as documented in a copious number of notes in his famous *Philosophical Notebooks*. See for example his comments on J. Dietzgen's philosophical writings in *Philosophical Notebooks*, LCW, Vol. 19, 79–82.
14. The notion that Lenin's reading of Hegel has hidden epistemological or "theoretical-political" fault lines comes up—though in contradictory arguments—in the work of authors as significant as Roger Garaudy, *Lenin* (Paris: PUF, 1968); and Lucio Colletti, *Il marxismo e Hegel* (Rome and Bari: Editori Laterza, 1976); the English translation is by Lawrence Gamer, *Marxism and Hegel* (London: Verso, 1979). According to the latter, Lenin simply falls back upon Hegelianism from 1914 onward. The Hungarian author who wrote on the subject, Ádám Wirth, *Lenin a filozófus* [Lenin the philosopher] (Budapest: Kossuth, 1971), took the route of simply showing Lenin as a philosopher, according to the traditional scientifically held defini-

tion. And though Wirth quotes Lenin's comments on the subject, in which he denied that he was a philosopher, he took this for "mere humility" on the part of Lenin. On the other hand he did well to notice that reductionist, narrow interpretations of Lenin leave the path clear to a field of theoretical speculation. Wirth, *Lenin a filozófus*, 30–31.

15. Chronologically speaking, "Leninism was born," according to Neil Harding, at the moment of this Hegelian turn. See Harding, *Leninism*, 234–42.
16. Kevin Anderson, *Lenin, Hegel and Western Marxism: A Critical Study* (Urbana: University of Illionis Press, 1995); Harding, *Leninism*. An interesting controversy issued around Anderson's cited Hegelianizing volume—which followed the trend begun by Raya Dunayevskaya—with the participation of Paul Le Blanc, Neil Harding, Michael Löwy, and of course Anderson himself, in the mid-1990s. Paradoxically, with Anderson's approach of separating Lenin's "good" and "evil" side it was the dialectical method he was so intent upon that suffered. See a summary of the debate at http://www.newsandletters.org/Issues/1997/Nov/1197pd.htm.
17. This school of thought dominates the last two volumes of Robert Service's here repeatedly cited three-volume work.
18. See the online debate on Anderson's book (n. 16).
19. An excellent description of these approaches and their inner contradictions is in Robert Mayer, "Lenin and the Practice of Dialectical Thinking," *Science and Society* 63/1 (Spring 1999): 40–62.
20. LCW,Vol. 18, 582.
21. "The dialectics of history were such that the theoretical victory of Marxism compelled its enemies to disguise themselves as Marxists." Ibid. No doubt, the historical moment for the Bernsteinist wing to make the Social Democratic Party the party of the "middle class" had not yet come. Let us not forget that in the Russia of 1913 the growth of the strike movement and a burgeoning workers movement was under way, swept aside for a few years by the outbreak of war.
22. LCW, Vol. 19, 21–28.
23. Ibid., 25.
24. Ibid., 28.
25. LCW,Vol. 19, 554.
26. LCW, Vol. 38, 179.
27. See Wirth, *Lenin a filozófus*, 23. In a letter written by Krupskaya to M. A. Ulyanova on 20 June 1899, it becomes clear that Lenin had made a serious study of philosophy even in exile: "We are all the same as ever. Volodya is busy reading all kinds of philosophy (that is now his official occupation)—Holbach, Helvetius, etc. My joke is that it will soon be dangerous to talk to him because he has soaked up so much philosophy." LCW,Vol. 37, 579–80. Lepeshinsky's memories also serve to underscore that he had been reading Hegel's *Logic* in exile: "In the evenings Vladimir Ilyich would normally read philosophy books—Hegel, Kant, and the French materialists." See *Vospominaniya*, vol. 1, 87; and *Találkozások Leninnel* [Encounters with Lenin] (Budapest: Kossuth, 1970), 30.
28. See *Leninskii sbornik* IX (Moscow–Leningrad: Giz, 1931), 3. In English: LCW,Vol. 38, 85–241.
29. Eric Hobsbawm, *The Age of Extremes: The Short Twentieth Century, 1914–1991* (New York: Pantheon Books, 1994), 1–10.
30. See *Leninskii sbornik* IX, 177 and 181. The careful investigation of "transitions" from the "general to the individual" and the "individual to the general," as well as thorough reflection on the correlations between "form and content," "method and science," "perception and reality," "theory and practice," are well presented in his notes on his reading of Hegel. He thinks through the importance and practical relevance of dialectics from more than one

point of view, as for example: "It is impossible completely to understand Marx's *Capital*, and especially its first chapter, without having thoroughly studied and understood the *whole* of Hegel's *Logic*. Consequently, half a century later none of the Marxists understood Marx!!" and "Hegel actually *proved* that logical forms and laws are not an empty shell, but the *reflection* of the objective world. More correctly, he did not prove, but *made a brilliant guess*." For his commentary on the correlation between *abstract* and *concrete* concepts in the context of the problem of how to formulate concepts, see *Leninskii sbornik*, 183, and 185; LCW, Vol. 38, 180–81.

31. Convincingly underscored by Mayer, "Lenin and the Practice of Dialectical Thinking," 42.
32. See *Leninskii sbornik* IX, 187–89, 219, 253, 271, 287.
33. Lenin, *Karl Marx*, LCW, Vol. 21, 88. Written between July and November 1914, and first published in 1915 in the 7th ed. of the *Granat Encyclopaedia*, Vol. 28.
34. Gramsci, "Hegemony, Relations of Force, Historical Bloc," in David Forgacs, ed., *The Gramsci Reader: Selected Writings 1916–1935* (New York: NYU Press, 2000), 192.
35. See Hermann István, "Marxizmus és totalitás" [Marxism and totality], in *A gondolat hatalma* [The power of thought] (Budapest: Szépirodalmi, 1978), 172–73, 182.
36. Robert Service turns Lenin's whole theoretical position inside-out and pulls the whole coherent system of his thought down to his own empiricist position when he measures the concept of the "revolutionary moment" only to his own logic, interprets the concept as an unstructured state of being, and shows little concern for Lenin's real position. See Service, *Lenin,* Vol. 2, 83–84. Lenin's real discovery was not the "proclamation" of the revolutionary situation that Service writes about, but that the war creates a revolutionary situation, because it decimates millions of people, and destabilizes, arms the proletariat, etc. Lenin was not fooled by the soldiers' singing as they marched off to war; that is how it usually was to begin with, disillusionment following inevitably in its footsteps. Finally, as we know, revolutions raged in many countries after the war.
37. This document was presented to the reading public as early as 1922, by the famous Russian historian E. V. Tarle, in "Germanskaya orientaciya i P. N. Durnovo," *Biloe* (1922) 19:161–62. Tarle did suggest that Durnovo, similarly to Engels in his time, equated the defeat in the war with the inevitable onslaught of the revolution. For more on this, see R. S. Ganyelin and M. F. Florinskiy, "Rossiyskaya gosudarstvennosty i pervaya mirovaya voyna" [Russian statehood and World War One] in *1917 god v sudbah Rossii i mira. Fevralskaya revoluciy:. Ot novikh istochnikov k novomu osmisleniyu* [The year 1917 in Russian and world history: The February Revolution, from the new sources to a new interpretation], ed. P. V. Volobuyev (Moscow: Instyitut Rossiyskoy Istorii RAN, 1997), 7, 31.
38. For example, in the following Lenin document, the *Appeal on the War*, he wrote: "The conscious or unwitting servants of the bourgeoisie are lying when they wish to persuade the people that the revolutionary overthrow of the tsarist monarchy can lead only to victories for and consolidation of the German reactionary monarchy and the German bourgeoisie." He goes on to indicate that the left wing of the German Social Democrats share his point of view, namely that the revolutionary struggle against "their own bourgeoisies" will bring the defeat of both monarchies. LCW, Vol. 21, 367–68.
39. A clear denunciation of the war appeared early in the party document written by Lenin on 24 August (6 September) 1914, *The Tasks of Revolutionary Social-Democracy in the European War*, LCW, Vol. 21, 15–19. The first full, thoroughly researched pamphlet from a theoretical, political, and organizational standpoint was *Socialism and War*, which was published in August 1915, virtually at the time of its completion as a party document. Ibid., 295–338.
40. LCW, Vol. 21, 19, 32–33, 160.
41. LCW, Vol. 21, 378–79. In other writings of the period he spoke about how the "*objective* con-

ditions in Western Europe are ripe for socialist revolution," while not emphasizing the direct "subjective" ripeness of the revolution. Ibid., 419. (Author's italics.)

42. The question came up right at the start of the war in a speech discussing Plekhanov's presentation at the local council of the Mensheviks in Lausanne on 28 September 1914. Ibid., 34.
43. "Everywhere the bourgeoisie vanquished the proletariat for a time, and swept them into the turbid spate of nationalism and chauvinism.... This state of affairs patently indicates the task of the proletariat... a struggle that will sweep along in its wake all the democratic masses, i.e., mainly the peasantry." LCW, Vol. 21, 418.
44. See the history of the conference in János Jemnitz, *A nemzetközi munkásmozgalom*, 334–58; for more on the Zimmerwald Conference and Lenin's role in it see Sándor Vadász, *Lenin és a zimmerwaldi baloldal* [Lenin and the Zimmerwald left] (Budapest: Akadémiai, 1971).
45. Lenin's irreconcilability did not, of course, extend to the Bolsheviks' ignoring Zimmerwald. Quite the opposite—Lenin's views became focal to the debates, even though no more than a dozen of the thirty European Social Democratic Party delegates were on his side in September 1915. Rosa Luxemburg and Karl Liebknecht were in prison at the time.
46. Lenin, "Revolutionary Marxists at the International Socialist Conference, September 5–8, 1915," *Sotsial-Demokrat*, 11 October 1915. LCW, Vol. 21, 389–93.
47. Ibid., 390, 392. Later on it was Gramsci, in Mussolini's jails, who discussed the range of problems raised by the notion of foresight, in his writings dealing with Lenin's legacy. Gramsci gave an exacting formulation of "prediction" according to which "prediction reveals itself thus not as a scientific act of knowledge, but as the abstract expression of the effort made, the practical way of creating a collective will." Gramsci, *Selections from Prison Notebooks*, 438. As a result, "prediction" is a "solely ideological" act, and as such plays an important role in history. Eric Hobsbawm set forth similar thoughts, well worth pondering in Eric John Hobsbawm, "The Present as History," in *On History* (New York: New Press, 1997), 228–40.
48. See Lenin, *Kautsky, Axelrod and Martov—True Internationalists*, LCW, Vol. 21, 394–400.
49. See Lenin, *The War and Russian Social-Democracy*, LCW, Vol. 21, 25–34.
50. Ibid., 32–33; as well as *The Collapse of the Second International*, LCW, Vol. 21, 205–59.
51. Lenin, *We Are Thankful for Such Frankness*, LCW, Vol. 21, 370–71.
52. See János Jemnitz, *A nemzetközi munkásmozgalom*, 15, 17, 34, 38. This work by Jemnitz is the best and most detailed discussion of the subject to my knowledge. See also on the same subject, S. V. Tyutyukin, *Voyna, mir, revoluciya* [War, peace, revolution] (Moscow: Misl, 1972).
53. Nikolai Bukharin, *Imperialism and World Economy* (New York: International Publishers, 1929).
54. On the subject, see Géza Ripp, *Imperializmus*, 185–204.
55. LCW, Vol. 21, 229.
56. Lenin, *Preface to N. Bukharin's Pamphlet, Imperialism and the World Economy*, LCW, Vol. 22, 103, 105, 106. "Inevitably imperialism will burst and capitalism will be transformed into its opposite *long before* one world trust materializes, before the 'ultra-imperialist,' worldwide amalgamation of national finance capitals takes place." Ibid., 107.
57. "But while the slogan of a republican United States of Europe—if accompanied by the revolutionary overthrow of the three most reactionary monarchies in Europe, headed by the Russian—is quite invulnerable as a political slogan, there still remains the highly important question of its economic content and significance. From the standpoint of the economic conditions of imperialism—i.e., the export of capital arid the division of the world by the 'advanced' and 'civilized' colonial powers—a United States of Europe, under capitalism, is either impossible or reactionary." Lenin, *On the Slogan for a United States of Europe*, LCW, Vol. 21, 339–43.
58. RGASZPI, f. 2, op. 5, dyelo 596, 1–2.
59. "Finance capital does not want freedom, but domination." Rudolf Hilferding, *Finance Capi-*

tal. A Study of the Latest Phase of Capitalist Development, edited by Tom Bottomore (London: Routledge & Kegan Paul, 1981), 334.

60. LCW, Vol. 23, 43.
61. Ibid., 43–45, 47–48.
62. Lenin, *Appeal on the War*, LCW, Vol. 21, 367–69.
63. See François Furet, *The Passing of an Illusion: The Idea of Communism in the Twentieth Century*, trans. Deborah Furet (Chicago: University of Illinois Press, 1999).
64. For more on Furet's book, see a detailed critique by Gizella Horváth, "A fasizmus és a kommunizmus összefüggéséről: François Furet titkai" [On the correlation between fascism and communism: The secrets of François Furet], *Eszmélet* 47:33–44. Furet solves the puzzle of the "Leninist mode of speech" without examining Lenin's works. This applies to the Leninian analysis of the war as well. These are "unimportant motives," and do not fit into the narrative of the *terror*. Therefore a "narrative shift" is required.
65. Lenin also quotes Kautsky in his work, *A Caricature of Marxism and Imperialist Economism: Neue Zeit* (1910) 28, 2:776. LCW, Vol. 23, 3.
66. LCW, Vol. 21, 442.
67. Ibid., 442.
68. Ibid., 448.
69. Ibid., 453.
70. He brought up the problem especially frequently in 1916 to combat the effect of the official national propaganda, indicating the nationalist, "social-chauvinist" message of the slogan. See in this regard his *Reply to P. Kievsky (Y. Pyatakov)*, written in August–September 1916, LCW, Vol. 23, 22–27; as well as *A Caricature of Marxism and Imperialist Economism*. Ibid., 28–76.
71. See the Party Resolutions. LCW, Vol. 21, 59–60.
72. LCW, 23, 13–21, esp. 18. "The present war unites and 'merges' nations into coalitions by means of violence and financial dependence. In our civil war against the bourgeoisie, *we* shall unite and merge the nations *not* by the force of the ruble, *not* by the force of the truncheon, not by violence, but by *voluntary* agreement and solidarity of the working people against the exploiters." Ibid., 27.
73. See *A Caricature of Marxism and Imperialist Economism*, LCW, Vol. 23, 61.
74. LCW, Vol. 22, 331. See also his pamphlet *Socialism and War*, LCW, Vol. 21, 295–338.
75. LCW, Vol. 23, 73.
76. A great deal of literature is available for further analysis of the subject; see, for example, Emil Niederhauser, *A nemzeti megújulási mozgalmak Kelet-Európában* [The movements for national renewal in Eastern Europe] (Budapest: Akadémiai Kiadó, 1977), 385; and by the same author, *Kelet-Európa története* [The history of Eastern Europe] (Budapest: MTA Történettudományi Intézete, 2001); and Eric Hobsbawm, *Nations and Nationalism since 1780: Programme, Myth, Reality* (Cambridge: Cambridge University Press, 1990).
77. The background of this issue was the subject of closer study in an earlier book by Tamás Krausz, *Bolsevizmus és nemzeti kérdés: Adalékok a nemzeti kérdés bolsevik felfogásának történetéhez* [Bolshevism and the national question: Toward a history of the Bolshevik approach to the national question] (Budapest: Akadémiai Kiadó, 1989). Russians not only made up the most numerous group of people, but also the most "widely spread out" nationality. Citizens of Russian nationality made up more than 50 percent of the total population, and this was nearly 10 percent above the proportion they represented at the turn of the century. The second largest national group, Ukrainians, had decreased somewhat within the whole population. The seventh largest national group, after the Byelorussians, Uzbeks, Kazakhs, and Tatars, was formed by the Jews. (In the last year of peace preceding the First World War, the total population for the whole of Russia came to 139.3 million.)

78. István Dolmányos, *A nemzetiségi politika története a Szovjetunióban* [The history of ethnic policy in the Soviet Union] (Budapest: Kossuth, 1964), 17. In Vilnius, toward the end of the nineteenth century, the "original" nationality—Lithuanians—formed an insignificant minority. Living beside 61,844 Jews, 47,641 Poles, and 30,919 Byelorussians, 3,231 Lithuanians are noted by the Hungarian author.
79. Emil Niederhauser, *Lenin i natsionalniy vopros* (Budapest: 1970).
80. An exploration of the principle of the right of nations to self-determination from the French Revolution in 1789 to the October Revolution. The principle had already been included in the program of the First International (in 1865) after the Polish uprising of 1863, an expression of protest against the tsar's (ethnic) policy. See Edward Hallett Carr, *The Bolshevik Revolution, 1917–1923,* Vol. 1 (London: Macmillan, 1960), 411–17.
81. In Russia and Poland, the All-Jewish Workers Union positioned itself on a platform with the Austro-Marxists for cultural autonomy. For the debate at the Congress see *Protokoli 2-ogo*, 1959, 50–107.
82. *Az SZKP kongresszusainak, konferenciáinak és KB plénumainak határozatai* I. rész [Resolutions of the congresses, conferences, and central committee plenary meetings of the Communist Party of the Soviet Union Part 1] (Budapest: Szikra, 1954), 51, 64.
83. See Lenin, *Critical Remarks on the National Question* (October–December 1913). The article was preceded by lectures on the national question that Lenin delivered in a number of Swiss cities in the summer of 1913 and of course the autumn report at the "August" (Summer) Conference of the Central Committee of the RSDLP.
84. LCW, Vol. 20, 27.
85. See the theses, in LCW, Vol. 22, 150–51.
86. In his work *A Caricature of Marxism* (LCW, Vol. 23, 46–47, 58–59), Lenin suggests that P. Kievsky (Pyatakov) read in Engels's letter to Kautsky of 12 September1882 (MECW, Vol. 46, 320–23) that "to dream of the 'united action of the proletarians of *all* countries' means postponing socialism to the Greek calends, i.e., forever." *Reply to P. Kievsky (Y. Pyatakov)*, LCW, Vol. 23, 22–27.
87. "The principle of nationality is historically inevitable in bourgeois society and, taking this society into due account, the Marxist fully recognizes the historical legitimacy of national movements. But to prevent this recognition from becoming an apologia of nationalism, it must be strictly limited to what is progressive in such movements." LCW, Vol. 20, 34.
88. Lenin, *The Junius Pamphlet*. LCW, Vol. 22, 305–19.
89. Lenin engaged in polemics with a study of Rosa Luxemburg's that had appeared in Polish in 1908–9, in which Luxemburg rejects the right of nations to self-determination as a "bourgeois" category.
90. See *The Right of Nations to Self-Determination*, LCW, Vol. 20, 393–454.
91. "There is the Great-Russian culture of the Purishkeviches, Guchkovs and Struves—but there is also the Great-Russian culture typified in the names of Chernyshevsky and Plekhanov. There are the same two cultures in the Ukraine as there are in Germany, in France, in England, among the Jews, and so forth." *Critical Remarks on the National Question*, LCW, Vol. 20, 32.
92. LCW, Vol. 20, 25.
93. LCW, Vol. 21, 318.
94. Lenin, *On the National Pride of the Great Russians*, LCW Vol. 21, 104.
95. Lenin's letter of 6 December 1913 to S. G. Shahumyan. Lenin was very fond of Shahumyan, whose earlier letter he called "especially pleasurable," because "[o]ne feels less isolated when one receives letters like this." LCW Vol. 19, 499–502.
96. LCW, Vol. 20, 41.
97. Shahumyan argued that the official state language should be Russian. Lenin took a position

against the demand for a "state language," accepting that "the *Russian* language has undoubtedly been of progressive importance for the numerous small and backward nations. But surely you must realize that it *would have been* of much greater progressive importance had there been no compulsion." Lenin underscored the role of the *psychological* factor in his argument, because any form of compulsion or force only deepens hatred: "The economy is still more important *than* psychology: in Russia we *already* have a *capitalist* economy, which makes the *Russian* language essential." But he interpreted making it compulsory as wanting to "prop it [the economy] up with the crutches of the rotten police regime. . . . Will not the collapse of the wretched police regime multiply tenfold (even a thousand fold) the number of voluntary associations for protecting and spreading the Russian language?" LCW. Vol. 19, 499–500.

98. The resolution of the Porino Council of the Bolshevik Central Committee in August 1913, prepared by Lenin, emphasized that the "partitioning of education according to nationalities is reactionary, from the aspect of democracy in general, and especially the class-struggle of the proletariat." *Az SZKP kongresszusainak, konferenciáinak és központi bizottsági plénumának határozatai* 1. köt. 1898–1924 [Resolutions of the congresses, conferences, and central committee plenary meetings of the Communist Party of the Soviet Union Part 1] (Budapest: Szikra, 1954), 363.

99. "If we do not want to betray socialism we *must* support every revolt against our chief enemy, the bourgeoisie of the big states, provided it is not the revolt of a reactionary class." LCW, Vol. 22, 333.

100. *The Discussion on Self-Determination Summed Up*, LCW, Vol. 22, 320–60, see 325.

101. LCW, Vol. 23, 55–56.

102. "We will *not* support a struggle of the reactionary classes against imperialism; we will *not* support an uprising of the reactionary classes against imperialism and capitalism." Ibid., 63. In opposition to Kievsky (Pyatakov) Lenin drew attention here to the fact that where a labor movement was not to be found, the slogans of the labor movement must be reformulated for the "millions of working people." This was Lenin's break with the sectarianism of "abstract internationalism" which, in regard to the colonies, was unable to contend with the social forces that could achieve the right of nations to self-determination in the interest of the progressive anti-imperialist struggle.

103. Ibid., 68.

104. *The Nascent Trend of Imperialist Economism*, LCW, Vol. 23, 13, and LCW, Vol. 20, 49; A *Caricature of Marxism and Imperialist Economism*, LCW, Vol. 23, 28–76. This group (Bukharin, Pyatakov, Bosh and others) was formed through efforts to establish the short-lived journal called *Communist*. The editors of *Sotsial-Demokrat* began the publication and financing of the journal in Spring 1915. Besides Pyatakov's article, Lenin also aligned the article by Radek, *A Quarter of a Century of Development of Imperialism*, with this trend. Finally Pyatakov, Bogrovsky, Bukharin, and Bosh announced the end of the journal as well as the group that had formed around it in a letter to Lenin and Zinoviev from Stockholm, dated 3 December 1915. RGASPI f. 2, op. 5, dyelo 620, 1.

105. Lenin, *The Discussion on Self-Determination Summed Up*, LCW, Vol. 22, 320–60.

106. Ibid., 326. Accordingly, if, similar to many other demands of democracy, the national right to self-determination is impossible to achieve under capitalism, this does not entail that the Social Democrats should cease their struggle for this extension of democracy.

107. Ibid., 341.

108. Ibid. Italics in original.

109. Ibid., 345.

110. Ibid., 346.

111. Ibid., 356–57. "It is the misfortune of the Irish that they rose prematurely, before the Eu-

ropean revolt of the proletariat had had time to mature. Capitalism is not so harmoniously built that the various sources of rebellion can immediately merge of their own accord, without reverses and defeats." Ibid., 358.

112. Ibid., 359.
113. *The Russian Provisional Government, 1917: Documents*, ed. Robert Paul Browder, Aleksandr Fyodorovich Kerensky (Stanford, CA: Stanford University Press, 1961), 317. In Russian: *Revolyucitsia i nacionalniy vopros: Dokumenti i matyeriali po istorii natsionalnogo voprosa v Rossii i SSSR v XX veke,* vol. 3, 1917, fevral–oktyabr, ed. S. M. Dimanshteyn (Moscow), 53–54, 56.
114. The organizational structure of the new state was conceptualized in many different ways. Stalin, who gained a name among Bolsheviks on the issue of the national question, next to Shahumyan and Zinoviev, following his paper, *Marxism and the National Question* of 1913 (though Lenin himself never quoted the paper he had encouraged Stalin to write), resolutely rejected the federal concept in "Abolition of National Disabilities" in issue no. 17 of *Pravda* in March of 1917 (25 March), and took up the cause of autonomy: "It is therefore necessary to proclaim: 1) political autonomy (not federation!) for regions representing integral economic territories possessing a specific way of life and populations of a specific national composition, with the right to conduct 'affairs' and 'education' in their own languages; 2) the right of self-determination for such nations as cannot, for one reason or another, remain within the framework of the integral state. This is the way toward the real abolition of national oppression."
115. *Szedmaya (Aprelskaya) Vserossiyskaya konferenciya RSDRP (bolshevikov): Protokoli* (Moscow, 1958), 212.
116. Ibid., 215. Italics in original.
117. LCW, Vol. 24, 299–300.
118. See more on this platform in *Ocherki po istorii oktyabrskoy revolyucii,* vol 2 (Moscow, 1927). From an abridged form of the text: "The struggle against national oppression cannot be different . . . from the struggle against capitalism in general." Their platform continued not to consider a possible progressive role for the national movements. In relation to the oppressor and oppressed nation, "our task—our priority—is to mobilize the forces of the proletariat of both nations (together) under the banner of the civil war on class and in support of the socialist propaganda, to counter the forces gathering under the slogan of the 'right of nations to self-determination.'" *Revolyutsia i natsionalniy vopros,* 30.
119. See Bukharin's letter to Lenin: "Dear Vladimir Ilyich, In spite of all our conflicting views and etc, etc. I think that on the large scale we will continue to work together." RGASPI f. 2, op. 5, dyelo 721, 1.
120. Lev Kamenev, "Plodi prosveshcheniya," *Pravda,* 14 June 1917.
121. *Revolyutsia i natsionalniy vopros,* 91–93.
122. Ibid., 96, 451–55.
123. For details of the controversy, see Krausz, *Bolsevizmus és nemzeti kérdés,* 22–28.
124. Finally the resolution formulated by Stalin and supported by Lenin and Zinoviev won the vote at the conference (56 for, 6 against, 18 abstentions). Eleven delegates voted for Pyatakov's proposal, 48 against, and 19 abstained. Ibid., *Sedmaya*, 1958, 210–12, 214 and 227.

CHAPTER 5—THE STATE AND REVOLUTION

1. This was Louis Fischer's opinion in the late 1960s in his *The Life of Lenin*, 113.
2. There are those authors who profess that the main aim even of this work by Lenin, written in deep illegality, is some sort of personal ambition for power. "Among Lenin's main goals as a Marxist, was to prove the correctness of his own ideology." This statement holds that consid-

erations of wielding power was the driving force behind the writing of this book as well. See Service, 2:216–17.

3. Tibor Hajdu made an attempt to restore the original theoretical and historical perceptions of this work. *The State and Revolution* appeared as a kind of "unnecessary" or "outdated" literature in the practice of Stalinist, state socialist ideology. Tibor Hajdu, "A szocialista állam elméletének történetéhez" [On the history of the socialist state], *Magyar Filozófiai Szemle* [Hungarian philosophical review] 2 (1970): 205–33. In regard to the contrary "bias" see Ottó Bihari, *A szocialista államszervezet alkotmányos modelljei* [The constitutional models of socialist state structure] (Budapest: Közgazdasági és Jogi Könyvkiadó, 1969). It is clear from Bihari that Lenin's work was not suitable for the market reforms of 1968. Hajdu was right in noting in his reconstruction that "even bourgeois sociology prefers to examine the structure, efficiency, and administrative functions of the state than what is crucial to Marxism: the relationship of the state and the classes." And let us add that this is what *The State and Revolution* is really about.

4. In this lecture of Bukharin's—an excellent student of Lenin by that time—while discussing the issue of the state acknowledged the historical role of Lenin, saying that "he was the first who conducted archeological explorations into Marx's theories, cleansing them from the layers of dirt left on them by their interpreters and commentators, such as Kautsky and Plekhanov." *Lektsiya N. Buharina: Razvitije kommunyizma ot Marksza do Lenina*, RGASZPI f. 329, op. 1. dok. 40. 2–3.

5. Lenin paid close attention to the fate of his pamphlet after the October Revolution. The postscript of 30 November 1917 indicates that the publication was not yet fully finished: "This pamphlet was written in August and September 1917. I had already drawn up the plan for the next, the seventh chapter, 'The Experience of the Russian Revolutions of 1905 and 1917.' Apart from the title, however, I had no time to write a single line of the chapter; I was 'interrupted' by a political crisis—the eve of the October Revolution of 1917.... It is more pleasant and useful to go through the 'experience of revolution' than to write about it." LCW, Vol. 25, 492. The "blue-colored notebook," the birth of which Kazakevitch related to in a nice little booklet, contained the notes that Lenin had prepared at the beginning of March in Zurich. In its own time, Y. Berzin, the envoy of Soviet Russia in Switzerland, played a major role in spreading this work abroad, with Lenin's expression of gratitude for a German edition recorded in a letter dated 1 November 1918. When the French translation of *The State and Revolution* was ready, he also asked Berzin in the postscript of the same letter to criticize both Kautsky and Vandervelde in the publisher's preface, as he was himself about to address some criticism to them, and finally he gave instructions on the distribution of the book in Berlin. LCW, Vol. 44, 160–61. The French edition was finally published in 1919 in Moscow.

6. On the one hand, see Neil Harding, *Lenin's Political Thought,* Vol. 2; Kevin Anderson, *Lenin, Hegel and Western Marxism* (Urbana: University of Illinois Press, 1995); on the other hand, see A. J. Polan, *Lenin and the End of Politics* (London: Methuen, 1984); and R. Service, *Lenin,* Vol. 3, 379–80. This latter critique, with no minor distortion of facts, "contextualized" *The State and Revolution* on the basis of Kautsky's (*The Dictatorship of the Proletariat*) and Martov's writings of 1918–19, and essentially presented a literary justification of the evolving civil war and terror.

7. A. J. Polan, *Lenin and the End of Politics*, 49.

8. An apt critical analysis by Jules Townshend, "Lenin's *The State and Revolution*: An Innocent Reading," *Science and Society* 63/1 (1999): 63–82.

9. Lenin, *The Three Sources and Three Component Parts of Marxism*, LCW, Vol. 19, 21–28.

10. See Márton Szabó, *Politikai idegen* (Budapest: L'Harmattan, 2006), 129. It is almost to be expected that in this substantial volume the author is nowhere able to refute or even contest

Lenin's concrete remark regarding politics. It is a typical feature of our times that the main concern of a political scientist and his "value-exempt" textbook, strangely, was to distance himself from a worldview and the political attitude of a party, with Lenin emerging merely as a tool of this objective.

11. Townshend, 72.
12. LCW, Vol. 26, 113.
13. Bukharin's interest in theory had been well known in the party for years. This fact was evinced by his review of the first volume of Marx's *Capital* from 1914, which was published in Stuttgart under Kautsky's "popular" editorship after "the copyright for Marx's works expired" on 1 January 1914. RGASPI F. 329, op. 1. d. 2. The expertise, both in the theoretical and literary sense, and his analyses of Ryazanov's indicators and annexes all revealed the competence of Bukharin, who was still in his twenties at the time.
14. See Bukharin's letter of autumn 1915, which he wrote to Lenin and Zinoviev under the pseudonym V. S. Dovgalevsky (from Stockholm to Bern). This document brilliantly reflects the "confused" ideas circulating even in Lenin's close environment about the state. RGANI, 2. f. 5. op. 573. dok., 4. See Lenin's letter of September 1916 to Shlyapnikov. The first serious historiographic study dealing with Bukharin's lifework is S. F. Cohen, *Bukharin and the Bolshevik Revolution: A Political Biography 1888–1938* (New York: Oxford University Press, 1973). See also Neil Harding, *Lenin's Political Thought*, Vol. 2, 83–141.
15. RGANI 2. f. 5. op. op. 573. dok., 4.
16. Ibid. "3rd point: The 'defense of the revolution.' Earlier I had thought that in the place of the word 'defense,' 'propagation [*rasprostraneniye*] should be used … but I transcribed this word with caution."
17. Ibid., 2–3.
18. See N. Bukharin, "Teoriya proletarskoy diktaturi" [Theory of the dictatorship of the proletariat], in *Ataka* (Moscow: Gosizdat, 1924), 91–114.
19. See for example, József Bayer, *A politikai gondolkodás története* [The history of political thought] (Budapest: Osiris, 1998), 321.
20. LCW, Vol. 25, 458.
21. Lenin noted: "The only difficulty that may perhaps arise will be in regard to the term. In German there are two words meaning '*obshchina*' of which Engels used the one which does not denote a single community, but their totality, a system of communities. In Russian there is no such word, and we may have to choose the French word 'commune,' although this also has its drawbacks." Ibid., 440–41, 490–91.
22. Ibid., 457.
23. Lenin's numerous notes on the works of Marx, Engels, and Kautsky indicate that bureaucracy, which, as a trait of modern capitalism, had grown both quantitatively and in terms of institutional influence during the war, interested him essentially as a question of politics and power. Lenin deals with this issue in regard to Marx's writings, *The Eighteenth Brumaire*, *The Civil War in France*, and *Revolution and Counterrevolution in Germany* or the letter Marx wrote to Kugelman in 1871, during the days of the Commune. See "Marksizm o gosudartstve. Materiali po podgotovke broshuri 'Gosudarstvo i revolyutsiya': January–February 1917," in *Leninsky Sbornik* XIV (Moscow and Leningrad: Gos. Izdat., 1930), 210–385.
24. LCW, Vol. 33, 212.
25. LCW, Vol. 1, 177.
26. Ibid., 180.
27. Fore more on this see Tamás Krausz, *Pártviták és történettudomány*, chaps. 2 and 3.
28. While taking notes on Marx's writings in the "blue notebook," in his notes in the margin Lenin referred several times to the people's "superstitious faith in the state," mentioning

"the blind, narrow-minded faith" with which people relate to the state. LCW, Vol. 31, 182–83.

29. In Hungary, László Tütő described various economic theories along this divide in greater detail. He pointed out that both Bernstein and Stalin approached socialism from the dimension of distributional relationships; both of them, so to speak, identified socialism with state distribution, their starting point not being production and the division of labor. See László Tütő, "Gramsci és a gazdasági demokrácia kérdése" [Gramsci and the question of economic democracy], in *Tanulmányok Gramsciról* [Studies on Gramsci], ed. József Banyár (Budapest: MKKE Társadalomelméleti Kollégium, 1987), 85–111, esp. 85–90.
30. On this subject, see G. Volkova, "Istoricheskiy vibor" [Historical choice], in *Leninskaya kontseptsiya sotsializma* (Moscow: Izdat. Polityicheskoy literature, 1990), 69–70.
31. LCW, Vol. 10, 17–28. He defined his own position as that of an outsider, alluding to the fact that he was not an immediate partaker of events and thereby leaving open the option of changing his political stance at a later stage. His approach nevertheless showed such methodological and theoretical features, which demonstrated long-term analytical tendencies applicable to later periods as well, and independence from political "eventualities."
32. Ibid., 21.
33. Ibid., 26–27.
34. Lenin, "The Boycott of the Bulygin Duma, and Insurrection," *Proletary*, No. 12, 16 August (3), 1905. LCW, Vol. 9, 184. A few weeks later, in another article, he raised the issue once more: "In the measure that the Kerch Municipal Council has, of its own free will, extended the scope of the powers it is entitled to by law, and in the measure that it is participating in the revolutionary life of the whole country, it is embarking upon really 'revolutionary self-government.' But where are the *guarantees* that that self-government will turn into one by the *people?* And should we Social-Democrats emphasize this 'piece of revolution' as the main slogan of agitation, or speak of a complete and decisive victory of the revolution, which is impossible without an uprising?" "On the Current Moment," *Proletary*, No. 18, September 26 (13), 1905; LCW, Vol. 9, 287.
35. "The Zemstvo Congress," *Proletary*, No. 19, 3 October (20 September) 1905; LCW, Vol. 9, 306.
36. The article was originally written from a record of Lenin's speech, and appeared in *Zagranichnaya Gazeta*, No. 2, 23 March 1908. Lenin gave this speech on 18 March, to the international meeting of the Social Democrats convened for the anniversary of the Commune. LCW, Vol. 13, 475–78.
37. Ibid., 476.
38. Ibid., 477.
39. In writing about the revolution, Lenin mentions that the Russian proletariat "was mindful of the lessons of the [Paris] Commune." It would have been more exact to say it had rediscovered them. He did have a point in that the Russian workers summed up the results of their earlier demonstrative movements in realizing the armed uprising (Krasnaya Presna). Elsewhere Lenin goes a long way to emphasize the resourcefulness and ingenuity of the Russian proletariat in bringing forms of communal life into being. LCW, Vol. 13, 477–78.
40. Lenin, "Marksizm o gosudarstve," *Leninskii Sbornik* XIV, 222; LCW, Vol. 39, 602–4.
41. One kind of anarchism, the one most worked out in terms of theory, which may be tied to Kropotkin's name, could not gain an influence in respect of the social democratic labor movement involved in the class struggle—and even less so with Lenin—primarily because of its moral orientation. Kropotkin counterposed "mutual assistance" with "mutual struggle," and left politics, as a relatively amoral field of action, out of consideration, as in his opinion the "inclination," the moral necessity for solidarity and association that had developed among

laborers, only takes shape in "civil" organizations. See P. Kropotkin, *Mutual Aid: A Factor of Evolution*, ed. with an introduction by Paul Avrich (New York: New York University Press, 1972), 246–51.

42. Julius Martov, *Obshchestvennie i umstvenniye techeniya v Rossii*, 23–25.
43. I. K. Pantin was the first in the Soviet Union to position the Bakuninian legacy within the history of European and Russian socialist thought and took the first serious steps from unveiling the subject to scientific processing. See Igor K. Pantin, *Sotsialisticheskaya misl v Rossii: Perehod ot utopii k nauke* (Moscow: Polit. Izdat, 1973), 240–44.
44. LCW, Vol. 23, 45–46.
45. "How to Guarantee the Success of the Constituent Assembly—On Freedom of the Press," *Rabochy Put,* No. 11, September 28 (15), 1917; LCW, Vol. 25, 375–76. "Indeed, take, say, the Petrograd and Moscow newspapers. You will see at once that it is the bourgeois papers . . . that have by far the largest circulation. What makes for this prevalence? Not at all the will of the majority, for the elections have shown that in both capitals the majority (a gigantic majority, too) favors the democrats, i.e., the S.R.s, Mensheviks, and Bolsheviks. These three parties command from three-quarters to four-fifths of the votes, while the circulation of the newspapers they publish is certainly less than a quarter, or even less than one-fifth, that of the whole bourgeois press.... Why is that so? Everyone knows very well why." In order to bring this dominance down, Lenin proposed the "state monopoly on private press advertisement" following the seizure of power: "State power in the shape of the Soviets takes *all* the printing presses and *all* the newsprint and distributes them *equitably*: the state should come first—in the interests of the majority of the people, the majority of the poor, particularly the majority of the peasants, who for centuries have been tormented, crushed and stultified by the landowners and capitalists." LCW, Vol. 25, 377–78.
46. Exit from the war was not a preferred option on the bourgeois side where power politics was concerned. In 1917, from Miliukov, the leader of the bourgeois liberal party, to Max Weber, and across Europe the notion that the war was a force for stabilization held strong, arguing that it "cemented patriotic fervor," which brings society together under the leadership of bourgeois governments. (The peasants could also be kept away from home and the land occupier movements by continuing the war.) See N. G. Dumova, *Kadetskaya partiya v period pervoy mirovoy voyni i Fevralskoy revolyutsii* (Moscow: Nauka, 1988), 147–48.
47. Mainstream historical literature evades this criticism by the qualification of the work as a "utopia." This is a misrepresentation, in which both methodology and content are concerned. For mainstream history compares the way parliamentary democracy in the West has firmly come to function over the centuries and its crystallized mechanisms and theories to the moral-theoretical and future-oriented premises of Lenin's work, such as, for example, the innovative form of linking, and "socially overseeing" the legislative, executive, and legal institutions. See Service, *Lenin: A Biography*, 189–90 and 195–96.
48. LCW, Vol. 25, 490–91.
49. Ibid., 413.
50. Ibid., 424.
51. Ibid., 460.
52. "Marx, referring to the example of the Commune, showed that under socialism functionaries will cease to be 'bureaucrats,' to be 'officials'; they will cease to be so in proportion as—in addition to the principle of election of officials—the principle of recall at any time is also introduced, as salaries are reduced to the level of the wages of the average workman, and as parliamentary institutions are replaced by 'working bodies, executive and legislative at the same time.' As a matter of fact, the whole of Kautsky's argument against Pannekoek ... is merely a repetition of Bernstein's old 'arguments' against Marxism in general. In his renegade book,

The Premises of Socialism, Bernstein combats the ideas of 'primitive' democracy, combats what he calls 'doctrinaire democracy': binding mandates, unpaid officials, impotent central representative bodies, etc." LCW, Vol. 25, 487.

53. Ibid., 484.
54. Ibid., 437. He argues elsewhere with the anarchists along the following lines: "There is no trace of utopianism in Marx, in the sense that he made up or invented a 'new' society.... He 'learned' from the Commune.... Abolishing the bureaucracy at once, everywhere and completely, is out of the question. It is a utopia.... We are not utopians, we do not 'dream' of dispensing at once with all administration, with all subordination. These anarchist dreams, based upon incomprehension of the tasks of the proletarian dictatorship, are totally alien to Marxism, and, as a matter of fact, serve only to postpone the socialist revolution until people are different." Ibid., 425–26.
55. Ibid., 436–37. Lenin commented on Engels's critical opinion of the anarchists as expressed in his article *On Authority*. The anarchists "demand that the political state be abolished at one stroke, even before the social relations that gave birth to it have been destroyed." MECW, Vol. 22, 422–25.
56. LCW, Vol. 25, 484.
57. For an anarchist view on this see Volin's (V. M. Eykhembaum) introduction to Petr Arsinov, *The History of the Makhnovist Movement: 1918–1921* (London: Freedom Press, 1987), 7–24; Nestor Makhno, "My Interview with Lenin," in *My Visit to the Kremlin* (Berkeley, CA: Kate Sharply Library, 1993).
58. An example of such projection to the earlier period can also be found in Robert Service, *Lenin: A Biography*, 195.
59. Ibid., 197.
60. Ibid.
61. Recent historiography leans toward the interpretation—suggesting a number of reasons for each point of view—that the February Revolution signaled the beginning of a new revolutionary *process*, a process that could not be halted "artificially." See, for example, C. Hashegava, "Fevralskaya revolyuciya: kontsensus s issledovateley?" and V. P. Buldakov, "Istoki i posledstviya soldatskogo bunta: k voprosu o psihologii 'cheloveka s ruzhyom'," both in *1917 god v sudbah Rossii i mira. Fevralskaya revolyutsiya: Ot novih istochnyikov ko novomu osmislenyiyu*, ed. P. V. Volobuyev (Moscow: RAN, 1997), 107–8, 208–17. The editor found both studies "at fault" in exaggerating the "military aspect." Modern literature on Lenin is also sensitive to the fact that a unified process is in question here. *The State and Revolution* documents how Lenin gave up his earlier concept of a "multiple phased" revolution due to this process. See Statkis Kouvelakis, "Lenin as Reader of Hegel: Hypotheses for a Reading of Lenin's Notebooks on Hegel's The Science of Logic," in *Lenin Reloaded*, 195.
62. Service, *Lenin: A Biography*, 197–98.
63. See Eric Hobsbawm, "Looking Forward: History and the Future," and "Can We Write the History of the Russian Revolution?" in Hobsbawm, *On History*, 37–55, 241–52.
64. Tamás Krausz, *A cártól a komisszárokig* [From the Tsar to the commissars] (Budapest: Kossuth, 1987), 164–222.
65. On the subject, see Dmitry Churakov, "A munkásönkormányzatok közösségi aspektusai az 1917-es orosz forradalomban" [Community in the laborers' local governments of the Russian Revolution of 1917], in *1917 és ami utána következett* [1917 and what followed], ed. Tamás Krausz (Budapest: Magyar Ruszisztikai Intézet, 1998), 53–67; Vladimir Bukharayev, "1917—az obscsinaforradalom pirruszi győzelme" [1917—The pyrrhic victory of the obshchina revolution], in ibid., 37–52.
66. Włodzimierz Brus, *The General Problems of the Functioning of the Socialist Economy* (Lon-

don: Oxford University Press, 1961); László Szamuely, *Az első szocialista gazdasági mechanizmusok* [The first socialist economic mechanisms] (Budapest: Közgazdasági és Jogi Könyvkiadó, 1971); E. G. Gimpelson, *Voyenniy kommunism: politika, praktika, ideologiya* (Moscow: 1973). In the necrology he wrote for W. Brus ("Wlodzimierz Brus: Economist committed to market reforms and democracy in Poland," *Guardian*, November 13, 2007), Jan Toporowski noted that in 1951–52, Brus spoke highly of Stalin's book, *Economic Problems of Socialism in the U.S.S.R.*, in which Stalin outlined the thought of market socialism for the first time, a momentum duly recognized in its own time by Ferenc Tőkei. For more on this, see Tamás Krausz, "A 'sztálini szocializmus'" [Stalinist socialism], in *Lenintől Putyinig* [From Lenin to Putin] (Budapest: La Ventana, 2003), 98–99.

67. Lenin, *The Tasks of the Proletariat in the Present Revolution*, LCW, Vol. 24, 19–26.
68. Ibid., 21–22.
69. Ibid., 23.
70. Ibid.
71. Ibid., 22–24. With a change in the name of the party (to Communist Party), a new aspect of the revolutionary program was seeking to distance itself from "centrist," war-party social democracy and the national defense, which "had sided with the bourgeoisie." Lenin, at the same time, proposed the founding of a new "Revolutionary International." Among his international revolutionary allies he mentions only Rosa Luxemburg, who "on August 4, 1914, called German Social-Democracy a 'stinking corpse,'" in the *April Theses*. The new revolutionary rule, which would be able to realize this revolutionary antiwar policy, would embark on a "revolutionary war"—as he then supposed—in case the offer of democratic peace came to be rejected internationally: *"And that in the event of the German, British, French and other capitalists declining such a peace, we would ourselves start a revolutionary war, and call upon the workers of all countries to join us."* LCW, Vol. 24, 165. Later, at Brest-Litovsk, the thesis of revolutionary war would have to be replaced by the practical implementation of the "defensive war."
72. Ibid., 327–29.
73. Ibid., 329.
74. Lenin, *From a Publicist's Diary (Peasants and Workers)*, LCW, Vol. 25, 275–76. He summarized the unification of the various strata of the revolution as follows: "A mass Social-Democratic workers' movement has existed in Russia for more than twenty years (if we begin with the great strikes of 1896). Throughout this long span of time, through two great revolutions, through the entire political history of Russia, runs the issue of whether the working class is to lead the peasants forward, to socialism, or whether the liberal bourgeoisie are to drag them back, to conciliation with capitalism." Ibid., 277.
75. Viktor I. Miller, "Revolyutsiya v Rossii 1917–1918" [Revolution in Russia 1917–1918], a lecture based on the author's PhD diss., in *Ostorozhno: istoriya!* (Moscow: ETC, 1997), 47–48. A memorial volume of his writings was published posthumously.
76. Miller, *Ostorozhno: istoriya!*, 33–37. In Russia, recent historical research puts the number between 10,000 and 24,000 on the eve of the February Revolution. The number of party members in the period of the April Conference (*Sedmaya Aprelskaya*, 1934 *Vserossiiskaya i Petrogradskaya obshchegorodskaya konferentsii R.S.D.R.P.(B.). Aprel 1917*, Moscow: 1934, 149) can be set at around 50,000; by May the Menshevik membership had reached 100,000. At the Sixth Party Congress in August 1917, the number of Bolshevik members would have been 200,000, and risen to 350,000 on the eve of October. Menshevik membership stagnated at the end of 1917, stayed at about 200,000, and then began to decrease.
77. This polemic work by Lenin records a debate with Sukhanov, a Menshevik intellectual, "one of the best rather than worst representatives of petit-bourgeois democracy," who wrote for *Novaya Zhizn*, and who incidentally lent his flat a few weeks later for the decisive meeting of

the Bolshevik Central Committee, as his wife was a Bolshevik. *Rabochy* No. 10, 14 (1) September 1917; LCW, Vol. 25, 294–304.

78. For more on this, see E. G. Gimpelson's reconstruction dating back a number of years. Efim Gilevich Gimpelson, *Sovietskii Rabochii Klass 1918–1920* [The Soviet working class 1918–1920] (Moscow: Nauka, 1974), 14–20, 26–27. This historiographic overview shows how wide the scope of research carried out on the subject was in the Soviet period, in spite of ideological restrictions.

79. See Miller, *Ostorozhno: istoriya!*, 7–67; P. Volobuyev, *Proletariat i burzhoaziya Rossii v 1917* [Russian proletariat and bourgeoisie in 1917] (Moscow: 1964), 15.

80. See L. S. Gaponenko, *Rabochii Klass Rossii v 1917* (Moscow: 1970), 43, 71–72.

81. LCW, Vol. 30, 260–61. Approximately 11 million persons served in the army and the navy, i.e., 7.2 percent of the population, of whom close to two-thirds were peasants, one-fifth workers, and a similar proportion middle class. Of the 11 million employed by the army, 53 percent, i.e., 5.8 million, were Russian. It is clear that the political battle that erupted within the army concerned the fate of the *whole* of society. The organizational level of the military masses was very high, and of the 20.3 million people represented at the Second All-Russian Congress of the Soviets 5.1 million were workers, 4.24 million were peasants, and 8.15 million were soldiers. Furthermore, soldiers comprised over half the membership of the S.R. party, one-third of the Bolshevik party, and one-fifth of the Menshevik party. See Miller, *Ostorozhno: istoriya!*, 20–21, 23.

82. Nikolay Berdaev, for example, correctly registered that the Bolshevik Marxists were more deeply bound up with the old Russian revolutionary tradition than the Mensheviks, who were more intellectual in Marxism. The folk mentality was in support of the Bolsheviks, rather than the other socialist parties that wished to experiment further with capitalism. See Berdaev, *Istoki i smisl russkogo kommunizma* (Moscow: 1990), 86 (repr. ed.).

83. Lenin had already highlighted in his Political Report of the Central Committee at the Extraordinary Seventh Congress of the R.C.P.(B.) on 7 March 1918 the international development of the revolutionary process: "The revolution will not come as quickly as we expected. History has proved this, and we must be able to take this as a fact, to reckon with the fact that the world socialist revolution cannot begin so easily in the advanced countries as the revolution began in Russia—in the land of Nicholas and Rasputin—the land in which an enormous part of the population was absolutely indifferent as to what peoples were living in the outlying regions, or what was happening there. In such a country it was quite easy to start a revolution, as easy as lifting a feather." LCW, Vol. 27, 98–99, as well as 102.

84. LCW, Vol. 26, 21, 40–41.

85. *Marxism and Insurrection: A Letter to the Central Committee of the R.S.D.L.P.(B.)*, discussed and adopted at the meeting of the Central Committee on 15 (28) September. LCW, Vol. 26, 22–23. See also *Letter to I. T. Smilga, Chairman of the Regional Committee of the Army, Navy and Workers of Finland*, of 27 September (10 October) 1917. This was also not a letter meant for public perusal, and was only published in 1925. With this letter he is engaged in arranging a conspiratorial meeting, with plans for his return to Petrograd for the immediate start of preparations for armed insurrection. Ibid., 72–73.

86. Lenin even tendered his resignation from politics in case of failure of an immediate start to the insurrection: "I am compelled to *tender my resignation from the Central Committee*, which I hereby do, reserving for myself freedom to campaign among the *rank and file* of the Party and at the Party Congress." LCW, Vol. 26, 84. The famous sentences above were written in a letter following the critical Central Committee meeting of 10 October; see *Letter to the Central Committee, The Moscow and Petrograd Committees and the Bolshevik Members of the Petrograd and Moscow Soviets*, 1 (14) October 1917, ibid., 140–41.

87. It is customary to refer on this point to the document in which he describes the role of the Bolshevik Party in regard to the question of seizing power. See *Can the Bolsheviks Retain State Power?,* LCW, Vol. 26, 87–136, written the end of September to 4 October 1917: "But let me begin with a word or two about the first of the questions mentioned—will the Bolsheviks dare take over full state power alone? I have already had occasion, at the All-Russia Congress of Soviets, to answer this question in the affirmative in no uncertain manner by a remark that I shouted from my seat during one of Tsereteli's ministerial speeches [4 (17) June, 1917, 'There is!']. And I have not met in the press, or heard, any statements by Bolsheviks to the effect that we ought not to take power alone. I still maintain that a political party—and the party of the advanced class in particular—would have no right to exist, would be unworthy of the name of party, would be a nonentity in any sense, if it refused to take power when opportunity offers."

88. Lenin considered the alternatives in *Revision of the Party Program*: "We do not know whether our victory will come tomorrow or a little later. (I personally am inclined to think that it will be tomorrow—I am writing this on October 6, 1917—and that there may be a delay in our seizure of power; still, tomorrow is tomorrow and not today.) We do not know how soon after our victory revolution will sweep the West. We do not know whether or not our victory will be followed by temporary periods of reaction and the victory of the counterrevolution—there is nothing impossible in that—and therefore, after our victory, we shall build a 'triple line of trenches' against such a contingency." LCW, Vol. 26, 171.

CHAPTER 6—DICTATORSHIP AND DEMOCRACY IN PRACTICE

1. Robert Service writes that "the Bolsheviks promised a government elected by the people, but dissolved the Constituent Assembly." See Service, *Lenin*, Vol. 3, 1. Matters were more complex, and could be discussed on various levels. An analysis of greater acuity, which sees the events from the environs of the class struggle, would demonstrate this. As an example, Service does not even allude to a fact long held in evidence: documents excavated from the archives of the S.R. Party clearly show that at the time of the election campaign, late December 1917, the right-wing leaders of the S.R. Party were already planning that in the event of victory they would bring a counterrevolutionary turn to pass, in alliance with the Rada of Kiev, Kaledin in the Don region, and nationalist organizations and groups in the Caucasus and Volga regions. Parallel to this there were also the well-known activities of the Kadets and armed counterrevolution. See E. N. Gorodetsky, *Rozhdeniye sovetskogo gosudarstva 1917–1918* (Moscow: Nauka, 1987), 273–81.

2. Lenin, *Constitutional Illusions,* in *Rabochy i Soldat* Nos. 11 and 12, 29 July (5August), 1917, LCW, Vol. 25, 198. In his article, "They Do Not See the Woods for the Trees," Lenin argued with Martov, who changed his evaluation of the July days when he was still pushing for the soviets' takeover of power. Martov explained his shift with the argument that now this could only take place "in the course of a civil war." Lenin refuted him by saying that the civil war had in fact begun, during the July days. Lenin also differentiated between the monarchist and the bourgeois counterrevolution, saying that the "Bonapartist government that constitutes a government of the counterrevolutionary bourgeoisie" was actually embodied in the measures taken by the Provisional Government to force the Bolsheviks underground. In *Proletary* No. 6, 1 September (19 August) 1917. Signed: *N. Karpov*. Ibid., 252.

3. Ibid., 196–97.

4. *On Compromises*, ibid., 306. *Rabochy Put* No. 3, 19 (6) September 1917.

5. LCW, Vol. 26, 71. Lenin repeats the thesis in the document "Letter to the Central Committee the Moscow and Petrograd Committees and the Bolshevik Members of the Petrograd and Moscow Soviets" of 1 (14) October 1917: "Together with the Left Socialist-Revolutionaries we have an *obvious* majority *in the country*. . . . The Bolsheviks have no right to wait for the

Congress of Soviets, they must *take power at once.*" Ibid., 140–141. See also *Meeting of the Central Committee of the RSDLP(B) October 16 (29), 1917*. Speeches in Discussion Minutes, ibid., 192–93. The closer Lenin came to the insurrection, the less optimistic he was about the elections, but he did not deny the necessity of holding them: "It is senseless to wait for the Constituent Assembly that will obviously not be on our side, for this will only make our task more involved." Ibid., 189. His more pessimistic (realistic) "tone" was because he found winning over the leftist S.R.s difficult, as they had not even come to form a party as yet.

6. Among others in Russia, L. G. Protasov in his work exploring the All-Russia Constituent Assembly of 5 January 1918, *Vserossiyskoye uchreditelnoye sobraniye, istoriya, rozhdeniya i gibeli* [The All-Russia Constituent Assembly: Its history, formation and demise] (Moscow: ROSSPEN, 1997), argues that the Constituent Assembly was a precursor to the "westernization" of 1991, and both were a part of the progressive "civilizational turn" in history. The author, loyal to the West, went so far in his admiration as to proclaim the Constituent Assembly itself as an axiom, the highest rung in the ladder of democracy, as if an institution could be identical to the network of governing relations.
7. See I. Ya. Froyanova, *Oktyabr semnadkatogo (Glyadya iz nastoyashchego)* [October 1917 (From a current perspective)] (St. Petersburg: S P. Univesiteta, 1997).
8. In the commemorative publication prepared by pupils and colleagues for the 70th anniversary of his birth, he was termed a historian of Russia: *Istorik i revolyutsia* [The historian and the revolution] (St. Petersburg: Dmitry Bulanyin, 1999). See also, L. Ye. N. Gorodetsky, *Rozhdeniye sovetskogo gosudarstva* [The birth of the soviet state].
9. O. N. Znamensky, *Vserossiyskoe uchreditelnoe sobranie: Istoriya soziva i politicheskogo krusheniya* [The All-Russia Constituent Assembly: A history of its convention and political collapse] (Leningrad: 1976). By the same author, *Intelligentsia na kanune Velikogo Oktyabrya (fevral-oktyabr 1917)* [The intelligentsia on the eve of great October] (Leningrad: 1988). Following the change of regime, the question was hotly debated with him by L. G. Protasov, who portrayed the Constituent Assembly as "the central principle of the creed of Russian nationhood," to which every party from the moment of its establishment—that is, from the turn of the century, or the first Russian revolution at the latest—had been committed to, or at least demanded, its convening. The only "little" problem was that almost every political party and organization thought of the function and nature of this assembly differently.
10. See the report from 1994 of the Gulbenkian Commission under the chairmanship of Immanuel Wallerstein, *Open the Social Sciences: Report of the Gulbenkian Commission on the Restructuring of the Social Sciences* (Stanford, CA: Stanford University Press, 1996).
11. Iván Harsányi touches upon the problem of system definitions in historiography in his examination of Spanish liberalism, "A spanyol liberalizmus történeti útja" [The historical path of Spanish liberalism], *Múltunk* 3–4 (1998): 299–343. It seems generally valid that in semi-peripheral countries, from Russia to Spain, that during critical historical situations and periods of civil war liberalism seems to lose its footing completely. It ceases to exist as an independent political force, as its existence depends largely on the bourgeois democracies of the central countries, the role they play, and the interests they have in the periphery.
12. A few years ago the old questions, characteristic of the region, came up at the annual session of the Politikatörténeti Intézet [Institute of Political History] using current historiographic concepts and arguments. An edited version of the minutes taken at this session were published by Levente Sipos, "A huszadik század az 1945 utáni történetírásban" [The twentieth century in post-1945 historiography], *Múltunk* 2 (1999): 223–257. For the matter under discussion, the contributions of Péter Sipos and Ignác Romsics are of interest; see 244–257. Romsics highlighted the fact that, not considering its "beginning and end," the Horthy system could not be considered a repressive system based on terror. The question this posed (256) was when

was the "beginning" and "end" of the period. Sipos was concerned about oversimplification. Would the rule of the gendarmerie in rural Hungary, which kept the "three million beggars" of the nation at bay for the ruling classes, the execution of Sallai and Fürst, the anti-Jewish laws, the aggression against Yugoslavia, the aggression on the Soviet Union and murders in Ukraine, the holocaust of Körösmező, etc., belong within the definition of a "repressive system of terror" or not? True, the Horthy system was not a fascist dictatorship, but fits easily into the bracket of a "parliamentary dictatorship," in which the parliament is more or less a caricature of a parliament in Western Europe. The Italian fascist dictatorship functioned within the framework of a "multiparty" parliament until 1926, yet this did not make much of a dent on the actual nature of the system. The number of parties therefore does not weigh much in the matter of democracy or dictatorship, especially if the variety of forms taken by dictatorships and democracies is kept in mind—not to mention that democracies also have dictatorial traits not only in the political, but also in the economic and social, spheres.

13. A reference can be made at this point to the system under Yeltsin, which destroyed the legitimate parliament through armed attacks, which may be seen as a particular combination of authoritarian and elitist parliamentarianism, whose character traits cropped up in various degrees in other East-European arrangements for regime change. For more on this, see Tamás Krausz, "A jelcinizmus" [What is yeltsinicism], in *Jelcin és a Jelcinizmus* [Yeltsin and Yeltsinism], edited by Tamás Krausz, Ákos Szilágyi (Budapest: Magyar Russzisztikai Intézet, 1993), 67–92; and *Konyec Jelcinscsini* [Konyets Yeltsinshchini] (Budapest: Magyar Russzisztikai Intézet, 1999).

14. This aspect of the historical moment is most aptly described by Alexander Rabinowitch in his excellent history of the revolution: "For it bears repeating that the Petrograd masses, to the extent that they supported the Bolsheviks in the overthrow of the Provisional Government, did so not out of any sympathy for strictly Bolshevik rule but because they believed the revolution and congress to be in imminent danger. Only the creation of a broadly representative, exclusively socialist government by the Congress of Soviets, which is what they believed the Bolsheviks stood for, appeared to offer the hope of ensuring that there would not be a return to the hated ways of the old regime, of avoiding death at the front and achieving a better life, and of putting a quick end to Russia's participation in the war." Alexander Rabinowitch, *The Bolsheviks Come to Power: The Revolution of 1917 in Petrograd* (New York: W. W. Norton, 1976), 314.

15. Rosa Luxemburg, *The Russian Revolution*, trans. Bertram David Wolfe (New York: Workers Age, 1940). The study by Luxemburg will be discussed in greater detail later in this book; I note here only that its critique was felt. The institutions of the revolutionary dictatorship (the dictatorship of the Bolshevik Party) and the labor self-government already existed in parallel, complementing each other's power and interlocking, but at the same time also in opposition.

16. For more on this see a document from September in *Uchreditelnoye sobraniye: Rossiya 1918* [Constituent Assembly Russia 1918] (Moscow: Nedra, 1991), 25–27.

17. Ibid. See also "Zapis osoboy komissii po sostavleniyu proyekta osnovnih zakonov pri vremennom pravitelstve" [Memo of the Special Committee for the collection of the fundamental laws overseen by the provisional government], *Zasedaniye 14 oktyabrya 1917 goda* (no. 2), 35–36.

18. Protasov explored the day in question extensively, especially in his *Vserossiyskoye uchreditelnoye sobraniye*, 305–8.

19. There is no proof that the central authority of the Bolsheviks gave orders for this act, which was not in its interests, as the Soviet government was seeking to prove its peaceful, nonviolent intentions during the period of assembly. According to the contemporary documents of protest composed by the Mensheviks and S.R.s, the demonstration of 5 January was shot down by "fratricidal" Red Guardists, they spoke of scores of victims, and placed responsibility for

the violence squarely on Lenin. See *Mensheviki v Bolshevistkoy Rossii 1918–1924*. [Mensheviks in Bolshevik Russia], *Mensheviki v 1918 godu. Dokumentalnoye naslediye* (Moscow: ROSSPEN, 1999), 92–102.

20. LCW, Vol. 44, 53[b]-54[a].
21. Ibid., 54[b].
22. Ibid., 54[c]–59[c].
23. On the social backdrop to the civil war see D. P. Koenker, W. G. Rosenberg and R. G. Suny, eds., *Party, State and Society in the Russian Civil War: Explorations in Social History* (Bloomington: Indiana University Press, 1992). An expressive portrayal and rich material on the tendencies and sources for the overflow of mass scale violence among the full array of peoples can be found in Vladimir Buldakov, *Krasnaya smuta* [Red time of troubles], (Moscow: ROSSPEN, 1997).
24. See A. Nenarokov, D. Pavlov, U. Rozenberg, "V usloviyah ofitsialnoy i poluofitsialnoy legalnosti. Yanvar–dekabr 1918 g," in *Mensheviki v bolshevistskoy Rossii*, 25.
25. Protasov, *Vserossiyskoye uchreditelnoye sobraniye*, 12–20.
26. The tactical position was in the period of revolutionary unrest determined by which force would be able to put the Constituent Assembly to use in its own interests. For it was plainly obvious that a Constituent Assembly, inasmuch as it stood for a republic, could not be convened under tsarist rule, for it would mean the end of the autocratic regime. Of course there were utopists that proclaimed the liberal ideal of constitutional monarchy, which signaled their existence in Russia, acting as if the process of English development could be transplanted into Russia. The most influential representative of this manner of thinking was Miliukov, the foreign minister of the Provisional Government and a well-known historian.
27. For the data and analysis see, for example, Gorodetsky, *Rozhdeniye sovetskogo gosudarstva*, 268–69.
28. Lenin, *On Compromises*, LCW, Vol. 25, 306–7.
29. Ibid., 310.
30. See Miller's convincing argument in "Grazhdanskaya voyna: Istoricheskiye paralleli" [The civil war: Historical parallels], in *Ostorozhno: istoriya!* [Watch out! History], 143–52.
31. The noted historian this field, Gennady Bordugov, described the lack of alternative at this historical juncture: In 1917 "two alternative legal forms of democracy took the stage: the as yet unknown soviet type, and the 'constituent' type, which was related to the traditions grounded in the Duma and found in European examples. . . . History gave both sides—the Bolsheviks, and their political opponents—a chance to prove the truth of their own position. It can be observed that the democratic ideals soon lost the support of the masses. Since they could not come to an understanding or reach a compromise, both the soviet, and the 'constituent' form entered a crisis and had to surrender their place to forms that everyone had long considered outdated. As a result, rather than being left with a choice of the soviet or 'constituent' forms of democracy, the country had to choose between a 'red' or 'white' dictatorship. Soviet democracy had subordinated its principles to the dictatorship of the one-party system, which was woven through-and-through with the rough threads of militarism. Adherents of the Constituent Assembly cooperated with the White generals, and then subordinated their ideas irrevocably to the drive for restoration." See Gennady Bordugov, "A 'különleges rendszabályok és a rendkívüli állapot' a Szovjet Köztársaságban és a többi államalakulatban Oroszország területén 1918–1920-ban" ["Special regulations and the state of emergency" in the Soviet Republic and other state formations in the territory of Russia in 1918–1920], in *1917 és ami utána következett*, 19.
32. Ibid., 19–20. See the systemic history of the dictatorships of the generals by Iván Halász, *A tábornokok diktatúrái—a diktatúrák tábornokai: Fehérgárdista rezsimek az oroszországi*

polgárháborúban 1917–1920 [The dictatorships of the generals—the generals of the dictatorships: The White Guard regimes during the Russian civil war 1917–1920] (Budapest: Magyar Ruszisztikai Intézet, 2005).

33. For more on this see G. I. Zlokazov and G. Z. Joffe, *Iz istorii borbi za vlasty v 1917 godu: Sbornik dokumentov* [Historical excerpts from the struggle for power in 1917: Documents] (Moscow: IRI RAN, 2002), 44–46. See also the introduction for more.
34. After the Soviet government set the date for the election on 27 October for 12 November, as if in a rush to get it over, the Central Executive Committee proclaimed in the name of real democracy and real representation of the people in a decree of 21 November that "the electors have the right to recall their delegates," which is a "fundamental thesis of democracy." *Uchreditelnoye sobraniye*, 54, 56.
35. Ibid., 57.
36. "The enemies of the people, the landlords and the capitalists should not be given seats in the Constituent Assembly. Only a Constituent Assembly made up of representatives of the working and exploited classes of the people can save the country." Ibid., 59. At the end of 1917, a decree ordering the arrest of the Kadet leaders of the Constitutional Democratic Party and the striking clerks was passed. See *Dekreti Sovetskoy Vlasti*, vol. 1 (Moscow: 1957), 161–62, 540.
37. *Uchreditelnoye sobraniye*, 61.
38. Ibid., 62.
39. Ibid.; and LCW, Vol. 26, 423–25.
40. See Carr, *The Bolshevik Revolution*, Vol. 1, chap. 5.
41. For a proper documentation of the event in the memo, see *Uchreditelnoye sobraniye*, 68–69.
42. Ibid., 69.
43. Ibid., 140–41.
44. The decree of the Central Committee of the Soviets provided the legal grounds for the dissolution. Ibid., 66.
45. Ibid., 67.
46. LCW, Vol. 26, 435.
47. Ibid., 437–39. "When I hear the enemies of the October Revolution exclaim that the ideas of socialism are unfeasible and utopian, I usually put to them a plain and simple question. What in their opinion, I ask, are the Soviets? What gave rise to these organisations of the people, which have no precedent in the history of the development of world revolution?" Ibid., 437–38. "We are now 'dissolving' the Constituent Assembly although at one time we defended it. . . . But as long as Kaledin exists, and as long as the slogan 'All power to the Constituent Assembly' conceals the slogan 'Down with Soviet power,' civil war is inevitable. For nothing in the world will make us give up Soviet power!" *Speech on the Dissolution of the Constituent Assembly Delivered to the All-Russia Central Executive Committee, January 6 (19), 1918*. Ibid., 439–41.
48. Lenin had various explanations for the relatively poor performance of the Bolsheviks in the elections. He interpreted the S.R. majority as a result of electoral lists based on political relations that preceded the revolution, meaning that left-wing S.R.s were not even on the lists. Whatever the case may have been, soviet power and bourgeois democratic parliamentarianism were irreconcilable regimes for Lenin and the Bolsheviks, and were to remain so in the future.
49. The most widely known summary of this position can be seen in his debate with Kautsky, where this contradiction is presented almost paradigmatically. See Lenin, *The Proletarian Revolution and the Renegade Kautsky*, LCW, Vol. 28, 227–325. This political disputation was an answer to Kautsky's pamphlet *The Dictatorship of the Proletariat*, which pointed out the contradictions of political oppression. In his answer citing *State and Revolution*, Lenin condemned the bourgeois liberal "degeneration" of Kautsky and the leaders of the 2nd In-

ternational, though he defended the suppression of the labor demonstrations in Russia, as if the dictatorship of the proletariat could be used against the proletariat itself, and referred historically to how "dialectics are concrete and revolutionary and distinguish between the 'transition' from the dictatorship of one class to the dictatorship of another and 'transition' from the democratic proletarian state to the non-state ('the withering away of the state')." But can the transition to a "non-state" be made against the resistance of a good proportion of the proletariat? Ibid., 323.

50. For more on the anti-regime traditions of labor self-organization, see Dmitry Churakov, "Protestnoye dvizheniye rabochih v period skladivaniya sovyetskogo gosudarstva," [Workers' protest movements in the period of soviet state formation], *Alternativi* 2 (1999): 98–101.
51. The facts of everyday life and the social, economic, and political nature of the famine are explored in A. A. Ilyuhov, *Zhizny v epohu peremen: Materialnoye polozheniye gorodskih zhitelev v godi revolyutsii i grazhdanskoy voyni* [Life in the period of change: The material situation of urban dwellers in the period of revolution and civil war] (Moscow: ROSSPEN, 2007). The unheard-of wealth in data cited by Ilyuhov is not spoiled by the passionate anti-communism typical today, often ruffling the surface, in that it is easily comparable with the compulsory "ideological drift" of interpretations in the Soviet period.
52. Even then, the specific form of slogan typifying this nostalgia had been put into words, such as "Down with the Bolsheviks and horse-meat, long live the Tsar and beef." True, before October a majority of workers were very much behind the slogan of the Constituent Assembly, considering it something that would save Russia from absolutism and deprivations, and distribute land among the peasants, etc. But they did not place the Constituent Assembly in opposition to the soviets, and approached it as some sort of "revolutionary people's center." But because agrarian reform was carried out by the Soviet government and not the Constituent Assembly, it took a great deal out of the people's positive disposition toward the Constituent Assembly, even rurally; after all, the majority of the rural population had not even gone to cast a vote.
53. See Churakov, "Protestnoye dvizheniye rabochih."
54. Ibid.
55. For decades, Soviet historiography portrayed the rebellion as if the White Guard or the "Menshevik-S.R. counterrevolution" had organized it. Their premise and conclusion was that the rebellion would have led to the "victory of the counterrevolution." See, for example, Yu. A. Setinov, "Melkoburzhoaznie partyi v Kronshtadtskom myatyezhe 1921 goda" [The petit-bourgeois parties in the Kronstadt revolt of 1921], *Vestnik Moskovskogo Universiteta* 3 (1974): 28. According to the data available there were 27,000 sailors and 30,000 civil residents of Kotlin Island, among them 2,200 Communist Party members.
56. "Call of the Provisional Revolutionary Committee to the Peasants, Workers and Red Guard Soldiers," Vladimir Pavlovich Naumov, Aleksandr Albertovich Kosakovsky, eds., *Kronstadt, 1921: Dokumenti o sobitiyah v Kronstatye vesnoy 1921 goda* [Kronstadt 1921: Documents of the spring events in 1921] (Moscow: Demokratiya, 1997), 55–56.
57. On the basis of archival sources, see S. V. Yarov, "Rabochiye i Uchreditelnoye sobraniye: 1921" [Workers and the Constituent Assembly], in *Istorik i revolyutsiya* (St. Petersburg: 1999), 201–14.
58. Luxemburg, *The Russian Revolution* (Ann Arbor: University of Michigan Press, 1961).
59. For a historical exposition of the problematic field in question, see Tamás Krausz, *Szovjet Thermidor*.
60. Records of Dan's interrogation in Naumov, *Kronstadt, 1921*, 266–7.
61. Luxemburg, *The Russian Revolution*, 15, 36.
62. Ibid., 40.
63. Ibid., 38–39. The economic issues shall be addressed in chapter 8.

64. Ibid., 45.
65. For details see G. Z. Joffe, *Kolchakovskaya avantyura i yeyo krakh* [Kolchak adventure and its collapse] (Moscow: Misl, 1983), 56–63; and Tamás Krausz, "Az Összorszországi Alkotmányozó Gyűlés és a bolsevikok" [The All-Russia Constituent Assembly and the Bolsheviks], in *Dél-Európa vonzásában. Tanulmányok Harsányi Iván 70: Születésnapjára* (Pécs: Special Edition, 2000), 1–15.
66. Joffe, *Kolchakovskaya avantyura*, 60–63. Various groups of the Constituent Assembly gathered in various places throughout Siberia (Ural, Omsk, etc.) following the city of Samara, and S.R. governments were formed on a territorial basis elsewhere, when soviet power was defeated. Only the Samara "government" had all-Russian demands, however, as these formations usually became peripheral and fragmented at great speed, unable to bring any sort of middle ground between the far-right and the left. See Susan Zayer Rupp, "The Struggle in the East: Opposition Politics in Siberia, 1918," in *Carl Beck Papers* No. 1304 (Pittsburgh: Center for Russian and East European Studies, 1998).
67. Protasov takes the future of democratic production among the democratic objectives of the Constituent Assembly seriously (Protasov, *Vserossiyskoye uchreditelnoye sobraniye*, 324), though it had originally been an integral part of the theoretical Bolshevik program in *State and Revolution*. Protasov does not seem to comprehend that no form of democratic production can be conceived under the reign of capitalist ownership.
68. See, for example, the document adopted on 3 January, *Declaration of Rights of the Working and Exploited People*, which filled in as a constitution, drawn up in the name of the Central Executive Committee and rejected by the Constituent Assembly.
69. LCW, Vol. 27, 140.
70. A wealth of material on this historical matter may be found in E. G. Gimpelson, *Sovyeti v godi interventsii i grazhdanskoy voyni* [The soviets in the years of intervention and civil war] (Moscow: Nauka, 1968).
71. LCW, Vol. 42, 100[b].
72. The history of Stalinism and the demise of direct democracy is not a subject of this volume. I have attempted to throw light on these developments a number of times, for example, in my earlier cited book, *Államszocializmus* [State socialism].
73. I addressed the question of Rozhkov's concept of Russian history some years ago in Krausz, *Pártviták és történettudomány*, 113, 62–65, 119, 143–45; but the fact that Rozhkov, a Menshevik, was active in politics after 1917 has not been widely commented on.
74. Rozhkov was deported from Petrograd to Pskov on Lenin's suggestion in 1922, where he worked as professor until his passing away in 1927. See Lenin's letter to Stalin in this matter, also left unpublished in the Soviet period, in *V. I. Lenin, Neizvestnye dokumenty. 1891–1922*, 545 and 579–80.
75. Ibid., 268–69. Also see Rozhkov's letter "Pismo N A. Rzhkova, Petrograd, 11 January 1919" in *Mensheviki v bolshevistkoy Rossii: Mensheviki v 1919–1920* [The Mensheviks in Bolshevik Russia] (Moscow: ROSSPEN, 2000), 78–79.
76. *V. I. Lenin, Neizvestnye dokumenty. 1891–1922*, 268.
77. Enormous archival material documents this group of phenomena: *Obshchestvo i vlasty. Rossiyskaya provintsiya,* Vol. 1, 1917-seredina 30-h godov (Moscow, Nizhniy Novgorod, Paris: 2002). For an example of the difficulties faced by the new regime in regard to the requests for armed support in dealing with chaos, banditry, and "the fight against the kulaks," a good example can be found in the report of the communards of Voskresensk city, on 30 September 1918. Ibid., 65–69.
78. Ibid.
79. "Keep your distribution apparatus going, and protect it, but do not monopolize trade even in

any produce, not even grain. . . . If you will not do it, your enemies will. . . . It is impossible to transform the country into closed, local market conglomerates in the twentieth century: within the current borders of Soviet Russia this was natural in the medieval period, when the populace numbered one-twentieth of its size today. This is the greatest stupidity to try it today." Ibid.

80. Ibid.
81. For more details see Krausz, "Szovjet Thermidor," 52–53.
82. "Document 33, Letter to N. A. Rozhkov," 29 January 1919, in Pipes, *The Unknown Lenin*, 62–63; Russian original in "Pismo Rozhkovu, 29 January 1919," *L. V. I. Lenin: Neizvestniye dokumenti*, 266–67.
83. Lenin answered Rozhkov's proposals in a very courteous tone in his reply: "Nikolai Aleksandrovich! I was very glad to get your letter—not because of its contents but because I am hoping for a rapprochement on the general factual basis of soviet work." Pipes, *The Unknown Lenin*, 62; *Neizvestniye dokumenti*, 266.
84. *Speech Delivered at a Meeting in the People's House, Petrograd, 13 March 1919,* newspaper report, LCW, vol. 29, 47–53; "Rech na mitinge v zheleznom zale narodnogo doma v Petrograde," *Neizvestniye dokumenti*, 270–76.
85. Pipes, *The Unknown Lenin*, 62; *Neizvestniye dokumenti*, 267.
86. Pipes, *The Unknown Lenin*, 62–63; *Neizvestniye dokumenti*, 267.
87. *Neizvestniye dokumenti*, 269.
88. See Loginov, *Poslesoviye*, 584.
89. Not surprisingly, Lenin returned to the subject: he wrote an extensive disputation on the Constituent Assembly in 1919 for the December issue of *Kommunistichesky Internatsional*, in which he explained the reasons for the victory of the Bolsheviks in light of electoral data. What he was certainly right about was that the fate of the revolution was decided not by the elections, but by the final outcome of the civil war. See Lenin, *The Constituent Assembly Elections and the Dictatorship of the Proletariat*, LCW, Vol. 30, 253–75.
90. Y. O. Martov's letter to S. D. Shupak (Berlin, 23 December 1921), in *Mensheviki v 1921–1922*, 393.
91. Luxemburg, *The Russian Revolution,* 79–80.
92. MECW, Vol. 25 (New York: International Publishers, 1987), 171.
93. Expanding on the latter subject, see the extensive volume edited by Tamás Krausz, *GULAG: A szovjet táborrenmdszer története: Tanulmányok és dokumentumok* [GULAG: The history of the Soviet camp system: Studies and documents] (Budapest: Pannonica, 2001).
94. See Leon Trotsky, *The Young Lenin*, trans. from the Russian by Max Eastman, ed. and annotated by Maurice Friedberg Stacks (Garden City, NY: Doubleday, 1972); later published in Russian after the change of regimes. See also Lev Trotsky, *Dnevniki i pisma*, ed. Yuriy Felshtinsky (Harvard: Houghton Library, Hermitage, 1986), 190–91.
95. LCW, Vol. 11, 167–69.
96. *V. I. Lenin, Neizvestnye dokumenty. 1891–1922*, 27.
97. For more on this, see Vladimir Buldakov, *Kransnaya Smuta*.
98. On this subject see N. Yevreinov, *Istoriya telesnih nakazaniy v Rossii* [The history of physical disciplining in Russia] (Moscow: 1911).
99. See Vladimir Buharayev, "1917—Az obscsina-forradalom pirruszi győzelme" [1917—The Pyrrhic victory of the obshchina revolution], in *1917 és ami utána*, 47–48. Writing about the roots of the traditional peasant way of life, the author says that, in 1917, "ethical considerations with regard to livelihood were validated: their 'own' landlords, of course, they did not spare. The obshchina village was pitiless toward anyone who did not use land for its traditional, natural purposes but expected income from it, whether merchants, banks or those who

did not cultivate their land themselves." One might add however, that though pitiless, it was no more pitiless than the ruling landowning class was with the Russian *muzhik*, over centuries of domination.

100. Yuriya Felshtinsky, a historian who gained fame in the 1980s and who was an affiliate of the Trotsky Archives at the Houghton Library, traced the Red Terror back to the revolution, and some form of inexplicable, pathological mania for power—or simply evil—shown by Lenin and the Bolshevik Party. See Yuriya Felshtinsky, "O terrore i amninstiyah pervih revolyutsionnikh let" [On terror and amnesty in the first years of the revolution], in *VCHK—GPU: Dokumenti i materiali*, ed. Yu. G. Felshtinsky (Moscow: Gumanitarnoy Leteraturi, 1995), 3–25.
101. See G. Z. Joffe, *Beloye Delo: General Kornilov* [White matter: General Kornilov] (St. Petersburg: Publishing House M. Nauka, 1989), 233.
102. V. Miller noted in his earlier cited work that violence and terror put down such deep roots during the civil war that the war's "aftereffects" could still be felt decades later, in such happenings as the bloodshed of Katyn, or numerous events of the Great War of home defense; for example, the acts of Krasnov or Vlasov's units fighting for the Wehrmacht. See Miller, "Grazhdanskaya voyna: istoricheskiye paralleli" in *Ostorozhno: istoriya!*, 62.
103. Mikhael Bakunin, "K ofitseram Russkoy armii" [To the officers of the Russian army], in *Revolyutsionniy radikalizm v Rossii: Vek devyatnadsadtiy* (Moscow: 1997), 280. Excerpts in English: *The Hague Congress of the First International September 2–7, 1872* (Moscow: Progress Publishers, 1976), 64.
104. LCW, Vol. 44, 56[c]–57[a] and 57[c]–58[a].
105. Vast archival documents and resources are available today to prove this. For the more recent publications, see *"Sovershenno sekretno": Lubyanka—Stalinu o polozhenii v strane (1922–1934 gg)* ["Top secret": Lubyanka—for Stalin on the situation in the country], vol. 1, chap. 1 (Moscow: Institut Rossiyszkoy Istorii RAN, 2001; New York/London, CAN: Edwin Mellen Press, 2001). Lenin was provided a copy of the first summary reports of the Cheka-OGPU, which gave an impression of wide swaths of the population characterized by resistance against Soviet power, malcontented on account of famine, chaos, and lack of security.
106. "Letter to the Military Revolutionary Committee: Has there been a note from the Military Revolutionary Committee to the effect that spirits and wine should not be poured out, but immediately sold in Scandinavia? One must be written immediately. 9 (22) November 1917. *Lenin.*" A resolution was passed the same day by the MilRevCom: "The confiscated (30,000 buckets) of wine must be transported abroad at once." See *Voprosi. Istorii KPSS* (1960): 3.
107. Lenin's dispatch to the People's Commissar for Food, A. D. Tsryupa, on 10 August 1918: "I propose that 'hostages' should not be taken but designated by name for each volost. The purpose of designating them: it is the rich peasants who, in the same way as they answer for contribution, will answer with their lives for the prompt collection and delivery of grain surpluses.

    An instruction to this effect (to designate 'hostages') to be given

    (a) to the Poor Peasants' Committees,

    (b) to all food detachments." LCW, Vol. 44, 127.
108. LCW, Vol. 44, 200[c]–201[a].
109. *Lenin Miscellany,* Vol. 24, 173; quoted by Krupskaya, in *Reminiscences of Lenin*, trans. Bernard Isaacs (New York: International Publishers, 1970).
110. Letter to G. Y. Zinoviev, also to Lashevich and other members of the Central Committee, 26 June 1918:

    "Comrade Zinoviev, Only today we have heard at the C.C. that in Petrograd the workers wanted to reply to the murder of Volodarsky by mass terror and that you (not you personally, but the Petrograd Central Committee members, or Petrograd Committee members) restrained them. I protest most emphatically! We are discrediting ourselves: we threaten mass terror, even in resolutions of the Soviet of Deputies, yet when it comes to action we obstruct the revolutionary initiative of the masses, a quite correct one. This is impossible! The terrorists will consider us old women. This is wartime above all. We must encourage the energy and mass character of the terror against the counterrevolutionaries, and particularly in Petrograd, the example of which is decisive." Vol. 35, 336.

Tsaritsyn to People's Commissar Stalin, 7 July 1918, 1 a.m.:

"Today at about three p. m. a Left Socialist-Revolutionary killed Mirbach with a bomb. This murder is obviously in the interests of the monarchists or Anglo-French capitalists. The Left S.R.s, not wanting to surrender the assassin, arrested Dzerzhinsky and Latsis and began an uprising against us. We are liquidating it mercilessly this very night and we shall tell the people the whole truth: we are a hair's breadth from war. We have hundreds of Left S.R.s as hostages. Everywhere it is essential to crush mercilessly these pitiful and hysterical adventurers who have become tools in the hands of the counter-revolutionaries." LCW, vol. 27, 523.

111. LCW, Vol. 44, 245[b]. See also Felshtinsky, *VCHK—GPU: Dokumenti i materiali*, 19.
112. In the extreme historical situation the mass terror came to use tools "crystallized" in the course of the First World War, such as the concentration camp (which is of course not identical with the Stalinist, nor Hitler's camps), which was developed to isolate war prisoners: "Essential to organise a reinforced guard of selected and reliable people, to carry out a campaign of ruthless mass terror against the kulaks, priests and whiteguards; suspects to be shut up in a detention camp outside the city. Get the office working." LCW, Vol. 36, 489.
113. LCW, Vol. 44, 209[a], 504.
114. To give some examples, one may read his letters to N. P. Bryukhanov, written in 1919, LCW, Vol. 44, 195[b]; as well as his letter to the Yaroslav Gubernia Executive Committee, etc., *Lenin Miscellany Vol. 24*, 171–72.
115. See party documents on the organization of the OGPU in *Lubyanka. Stalin i VCHK-GPU-OGPU-NKVD. Yanvar 1922–dekabr 1936*, ed A. N. Yakovlev (Moscow: ROSSPEN, 2003), 10–27.
116. LCW, Vol. 42, 419.
117. See Terence Martin's introduction to *"Sovershenno sekretno,"* Vol. 1, 22.
118. The monthly report that informed the Soviet leadership about the mood of the nation was a new form of economic and political information provided by the state security services from the second half of 1921. It was prepared from press reports and operative information from institutions of the state, party, labor unions, local governments, and governorates, as well as the GPU and police. The "summaries" (*svodki*) were also regularly sent to Lenin's address, and a collection in chronological order remains in his archives. The 3rd All-Russia Conference of Executive Committees (June 1919) vested the responsibility of collecting politically sensitive information on the secret department of the Cheka. The Department for Information (INFO) was established within the Secret-Operative Department in December 1921. This system was further chiseled at the inception of the GPU: "The mood of every group in society had to be reflected, and especially factors that stood in relation to the measures taken by the Soviet government." See V. K. Vinogradov, "Ob osobennostyah informatsionnikh materiaov OGPU kak istochnika po istorii sovetskogo obshchestva," in *"Sovershenno sekretno,"* Vol. 1., 31, 33, 43, 45.
119. LCW, Vol. 30, 180–82.
120. Lenin and Trotsky often referred explicitly in their writings and official documents to the fact that the NEP, absolutely objectively, established the "new" social and political opponents of the Soviet system. Trotsky's letter from the period shows a recognition of this relationship between the party and the state. "Pometka na pisme L. D. T chlenam Politburo CK RKP(b)

Trotskogo," *V. I. Lenin. Neizvestniye dokumenti*, 513–14. See also, with regard to affairs of the church, documents no. 369 and 370, 516–23, and with regard to the expatriation of groups of intellectuals, see 544–47 and 550–59.

121. The introduction of the Red Terror in the summer of 1918 was also connected to definite events, a particular "psychosis," as reflected in how the fortunes of the family of the tsar fared. After all, the fate of the tsar did not turn out as planned; spontaneous factors played a rather important role. The execution of the tsar's family (on 17 July 1918) is generally used as evidence of a "vindictive Lenin," though Lenin and Soviet leaders wanted to lay bare the crimes of the tsar in a public legal trial. The lack of a trial is explained given the political circumstances. Besides, there is no evidence that Lenin personally gave an order for the execution of the family of the tsar. The decision was made on the basis of the actual political-military situation, for there was a danger that the tsar and his heirs might gain liberty, and thereby become emblematic figures of the counterrevolution. Not much later the Whites did indeed capture Yekaterinburg. The document of the execution was signed by Beloborodov, the chairman of the Executive Committee of the Ural Soviet in Yekaternburg, where the family was kept in detention. The document informed the public that "the onetime Tsar and autocratic ruler had been shot dead on 17 July 1918, upon the order of the Executive Committee and Revolutionary Branch of the Worker, Peasant and Army Soviet of the Urals." Words pertaining to the family of the tsar have been crossed out on the document, which indicates that the Bolsheviks of the Urals also considered the execution of the children as information to be withheld, were ashamed of the act, and that the matter was never to be discussed in Soviet historiography. The document of the execution has been commonly known for a long time because the easily legible color photo was published decades ago. See *Bildung der Russischen Revolution* (Berlin and Frankfurt: 1978; repr. 1979), 179.
122. See, on the issue of the famine, Ilyuhov, *Zhizny v epohu peremen*, 184–85.
123. LCW, Vol. 44, 224–26[a].
124. Y. A. Berzin, secretary of the Comintern executive committee and representative of the Soviet Federation in England, was critical of the arrest of the members of the committee on the grounds of desiring a more positive international view of Soviet Russia. Lenin reacted harshly in a personal letter, pointing out that Noulence, the French ambassador in Moscow and president of the "International Committee Fighting the Famine," had to be slapped in the face, expressly in order to strengthen "international standing." See Lenin's letter of 8 September 1921, in *V. I. Lenin, Neizvestnye dokumenty. 1891–1922*, 468.
125. A vast array of documents on the expropriation of church treasures has become available, thanks in significant measure to the work of A. N. Artizov and his colleagues. See his *Ochistim Rossiiu nadolgo: Lenin (Ulianov) Repressii protiv inakomysliashchikh Konets 1921–1923*, ed. A. N. Artizov (Moscow: ROSSPEN, 2008). The volume of more than 800 pages presents a comprehensive documentation of expropriation and includes 377 archival papers. See also Artizov, "'Ochistim Rossiiu nadolgo.' K istorii visilki intelligentsii v 1922 g.," in *Otechestvennie arhivi* (2003/1), 65–97.
126. N. N. Pokrovsky, who published the documents related to the Soviet government and the church with ROSSPEN, examines the circumstances of the expropriation of the church treasures in his introduction. See N. N. Pokrovsky, *Politburo i tserkov 1922–1925* [The Politburo and the church] (Moscow: ROSSPEN, 1997); and "Istochnikovedeniye sovetskogo perioda. Dokumenti Politburo pervoy polovini 1920-h godov" [Archival research in the Soviet period], in *Arheograficheszky Yezhegodnik za 1994* (Moscow: 1996), 18–46.
127. In spite of all his differences with the church and religion, Lenin took a vocal stand against local intrusions on a number of occasions, such as his letter of 2 April 1919, written to V. Balakhov, who was the delegate of the temple builders of Cherepovets county, Yaganov district.

The peasants asked for permission to complete their church, which they had begun building in 1915. "Completion of the church is permitted, of course; please call on the People's Commissar of Justice, comrade Kursky, whom I have telephoned, for instructions." LCW, Vol. 50, 273; quoted in A. Barmenkov, *Freedom of Conscience in the USSR*, trans. Dmitry Sventitsky (Moscow: Progress Publishers, 1983), 57 (http://leninist.biz/en/1983/FCU180/index.txt).

128. LCW, Vol. 44, 239[a].

129. Lenin, incidentally, thought of the institution of the theater as a replacement for the church—theater being a place that could provide intellectual and moral "renewal," "growth," and atheist enlightenment of the individual and society. He looked similarly upon film and the cinema, which he intended not to merely function as agitative, but dreamed of them having a role that eventually television played in the fields of social education and "self-education."

130. See Lenin's "top secret" letter to Molotov dated 19 March 1922, in *V. I. Lenin, Neizvestnye dokumenty. 1891–1922*, 518–19. Patriarch Tikhon's fate shortly took a sharp turn, and instead of excommunicating the Soviet government, he laid emphasis on recognition of something that caused quite a stir at the time. A diary entry from 11 July 1923 by the great writer M. Bulgakov reflects this perfectly: "Patriarch Tikhon unexpectedly gave a statement in which he recants his earlier erroneous views on the Soviet government, and declares that he is no longer its enemy, etc. So he is let free. All sorts of conjectures are being made in Moscow, the White newspapers abroad are in complete disarray on this. . . . In a nutshell: the Patriarch is now a friend of the Soviet government. No Church reform is required, only the new grammar and use of language." Mikhail A. Bulgakov, *Sárba taposva: Naplók, levelek 1917–1940* [Stamped into the mud: Diaries, letters 1917–1940] (Budapest: Magvető, 2004), 13.

131. See "Telegramma V. I. Lenina i V. M. Molotova vsem gubernskim i oblastnim komitetam RKP(b), 30 July 1921," in *V. I. Lenin, Neizvestnye dokumenty. 1891–1922*, 463–64; or for the English translation, Pipes, *The Unknown Lenin*, 130–31. The drought affected such large areas as would have led to catastrophe even had the economy been fully operational, not to mention the chaotic conditions of a just-ending civil war.

132. Russian original in "Pismo V. M. Molotovu dlya chlenov CK Politburo CK RKP" [Letter to Comrade Molotov, for members of the Politburo], 19 March 1922; top-secret document no. 370, in *V. I. Lenin, Neizvestnye dokumenty. 1891–1922*, 516–19. English translation: *Revelations from the Russian Archives,* Library of Congress, http://www.loc.gov/exhibits/archives/ae2bkhun.html; or Pipes, *The Unknown Lenin*, 152–55.

133. The main motivator of the organizational action was Trotsky, with the immediate support of Lenin above all, and also Stalin. Molotov tried to mitigate Lenin and Trotsky's plans, which aimed essentially at the total elimination of the church in political terms. For details, see N. N. Pokrovsky, "Istochnikovedeniye sovetskogo perioda," 28–31.

134. See in *V. I. Lenin, Neizvestnye dokumenty. 1891–1922*, 518–19. He considered the arrest of Patriarch Tikhon unnecessary, "though he undoubtedly headed this whole revolt of slaveholders." Also see Nedava, 120; and Tamás Krausz, "Kutatás közben. Megjegyzések a Lenin-tematikához az 'új' dokumentumok fényében" [In the course of research. Comments regarding the Lenin topic in light of the "new" documents], in Krausz, *Lenintől Putyinig* [From Lenin to Putin] (Budapest: La Ventana, 2003), 15–27.

135. According to official sources, the value of the confiscated treasures until 1 November 1922 amounted to 33 poods and 32 Russian pounds of gold, 23,997 poods and 23 Russian pounds of silver, 35,670 diamonds, etc., as well as 964 "antique items" not taken into account, which altogether was worth 4,650,810 golden rubles. This was way below Trotsky's expectations; he had estimated the value of the church's treasures at several billions of rubles. Trotsky's explanation for the meagerness of the amount was that during the years of the civil war the Whites—collaborating with the priesthood—had already smuggled the majority of the trea-

sures out of the country. N. N. Pokrovsky says that they were pillaged by the parties at war. With this the Russian historian contradicts his own thesis, which states that the expropriation of treasures was an Old Russia bargain sale. As Trotsky suggested, out of this amount one million was spent on grain for the starving, and a significant amount was consumed by the campaign itself. See *Tserkov i politburo,* document nos. 23–54; and N. N. Pokrovsky, "Istochnikovedeniye sovetskogo perioda," 12–14 and 80.

136. *V. I. Lenin, Neizvestnye dokumenty. 1891–1922,* 518–19.

137. There were cities, governorates, and factories where the workers were against the expropriation. In a number of factories in Moscow and Petrograd workers protested against the confiscation of the church treasures. "After the 28 March convention of believers in the Revolutionary Estrade Theatre the crowd walked down Liteyny Prospect singing psalms, and invited people they met to meetings, protesting against the requisitioning of church treasures." See "Gosinformsvodka za 1 i 2 aprelja No 29/293," in *"Soversenno sekretno,"* 132.

138. The committee established under a decree of the Central Executive Committee passed on 23 February (*O porjadke izyatiya tserkovnih tsennostyah, nahodyashchihsya v polzovanii grupp veruyushchih*) announced the expropriation of the treasures on 13 March. However, due to the protests by enraged followers, the requisitioning was postponed to 15 March. A day before, on 14 March, the assets of the synagogue were expropriated under calm circumstances. A huge crowd gathered on the square in front of the basilica on 15 March, which welcomed the mounted police with threats and stones, but the police were followed by approximately half a company from the Red Army infantry. There were shots fired from the crowd, which was followed by the commander's order to the soldiers to shoot in the air, though then they shot into the crowd, which scattered. Four people were murdered, and ten injured. In the course of a central investigation, 10 poods of silver, gems, pearls, and other treasures were collected. A group of high-placed officials were sent to Shuia to form an investigation committee, which reported on 23 March that all expropriatory actions were legal, and called for the local authorities to find those responsible and the Revolutionary Court to impose charges on them.

139. Following this, Lenin gave validity to the Politburo's telegram temporarily halting expropriation. Let the enemy think "that we are vacillating . . . that they managed to scare us." Meanwhile he provisioned strict punishment for the people responsible for the Shuia events. "I think it is expedient for us not to touch Patriarch Tikhon himself, although he is undoubtedly heading this entire rebellion of slaveholders. Regarding him, a secret directive should be issued to the GPU, so that all of this figure's connections are carefully and scrupulously observed and exposed, precisely at this moment. Dzerzhinsky and Unshlikht should be required personally to report on this to the Politburo weekly." Pipes, *The Unknown Lenin,* 154; *V. I. Lenin, Neizvestnye dokumenty. 1891–1922,* 518.

140. *V. I. Lenin, Neizvestnye dokumenty. 1891–1922,* 517.

141. Krasin, the People's Commissar of Foreign Trade tried to take the lead in selling the treasures abroad illegally, and he criticized Trotsky for his exaggerated expectations about the envisaged profits. Even members of the Comintern were engaged in these sales, and used such revenues for supporting the international revolutionary movement. Pokrovsky's assessment, in its extremism, goes as far as to say that with this "the Bolshevik leaders showed themselves ready to destroy their own country completely, with absolute faith in the spirit of permanent world revolution." See Pokrovsky, 12–14. In reality, treasures of museum value were never placed on the market. A special decree ordered that religious assets of historical and artistic value must be protected: in accordance with the "regulations governing the expropriation of church treasures used by religious congregations," those articles "that were of unequivocal museal value were delivered into the care of various departments at museums, and those articles to be expropriated, but also required for the practice of faith were replaced with less valuable ones."

See Nina Dmitrieva, "Lenin és az orosz értelmiség: 1922" [Lenin and the Russian intelligentsia: 1922], *Eszmélet* 19/76 (2007 Winter).

142. Researchers reference several works. N. N. Pokrovsky, for example, mentions these: L. Regelson, *Tragediya Russkoy Tserkvi. 1917–1945* (Paris: 1977), 285; and V. A. Alekseyev, *Illyuzii i dogmi* (Moscow: 1991), 204. In 1922 they estimated the number of bloody incidents related to the expropriation at 1,414. It is presumed that 8,100 persons became victims of the national campaign during the clashes and court sentences. Other literature (such as D. V. Pospelovskiy, *Russkaya Pravoslavnaya tserkov v XX veke* [Moscow: 1995], 106) mentions 231 court cases in which 732 people were found guilty. On 8 May 1922, the Moscow Court imposed death sentence on eleven persons (priests, religious officials, laymen) among the organizers of the riots, and four were given five-year prison sentences, thirteen were sentenced to three years, and ten for one year. Those sentenced to death turned to the Supreme Court, which forwarded their appeal to the Central Executive Committee with a recommendation for mitigation. The sentence on five priests remained unchanged, and in the case of the other six, they modified the death sentence to five years of imprisonment. Kamenev tried to move decisions toward mitigation from the beginning, but a halfway standpoint gained dominance. See *Neizvestniye dokumeti,* 522–23.

143. "Gosinfsvodka za 4 aprelja No. 31/296," in *"Soversenno sekretno,"* Vol. 1, chap. 1, 148. In the governorate of Ivanovo-Voznesensk, "Shuia saw no further protests on the part of the priesthood or believers of the church against the expropriation of church treasures after the events of 14 March." "Gosinformsvodka za 1 i 2 aprelja No 29/293," in ibid., 132–33. According to data related to the expropriation of church treasures in the northern governorates: "The work of the committees proceeds smoothly." In the governorate of Pskov: "The work of the committee dealing with the expropriation of church treasures goes on without greater conflicts. The majority of priests have a passive stance on the requisitions. Some of the priests and anti-Soviet elements carry on hidden propaganda among large groups of the populace, which means that a majority of the population does not look well upon thc expropriations." Ibid.

144. V. G. Makarov and V. S. Hristoforov, "Predislovie," in *Visilka vmesto rasstrela. Deportatsiya intelligentsii v dokumentah VCSK-GPU 1921–1923* (Moscow: Russkiy puty, 2005), 41.

145. LCW, Vol. 33, 227–36.

146. A. N. Artizov, *Repressii protiv inakomislyashchih konets 1921*, 65–67.

147. S. A. Fedukin, *Velikiy Oktyabr i intelligentsiya. Iz istorii vovlecheniya staroy intelligentsii v stroiteltstvo sotsializma* (Moscow: Nauka, 1972), 286–88. It is obvious that Fedukin could only have known a fraction of the documents included in the volume edited by Artizov, and thus his data and point of view are outdated.

148. A GPU note for the Politburo "On the anti-Soviet groups forming among the intellectuals." Published by A. N. Artizov, *Otechestvenniye arkhivi*, 2003/1. 76. For more on this, see Dmitrieva, "Lenin és az orosz értelmiség: 1922."

149. B. N. Losskiy, "On the 'deportation of the men of thought' in 1922," *Stupeni: Filosofsky zhurnal* ¼ (St. Petersburg: 1992): 62, quoted by Dmitrieva, "Lenin és az orosz értelmiség: 1922".

150. "'Cleaning up the country for a long while.' Toward a history of the intellectuals sent into exile in 1922," annotations and an introduction, as well as preparation of the documents for publication by A. N. Artizov, in *Otechestvennoye arkhivi* 2003. no. 1, 75. Also see the Introduction to the volume of documents by Artizov, 6–7.

151. Lincoln Steffens, *The Autobiography of Lincoln Steffens* (New York: Harcourt, Brace, 1931), 797–98. Quoted in Dmitiriyeva, 166–67.

152. See A. N. Artizov, *Otechestvenniye arkhivi*, 66–67.

153. Artizov, Makarov, and Hristoforov, "Introduction," in *Ochistim Rossiiu nadolgo*, 11.

154. Gorky's letter to N. I. Bukharin, 22 June 1922, in RGASPI F. 329. op. 2. d. 4. 9.

155. Dmitriyeva, n. 94.
156. LCW, Vol. 28, 207–8.
157. These Cheka-GPU objectives were of course comprehended by those Mensheviks arrested and those protesting. Numerous documents testify to this: "Protest CK RSDRP vo VCIK v svyazi s rasshiryayushchessya politikoy repressiy protiv sotsial-demokratov" (Moscow, 8 December 1921); and "Zayavlenie v Prezidium VCIK gruppi sotsial-demokratov, zaklyuchonnikh butirskoy tyurmi" (12 December); and an endless series of documents in *Mensheviki v 1921–1922 gg.* (Moscow: ROSSPEN, 2002), 386–91.
158. *Sudebniy process nad sotsialistami-revolyutsionerami ijuny-avgust 1922 g. Sb. Dokumentov*, comp. and introduced by S. A. Krasilnikov, K. N. Morozov, I. V. Chubikin (Moscow: ROSSPEN, 2002), 512.
159. Ibid., 513.
160. Ibid., 778.
161. Lenin accepted the repeal of the death sentences but did not think that the continuation of three Internationals should be subordinated to the trial. Finally, as noted, death sentences were passed, but they were not carried out. Incidentally, Western European social democrat observers were invited to participate at the trial. See Lenin's article in *Pravda.* 11 April, *We Have Paid Too Much*. LCW, Vol. 33, 330–34.
162. All that the representative historical tome *Drama rossiskoy istorii* contains on the history of the pogroms is that the later memoirs of General Denikin—head of the Volunteer Army and responsible for a significant part of the massacres—mentions "the pogroms against the Jewish population" as a cause of their defeat. Volobuyev, *Drama rossiskoy Istorii*, 333.
163. Mikhail Bulgakov, *The White Guard*, trans. Michael Glenny (New York: McGraw-Hill, 1971), 289.
164. B. Pinkus notes that the intelligentsia were in absolute majority among the Jewish revolutionaries who joined the party, as they generally found an internationalist community in the centralized party, which accepted them completely, in line with the ideology of universal emancipation. See Benjamin Pinkus, *The Jews of the Soviet Union: The History of a National Minority* (Cambridge, New York, and Sidney: Cambridge University Press, 1989), 77–79.
165. See Joseph Nedava, *Trotsky and the Jews* (Philadelphia: Jewish Publication Society of America, 1971), 69.
166. An interesting study on the way Jewish messianism and revolutionary thought were joined is found in Michael Löwy, "Messianisme juif et utopies libertaires en Europe centrale (1905–1923)" [Jewish messianism and libertarian utopias in Central Europe (1905–1923)], *Archives de Sciences sociales des Religions* 51/1 (1981): 5–47. See also Michael Löwy, *Redemption and Utopia. Jewish Libertarian Thought in Central Europe: A Study in Elective Affinity* (Stanford, CA: Stanford University Press, 1992).
167. I have dealt with this question in greater detail previously, in Tamás Krausz, *Bolsevizmus és nemzeti kérdés,* esp. 49–80.
168. According to the data of the 1897 census, 5,215,805 subjects of Jewish origin lived in the tsarist empire. For a more detailed overview of the subject see Tamás Krausz, "Lenin és a zsidók" [Lenin and the Jews], in *Kelet-Európa: történelem és sorsközösség. Palotás Emil 70. születésnapjára* [Eastern Europe: History and a common lot. Commemorating the 70th birthday of Emil Palotás], ed. Tamás Krausz (Budapest: ELTE Kelet-Európa Története Tanszék, 2007), 149–87.
169. In the profusion of literature first see the comprehensive work by Yu. I. Gessen, *Istoriya yevreyskogo naroda v Rossii* (Leningrad: 1925), repr. Moscow and Jerusalem, 1993; on the literature see V. Kelner, "Russkaya intelligentsiya i 'yevreyskiy vopros' v nachale XX veka," in *Russko-yevreyskiy i istoriko-yevreyskiy literaturniy i bibliograficheskiy almanakh*, 2004, No.

4–5; J. Klier, *Imperial Russia's Jewish Question, 1855–1881* (Cambridge: Cambridge University Press, 1995).

170. See I. P. Traynin, *SZSZSZR i natsionalnaya problema. Po natsionalnim respublikam i oblastyam Sovetskogo Soyuza* (Moscow: 1924), 5–6; and O. V. Budnitsky, *Rossiyskie yevrei mezhdu krasnimi i belimi (1917–1920)* (Moscow: ROSSPEN, 2005), 30–33.

171. For an explanation of the episode, see Nedava, 51.

172. Lenin, *Does the Jewish Proletariat Need an Independent Political Party?* LCW, Vol. 6, 330–36. The Bund joined the RSDLP in 1898, but preserved its nation-based organizational structure.

173. The intensification of anti-Semitism at the beginning of the century in the southern governorates was related to steps taken by the government to increase the number of non-city settlements with the aim of resettling the poorest Jews, thereby reducing the concentration of poor Jews in urban centers. The measures had neither the effect of making the Jews more leftist nor easing social conflict, and still, or perhaps on these very grounds, the most merciless pogroms took place here (primarily in the governorates of Kiev and Bessarabia). For a recent examination of the problematic field, see L. S. Gatagova, "Mezhetnyicheskiye otnoseniya," in *Rossiya v nachale XX veka*, ed. A. N. Jakovleva (Moscow: Noviy hronograf, 2002), esp. 146–52.

174. Lenin, "Mobilizatsiya reaktsionnih sil i nashi zadachi" [The gathering of forces by the reactionaries and our tasks], first published in *Iskra* 3/41 (1 June 1903). Cited in *N. Lenin: O evreiskom voprose v Rossii* (Tel Aviv: Aticot, 1970); previously published in *Vvedenie S. Dimanshteyna*, Introduction by P. Lepesinszkij (Zaporozhye: Kommunar, Kooperativnoe Izdat. Proletary, 1924).

175. *N. Lenin: O evreiskom voprose v Rossii*, 11.

176. Ibid., 34–36. See also LCW, Vol. 6, 332–33, 322–33, 518–21.

177. The social foundations of the high level of organizational development in the Bund was determined primarily by the factor that in the multiethnic cities of Russia, the Jewish proletariat had made the "techniques" of class struggle its own from the beginning, though purely Jewish urban centers had never even existed. According to later data, after the victory of the revolution the urban ethnic Jewish population of Ukraine was set at 22.7 percent, and the Belorussian at 40.2 percent of all Soviet citizens. L. Zinger, *Dos benayte folk* (Moscow: 1941).

178. See S. Dimanshteyn's "Introduction" in *N. Lenin: O evreiskom voprose v Rossii*.

179. For the debate within the party upon this question, see *Vtoroy syezd RSDLP. Iyul–avgust 1903 goda* (Moscow: Protokoli, 1959), 51, 60–107.

180. Ibid., 89–90; LCW, Vol. 6, 479. They rejected the Bund's formulation proposed for the consideration of the Congress (organizational statue no. 2), which was put as follows: "The Bund is a social democratic organization of the Jewish proletariat which is not bound by any form of territorial confines in its activity and is member of the party as sole representative of the Jewish proletariat." Ibid., 473.

181. *Vseobshchiy Evreyskiy Rabochiy Soyuz v Litve, Polse i Rossii*, Bund Archives, New York.

182. *The Position of the Bund in the Party,* originally published in *Iskra* 51 (October 22, 1903), LCW, Vol. 7, 92–103.

183. See *Iskra* no. 42 and the separate reprint from it *The Kishinev Massacre and the Jewish Question*, 3.

184. LCW, Vol. 7, 99–101. (Emphases in the original.)

185. Nedava, 194 and 272.

186. Lenin, *Preface to the Pamphlet Memorandum of Police Department Superintendent Lopukhin*. LCW, Vol. 8, 202–5.

187. See Lenin, *To the Jewish Workers*. LCW, Vol. 8, 495–98.

188. See György Bebesi, *A feketeszázak* [The Black Hundreds] (Budapest: MRI, 1999).

189. Lenin, "The Black Hundreds and the Organisation of an Uprising," *Proletary* No. 14, 29 (16) August 1905. LCW, Vol. 9, pages 200–204.
190. I. V. Omelyanchuk, "Sotsialniy sostav chernosotyennih partiy v nachale XX veka" [The Black Hundreds Party and its social composition in the beginning of the twentieth century], *Otechestvennaya istoriya*, 2004/2, esp. 87–89.
191. See O. Budnitsky, *Rossiyskie yevrei*, 53.
192. *N. Lenin: O evreiskom voprose v Rossii*, 44. This writing by Lenin is missing in *Lenin's Collected Works*: the article should be in volume 9, though these thoughts also appear in other writings by him.
193. Lenin, *The Reaction Is Taking to Arms*, LCW, Vol. 10, 508–13.
194. Ibid.
195. This extremely important circumstance was emphasized by Dimanshteyn, publisher of Lenin's writings on Jewish themes, in his introduction from 1924, in N. Lenin, *O yevreiskom*, 13. "The dominance of the Bund among the Jews living in the Pale of Settlement was made possible by the low participation of Jewish labor in the large industrial production, the proximity to the petit-bourgeois segment of society through their artisanship, and the national oppression of the autocratic regime, as well as the fact that our party did not adapt to work among the Jews because of the language." (Russian Jews mostly spoke Yiddish.)
196. Emil Niederhauser, *A nemzeti újjászületési mozgalmak Kelet-Európában* [The movements of national rebirth in Eastern Europe] (Budapest: Akadémiai Kiadó, 1977); Emil Palotás, *A Balkán-kérdés az osztrák-magyar és az orosz diplomáciában* [The Balkan question in Austro-Hungarian and Russian diplomacy] (Budapest: Akadémiai Kiadó, 1972).
197. The Bolsheviks organized an illegal party conference with the leadership of Lenin in Poronino in 1913, dealing thematically with the question of nationalism. The resolution passed here emphasized the "reactionary nature of the separation of educational authorities based on ethnicity" based on a politics of "ethnically unconstrained class unity." See *Az SZKP kongresszusainak, konferenciáinak és KB plénumainak határozatai* I. rész [The resolutions of the congresses, conferences and Central Committee plenaries of the Soviet Communist Party, Part 1], 363.
198. See Lenin, *The Nationalisation of Jewish Schools*. LCW, Vol. 19, 307–8.
199. Lenin, *Critical Remarks on the National Question*. LCW, Vol. 20, 37–38. Also see W. Laqueur, *Chornaya sotnya* (Moscow: Tekst, 1994), 62–63; György Bebesi, *A feketeszázak*.
200. LCW, Vol. 20, 28.
201. Ibid., 26.
202. LCW, Vol. 23, 250.
203. Genocide in 1915 was itself a consequence of the First World War. It is a known fact that under conditions of total collapse, the Turkish army and armed personnal carried out the extermination of many hundreds of thousands of Armenians, or according to some data, one and a half million.
204. "Lenin presupposed that with regard to the effect of the imperialist war upon the October Revolution, a future researcher would not take into account the huge effect of certain factors, such as the evacuation of the factories from the Baltic region and other peripheral regions to central Russia, due to the war manoeuvres, which was followed by the evacuation of the Jewish populace to the center of Russia, in significant numbers, at least among the more active segment." See S. Dimanshteyn, "Introduction" in *N. Lenin: O yevreiskom*, 17.
205. "The policy of persecution against Jews was not only the personal anti-Semitism of Prince Nikolay Nikolayevich and his headman N. N. Yanushkevich. This policy functioned as a military theory; the officers received tuition on the harmful and useful elements of society in their schools and academies. . . The Jews were apt for the role of those who caused the military fail-

ures and unviable finances. A part of this was that they were completely defenceless." See O. Budnitsky, *Rossiyskie yevrei*, 286–87, 290. The most comprehensive collection of documents on the pogroms to date, required for researchers of the subject, is *Kniga pogromov. Pogromi na Ukrainye, v Belorussii i yevropeyskoy chastyi Rossii v period Grazhdanskoy voyni 1918–1922 gg.*, ed. L. B. Milyakova (Moscow: ROSSPEN, 2007).

206. See Budnitsky, *Rossiyskie yevrei*, 19. Budnitsky does not put sufficient emphasis on the fact that anti-Semitism, and the anti-Semitic pogrom in general, always counted as the most serious crime, whereas among the Petliurists, the Cossacks, and the Whites it was not even looked upon as a crime, unless one is to look upon Denikin's weak admonishments as "protest."

207. See G. V. Kostirchenko, *Taynaya politika Stalina. Vlasty i antisemitizm* (Moscow: M. O., 2003), 55.

208. The Commissariat for Jewish Matters operated within the framework of the People's Commissariat for Nationalities headed by Stalin, and was brought about by the Council of People's Commissars on 21 January 1918.

209. For more on this, see Tamás Krausz, *Bolsevizmus és nemzeti kérdés*, 52–53.

210. A. V. Lunacharsky, *Ob antisemitizme* (Moscow and Leningrad: 1929), 38; and V. Bonch-Bruyevich, "Ob antisemitizme," in *Protiv antisemitizma* (Leningrad: 1930), 13.

211. *Politika sovetskoy vlastyi po natsionalnomu voprosu za tri goda 1917–1920. Narodniy Komissariat po delam natsionalnostey* [The policy of the Soviet government for national issues, 1917–1920], (Moscow: Gos. Izdat, 1920), 31. The decree was signed by Lenin, Stalin, and Bonch-Bruyevich.

212. Upon a critical analysis of the latest data, O. Budnitsky published the following numbers based on an array of literature and sources: between 1918 and 1920 over 1,500 pogroms took place in 1,300 settlements. On the basis of various estimates the number of those killed is placed between 50–60,000 and 200,000. Approximately 50,000 women were widowed and 300,000 children were orphaned. Hundreds of the most horrific murders were committed, and thousands of women and young girls were raped. The torture and murders beyond human imagination leave only the Holocaust to compete for worse horrors. For more on the subject see *Bogrovaya knyiga*, with an introduction by Gorky (1922). See also L. B. Milyakova, "Vvedeniye," in *Knyiga pogromov*, III–XXVIII; and S. P. Pavlyuchenkov, "Yevreyskiy vopros v revolyutsii, ili o prichinah porozheniya bolshevikov na Ukrainye v 1919 godu," in *Voyenniy kommunizm: vlasty i massi* (Moscow: 1997), 251–63.

213. "Dokladnaya zapiska tsentralnogo Byuro Yevreyskih Kommunisticheskih Sektsii pri CK i Glavnogo Byuro Evreyskih Kommunisticheskih Sektsii pri CK KPU," in *N. Lenin: O evreiskom voprose v Rossii*, 86.

214. Budnitsky, *Rossiyskie yevrei*, 69–70, 268–71, 344–46, 354–61. The Kadet politicians and intellectuals surrounding Denikin accepted that the General's troops carried out over 200,000 pogroms in Ukraine alone, practically without a word. The liberals subjected everything to military victory, sacrificing their whole bourgeois democratic program to the interests of the military officers' dictatorship. For more on the subject see Aleksandr Usakov, "A zsidók és az orosz forradalom. Adalékok a kérdés felvetéséhez" [Jews and the Russian Revolution—Toward the formulation of questions], in *1917*, 160–68. It sometimes seems as if Usakov himself came under the influence of prejudices that were part of the propaganda of the White Guards, for he does not clarify that the greater proportion of Jews in the parties and even among the commissars is connected to the fact that due to well-known circumstances the proportion of literates and intellectuals was greater among them.

215. This situation is well documented in an article by the commissar of the 1st Mounted Regiment, I. Vardin, that appeared in *Pravda* on 14 May 1918, titled "Against the Jew—for the Tsar": "The battle with Jewry has become inseparably bound up with the battle against the

Soviet government, the party of the communists. 'Beat the Jew—save Russia, down with the communists and the commissars!' This cry resounds wherever the dark powers of the priests, landlords, the kulak and the shopkeepers rises to battle." He was also to write in the 12 June issue of the same year, "'Stinking Jew', that was the bone with which the Tsar and the landlords tried to stuff the hungry mouths of the workers and peasants," as quoted by Budnitsky, in *Rossiyskie yevrei*.

216. *N. Lenin: O evreiskom voprose v Rossii*, 16–17.
217. For the historical character of the dictatorships of the White generals and their leaders' aims, see Iván Halász, *A tábornokok diktatúrái—a diktatúrák tábornokai*, 109 and 246.
218. For more details, see Tamás Krausz, "Bolsevizmus és nemzeti kérdés" [Bolshevism and the national question], *Világosság* 1 (1980): 681–88. Incidentally, it is worth noting that the view that Lenin was a "cosmopolite," which crops up in historiography, does not rest on any sort of objective examination of the historical documents.
219. More details on this can be found in Kostirchenko, *Taynaya politika Stalina*, 60–87.
220. The decree of the People's Commissariat for Nationalities on the support to be provided to Setmass (All-Russia Alliance of Jewish Working Masses). *Zhizhny natsionalnostyey*, 1 August 1920; and *Politika sovyetskoy vlastyi*, 34–35.
221. Those days were past when the Bund, following the February Revolution, supported—as previously—the politics of the Menshevik wing of the RSDLP against that of the Bolsheviks, thereby proposing cooperation with the Provisional Government. They came over to the Bolshevik side, pushed by the White Guard counterrevolution, the pogroms, and persecution of Jews.
222. See Tamás Krausz:, *Bolsevizmus és nemzeti kérdés*, 52–54.
223. *Sedmoy vserossiyskiy syezd sovetov rabochih, krestyanskih i kozachyih deputatov. Stenograficheskiy otchot* (Moscow: 1919), 5–9, and (Moscow: 1920), 22–24.
224. Ibid., 24–28.
225. László Béládi, "A bolsevik párt kongresszusai a számok tükrében 1917–1939" [The Congresses of the Bolshevik Party seen through the figures], *Világtörténet* 3 (1983): 86–89. Between 1918 and 1923 ethnically Jewish delegates made up 15 percent of the congresses. But a majority of the Communist Jewish leaders no longer even spoke the common Jewish language, Yiddish, including Dimanshteyn himself, who had begun his career around the turn of the century as a rabbi. For more on this tendency, see S. Agursky, *Yevreyskiy rabochiy v kommunistyicheskom dvizhenii* (Minsk: Gosizdat, 1926).
226. Speaking about the political representation of Jews, Budnitsky writes: "According to my calculations—leaving room for all contingencies—somewhat over 3,000 individuals belonged to the Russian political elite in 1917 and the first half of 1918. The elite includes the representatives of the Constituent Assembly, members of the VCIK, participants of the Democratic Council, members of the Provisional Government of the Russian Republic (pre-parliament), members of the central committees of the country-wide parties. The chronological framework is provided by the February Revolution at the start and the creation of the one-party dictatorship in the summer of 1918, at the end. Over 300 Jews entered the political elite, participating in the full spectrum of political parties and trends, from the extreme left (Bolsheviks, anarchists) to those positioned on the right wing of the Kadets. Jews were present in the central committee of virtually every significant party. Besides, Jews composed up to one-quarter or one-third of the central committees of the membership in the central committees of the parties on the left (Bolsheviks, S.R.s)." Budnitsky, *Rossiyskie yevrei*, 77. See also Ushakov.
227. Though the Soviet government needed to employ Jews in the Cheka because barely 1 percent of those working there had completed higher education, the employees were recruited "by chance"—and often even included criminals. In September 1918, the VCHK central appa-

ratus in Moscow had 781 employees and officials, of whom 3.7 percent were Jews. Their presence among the directors was stronger (at 8.6 percent). At the end of 1920 approximately 50,000 employees worked for the Cheka in all the governorates, with Russian composing 77.3 percent of the workforce, Jews making up 9.1 percent, Latvians 3.5 percent, Ukranians 3.1 percent, Poles 1.7 percent, Germans 0.6 percent, and Byelorussians 0.5 percent. About the same figures apply for the Soviet apparatus. See Budnitsky, *Rossiyskie yevrei.*

228. The Politburo discussed the report submitted by the People's Commissar of War at its meeting in the beginning of April 1919: "A large percentage of the Cheka near the frontlines are Jews, and a large percentage of Latvians and Jews make up the workers of Executive Committees and central Soviet institutions near the front and in the backcountry; on the front itself this proportion is not high, and chauvinistic agitation on this account is strong among the Red soldiers, which does find some reciprocation; according to comrade Trotsky there is a need for a reshuffling of the party forces for a more equal distribution of workers from every ethnic background." *The Trotsky Papers,* Vol. 1 (The Hague and Paris, 1971), 730; also see Chicherin's letter to Lenin, 2 October 1919, ibid., 722–24.
229. *N. Lenin: O evreiskom voprose v Rossii*, 7. It must nevertheless be pointed out in relation to Dimanshteyn, Agursky, and other Bolshevik leaders that though the internationalists who were Jews or of Jewish origin did indeed take a role in the struggle against religion and Russian Orthodoxy, no one in Soviet Russia fought the Jewish religious establishments that "dampened class consciousness," or Zionism for that matter, with greater determination than they did, often bordering on fanaticism and even overstepping the limit.
230. *N. Lenin: O evreiskom voprose v Rossii*, 17.
231. Ibid., 18.
232. *Iz literaturnogo naslediya: Gorky i yevreyskiy vopros* [From the literary legacy: Gorky and the Jewish question], ed. M. Agurskiy and M. Shklovskaya (Jerusalem: 1986), 275. Apart from this book, Gorky's and in part Lenin's relationship to the Jews is approached analytically by M. Agursky in "Gorky i yevreyskiye pisateli" [Gorky and Jewish writers], *Minuvsee. Istoricheskiy almanakh,* Vol. 10 (Moscow and Leningrad: SPb, 1992), 184–192.
233. Agursky, *Yevreyskiy rabochiy v kommunistyicheskom dvizhenii*, 185–87.
234. For example, Gorky succeeded—with Lenin's support—in securing a "state distinction" for the Jewish theater Habima, against the wishes of the "Jewish Section" of the Central Committee (Yevsektsia). Agursky, *Yevreyskiy rabochiy v kommunistyicheskom dvizhenii*, 187. Gorky later managed to solicit permission from Lenin to allow abroad the well-known Jewish poet Byalik, as well as others, but Lenin's relationship with the leaders of the Jewish Section became increasingly strained. See ibid., 191.
235. LCW, Vol. 29, 252–53.
236. Ibid.
237. See Tamás Krausz, *Bolsevizmus és nemzeti kérdés*, 54; and Budnitsky, *Rossiyskie yevrei*, 185–86.
238. On this, see Tamás Krausz, "Lenin és a lengyel-szovjet háború" [Lenin and the Polish-Soviet war], in Életünk Kelet-Európa, 120–26.
239. Many records tell the story of the bloodbaths committed by occupying units of the Polish army in Ukraine and Byelorussia, *Kniga pogromov*, e.g. 631–62, but accounts of horrors can be found on many more pages of the volume.
240. A significant amount of material is made available on this subject by the book *Kniga Pogromov*; see the statistics on the pogroms committed as shown in the quoted introduction. For the reports on the pogroms of the 1st Cavalry Army's 6th Cavalry detachment, see 424–28. Levenberg's announcement, ibid., 530, gives information on the pogroms, murders, violence committed. There were some Makhnoists—or, more precisely, pogromists of the cavalry who

laid claim to "batyko Makhno" [brother Makhno]—who agitated their fellows with the following slogans: "Come on, let's cleanse the backcountry of Jews," "Come, let's unite with Batyko Makhno," "Beat the Jews, the Commissars, the communists." Ibid., 425.

241. *The Unknown Lenin: From the Secret Archives*, ed. Richard Pipes (New Haven and London: 1996), 117–18. For a detailed critical appraisal of Pipes's views see O. Budnitsky, "Jews, Pogroms and the White Movement: A Historiographical Critique," *Kritika: Explorations in Russian and Eurasian History* 2/4 (Fall 2001): 752–53.
242. Se *Krasny Kavallerist*, 10 October 1920. In Hungarian, *Zsidók Oroszországban*, 77.
243. *"Soversenno sekretno."* For an analysis of the GPU archives in relation to these questions see Tamás Krausz, *The Soviet and Hungarian Holocausts: A Comparative Essay*, Hungarian Authors Series No. 4, trans. Thomas J. DeKornfeld and Helen D. Hiltabidle (Boulder, CO: Social Science Monographs; Wayne, NJ: Center for Hungarian Studies and Publications; New York: Columbia University Press, 2006), 13–14; for the Hungarian original, *Antiszemitizmus—holokauszt—államszocializmus* [Anti-Semitism—Holocaust—state socalism] (Budapest: Nemzeti Tankönyvkiadó, 2004), 23–40.
244. See *Zsidók Oroszországban*, 80.
245. See *Neizvestniye dokumenti*, document nos. 257 and 258, two notes to E. M. Sklansky, end of October–November, 399–400.
246. Ibid.
247. Ibid.
248. Ibid., 586.
249. For documents relating the horrors committed by Balahovich and his troops, see *Kniga pogromov*, 609–11, 619, 623, 630–59.
250. The noted writer is also correct in saying that the Nazis arrived at the Holocaust on their own; they needed no guidance from the Russian extreme right—a mistaken notion that found its way into the work of Pipes and Walter Laqueur. The "Russian connection" is only required by Pipes—following Nolte's logic—to root Nazism and even the Holocaust in the Russian Revolution, as if this had been Lenin's legacy, and not the exact opposite. See Tamás Krausz, "Lenin marxizmusa" [Lenin's Marxism], *Eszmélet* 76 (Winter 1997).

CHAPTER 7—WORLD REVOLUTION

1. Eric Hobsbawm's description of the universal and European historical conditions for the revolution, the concrete prospects of its unfolding and course in Europe, in a number of his books is of lasting relevance. "The revolutions of 1848 thus require detailed study by state, people and region. . . . Nevertheless they had a great deal in common, not least the fact that they occurred almost simultaneously, that their fates were intertwined, and that they all possessed a common mood and style, a curious romantic-utopian atmosphere and a similar rhetoric, for which the French have invented the word *quarante-huitard*. Every historian recognises it immediately: the beards, flowing cravats and broad-brimmed hats of the militants, the tricolours, the ubiquitous barricades, the initial sense of liberation, of immense hope and optimistic confusion." E. J. Hobsbawm, *The Age of Capital 1848–1875* (London: Abacus, 1975), 26.
2. Karl Marx, *Grundrisse*, trans. Martin Nicolaus (New York: Random House, 1973), 539–40.
3. Ibid., 749–50.
4. MECW, Vol. 5, 49.
5. LCW, Vol. 26, 167. Italics of the author.
6. "An ominous, gloomy kind, the Hungarian, / To have lived the revolution, but spun / Into War, that Horror, sold as a cure / By scoundrels accursed in their graves." Endre Ady, "Üdvözlet a győzőnek» [A Welcome to the Victor].

7. Lenin said in October 1914 that the war was "distracting the attention of the working masses from the internal political crises in Russia, Germany, Britain and other countries, disuniting and nationalist stultification of the workers, and the extermination of their vanguard so as to weaken the revolutionary movement of the proletariat—these comprise the sole actual content, importance and significance of the present war." LCW, Vol. 21, 27.
8. Tibor Hajdu, *Közép-Európa forradalma 1917–1921* [The revolution of Central Europe 1917–1921] (Budapest, Gondolat, 1989). This work provides new information for a reevaluation of this subject, just as the international points of contact for the Hungarian revolution are also documented in, for example, Peter Pastor, "Hungary between Wilson and Lenin: The Hungarian Revolution of 1918–1919 and the Big Three," *East European Quarterly* (1976); Mihály Fülöp and Péter Sipos, *Magyarország külpolitikája a XX. században* [Hungarian foreign policy in the twentieth century] (Budapest: Aula, 1998), 56–62. See also Jenő Szűcs.
9. LCW, Vol. 23, 367–74.
10. In his telegram of 24 January (6 February) 1918 to Arthur Henderson, Lenin indicated that he could not accept the invitation to the peace conference of the socialist parties of the Entente to be held on 20 February, because not all socialist parties of Europe had been invited. "We object to division of the working class according to Imperialist grouping. If British Labour agrees to Russian peace aims, which are already accepted by the Socialist parties of the Central Powers, such division is still more unwarranted." LCW, Vol. 44, 60[b].
11. On the organizational structure of the Comintern during Lenin's time, see G. M. Adibekov, Z. I. Shahnazarova and K. K. Shirinya, *Organizatsionnaya struktura Kominterna 1919–1943* [The organizational structure of the Komintern 1919–1943] (Moscow: ROSSPEN, 1997), 7–89.
12. See Eric J. Hobsbawm, "Being Communist," in *Interesting Times*, 127–51.
13. The specific phenomenon is well depicted by Péter Hanák, "The Garden and the Workshop: Reflections on Fin-de-Siècle Culture in Vienna and Budapest," in *The Garden and the Workshop: Essays on the Cultural History of Vienna and Budapest* (Princeton: Princeton University Press, 1999), 63–97. In German: "Die Volksmeinung wahrend des letzten Kriegsjahres in Österreich-Ungarn," in *Die Auflösung des Habsburgerreiches: Zusammenbruch und Neuorientierung im Donauraum,* vol. 3 (Vienna, 1970), 58–66; and Hungarian: "Népi levelek az I. világháborúból," in *A kert és a műhely* (Budapest: Gondolat, 1988). This work even inspired E. J. Hobsbawm.
14. E. J. Hobsbawm, *Nations and Nationalism since 1870: programme, myth, reality* (Cambridge and New York: Cambridge University Press, 1992), 129–30.
15. Among literature on this subject from various periods, see István Lengyel, *A breszt-litovszki béketárgyalások* [The peace talks of Brest-Litovsk] (Budapest: Kossuth, 1975); Geoffrey Swain, *The Origins of the Russian Civil War* (Essex: Longman, 1996); Geoffrey Jukes et al., *The First World War. The Eastern Front 1914–1918,* Vol. 1 (Oxford: Osprey Publishing, 2002).
16. *Protokoli centralnogo Komiteta RSZDRP(b). Avguszt 1917–fevral 1918* (Moscow: 1958).
17. LCW, Vol. 35, 372.
18. See Lenin, *On the History of the Question of the Unfortunate Peace*, LCW, Vol. 26, 442–50; and *Speeches at a Meeting of the Central Committee OF THE RSDLP(B)* on 19 January, LCW, Vol. 35, 507–9.
19. Ibid., 452.
20. Ibid., 273.
21. For a concrete historical examination of the debates, see Tamás Krausz, "Bolsevizmus és nemzeti kérdés; Ideológiatörténeti adalékok a 20-as évekből" [Bolshevism and th national question; Material from the twenties, for the history of ideologies], *Világosság* 11 (1980): 681–88.

22. *The Chief Task of Our Day*, LCW, Vol. 27, 159.
23. LCW, Vol. 27, 162–63.
24. LCW, Vol. 29, 448–450.
25. Ibid., 294 and 270, *Greetings to the Hungarian Workers.*
26. LCW, Vol. 42, 245.
27. "To the CC of the RSDLP(B). Please include my vote *in favour of* getting potatoes and arms from the bandits of Anglo-French imperialism. *Lenin.*" 22 February 1918, LCW, Vol. 44, 67[c].
28. Tibor Hajdu, *Közép-Európa*, 142–64.
29. Telegram to I. I. Vatsetis and I. S. Aralov, 21–22 April 1919, LCW, Vol. 44, 215[b].
30. In a note from G. V. Chicherin to Lenin, dated 15 July 1919, the following remarks are to be found: "It is absolutely inadmissible for this arrogant fellow to send such a telegram. After all, Rakovsky is not of the best figures of the International. And in the interest of the cause, it is not on the cards to get wild." The correspondence between Chicherin and Lenin concerns a harsh telegram written by Béla Kun to H. G. Rakovsky on the occasion of Radek's arrest in Berlin. Written by Lenin to Kun: "Dear Comrade Bela Kun, Please do not worry too much and do not give way to despair. Your accusations or suspicions against Chicherin and Rakovsky have absolutely no foundation whatever." LCW, Vol. 44, 271[b].
31. "Telegramma Sovyeta Narodnikh Komissarov Ukraini G. Chicherinu, kopiya Predsedatelyu SNK V. Leninu o shifrovke B. Kuna. Kiyev, 14 ijulja 1919 goda," in *Komintern i ideya mirovoy revolyutsii* (Moscow: Nauka, 1998), 140.
32. Kun continued his disparagement of Rakovsky, the famous internationalist Ukrainian Soviet leader in a radio telegram sent to Lenin on 29 July 1919: "Rakovsky was forced upon the people of Ukraine against their will," and also criticized Lenin for, so to say, not supporting the Hungarian Soviet Republic in Bessarabia. *Komintern i ideya*, 144.
33. "I suggest," Lenin wrote to Chicherin in a note of 15 July, "that you reply in a dry, but harsh tone: (such and such) factors wholly refute the allegations brought up against Rakovsky and others, and if they keep writing in such a tone, they will be proclaimed not communists, but hooligans." *V. I. Lenin, Neizvestnye dokumenty. 1891–1922,* 294.
34. *Komintern i ideya*, 148.
35. A standard portrayal in terms of Soviet historiography may be found in *A polgárháború a Szovjetunióban, 1918–1922* [Civil war in the Soviet Union 1918–1922] (Budapest, Kossuth, 1964), which comes short of having portrayed the multidimensionality of the issue. N. Davies's *White Eagle, Red Star: The Polish-Soviet War, 1919–1920* (London: Random House, 1972), remains a very useful specialized work to this day. Studies in Hungarian also came out on the subject, among them Péter Sipos, "A Nemzetközi Szakszervezeti Szövetség és az 1920 évi lengyel-szovjet háború" [The International Association of Labor Unions and the Polish-Soviet War of 1920], in *El a kezekkel Szovjet-Oroszországtól* [Hands off Soviet Russia] (Budapest: Kossuth, 1979); Erika Somogyi, "Magyarország részvételi kísérlete az 1920-as lengyel–szovjet háborúban" [The Hungarian effort to participate in the Polish-Soviet War of 1920], *Történelmi Szemle* [Historical review] 2 (1986); István Majoros, "A lengyel–szovjet háború. Wrangel és a francia külpolitika 1920-ban" [The Polish-Soviet War. Wrangel and the French foreign policy of 1920], *Századok* 3 (2001): 533–67. Among more recent works see I. B. Mihutina, "Nekotorie problemi istorii polsko–sovetskoy voyni 1919–1920 gg." [Some of the problems of the history of the Polish-Soviet war], in *Versaly i novaya Vostochnaya Yevropa* (Moscow: 1996), 159–76; I. S. Yazhborovskaya and V. S. Parsadanova, *Rossiya i Polsa: Sindrom voyni 1920 g.* [Russia and Poland: The syndrome of the war of 1920] (Moscow: 2005); Jerzy Krasuski, *Tragiczna niepodległosc. Polityka zagraniczna Polski w latach 1919–1945* [Tragic independence. Polish foreign policy 1919–1945] (Poznań: 2000).
36. The documents were slow to find a place in new research, as quite palpable in investigations

in the field of the Polish-Soviet War and Lenin by Robert Service, *Lenin: A Biography,* Vol. 3 (London: Macmillan, 1995), 117–21.

37. Robert Service was terribly "surprised" at the large extent to which Lenin "misunderstood" the motives of Piłsudski when he approached the entire war as one dimension of the relationship between Moscow and Berlin. See ibid., 118. Actually Lenin—in contradiction to all post-fact wisdoms—fit the Polish-Soviet War into a pan-European constellation. Closer examinations of diplomatic history have proved the "pan-European" approach well founded, for example, see the quoted article by István Majoros.
38. Kun's letter in *Komintern i ideya*, 168–69.
39. Pipes, *The Unknown Lenin*, 90–92 in English; and in Russian, *Komintern i ideya*, 186.
40. *Komintern i ideya*, 187–88, and a report of the Polish agitprop office working with the CC of the RCP dated 21 April 1920, *Komintern i ideya*, 172–75. For a number of years the official Soviet historiography tried to suppress this position for reasons of "state interest," some politicians and historians going even further in certain periods by falsifying it.
41. See Service, *Lenin,* Vol. 3, 119; Davies, *White Eagle, Red Star*, 169–70.
42. The speech originally appeared in the first issue of *Istorichesky Arkhiv* in 1992; for the whole text, including the Central Committee report and the conclusion, see *V. I. Lenin, Neizvestnye dokumenty, 1891–1922*, 370–92. The complete argumentation could not have been known to historians earlier, because it only became public in 1999. In English: Pipes, *The Unknown Lenin,* 95–115.
43. Lenin refereed to the government proclamation of the Council of People's Commissar's on 28 January 1920, and its call of 2 February, which practically recognized Poland's territorial acquisition of more or less all of Belorussia and the right half of Poland with a population of around 4 million. See Dekreti sovyetskoy vlasti, Vol. 7 (Moscow: 1975), 141–42, 162–65. For an ethical approach, see Emil Niederhauser, "Lenin és a nemzeti kérdés" [Lenin and the national question], in *Nemzet és kisebbség* [Nation and minority] (Budapest: Lucidus, 2001), 65–83; Tamás Krausz, *Bolsevizmus és nemzeti kérdés.*
44. *V. I. Lenin, Neizvestnye dokumenty. 1891–1922*, 372–73; in English, see Pipes, *The Unknown Lenin,* 100–101.
45. Lenin explained the role of the British in this matter through his communications in the beginning of June with Trotsky, the People's Commissar for War: "Lloyd George's meetings with Krasin have demonstrated in *full clarity* that England is helping, and will continue to help the Polish and Wrangel. The line certainly has a unity." See LCW, Vol. 42, 229[b]; and *The Trotsky Papers,* Vol. 2, 358, 376, 378, 398; see also Tamás Krausz, *Bolsevizmus és nemzeti kérdés*, 80–81.
46. LCW, Vol. 44, 225–26; LCW, Vol. 31, 323–24.
47. Pipes, *The Unknown Lenin,* 97–98; *V. I. Lenin, Neizvestnye dokumenty, 1891–1922*, 373. The quotation includes a comment to the secretary in charge of keeping records.
48. Pipes, *The Unknown Lenin,* 98–99; *V. I. Lenin, Neizvestnye dokumenty, 1891–1922*, 374. Lenin stressed that this issue for conspiratorial reasons could not be discussed at the public congress of the Communist International.
49. For more details, see Tamás Krausz, *Bolsevizmus és nemzeti kérdés.*
50. Budnitsky, *Rossiyskie yevrei*, 478–79.
51. Pipes, *The Unknown Lenin,* 99; *V. I. Lenin, Neizvestnye dokumenty, 1891–1922*, 375.
52. Pipes, *The Unknown Lenin,* 99–100; *V. I. Lenin, Neizvestnye dokumenty, 1891–1922*, 375–76.
53. Pipes, *The Unknown Lenin,* 114; *V. I. Lenin, Neizvestnye dokumenty, 1891–1922*, 389.
54. The quotation of Radek's speech is based on his contribution at the 9th Party Conference, in *Komintern i ideya*, 202.

55. Ibid., 208.
56. Pipes, *The Unknown Lenin*, 99; *V. I. Lenin, Neizvestnye dokumenty, 1891–1922*, 374.
57. *Komintern i ideya*, 210–11. Bukharin also thought similarly. See his article from December 1920, "On the Tactics of Offence," ibid., 223–27. Orginally published in *Kommunistichesky Internatsional*, 15 December 1920.
58. See on this N. Valentinov's memoirs, *NEP i krizis partyi: Vospominaniya* (New York: Stanford University Press and Teleks, 1991), 20. (A facsimile of the original publication of 1971.)
59. Lenin, *Left-Wing Communism: An Infantile Disorder*, LCW, Vol. 31, 17–104. The wide renown of the pamphlet is reflected in its 22 languages and 106 editions published outside of the Soviet Union by the year 1960. The reasons for this are not to be found in theoretical values, but rather the political determination that the communist parties sideline the opponent "leftist radicalism" to the periphery.
60. Ibid., 103.
61. For details of the political history of this field see Gábor Székely, *A Komintern és a fasizmus 1921–1929* [The Comintern and fascism 1921–1929] (Budapest: Kossuth, 1980), 174–86.
62. LCW, Vol. 21, 561–63.
63. *Kommunismus* (Vienna: 1920).
64. Lenin, *"Left-Wing" Childishness and the Petit-Bourgeois Mentality*, LCW, Vol. 27, 323–34.
65. See Tamás Krausz and Miklós Mesterházi, *Műés történelem*, 75–79. See also the proclamation of the KIVB to the revolutionary workers of Germany, which called for a "brave, unified struggle to seize power, for a Soviet Germany." *Komintern i ideya*, 254–55.
66. See István Hermann, "Az elméleti vita feltételei. A messianisztikus marxizmus avagy az úgynevezett nyugati marxizmus" [The conditions of a theoretical debate. Messianistic Marxism or, so called, Western Marxism], *Világosság* 4 (1984): 214–15.
67. Ibid., 211. On the role of Béla Kun see György Borsányi, *Kun Béla* (Budapest: Kossuth, 1979), 240. On the roles of Zinoviev, Rákosi, and the Comintern in the German uprising, see Gábor Székely, "Az egységfront és a népfront vitája a Kominternben" [The argument between the unified front and the people's front in the Comintern], *Világosság* 4 (1984): 248–49; and by the same author, "Kun Béla a Kommunista Internacionáléban" [Béla Kun in the Communist International], in György Milei, ed., *Kun Béláról: Tanulmányok* [On Béla Kun: Essays], (Budapest: Kossuth, 1988), 490–91, 394–97.
68. *Komintern i ideya*, 256.
69. In regard to Béla Kun, two Lenin documents from 1921 emerged that remained unpublished until 1999, most probably on account of their harsh tone (Lenin later apologized for the coarse vocabulary). They did not want to bring the Hungarian leaders into a difficult situation in the Soviet period. In these documents Lenin scolded the leader of the Hungarian Soviet Republic; criticizing one of Kun's speeches he wrote: "I must loudly protest at the copying of semi-barbaric Russian methods by civilized Western Europeans. The aim is to make the 'whole speech' available to the audience, but stupidities, a complete muddle, a mess is published. I firmly distance myself from any responsibility. Publish the general content of the speech, this will be a European job, rather than an Asian one." *V. I. Lenin, Neizvestnye dokumenty, 1891–1922*, 480. The speech Lenin was concerned about could not be discovered. A copy of Lenin's letter can be found in the RCHIDNI archives, with the envelope on which Lenin wrote: "Archive (copy of the letter written to Béla Kun on 27 October 1921) about the German speech on ('Meaninglessness') and ('Method')." RCHIDNI, f. 2, op. 1. D. 21619, l. 2. The other document also concerned the criticism of a Kun speech that had been given at the extended meeting of the Comintern Executive Committee on 17 June 1921. See *V. I. Lenin, Neizvestnye dokumenty, 1891–1922*, 450–53. Lenin denounced Kun's attack on Trotsky, because the Hungarian communist had come

forward with ultra-revolutionary demands "of the 1919 sort" in reaction to the French occupation of the Ruhr region: "Trotsky says that if these types of left-wing comrades continue on the path they have struck out on, they will kill off the movement of the communists and laborers n France. (Applause.) This is also my deep conviction. That is why I have come here to protest against the speech by Béla Kun and etc. . . . The preparation of the revolution in France, one of the largest countries in Europe, cannot be carried out by a single party. The conquest of the labor unions by the French communists—that is news that gives me the most joy. . . . When I on occasion page through a French newspaper (and I honestly admit that this happens very rarely, as I do not have time to read newspapers) I am most impressed by the word 'ячейка' (*yacheyka*). It seems to me that this word cannot be found in any dictionary, because it is a purely Russian concept, which we have forged ourselves through our long struggle against tsarism, the Mensheviks, opportunism and the bourgeois democratic republic. It was our practice that brought this organization into being. These cells work in collective fashion within the parliamentary factions, the labor unions, or other organizations, wherever the seed of our movement exists. And if we come across a communist who makes mistakes, smaller ones than the stupidity done by Béla Kun, etc., we do not pat them on the back."

70. LCW, Vol. 31, 103–4. It is precisely a *methodological critique* of the subject that is missing from Péter Konok's book on "leftist radicalism"—not to mention the fact that the leftists simply misunderstood the actual alternatives offered by the historical situation they were witnessing. It seems as if the issue had been simply different political *assessments*, while the real historical and theoretical problem rests in their radically different approach to the world of politics. For more on this book see a critical review by Péter Konok, Eszter Bartha, Gábor Székely, "'. . . a kommunizmus gyermekbetegsége?' Baloldali radikalizmusok a 20. században. Beszélgetés Konok Péter könyvéről" [". . . an infantile disorder of Communism?" Leftist radicalism in the 20th century. A discussion of Péter Konok's book], *Eszmélet* 73 (2007 Spring): 141–54.

71. "The 'new materialism' of Lenin is the great instrument which is now used by the Communist parties in the attempt to separate an important section of the bourgeoisie from the traditional religion and idealistic philosophies upheld by the upper and hitherto ruling strata of the bourgeois class, and to win them over to that system of state capitalistic planning of industry which for the workers means just another form of slavery and exploitation. This, according to Pannekoek, is the true political significance of Lenin's materialistic philosophy." Karl Korsch, "Lenin's Philosophy," *Living Marxism* 4/5 (November 1938) and http://www.marxists.org/archive/pannekoe/1938/lenin/app-korsch.htm.

CHAPTER 8—THE THEORY OF SOCIALISM—POSSIBILITY OR UTOPIA?

1. The noted Menshevik author, David Dalin, after having thought through the problem from a point of view of "consistent Marxism," came to the conclusion that "the revolution, which Russia has lived through in the past five years was from the beginning and remains a bourgeois revolution. But this is only true in an objective sense. The revolution passed through whole stages that were decorated subjectively—by its leaders and participants—in the most varied range of colors. In other words, there has never been a greater chasm between the objective meaning of historical events and the objectives, hopes, and tasks of its participants than in the time of this revolution." And because he was able to take a more informed account of the Western European outlooks than Lenin, Dalin could see how the chances of *socialism* in Russia were eroded, though he was not able to transcend the "democratic" utopia, that is, the "bourgeois democratic" perspective of Russian development. David Dalin, *Posle voyn i revolyutsii* (Berlin: Grani, 1922), 7 and 52–62.

2. In my writings over the last decade, I have tried to explore in greater detail the context of this subject in terms of concrete theory and political history, but the confines of the present volume of course do not permit this, and so what follows has been based in part on these works: *Állam és demokrácia: Lenin és a húszas évek vitái*; "Szocializmus-képek a húszas években: Átmeneti korszak és szocializmus" [Socialist images of the world in the twenties: A transitional period and socialism], *Világosság* 4 (1984): 202–10; with László Tütő, "Lenin a szocializmusba való politikai átmenet időszakáról" [Lenin on the period of transition to socialism], *Társadalmi Szemle* [Social review] 6–7 (1984): 108–16; with Miklós Mesterházi, *Mű és történelem*; *Szovjet Thermidor*; "A szocializmusvita jelenlegi állásáról" [On the current position of the debate on socialism], in *Államszocializmus: Értelmezések - viták - tanulságok* [State socialism: Interpretations—debates—lessons], ed. Tamás Krausz and Péter Szigeti (Budapest: L'Harmattan and Eszmélet Foundation, 2007), 122–44; "'Stalin's Socialism'—Today's Debates on Socialism: Theory, History, Politics," *Contemporary Politics* 11/4 (2005): 235–38.
3. It was pointed out in the chapter "State and Revolution" that the defining and exclusive source of the idea of socialism was Marx and Engels. For an authentic philosophical-theoretical reconstruction of Marx's views on the period of transition and socialism, see László Tütő, "A 'kommunista társadalom első szakasza' Marx elméletében" [The "first phase of communist society" in Marx's theory], in *Egy remény változatai: Fejezetek a szocializmusgondolat történetéből* [Variations on hope: Chapters from the history of socialist thought], ed. Ágnes Kapitány and Gábor Kapitány (Budapest: Magvető, 1990), 56–99. See also Attila Ágh, "Társadalmi önszerveződés és szocializmus" [Social self-organization and socialism], in *Válaszúton* [Crossroads], ed. Tamás Krausz and László Tütő (Budapest: ELTE ÁJTK, 1988), 49–61.
4. *Sotsiologicheskaya smisl v Rossii. Ocherki istorii nemarksistskoy sotsiologii poslednie treti – nachala XX veka*, ed. B. A. Chagina (St. Petersburg: Nauka, 1978), 129.
5. LCW, Vol. 1, 184–85.
6. "There is nothing more primitive from the viewpoint of theory, or more ridiculous from that of practice, than to paint, 'in the name of historical materialism,' *this* aspect of the future in a monotonous grey. The result will be nothing more than Suzdal daubing." *A Caricature of Marxism and Imperialist Economism*, LCW, Vol. 23, 70.
7. LCW, Vol. 1, 263. See Lenin's earlier quoted notes to Kautsky's work, where Lenin frequently refers to the possibilities and workability of "socialization"; for example, "American communist agrarian cooperatives tended the land wonderfully." The fact that socialism occupied the position of an important theoretical problem in his thoughts from before the turn of the century is demonstrated by his debates with the liberal "deviations." See "Konspekt i kriticheskie zamechaniya na knigu S. Bulgakova," in *Leninskiy Sbornik XIX*, especially 118–19. He analyzed the works of Kautsky, Hertz, Bulgakov, Berdyaev, and others in the course of his studies of agrarian capitalism, and in the notes he prepared on these readings he enlarged upon the particulars of the general development of capitalism, with frequent allusions to the socialist perspective, and mentions social and cooperative ownership among various forms of state and private property. LCW, Vol. 41–42, 113. See also notes for a lecture by Lenin in *Leninskiy Sbornik*, 226–28.
8. LCW, Vol. 1, 169 and 171–72.
9. Ibid., 180.
10. Ibid., 187.
11. LCW, Vol. 20, 154.
12. LCW, Vol. 27, 90.
13. LCW, Vol. 25, 323–69. Written 10–14 (23–27) September 1917. Ibid., 327–28.

14. Kit Kitych is a rich, bloated merchant in Alexander Ostrovsky's comedy *Shouldering Another's Troubles.*
15. LCW, Vol. 25, 331.
16. Ibid., 299–300.
17. LCW, Vol. 27, 237.
18. Ibid., 238.
19. Ibid., 246, 248.
20. Ibid., 248–50.
21. Ibid., 254.
22. On this, see for example V. P. Dmitrenko, *Sovyetskaya ekonomicheskaya politika v pervie godi proletarskoy diktaturi* [Soviet economic policy in the first years of the dictatorship of the proletariat] (Moscow: Nauka, 1986). On the issue in question, see 21–29.
23. Production for the market and directly for state requirements raised the issues of disciplined work and remuneration. The Council of Labor Unions introduced strict rules of conduct at state-owned enterprises in April 1918, and after the October Revolution performance-based pay replaced work hours–based pay, meaning that a quarter of the workers at the companies in Petrograd received performance-based pay by July. LCW, vol. 27, 583. See also László Szamuely, *Az első szocialista gazdasági mechanizmusok*; and Tamás Krausz, "Szocializmus-képek a 20-as években," 202–10.
24. LCW, Vol. 25, 330.
25. LCW, Vol. 27, 259.
26. Ibid., 274–75.
27. A frequently posed idea in the literature is that the formation of the poor peasant committees for the compulsory delivery of grain was some sort of "refined" step taken to intensify the class struggle in the villages. The objective was in fact to provide the cities and the workers with at least enough grain to save them from starving to death or leaving the cities, and to disfuse urban discontent. The workers' brigades for state subsistence were sent from Petrograd in the beginning of June. Nonetheless, the activities of these brigades in the villages undoubtedly heightened social-group conflict between the poor and the well-to-do peasants, with consequences that are widely known—but the cause and effect are still not interchangeable.
28. LCW, Vol. 27, 392–93.
29. The history of war communism has been well known in the literature for decades. For more on this, see E. G. Gimpelson, *Voyenniy kommunizm: polityika, praktyika i ideologija* (Moscow: 1973); and his *Sovyetskiy rabochiy klass 1918–1920 gg.* (Moscow: 1974); László Szamuely, *Az első szocialista gazdasági mechanizmusok*; E. H. Carr, *The Bolshevik Revolution,* Vol. 2 (London: Pelican, 1966).
30. Dmitrenko, *Sovyetskaya ekonomicheskaya politika,* 109–12.
31. Nikolai Bukharin and Evgeniy Preobrazhensky, *The ABC of Communism*, translated from the Russian by Eden and Cedar Paul (Harmondsworth, Middlesex: Penguin Books, 1969), 209; in Russian, Nikolai Bukharin and Yevgeni Preobrazhenskiy, *Azbuka kommunizma* (St. Petersburg: Gosizdat Peterburg, 1920), 123–25.
32. LCW, Vol. 30, 506.
33. LCW, Vol. 25, 442.
34. LCW, Vol. 26, 468.
35. LCW, Vol. 25, 471.
36. Lenin could not have known that under the decades of "state socialist" and "existing socialist" rule hordes of writers who considered themselves Marxists would mix-and-match state and social property together—arm in arm with the (neo)liberals and neoconservatives. Not to mention the false explanations that have come to the fore since the collapse of

state socialism, the most typical and common of which is state socialism being called "communism."

37. LCW, Vol. 28, 172, 228–29.
38. Ibid., 300.
39. LVW, Vol. 29, 360.
40. See A. Slepkov, "K tretyey godovshchine kronstadtskogo myatezha," *Bolsevik* (1924): 1, 45.
41. See Vvedenyiye, in *Kronstadt*, 9.
42. See, for example, Gurevich's letter to the leadership of the German Independent Social Democratic Party, or the information of the *Gazeta pechatnikov* on the All-Russia Party Congress of the RSDLP, in *Mensheviki v bolshevistskoy Rossii 1918–1924: Mensheviki v 1918 godu* (Moscow: ROSSPEN, 1999), 672–73, 700. In Hungarian, for a more detailed approach, see *Szakszervezetek és államhatalom: Dokumentumok a szovjet-oroszországi szakszervezetek történetéből 1917–1923* [Trade unions and state power: Documents from the history of trade unions in Soviet Russia, 1917–1923], ed. Béládi László (Budapest: ELTE ÁJTK, 1985), as well as the introduction by Tamás Krausz.
43. See Lenin's speech at the 11th Congress in March 1922. LCW, Vol. 33, 279.
44. Studies, books, and publications of sources related to the NEP can hardly be followed in recent years. See among more recent works the book under the name of A. N. Yakovlev, and written by colleagues, which contains an extensive large collection of material, *Rossiya nepovskaya* (Moscow: Noviy hronograf, 2002).
45. For an overview of the issue, see the recent work by A. S. Senavskiy, "Novaya ekonomicheskaya politika: Sovremennie podhodi i perspektivi izuchenyiya" [The NEP: Current approaches and perspectives for further research], in *NEP: ekonomicheskie, politicheskie i sotsiokulturnie aspekti* (Moscow: ROSSPEN, 2006), 5–25. From the 1970s onward, works beyond those already mentioned by Szamuely and Brush were also available in Hungarian; take for example, *A NEP tapasztalatai a Szovjetunióban* [The empirical evidence of the NEP in the Soviet Union] (Budapest: Kossuth, 1975).
46. See E. G. Gimpelson, *Novaya ekonomicheskaya politika Lenina–Stalina: Problemi i uroki (20-e godi XX v.)* [The NEP of Lenin and Stalin: Problems and lessons] (Moscow: Sobranie, 2004). Gimpelson faults the Bolsheviks for stemming the bourgeois-capitalist growth of the NEP. According to the new interpretation, the Bolsheviks were caught in the trap of the socialist "utopia," with Lenin in tow, who could not comprehend that the task should have been a democratic capitalism (democratic, commodity-producing, market-oriented society) resting on bourgeois democracy and privatized state property, which Gimpelson says has not been achieved since 1991. (See ibid., 293–96.) Projecting the possibility of a "democratic capitalism" back by decades, Gimpelson assumed that a liberal market economy could be realized even without a serious social upsurge; to desire it would be enough. The assumption that Lenin would or should have carried through the reinstatement of the capitalist system is the "misunderstanding" that typifies presentist historiography.
47. N. Valentinov's description of Lenin's politics in his earlier memoir, bearing the authority of an actual eyewitness, indicates that Lenin planned for the NEP with its allowances for market economy to remain in place for a longer term, though, along with some others (and in contrast to Bukharin in particular), he was not willing to give more of an ideological explanation to the introduction of the NEP than was necessary. See N. Valentinov, *Krisis partii*, 30–31.
48. For more on this see *Szakszervezetek és államhatalom*.
49. He addressed the alienated, bureaucratic nature of apparatuses even in his last published writing, *Better Fewer, But Better*, with its final source traceable to the well-known, almost aphoristic expression that told the reader: "We have elements of knowledge, education and training, but they are ridiculously inadequate." LCW, Vol. 33, 487–52.

50. By the first half of the 1980s, works on the debate could be published in Hungary using "banned sources." See Tamás Krausz, *Állam és demokrácia*, 492–98.
51. LCW, Vol. 32, 20.
52. For more on this, see Tamás Krausz, "A szakszervezeti kérdés az OK(b)P X. kongresszusán (1921)" [The trade union issue at the Tenth Congress of the RCP(b) (1921)], in *A nemzetközi munkásmozgalom történetéből. Évkönyv 1981* [Toward a history of the international workers' movement. Annuary 1981] (Budapest: Kossuth, 1980), 156–66.
53. LCW, Vol. 32, 48.
54. LCW, Vol. 32, 25.
55. This was Ya. E. Rudzutak's position, who gave expression to his doubts in a letter of 10 January 1922 to Lenin. *Bolshevistskoye rukovodstvo. Perepiska. 1912–1927* [Bolshevik leadership. correspondence] (Moscow: ROSSPEN, 1996), 234. Zinoviev also sent an interesting report on the reception of Lenin's theses, see ibid., 236. Find Lenin's theses in LCW, Vol. 42, 374^{b}-386^{a}, esp. 375–76.
56. L. D. Trotsky, "Terrorizm i kommunyizm," in *Sochineniya* 12 (Moscow, 1925): 23–30, 40–41; in English, see Trotsky, *Terrorism and Communism* (Michigan: University of Michigan Press, 1961).
57. Mayer, "Lenin and the Practice of Dialectical Thinking," *Science and Society,* Vol. 63 No. 1 (1999): 55.
58. Ibid., 58–59.
59. Invaluable archival data and information about these events are published in I. M. Nekrasova, "Obzor i analiz istochnikov CAODM o zabastovkah i volneniyah rabochih proizvodstvennoy sferi v 1920-h godah" [Analysis of the plant council archives in relation to the worker strikes and demonstrations in the 1920s], in *Trudovie konflikti*, 75.
60. Of course, as Samson Madiyevsky, the once Soviet, now German, historian remarked in one of his reviews in manuscript form, if a Soviet citizen in Stalin's time would have ventured to use one of Lenin's more critical comments on bureaucracy or the communists publicly—e.g., "Commie lies"—he would shortly have found himself in the Gulag.
61. It is interesting that even the memoirs of N. Valentinov (Volsky), who had known Lenin for a long time, remained completely insensitive—as did a majority of the Mensheviks—to Lenin's efforts in the theoretical field, discussing the way the Communist Party related to the NEP, perceiving them virtually as power games exclusively. See N. Valentinov, *NEP i krizis partii. Vospominaniya* (New York: Teleks, 1991). Current historiography seems to go down the same track, sweeping aside the theoretical issues of socialism.
62. Nikolai Bukharin, *Ekonomika perehodnogo perioda* (Moscow: Gos. izdat, 1920); in English, "The Economics of the Transition Period" in *The Politics and Economics of the Transition Period*, ed. and with an introduction by Kenneth J. Tarbuck, trans. Oliver Field (London and Boston: Routledge & Kegan Paul, 1979), 59–250.
63. LCW, Vol. 42, 376. Examining Lenin's conceptualization of socialism, Gábor Székely does not share the view that the concept of "state capitalism" could be applied to the NEP as a valid theoretical category. See Gábor L. Székely, "Lenin és a szocializmus" [Lenin and socialism], *Múltunk* (2001): 2–3, 130–78.
64. Lenin, *On Cooperation*. LCW, Vol. 33, 472.
65. *Speech at the Eleventh Congress of the R.C.P.(B.)*, LCW, Vol. 33, 277–78. For greater detail, see Tamás Krausz, *Szovjet Thermidor*, 123–24.
66. LCW, Vol. 33, 420.
67. Ibid., 478–79.
68. Ibid., 160.
69. This link is a returning leitmotif of the ideological masterwork of the Stalinist period, *Kratki*

Kurs [The short course] (Moscow: 1938). For more on this work, see Tamás Krausz, "A 'Rövid tanfolyam' és a történelem" [The "short course" and course of history], *Világosság* 3 (1989): 174–79.

70. N. V. Ustryalov, "*Smena Vekh*, 12 November 1921, 3/1," in *V borbe za Rossiyu* (Harbin: 1920). This volume contains Ustryalov's articles written in the spring and summer of 1920, after Kolchak's defeat.
71. See ibid.; and Krausz, *Szovjet Thermidor*, 105–17. For more on the programs of the White generals see Iván Halász, *A tábornokok diktatúrái – a diktatúrák tábornokai. Fehérgárdista rezsimek az oroszországi polgárháborúban 1917–1920* [Generals leading dictatorships—dictatorships leading generals. White guard regimes in the Russian civil war 1917–1920] (Budapest: Hungarian Institute for Russian Studies, 2005].
72. LCW, Vol. 33, 285–87.
73. N. Bukharin, "Tsezarizm pod maskoy revolyutsii" [Caesarism in a revolutionary mask], *Izd. "gazeti Pravda"* (Moscow, 1925), 5–45.
74. Ibid., 43–45.
75. Ibid., 44.
76. The most recent work to exculpate Stalin, a thick book that belongs largely in the realm of conspiratorial fantasy, does not question the authenticity of the Lenin manuscript under examination, though the author believes that Lenin was misled by Trotsky's followers (Gorbunov, Fotieva, Glyasser) as of 1922. The author outlined the structure of a whole conspiracy. The case for Lenin not having been sufficiently informed of the Georgian conflict has also not been convincingly set forth. See V. A. Sakharov, *"Politicheskoe zaveshchaniye" Lenina. Realnosty istorii i mifi politiki* (Moscow: Izdat. Moskovskogo Universiteta, 2003), 345–62.
77. The history of these debates were examined in greater detail by Krausz, *Bolsevizmus és nemzeti kérdés*; for details, see 107–25.
78. LCW, Vol. 36, 607–8.
79. Ibid., 609–10.
80. *Pages from a Diary*. LCW, Vol. 33, 463.
81. Returning to his village of birth after the civil war, Pavel, the Red soldier—no longer illiterate—founded a theatre, wrote a play, and performed the "heroic ballad of revolution" to the huge but peculiar interest of the locals, who were invited with posters. "He applied special artistic twirls to this part of the poster: Written by Pavel Teretevich Mohov, Red machine-gunner, author of the collective. Below, the exhortations followed: ... "No *spitting* please! We request that all private conversations during the performance are avoided! Please avoid using dirty expressions in the intermission! With respect, Mohov, the playwright." Vyacheslav Shishkov, "Színielőadás Ogrizovo faluban" [Theatre performance in the village of Ogrizovo], in *A négylábú tyúk: Mai szovjet szatírák* [The four legged hen: Contemporary Soviet satires], selection and postscript by László Bratka (Budapest: Szépirodalmi Könyvkiadó, 1984), 33.
82. LCW, Vol. 33, 487.
83. Ibid., 488.
84. Ibid., 476.
85. Ibid., 477.
86. Ibid., 479.
87. Even at the very end of his creative life Lenin kept emphasizing in *Pages From a Diary* that direct organization and indoctrination of the peasantry on a village level is ruled out: "I said 'communist,' but I hasten to make a reservation for fear of causing a misunderstanding, or of being taken too literally. Under no circumstances must this be understood to mean that we should immediately propagate purely and strictly communist ideas in the countryside.

As long as our countryside lacks the material basis for communism, it will be, I should say, harmful, in fact, I should say, fatal, for communism to do so." 2 January 1923, LCW, Vol. 33, 462–66.

88. *Re the Monopoly of Foreign Trade*, ibid., 455–59.
89. Ibid., 334.
90. Ibid., 335–36.
91. These phenomena affected the immediate conditions of everyday life, of "survival." To get a feel of this it is worth alluding to the diary entries of Mikhail Bulgakov, which captured the situation graphically: "30 September 1923. Moscow is still a peculiar cloaca. Everything is madly expensive, with everything counted no longer in banknotes, but only gold. The chernovets today cost 4,000 rubles in 1923 banknotes (4 billion)." Another entry: "18 October 1923, Thursday night. By the grace of god the chernovets today was 5,500 (5 and a half billion) rubles. The French buns cost 17 million, and a pound of white bread was 65 million. A score of eggs cost 200 rubles yesterday. Yesterday they restarted the tram on line no 24 (Ostozhenka)." Bulgakov, *Sárba taposva*, 20, 23–24.
92. *A NEP tapasztalatai a Szovjetunióban*, 161.
93. Ibid., 171–73. For more on this field see the works of Brush, Szamuely, Senavsky.
94. For an investigation of the way economic sectors were related to one another in an economic and economic history context, see Andrey Kolganov, *Puty k sotsializmu. Tragediya i podvig* (Moscow: Ekonomika, 1990), 4–50.
95. LCW, Vol. 33, 287.
96. Tamás Krausz, "A 'sztálini szocializmus,'" in *Lenintől Putyinig*, 87–106. A rich store of historical material has piled up detailing the coexistence of the community sectors, with research ongoing since the 1970s. See I. Ye. Zelenin, *Sovkhozi v pervoye desyatiletiye sovyetskoy vlaszti 1917–1927* [The Sovkhovs in the first decade of Soviet rule] (Moscow: Nauka, 1972).
97. A. S. Senavsky, whose rather clear picture of the internal contradictions of the NEP has been useful in providing insights here, has surprisingly relegated "democratic socialism" and "self-governing socialism" to the world of liberal illusions: "Those sorts of ideas regarding 'democratic socialism' and 'cooperative' socialism were mere 'mental games,' the illusions of liberal intellectuals." See Senavsky, *NEP: Ekonomicheskie* (2006), 14.
98. *On Cooperation*, LCW, Vol. 33, 467–75.
99. Ibid., 467.
100. "The cooperatives must be granted state loans that are greater, if only by a little, than the loans we grant to private enterprises." (The cooperative order as socialism.) "But it will take a whole historical epoch to get the entire population into the work of the cooperatives through NEP." Ibid., 469–70.
101. Ibid., 472–73.
102. Ibid., 474.
103. Trotsky, *Sochineniya,* Vol. 12, 327. Trotsky at the same time argued against the validity of using the concept of state capitalism, for which he would soon put blame on Zinoviev (with Zinoviev being most likely in the right, on this occasion). See G. Zinoviev, *Leninizm:. Vvedeniye v izucsenyie lenyinyizma* (Leningrad: Gosz. Izdat., 1925), 254–58. In December 1924, when Stalin declared his thesis of "socialism in one country," both considered it a theoretical impossibility.
104. For more on this, see Krausz, *Átmeneti korszak*, 208–9. On the basis of the *Critique of the Gotha Program*, Preobrazhensky identified socialism with a form of planned production in which the management of autodynamic associations is not regulated by the anarchic markets but by social accounting. He captured the essence of socialist distribution in "exchanges in equal value, the equality of how labor intensity is measured." See J. Preobrazhensky, "Sotsialisticheskiye

i kommunisticheskie predstavleniya o sotsializme," *Vestnik Kommunisticheskoy Akademii* (1925): 12, 56, 60–61.

105. The regulatory role of the market—following production—could not apply because the traditional commercial relations had broken down in the chaos of civil war. As the NEP was introduced, demand was so high that there was hardly an article on the market that would not find a buyer. Concepts for state planning were only at the stage of inception at that point. The introduction of a planned state economy came up at the beginning of the 1920s, as institutionally manifested in the establishment of the Gosplan (State Planning Committee), initiated by Trotsky and supported by Lenin, in 1922.
106. István Mészáros, *Beyond Capital* (London: Merlin Press, 1995).
107. LCW, Vol. 33, 96.
108. Such a historical interpretation of Lenin can be found in a number of recent publications, among them Yu. Burtin, *Drugoy sotsializm: "Krasniye holmi"* (Moscow: 1999); as well as Yu. M. Ivanov, *Chuzhoy sredi svoih: Posledniye godi zhizni Lenina* (Moscow: 2002).
109. Two of my works, both in English, address the transformations "market socialism" went through over historical time. See "Stalin's Socialism" and "Perestroika and the Redistribution of Property in the Soviet Union: Political Perspectives and Historical Evidence," *Contemporary Politics* 13/1 (March 2007); as well as, in Hungarian, "A peresztrojka és tulajdonváltás. Politikai koncepciók és történelmi valóság," in *Peresztrojka és tulajdonáthelyezés. Tanulmányok és dokumentumok a rendszerváltás történetéből a Szovjetunióban (1985–1991)*, ed. Tamás Krausz and Zoltán Sz. Bíró (Budapest: MRI, 2003), 52–102; *Válaszúton* [Crossways], in the series *Politikatudományi Füzetek* no. 7, ed. Tamás Krausz and László Tütő (Budapest: ELTE ÁJTK, 1988).
110. See Mészáros, *Beyond Capital*, 823–50.
111. Apart from István Mészaros's work, this tradition is also honored in part by the Trotskyist heritage in Western Europe, in part by the Russian "self-governors" who are gathered largely around the journal called *Alternativu*, which is related in its positions to the Hungarian journal *Eszmélet*. See also *Önkormányzás vagy az elitek uralma* [Self-government or the reign of the elites], ed. Tamás Krausz and László Tütő (Budapest: Liberter Kiadó, 1995); and *Államszocializmus*.
112. Trotsky, who defended state property as the precondition of socialism even in the 1930s, was later the recipient of sharp criticism from Marxists as well, for becoming a protector of Stalinism. These critics forgot that Trotsky's precise notion was that it will be easier to socialize Soviet state property in a "revolutionary turn," than if the bureaucracy and capital alienates state property from those who created it by way of private expropriation. For more on this, see Krausz, *Szovjet Thermidor*, 227–30.
113. *Novaya ekonomicheszkaya politika Lenina-Stalina*, the work by the originally regime-friendly, turncoat, right-wing writer Gimpelson, also looks upon Lenin as a barbaric gravedigger of capitalism.

SUMMARY COMMENTS IN PLACE OF A POSTSCRIPT

1. This implication of Lenin's activities was understood by Gramsci many decades earlier. See Antonio Gramsci, *Selections from the Prison Notebooks*, trans. Quintin Hoare and Geoffrey Nowell Smith (London: ElecBook, 1999), 688–90.
2. "Theses on Feuerbach," *Marx/Engels Selected Works*, Vol. 1, translated from the German by W. Lough (Moscow: Progress Publishers, 1969), 13–15.
3. Lenin sought the way out from four such collapses: 1) the collapse of traditional Russia and the rise of Russian capitalism at the turn of the century; 2) the Russo-Japanese war and the Revolution of 1905; 3) the Great War; 4) the revolutions of the year 1917, the collapse of autocracy, and the destruction wrought by the civil war.

4. A rich plethora of ideas and arguments on this issue from the perspective of the new era can be found in Savas Michael-Matsas, "Lenin and the Path of Dialectics," in *Lenin Reloaded*, 101–19; and Stathis Kouvelakis, "Lenin as Reader of Hegel: Hypotheses for a Reading of Lenin's *Notebooks* on Hegel's *The Science of Logic*," 164–204.
5. The transfer of Lenin's ideas into the twenty-first century according to the leftist critique of the regime is not a matter of individual endeavor or experiment. It is an international phenomenon, involving a group of renowned theoreticians, whose works have been collected under the appropriate title *Lenin Reloaded*, ed. Sebastian Budgen, Stathis Kouvelakis, Slavoj Žižek, and David Fernbach (Durham, NC: Duke University Press, 2007).
6. Although the cult of Lenin existed in his homeland, sponsored by Stalin and sometimes showing quasi-religious overtones continued in the "official" Communist Party and beyond, Lenin's heritage gave rise to very little serious *theoretical* analyses and systematic approaches in regard to its historical significance or relevance for the present. As for monographs, however, there were a few outstanding books published with the aim of presenting Lenin's authentic human face, contrasting starkly with an abundance of, as V. Loginov put it, "Lenin-devouring" literature.
7. He reached this development largely by assimilating Kautsky's earlier, pre-reformist concepts. Particularly in regard to class consciousness, land reform, the issue of nationalism (see *Der Weg zur Macht*, etc.), but "returned" to Marx and turned against Kautsky in the period when World War One broke out.
8. Regarding the historical reconstruction of the debates about Lenin's heritage, see Tamás Krausz and Miklós Mesterházy, "About Lenin's Heritage," in *Mű és történelem*, chap. 4, 101–29.
9. The Soviet Russification of Lenin, veiled in an abstract universalism, reinforced the "bourgeois" Russification that was its very opposite (in theory at least), and which deprived Lenin's Marxism of its universal application, dismissing it as some kind of "local manifestation."
10. The later systematizations aiming at legitimizing his ideas did not admit this fact because, after all, state socialism appeared to be the incarnation of socialist theory; behind this process we can perceive the trickery, meant to legitimize the political ideology, making state property appear as public property. It should be noted that in Marxist circles, not only in Western Europe but even in Hungary, there were attempts to show the opposite, mainly from the mid-1980s on.
11. According to Krupskaya's testimony, when Trotsky, shortly before Lenin's death, compared him to Marx, Lenin felt flattered, but felt it was an exaggeration, since he had never elaborated a scientific methodology of his own, nor any theory that differed from Marxism. Bureaucratic systems were alien to Lenin, as noted by even such original interpreters of his work as Gramsci. The Italian philosopher, in his critique of Bukharin's anti-dialectical "system generation," also rejected by Lenin, remarked, in arguing against the formal creation of systems: "But the vulgar contention is that science must absolutely mean 'system,' and consequently systems of all sorts are built up which have only the mechanical exteriority of a system and not its necessary inherent coherence." Antonio Gramsci, *Selections from the Prison Notebooks of Antonio Gramsci*, ed. and trans. Quintin Hoare and Geoffrey Nowell Smith (New York: International Publishers, 1971), 434.
12. Georg Lukács, "Towards a Methodology of the Problem of Organization," in *History and Class Consciousness* (Cambridge, MA: MIT Press, 1971), 305.
13. Georg Lukács, *A társadalmi lét ontológiájáról* [The ontology of social being], Vol. 3: *Prolegomena* (Budapest: Magvető könyvkiadó, 1976), 270.
14. Ibid.
15. Ibid. It might be noted that Lukács was exaggerating somewhat. It was only in the countries of the center that "relative surplus value" became dominant.

16. Lukács accurately noted the serious, even "fatal consequences" of this hiatus for later times: "The ideological generalization [of Lenin's formulations from this period] gave Stalin and his followers the opportunity to present their own ideology, which is the exact opposite [of Lenin's] in every significant respect, as its direct continuation." Ibid., 279.
17. Tamás Krausz, "Ami a wallersteini elméletből 'kimaradt': Néhány megjegyzés" [The theory of Wallerstein: All that has been "left out"], *Eszmélet* 91 (2011).
18. In general Lenin neglected to study methodically the bourgeois sociology and philosophy of his times because he conceived of these as merely apologies for the existing order. He only reacted to them when they made inroads into social democratic ideas or politics. He spent more time delving into an examination of tendencies within Marxism and social democracy (Plekhanov, Bernstein, Kautsky, Hilferding). He overcame these limitations in his historical studies, learned a great deal from bourgeois science and accepted some of its findings from the "progressive period," as he called it, which ended with the Great War. At that point, the *ancien regime* crossed over into its negative, degenerating stage.
19. See Péter Szigeti, *Világrendszernézőben* [Examining Weltanschauungen], 37. Szigeti is correct in arguing that the real and very important problem of unequal development should not be overgeneralized, and equal development should not be overlooked. In this sense Lenin and the Marxism of the entire communist movement got stuck in relative backwardness, in the historical terrain of having to "catch up."
20. After the collapse of the Soviet Union, it is once again the Hegelian methodology that dominates much of Marxist-Leninist thinking—often disabused nowadays—and historians convert to Bernsteinianism and revisionism. Once again this provides for a Hegelian coexistence with reality, only nowadays it comes in the form of "validation of revisionism." A typical example of this would be T. I. Oyzerman, *Opravdanyije revizionyizma* (Moscow: Kanon, 2005).
21. For the most recent contribution of an old representative of this discovery see Kevin B. Anderson, "The Rediscovery and Persistence of the Dialectics in Philosophy and in World Politics," in *Lenin Reloaded*, 120–147. Perhaps this discovery first appeared in the work of Henri Lefebvre, in his "La pensée de Lénine," first published in 1957, reprinted in *Lenin Reloaded*, 138. But the Bolsheviks were already debating the significance of dialectics in Lenin's work not long after Lenin's death. Whether the reading of Hegel by Lenin in 1914 revealed an epistemological or an ideological break, is mentioned, albeit in the opposite sense, by such well-known authors (not too surprisingly in the late 1960s) as Roger Garaudy, *Lenin* (Paris: PUF, 1968), and L. Coletti, *Il Marxismo e Hegel* (Bari: Laterza, 1976). See, from the same period, Marcel Liebman, *Leninism under Lenin*. From the 1980s and 1990s, see Kevin Anderson, *Lenin, Hegel and Western Marxism: Critical Studies* (Urbana: University of Illinois Press, 1995), as well as Neil Harding's *Leninism*. There was an interesting debate about Anderson's "Hegelian" book in the mid-1990s, upon the initiative of Raya Dunayevskaya. We would be remiss if we failed to note that in Hungary the work of István Hermann and György Szabó András also made important contributions. Adam Wirth published an entire monograph titled *Lenin, a filozófus* [Lenin, the philosopher] (Budapest: Kossuth, 1971), albeit it was written from the old professional point of view.
22. This concept is broached in *The State and Revolution*. In his theoretical introduction Lenin activates certain, almost forgotten, views of Marx: socialism was the outcome of a protracted historical process; as the first phase of communism, which functions as the possibly universal evolution toward the future; as the "community of associated producers"; as the global freedom of civilized humanity.
23. An effort to frame an ideology for the unplanned developments of state socialism is completely absent from Lenin's ideas, and this absence was one of the theoretical sources in the lively debate engaged in by Trotsky and his comrades, joined later by others (including J.-P. Sartre),

challenging the coherence and meaning of the Stalinian thesis of "socialism in one country."

24. I. K. Pantin wrote in connection with the already mentioned work by L. Oyzerman, "Istoricheskiye sugybi marxizma," in *Vestniik Rossiyskoy, Akademii Nauk* (2006 August): 747–53.
25. Nikoilai Ustrialov, *Nacional-Bolshevizm* (Moscow: Algoritm, 2003), 372–76.
26. Slavoj Žižek , *13 opitov o Lenine* (Moscow: Izdatielstvo Ad maginem, 2003), 252–53.

Index